A Celebration of Sligo
First Essays for Sligo Field Club

Edited by

Martin A. Timoney

2002

Published by Sligo Field Club, Co. Sligo, Ireland
A Celebration of Sligo
First Essays for Sligo Field Club
Edited by Martin A. Timoney

Articles © Sligo Field Club and Authors, 2002
Design and Layout © Martin A. Timoney, 2002

© Title, *A Celebration of Sligo, First Essays for Sligo Field Club,*
and variations thereof, © Martin A. Timoney, 2002

No part of this work may be printed, copied, reproduced, stored in a retrieval system or transmitted in any form or by any means, electronic, mechanical, photocopying, recording or otherwise, now known or hereafter invented, without the prior written permission of the publishers and the author(s).

While every care has been taken by the Authors and the Editor on behalf of Sligo Field Club to ensure that the information presented here is correct at time of going to press no responsibility whatsoever is accepted for any loss, inconvenience or damage arising from errors, inaccuracies or interpretations which may be expressed here.

The views and interpretations expressed here are not necessarily those of the Editor nor of Sligo Field Club

ISBN 0 9528091 0 9 Hardback
ISBN 0 9528091 1 7 Paperback

Cover Design: Mary B. Timoney using images by
An Early Christian Sculptor, William Frederick Wakeman and Tony Toher
Cover Design Computerisation: Maghnus O'Brien, Carol McGowan

Maps based on Ordnance Survey of Ireland are by Permission of the Government,
Permit No. 6785 © Government of Ireland

Printed by Carrick Print 2000 Ltd., Carrick-on-Shannon, Co. Leitrim, Ireland

A CELEBRATION *OF* SLIGO

CONTENTS

Presidential Foreword
Patrick Heraughty, John J. Flynn,
Brían Ó Súilleabháin, Desmond Smith†,
Martin Enright, Frank O'Connor,
John McTernan, Brendan Rooney,
Tony Toher and Larry Mullin ... 1

Editorial
Martin A. Timoney ... 3

The Surroundings of Truskmore
Patrick Tohall† ... 5

Benbulbin - Geology and Scenery
Richard Thorn ... 13

*The Natural History of The Bricklieves,
Co. Sligo*
Don C. F. Cotton ... 17

Eels and Eel Fishing in County Sligo
Christopher Moriarty ... 31

Note on Hut-Sites at Aughris, County Sligo
Finlay Tower Kitchin† ... 37

Aughris, Portavaud, Lackan and Kilcummin
Martin A. Timoney ... 41

*Monuments Of Meaning, Role and symbolism
of passage tombs in Cúil Irra, Co. Sligo.*
Stefan Bergh ... 65

*The Search for an Irish Paleolithic:
Rosses Point Revisited*
Peter Woodman ... 73

*Pollen Analytical Investigations
in the Sligo Area*
Hans Göransson ... 85

New Barrow Types Identified in County Sligo
Jean Farrelly and Margaret Keane ... 97

*The Promontory Fort, Inhumation Cemetery
and Sub-Rectangular Enclosure at
Knoxspark, Co. Sligo*
Charles Mount ... 103

*A Curious Inhumation Burial from
Dernish Island, Co. Sligo*
Victor M. Buckley, Laureen Buckley
and Finbar McCormick ... 117

*The Irish in War and Peace,
A.D. 400 - 800*
Etienne Rynne ... 121

Ogam Stones in Sligo and their Context
Catherine Swift ... 127

Carrowntemple, Co. Sligo, A Review
Martin A. Timoney ... 141

*St. Feichin's, Ballisodare, Co. Sligo:
Discoveries and Rediscoveries*
Mary B. Timoney ... 149

*A Romanesque Sculpture found
at Carrowculleen, Skreen, Co. Sligo*
Martin A. Timoney ... 161

Sligo Castle
Kieran Denis O'Conor ... 183

*Archaeological Excavation at Sligo
Town Hall Gate Lodge, June 2002*
Eoin Halpin ... 193

*Sligo's de Burgo Castle of 1310:
An Addendum*
Patrick E. O'Brien and
Martin A. Timoney ... 195

*Archaeological Site Assessment,
1993-1994, Rockwood Parade, Sligo*
Eoin Halpin ... 199

Silver Pennies of Edward I from Tubbercurry, Co. Sligo Michael Kenny	213
Irish Dominican Medieval Architecture Fr. Patrick Conlan, O.F.M.	215
Archaeological Site Assessment west of The Green Fort Eoin Halpin	229
Downing's Description of County Sligo, c. 1684 Nollaig Ó Muraíle	231
The Antiquities of Sligo in 1779 as seen by Lewis Irwin of Tanrego House Peter Harbison	243
George Gabriel Stokes, A Sligo-born Scientist John O'Dea	247
A Northern Scholar in County Sligo Ernan Morris	251
The Arrival At Sligo, Early approaches to Sligo in the 19th century Derry O'Connell	257
The Origins of Technical Education in Sligo Town, 1904-1912 Larry Mullin	263
Environmental Education at The Institute of Technology, Sligo William FitzGerald	267
Archaeological Survey in Sligo Olive Alcock and Mary Tunney	269
A Practitioner's Perspective on the Development Conflict John O'Dwyer	273
'Sligo Antiquarian Society, 1945-1946, and Sligo Field Club, 1946-1947, 1954 – 2002 Martin A. Timoney and Patrick Heraughty	275
Authors	331
Tabula Gratulatoria	333

Special Pictorial Pages
    12, 30, 36, 84, 96, 160, 212, 257, 262, 331, 332

Tawnatruffaun Portal Tomb, Co. Sligo. Sligo Field Club Collection.

PRESIDENTIAL FOREWORD

Sligo Field Club seeks to promote interest in our natural and man-made environment among people of all walks of life. Sligo Field Club holds lectures of the highest standard and guides field trips, and it records and protects field monuments and landscape. It also provides guides to visiting groups, assists students and academics and encourages national and international scholars to study Sligo and its place in Ireland and Europe.

Archaeology, history, folklore, folklife, natural history, botany, ornithology, geology, industrial, architectural and engineering history, fine arts, the quality of the environment and planning have all been of interest to us down the years.

We aspire through education, in the broadest sense, to instill pride, principle and perception into all concerned with our heritage. Seeing so many families at our lectures and particularly at our outings gives hope for a new generation of enthusiasts - the conservation ideal can not be instilled too early!

Sligo Field Club has a national and international reputation as a fieldwalking society, one which shares the knowledge of its discoveries with those genuinely motivated. Our own State, County, Planning and Tourist agencies, visiting societies and universities from all over Ireland, Britain and other parts of Europe have drawn on our knowledge. Most of us have no formal training but we are professional in all we do. As a local voluntary organisation we have very good relationships with The National Museum of Ireland, The Ordnance Survey, Dúchas -the Heritage Service, formerly The National Monuments Service and The National Parks and Monuments Branch and The Wildlife Service of The Office of Public Works, our own Local Authorities and other like-minded societies.

Sligo Antiquarian Society was founded in 1945. The name was changed to Sligo Field Club in 1946. There is no record of any organised public activities from mid-1947 until it was revived in 1954 though some members were individually active throughout that period. Since then it has been in continuous existence, arranging lectures, guiding outings and helping those studying particular aspects of the heritage of Co. Sligo. The idea of a Sligo Field Club publication was floated in 1955 and again in 1956 and 1959. Despite this being a period of new *Journals* across the 'drumlin belt' of Ireland, the members of Sligo Field Club devoted their energies to productive fieldwalking. The results of this work has benefited us all and much of it is included in *The Megalithic Survey of Ireland, Vol. 5, Co. Sligo*, The Sites and Monuments Record and The Record of Monuments and Places.

To commemorate its own successful past the Members decided in 1994 to publish a volume of essays. The volume on aspects of Sligo, past and present and with a glance to the future, in a national and European context, would help to expand, clarify and spread the story of Co. Sligo. It would also encourage debate and we hope that it would encourage prudent use of our inheritance.

We, the eleven Presidents who have held office since 1961, thank the authors, several of whom are members of Sligo Field Club, for their devotion, time and energy in giving of their knowledge of our part of the heritage of Europe and its place in the story of Ireland. Some of the authors have entertained us with lectures and outings. The quality of the material is reflective of their interest in, enthusiasm for, and dedication to the work of Sligo Field Club.

We acknowledge the contribution of members who have supported us over the years through their membership fees, attendance at lectures and outings and most importantly the time they have freely given. We particularly acknowledge the work done by the eighty-nine people who have served on the committee. Some individuals have served for over a quarter of a century, giving unstintingly of their talents, time and energy. Sligo Education Centre, formerly Sligo Teachers' Centre, has provided us with a venue for our lectures since 1975. Sligo Corporation, Sligo County Council, E.S.B. and Telecom Eireann, now Eircom, sponsored some of our lectures over several years. Private landowners, who are privileged to own the greater proportion of our heritage, kindly allowed us access to their property to study that heritage. All of these are in our debt.

A CELEBRATION *OF* SLIGO

The publication of this volume would not have been possible without the support and the assistance of many people and institutions.

Firstly we mention our sponsors, particularly the former Director Brendán Mac Connamhna of Sligo Regional Technical College, now The Institute of Technology, and his staff. Sligo, Sligo County Council, Sligo Corporation, The Town of Sligo Vocational Education Committee, Dúchas - The Heritage Service, formerly the Office of Public Works, Sligo Education Centre, formerly Sligo Teachers' Centre, Sheela Kitchin, the Morris family, and Patrick F. O'Donovan provided sponsorship at the early stage. These together with those who provided sponsorship or became subscribers at the closing stages are acknowledged in the *Tabula Gratulatoria*. Several teachers at the Convent of Mercy, Castlerea, later to become Castlerea Community School, provided computer assistance in the early stages of production.

Sligo County Library, The National Library of Ireland, The National Museum of Ireland, The Royal Irish Academy, The Ordnance Survey of Ireland, Patricia Curran-Mulligan, Verity Swan, Sligo County Council, The National Museums of Scotland and Musée National du Moyen Age au Thermes de Cluny in Paris gave permission to use illustrations or maps in their care. Michael Yeats gave permission to use extracts from the poetry of his father, William Butler Yeats. Tom and Trudy Bourke, Westprint, Inishcrone, set up some of the articles at the early stage. Della Dwyer Beirne, Carol McGowan and all the staff at Carrick Print 2000 meticulously turned three dozen typescripts into this magnificent book. We were honoured that Professor Seamus Caulfield was pleased to launch the book.

Martin A. Timoney, as Editor, and his wife, Mary, gave long hours of voluntary and patient work.

Jack Flynn and Larry Mullin took care of the initial financial worries by securing sponsorship. John McTernan, Dr. Don C. F. Cotton and Brendan Rooney were also involved at the early stages. Aidan Mannion, Patrick E. O'Brien, Martin Wilson, Margaret McBrien, Larry Mullin and Joyce Enright saw the final financial arrangements through.

To all these and many others who have helped in lesser but significant ways, we tender our sincerest thanks.

This volume is, and will remain, a lasting tribute to the enthusiasm for and dedication to the work of Sligo Antiquarian Society and Sligo Field Club members since 1945. It has been an honour for us to be associated with it. We have no doubt that it will prove to be uplifting and of absorbing interest to Sligo people in particular and be of benefit to those interested in Sligo and its heritage.

Sligo Field Club Presidents

Patrick Heraughty	1961-1982	John McTernan	1992-1993
John J. Flynn	1983	John J. Flynn	1994-1995
Brían Ó Suilleabháin	1984-1985	Brendan Rooney	1996-1997
Des Smith	1986-1987	Tony Toher	1998-1999
Martin Enright	1988-1989	Laurence Mullin	2000-2001
Frank O'Connor	1990-1991	Martin A. Timoney	2002

EDITORIAL

The idea of a Sligo Field Club publication was mentioned by joint Hon. Secretaries Guy Perrem and Mary F. Ryan in the 1955 Annual Report. Again in 1956 and 1959 the topic was raised by Mary F. Ryan but Sligo Field Club Members devoted their energies to fieldwalking, adding sites to the maps and assisting academics as well as organising lectures and outings of the highest standard and fighting the occasional battle. They were primarily concerned with sites of all periods for one county; finding sites and objects is the stuff of local societies. It was not until fifty years after our own foundation and the upcoming of the Sligo 750 Celebrations in 1995, a date based on the 750th anniversary of Sligo's first castle, that the current publication was initiated. The Celtic Tiger must take the blame for the delay this time! That the work has finally come to fruition in the year of the 750th anniversary of Sligo Abbey is purely coincidental.

This volume will spread knowledge of some of the culture and heritage, both natural and manmade, of Sligo, Town and County, now becoming City and County, to the people of Sligo, Ireland and beyond. References to published works up to the middle of 2002 are included. It will inform those who guide this county, at local, national and European Union level, that we exist, that we have all this heritage resource, that Sligo Field Club has provided a service to the county because of our long-term wide and deep knowledge of our county, and we want to celebrate it! Sligo Field Club seeks to give a greater sense of local identity and a boost to local pride to the people of this county. We are justly proud, but prejudiced as to the important heritage we have on our doorstep, and we invite the people in Sligo to join us on our voyages of discovery. Primarily this book, like the heritage we have in the county, is for the people of Sligo.

Sligo Field Club is recognised, not just nationally, but internationally, as one of the most successful fieldwalking societies, being most willing to share their knowledge with those genuinely and respectfully seeking assistance. Fieldwalking in itself can be very satisfying and discoveries of sites not previously noted drives one on. Fieldwalkers expect recognition for their discoveries, but if others publish our discoveries without acknowledgement then the flow of knowledge ceases. This is akin to the concept of intellectual property. The local fieldworker is often the eyes and the ears for the process of academic research. We regret that Sligo does not, on occasions make as much use of us as it could. The story of Sligo Antiquarian Society and Sligo Field Club as laid out elsewhere in this volume gives an indication of our scope of knowledge and ability. However, we need many more members throughout the county.

Our members have been watchdogs for our heritage and so a county-wide presence is important. A major objective for us, as it is for all local societies, is to ensure that the authorities observe the rules and regulations and that in the words of the Supreme Court they "will not shirk from enforcing these objectives on themselves". But which is more important, protection of rules, regulations and law, or protection of the heritage? W.B. Yeats asked in 1938 *Have I . . . Spoilt what old loins have sent.* Hopefully we will be judged as having been successful in wisely using the heritage our ancestors handed on to us without spoiling it.

While these assets are a blessing to the county they are a major problem for us all today who live here, particularly developers and planners. Is Sligo to become part of a living museum for those who live on the other side of this island? Are these riches to be an obstacle to progress in Sligo?

'Discover, Record, Illustrate, Preserve' could well be the motto of local archaeological and historical societies. These we have been doing, quite often individually more so than collectively, for decades, but now by publishing we are reaching a further stage of completion. Sligo is endowed with more monuments than even the most determined fieldworker could visit and comprehend in a lifetime. The 1995 Recorded Monuments list comes to almost 5,000 sites and monuments of pre-1700 AD date belonging to 175 categories. Perhaps new categories need now be added. If big houses, folklife sites, industrial sites, *etc.*, are included then the total must be in the region of 8,000. Many of these monuments are well past their period of original use and some have been reused more than once, making them more interesting. Their recycling in later times, as happened at Carrowmore, Inishmurray and Sligo Abbey, makes their stories even more interesting. We are only beginning to understand just how much our ancestors used this county and for how long. The name of the county, Sligo – *Sligeach*, derives from man's use of oysters and cockles that abound along our shores and have been used as a food resource for five thousand years. In addition to monuments the county is blessed with huge areas of natural heritage and of scientific interest on a beautiful landscape. In the words of a group of Swedish students I took around Sligo some years ago,

*God, Have mercy on us sinners, Who must walk, With no dinner, No gravy and no grub.
No showers either, Only those that fall from the Sligo skies, Only sites and pubs!*

Our heritage deserves a focal point. Sligo Museum has some items of immense importance but it does not have a full time Curator to actively draw in the associated objects of our heritage. This is a major omission in the cultural, tourist and economic infrastructure of Co. Sligo. The potential benefits to Sligo from heritage can easily be seen when one looks at Co. Clare. The educational potential for those studying art, history and geography is enormous. If we do not provide a place for storage and display of our movable heritage then, as has happened in the past, it will be moved beyond our shores and will be a loss to the nation.

In the early days the membership was professionals in all but title. It was all *terra incognita*, a voyage of discovery. Today, not so often do we come home really chuckling with satisfaction when we have found some 'new' site or seen an 'old' site in a new light. Often in the past a visit to a megalithic tomb or an earthwork was concentrated on the monument itself. Today we examine much more, the landscape, the adjoining field pattern, the relationship of other monuments, even the distribution of the flora, to put the monument in context or to interpret its features.

Further, but much slimmer, volumes are in the Editor's thoughts. Listings of lectures, places visited on outings and persons associated with Sligo Field Club either as members or as guests, *etc.,* as well as responses to some of the works in this volume and new material need a place for publication.

We have endeavoured to provide as much local knowledge to the authors and to check our facts as far as humanly possible. It is most likely that others may wish we had given more information, or perhaps less. They may wish we had expressed different opinions and expressed opinions differently. The opinions expressed are those of the authors and are not necessarily those of The Editor nor of Sligo Field Club.

There is not a total consistency of style between the authors who are from a diverse range of academic backgrounds. Orthography is, hopefully, consistent except in a few cases. Ballisodare or Ballysodare, Benwisken or Benwiskin, Ben Bulbin or Benbulbin, Drumcliff or Drumcliffe, Eniscrone or Iniscrone, and Keash, Kesh, Keshcorran or *Ceis Chorainn* are some of the variants.

The cover design was conceived by Mary B. Timoney and computerised by Maghnus O'Brien using images by an Early Christian sculptor, by William F. Wakeman from 1882 and Tony Toher from 1945. The title, *A Celebration of Sligo, First Essays for Sligo Field Club,* was the combined effort of Nicholas Prinz, Mary B. Timoney and Martin A. Timoney.

Thirty-six authors have given of their time and dedication and have been patient with my many demands during the long period of gestation. In addition there has been a back-room staff of hundreds, such as Pat Hurley, Martin Dunbar, Tony Toher, Elaine Cotton, Dr. Richard Thorn, Raghnall Ó Floinn, Mary Cahill, Elizabeth Kirwan, James O'Shea, Francis Hegarty, Pat Gannon, Anna Shannon-Conlan, Frances Dolan, Ultan McNasser, Lisa McMonigle, Gabriel Brown, John O'Hara, Paul O'Dwyer, John Mahony, Declan Forde, Hugh Sheils, James Reidy, Catherine Brennan, Frances Stroker, Yvonne Hanbury, John Gornall, Tom, Trudy and Paul Burke, to mention only the most pressed upon who were not found wanting when called on. Two research assistants, Siobhán de hÓir in Dublin and Mary B. Timoney at home, are especially thanked.

Prof. Etienne Rynne, Dr. Harman Murtagh, Raghnall Ó Floinn, the late Noel Cassidy, John Bradley, Sheila Mulloy, Chris Corlett and Con Manning, who have been down the editorial road before me, gave me so much encouragement and advice. The staff of the County Libraries of Sligo, Mayo and Roscommon, The National Library of Ireland, The National Museum of Ireland, Dúchas, The Royal Irish Academy, Trinity College Dublin, The Royal Society of Antiquaries of Ireland, The National University of Ireland at Galway, Cork, Maynooth and Dublin have been extremely helpful.

Jack Flynn and Larry Mullin took care of the initial financial worries by raising sponsorship. John McTernan, Dr. Don C. F. Cotton and Brendan Rooney were also involved at the early stages. Aidan Mannion, Joyce Enright, Larry Mullin, Patrick E. O'Brien, Margaret McBrien and Martin Wilson saw the final financial arrangements through.

Mary B. Timoney, and our children, Martin J., Catherine and Bridget, who lost their Dad among piles of papers on many occasions over the last few years, have often rescued him when things went wrong; their help has been immense.

I thank all these for all their help, dedication, knowledge and patience. Hopefully those who have gone before us would have approved of our endeavours.

Martin A. Timoney
Bóthar an Chorainn, Keash, Co. Sligo.
29th November, 2002

A CELEBRATION *OF* SLIGO

THE SURROUNDINGS OF TRUSKMORE

Patrick Tohall†

EDITORIAL NOTE: In April 1962 Patrick Tohall[1], founder member of Sligo Antiquarian Society and Sligo Field Club, then of 13, Moore Park, Newbridge, Co. Kildare, wrote the three articles and collectively called them THE SURROUNDINGS OF TRUSKMORE. He sent them to Telefís Éireann, who had recently erected the T.V. transmitter on Truskmore, with the idea that they be used in a programme about the glaciation, scenery, farming, archaeology and folklore of the area surrounding the mountain. Telefís Éireann chose not to use the scripts and they were returned some months later.[2]

PART 1
THE TOUR AROUND THE PLATEAU

INTRODUCTION

Trosc-Mor ("Hunger Summit")[3] at an altitude of 2,113 feet is the restricted capping of Sandstone-on-Shale, which gives the final altitude to the otherwise Limestone surface of the "barr" (plateau) of Sliabh-Cairbre, situate in the counties of Sligo and Leitrim. From the landward side, the massif starts three miles west of Manorhamilton as a gentle sloping salient, progressing in altitude from the fenced fields to the "Tulai" (mountain slope) to form the elevation between two valleys, each of which is about eight miles long.

THE VALLEYS OF GLENCAR & GLENADE

To the traveller heading for Sligo through Glencar or to Bundoran through Glenade, the gentle side-slope of Sliabh Cairbre develops to majestic rocky scarps. In Glencar two slices of the mountain have slid down to form side prisms now decked with forest, while the rock-slides of Glenade have accomplished a fall of some four hundred feet with such aplomb that the main group appears as three gigantic pillars, spaced well forward from the mountain and visible from the coast road four miles away. They are called Tiompán Mor, Tiompán Lár and Tiompán Rua.

The portal of Glenade from Dartrai, hitherto unrecorded, is shown on accompanying map as "Trosc-corrach" (Hunger Curve). The interpretation of the opposite portal of Sorgagh Dearg is uncertain except for one suggestion of Sorg as "a mountain plant that spreads after fires". The Gaelic names are from Oyan Mac Con-choille (Woods) of Largydonnell, and the suggestion from Co. Donegal.

EMERGENCE ON THE FRONTAL PLAIN

The two Glens emerge about ten miles apart on the open grassy plain fronting the Atlantic Ocean and backed by the towering scarps of Sliabh Cairbre. The Northern portal of Glencar is the rocky prow of Benbulbin, the beauty of which in the year 1813 fascinated the brilliant English Economist, J. C. Curwen, in contrast to his depression over the squalor of the rack-rented smallholdings. How he might rejoice today to view the farmsteads of Cairbre as seen from the shoulder of Sliabh Calrai on the Sligo-Glencar road. The opposite portal of Glencar is Benbulbin, and continuing northeast one journeys past the long recess of Ardnaglass to come level with Ben Wiskin (Beann Bhaoiscín) which rivals Benbulbin. Round the corner is Gleniff which is really a "cúm", having the circular recess with perpendicular rockface which tells of the solid mass of ice separated from the mountain by a crevasse where lumps of ice and boulders churned together, continually eroding the solid mountain, especially in periods of thaw, in the spurts of the Glacial epoch which lasted off and on for nearly a million years, after gaining the first foothold to Gleniff in what may be a long narrow underground fissure penetrating to Glencar, at the present barytes mines.

THE ROCK FORMATION

Sligo Field Club has had the privilege of excursions led by Mr. F. M. Synge, including the introduction of the work of D.H. Oswald on "The Carboniferous Rocks between Ox Mountains and Donegal Bay". The amateur can grasp the horizontal layers of Benbulbin as topped by about 900 feet of Limestone constituting the picturesque prow and which rests on the triple base composed of Sandstone sandwiched between two beds of Shale:- layers of compressed black mud, variously enlivened in composition.

To round off the picture there is another great layer of Limestone buried underneath, so that there is a humble layer of Sandstone sandwiched between two beds of Shale, the three uniting to divide the magnificence of the two Limestone kingdoms.

ICE INTERVENES TO FERTILIZE IRELAND

The Limestone which is the priceless source of the loams, clays and tills of Ireland, was laid down more than 200 million years ago and still floors about half the country, but the loam was eventually fructified by the great glaciers which repeatedly arrived, expanded, dwindled and spread again in the course of the last million years until the residual congealed masses, buried in their clays, melted about 7,000 years ago. The glaciers not only spread the fertile clays over quartzites and schists, but cladded Limestone surfaces which otherwise might have remained as rugged as the present Burren of County Clare.

The Glaciation of the coastal plain of North Sligo and the Erne remained a puzzle till the joint research of Professor H.A.K. Charlesworth and Professor J.K. Charlesworth was published in the *Irish Naturalists Journal* of October 1955. The amateur is pleased to learn of the first glaciation emerging from inland through our two Glens, thus confirming his tentative picture of the glaciers grinding away the opposing precipice on the County Leitrim approach to Sliabh Cairbre while they accentuated the western precipices over which they finally dropped, or along which they rubbed.

On the other hand, the casual rambler had failed to interpret any pattern in the sweeping curves of the surface of the plain of Cairbre which are now shown as created by a Glacier-front lying across the strand and moving from the Erne to Drumcliff River, the main line of forward pressure. The results crown the monumental series of Charlesworth research continuing steadily since 1924.

THE SUMMIT OF TRUSKMORE

The new road from Gleniff provides wheeled access to the plateau heretofore accessible only by a laborious climb. From Glencar or Gleniff one reached the general level with its pleasant limestone surface and mountain herbage, but the summit was still distant. To visit Truskmore one day in late August the route chosen was from Glenade valley, whence a track winds upwards from Cloontyprughlish heretofore providing the shortest route to the summit, which showed the sombre surface to be expected from the Shale and Sandstone capping. The only growth casually observed was what appeared to be a "Bent" growing as isolated rods spaced about a yard apart: it may be the flatteringly-titled "Deer-Grass" mentioned by Scottish naturalists for the top level of plant-life in Britain.

THE VIEW

But who would waste time on the sombre ground once he glanced the uplands visible all round this commanding elevation? - the hills to the east stretching across the Counties of Leitrim, Fermanagh, Monaghan and unto Tyrone, with a still higher summit showing in the county of Cavan. And what matter the platform underfoot when one realizes that Limestone is the prevailing rock in view? - the life-giver besides which the Philosophers Stone is dross. The limestone does not preponderate in the view westward but there is compensation in the inspiring scenery of the long ride of the Sliabh Gamh (Ox mountains) leading the eye to the Mayo Coast and in favourable weather to the great bulk of Nephin, while only a very rare blink of clear atmosphere discloses the cone of Croagh Patrick.

THE GOLD OF BEANNA-BÓ

When John O'Donovan visited Leitrim in 1836, the tradition of gold in Benbo was still strong.

"Is saidhbhre Beanno-bó
ná Eire fa dó"

that is, more feebly,

"There is twice the gold within Benbo
than the treasuries of Ireland can put on show."

Benbo is the eastern salient of Sliabh Gamh, the County Sligo outcrop of the Scandinavian Chain, the back-bone of N.W. Europe.

Early generations must have picked up an occasional nugget on this range, though in our day the best a schoolboy can expect is a lump of mica, the substance which was commercially mined at Moidart from the Scottish outcrop of the Scandinavian Chain during the last Great War, when African supplies ran short.

PART 2
THE HABITATION PLAINS AROUND TRUSKMORE

RATHS, CASHELS AND SOUTERRAINS.

The fifty odd square miles of plain between Sliabh Cairbre and the ocean is nearly all light healthy loam, but "It's no onion bed". In Dartrai which lies North of the mountain the glacial soils are more raw, especially ridges of "ioscar" near the mountain and continuing westward. Glenade and Glencar are no better than the rest of County Leitrim, the area historically known as "Garbh-thrian Connacht" (The Rough Third of Connacht). The plantations are being gradually restored to the side-slopes: one wonders whether windborne Birch seeds will take root in some of the sheltered nooks above the 500feet contour which bear titles attesting to the little groves stripped by the smallholders of the Famine days, and by overstocking with sheep. The youth of Glenade and Glencar still delight in the sporting hazard of gaining access to a perpendicular scarp to rescue a sheep helpless on a narrow shelf: "It's for who'll be the first man to face the rock".

LIOS TRANSFORMED TO CAISEAL

An outstanding feature of the plains is the number of "early habitation sites", some large enough to enclose an efficient farmstead and its appurtenances. Professor Gerhard Bersu, the German who had availed of the War Period to excavate and study similar habitations on the Isle of Man, came later for a few days' tour of our Sligo habitation-circles. Travelling with him, one revelled in the thrill of his decisive observation of the almost universal adaption of lios to caiseal by substituting stone rampart for earthen Rath. One journey with him and the late Richard Kirwan of Sligo started on the road to Tobercurry, the first halt being at Carrowntawy where the Professor immediately identified the typical reconstruction. More obvious were those on the southern slope of the Sliav Gamh from Kilmacteige to Letterbrone where the land is semi-mountainous. It is usually assumed that the key-period of Liss-construction was around the Christian Era when farming developed under the strong Central and Provincial Rule summarized as the "Pax Gaedilica", which lasted until disturbed by the Norse raiders in the period around 800 A.D., so that there then was a phase of general alteration of the Lis to the defensive Cashel, especially on coastal plains such as Cairbre-Connacht.

LISNALURG

Yet one of the finest and pleasantest Lisses in Ireland is to be seen on the Rowlette farm of "Lisnalurg", about four miles North of Sligo town, to the west side of the Bundoran road. Close to the modern farmhouse is a widely spaced grassy double Rath. The hollow between these twin Raths has its own well and pump, and presumably served for dry-stock; whereas the great inner circle shows traces of the rectangular structures which presumably served as dwellings and grain-stores. The whole complex occupies several acres and could have served a farm of about 500 acres or more. One is surprised at the lack of defensive stonework for a centre so important, but part of the inner Rath does show stone revetting externally, whether or not this was continuous. The possibility that such rampart existed appears likely from the fine stone walls fencing the adjoining fields, for which the stones of demolished fortifications would have been so handy. In fact a system of stone-fenced modern fields is often a clue to the existence of historic monuments completed demolished. On the other hand, the term Lis in Lissnalurg either denies, or is not contemporaneous with the stone fortification, and such development would have been an enormous task in case of a Lis so large.

CAISLEAN BÁN

Still travelling towards Bundoran and halting only at "Habitation Sites", one passes Drumcliffe Bridge. Three good miles ahead is the cross-roads of "Cashelgarn":- Caislean g-Carn: the Cashel among the Carns of Artificial Heaps of Stones. The dominant feature is the circular stronghold of CAISLEAN-BÁN topping the rocky knoll which fortuitously marks the sharp change of gradient between Benbulbin in its rear and the grassy water-shed which bisects the plain:- from the slender scarp such as inspired Greek sculptors, to the gentleness of the vegetation. Turning into the bye-road, the short walk to Cashel-bawn is up a slope to the vestigial outer earthen ring and the half-filled fosse fronting the stonewalling of the inner fortification, which is still majestic even in its reduced height. In the fosse there is an inviting "Sallyport" leading inwards under the rampart. The Sallyport can be entered for a rewarding glance of the walling and, though lightly blocked further on to exclude sheep, it ascends to the complex of passages which is just below the floor of the Cashel and is clearly traceable.

The main entrance to the Cashel is merely a gap in the rampart having surely been denuded of its specially prepared stone jambs.

THE REFUGE FOR NON-COMBATANTS

Most intriguing of all is the fine souterrain about 200 yards to the south which was obviously a refuge for non-combatants when danger threatened. Incidentally both structures are on lands belonging to the two Haran families whose shop and house are respectively below and on the main road: the shop has been handy for courteous enquiries. The souterrain is as perfect as the day it was excavated possibly a thousand years ago. It entailed the excavation of a pit some 40 feet square and 14 feet deep to take first drainage layer three feet deep, consisting of round stones, which floor the two clean, wholesome chambers with their sidewalls carrying a stone roof formed of "Corbels" topped by a row of stone lintels. Access from the first to the second chamber is at floor level by a long "creep", so small that an intruder's head would be fatally vulnerable. The inner chamber is ventilated by a roofshaft even more inconspicuous externally than the little pit which forms the entrance to the outer chamber. A stranger could pass dozens of times over the grassy roof and fail to distinguish anything structural.

REFUGES REVIVED IN 1921

When the stranger admired the souterrain he was told of many similar ones round about:- "Ask Mr. Feeney in the house beyond the main road: he used to sleep in the cellar on his own land every night when the Black-and-Tans were interning the young men. He'll tell how airy it was and how his sister was able to hand him in an early cup of tea through the ventilator. A couple more lads used it off and on as well". The demand for such refuges revealed so many that it finally appeared that every knoll held a souterrain. The Siggins farm has one in the northeast angle of the main crossroads.

SOUTERRAINS PLEASANTLY ACCESSIBLE TODAY

But for mazes of underground chambers the place is Maherow peninsula - just west of Lissadill Demesne. Here the townland of Cloghboley takes the cake: near the cross-roads west of Maherow Church, the fields are a menace to exasperated tractor-drivers.

Incidentally if you are the parent of small boys and girls bent on visiting a souterrain there are delightfully clean airy, passages under the Lis on Mitchell's farm in Cloghboley about a half-mile south of the crossroads and backing on Lissadill Demesne. Here also there is a long escape passage into which a plough dropped, although fifty yards from the Lis itself. Another passage right beside the main road is the Sallyport from the Lis near Lissadill Church and School.

THE RAT WAS THE WORST INVADER

What a picture develops of the strategy of the local residents to whom the escaping Spanish seamen of the Armada appeared as so many pirates such as those of the shipping against which they and their ancestors had developed these hide-outs both for defence and retaliation! Evidence is still wanting as to the arrival of the other pirate: the Rat, which has no Gaelic name but is called "Francisco" indicating his modern arrival from the Continent. This pest probably introduced the Black Death of 1350 into England; but is not found on Tory or Inishmurray Islands, otherwise the inhabitants could have been exterminated as were the people of a Scottish island in a Winter about 1780, when rats from a wreck ate the Island's store of oatmeal which had been packed in goat-skins and stored in underground stone chambers. When the first ship from the outer world arrived in Spring every one of the inhabitants had consequently died of starvation. And all the rats had also died of starvation after their phase of gorging. For Irishmen who as boys had to set lines of rat-traps every night, the possible loss of the Georgian facades is compensated by the rat and mouse-proof quality of Cement-Concrete. But why not have Concrete walling combined with the dignity and comfort of sash-windows.[4]

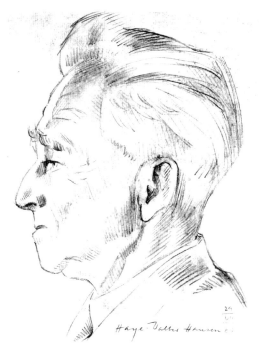

Patrick Tohall

PART 3
THE MAN-KILLING DOBHAR-CHÚ OF GLENADE

THE TOMB-STONE IN CONWALL CEMETERY

In the ancient cemetery of Conwall (Congbháil) near the northern end of Glenade is the recumbent tombstone of Grainne O'Connley wife of Traelach MacLoghlin as already recorded in the *Journal of the Royal Society of Antiquaries of Ireland* for December 1948. The text can still be fairly deciphered as "Here lyeth the body of Grace Connly wife to Ter. MacLoghlin who dyd September 24th Anno Domini MDCCXX11" - that is Year 1722". Although documented here as "Grace", she is still traditionally spoken of as "Grainne". The English text must have been the effort of one of the contemporary Catholic clergy of the district, everyone of whom was officially classified linguistically as "gaedilice et latine loquitur" with no mention of "anglice". Above the text is a panel 17.5 by 7 inches, showing in low relief a four legged animal pierced by a barbed spear or spit gripped in a human fist, the weapon entering the upturned throat and reappearing below the ribs. The head and neck are those of an otter but the strong body, limbs and tail have the coarser members and more decided joints of a canine. One might surmise that the sculptor, working from descriptions, showed the fore-parts of an otter and then, balking at the attempt of picturing a hybrid, he endowed the creature with outright canine body, legs and tail, all emphasising strength.

The people around Glenade Lough such as James Roonian of Sracleighreen (born about 1870) are clear and objective in their description of the events of 24th of September 1722: of the morning when Traelach McLoghlin and his wife Grainne O'Connley parted from their house in Creevelea townland on the northwest corner of Glenade Lough - he to his routine farming and she to wash her soiled clothes on the lakeshore. When Traelach returned he found the house empty, and with mounting anxiety made for the shore, where he was shocked to see the gory corpse of his wife, with the revolting spectacle of a great otter lying asleep on her chest. Traelach, who must have been possessed of exceptional coolness crowned by the skill of a hunter, slid back home for his fish-spear, and arriving silently he plunged the weapon right through the breast of the sleeping Do'ar-chu.

A whistle emitted by the dying animal was answered by another whistle from the island on the Loch, from which a second Do'ar-chu appeared swimming to succor his mate. The lakesiders complete the tale by relating how the animal attacked Traelach, who dispatched this

Fig. 1

DIAGRAM OF SCULPTURE (Patrick Tohall)

Fig. 2

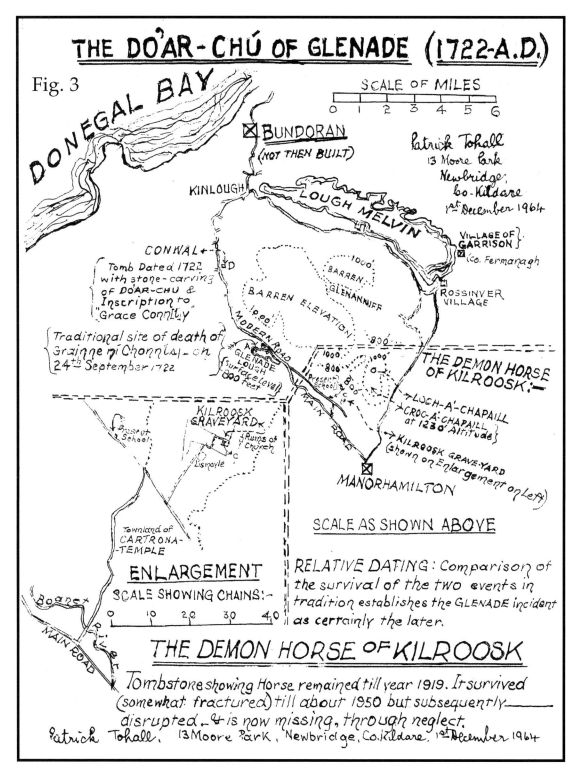

second attacker, with the help of his brother. On this highlight ends the tale as told by the descendants of the group concerned, with their feeling for the darling young woman of their own race, and of how manfully her death was avenged by the husband, as far as could be done. The sadness for the beloved one remained, and still survives in the minds of mourners at the funeral of a young woman.[5]

A PREVIOUS KILLING IN GLENADE

Paradoxically it was the general population of north Leitrim who made a public sensation of the case, in progressive ripples of terror which spread further and further abroad. There had been a similar slaughter of another woman on the same lake, killed when washing "a roll of newly-woven cloth at the boundary between Sracheighreen and Gubinea". A tombstone had been erected over her grave in Killroosk Cemetery, but it had been split in two, and the pieces were lost. People who saw this particular monument hold that the animal shown as headpiece "looked like a horse".

THE DEMON HORSE AND "THE LOUGH NESS MONSTER"

There is the frequent tradition of a lone human whose dead body is found on the edge of a mountain lake, so mangled that it is assumed to be the work of a Demon-Horse. Thus "Loch-a'chapaill" is the name given to several local mountain lakes. But for the arrival and decisiveness of Traelach Mac Loghlinn, the death of Grainne his wife would have been another puzzle and a continuance of the series of demon-killers with all the delightful befuddlement akin to the tales of the "Lough Ness Monster", which is now decided as a mass of gasified weeds, described by Dr. Maurice Burton in *The Elusive Monster* (Harte-Davis 1962)

Naturalists find that otters have a wide range in size, from about 25 to over 40 lbs. in weight, the colour usually being darker in the larger specimens. The term Dobhar-chu (Water hound) appears to have been standard for otters in both Irish and Scots Gaelic until modern times.

Seán Ó hEochaidh, the Tír-Conaill corespondent of Beal-oideas Eireann (Folklore), finds that the everyday otter of the streams is now known in the Gaeltacht as "Mada-Uisge" (Waterdog), the term "Dobhar-chú" being reserved for the fabled animals of Folk-lore; but there is also the tradition that the Dobhar-chu is the "seventh cub of the Mada-uisge".

But for sensational tales of the "Do'ar-chu of Glenade", the summit of imagination is the pursuit along the ancient narrow road skirting Sliabh Cairbre northward from Glenade Lough and then West round the Dartrai facade until it turns southwest at Gleniff into the plain of Carbrai, and finally reaches its climax close to Cashelgarn. The two McLoghlin brothers are described as galloping along on horseback with the avenger Do'ar-chu in pursuit: they pass below the three towering rock-pillars, Tiompán Mor, Tiompán Lár and Tiompán Rua, before emerging at Trosc-corrach on the plain of Dartai where the plateau slopes down precipitous but grassy above the gallopers; on past the entrance to Gleniff and turning southwest below the scarp of Benweeskin till they reach Cashelgarn where the "Seanchai" allows them to make their stand against the Do'ar-chu. According to some versions the animal now turns out to be armed with a frontal horn, like that of the unicorn, with which he pierces one horse and himself follows through the aperture, but just as he emerges one of the two men stabs him mortally. All this entails a journey of about sixteen miles, so little wonder that the monumental sculptor endows the Do'a-Chu with a Hound's legs! - instead of the swimmer's short lithe limbs and webbed paws.

THE SCENERY

The holiday-maker of our day can motor pleasantly over the same route for one of the most stirring of journeys, and enjoy it all the more on modern roads, with short detours to the rock-pinnacles and the Cúm of Gleniff, finishing with the expansive view of the panorama of grassy plain, sandy beach, white foam and blue sea, which stretch away in glory below the dominating height of Caiseal Bán.

1. Died 25 June, 1973, aged 86.
2. The articles are published here with the permission of his daughter, Elis Ó Muire, 29, Moore Park, Newbridge, Co. Kildare, in whose posession the original text is. The articles are published without comment as a tribute to Tohall's dedication in the early years of Sligo Antiquarian Society and Sligo Field Club. Only alterations in presentation have been made.
3. In his letter to Telefís Éireann he pointed out that Connemara Gaelic was his household vernacular.
4. This last line is crossed out in the typescript.
5. Tohall published the "Dobhar-Chu" story in *J. Roy. Soc. Antiq. Ireland*, 78 (1948), 127-129, under the title "The Dobhar-Chu Tombstones of Glenade, Co. Leitrim (Cemeteries of Congbhaill and Cill-Ruisc)". The essentials of this story were published by Miss L. A. Walkington under the somewhat misleading title "A Bundoran Legend" in the Miscelenea in *J. Roy. Soc. Antiq. Ireland*, 26 (1896), 84. Patrick Tohall does not refer to this in his 1948 or his 1962 articles.

Clasaí Mór, Inishmurray, Co. Sligo.

Knocklane, Co. Sligo

BENBULBIN - GEOLOGY AND SCENERY

*Richard Thorn,
Director Institute of Technology, Sligo.*

Although I have spent twenty years living and working in and around Sligo and, for a number of years before that, brought students from Dublin to Sligo and Donegal on geological and geomorphological field excursions, the sight of Benbulbin as you drive from Sligo out through Grange and Cliffoney - like the bowsprit of some leviathan facing into the Atlantic - still manages to inspire wonder.

Although it may appear as if Benbulbin is geologically distinct from the area surrounding it this is not so and any understanding of the why? and the when? of Benbulbin must draw on an understanding of the wider area.

The geology of north Sligo is dominated by two types of materials; the rocks and sediments of the Carboniferous and Quaternary Periods respectively.

The Carboniferous Period in Ireland began about 360 million years ago and lasted until about 290 million years ago. The main feature of this time was the movement northwards of a tropical ocean and the deposition on the underlying rocks of a range of materials; sands near the edge of the ocean and limestones and shales in deeper water. The movement (or transgression) northwards is clearly marked in the rocks of Benbulbin and the surrounding areas; Figure 1 is a geological map showing the different groups of rocks in the area.

The Basal Sandstones are near-shore deposits which were laid down as the waters of the transgressing ocean lapped the land and these are overlain sequentially by the Ballyshannon Limestone and the Bundoran Shale which both indicate a deepening of the water. The Mullaghmore Sandstone consists of siltstones, sandstones and shales, arranged in such a manner as to indicate that they were deposited in a delta by a river flowing in from the land to the north. On top of the Mullaghmore Sandstone are the Benbulbin Shales and the Glencar and Dartry Limestones respectively, all of which indicate a return to deeper water conditions. The Glencar limestone is best known for its 'cabbage stalk'
fossils (Siphonophyllia caninia) which are best seen on the foreshore at Streedagh. The Dartry Limestone is host to a metre wide vein of barytes which has been worked intermittently for many years. The barytes (barium sulphate) is creamy white in colour and is very dense. In the past it was used mainly in plasters and paints but more recently it has found use in the drilling industry as a 'drilling mud' that is used to cool drilling bits and carry rock chippings to the ground surface. The final two groups of rocks are the Meenymore Formation and the Glenade Sandstone which indicate a final shallowing of the ocean and are the youngest Carboniferous rocks in the area. These rocks are best seen around Truskmore and consist of evaporitic deposits and laminated rocks both of which indicate deposition in a very shallow, tropical marine environment.

As Figure 1 shows the Carboniferous rocks are traversed by a series of faults which were formed during a period of mountain building between 290 and 270 million years ago.

The other group of deposits seen in the area were laid down by glaciers and melting ice sheets during the Quaternary Period. Figure 2 shows that ice moved out from the Lough Erne area and moved southwestwards down Donegal Bay. Ice also moved from the midlands through the Glenade and Glencar valleys and from corries within the Benbulbin plateau. During retreat and melting of the ice masses a range of landforms were created including kames (hills of sand and gravel), glacial striae (scratches on rocks caused by the passage of rock-filled ice over them) and 'crag and tails' (streamlined mounds orientated in the direction the ice moved and shaped by the ice). The locations of some of these features are seen in Figure 2.

Although the foregoing comments deal with the nature of Benbulbin they do not answer the question why it is like it is?

Although the Benbulbin plateau is bounded by steep sided valleys a cursory examination of a topographic map of the north

A CELEBRATION OF SLIGO

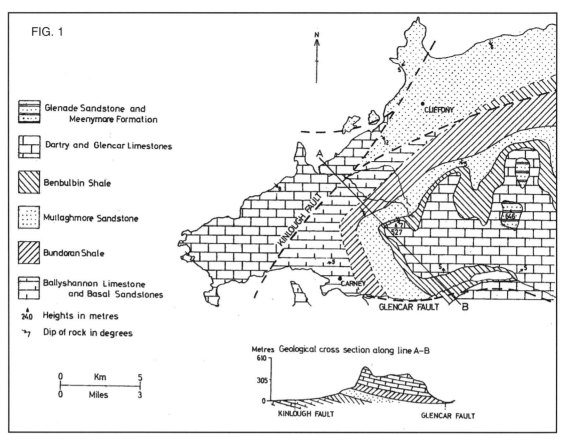

Fig. 1 - Geology map and cross section of the Benbulbin area. (After Thorn 1984)

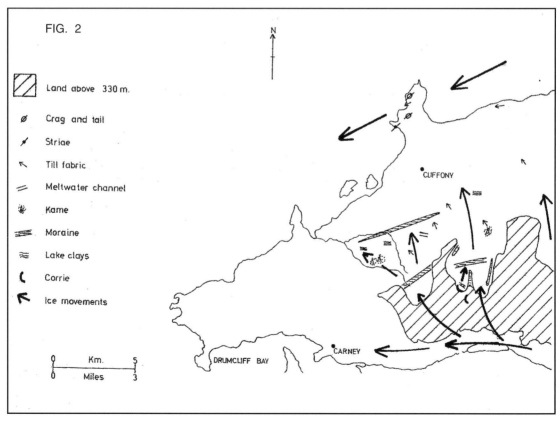

Fig. 2 - Sketch map showing the direction of ice movements in the Benbulbin area and the associated features. (After Thorn, 1984)

Sligo - north Leitrim area shows that the plateau is just one of a series which were originally contiguous. The means whereby the plateau was dissected, so forming Benbulbin, is far from clear but two hypotheses are offered.

One of the curious aspects of Ireland's geological heritage is that with the exception of the north-east of the country there are almost no rocks that straddle the gap between the Carboniferous and the Quaternary Periods; so there is a hiatus in the geological record of approximately 290 million years. The evidence that is available suggests that during this gap there was indeed a thick cover of rocks but which was subsequently removed by large scale erosion during the Tertiary Period (63 to 2 million years ago).

The presence and subsequent removal of these rocks is the basis for the first hypothesis as to the formation of Benbulbin. There is evidence that the present rivers on the Slieve League peninsula may have evolved as a result of superimposition from a southerly dipping surface (the missing rocks referred to above) onto the underlying rocks (Carboniferous and older) following prolonged Tertiary erosion (Dury 1964). One might, for the Benbulbin area, similarly imagine southwards flowing rivers and their tributaries being superimposed on the underlying rocks. The rivers and their tributaries would undoubtedly exploit existing lines of weakness, e.g. faults, and so a valley like Glencar could have been initiated as a tributary of a southerly flowing river developing along the line of a fault (see Figure 1).

An alternative hypothesis has been proposed by Davies and Stephens (1978) who argue that because the very old rocks around the rim of Ireland stand proud of the land surface, while in the midlands the same rocks lie buried, uplift of the rim of the island must have occurred. Davies and Stephens suggest that the uplift took place during the Tertiary and maintain that rivers flowing from the midlands were gradually incised into the uplifting rocks of the rim of the island. Thus, in the case of the north Sligo - north Leitrim area the inception of the Glenade and Glencar valleys would have resulted; fault-control of the rivers would, as with the first hypothesis, be likely.

Whatever mechanism caused the initial dissection of the plateau its completion was almost certainly due to erosion by ice movement following pre-glacial channels during the Quaternary. Thus, it would appear, was Benbulbin formed.

References
Davies, G.L. Herries, and Stephens, N. 1978: *The Geomorphology of the British Isles - Ireland*, Methuen and Co., London.
Dury, G.H. 1964: "Aspects of the geomorphology of the Slieve League Peninsula, Donegal". *Proceedings of the Geological Association*, 75, 445-459.
Thorn, R.H. 1984: "Aspects of the geology and geomorphology of the north Sligo/north Leitrim border". *Geographical Viewpoint*, 13, 46-53.

Benbulben, Co. Sligo.
Sketch by George Petrie about 1836. R.I.A. MS.23L44 f.32.
Copyright Royal Irish Academy

A CELEBRATION *OF* SLIGO

Benbulben, Co. Sligo

Benbulben, Co. Sligo

THE NATURAL HISTORY OF THE BRICKLIEVES, CO. SLIGO

Don C.F. Cotton,
Institute of Technology, Sligo.

ABSTRACT: The small and well-defined uplands of the Bricklieve Mountains and Kesh Corann have geological, geomorphological, botanical, zoological and archaeological features of considerable interest and heritage value. They are designated as both a Natural Heritage Area and as a Special Area of Conservation because of their wildlife value, but such listings mean little to most people unless information about what they contain is made more widely available. This article briefly describes aspects of the geology, botany and zoology that can be seen by a visitor to the Bricklieves and makes reference to publications where more detailed information may be obtained. An appendix lists 400 species of organisms authentically recorded from this area.

INTRODUCTION

The Bricklieves are a very distinctive group of hills lying close to the southern boundary of County Sligo. They are often referred to as the Bricklieve 'Mountains' although in fact they only cover an area of about 25 square kilometres and include just two major hills, namely Carrowkeel (321m) and Kesh Corann [*alias* Kesh and Keishcorran] (359m). The nearest town is Ballymote lying to the north-west, but access is most commonly gained from the north-east by leaving the main Dublin-Sligo road at the village of Castlebaldwin from where the route to the megalithic cemetery is clearly signposted and this brings one right to the heart of the Carrowkeel area.

This is an extraordinarily interesting place from several points of view. The scenery in this small area is very special, offering many views and prospects with a landscape of limestone cliffs and rocky outcrops, steep grassy or lightly wooded scree slopes, flat heathery hill tops and some rock pavements. The views from the summits are also very beautiful giving panoramas across Lough Arrow and distant vistas of the Ox Mountains and of Ben Bulben in the Dartry range. It is not surprising that this area is included in the 'Inventory of Outstanding Landscapes' (An Foras Forbartha 1977) and is identified in the County Development Plan as a "Sensitive Rural Landscape" with "Visually Vulnerable" areas (Sligo County Council 1999). The scientific value of this area has also been recognised in various reports as it was originally listed as an Area of Scientific Interest (ASI) for botanical and ecological reasons (Watts 1969; An Foras Forbartha 1972; 1978; 1981) and has more recently been designated as a Natural Heritage Area (NHA) under the Wildlife (Amendment) Act 2000 and most importantly as a Special Area of Conservation (SAC) under the EU Habitats Directive (92/43/EEC). The archaeological importance of the Bricklieves is generally better known than the natural history, with the megalithic cemetery (Macalister *et al.* 1912; Bergh 1995, 46-54) and the Caves of Kesh being sites of a national importance (Scharff *et al.* 1903; An Foras Forbartha 1974; Archaeological Survey of Ireland 1990).

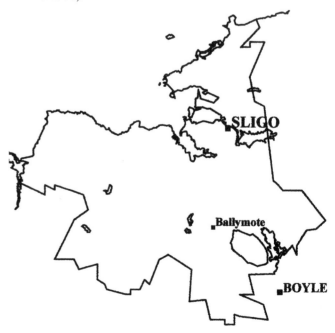

Fig. 1 - County Sligo showing the Bricklieves lying between Ballymote and Boyle

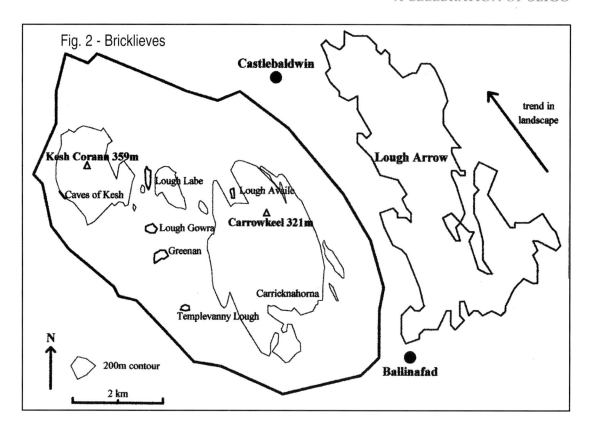

Fig. 2 - Bricklieves

GEOLOGY AND GEOMORPHOLOGY

These hills are composed of a hard limestone rock, with a 335m thick sequence of sediments which were deposited during the Lower Carboniferous (Viséan), a little more than 300 million years ago (Dixon 1972). They were laid down in a shallow marine basin that lay between two parallel island ridges running from south-west to north-east, now known to us as the Curlew Mountains and the Ox Mountains. This basin was a small part of a much larger tropical sea with extensive coral reefs. Rocks of the same age and origin were deposited in a similar marine basin to the north of the Ox Mountains and include Knocknarea and Ben Bulben which form the Dartry Mountains of Sligo and Leitrim and then continue eastwards into the Marble Arch area of Fermanagh. The limestone rock we now see is rich in fossil corals, the shells of brachiopods and the stems of crinoids, which occasionally form reefs; and it also contains chert, which is a hard mineral similar to flint.

It is surprising to find that the beds of this sedimentary rock still form a nearly horizontal plateau in the Bricklieves even though they have been subjected to a long geological history. However a great deal of chemical weathering did occur during the period between 100 and 60 million years ago resulting in the opening up of rifts, solution depressions, sinkholes and even small caves, creating a karst topography. The chemical weathering process ceased but was replaced by physical weathering processes during the last two million years when the ice ages left their mark. Towards the end of the last ice advance, ice sheets and glaciers, spreading from the Irish Midlands, further eroded the rock and enhanced the south-east to north-west trend of the rifts, giving Carrowkeel its very distinctive series of cliffed ridges and valleys that make the landscape so very attractive. Looking eastwards from the plateau of Carrowkeel, one can see the same trend in the landscape continued right across Lough Arrow, where the lake's islands are glacial deposits called drumlins, and on to the hills of Highwood on the eastern side of the lake which are a miniature manifestation of the Bricklieves scenery. The higher areas were thus stripped of rocks and laid bare, and are consequently poor for agriculture, whilst the low-lying areas received deposits of glacial till, and have a soil suitable for intensively managed grassland. The karst topography of the Bricklieves is thus the combined result of deep chemical weathering processes opening up rifts and caves below the ground, and physical glacio-karstic processes leaving a limestone pavement on the flat summits after the surface had been stripped by glaciers.

The weathering processes continue today but at a slower rate as water sinks through the surface rock to flow underground leaving dry valleys and sink holes on the surface. The rate of weathering on Kesh Corann has been estimated at 30mm per thousand years (Corbel 1957 quoted in Williams 1970). Karst limestone landscapes are generally very beautiful and hold a lot of interest for geologists and cavers. This means that a good deal tends to be written about karst limestone districts, and the great Sligo-Fermanagh caving area, as described by

Fig. 3 - Valley at east side of Carrowkeel, Co. Sligo.
Photo: Don C.F. Cotton.

Chapman (1993), includes the Bricklieves. Unfortunately, the Bricklieves have been somewhat neglected in this publication because they do not appear to contain any active cave systems and only exhibit dry caves that date far back to the pre-glacial period of deep chemical weathering. Cruise (1878), Coleman (1955; 1965) and Knibbs (1967) all made some reference to the most obvious old dry caves in these hills; namely the Caves of Kesh, two small caves called School Cave and Pollnagaddy situated on the east side of Kesh Corann and the large sink hole of Pollnagollum on Carrowkeel. There is also mention that there are numerous other sink holes in the peat-covered summits. A much more thorough investigation of this karst area was carried out by Thorn, Drew and Coxon (1990) who summarised most of the available information, identified some additional caves, and also carried out some water-tracing experiments in small active systems involving sinks and springs (Coxon & Thorn 1989).

EARLIEST INHABITANTS

As the last glaciers of the ice age retreated, from about 12,000 years ago, the shallow Caves of Kesh on the west side of Kesh Corann were occupied by wild animals. As previously indicated, these caves have little significance from a geomorphological or speleological point of view, and indeed, throughout the 19th century they were regarded as a place for an excursion for their curiosity and scenic value (*e.g.*, Anon 1840, 9-10; Hardman 1892). However, all this changed from around 1895 when the great cave explorer, Edouard Martel, visited Fermanagh and Mitchelstown, Co. Cork, and stimulated a new interest in serious cave research. The Mitchelstown Caves were excavated and revealed late ice-age animal remains and the search was then on for other suitable locations. A list of Irish caves was compiled and in a supplement the Caves of Kesh were added with the observation that a bear skull (scientific names of all species mentioned in text supplied in Appendix) had been recovered from deposits in 1887 (Scharff 1895; Praeger 1896). An expedition was mounted in 1901 with a preliminary survey by Drs. Scharff and Praeger in April, followed by serious excavation work from late May, through June and July (Anon 1901a; Anon 1901b). The announcement that bones of the Arctic lemming had been found for the first time in Ireland was of very great interest (Ussher 1902; Anon 1903a; Anon 1903b; Ussher 1906), and eventually the full results were published in a detailed report (Scharff *et al.* 1903).

The excavations found signs of human habitation along with the bones of ox, goat, pig, horse and marine shells in the superficial layer which was considered to have formed long after the ice-age. Below this was a distinctive layer without any human influence believed to date from late-glacial or immediately post-glacial times and containing many bones of bears, and also some Arctic lemming remains as well as red deer, wolf, hare and pig bones. Lists of other animals including snails, fish (trout), frog and many birds are also included in the report, but again, most of these remains were from the more recent surface layers. However, the bones of little auk, common scoter and smew, which are uncommon or rare in Sligo today, came from older deeper layers associated with lemming bones, and probably represent a late glacial bird fauna.

In the report of the 1901 excavations it was not possible to put dates on the finds, apart from to say that the animals must have lived in Ireland since the ice-age and in some cases were now long extinct. A further dig was carried out in 1929 which did little to advance the knowledge of the first exploration (see Gwynn, Riley & Stelfox 1940; Coleman 1947), but in more recent times new information has become available about the ages of some of the bones due to the development of the "Accelerator Mass Spectrometry Carbon-14" (AMS C14) dating method. Four samples of bone from the 1901 dig gave results (Woodman & Monaghan 1993) that confirm a late glacial date for the lower layers :-

Brown bear	11,920	±	85 BP
Red deer	11,790	±	120 BP
Wolf	11,150	±	90 BP

and a relatively recent origin for the surface layers :-

Horse	1,580	±	55 BP

These caves have thus been important in providing a rare glimpse into the late glacial fauna of Ireland (Stuart & Wijngaarden-Bakker 1985) and have shown that since 12,000 years ago, mammals (including brown bears, wolves, arctic lemmings and reindeer) that were once native in the Bricklieves, are now completely extinct in Ireland.

Since the ice ages different peoples have come and gone, they have hunted, farmed and altered their environment in different ways. Once again the Bricklieves provide a most important record of some of the earlier inhabitants because the passage tombs and hut circles which are found spread widely over the dissected plateau, are a superbly preserved record of stone age and bronze age activity of this area dating from approximately 6,000-3,500 years ago. There is much yet to be learnt from these remains but a start was made upon their exploration in 1911 (Macalister, Armstrong & Praeger 1912), although modern archaeologists are horrified at some of the methods adopted during that dig! The history of the people who lived and worked in the Bricklieves is a story for the archaeologists and historians to tell, but their influence can not be ignored by naturalists because they have largely determined land use, and thus what is left for nature to adapt and shape within the constraints of farming practices.

FLORA AND FAUNA

PREVIOUS STUDIES

The flora and fauna of the Bricklieves that we see today is yet another treasure of this important area. Over the years these hills were visited by naturalists such as Foot (1871), Colgan (1902) and the famous R.Ll. Praeger who made botanical records in 1896, and was involved in cave and archaeological excavations in 1901 and 1911. The naturalist Robert Welch took photographs of the flora at Kesh Corann in 1901 (Hackney *et al.* 1983). In the late 1940s the botanist D.A. Webb made a special study of Carrowkeel (Webb 1945; 1947a; 1951; 1952) and Roger Goodwillie visited and prepared a short report on the area in the early 1970s (An Foras Forbartha 1972 which was very slightly modified in 1978). Webb (1947a) enumerated about 240 species of ferns and flowers on Carrowkeel and commented that;

"Such a number of species for an area some 890 hectares is by Irish standards very high, if it is remembered that most of the area is over 150 meters above sea level, that it contains virtually no streams and rivers and only one small lake, and that the survey was restricted so as to exclude artificial habitats such as ploughed fields, roads and walls".

Most recently, I led a Botanical Society outing to Carrowkeel in 2001 and the flora greatly impressed the participants (Cotton 2002). A database of all plants and animals authentically recorded from this range of hills is held by the author, and a list of 400 species derived from this database is presented in an appendix.

It was in recognition of their botanical richness as described by Webb, that the Bricklieves were designated as an Area of Scientific Interest (ASI) of National Importance in 1972; a designation that has since been superseded by them being declared a Natural Heritage Area (NHA) for their ecological interest and added to the list of Special Areas of Conservation (SAC) under the Habitats Directive of the European Union (Heritage Service 1997).

THE CURRENT SITUATION

It is a sad fact that in recent times the rate of change in the environment has greatly accelerated, usually to the detriment of wildlife. Consequently places formerly recognised as being ecologically interesting have been partly or wholly destroyed without the knowledge of

Fig. 4 - Doonaveeragh viewed from Carrowkeel, Co. Sligo.
Photo: Don C.F. Cotton.

wildlife experts. Against this background, new survey work has been undertaken in the Bricklieves in recent years (*e.g.,* Goodwillie *et al.,* 1992, Cotton 2002), and the following account is an integration of new and old observations.

It is good to report that most species formerly recorded from the area are still present at the beginning of the 21st century, and that recent fieldwork has discovered the presence of some uncommon and rare species not previously noted. It has also been apparent that descriptions made over 50 years ago in the detailed paper of Webb (1947a) are still valid, which is a very welcome observation. It can be concluded that the diversity of habitats and species we see today in the Bricklieves are easily good enough to rate the area as being of international ecological interest.

SOME GENERAL COMMENTS

Almost all natural history study in the Bricklieves has been concerned with the recording of plant species and their distributions. Some new information is included in the following account concerning snails, moths, butterflies, birds and a few other invertebrate groups, but this is very selective and really does not do justice to the animal kingdom. It should be pointed out that this situation is typical of the national position for our knowledge of animal groups.

An understanding of the major environmental influences on the flora of the Bricklieves must begin with the limestone, which has so little glacial drift that it frequently outcrops, and is rarely far below the ground surface. Plants that like lime-rich soils are termed calcicole, and one would expect that many such species should be present in a limestone district. However, whilst there are some calcicole species growing here, the resistant nature of this old limestone to weathering, and the strong influence of rainfall in leaching calcium down and away from the plant roots, has often resulted in lime-hating (calcifuge) plants living in a thin acid soil just a few centimetres above pure limestone rock.

The high rainfall, large number of rain days, high humidity and the mild nature of the climate have also come together to have a major influence on the flora. Many species that might otherwise seek the damp protective shelter of woodland are found growing out in the open. The ferns are particularly diverse and twenty-one species have been recorded from this area (see Appendix). Wind is also a major factor in such a high and exposed place in the west of Ireland. Trees are particularly affected, to the extent that vigorous tree growth can be restricted to sheltered eastern slopes and they may find it impossible to take hold on the plateau areas in situations where wind and light grazing by stock conspire to eliminate them.

Finally the activities of man, in farming the area for much of the last six thousand years, has been one of the most important factors in influencing vegetation. The burning of heather and scrub, and the grazing of cattle must have been practised for hundreds, if not thousands of years (Bergh 1995; Göransson, this volume) and it may be that the Bricklieves have changed very little in that long time span.

The flora and fauna of these hills will now be described, but in order to simplify the environment, it is considered best to divide it into descriptive units. Several major habitats can be readily identified in this beautiful area, which are now listed with notes on some of their principal and special species, where they occur and their conservation value.

WOODLAND AND SCRUB

If the influence of man had never been felt in this region it is believed that the natural 'climax' habitat would be deciduous woodland with a more bushy or scrubby habitat on the exposed hill tops. Today the woodland and scrub is confined to places where grazing by large herbivores has been lessened by difficult cliffy terrain, or prevented by fences. The result is that woodland is mainly localised to narrow strips along the bases of some of the larger cliffs, particularly along the east-facing cliffs that offer shelter from westerly winds which are also a major factor in restricting the growth of trees. The woodland is principally composed of hazel scrub with ash, rusty-willow, hawthorn, blackthorn, rowan, birch and holly as lesser members of the tree community. The ground flora includes wood rush, herb-Robert, wood sorrel, primrose, lesser celandine and many other shade-tolerant species. More interesting and much rarer members of the woodland flora include whitebeam, guelder rose, spindle, midland hawthorn (the only known place for it in Sligo), and goldilocks buttercup. Little has been done to study the fauna of these wooded areas but uncommon butterflies like the silver-washed fritillary and Real's wood white are here, with long-eared owl hunting wood mice and spotted flycatcher flying out from sunny perches along woodland edges.

The woodland here is very similar to that in hills above the northern shore of Lough Gill and in the Highwood area where hazel scrub has developed on a thin limestone soil after the exclusion of cattle and sheep. Webb (1947a) found the woodland flora of Carrowkeel to be more similar to acid oak woodlands described for Britain than that which might be expected of a limestone district and he concluded that the high rainfall of the area was to some extent over-riding the influence of the rock-type.

Grassland

This is almost certainly a man-made habitat of considerable antiquity, that came into being after the original tree and scrub cover was removed and domestic grazing animals were allowed to browse and thus keep the scrub from reinvading. As in The Burren of County Clare, it is likely that after clearance much of the soil would have washed down through cracks in the limestone and the remaining thin soil then supports a diversity of herbs, including some exclusively lime-loving (calcicole) species. In the Bricklieves the herb-rich limestone grassland is mainly found on the steep scree slopes leading up to the plateau but some of the flat tops have a limestone pavement habitat akin to that of The Burren. Grassland species such as bird's-foot trefoil, quaking grass, thyme, eyebright, common spotted orchid, lady's mantle, harebell and bulbous buttercup are often quite common, but there are also less common species like frog orchid, common twayblade and mountain cudweed.

A feature that greatly interests botanists about some Irish grasslands and hedgerows is the fact that some herbs, only found in woodland on the continent, are out in the open in places like the Bricklieves. Primrose, pignut and bluebell are examples of such species, and the explanation for this curious situation lies in the high and frequent rainfall of such regions creating humid conditions, that are only associated with shady woodland elsewhere. Butterflies such as the meadow brown, common blue and small heath are associated with the grassland areas, as is the 'beautiful yellow underwing' moth and a scarce woodlouse that has no common name but is known to scientists as *Haplophthalmus mengei*.

Another interesting fact about the herb-rich grasslands in the Bricklieves and certain other parts of Sligo and Leitrim, is the way in which the limestone grasslands intergrade into moorlands via an intermediate habitat that is sometimes called limestone heath. In most places this intermediate habitat is more common than the limestone grassland and it includes wild flowers such as lady's bedstraw, tormentil, common milkwort, common lousewort, heath spotted orchid and even the rare small white orchid is found at two localities (Cotton, Cawley & Roden 1994; Cotton 2002). This is a red data book species (Curtis & McGough 1988) and is listed in the Flora Protection Order of 1987. The transition from limestone grassland to heath is often quite gradual so that as one ascends a slope, patches of limestone heath are found growing where limestone outcrops near the surface or where there are limestone boulders, and further up the limestone heath merges in to acid heath with heathers, bilberry and hard fern, at first in patches, before it takes over and blankets the ground. In these patchwork situations it is really strange to see lime-loving and lime-hating plants growing side-by-side.

The survival of these herb-rich grasslands is largely due to the unsuitable nature of the terrain for the mechanical application of fertilisers or the possibility of getting in and ploughing and re-seeding the areas. These operations are made difficult due to the many rocky outcrops and the steepness of many slopes, some of which are founded on old scree or lateral moraine deposits.

Moorland and bog

The high rainfall of this region coupled with a mild climate and a reduction in grazing pressure are the ingredients that allow moorland and bog habitats to take over from herb-rich grassland. These are now the dominant habitats of most of the flat ground on top of the plateau and some of the flat valley areas found between the major ridges can often be quite wet and develop from rushy pastures into blanket bog.

The flora of these places is not very diverse and is quite typical of what one can expect over large parts of western Ireland. In the drier places ling (common heather) dominates with some bell heather, bracken and bilberry being obvious. A closer look will reveal smaller herbs such as tormentil, heath milkwort, heath bedstraw and occasionally there is cow-wheat and the lesser twayblade orchid. Wet pastures tend to have clumps of soft rush, and as the peaty soil begins to accumulate then sedges, purple moor-grass and cottongrasses begin to take over. Very wet places may have round-leaved sundew and bog asphodel in their flora.

Birds of these boggy places include the snipe in the very wet spots, but meadow pipit is the most common species and cuckoo is an occasional visitor, being a parasite on the meadow pipit. The common heath moth and Northern eggar moth are also typical of these areas; the latter generally being spotted whizzing across the bog from a long distance!

Small lakes and marshes

These habitats are very restricted due to the porous nature of the limestone rock which means that most water flows underground. The main area for wetlands lies between the hills of Kesh Corann and Carrowkeel where running from north to south, Lough Labe (at 144m) feeds into Lough Gowra (at 112m) and then into a turlough-like area at Greenan (at 105m). A little lower down, and in the same alignment, there is Templevanny Lough (at 84m) which has no obvious inflowing stream and must be primarily fed from ground water flowing south from Greenan.

In karst areas such as this, springs tend to be very lime rich even though the high rainfall can result in the formation of acid bog on the ground surface. Lough Labe is surrounded by blanket bog at its northern end and poor pasture at its southern end so at first sight it might appear to be an acid lake. However this is far from the truth because Webb (1947b) analysed about 250 samples of surface water from around Ireland and astonishingly found that the most alkaline reading he obtained was pH8.75 and this came from Lough Labe which is therefore spring fed. He also commented that the effluent stream from this lake vanishes after about a mile (1600m) in a swamp (Greenan) in which constant precipitation of calcium carbonate is taking place. A biological consequence of this high alkalinity is a thriving population of white-clawed crayfish in Lough Labe which is one of the few species of invertebrate protected under national legislation. The otter which feeds upon crayfish is also present in this lake and this is a red data book species (Whilde 1993) which is likewise protected by law.

The Inland Fisheries Trust surveyed Lough Labe in the 1950s and found it to be over 20m deep in one place. Because they found it had poor fish stocks and was in a catchment with no surface outflow they put in the North American rainbow trout which fished well for about 20 years but although they are reported to have spawned (Whelan 1989) fish populations have once again diminished and the Regional Fisheries Board were considering whether to re-stock the lake. Unfortunately, the steep sides to Lough Labe mean that there is no significant marsh flora and the deep water and lack of vegetation cover result in only occasional wildfowl being seen on the surface.

Lough Gowra is being used as a storage reservoir for a local water scheme and consequently has fluctuating water levels with quite low levels in the summer that expose large areas of marsh and mud around the shore. In the winter this small lake is frequented by about fifty duck including mallard, wigeon, teal and tufted duck. The flora around this lake has a poor diversity and appeared to lack interest until in June 2000 I discovered thousands of plants of fen violet in a band at a particular level all around the lake shore. It would seem that the fluctuating water levels have created a very special habitat for this species and its associated community of plants. The fen violet is a red data book species (Curtis & McGough 1988) with a very local and threatened Irish distribution and this is the first record of it in County Sligo. In Great Britain it is in danger of becoming extinct and stringent conservation measures are being taken at its three known sites (Anon 2001). This is yet another special species that adds to the interest and wildlife importance of the Bricklieves and it makes one wonder what other species might await discovery here.

Greenan is quite a different story because the fenny marsh is floristically very diverse with a patchwork of habitats reflecting the different degrees of flooding and inundation. For example there is a distinctive area of large tussocks typically formed by sedges that are subjected to regular flooding. Here the common sedge and bottle sedge are dominant with some greater tussock sedge, brown sedge, lesser-pond sedge, marsh willowherb and common marsh-bedstraw. An island of drier habitat is sandwiched between this flood-sedge and an open water area which has a small number of willows beneath which there is tufted sedge, but also a clump of the greater spearwort and slender tufted-sedge which are very scarce in Sligo. The more permanent water has a flora that includes mare's-tail, branched bur-reed, thread-leaved water-crowfoot, amphibious bistort, water forget-me-not, water mint and the uncommon lesser marshwort. This site was considered to be worthy of 'Area of Scientific Interest' status by Goodwillie *et al.* (1992) and some records from it were published by Douglas *et al.* (1993). The wintering wildfowl at Greenan are also important with over 150 duck often being present with occasional whooper swans which is a priority species listed in the EU Birds Directive (79/409/EEC).

Templevanny Lake is also of some interest as there is a small population of marsh fritillary butterflies here (a species protected by the EU Habitats Directive), smooth newt is nearby (a red data book species), the marsh flora is diverse and interesting, and small numbers of duck overwinter here.

There used to be a small lake in the heart of

Carrowkeel which is still shown as Lough Availe on the Ordnance Survey map. Webb (1947a) described the flora of this lake in some detail from observations made in 1942-1945, but in 1946 G.F. Mitchell observed that the lake had been drained. Recent visits show that there is no longer a lake here, in that there is no open water, but upon traversing the area it is obvious that there is a thick layer of vegetation floating on a closed lake, a habitat that is often referred to as a 'scraw bog'. The vegetation here is still quite interesting with plants typical of both acid and alkaline conditions occurring in different parts of the quaking marsh. The most interesting species are the Royal fern and broad-leaved cottongrass. The protected marsh fritillary butterfly is present here in association with its food plant, devil's-bit scabious.

Rock outcrops

Limestone cliffs abound in this region and offer ledges as sanctuary from grazing animals such as cattle and sheep. The walls of the sink holes, most notably of Pollnagollum on Carrowkeel, also offer a safe haven for a similar, but more luxuriant, flora. The vegetation of these places is an extension of the limestone grassland community with many species being calcicole.

There are many interesting and quite rare species to be found in these habitats and the list would whet any botanist's appetite; hairy rock-cress, hoary whitlowgrass, mossy saxifrage, black spleenwort, brittle bladder fern, early purple orchid, Welsh poppy, wall rue, maidenhair spleenwort, hard shield fern, water avens, fairy flax and stone bramble. An uncommon fern not seen in recent years is the green spleenwort (noted on Kesh Corann by Foot 1871).

A related habitat is offered by the megalithic cairns, and it is particularly interesting to see the similar-looking species of common whitlowgrass, hairy rock-cress and hoary whitlowgrass growing together, especially as the last two are not at all common with hoary whitlowgrass being a red data book species (Curtis & McGough 1988). Biting stonecrop and shining crane's-bill are also typical of the stone cairns but are uncommon elsewhere.

The fauna of the cliffs also has some specialities of the creepy-crawly variety, although they have never been properly surveyed, namely *Megabunus diadema* - a harvest-spider, *Armadillidium pulchellum* - a woodlouse, and *Acicula fusca* which is a tiny snail. Birds using the cliffs and rock cervices include wheatear, peregrine and raven. Unfortunately the peregrines are considered quarry by some 'sportsmen' and reports indicate that on at least one occasion a bird has been shot to be made into a trophy for a local public bar.

LOOKING TO THE FUTURE

The Bricklieves are a small but important area of great heritage value. They offer a fascinating landscape of cliffs, bogs, herb-rich grasslands and limestone pavement through which a walker may find solitude and great natural beauty. Many surprises and delights await discovery with geological features, archaeological monuments and a diversity of wild flowers and animals that together give a unique blend of interest for the natural history

Fig. 5 - Valley at Carrowkeel, Co. Sligo. Photo: Noel Murphy

student and the rapidly increasing numbers of environmentally aware local people and tourists.

The area has been modified by thousands of years of human history and yet remains largely unspoilt. However, the next hundred years might prove to be the most traumatic in its long history because rapid changes in land use, driven by environmentally blind economic forces, are happening all over Ireland. Sheep grazing has already proven to be a problem on Kesh Corran with changes in the floral composition of the grasslands over vast areas being obvious on close inspection. No longer are the herb-rich pastures clothing the hillsides or the heathery tops so prevalent as they were just 10 years earlier. Another threat could be from grant-aided forestry, that can be planted over large tracts of land in a few weeks, and although the effects are not immediately apparent, the existing flora is doomed from that moment onwards.

Introduced species of flora and fauna can also cause severe problems. The mountains of Sligo have been invaded by the New Zealand willowherb over the last twenty years and recently this species has been noted in the Bricklieves. Who knows how it will compete with native plants, especially on the limestone cliffs and ledges? Similarly, small leaved *Cotoneaster* is present in an area of limestone pavement in the Bricklieves and may well become rampant as it has invaded other areas of limestone heath in Sligo.

Uncontrolled tourism may also be a threat to such a sensitive landscape. Large numbers of tourists may seem like a dream scenario to local enterprise, but without careful forward planning, the very attraction of the wild places can be destroyed by a development such as a road leading too far into the original pristine resource. What are today beautiful hill-top views may be permanently scarred by eroded footpaths, tracks and litter, just as has happened in many other places in Europe where the clock can not be turned back. As an area opens up pressure comes on for the development of holiday homes, at first around the edge of the area and gradually further and further in to the area as roads are improved. The Bricklieves may be saved this fate due to the lack of potable water, but every house poses a threat in such an area from the disposal of septic tank waste going straight in to the groundwater and from its impact on the scenery. In 2001 a local water scheme at Carricknahorna East was upgraded which included 'improving' a mountain track with heavy earth-moving equipment, building a concrete sump over a species-diverse natural spring and diverting another spring down pipes with the drainage and loss of a herb-rich fen, all within the boundaries of the SAC. If such damage is to be avoided then environmentally aware people must be very vigilant and ecologists must be consulted to help find ways of developing such schemes without the negative environmental impact.

Let us hope the Bricklieves survive the 21st century through good planning and environmental management. Such a plan has been proposed as a part of a Masters thesis (Brakspear 1996) which combines the archaeological and ecological interest in the Bricklieves using principles of sustainable-tourism, so hopefully the recommendations will be used and the report will not just gather dust. A new field studies centre is built and will be functioning very soon at Ballinafad on the south-east margin of this area which could bring 'eco-tourism' to this area in a big way. Let us hope that these hills are enjoyed by an increased number of people because it is going to be through love and understanding that their eventual security will be won for all time!

FURTHER READING

The following publications, used in the preparation of this article, can be obtained by those wishing to delve more deeply into the science of the Bricklieves :-

An Foras Forbartha 1972: *Heritage Inventory Reports for Co. Sligo. Areas of Scientific Interest in Co. Sligo.* (Preliminary report), An Foras Forbartha, Dublin, (Unpublished report).

An Foras Forbartha 1974: *Heritage Inventory Reports for Co. Sligo. Monuments of Archaeological Interest.* An Foras Forbartha, Dublin. (Unpublished report).

An Foras Forbartha 1977: *Inventory of Outstanding Landscapes,* An Foras Forbartha, Dublin.

An Foras Forbartha 1978: *Heritage Inventory Reports for Co. Sligo. Areas of Scientific Interest in Co. Sligo.* (Revised and expanded report), An Foras Forbartha, Dublin. (Unpublished report).

An Foras Forbartha 1981: *Areas of Scientific Interest in Ireland,* An Foras Forbartha, Dublin.

Anon 1840: The caves of Kish-Corran, *The Irish Penny Journal,* 1(2), 9-10.

Anon 1901a: News gleanings. The cave committee's work, *Ir. Nat.,* 10, 141-142.

Anon 1901b: Notes. Geology. Exploration of the Keish caves, *Ir. Nat.,* 10, 256.

Anon 1903a: Proceedings of Irish Societies, Belfast Naturalists' Field Club. *Ir. Nat.,* 12, 19-21.

Anon 1903b: Proceedings of Irish Societies, Belfast Natural History and Philosophical Society, *Ir. Nat.,* 12, 51.

Anon 2001: Species Recovery Programme. Fen violet *Viola persicifolia, Flora English Nature,* Winter 2001:9.

Archaeological Survey of Ireland 1990: *County Sligo Sites and Monuments Record,* The Office of Public Works, Dublin.

Bergh, S. 1995: *Landscape of the Monuments. A study of the Passage Tombs in the Cuil Irra region, Co. Sligo, Ireland,* Arkeologiska undersokningar. Skrifter nr 6. Riksantikvarieambetet, Stockholm.

Brakspear, R. 1996: *Archaeology and Nature Conservation: Implications for the management of ancient monuments and historic landscapes in Ireland,* M.Sc. thesis, University College, North Wales.

Caldwell, W.G.E. & H.A.K. Charlesworth 1962: Visean coral reefs in the Bricklieve Mountains of Ireland, *Proc. Geol. Assoc.,* 73, 359-382.

Chapman, P. 1993: *Caves and Cave Life,* The New Naturalist, HarperCollins, London.

Coleman, J.C. 1947: Irish cave excavations, *J. Roy. Soc. Antiq. Ireland,* 77, 63-80.

Coleman, J.C. 1955: Notes on the cave region of North West Ireland, *Cave Research Group Newsletter,* No. 52, 25-28.

Coleman, J.C. 1965: *The Caves of Ireland,* Anvil Books, Tralee.

Colgan, N. 1902: Notes. Botany. Some new county records, *Ir. Nat.,* 11, 184.

Cotton, D.C.F., M. Cawley & C. Roden 1994: Botanical note. On the occurrence of *Pseudorchis albida* in Sligo (H28), Leitrim (H29) and Galway (H15, H16 and H17), *Ir. Nat. J.,* 24(11), 468-471.

Cotton, D.C.F. 2002: Reports of field meetings - 2001. O'Rourke's Table, Co. Leitrim (v.c. H29). & Cullentra Wood, Bricklieve Mountains & Unshin River, Co. Sligo (v.c. H28) 16th & 17th June, *BSBI News,* No.89:60-61.

Coxon, C. & R.H. Thorn 1989: Temporal variability of water quality and the implications for monitoring programmes in Irish limestone aquifers. Pages 111-120 in: *Groundwater Management: Quantity and Quality,* Proceedings of the Benidorm Symposium, IAHS Publication no. 188, 1989. Cruise, R.J. 1878: *Explanatory memoir to accompany sheets 66 and 67 of the maps of the Geological Survey of Ireland illustrating part of the Counties of Sligo, Leitrim, Roscommon and Mayo,* Memoirs of the Geological Survey, Dublin.

Curtis, T.G.F. & H.N. McGough, 1988: *The Irish Red Data Book. 1. Vascular Plants,* Stationery Office, Dublin.

Dixon, O.A. 1972: Lower Carboniferous rocks between the Curlew and Ox Mountains, Northwestern Ireland, *J. Geol. Soc.,* 128, 71-101. (12 figures).

Douglas, C., R. Goodwillie & E. Mooney 1993: Botanical notes. Notes on the flora of the Owenmore catchment Cos. Sligo (H28) and east Mayo (H26), *Ir. Nat. J.,* 24(5), 218-220.

Foot, F.J. 1871: On the occurrence of *Hymenophyllum Wilsoni* in the neighbourhood of Boyle; with notice of new stations for some of our rarer plants in the surrounding district, *Proc. Nat. Hist. Soc.* Dublin (for the sessions 1865-1869), 5, 16-17 [discussion of paper 17-20].

Goodwillie, R., Buckley, P. & C. Douglas 1992: *Owenmore River. Proposed Arterial Drainage Environmental Impact Assessment. Botanical and Ornithological Surveys,* A report for National Parks and Wildlife Service, Office of Public Works. (Unpublished report).

Goransson, H. 2002: Pollen analytical investigations in the Sligo area, In Timoney, M.A. (ed.) *A Celebration of Sligo.* Sligo Field Club, Sligo.

Gwynn, A.M., F.T. Riley & A.W. Stelfox 1940: Report on a further exploration (1929) of the caves of Keshcorran, Co. Sligo, *Proc. R. Ir. Acad.,* 46B, 81-95.

Hackney, P.; K.W. James & H.G.C. Ross 1983: *A list of the photographs in the R.J. Welch Collection in the Ulster Museum. Volume 2 Botany, Geology and Zoology,* Ulster Museum, Belfast.

Hardman, E.J. 1892: The limestone caves of Sligo. Volume 3, Appendix A: 375-378 in Wood-Martin, W.G. *History of Sligo.* Hodges, Figgis & Co., Dublin.

Heritage Service 1997: *Co. Sligo. Proposed Natural Heritage Areas (pNHA) and proposed Candidate Special Areas of Conservation (pCSAC),* Map 19. National Parks & Wildlife, Heritage Service, Dublin.

Knibbs, A.J. 1967: Ireland - 1962, *J. Mendip Caving Group,* Volume 4.

Macalister, R.A.S., E.C.R. Armstrong & R.L. Praeger 1912: Report on the exploration of bronze age carns on Carrowkeel Mountain, Co. Sligo, *Proc. R. Ir. Acad.,* 29C, 311-347 with 16 plates.

Praeger, R.Ll. 1934: *The Botanist in Ireland,* Section 382. Hodges, Figgis & Co., Dublin.

Scharff, R.F. 1895: Cave at Ballymote, Co. Sligo, *Ir. Nat.,* 4, 94.

Scharff, R.F., G. Coffey, G.A.J. Cole, R.A. Ussher & R.L. Praeger 1903: The exploration of the caves of Kesh, County Sligo, *Trans. R. Ir. Acad.,* 32(B), 171-244. Plates 9-11.

Sligo County Council 1999: *Development Plan for the County of Sligo 1999-2004,* Sligo County Council, Sligo.

Stuart, A.J. & L.H. van Wijngaarden-Bakker 1985: Quaternary Vertebrates. Chapter 10: 221-249 in Edwards, K.J. & P. Warren (eds.), *The Quaternary History of Ireland,* Academic Press, London.

Thorn, R., D. Drew & C.Coxon 1990: The hydrology and caves of the Geevagh and Bricklieve karsts, Co. Sligo, *Ir. Geog.,* 23(2), 120-135.

Ussher, R.J. 1902: The British Association in Belfast. Report of the committee appointed to explore Irish caves, *Ir. Nat.,* 11, 272-273.

Ussher, R.J. 1906: Discoveries in Irish and other bone caves, *J. Waterford and south east Ireland Arch. Soc.,* 9, 1-11, with illustration of Keish cave Co. Sligo.

Watts, W.A. 1969: 1. Map of Areas of Scientific Value in Ireland. Appendix 3 in : Anon (1969) *The Protection of the National Heritage,* An Foras Forbartha, Dublin.

Webb, D.A. 1945: Botanical notes. Some new county records, *Ir. Nat. J.,* 8, 313-314.

Webb, D.A. 1947a: The vegetation of Carrowkeel, a limestone hill in NW Ireland, *J. Ecol.,* 35, 105-129.

Webb, D.A. 1947b: Notes on the acidity, chloride content, and other chemical features of some Irish fresh waters, *Scientific Proceedings of the Royal Dublin Society* 24(24):215-228.

Webb, D.A. 1951: *The vegetation of Carrowkeel, reproduced notes,* Botany School, Trinity College Dublin 5(2), 23-49, with figures.

Webb, D.A. 1952: Botanical notes. *Alchemilla vulgaris* agg. in Ireland: a preliminary report, *Irish Naturalists' Journal* 10:298-300.

Whelan, K. 1989: *The Angler in Ireland. Game, Coarse and Sea,* Country House, Dublin.

Whilde, A. 1993: *Threatened Mammals, Birds, Amphibians and Fish in Ireland. Irish Red Data Book 2: Vertebrates,* HMSO, Belfast.

Williams, P.W. 1970: Limestone morphology in Ireland. Chapter 7: 105-124 in Stephens, N & R.E. Glasscock (eds.) *Irish Geographical Studies,* Department of Geography, Queen's University of Belfast.

Woodman, P.C. & N. Monaghan 1993: From mice to mammoths. Dating Ireland's earliest faunas, *Archaeology Ireland,* 7(3), 31-33.

> **Appendix:** Species of organisms recorded from the Bricklieves that are on the database of the author.
> * species mentioned in text
> + species known from archaeological deposits

SCIENTIFIC NAMES	COMMON NAMES
MOSSES & LIVERWORTS	
Rhytidiadelphus squarrosus	Springy turf-moss
Sphagnum capillifolium rubellum	Red bog-moss
Thuidium tamariscinum	Common tamarisk-moss
Calliergon cuspidatum	Pointed spear-moss
Hypnum spp.	Plait-moss spp.
Rhytidiadelphus squarrosus	Springy turf-moss
Conocephalum conicum	Great scented liverwort
HORSETAILS	
Equisetum fluviatile	Water horsetail
Equisetum arvense	Field horsetail
FERNS	
Osmunda regalis	Royal fern*
Polypodium vulgare	Common polypody
Polypodium interjectum	Intermediate polypody
Polypodium cambricum	Southern polypody
Pteridium aquilinum	Bracken*
Phyllitis scolopendrium	Hart's-tongue fern
Asplenium adiantum-nigrum	Black spleenwort*
Asplenium trichomanes	Maidenhair spleenwort*
Asplenium trichomanes-ramosum	Green spleenwort*
Asplenium ruta-muraria	Wall-rue
Ceterach officinarum	Rustyback
Athyrium filix-femina	Lady-fern
Cystopteris fragilis	Brittle bladder-fern
Polystichum setiferum	Soft shield-fern
Polystichum aculeatum	Hard shield-fern*
Dryopteris filix-mas	Male-fern
Dryopteris affinis	Scaly male-fern
Dryopteris aemula	Hay-scented buckler-fern
Dryopteris carthusiana	Narrow buckler-fern
Dryopteris dilatata	Broad buckler-fern
Blechnum spicant	Hard fern*
FLOWERING PLANTS	
Caltha palustris	Marsh marigold
Anemone nemorosa	Wood anemone
Ranunculus acris	Meadow buttercup
Ranunculus repens	Creeping buttercup
Ranunculus bulbosus	Bulbous buttercup*
Ranunculus auricomus	Goldilocks buttercup*
Ranunculus lingua	Greater spearwort*
Ranunculus ficaria	Lesser celandine*
Ranunculus trichophyllus	Thread-leaved water-crowfoot*
Mecanopsis cambrica	Welsh poppy*
Ulmus glabra	Wych elm
Urtica dioica	Common nettle
Quercus robur	Pedunculate oak
Betula pubescens	Downy birch*
Corylus avellana	Hazel*
Alnus glutinosa	Alder
Montia fontana	Blinks
Arenaria serpyllifolia	Thyme-leaved sandwort
Stellaria holostea	Greater stitchwort
Stellaria uliginosa (=*alsine*)	Bog stitchwort
Stellaria media	Common chickweed
Stellaria graminea	Lesser stitchwort
Cerastium fontanum	Common mouse-ear
Sagina procumbens	Procumbent pearlwort
Lychnis flos-cuculi	Ragged-robin
Rumex acetosella	Sheep's sorrel
Rumex acetosa	Common sorrel
Rumex crispus	Curled dock
Rumex obtusifolius	Broad-leaved dock
Persicaria amphibia	Amphibious bistort*
Hypericum androsaemum	Tutsan
Hypericum pulchrum	Slender St.John's-wort
Drosera rotundifolia	Round-leaved sundew*
Viola riviniana	Common dog-violet
Viola persicifolia	Fen violet*
Salix viminalis	Osier
Salix caprea	Goat willow
Salix cinerea oleifolia	Rusty willow*
Salix aurita	Eared willow
Salix repens	Creeping willow
Alliaria petiolata	Garlic mustard
Rorippa nasturtium-aquaticum	Common water-cress
Rorippa palustris	Marsh yellow-cress
Cardamine pratensis	Lady's-smock
Cardamine flexuosa	Wavy bitter-cress
Arabis hirsuta	Hairy rock-cress*
Draba incana	Hoary whitlowgrass*
Erophila verna	Common whitlowgrass*
Calluna vulgaris	Ling (common heather)*
Erica tetralix	Cross-leaved heath
Erica cinerea	Bell heather*
Vaccinium myrtillus	Bilberry*
Primula vulgaris	Primrose*
Lysimachia nemorum	Yellow pimpernel
Ribes nigrum	Black currant
Umbilicus rupestris	Wall pennywort
Sedum acre	Biting stonecrop*
Sedum album	White stonecrop
Saxifraga hypnoides	Mossy saxifrage*
Chrysosplenium oppositifolium	Opposite-leaved golden-saxifrage
Parnassia palustris	Grass-of-Parnassus
Filipendula ulmaria	Meadowsweet
Rubus fruticosus agg.	Common bramble
Rubus saxatilis	Stone bramble*
Rubus idaeus	Raspberry
Potentilla palustris	Marsh cinquefoil
Potentilla anserina	Silverweed
Potentilla erecta	Tormentil*
Potentilla anglica	Trailing tormentil
Potentilla sterilis	Barren strawberry
Fragaria vesca	Wild strawberry

SCIENTIFIC NAMES	COMMON NAMES
Geum rivale	Water avens*
Geum urbanum	Wood avens
Alchemilla filicaulis	Hairy lady's-mantle (undiff.)*
Alchemilla glabra	Smooth lady's-mantle*
Rosa pimpinellifolia	Burnet rose
Rosa canina	Dog-rose
Prunus spinosa	Blackthorn*
Sorbus aucuparia	Rowan*
Sorbus aria agg.	Whitebeam*
Sorbus rupicola	Rock whitebeam
Cotoneaster microphyllus agg.	Small-leaved cotoneaster*
Crataegus monogyna	Hawthorn*
Crataegus laevigata	Midland hawthorn*
Anthyllis vulneraria	Kidney vetch
Lotus corniculatus	Bird's-foot trefoil*
Lotus pedunculatus	Greater bird's-foot trefoil
Vicia cracca	Tufted vetch
Vicia sepium	Bush vetch
Lathyrus linifolius	Bitter-vetch
Lathyrus pratensis	Meadow vetchling
Trifolium repens	White clover
Trifolium pratense	Red clover
Ulex europaeus	Gorse
Lythrum portula	Water-purslane
Epilobium montanum	Broad-leaved willowherb
Epilobium palustre	Marsh willowherb*
Epilobium brunnescens	New Zealand willowherb*
Chamerion angustifolium	Rosebay willowherb
Circaea lutetiana	Common enchanter's-nightshade
Euonymus europaeus	Spindle*
Ilex aquifolium	Holly*
Linum catharticum	Fairy flax*
Polygala vulgaris	Common milkwort*
Polygala serpyllifolia	Heath milkwort*
Acer pseudoplatanus	Sycamore
Oxalis acetosella	Wood-sorrel*
Geranium lucidum	Shining crane's-bill*
Geranium robertianum	Herb-Robert*
Hedera helix	Ivy
Sanicula europaea	Wood sanicle
Anthriscus sylvestris	Cow parsley
Conopodium majus	Pignut*
Apium inundatum	Lesser marshwort*
Angelica sylvestris	Wild angelica
Heracleum sphondylium	Common hogweed
Gentianella campestris	Field gentian
Myosotis scorpioides	Water forget-me-not*
Myosotis secunda	Creeping forget-me-not
Myosotis laxa	Tufted forget-me-not
Myosotis discolor	Changing forget-me-not
Stachys sylvatica	Hedge woundwort
Teucrium scorodonia	Wood sage
Ajuga reptans	Bugle
Glechoma hederacea	Ground-ivy
Prunella vulgaris	Selfheal
Thymus polytrichus britannicus	Wild thyme*
Mentha aquatica	Water mint*
Hippurus vulgaris	Mare's-tail*
Plantago major	Greater plantain
Plantago lanceolata	Ribwort plantain

SCIENTIFIC NAMES	COMMON NAMES
Fraxinus excelsior	Ash*
Scrophularia nodosa	Common figwort
Mimulus guttatus	Monkeyflower
Digitalis purpurea	Foxglove
Veronica serpyllifolia	Thyme-leaved speedwell
Veronica officinalis	Heath speedwell
Veronica chamaedrys	Germander speedwell
Veronica scutellata	Marsh speedwell
Veronica beccabunga	Brooklime
Melampyrum pratense	Common cow-wheat*
Euphrasia agg.	eyebright sp.*
Rhinanthus minor	Yellow-rattle
Pedicularis sylvatica sylvatica	Common lousewort ssp.*
Pinguicula vulgaris	Common butterwort
Campanula rotundifolia	Harebell*
Galium odoratum	Woodruff
Galium palustre	Common marsh-bedstraw*
Galium verum	Lady's bedstraw*
Galium saxatile	Heath bedstraw*
Galium aparine	Cleavers
Viburnum opulus	Guelder-rose*
Lonicera periclymenum	Honeysuckle
Valeriana officinalis	Common valerian
Succisa pratensis	Devil's-bit scabious*
Arctium minus	Lesser burdock
Cirsium vulgare	Spear thistle
Cirsium palustre	Marsh thistle
Cirsium arvense	Creeping thistle
Lapsana communis	Nipplewort
Hypochoeris radicata	Cat's-ear
Sonchus oleraceus	Smooth sow-thistle
Sonchus asper	Prickly sow-thistle
Taraxacum agg.	Dandelion
Pilosella officinarum	Mouse-ear hawkweed
Hieracium anglicum	hawkweed
Antennaria dioica	Mountain cudweed*
Bellis perennis	Daisy
Achillea millefolium	Yarrow
Senecio aquaticus	Marsh ragwort
Arum maculatum	Wild arum
Juncus squarrosus	Heath rush
Juncus bufonius	Toad rush
Juncus articulatus	Jointed rush
Juncus acutiflorus	Sharp-flowered rush
Juncus bulbosus	Bulbous rush
Juncus effusus	Soft rush*
Juncus conglomeratus	Compact rush
Luzula sylvatica	Great wood-rush*
Luzula campestris	Field wood-rush
Luzula multiflora congesta	Congested heath wood-rush
Eriophorum angustifolium	Common cottongrass
Eriophorum latifolium	Broad-leaved cottongrass*
Eriophorum vaginatum	Hare's-tail cottongrass
Trichophorum cespitosum	Deergrass
Eleocharis palustris	Common spike-rush
Carex paniculata	Greater tussock-sedge*
Carex disticha	Brown sedge*
Carex ovalis	Oval sedge
Carex echinata	Star sedge
Carex acutiformis	Lesser pond-sedge*
Carex rostrata	Bottle sedge*
Carex sylvatica	Wood sedge

SCIENTIFIC NAMES	COMMON NAMES
Carex flacca	Glaucous sedge
Carex panicea	Carnation sedge
Carex binervis	Green-ribbed sedge
Carex caryophyllea	Spring-sedge
Carex acuta	Slender tufted-sedge*
Carex nigra	Common sedge*
Carex elata	Tufted-sedge*
Carex pulicaris	Flea sedge
Nardus stricta	Mat-grass
Festuca rubra	Red fescue
Festuca ovina	Sheep's-fescue
Lolium perenne	Perennial rye-grass
Cynosurus cristatus	Crested dog's-tail
Briza media	Quaking grass*
Poa annua	Annual meadow-grass
Glyceria fluitans	Floating sweet-grass
Glyceria notata	Plicate sweet-grass
Helictotrichon pubescens	Downy oat-grass
Arrhenatherum elatius	False oat-grass
Trisetum flavescens	Yellow oat-grass
Koeleria macrantha	Crested hair-grass
Deschampsia flexuosa	Wavy hair-grass
Holcus lanatus	Yorkshire-fog
Holcus mollis	Creeping soft-grass
Aira caryophyllea	Silver hair-grass
Aira praecox	Early hair-grass
Anthoxanthum odoratum	Sweet vernal-grass
Phalaris arundinacea	Reed canary-grass
Agrostis capillaris	Common bent
Agrostis stolonifera	Creeping bent
Alopecurus geniculatus	Marsh foxtail
Danthonia decumbens	Heath-grass
Molinia caerulea	Purple moor-grass*
Sparganium erectum	Branched bur-reed*
Typha latifolia	Reed-mace
Narthecium ossifragum	Bog asphodel*
Hyacinthoides non-scripta	Bluebell*
Allium ursinum	Wild garlic
Iris pseudacorus	Yellow iris
Listera ovata	Common twayblade*
Listera cordata	Lesser twayblade*
Platanthera chlorantha	Greater butterfly-orchid
Platanthera bifolia	Lesser butterfly-orchid
Pseudorchis albida	Small white orchid*
Gymnadenia conopsea	Fragrant orchid
Coeloglossum viride	Frog orchid*
Dactylorhiza fuchsii	Common spotted orchid*
Dactylorhiza maculata	Heath spotted orchid*
Orchis mascula	Early-purple orchid*

SNAILS

Acicula fusca	*
Pyramidula rupestris	
Trichia hispida	Hairy snail
Cepaea nemoralis	Dark-lipped snail

EARTHWORMS

Allolobophora chlorotica
Aporrectodea caliginosa
Lumbricus rubellus
Satchellius mammalis

CRUSTACEANS

Gammarus duebeni	a freshwater shrimp

SCIENTIFIC NAMES	COMMON NAMES
Armadillidium pulchellum	a woodlouse*
Haplophthalmus mengei	a woodlouse*
Trichoniscus pusillus	a woodlouse
Austropotamobius pallipes	White-clawed crayfish*

MILLIPEDE & CENTIPEDES

Glomeris marginata	Pill millipede
Lithobius variegatus	a centipede
Lithobius borealis	a centipede

DAMSELFLIES & DRAGONFLY

Pyrrhosoma nymphula	Common red damselfly
Enallagma cyathigerum	Common blue damselfly
Ischnura elegans	Blue-tailed damselfly
Aeschna juncea	Common hawker dragonfly

GRASSHOPPER

Omocestus viridulus	Common green grasshopper

EARWIG

Forficula auricularia	Common earwig

MOTHS & BUTTERFLIES

Zygaena filipendulae	6-spot burnet
Leptidea reali	Real's wood white*
Pieris napi	Green-veined white
Anthocharis cardamines	Orange-tip
Lycaena phlaeas	Small copper
Polyommatus icarus	Common blue*
Vanessa atalanta	Red admiral
Aglais urticae	Small tortoiseshell
Argynnis paphia	Silver-washed fritillary*
Eurodryas aurinia	Marsh fritillary*
Pararge aegeria	Speckled wood
Maniola jurtina	Meadow brown*
Coenonympha pamphilus	Small heath*
Aphantopus hyperantus	Ringlet
Lasiocampa quercus callunae	Northern eggar*
Xanthorhoe montanata	Silver-ground carpet
Lomaspilis marginata	Clouded border
Ematurga atomaria	Common heath moth*
Tyria jacobaeae	Cinnabar moth
Anarta myrtilli	Beautiful yellow underwing*
Callistege mi	Mother shipton

HOVERFLY

Eristalis abusivus

WASP & BUMBLEBEES

Dolichovespula sylvestris	Tree wasp
Bombus lucorum	
Bombus magnus	
Bombus pratorum	
Bombus muscorum	
Bombus pascuorum	

LADYBIRD BEETLE

Coccinella 7-punctata	7-spot ladybird

SCIENTIFIC NAMES	COMMON NAMES
HARVESTMEN & SPIDER	
Nemastoma bimaculatum	
Oligolophus tridens	
Paroligolophus agrestis	
Mitopus morio	
Phalangium opilio	
Megabunus diadema	*
Rilaena triangularis	
Leiobunum rotundum	
Nelima gothica	
Meta menardi	Cave spider
FISH	
Esox lucius	Pike
Gasterosteus aculeatus	Three-spined stickleback
Perca fluviatilis	Perch
Salmo trutta	Trout+
Oncorhynchus mykiss	Rainbow trout*
AMPHIBIANS	
Triturus vulgaris	Smooth newt*
Rana temporaria	Common frog*
BIRDS	
Tachybaptus ruficollis	Little grebe
Podiceps cristatus	Great crested grebe
Cygnus olor	Mute swan
Cygnus cygnus	Whooper swan*
Anser albifrons	White-fronted goose
Anas penelope	Wigeon*
Anas crecca	Teal*
Anas platyrhynchos	Mallard*
Anas acuta	Pintail
Aythya fuligula	Tufted duck*
Aythya marila	Scaup
Melanitta nigra	Common scoter+
Bucephala clangula	Goldeneye
Mergus albellus	Smew+
Mergus serrator	Red-breasted merganser
Falco tinnunculus	Kestrel
Falco peregrinus	Peregrine*
Perdix perdix	Grey partridge
Crex crex	Corncrake
Gallinula chloropus	Moorhen
Vanellus vanellus	Lapwing
Gallinago gallinago	Snipe*
Scolopax rusticola	Woodcock
Numenius arquata	Curlew
Tringa totanus	Redshank
Tringa hypoleucos	Common sandpiper
Larus fuscus	Lesser black-backed gull
Plotus alle	Little auk+
Cuculus canorus	Cuckoo*
Asio otus	Long-eared owl*
Alauda arvensis	Skylark
Hirundo rustica	Swallow
Anthus pratensis	Meadow pipit*
Troglodytes troglodytes	Wren
Erithacus rubecula	Robin
Saxicola rubetra	Whinchat
Saxicola torquata	Stonechat
Oenanthe oenanthe	Wheatear*
Turdus merula	Blackbird

SCIENTIFIC NAMES	COMMON NAMES
Turdus pilaris	Fieldfare
Turdus philomelos	Song thrush
Turdus iliacus	Redwing
Turdus viscivorus	Mistle thrush
Phylloscopus trochilus	Willow warbler
Regulus regulus	Goldcrest
Muscicapa striata	Spotted flycatcher*
Garrulus glandarius	Jay
Pica pica	Magpie
Corvus monedula	Jackdaw
Corvus frugilegus	Rook
Corvus corone cornix	Hooded crow
Corvus corax	Raven*
Passer domesticus	House sparrow
Fringilla coelebs	Chaffinch
Carduelis chloris	Greenfinch
Carduelis carduelis	Goldfinch
Carduelis cannabina	Linnet
Acanthis flammea	Redpoll
Pyrrhula pyrrhula	Bullfinch
MAMMALS	
Oryctolagus cuniculus	Rabbit+
Lepus timidus	Irish hare
Lemmus lemmus	Arctic lemming+
Rattus norvegicus	Brown rat+
Apodemus sylvaticus	Wood mouse+
Ursus arctos	Brown bear+
Canis lupus	Wolf+
Canis familiaris	domestic dog+
Vulpes vulpes	Fox
Mustela erminea	Stoat+
Meles meles	Badger+
Lutra lutra	Otter*
Sus scrofa	Wild boar / pig+
Capra (domestic)	feral goat*
Ovis aries	domestic sheep+
Equus asinus	domestic donkey / ass+
Equus caballus	domestic horse+
Bos taurus	domestic cattle / ox+
Cervus elaphus	Red deer+
Rangifer tarandus	Reindeer+

EELS AND EEL FISHING IN COUNTY SLIGO

*Christopher Moriarty,
Zoology Department, Trinity College, Dublin.*

ABSTRACT: Official historical records of eel fishing in Sligo date to the 1862 Report of the Inspectors of Fisheries For Ireland when it was noted that five eel licences were issued in the Sligo Fishery District. The first scientific references to eels in the county were made in 1905. Statistics published in the official Reports on fisheries trace the fortunes of the Sligo eel fishery until the 1980s. The value of eels caught in the county in the 1980s was in the order of £30,000 per year in 1995 values. Comparison of the results of studies in Lough Gill and Lough Arrow with data from other lakes throughout Ireland suggested that, with proper management, the Sligo lakes could yield 50 tons of eel per year with a value of £150,000.

INTRODUCTION

The eel *Anguilla anguilla* (L.) is one of the most valuable fishes in Europe. The Lough Neagh eel fishery in Northern Ireland provides a livelihood for some 400 fishermen and eel fishing in the lakes of the River Shannon has been developed by the Electricity Supply Board to provide jobs for between 50 and 100 people. Eel is not a popular food fish in Ireland and the entire commercial catch is exported, formerly to England but, since the 1960s, mainly to Germany and the Netherlands.

Production of eel depends largely on the extent of suitable lakes and, in Co. Sligo, interest is concentrated in Loughs Gill and Arrow. While eel thrive in rivers, production of sufficient quantities for commercial fishing is confined in Ireland to the larger, lowland streams of the southern half of the country. Those rivers of Co. Sligo which do not flow through lakes are unlikely to yield significant catches - except for sport fishing. The usual size of eel caught in commercial fisheries in productive lakes ranges from 30 cm to 55 cm and in weight from 40 g to 500 g. Much bigger specimens, to more than 1 metre in length and weighing up to 5 kg are caught from time to time.

LIFE HISTORY OF THE EEL

The life history of the eel, first studied by Aristotle, was not clearly understood until 1923 when Johannes Schmidt published his discovery that the eels of Europe all spawned in the Sargasso Sea and nowhere else (Schmidt, 1923).

Later research work has shown that the breeding area is much larger than Schmidt had observed - though still in the single region of the Sargasso. It was also shown that the larval eel crosses some 3,000 miles of ocean in about a year, rather than the two and a half years which he had postulated.

An important contribution to Schmidt's search for the breeding place was the first capture in 1904 of eel larvae in the Atlantic Ocean. Two specimens were secured, one by the Danish research vessel *Thor*, off the Faeroes the other by G P Farran on the Irish research vessel *Helga* off Co. Mayo. The identification of these specimens, at points so far apart, indicated that the larval eel was very widely distributed in the ocean. While the *Thor* during the next two seasons hunted for larvae in deep water, the *Helga* surveyed inshore water on the Irish coast and caught relatively few. This negative result was important in locating the area where the larval eels metamorphosed into elvers.

At a considerable distance offshore, the larval eel metamorphoses from an ocean fish, with a body shaped like a willow leaf, to a small but recognisable eel. The body is transparent at first, and the fish is known as a 'glass eel'. The glass eels migrate inshore, reaching the coast in November and December and remaining in tidal water until the spring. In April or May pigment develops so that the little eel loses its transparency. The term 'elver' is loosely applied both to glass eels and small, pigmented, ones. In the early scientific literature and also in the Fisheries Acts the young eels are referred to as 'fry'.

The migration of the elvers into fresh water is often very conspicuous. They prefer to migrate under cover of darkness and, being true fish, attempt to stay in the water. When great numbers are present and an obstacle such as a waterfall impedes their progress, the elvers leave the water and wriggle over damp stones or moss to reach their destination. Occasionally, they are so numerous that the elvers swimming in a river resemble a black ribbon. They are therefore easy to see and well known to fishermen and fishery protection workers. This partly explains why it was possible to make a nation-wide survey of the migration early in the century.

After this initial migration, however, the eel effectively disappears until it has grown large enough to be of interest to the fishing industry. The great majority rest in the daytime, often burrowing into lake or river mud. They usually hunt at night and are seldom caught by casual fishermen so that they remain relatively unknown until their capture by special eel-fishing gear. The eel in fresh water feeds and grows until it reaches maturity. Then it stops feeding and migrates downstream, usually in autumn, heading back to the breeding ground. This is a once-in-a-lifetime event. The growing eels are coloured yellowish brown and are known as 'yellow eels' or 'brown eels'. The migrating form is bronze-black on its upper parts, white below and is called a 'silver eel'.

CATCHING METHODS

Two kinds of eel fishing gear have been used in Sligo since the 19th century or before: the long-line and the coghill net. The long-line can measure up to a mile and a half in length and carries a thousand or more hooks. Each hook has to be baited daily, the most popular bait being an earthworm. Long-lining is therefore labour-intensive. The line is set on the bed of a lake at dusk and lifted at dawn the following morning. The season is self-regulating because the yellow eels are active only in the warmer months, from mid-April to October or, occasionally, into November.

The coghill net, (from the Irish *cuideal*) used in rivers to capture silver eels, is conical in shape with a wide mouth, tapering to a narrow, cylindrical end which is closed by tying with string. The nets vary in size, but a length of 10 metres is widely used. The opening of the net is big enough to allow it to extend from surface to bed of the river. It is set with the opening facing upstream to intercept the migrating silver eels travelling towards the sea. On a slack night, when few eels are migrating, the net may be put in position at dusk and left to fish until the following morning. When there is a heavy run of eels, the nets have to be lifted two or three times per hour and, although the run usually ends about midnight, it can continue until morning.

The silver eel migration is seasonal and also subject to the weather and the moon's phase. In Ireland migration on a large scale begins in September and, depending on the length and complexity of the river catchment, may continue until the following April. In smaller catchments the season is much shorter, seldom extending later than November. Migration takes place at night, usually in the first hours after sunset. Peak activity is associated with dark conditions, the darkest being about the time of new moon when the river is in high flood.

EARLY RECORDS OF SLIGO EELS

Went (1969) quotes from the Civil Survey of 1654-1656 to the effect that the Ballysodare River had 'no commodity of fishing except some few eels of noe great moment'. Letters Patent were issued to John Browne in 1684, granting 'the Several Fishing of Salmon, Pyke, Eels and other fishings in the water or river near Wine Island'. Fishing rights between Lough Gill and the sea were purchased for Abraham Martin in 1801. Eel fishing in Sligo is mentioned in the deed of 1801 and again in a lease dated 1851 (McTernan, 1995) but neither document specifies the methods used. This right in the River Garvogue is still held by a descendant of the Martins, Richard Wood-Martin, who continues to operate a fishery for silver eels.

In 1862 the Reports of the Inspectors of Fisheries of Ireland began to record the numbers of eel licences sold each year throughout the country. These referred to coghill nets set for silver eels. An eel fishery can operate with one or more such nets so that the number licensed does not actually tell how many fisheries there were nor how many people might have been engaged in the work. Two people are usually needed to lift the net, but a crew of two can take care of several nets in the one fishery. Five licences were issued for the Sligo District in 1862 and 11 in 1871 and throughout the 19th century the numbers varied between 4 and 11. Between 1904 and 1919, 6 licenses or fewer were issued and from 1920 to 1959 licensed fishing ceased, with the exception of 1934 when 2 licenses were issued.

The annual reports of the Fisheries Branch of the Department of Agriculture and Technical Instruction for Ireland began to include references to eel fishing in 1904 and mention the Sligo Fishery District for the first time in 1905. This District includes both Lough Arrow and Lough Gill and the Unshin and Garvogue Rivers which flow from them. Unfortunately, the reports make no reference to the individual lakes or rivers. Eel fishing was bad in 1905, fairly good and improving in 1906 but was not mentioned in 1907. Between 1908 and 1913, when the regular reporting ceased, it was estimated that from 12 to 14 people were engaged in the fishery and that both nets and long-lines were used. The catch was exported to Billingsgate by rail and ferry.

In 1905 the Fisheries Branch issued a questionnaire to collect data on the arrival times of the 'eel fry' in rivers and estuaries. Holt (1908) in the first report of this survey mentions the Ballysodare Falls as one of the few places in Ireland where the immigration of elvers to fresh water is obstructed by a waterfall. He observed that some elvers made use of the salmon ladder. In the Garvogue, they used the salmon ladder at Victoria Bridge, now Hyde Bridge. Subsequent reports, issued up until 1910, mention elvers ascending the Garvogue but have nothing to say about the Ballysodare falls. The migration into fresh water usually began in May, but elvers were recorded in tidal parts of the Garvogue as early as February.

The Fishery Act of 1939 prohibited the use of 'fixed engines' in inland waters with the exception of those which had been in operation in any of the years 1936, 1937 or 1938. This should have disqualified the Sligo nets but two sites were subsequently used - even though there is no record of their proprietors holding licences. Both are in the Garvogue close to Sligo town. This prohibition was relaxed in 1959 and, from that time onwards, one or two licences have been issued in most years. Records of the issue of licences for long-lines began to be published regularly in 1928. Long-line fishermen usually operate in pairs and each licence therefore represents two people employed. Three licenses or fewer were issued in the Sligo District from 1920 to 1942 with a sudden increase to 7 in 1943, 9 the following year and 11 in 1946. Thereafter the numbers fell to 4 or fewer, except for 1969 when 10 were issued and between 1974 and 1980 when the numbers varied between 3 and 20, with the maximum being issued in 1976. Publication of the numbers of licences issued in the Sligo Fishery District ceased in 1980.

In 1947 records of the quantities of eels caught were collected. Forms were issued annually to all licensees requiring them to submit a return of their catch to the Fisheries authorities. Many complied with the requirement and it is likely that a majority of these presented an accurate record. However, a minority clearly made a rough estimate and many made no returns. The reported catch in the Sligo District from 1947 to 1959 was usually more than 1 ton with a maximum of 11 tons. Between 1961 and 1985, when the last official figures were published, catches of up to 7 tons were reported. Because of under-reporting, the only meaningful figures are the high ones and it seems likely that the usual catch in the District lay between 7 and 11 tons. The low catches are likely to be under-estimates or under-reporting. The highest give an indication of the potential yield for the District.

STUDIES OF EEL IN LOUGH GILL AND LOUGH ARROW

The first scientific study of eels in Sligo - as opposed to circulation of a questionnaire - was conducted by the Inland Fisheries Trust in Lough Arrow in 1954 and 1955 (Anon. 1956). A principal duty of the Trust at the time was to develop brown trout stocks and fishing and the aim of their eel study was to decide whether eel stocks and eel fishing operations were compatible with a good trout fishery. Using earthworms or perch fry for bait and setting their lines in a variety of habitats, including 'trout shallows', they caught 546 eels, 10 perch, one pike and no trout. Examination of the food in the stomachs of specimens showed that the eels ate a variety of food organisms of which the water louse *Asellus* was the most important, followed by shrimp *Gammarus* and small bivalves. Overlapping in the diet of trout and eel was not extensive and there was no evidence that either was a serious competitor for food. The conclusion was that neither the eel nor the activities of the eel fishermen was likely to conflict with the interests of trout and anglers.

Using fyke nets, the author sampled yellow eels in Lough Gill in 1972, in Lough Arrow in 1974 and in both lakes in 1979. Fyke nets, designed specifically for the capture of eels, are set in trains on the bed of the lake and left in position overnight. They are very effective and have the particular advantage that only

Fig. 1 - The Falls at Ballisodare, Co. Sligo. Photo: M.A. Timoney

TABLE 1	Number of nets used	Number of eels per net	Length (cm)			Age (years)			Growth (cm/year)	Principal food organisms				
			Minimum	Maximum	Mean	Minimum	Maximum	Mode		Asellus aquaticus	Ephemeroptera	Gammarus duebeni	Trichoptra (larvae)	Fish
L. GILL														
19-23 July 1972	104	1.2	31	72	41	7	28	10	2.3	*	***	**	***	***
19-20 July 1979	28	1.2	31	62	41	8	17	12	2.5					***
L. ARROW														
19-23 August 1974	56	1.0	34	73	49	8	34	11	3.0	***	**	**	***	*
30 July-3 Aug 1979	52	2.4	27	77	49	6	16	9	3.0	***		*		*

Table 1. Summary of data from L. Gill and L. Arrow eel samples.

negligible numbers of other fish are caught and these can be released unharmed. Details of the methods used and results of the Lough Gill study in 1972 are given in Moriarty (1974). The data collected in each of the four sampling studies comprised number of eels per net, lengths, ages and food of representative sub-samples. A summary of the results is given in Table 1.

The figures for Lough Gill, giving equal catch per net and equal mean length, indicate a stable population, with little variation in the course of the 7 years between successive samplings. The differences in growth rate are not significant. The stomachs of the Lough Gill eels contained very few water louse *Asellus* but many fish. In Lough Arrow, the numbers of eel caught per net showed a marked increase between 1974 and 1979. This, however, may have been influenced by the fact that in 1979 a known productive area was selected to maximise the catch while in 1974 the nets had been set at random. The Lough Arrow eels fed mainly on water louse and ate very few fish. Their growth rate was considerably greater than that of the Lough Gill eels and their average size larger.

The differences in food preference and growth rate closely resemble variations recorded between the Shannon lakes and Lough Corrib (Moriarty, 1979). The water louse diet is typical of Lough Key and other Shannon lakes while a diet of small fish and a wide variety of invertebrates seems to be associated with relatively poor feeding conditions as recorded elsewhere in Lough Corrib and Lough Conn.

In the autumn of 1979 Wood-Martin (1980) made a study of the size and behaviour of silver eels caught in a fyke net on the Garvogue just upstream of Sligo town. They ranged in length from 34 to 59 cm and in weight from 91 to 403 g. Her observations on the numbers of eels migrating each night showed that peak activity coincided with peak microseisms - the earth tremors associated with heavy wave action on the coast. Previous research had suggested that their sensitivity to microseisms would give the eel an early indication of climatic depressions over the Atlantic and a chance of prolonged stormy weather. Silver eels prefer to migrate during high floods.

Wood-Martin also made an experiment of tagging eels caught in the Garvogue and in the Burrishoole River in Co. Mayo. Of the 40 eels tagged in each river, 20 were released again in upstream lakes on their own rivers, through which they had already journeyed. The remaining 20 were transferred to the opposite river. The Sligo eels transferred to the Burrishoole made their way downstream much faster than did the local eels brought upstream in their own river. Unfortunately the parallel experiment, in which Burrishoole eels were taken to Sligo, failed because the net was damaged during severe floods. The results supported the theory that eels which have once made their way through a particular lake may be seriously disorientated if they are required to do it a second time.

ELVERS

In Ireland the capture or possession of elvers is forbidden by law. In spite of this, small numbers are used illegally as a very effective bait for trout. However, an authorisation can be issued under Section 14 of the Fisheries Act of 1959 to permit the capture of the elvers. Although elvers command a very high price in the market - £80 per kg or more - their capture is permitted only for transfer from the lower waters of a river system to the lakes upstream. Overland transportation of the elvers began in Germany in the 19th century. It was adopted by the ESB for the development of the Shannon eel fishery in 1959 and jointly by the ESB and the Department of Agriculture for Northern Ireland at Ballyshannon the following year for enhancement of the eel stocks in the Erne lakes.

The author conducted a wide-ranging search for elvers in Irish rivers in 1974 and 1975 during which it was observed that they were usually plentiful at Ballysodare and scarce on the Garvogue. The study was far from exhaustive but the results were in line with a general observation that the greatest numbers of elvers gathered at the rivers which had the longest estuaries. Ballysodare Bay gave the impression of being a good collecting ground for them.

For some years in the 1980s an authorisation to capture the elvers of the Ballysodare River was issued. It allowed 50% of the catch to be supplied to an experimental eel rearing facility in Kerry, provided the remaining 50% were released in Lough Arrow. The reasoning behind this arrangement was that the natural mortality possible at the bottom of the falls and moving half the catch to the lake would result in more of the elvers attempting to climb the Ballysodare falls would be very high. Catching as many as elvers reaching the lake than would be possible if they were left to fend for themselves.

CONCLUSIONS

While official historical records of professional fishing for eels date only to the mid 19th century, it is likely that a subsistence fishery has existed in Sligo for very much longer. Both long-line and coghill net fisheries continue, though on a relatively small scale. The recent historical figure in the 1980s of 10 tons per annum is likely to be a reasonable estimate of the potential of the eel fishery in Sligo and represents a potential income to the fishermen of £30,000. The managed fishery of Lough Neagh yields 20 kg of eel per hectare. In theory, operation of a management plan to take in all the lakes of County Sligo could attain such a yield, increasing the annual catch to 50 tons and a value of £150,000 - without conflicting with the interests of trout or of anglers.

References

Anon. 1956: Eel investigations, L. Arrow: preliminary report. *Inland Fisheries Trust Annual Report 1956*, 8-18.

Holt, E. W. L. 1908: Summary of reports relative to eel fry, 1905-1906. *Fisheries, Ireland, Scientific Investigations 1906*, 8, 3-11.

McTernan, John C. 1995: *Olde Sligoe, Aspects of Town and County over 750 years*. Sligo, Avena Publications.

Moriarty, C., 1973: Studies of the eel *Anguilla anguilla* in Ireland. 2. In Lough Conn, Lough Gill and north Cavan lakes. *Irish Fisheries Investigations*, Series A, No. 13.

Moriarty, C., 1979: "Biological studies of yellow eels in Ireland," *Rapports et Proces verbaux du Conseil internationale pour l'Exploration dè Mer*, 174, 16-21.

Schmidt, J. 1923: The breeding places of the eel. *Philosophical Transactions of the Royal Society*. 211, 179-208.

Went, A. E. J. 1969: Historical Notes on the Fisheries of the Two County Sligo Rivers. *Journal of the Royal Society of Antiquaries of Ireland*. 99, 55-61.

Wood-Martin, A. 1980: *A study of 2 silver eel* Anguilla anguilla *(Linnaeus) 1758 populations in the west of Ireland*. Moderatorship thesis, Trinity College, Dublin.

Wood-Martin, W. G. 1892: *History of Sligo*, Vol. 3, Dublin, Hodges Figgis.

'His Majesty' Photo: Noel Murphy

Church Island, Lough Gill, Co. Sligo. Photo: Dúchas, The Heritage Service

"Swans at Nest" - Photo: Noel Murphy

NOTE ON HUT SITES AT AUGHRIS, COUNTY SLIGO

Finlay Tower Kitchin[†]

ABSTRACT: Attention is drawn to a large group of small earthen enclosures, considered to be temporary habitation sites, at Aughris, Co. Sligo, and a few identical ones 8 km to the east at Portavaud, Co. Sligo.

In the area immediately to the west of the promontory fort on the cliff edge at Aughris (O.S. 6" Sligo sheet 12; 84.4 cm. from W., 37.6 cm. from E.) is a remarkable concentration of what appears to be hut sites. The first field to the west of the fort (unfortunately since rotovated) revealed some forty or fifty of these sites and the adjoining field to the west of that contains a somewhat lesser though nonetheless significant concentration. In addition individual sites of this nature are to be found over the greater part of the Aughris promontory.

The sites are of a more or less standard character and consist of a slightly raised central platform varying in shape from a rectangle (normally with rounded corners) to an oval or pear shaped pattern. This is encircled by a narrow and shallow depression, hardly qualifying to be described as a ditch, which in turn is surrounded by a miniature bank. The overall internal dimensions of these sites (by the unreliable yardstick of memory) varies from a maximum of approximately 3 m. by 2 m. to something substantially less. The encircling depression was presumably designed to drain the central area and the spoil arising from its excavation, would seem to have provided the material for the outer bank as well as perhaps some raising of the level of the central area.

When Mr. Marcus Ó hEocháidhe, the former Assistant Inspector of National Monuments with the Office of Public Works, was shown these sites he immediately identified them as identical in plan and character with the medieval booley sites which he himself had excavated at Slieve Breagh, Co. Meath.

While on this identification it seems probable that these sites are medieval in date and (by analogy with all booley sites) temporary in nature the question of their presence on Aughris Head, particularly in such numbers, remains to be answered. That they were true booley sites is most improbable. In the first place, the essence of the booleying system was the removal of stock in summer to mountain or other high altitude pastures (far removed from the farms to which they belonged) which could not be used at other times of year. Here not only is the land not of the best quality, but the area is no more than a mile or so from some of the best fattening land in the county. Secondly, the presence in total of perhaps some 150 to 200 sites scattered in a space of less than a square kilometre would suggest more herdsmen than cattle.

Fig. 1 - Enclosure at Aughris, Co. Sligo. Photo: Martin A. Timoney.

Fig. 2 - Enclosure Aughris, Co. Sligo. Photo: Martin A. Timoney

What then is the reason for the presence of these sites in such numbers? It has been suggested that they might have been the temporary homes of persons engaged in salt panning but that form of activity was not normally conducted from the top of a 120-foot cliff. In this context it may be mentioned that five or six sites of the same type are to be found close to the shore of the tidal lagoon at Portavad near the entrance to Ballisodare Bay and this location could well suggest a salt panning connection.

The most probable explanation lies in the suggestion made by Dr. Seán Ó Nualláin, Archaeologist to the Ordnance Survey, who refers to *The Festival of Lughnasa* by Máire Mac Neill (Oxford University Press 1962). Regarding Aughris McNeill (1962, 112-113) mentions that in former times a *patrún* was held on Garland Sunday, the last Sunday in July, at St. Patrick's Well, which is not far from the promontory fort. This *patrún* was attended by people from all over the Baronies of Leyney and Tireragh and she records that many from Lyney arrived the day before. That fact, coupled with the probability that the fringe activities of sports, dancing, matchmaking and drinking often associated with those occasions would involve a period of two or three days and necessitated the provision of some form of temporary accommodation. In the absence of any more convincing explanation this Garland Sunday connection may be accepted as at least the most probable.

EDITOR'S NOTE

Finlay Tower Kitchin, popularly Pat, of Newpark, Ballymote, and later of Ballisodare, Co. Sligo, was an enthusiastic fieldwalker and very active member of Sligo Field Club from the mid 1950s right up until he passed to his eternal reward on 30[th.] September, 1986. Biographical notes on his involvement in Sligo Field Club are to be found in Timoney and Heraughty (this volume). Like his contemporaries in Sligo Field Club he devoted his energies to fieldwalking, furthering the protection of monuments and reporting discoveries to higher authorities rather than to publication. The Carrowmore, Co. Sligo, passage tomb cemetery took up much his time and energy. He was responsible, through the good offices of Prof. Michael J. O'Kelly of Cork, for Dr. Göran Burenhult becoming involved in the Carrowmore cemetery. He published a record of the cemetery as it was in the 1970s in the *Proceedings of the Prehistoric Society* (Kitchin 1983).

Fig. 3 - Enclosure at Aughris, Co. Sligo. Photo: Martin A. Timoney

Fig. 4 - Enclosure Portavaud, Co. Sligo. Photo: Martin A. Timoney.

Fig. 5 - Enclosure Portavaud, Co. Sligo. Photo: Martin A. Timoney.

The enclosures at Aughris were first noticed before 1965 by his wife, Sheela, who also first noticed those at Portavaud somewhat earlier; both locations are included in a list of sites drawn up in 1965 for Sligo County Council. Kitchin's undated three-page manuscript, written about 1972, is published here with the permission of Sheela.

Kitchin and his colleague, Michael Cahalane, encouraged every archaeologist and folklife enthusiast they met to visit Aughris and Portavaud. Thus the Editor became involved and carried out some initial fieldwork and library research on Aughris and Portavaud. Further enclosures at Lackan, Co. Sligo, and Kilcummin, Co. Mayo, have come to notice since Kitchin's death. Descriptions of sample enclosures at the four locations, other material and discussion, is to be found in Timoney (this volume).

It was on a fieldwalking expedition to Aughris on the Sunday following Kitchin's death that Jack Flynn, sometimes President of Sligo Field Club, suggested we have an annual memorial lecture for Kitchin and his colleague, Michael Cahalane. This memorial lecture now honours all our outstanding fieldwalkers since our foundation as Sligo Antiquarian Society in 1945.

References:

Kitchin, Finlay Tower, 1983: 'The Carrowmore Megalithic Cemetery, Co. Sligo', *Proc. Prehistoric Soc.*, 49, 151-175.

Timoney, Martin A., 'Aughris, Portavaud, Lackan and Kilcummin' in Timoney, ed., 2002.

Timoney, Martin A., and Heraughty, Patrick, 2002: 'Sligo Antiquarian Society and Sligo Field Club, 1945-2002' in Timoney, ed., 2002.

Timoney, Martin A., ed., 2002: *A Celebration of Sligo, Essays for Sligo Field Club*, Sligo, Sligo Field Club.

Group photograph taken at the launch of *The Megalithic Survey of Ireland, Vol. V, Co. Sligo* in 1989.

Front Row: Joyce Enright, Sheela Kitchin, Mary B. Timoney, Senator William Farrell Chairman of Sligo County Council, Frank O'Connor.
Back Row: Dr. Patrick Heraughty, Pat Hurley, Martin Enright, Br. Angelo, Mayor Roderick McGuinn, Vincent Jordan, Dr. Seán Ó Nualláin who wrote the volume, Seán Daly, Larry Mullin, Brendan Rooney, Aodhán O'Higgins, Martin A. Timoney, Leo Mattimoe, Jack Flynn, Brendan Byrne Sligo County Secretary.

AUGHRIS, PORTAVAUD, LACKAN AND KILCUMMIN

Martin A. Timoney
Sligo Field Club

ABSTRACT: Three locations in Co. Sligo, Aughris, Portavaud and Lackan, and one in Co. Mayo, Kilcummin, are linked by the presence of small earthen sub-rectangular enclosures similar in shape to playing cards. Many suggested interpretations of these enclosures are discussed. Associated place-names and folklore, historical references to the Augustinian priory of Aughris and the French landing at Kilcummin in 1798 are included, as is architectural and historical evidence for towered churches in Co. Sligo.

INTRODUCTION

This article, initially titled 'Earthen sub-rectangular enclosures at Aughris, Portavaud and Lackan, Co. Sligo, and Kilcummin, Co. Mayo, together with notes on these four sites', (Fig. 1) follows from a three-page manuscript note[1] written by Finlay Tower Kitchin, *alias* Pat, about 1972 (Kitchin 2002) which dealt with small earthen enclosures at Aughris which had been first noted before 1965 by his wife, Sheela. He compared them with enclosures at Portavaud which previously also had been first noted by Sheela Kitchin. His interpretation was that they were habitation sites.

The purpose of this article is to draw further attention to the enclosures but not to provide a comprehensive survey of them, to discuss suggested functions and to put on record information on these sites, more particularly Aughris which was a place of assembly of great antiquity.

In preparing the article for publication Aughris Head and Portavaud were visited many times in 1996 and more enclosures were discovered at both locations. Tom Condit of The Sites and Monuments Record Office had drawn my attention by 1991 to the enclosures at Kilcummin, Co. Mayo, which he had recently discovered and which from aerial photographs seemed to him to be of the same type. This proved on inspection to be so. Victor Buckley of the Archaeological Survey of Ireland drew my attention to the Lackan examples and Patrick Tuffy, Lackan, Inishcrone, gave me further information about these. The enclosures were discussed with many people in the barony of Tireragh, particularly in the Aughris and Portavaud areas and with many archaeologists. In 2001 Dr. Elizabeth FitzPatrick excavated one enclosure at the west end of Aughris.

THE ENCLOSURES

The monuments under consideration are small earthen enclosures of a more or less standard character, varying in shape from sub-rectangular, normally a rectangle with rounded corners, i.e., a shape like that of a playing card, though varying in proportions, to an oval or pear-shaped pattern. They consist of a slightly raised central area, seldom more than 25cm above the height of the surrounding field. This is surrounded by a shallow ditch, which in turn is surrounded by a bank, seldom of greater height than the interior. Only in those with low banks are the banks of a relatively consistent height for the full circuit.

The enclosing ditch was presumably designed to drain the central area. The soil arising from its excavation would have provided some material for the outer bank as well as perhaps some raising of the level of the central area. In no case

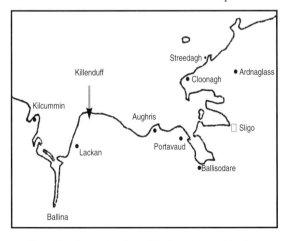

Fig. 1: Map showing locations of Aughris, Portavaud, Lackan, Ardnaglass and Cloonagh Co. Sligo, and Kilcummin, Co. Mayo.

is there anything that could be described as a definite entrance. Where the axial dimensions are close to being equal the enclosures look somewhat circular. The lesser dimension of all normal enclosures, be they big or small, is fairly consistent at 3m to 3.6m internally and 6m to 7m overall.

Without the benefits of a full survey of Aughris, Portavaud and Kilcummin, there is no apparent difference between the enclosures at the locations.[2] The Lackan enclosures no longer exist above ground.

AUGHRIS

Aughris Head[3] stands out on the coast of west Sligo in the way that The Cliffs of Moher do on the coast of Co. Clare. The very steep Lower Carboniferous limestone cliffs are renowned for their ornithological colonies.

The cliffs are just over 115 ft. (35m) high at most but are no more than a few feet high in some places. The coast is very rugged below the cliffs (Fig. 2; Bunn 1997, Pl. on 146-147). Near the west end of the cliffs the Atlantic drives into The Corragh dTonn sea cave (Fig. 3) with great power, creating great sound, sound which can be heard many miles away (Greer 1924, 124; Cowell 1989, 181). The headland has a maximum height of 146 ft. (45m) at which point there is a World War II lookout. Its majestic 35m cliffs with its enormous bird colonies and seals can be best seen from out at sea. At the east end is Aughris Pier. No doubt past peoples partook of the riches of the sea here as they do today. The cliff edge walk from Aughris Pier towards the promontory fort has recently been re-established (Canning & Dalby 1998, 14) and Aughris has received mention in at least one foreign produced tourist guide (Greenwood, Connolly and Wallis 1999, 417). Dúchas – The Heritage Service is currently proposing to declare Aughris Head a Special Protection Area, number SPA 004133, due to the importance of its ecology and international importance for wild birds.

At the east end of the headland[4] is a triple banked[5] cliff-edge or promontory fort (Condit 1997, Pl. 6; 1998, 30)[6] known locally as 'O'Toole's Castle', set over 20m directly above the pounding Atlantic which has severely eroded it. Nimo (1824, 27) recorded this as "the remains of a triple entrenchment called Toole's Castle".

The recently re-built St. Patrick's Well, an altar of stone slabs, and a small cairn are some fields to the west of the fort. There are wooden crosses on both the altar and the cairn. Towards the west end of Aughris Head there is a large mound, known locally as Healy's Round Hill, and a

Fig. 2: The sea cliffs of Aughris Head, Co. Sligo, looking west. Photo Martin A. Timoney.

Fig. 3: *The Corragh dTonn* sea cave, looking south. Photo Martin A. Timoney.

cashel and hut hollows (Sl.12:17). Somewhere hereabout are "the graves of drowned sailors" (William Kennedy, pers. comm.; possibly they are of a shipwreck of 1822 or 1843 at Pollgorm referred to by Bourke (1994, 198) citing *Ireland's Own*, 39 (1922), 347). Further west in Kilrusheighter is an unusual mound (Sl.12:18) and the remnants of a probable burial site, possibly a megalithic tomb (Grid Ref. 1484.3350) discovered in 1996 by the author and perhaps what was been referred to by MacNeill (1961, 112). To the south in Aughris is an enclosure (Sl.12:108) and a Fullacht Fiadha site (Sl.12:113).

There are at least two parallel and superimposed systems of earthen field banks on the Head,[7] the general alignment of which is about 10 degrees west of the line of the slope of the higher part of the Head. The banks are of varying height and current usefulness, some being severely eroded down.

There are more subdivisions of the land today than are indicated on the 1837 O.S. 6" Sligo sheet 12, though some that were there in 1837 are now no more than very low banks.[8] There are at least five rectangular plots, which could be called small fields, mainly set askew to the field systems. In one of the Michael Gibbons aerial photographs[9] there appears to be the cropmark of a further rectangular plot and a possible circular one. There are two banked trackways running generally northwards across the Head.

These are 2.50m wide with a fosse either side and a bank outside that again. There are several areas of cultivation ridges on the Head. Some pieces of folklore and tradition relating to Aughris are given in Appendix I.

There are large numbers of these intact, low, faint or ploughed down enclosures (Figs. 4 to 10) scattered over an area of 2.2km by 300m across Aughris Head. A major survey would be needed to do full justice to them. The measurements of fourteen sample enclosures out of "in total of perhaps some 150 to 200 sites", to use Kitchin's phrase, are given. One survey drawing of two adjacent enclosures **(Fig. 4)** and a number of photographs will suffice to illustrate their character.

STANDARD ENCLOSURES.

A1: One standard large enclosure (Fig. 5) measures 12.40m by 6.60m overall with the slightly domed interior measuring 7.60m by 2.90m. The fosse is 0.80m to 1.0m wide and the bank is 1.10m to 1.40m wide and at most 0.25m high. It has rounded corners.

A2: One standard small enclosure measures 7.20m by 6.50m overall with the interior measuring 4.10m by 3.50m. The fosse is 0.50m to 0.60m wide and the bank is 0.80m to 1.10m wide and at most 0.40m high. It also has rounded corners but, because of the near equality of dimensions, it looks somewhat circular.

A3: The smallest enclosure noted measures 5.60m by 5.80m overall making it almost circular.[10]

A4: The widest regularly shaped enclosure is south-east of Healy's Round Hill near the west end of the distribution. It measures 10.80m by 4m internally and with the normal width ditch and bank it comes to 15.60m by 8.30m overall.

A5: A large enclosure measures 16m by 8.80m overall with the interior measuring 10.40m by 3.6m. The fosse is 0.80m wide at the sides and 1.10m wide at the ends. The bank is 1m to 1.60m wide and at the N corner is 0.45m higher than the fosses beside it. The interior is 0.40m higher than the ditch near the W corner. It has rounded corners but is quite rectangular overall. While its south end is somewhat flattened the bank around its north end is in better condition than the banks on most other enclosures.

A6: Two adjacent enclosures in the SW corner of the field SW of the promontory fort were surveyed with a total station (Fig. 4). These enclosures touch corner-to-corner.

The southern enclosure measures 10.90m by

Fig. 5: Aughris Head, Co. Sligo, a standard large enclosure, looking W.   Photo: Martin A. Timoney.

6.80m overall with the interior measuring 6.20m by 2.90m. The fosse is 0.90m to 1.20m wide and the bank is 1.10m to 1.40m wide and at most 0.30m high. It has rounded corners. The northern end is somewhat flattened.

The northern enclosure, which is more flattened than its neighbour, measures 10m by 8m overall with the interior measuring 5.40m by 3.60m. The fosse is 0.90m to 1.30m wide and the bank is 1.00m to 1.50m wide and at most 0.20m high. It has rounded corners to the extent that it is more oval than sub-rectangular.

Fig. 4: Plan of side-by-side sites SW of Aughris fort. Plan: Thomas Gallagher.

Fig. 6: Aughris Head, Co. Sligo, an enclosure with two unequal internal areas, looking W.   Photo: Martin A. Timoney.

MULTIPLE ENCLOSURES

Towards the higher part of Aughris Head there are a few examples of double enclosures and one example of a treble enclosure. In the cases of two side-by-side enclosures and the three side-by-side enclosures the individual enclosures are basically of the standard dimensions. It is not clear as to whether we are dealing with consecutive or contemporary enclosures, though the former is more likely.

A7: One side-by-side enclosure consists of a complete enclosure and a parallel contiguous enclosure that it is lacking its longer common western side.

A8: In the case of the three side-by-side

enclosures the three enclosures are parallel, with the western enclosure being about 1.5m downhill, half the length of the enclosure, of the other pair but otherwise contiguous with the central enclosure.

COMPLEX ENCLOSURES

Most of the enclosures are of a standard nature but there are variations.

A9: Towards the eastern end of the distribution a number of standard enclosures have a C-shaped bank and ditch formation of the same nature set against one side (Fig. 6), as if the main enclosure was constructed over and at right angles to an earlier enclosure, though they could represent an annex to the main enclosure.

A10: There are at least three examples of regular enclosures with two unequal internal areas separated by a slightly shallower ditch (Fig. 7). It is not clear if this pattern was primary or if it is the result of subdivision or of extension. One of these measures 14m by 8.60m overall. Its bank stands 0.60m above the base of a deep wet fosse.

Fig. 7: Aughris Head, Co. Sligo, an enclosure with C-shaped bank and ditch formation of the same nature set against one side, that nearest the camera. Further sites in the background, looking SW. Photo: Martin A. Timoney.

A11: A large enclosure measures 14m by 7.60m overall with the interior measuring 9.30m by 3m. The fosse is 0.70m wide, the bank is 1.50m to 1.80m wide and at most 0.20m high. It has rounded corners but is quite rectangular. Set at an angle of 45 degrees to its south-west corner is another enclosure whose overall dimensions are 7.80m by 4.50m. It is not clear if the larger enclosure 'cuts into' the smaller enclosure and so may overlie it or if the smaller enclosure is an annex.

There is a fine enclosure west of a stone wall SW of cliff-edge or promontory fort (Figs. 8 and 9).

NON-STANDARD SHAPED ENCLOSURES

There are some odd shaped enclosures among the many at Aughris.

A12: The largest odd shaped enclosure is 18m by 11.20m, but its bank and ditch are hardly discernible; it is west of a trackway.

A13: In only one case, near the World War II lookout on top of the hill, is the central area below that of the surrounding field; this particular example is pear-shaped and is different from the others.

These fourteen descriptions cover all the types noted so far within the "total of perhaps some 150 to 200" enclosures on Aughris Head.

COUNT & DISTRIBUTION

The enclosures are spread out over an area 2.2km by 300m. None seem to survive to the south of the crest of the ridge of Aughris Head, except at the western end, perhaps because of greater agricultural activity here. One enclosure is very close to the present shore. In the area immediately to the west of the promontory fort there is a remarkable concentration of enclosures. Kitchin (2002) records that the first field to the west of the fort, rotovated in the 1970s, revealed some 40 or 50 of these enclosures.[11] Many enclosures still survive in this field, some only as mere cropmarks seen in Gibbons' aerial photograph (Condit 1997, Pl. 6; 1998, 30) and several more that I detected on the ground. The adjoining field to the west of that contains a somewhat lesser, though nonetheless significant, concentration. Other fields to the west again show further concentrations and so on right up across the highest part of the headland as one goes westward. The area west of the highest part of the headland seems to have fewer enclosures but further west again the distribution intensifies again. Here there are several good examples in the area near Healy's Round Hill. In addition to the concentrations of enclosures individual enclosures of this nature are to be found over the greater part of Aughris Head. Their distribution is continuous but not even. There are no rows of enclosures and nothing that could be called a linear pattern. Without a survey it would <u>appear</u> that the enclosures on the higher part of the Head are generally longer than those towards the promontory fort end.

The total was "perhaps some 150 to 200" enclosures. This is about four times the "40 to 50" figure attributed by Condit (1998, 29) to the writer. Their true count and distribution can not

Fig. 8 - Enclosure SW of cliff-edge or promontory fort at Aughris, Co. Sligo, looking S. Photo: Martin A. Timoney.

Fig. 9 - The same enclosure SW of cliff-edge or promontory fort at Aughris, Co. Sligo, looking SE. Photo Martin A. Timoney.

Fig. 10 - Enclosure close to Healy's Round Hill during excavation, 01E0700, in 2001 by Dr. Elizabeth FitzPatrick, looking SW. Photo: Martin A. Timoney.

be established without early Spring aerial photography of the entire headland. After the growth of grass enclosures become very difficult even to relocate, never mind discover. The relationship of these small earthen enclosures to each other or to the other features on Aughris Head is not clear. One is cut by the banked trackway, a few are cut by field banks. Some are at right angles to others not far away. None seem to be aligned on any specific feature and there is no apparent standard orientation.

The banks and interiors of some enclosures in one field at the eastern end of Aughris Head were levelled in 1995.

PORTAVAUD

Portavaud, 8 km. to the east of Aughris, is near the entrance to Ballisodare Bay and opposite the sandspit south of Strandhill. Here the enclosures (Figs. 11-14) are on a sandspit that is 1.5km long and varies in width from 15m to 90m. On the landward side of it there is a tidal lagoon. There is a possible ringfort or enclosure (Sl.13:86) at the east end of the spit and a raised ringfort and an ringfort or enclosure (Sl.13:78 and Sl.13:79) just south of the neck of the spit.

stones. The seven enclosures so far located on the ground are generally in a near linear fashion over an area measuring less than 200m E-W by 30m N-S. Their general E-W alignment reflects the alignment of the storm beach ridges. All the enclosures so far located at Portavaud are close together in an area where the vegetation is very low. There may be further enclosures concealed by the longer grass to the west and by the marram grass to the east and the build-up of sea sand along the north side of the sandspit may conceal other enclosures.

Kitchin referred to 'five or six' enclosures here but fieldwork, aerial photography and the Recorded Monuments listing combined suggest at least nine enclosures.[13] There are no complex enclosures at Portavaud.

The measurements of the seven enclosures, from west to east, are as follows.

P1: The westernmost enclosure is 10.30m by 5.90m overall with the interior measuring 6.30m by 2.20m. The fosse is 0.60m to 1m wide and the bank is 0.90m to 1.50m wide. The interior appears to be raised but only because it is cut into a slight ridge. It is not quite rectangular but

Fig. 11 - Portavaud, Co. Sligo, enclosures on south side of sandspit, looking E. Photo Martin A. Timoney.

The enclosures are close together near a modern marker cairn on the sheltered landward side of the sandspit (Fig. 11).[12] This area would be covered by the sea at only very high tide. Some enclosures are cut into the old storm beach ridges which contain many small sea rolled

is slightly wider at its SE end due to the curvature of the ridge on which it is. It has rounded corners.

P2: This enclosure is 15m to the east and measures 4.30m by 4.20m overall making it almost circular. The interior measures 2m by 1.30m. The fosse is 0.30m to 0.60m wide and the bank is 0.50m to 1m wide. It is barely discernible on the south side of a ridge.

P3: There may be a very small enclosure, of similar dimensions to P2, a further 50m to the east.

P4: This enclosure (Fig. 12), 40m further east again, measures 12.50m by 9m overall with the interior measuring 8.80m by 5.10m. The fosse is 0.70m to 0.80m wide and the bank is 1m to 1.50m wide. The interior appears to be raised but only because it is cut into a slight ridge. It is rectangular with rounded corners.

Fig. 12 - Portavaud, Co. Sligo, enclosure P4 cut into a slight ridge, looking W. Photo: Martin A. Timoney.

P5: Beside P6 is a small enclosure measuring 5m by 5.60m overall with the interior measuring 2.10m by 3m. The fosse is 0.40m to 0.60m wide and the bank is 0.60m to 1.10m wide. The interior is no higher than the surrounding ground. There are many small sea-rolled stones exposed in the bank where the sod is disturbed.

P6: The southernmost enclosure (Fig. 13) measures 11.20m by 8.20m overall with the interior measuring 6.30m by 4.40m. The fosse is 0.50m to 1m wide and the bank is 1m to 1.50m wide. It is rectangular with rounded corners.

Fig. 13 - Portavaud, Co. Sligo, the southernmost enclosure, P6, looking SW. Photo: Martin A. Timoney.

P7: The easternmost enclosure (Fig. 14), 40m east of P6, measures 9.90m by 7.30m overall with the interior measuring 5.70m by 3.20m. The fosse is 0.80m to 1m wide and the bank is 1.10m to 1.30m wide. The interior is 0.70m above the base of the clear-cut unbroken fosse. The interior looks to be raised but only because it is cut into a slight ridge. It is rectangular with rounded corners.

Fig. 14 - Portavaud, Co. Sligo, the easternmost enclosure P7 cut into a slight ridge, looking N. Photo: Martin A. Timoney.

LACKAN

North of the village of Inishcrone, Co. Sligo, is the magnificent multi-banked coastal cliff-edge fort, 'Cahermore', in Carrowhubbuck North. To the north of this again the Atlantic is severely eroding out a bay in the townland of Lackan, *alias* Lacken. Here close to the shore, and close to the earlier first millennium A.D. burial known as 'The Fisherman's Grave' (Buckley *et al.* 1991-1992), there were two L1 and L2, and possibly more, of these enclosures (Fig. 15), surviving until recent times (Buckley 1998). We are indebted to Patrick Tuffy of this townland for details of these sites. They are Recorded Monuments Sl.16:77 and Sl.16:78. Because of the severe erosion of this part of the coast we must allow for the possibility of other examples hereabouts.

Fig. 15 - Lackan, Co. Sligo, mound part of possible enclosure, looking W. Photo: Patrick Tuffy

L1: This was just north of 'The Fisherman's Grave' in a shallow depression inside of the storm beach. Only the faintest indications remain. With the eye of faith one can see the remnants of the surrounding bank and an internal ditch. Overall it would have been 12m by 8m.

L2: This was further north again, above a five metre rock cliff. It is remembered as being as much as 18m by 12m and larger than L1; it was more oval than rectangular. All above ground indications have been levelled.

KILCUMMIN

On the Co. Mayo side of Killala Bay, opposite Inishcrone, is Kilcummin promontory, standing at 50 to 100 ft. above sea level and surrounded on three sides by rocky cliffs. It is between Lackan Bay and Rathfran Bay and to the north of Killala. The point of the headland is Benwee Head. There was a Garland Sunday *patrún* at *Tobar Chuimín*, Ballinlena, the next townland to the south east of Kilcummin (MacNeill 1962, 498, 611-612). Just south of here again is Pollaclogher where the French landed in 1798 (See footnote 19).

South of Benwee Head in Kilcummin,[14] an area, numbered Ma.8:9 on the Recorded Monuments and Places maps, is boxed off and is listed as 'Barrow-Group Possible' (Gibbons *et. al.*, 1991). The SMR file notes up to 18 oblong ditched enclosures possibly a form of ring barrow identical to those at Aughris. Most regrettably, the largest field (Fig. 16) within this boxed off area has been re-seeded, probably between 1994 and 1998, obliterating all surface remains of pre-existing features; two major south-to-north drains have been dug along the sides of the field. Fieldwalking in 1997 and 1998 by the Timoney family located enclosures (Figs. 16-17) of the same type as those at Aughris and Portavaud in the fields to the west and south of this.

Subsequent to my first visit Noel O'Neill provided me with an aerial photograph of the central area of the distribution (Pl. 16; Condit 1998, 29, top) taken on 18th. Feb., 1994, prior to the re-seeding. In the two photos one can count 23 definite enclosures, 17 of which are excellent examples, and there are a further 17 possible enclosures here.[15] There are other enclosures beyond the limits of the photos. There is a minimum of 40 enclosures here. Ten of the enclosures were in the field that has been re-seeded.[16] The enclosures are scattered at random, with no pattern of orientation, among degraded field banks of at least three periods. In the aerial photographs one can see a few enclosures that are of the almost square variety and at least two instances, perhaps three, of almost contiguous enclosures. Complex enclosures of the types we have at Aughris have not yet been recognised at Kilcummin. Cultivation ridges overlie one enclosure at the top, *i.e.*, south, of the photo (Fig. 16).

The measurements of the five sample enclosures are as follows.

K1: The largest measured enclosure (Fig. 17) is rectangular with rounded corners and measures overall 13m by 7.60m.

Fig. 16 - Kilcummin, Co. Mayo, 18th. Feb., 1994, of the central part of the distribution of enclosures, looking S. The field to the left has since been re-seeded. Enclosures K1 to K4 are in the central field. Photo: Noel O'Neill.

Fig. 17 - Kilcummin, Co. Mayo, enclosure K1, a standard large enclosure, looking W. Photo: Martin A. Timoney.

K2: Another large enclosure of similar dimensions is very low on the ground.

K3: The smallest enclosure is somewhat oval in plan and measures overall 9.50m by 7.20m. It is truncated by a very degraded bank.

K4: This enclosure is 7.50m wide and has a current field bank built across it, beyond which the deep drain has removed the NE end of it.

K5: This enclosure measures 9m by 2.3m internally, has a ditch 0.5m to 1m wide and a 1m wide external bank.

COMMENT

The rectangular enclosures under consideration consist of a slightly raised central area surrounded by a shallow ditch and a low bank. They are found at four locations, Aughris with some "150 to 200" enclosures, Portavaud with at least nine enclosures, Lackan with at least two enclosures, and Kilcummin, with at least forty enclosures.[17]

Aughris and Kilcummin, promontories at 20m to 35m above sea level, show evidence of past tillage and degraded field banks of several periods and both have World War II lookouts. Portavaud and Lackan are almost at sea level.[18]

There is no strong folk tradition relating to the Aughris enclosures; the last inhabitants of the now-deserted Aughris village could shed no light on them. Some folklore relating to the Aughris area is recorded in Appendix I. Vague suggestions of there having been a camp up on Aughris Head are the normal response of the locals to questions about these enclosures. None of the locals seemed to be aware of the just how great are the numbers of enclosures there.

History is also silent on the matter. The battle of Aughris, fought in 598 (Wood-Martin 1882, 142) or in 602 (=603) (Byrne 1972, 75; 1973, 239), at which the *Cinel Cairbre*, of Carbury, defeated the *Cinel Fiachrach of Muirsc*, part of Tireragh, may have taken place on this headland. Mulligan (1942), in his topographical notes on the parish of Templeboy, records that the Men of Ulster, the Northerners, were beaten as far as the stream between Ballygreighan and Ballinphull further south in Templeboy Parish and finally defeated at *Awan a Vuai*, alias *Annawoe*, alias The River of Victory. MacNeill (1962, 587) refers to the local tradition, recorded in the Folklore Commission's schools manuscripts in 1934 by Michael Keane, that the Danes were the losers in a battle at or near a fort in Bernie Gilhool's land. There is no proven link between these enclosures and the Augustinian monastery of Aughris, whatever the location of that building be (See Appendix II).

There seems to be no local awareness of the Portavaud enclosures other than from Finlay Tower Kitchin or Sligo Field Club sources. The Lackan enclosures were discovered by Patrick Tuffy. It is suggested in the Kilcummin area that the enclosures were camp sites associated with the French landing of 1798, an apparently unfounded idea, though one frequently advanced in the bicentennial year, 1998, of that event.[19]

FUNCTION

What then is the reason for the presence of these enclosures and at Aughris, Portavaud, Lackan and Kilcummin? There seems to be nothing directly comparable to these enclosures in the published archaeological record.

Over the years Sligo Field Club members brought visiting experts in archaeology and folklife to Aughris to see if they could shed light on their nature. Their suggestions as to the function of the enclosures and those of people who have only seen photographs of them are now examined and reasons for their dismissal are given where appropriate. The arguments are applicable to the Portavaud, Lackan and Kilcummin enclosures also.

1. The Aughris and Portavaud complexes are both listed by Raftery (1974, 95) under **'habitation sites'** which was the opinion of Sligo Field Club, particularly Kitchin, at that time (see Kitchin 2002).[20]

2. They might have been the temporary dwellings of persons engaged in salt panning. Their location on high cliffs without easy access to the sea and in such numbers at Aughris and Kilcummin defeats this suggestion. In this context, the enclosures at Portavaud are in a location, close to the shore of the tidal lagoon, which could well have a salt panning connection but there is no evidence for such there.[21]

3. Marcus Ó hEochaidhe,[22] immediately on seeing them identified them as identical in plan and character with the medieval booley sites [23] which he himself had excavated at Slieve Breagh, Co. Meath. Perhaps these are the Group 'C' earthworks as defined by de Paor and Ó hEochaidhe (1956, 100) who conducted some excavations. The record of these excavations does not seem to have been available to Moore (1987). None of Moore's descriptions of the sites on Slieve Breagh seem to match any of the types of enclosure at Aughris, Portavaud, Lackan and Kilcummin. If Ó hEochaidhe's comparison for these enclosures was correct they would be medieval in date and, by analogy with all booley sites, temporary in nature. That they were true booley sites associated with cattle herding is most improbable at the locations in question. In the first place, the essence of the booleying system was the removal of stock in summer to mountain or other high altitude pastures, pastures often far removed from the farms to which they belonged. Aughris Head is no more than a mile or so from some of the very best cattle fattening and tillage land in the county, an area described in past centuries as 'The Granary for the Counties of Leitrim and Fermanagh' with 'a considerable store still left for exportation, sometimes 30,000 barrels of barley are exported from the port of Sligo in one year' (Henry 1739, 349).[24] Secondly, the presence of "in total of perhaps some 150 to 200" enclosures randomly scattered in a space 2.2 km by 300m, less than a square kilometre, would suggest that herdsmen would have outnumbered cattle![25] Furthermore the idea of booley huts at Portavaud, Lackan and Kilcummin seems equally illogical.

4. Maire MacNeill refers to the Aughris patrún that was held in former times on Garland Sunday, the last Sunday in July, at St. Patrick's Well to the west of the promontory fort on Aughris (MacNeill 1962, 112-113; 'Portholanus' 1861-1862, 72; Kitchin 2002).[26] This patrún was attended by people from all over the Baronies of Leyney and Tireragh and she records that many people from Leyney arrived the day before.[27] That fact, coupled with the probability that the fringe activities of sports, dancing, matchmaking[28] and drinking often associated with these occasions would involve a stay of a period of two or three days, and the argument was that this necessitated the provision of some form of *temporary accommodation*, hence the enclosures. The local people recall that the visitors stayed in barns, outhouses, *etc.*, as well as in friend's houses. Questions that have to be raised with this suggested explanation for the enclosures are 'Why are the enclosures so scattered if connected with a patrún associated with the holy well, around which there is not any greater density of enclosures? Why are they at Portavaud and Lackan where there was no patrún? There was a Garland Sunday patrún at Tobar Chuimín, adjacent to Kilcummin (MacNeill 1962, 498, 611-612).

5. These enclosures are comparable with the *booley huts of late medieval*, 15th.-16th. century, date at Goodland, Co. Antrim. The publication of the Goodland complex (Case *et al.* 1969) concentrates on paleoecology, with the hut enclosures as such getting little specific attention. There is no description of a hut-site and the only close photograph of one (Case *et al.* 1969, Pl. 16a) shows a bank with there being no sign of a raised interior. From the report (Case *et al.* 1969, 41, 43, 44, 53, Pl. 15-16) these sites are not comparable to those at Aughris, Portavaud, Lackan and Kilcummin. McDonald (1992, figs. 17, 19B and 27) illustrates some Achill, Co. Mayo, booley houses. These have at least one entrance and the remains of the wall stands higher than the interior.

6. These enclosures were **habitation sites** of an unspecified period. The absence of anything resembling an entrance and the lack of indication

of back as opposed to front to any of the enclosures argues against their functioning as habitations. The small dimensions of the interior, not just of the smallest enclosures, further argues this case. Some enclosures at Portavaud are cut into the old storm beach ridges in a way that argues against them being for habitation. There is no evidence for an overall defensive feature at any of the four locations.

7. They had something to do with the **Augustinian Canons monastery** of Aughris. They are to be found at three other sites, each lacking a medieval monastic site. They are not known from other monastic locations.

8. They had something to do with **'O'Toole's Castle'**. They are to be found at two other sites, each lacking a castle. They are not known from other castle locations.

9. They are the bases for **reeks of hay.** Surely the building of reeks of hay would be totally illogical from a wind point of view on the exposed locations of Aughris, Lackan and Kilcummin and would not be logical from a sea level point of view on Portavaud sandspit. The material from the ditch would be better used to raise the interior to provide a dry platform rather than to build an unnecessary bank which would retain water in the fosse; this applies to several of the other suggested uses.

10. That they were **storage structures** can be dismissed for the same reasons.

11. They had something to do with the **World War II lookouts** at Aughris and Kilcummin. There is no foundation for this suggestion. There is no lookout at Portavaud and Lackan.

#12. Should one then turn to a **funerary function** for these enclosures and compare them with ring barrows? In common with ring-barrows they have a low central mound surrounded by a shallow ditch and a low bank. The essential difference is in their shape; they are basically sub-rectangular, as opposed to round, but have rounded corners, like playing cards. This suggested interpretation, that of barrows, was arrived at independently by Condit and by myself. The SMR file on Kilcummin suggests that the oblong ditched enclosures are possibly a form of ring barrow identical to those at Aughris. Two suggestions arose as a follow-up to Condit's 1998 article.

13. These enclosures have something to do with **kelp burning.** These enclosures would not be suitable for kelp burning. Dornan (2000, pl. 21, a & b) illustrates a kelp burner or kiln near Porteen na Laghta on Inishkea South, Co. Mayo, and he describes the process on pp. 143-144. Dornan (pers. comm.) has noted about thirty of these on the Inishkea Islands. See also below.

14. They were pillow mounds in a rabbit warren. None show any sign of rabbit burrowing and they are not really mounds.

FURTHER INTERPETATIONS

The recent classifications of these sites at the four locations are now mentioned. In the Sites and Monuments Record, Co. Sligo (Gibbons *et al.* 1989) the Aughris sites are included under the all-encompassing term of 'archaeological complex' and those at Portavaud are classified as "habitation site". The Lackan examples were not known to archaeologists in 1989. In the Sites and Monuments Record, Co. Mayo (Gibbons *et al.* 1991) the Kilcummin enclosures are classified as 'barrow group – possible'. In the Recorded Monuments and Places, Co. Sligo (1995) Aughris is again included under the term "archaeological complex" but the enclosures at Portavaud are classified as "mound". The enclosures at Lackan are classified as "barrow". Condit (1998, 30) suggests that we are dealing with a previously unrecorded type of barrow.

Rectangular barrows do not seem to be present in the Irish archaeological record. Foreign parallels are not forthcoming either. The rectangular, really sub-square, barrows of Iron Age Yorkshire, e.g., Wetwang Slack (Dent 1982, 440), Garton Slack (Brewster 1975, 111 & 113), and Rudston and Burton Flemming (Stead 1985, Pl. 91; 1991; 1996, Pl. 98) do not seem to invite comparison.

This is also the view of Dr. Ian Stead who, having read an earlier draft of this article and having seen some of the photographs, commented as follows in a letter of 10th Jan., 1997.

"In some ways they do resemble the Yorkshire square barrows, in overall size, low mounds, absence of entrances, grouping in 'cemeteries', and even the multiple-monuments. But they do seem to be distinctively rectangular, whereas the Yorkshire ones are square or squarish; the Yorkshire barrows do not have external banks, and the ditches are quarries for the mounds and not intended for drainage. Above all, of course, the Yorkshire barrows have central burials."

Neither the post-Roman square-ditched graves at Tandderwen, Clwyd, (James 1992, 92-93) nor the square-ditch barrows of the Pictlands of Scotland (Alcock 1992, 127-128) seem comparable. The Neolithic barrow, described as oval but really rectangular with rounded corners, beside the Abingdon causewayed enclosure in Oxfordshire (Bradley 1992, 131) is much larger than the largest of the Aughris enclosures and is not comparable.

Condit (1998, 30) surmises that the Aughris and Kilcummin enclosures are barrows of two of the largest barrow cemeteries in Ireland.

RESPONSES TO CONDIT

There was a considerable response to the article by Condit (1998) on the Kilcummin and Aughris sites from English fieldworkers. The general thrust of it is that there are similar features on the downlands of Bodmin Moor at 200m to 380m ASL, where about nine hundred and fifty have been identified, and on The Lizard at 65m to 110m ASL, where another nine hundred and fifty have been identified. These, it is argued, were steads for turf ricks, though some of the ideas about how turf is saved would not work in the west of Ireland. They also claim that they were used up to the middle of this century. Some of the respondents mention the possibility of these sites being for producing charcoal in medieval times or that they were prehistoric house platforms, though Quinnell as a *caveat* at the end of his report writes "Most platforms appear to be very old, under a pasture which has replaced the ultimate stripping of peat, and in more than one instance a platform is cut through by a tinner's leat".

This writer, while admitting that some of the English examples may well have been for **saving turf**, discounts this explanation for the Sligo and Mayo enclosures. Why construct a ditch and outer bank which would retain water close to the base of the turf you are trying to dry? Would a 30cm bank outside a shallow ditch protect the turf rick from animals? Certainly all our four locations are in windswept locations, good for drying turf but then the Sligo examples are frequently showered with sea spray from the pounding Atlantic! More to the point are questions of where was the turf coming from, and even more so, where was it being brought to? Aughris, Portavaud, Lackan and Kilcummin are places of isolation. If these enclosures were for turf why have we not found them along the edges of our many bogs? Such explanations are simply non-tenable!

One of the respondents to Condit (1998) referred to the publication of the excavation of Site 40, Trelan, Cornwall, (Smith 1984) in support of the turf drying theory. The site in question, which had been ploughed down, was an inner sub-circular ring ditch, 5.5m in diameter, within and later than an oval ring ditch. The single pottery fragment, despite being "too simple to be diagnostic" was thought "to fall within the post-Roman to Early Medieval bracket" (Smith 1984, 8). Radiocarbon dating of charcoal from a contemporary hearth gave a 13th. to early 15th. century date range (Smith 1988, 213). I mention it here for the sake of completeness of the response, even though the site is not comparable to our enclosures.

Perhaps, most telling of all is the comment in 1970 of an eighty year old turf cutter from Bolventor, Bodmin Moore, that he had "had no idea of what the platforms were" and was dubious of the suggested interpretation as turf drying platforms . . ."we don't cut or dry peat that way" (Quinnell in Smith 1984, 11-12).

Another suggestion from the English fieldworkers is that we these features are pillow mounds in a rabbit warren. None of enclosures show any sign of burrowing.

A separate theme was raised in response to Condit's article (1998) by Skeehan (1998, 40). He wonders about the usefulness of the banks and ditches of coastal promontory forts as defensive features against humans, as opposed to against carnivorous quadrupeds, and asks if promontory forts could have contained **excarnation platforms.**

AUGHRIS, A PLACE OF IMPORTANCE

Aughris has in recent times been a meeting place of major importance (see Appendix I). Greer (1924, 124-125), after describing the natural wonders of Aughris, writes "No wonder that Aughris has been on many occasions the trysting place for great and renowned gatherings of Tireragh. In days of old it was the gathering spot - the Tara of the barony. In modern times it has been so."

One must ask why so many assemblies for different purposes were held at Aughris. Aughris is an obvious landmark (Fig. 2) in the Tireragh landscape but it is not the most accessible location for major gatherings. It is a kilometre away from the coast road (Taylor and Skinner 1777; 1783, 224-225), which pre-dates the present main Ballisodare via Dromore West to Ballina road. This aspect on accessibility of course is as if we are looking at Aughris from the perspective of modern land transport. There is a pier at Aughris and if one considers travel by sea across Ballisodare, Sligo and Drumcliff Bays, and we have plenty of tradition for this, Aughris is much more central location within the combined baronies of Tireragh and Carbury. It also stands out in the landscape of Tireragh and the seascape of west Sligo.

Should we see Aughris as the equivalent of a

promontory fort or a hillfort, a hillfort of the non-defensive type?,[29] defined not by earthworks but by a combination of a stream and low ground to the south. Should we see the entire headland as a ritual promontory fort with a defensive promontory fort at one end and a large bowl barrow and a possible passage tomb at the other? If Aughris Head was a promontory fort or a hillfort, does this bring the enclosures into the Later Bronze Age or Iron Age date? and also the enclosures at Portavaud, Lackan and Kilcummin into that time span as well?[30] Essentially the enclosures at all four locations are of the same nature.

Few people today see the cliffs and its noisy sea caves, the bird colonies and the seals of Aughris Head (Fig. 2-3).[31] Did this add to the allure of the place, even have been its raison d'être as a place of assembly in past times?

RESEARCH & FIELDWORK BY FITZPATRICK

In 1999 **Dr. Elizabeth FitzPatrick,** Dept. of Archaeology, NUI Galway, began a survey of *Carn Inghine Briain*, the post-Norman inauguration site of the Ó Dubhda, and the surrounding area in Kilrusheighter, a townland to the southwest of Aughris. This survey was extended northwards to the west end of Aughris and included some earthen enclosures of the type described above. In 2001 FitzPatrick excavated one enclosure, 13 m by 7 m, about 50 m to the south-east of Healy's Round Hill at the west end of Aughris. In return for my giving Dr. FitzPatrick an earlier draft of this article she gave me a copy of her preliminary report for Dúchas on her excavation, 01E0700 (Fig. 10). In the report she sets out her reasons, including a transcript of an interview with William and Mary Kilgannon of Doonmmadden as to why she believes these enclosures, found on commonage areas under estate management in recent centuries, were for stacking wrack after it had dried out and before it was processed elsewhere with sea rods to make kelp; See Appendix IV for enclosures at Cloonagh and Ballyconnell and Appendix V for the modern *Fionnán* enclosures in Co. Kerry. These Aughris enclosures were not used for burning kelp. Kilgannon did not recollect any enclosures being built in his time, only of their being used.

The dating suggested for the enclosures by Dr. FitzPatrick is that they are nineteenth and early twentieth century. The finds are recent and these are from the base of the ditch of the enclosure. FitzPatrick reports that there are a dozen sites on *Eireaball Sionnaigh Racecourse*, whose limits are not clearly defined on the ground, but which is earlier we do not know.

Could this be an occasional re-use of this type of site? The Kilgannon's talk of 'round circles', as opposed to playing-card shaped, enclosures at Aughris. I find it rather strange that despite my questioning of John Stephen Kilgallon, Pat and Sean Finnegan and Willie Kennedy in the mid-1990s and members of SFC, Kitchin in particular, asking similar questions in the 1970s, there never has been a clear-cut interpretation offered as what these enclosures were for. Kitchin and colleagues was researching here when people were still using traditional farming methods in this area. They should have picked up traditions. They talked to old Mrs. Finnegan and they were provided with tea by the inhabitants of Aughris village and the hip-flask is remembered as having loosened many tongues over the years! The suggested usage of wrack drying has come from only one family only. The dominant local traditions were of a camp site.

FitzPatrick's paper on the archaeology and folklore of Aughris was published by the Royal Irish Academy in April 2002 (FitzPatrick 2001). In it she provides much detail of the west end of Aughris and many of the facts set out in my article are eloquently set against the background of folklore and medieval history on a national scale. She discusses the rectangular enclosures (FitzPatrick 2001, 85-90) and counts them at "over 250" (FitzPatrick 2001, 90) which is more than 50 over the highest figure suggested above. Several enclosures new to me show up in her Plates I and II and extend and intensify the distribution at the western end of Aughris. She comments that the "most recent use of the enclosures was allegedly for stacking wrack" and "the question remains as to whether these monuments had quite a different function originally and were used latterly as wrack steads" (FitzPatrick 2001, 90 and footnote 78). Perhaps we are both saying that the jury is still out on these enclosures!

CONCLUSION

The question of the presence of these enclosures at four coastal locations, Aughris, Portavaud, Lackan and Kilcummin, remains to be answered. Only the testimony of the spade may establish the true story of these enclosures and to other questions opened herein. Perhaps analysis of soil samples may provide pointers but then being so close to the sea the effects of frequent drenching with sea spray may not be significantly different to temporary piling of seaweed. Hopefully this article, prompted by that by Kitchin (2002) will lead to further work, consisting of a full survey of each of the locations and consequent total extensive excavation of several carefully chosen sample sites across the four locations. In the meantime we should preserve them, for they could be endangered by current Government farming grants and practices, and incorporate their locations into coastal walks.

APPENDIX I

Some Facts and Folklore of Aughris, Co. Sligo.

The lands of Tireragh are fertile and green,
Fit homes for brave peasants, blue eyed colleens,
From purple Ox Mountains right down to the sea,
No spot in old Erin could ere fairer be.[32]

In researching these enclosures at Aughris the writer has come across some pieces of folklore and tradition, worth putting on record together.

1. The 'imprints of a horse's hooves' near the top of the *Corragh dTonn* (Fig. 3) chasm were part of the folklore of Aughris, being variously attributed to the horse of Alexander the Great having failed to go further than the cliffs ('Portholanus' 1861-1862, 72; Wood-Martin 1892, 211; Cowell 1989, 181) and Countess Markievicz having jumped her horse over the yawning obstacle (Cowell 1989, 181). Mulligan (1943), in his topographical notes on the parish of Templeboy, connects the impression of the horse's hoofs with a chase between two white steads, one of an O'Dowd chief and that of an unnamed neighbour. Corragh na dTonn is the name for a proposed CD and book on the history of Irish music by Maura McDonnell Garvey, Dan Healy and Ciaran O'Raghallaigh.

2. The place-names *Belturlin, Lacknarookan, Pollnamaugagh, Coradun, Pollaphuca, Lackaphoery, Altbo, Carrickananfy, Pollaree, Clashcony, Clashnagall and Pollachurry* are indicated on the 1837 6" OS Sligo sheet 12. Appendix III contains explanations by Dr. Nollaig Ó Muraíle of these. Of these only Pollaphuca, the locality of the highest cliffs (Fig. 2) is referred to by Wood-Martin (1892, 382).

3. Several meetings were held at Aughris. The Garland Sunday patrún was a major event in the life of the barony of Tireragh. Parnell held a meeting there (William Kennedy, pers. comm.; Greer 1924, 125).[33] The Gaelic League held a feis there in 1898 (Mac Aodha 1943, 56). Dr. Douglas Hyde and Dr. J.P. Henry[34] addressed a great meeting in support of the Irish language movement there in Sept. 1901 (Anon. 1943, 60). Other meetings were held on Garland Sunday 1902 (John McTernan pers. comm.) and Garland Sunday 1903 (The Sligo Champion, 22nd Aug., 1903). An anti-conscription meeting was held here about 1915 (William Kennedy, pers. comm.).

4. "Eireaball Sionnaigh Racecourse" is the name applied to an area of the western part of the distribution, but the significance of this is no longer recalled.[35] Templeboy races were held at Aughris Head in June 1910 (The Sligo Champion, June 1910). Races were held on Dunmoran Strand immediately to the east of Aughris Head (Greer 1924, 124; Cowell 1989, 181).[36] A parish sports and a football match was held at Aughris on Garland Sunday 1940 (John McTernan pers. comm.). Meetings continued to be held at various fields at Aughris until about the mid-1950s.

5. How far back in time does this strong tradition of assembly at Aughris all go? Should one go back as far as the battle of Aughris of 598, recte 603, (Wood-Martin 1882, 142; MacNeill 1962, 587), at which the Cinél Cairbre of Carbury defeated the Cinél Fiachrach of Muirsc, to this list, or into prehistoric times as implied by some of the place-names (Ó Muraíle Appendix III).

APPENDIX II

The Augustinian Canons House at Aughris

Clearly from historical and cartographic sources there was an Augustinian church or monastery on Aughris. The Down Survey maps have separate churches in Aughris and Corcoran's Acres.

There is no archaeological or architectural evidence for locating the elusive Augustinian Cannons monastery of Aughris, alias Ackeross, Akeras, Eckrois or Kilmaltin, (Gwynne and Hadcock 1970, 153, 158; O'Rorke 1878, 12; O'Rorke 1889, II, 405-406; McHale 1990-1991, 37 & 41; Harbison 1991, 100) to the headland.

In the absence of such archaeological or architectural evidence the church ruins at Corcoran's Acres, a kilometre to the south-east, has occasionally been claimed to be the true location. The medieval parts of that church do not suggest an Augustinian monastery. The few pieces of loose sculpture within the building may well have been brought there, perhaps from Aughris.

During his visit to Sligo in 1699 and 1700 (McGuinness 1996) the Welsh antiquarian and naturalist Edward Lhuyd visited Aughris in 1700 (Campbell 1960, 224, citing TCD MS I.4.19) but he makes no mention of the Augustinian Cannons monastery nor of the enclosures for that matter.

In the rentals of 1633-1636 (Harlian Ms 2048; Wood-Martin 1889, 146) the townland name is given as Carowaghrish (= *Ceathrú Eachrois*) and is described as a peninsula in the sea, then owned by O'Connor Sligo and mortgaged to Mr. Ridge and worth £30 per annum.

The historical documentation assembled by Gwynn and Hadcock (1971, 153, 158) shows that there was an Augustinian priory of Aughris, founded before 1172 and dissolved c. 1584, and that it was a thriving establishment c. 1462. Expanding on O'Rorke (1889, II, 405) they note that an Inquisition of 1584 mentions that Aughris had a church with a steeple in the form of a castle, lands, and four vicarages, total value £15-15-0 (Irish) and an unvalued grange in Co. Fermanagh. Battersby (1856) does not include Aughris, by any name, in his work on Augustinian houses in Ireland. The abbey may well have gone out of use by 1577 (Nicholls 1972-1973). O'Rorke (1878, 12) and McHale (1985, 27-28; 1990-1991, 37 & 41 bis; 1991, 215-218 and passim) note historical mentions of the Aughris Augustinian priory. Until the 15th. century Aughris used the name *Insula Murray* (Gwynn and Hadcock 1971, 158; Harbison 1991, 100). Downing (Ó Muraíle 2002, ## 22) and McDonnell (1976, 12 & 14) record further information.

Many writers have had difficulty with the location of this site. O'Donovan (1844, 138, note s) says Aughris is a townland containing the ruins of an abbey. On "A Map of Hy-Fiachrach" (1844, frontispiece) he shows a structure on Aughris Head. O'Rorke (1889, II, 405-406) asserts that the priory of Aughris was "on the summit of the singularly bold headland" but that there was then "no trace of the structure". He records that opinions expressed at an Exchequer Inquisition of 1584, *campanile in forma castri aedificatum, i.e.,* "the belfry of the church had a castellated finish."

The Down Survey and other early maps indicate a structure, a castle or a church, on the headland. Most informative are the 1875 certified copies of the burnt original 1657 maps of the Down Survey in Sligo Library Local History Archive. Map 24 for the Parish of Templeboy, alias Corkagh, shows a towered building east of half way along the headland on lands owned by ~ane Smith while the church at Coraran's Acres is separately shown on lands owned by John Boswell. Map 20 of the Barony of Tireragh shows the church at Corcoran's Acres and a separate structure on Aughris headland north of Protestant lands. There is no trace of any medieval structure in Aughris townland today. In 1999 Michael Flatley indicated the south-east garden on the east side of the lane to the now-deserted Aughris village as being its location. The drawing of the structure shows what looks like the west end of a church with a higher building attached to its right side but such details should not be interpreted as a depiction. The opinion expressed at an Exchequer Inquisition of 1584, campanile in forma castri aedificatum, i.e., "the belfry of the church had a castellated finish", could be what is being referred to in the name "O'Toole's Castle" which John Stephen Kilgallen (pers. comm.) applied to the promontory fort. The published aerial photographs of Aughris promontory fort (Condit 1997, Pl. 6; 1998, 30) indicate a slightly raised area within the inner enclosure, the bulk of which survives but nothing of a masonry structure is to be seen.

Leask illustrates such a towered church at Taghmon, Co. Westmeath, (1928; 1960, 20 and Fig. 4) and refers to others at Newcastle, Co. Dublin, (1960, 18-19) and Kilpatrick, Co. Westmeath (1960, 21). Murtagh (1998, 5) discovered an oblong chapel adjoining and contemporary with a small late medieval towerhouse at Kilmurray, near Slieverue, Co. Kilkenny. Though now in very ruinous condition there may have been a tower at the west end of Moynoe church, Co. Clare (Recorded Monument Cl.29:3).

The towered churches at Taghmon, Co. Westmeath, (Leask 1928; 1960, 20 and fig. 4; de Breffney & Mott, 1976, 91-92, upper plate) has a tower at its west end.

While de Breffny and Mott (1976, 91) give a photo of Taghmon they also mention (1976, 90) Killeen, Dunsany and Rathmore as having narrow tower(s) at the west end and a tower-like structure at the north side of the eastern end (1976, 90, plate).

Further churches with residential towered features in Meath, Westmeath and Dublin are mentioned by Leask (1928, 109-110; 1960, 18-21; de Breffney and Mott 1976, 90-92).

FitzPatrick and O'Brien (1998, figs. 107, 116 and 127-131) illustrate such a feature in Co. Offaly churches and Conlan (this volume) in his article on Dominican architecture refers to parish churches with a residential tower at the western end.

There are indications of either a ground-floor room or a tower at the rear of several churches in

Co. Sligo. Only at Shancough (Sl.35:52) is there definite evidence that this was more than one story high. That evidence is in the form of the lower stones of a latrine shoot, 2.3 m above ground, on the south wall of the church. The room has a barrel vault with wickerwork centering. Grange More castle in Cashelboy (Sl.18:29) is a square towerhouse still standing to two storeys, and there was at least one further story, directly west of the west wall of the medieval church. Thomas McGettrick, past Vice-President of Sligo Field Club, maintained that the large quantity of masonry within the rear of Ballynaglough church (Sl.33:140) arose from a collapsed tower. Kilross (Sl.21:56) has the remnants of a barrel vault. Wood-Martin (1889, 299, Appendix H) in relation to Drumcliff quotes from an Inquisition of 26th April 1607 before Osbaldson, Maye and Brady, that "also a church and a house belonginge to the Parson of Dromclive, joining to the west end of the said church". This is a clear early seventeenth century indication of a house for a cleric at the west end of a church. Killaspugbrone (Sl.13:2) has a substantial barrel vaulted room. Toomour (Sl.40:140), Killery (Sl.21:11), Church Island (Sl.15:96) and Drumbcolumb (Sl.27:141) all have indications of a room at the rear of the church. Taylor and Skinner (1777, map 235) indicate three castles on the north side of the road between Ballygawley and Ballintogher, Co. Sligo. These are Castledargan, Sl.21:45, and Doonamurray in Drumcondra, Sl.21:68, with Kilross, Sl.21:56, between these. The cartographer has taken the church with a west tower as being a castle. There may have many other similar structures throughout the land.

APPENDIX III

Place-names at Aughris and Portavaud, Co. Sligo, and Kilcummin, Co. Mayo

Nollaig Ó Muraíle

The following are some examples of microtoponymy, or minor place-names, which have been abstracted from the 1837 first edition of the OS 6" map, Co. Sligo sheets 12 & 13 and, in the case of Kilcummin, Co. Mayo sheet 8, or have recently been recorded orally.

Such names are among the most vulnerable of our place-names heritage as they are often known to only a small number of (usually older) people and in many cases are unlikely to be handed on to future generations. They are also of particular interest because, as in this instance, they usually preserve relatively faithful and undistorted Irish forms and thus reflect the language and culture which were predominant in this area for perhaps two millennia down to quite recent times.

Many of the names in this list, as one might expect, refer to such coastal matters as the beach, rocks, types of fish, cliffs, a boat, and so on.

Apart from those marked by an asterisk (*), all the names below are to be found in the Ordnance Survey Namebooks for Co. Sligo (twelve in OSNB par. Templeboy, vol. 1, pp. 38-9, 43-9, and one in OSNB par. Skreen, vol. 1, p. 40) and Co. Mayo (OSNB par. Kilcummin). The names are given in the west to east order in which they occur at each location, rather than in alphabetical order.

AUGHRIS, Par. Templeboy

Belturlin: *Béal Tuirlinge,* 'mouth [=entrance] to (the) stony beach'. The word *tuirling* is also written *duirling;* another alternative form may occur in the Irish form of the name Porturlin, *Port Durlainne,* in north-west Mayo.

Lacknarookan: *Leac na Ruacan,* 'the flagstone of the cockles'. (*Ruacan Abhann* is a periwinkle.)

Pollnamaugagh: *Poll na Mágach,* 'the hole, or hollow or cave, of the pollock'. The last word is a variant form of the word *mangach.*

Ruball Sionnaigh Racecourse: *Eireaball Sionnaigh,* 'tail, or long strip of land, of (the) fox.'* *Ruball* and *drioball* are among Connacht dialectal variants of the word *eireaball.* Other forms include *earball* and *iorball.* The element occurs in the townland-names Rubball in the parish of Drumlease, Co. Leitrim, and Rubble in the parish of Killasser, Co. Mayo.

Coradun: *An Comhra Donn,* 'the brown or dark-coloured chest or locker', or *Comhra na dTonn,* 'the locker of the waves'? (Compare 'Davy Jones's Locker' = the ocean.). The 'Descriptive Remarks' on this name in OSNB (I, 46) describe it as 'A deep indent in the shore with precipitous sides, and having a cavern at its extremity'. (There is a place of the same name on, or off, the western shore of Clare Island, at the mouth of Clew Bay.)

Pollaphuca: *Poll an Phúca,* 'the hole, etc., of the pooka'. The pooka is probably the best-known of the supernatural creatures occurring in Irish folklore; the word is of Germanic origin and may well have been brought into Ireland both by the Vikings and the English. There are more than twenty other instances of the place-name *Poll an*

Phúca scattered throughout Ireland, including five in Waterford, four in Clare and two each in Galway, Tipperary and Wicklow, while up to a hundred further place-names conjoin the element *púca* with some word other than *poll* (Breatnach 1993, 68-77).

Lackaphoery: *Leac an Phaoraigh,* 'the flagstone of An Paorach [=Power]'. This Anglo-Normnan surname (de Paor) is quite rare in Connacht.

Aughris: *Eachros,* 'horse headland'. The name in its Irish form represents a name- structure which dates from a period prior to the seventh century, and may even belong to the pre-Christian era (Mac Giolla Easpaig 1981, 152). There is another townland of the same name in the parish of Cloonoghil, barony of Corran, S of Ballymote, Co. Sligo, (6" sheets 33 & 39) while there is double townland called Aughrus Beg and Aughrus More opposite High Island at the westernmost extremity of Co. Galway (6" sheet 21). Comparable name-structures include Aughrim (*Eachdhroim,* 'horse-ridge'), of which there are more than twenty instances throughout Ireland, and Muckros(s), Muckruss, etc., (*Mucros,* 'pig headland'), of which there are about a half-dozen instances.

Altbo: *Alt Bó,* 'cliff of (the) cow(s).'

Carrickananfy: *Carraig an Anfa,* 'the rock of the storm.'

Pollaree: *Poll an Fhraoigh,* 'the hole, *etc.,* of the heather'; or Poll *an Rí, … of* the king'? The latter is the form given in OSNB: I, 49. Since in Modern Irish the pronunciation of the two forms is virtually identical, there is really no way of deciding which of the two is the more correct. In a place such as this, one might think that a reference to heather would make more sense but, in view of Aughris having been the site of a battle in 602 or 603 in which Máel Cothaid, king of Uí Fhiachrach, was put to flight by Colmán, king of Cenél Coirpri, perhaps we should not dismiss the possibility that the place-name does indeed refer to a king - perhaps one who reigned all of fourteen centuries ago!

Clashcony: *Clais an Chonnaidh,* 'the trench, or gully, of the firewood'. A comparable name is *Clooncunny (Cluain Connaidh),* Cos. Limerick and Sligo.

Clashnagall: *Clais na nGall,* 'the trench, or gully, of the foreigners' (=Vikings or English, depending on the date at which the name was first applied). The final element in this name occurs more famously in the county-name *Dún na nGall,* Donegal. Other instances are *Baile na nGall* (Ballydavid in west Kerry) and *Cluain na nGall* (Clonegal, Co. Carlow).

Pollachurry: *Poll an Choire,* 'the hole, *etc.,* of the cauldron'. The last element also occurs in the name of the well-known Co. Sligo town, Tubbercurry, *Tobar an Choire.*

The Ruans: *Na Ruáin,* 'the red, or russet, places.'* Ruan is also the name of a parish in Co. Clare and of a townland in Co. Limerick, while there are townlands called Ruanes and Ruaunmore in Cos. Cork and Wexford respectively, Rooan in Co. Westmeath, Rooaun in Cos. Galway (twice), Offaly and Roscommon (twice), Rooaunalaghta in Co. Mayo, Rooaun Bog and Meadow in Co Roscommon, and Rooaunmore in Co. Galway (twice). Ruan also occurs as a fairly well-known minor name, not marked on any map, in the parish of Knock, Co. Mayo. The east fields of Ballybeg townland, Co. Sligo, (OS 6" 14) are known as The Ruauns. It is also found as a secondary element, for example, in Ballinrooaun and Ballinruan(e) in Cos. Galway (four), Wexford (four), Clare, Tipperary and Limerick.

PORTAVAUD, *Par. Skreen*

Loughanleagh: *An Lochán Liath,* 'the grey lakelet'* [?or An Lochán Léanach: 'the lakelet of the lowlying grassy place' - this being the form which occurs in the Namebook].

Portavaud: *Port an Bháid,* 'the landing-place of the boat.'

Carrigahommer: *Carraig an Chomair,* 'the rock of the meeting place.'* Among the various other meanings which dictionaries assign to the word *comar* (or *cumar*) are 'confluence of rivers', 'ravine (usually with a stream)', 'steep-sided inlet (or the sea)', 'channel, rut', 'promontory, or ravine', *etc.* The word occurs in the place-names Comber, Co. Down, and Cummer, Co. Galway.

KILCUMMIN, *Par. Kilcummin*

Benwee: *An Bhinn Bhuí,* 'the yellow peak, or cliff.'

APPENDIX IV

Searches Along Parts of the Coastline of Co. Sligo

On 30th March, 2001, Dr. Elizabeth FitzPatrick gave The Cahalane-Kitchin Memorial Lecture "Recovering A Lost Landscape of Assembly at Aughris, Co. Sligo" to SFC. Afterwards SFC member Mr. Leo Leydon of Cloghboley mentioned that there are small circular earthworks at Cloonagh and Ballyconnell on the Maugherow peninsula (Fig. 1). He also mentioned local tradition that these were for harvesting seaweed. Mr. Leydon guided fellow SFC members Jack Flynn, Pat O'Brien, Martin Wilson and the writer to this location on Feb.

Fig. 18 - Small circular earthwork at the Cloonagh-Ballyconnell boundary, Maugherow, Co. Sligo, looking W. Photo: Martin A. Timoney.

17th 2002. Here there are perhaps twenty of these heavily grass-covered circular earthworks, all close to easy passes down the adjacent cliffs to the rocks below. These circular earthworks (Fig. 18) have 4 m to 6 m diameter raised interiors, making them smaller that those elsewhere. These are surrounded by a bank of total width of about 0.80m and less than 0.50 m in height and a fosse of 0.90m in width and less than 0.40 m in depth. Some have an entrance through the bank. Physically these are totally different to the sub-rectangular playing-card shaped earthworks found at Aughris, Portavaud, Lackan and Kilcummin. Their positioning is also different in that these are directly in from the cliff edge whilst many of those at Aughris and Kilcummin are far back in on the land.

On 2nd March 2002 SFC members Pat O'Brien, Margaret McBrien, Martin A. and Mary B. Timoney searched the coastal commonage areas at Streedagh, Co. Sligo. On 3rd March 2002 SFC members Martin Wilson, Paddy Tuffy, Martin A. and Mary B. Timoney searched the coastal commonage areas at Killeenduff, west of Easkey, and Pollacheeney, north of Inishcrone. In none of these areas, where seaweed and sea rods grow abundantly on the rocks, there were no enclosures or features of any sort, rectangular or round.

The sub-rectangular playing-card shaped enclosures may have had the same function, at some time in their existence, as these Cloonagh and Ballyconnell enclosures, but they are certainly physically different. If they were related to seaweed harvesting then why are they not along other rocky coastlines of Sligo and Mayo, and elsewhere, where there is commonage along the shore? And why so many just to dry seaweed?, and why so far in from the edge of the sea?

APPENDIX V

Fionnán enclosures in Co. Kerry

O'Sullivan and Sheehan have discovered and published (1992) some several hundred small circular enclosures in several townlands at Gowlanes East and in the Macgillcuddy's Reeks Co. Kerry. These are usually 5 to 6 metres in diameter defined by a bank of about 0.50m and 0.80 m in height and a fosse of 1.00 m in width and 0.50 m in depth. The description of these Kerry sites could equally apply to the Cloonagh and Ballyconnell sites used for harvesting seaweed in Co. Sligo. These resemble certain categories of well known archaeological monuments. However, recorded oral traditions show these to be in fact post-17th century to first half of the 20th century platforms for harvesting *fionnán* grass, otherwise known as 'purple moore-grass'. This *fionnán* was used for bedding for farm animals and thatching and as a last-resort fodder. Thus, these 'what seemed to be archaeological monuments' are quite recent.

Is there a danger that since one potential type of archaeological monument the fionnán enclosures of Co. Kerry have been shown to be of recent centuries that we should be seeking a modern explanation for other problematic features, such as the enclosures at Aughris? Is there confusion at Aughris between two physically different types of sites, one 'round circular' and related to wrack harvesting and one rectangular with rounded corners whose use and date we are still not fully informed on? I fear for the safety of these enclosures from modern farming practices, at least until their nature has been established beyond doubt.

ACKNOWLEDGEMENTS

This article began as an updated publication by the writer of Finlay Tower Kitchin's note on the Aughris enclosures. Because of discoveries since Kitchin's death in 1986 it became necessary to separately publish Kitchin's note. This article, then, is derived from Kitchin's note. This article has benefited from several fieldwalking trips by Mary B., Martin J., Catherine and Bridget Timoney and Jack Flynn during 1996, 1997 and 1998, examination of Michael Gibbons' nine 1989 aerial photographs of Aughris, Noel O'Neill's 1994 aerial photographs of Kilcummin and my 1996 aerial photographs of Aughris and Portavaud. Local information relating to Aughris was got from Pat Finnegan, Sonny Finnegan, Mattie Golden, Patricia Scott, Noel, Kieran and Margaret Kennedy, but mainly from William Kennedy (+ 16 July, 1996) and John Stephen Kilgallen. Our information of the Lackan sites comes from Patrick Tuffy. Dr. Nollaig Ó Muraíle provided the information on the place-names in Appendix III.

For discussion and help I thank all these and Declan Forde, Mary Tunney, Victor Buckley, Charles Mount, Tom Condit, Neal McHugh, Raymond Gillespie, Dáthaí Ó hÓgáin, Connor Newman, Eamon Cody, Maura McDonnell Garvey, Dr. John Cowell, James Eogan, Brian K. Duffy, Celine Walsh, Michael Gibbons, Olive Alcock, Prof. Etienne Rynne, Dr. Elizabeth FitzPatrick, Joseph Fenwick, Gerry Walsh, Padraig Gorham, Gerry Bracken, Una Garvey, Maureen Feeney, Patricia Sweeney, Frances Stroker, Dan Murphy, Aodán Ó Higgins, Dr. Michael O'Connor, Queenie Dolan, Thomas McGettrick, Thomas Gallagher, Tobias Baudrey, Greg Daly, Patrick Finnegan, Helen Gormley, John McTernan, Nicholas Prins, Pat Hurley, Michael Flatley, Sean Finnegan, Davey Finnegan, Sean Tempany, Maureen McDermott, Dr. Patrick Heraughty, Jack Flynn, Des Smith, Brían Ó Súileabháin, Martin Wilson, Margaret McBrien, Hugh Shiels, Patrick E. O'Brien and Conor Brady. Martin Wilson made some useful amendments to the near-final version of the text. I further thank Mr. Noel O'Neill for copies of the responses from Tony Blackman, Perranporth, Cornwall, Peter Herring, Field Officer, Cornwall Archaeological Unit, Cornwall County Council (Herring 1998), Norman Quinnell, a former field investigator & surveyor with the Ordnance Survey and later with the Royal Commission on Historical Monuments (England), Exeter, Devon, and David McOmish, National Monuments Record, London, and for a copy of Smith (1984).

I acknowledge the permission of the National Archives of Ireland to quote from William Henry's 1739 manuscript (NAI MS 2533).

Finally I thank Mary B. Timoney for many comments on several drafts of an article publishing yet another archaeological conundrum from the Barony of Tireragh, and across Killalla Bay in Kilcummin in the Barony of Tirawley.

NOTES

1 Finlay Tower Kitchin, popularly known as Pat, passed to his eternal reward on 30th. Sep., 1986. He was an enthusiastic fieldwalker and very active member of Sligo Field Club, being on the Committee for twenty-four years, 1959-1982, and its Vice President in 1961 and 1962. His only published article (Kitchin 1983) is that on the state of the Carrowmore passage tomb cemetery as it was in the 1970s. It was on a fieldwalking expedition to Aughris by Jack Flynn, Des Smith, Aodán Ó Higgins, Brían Ó Súileabháin, Mary B. Timoney and the writer on the Sunday following Kitchin's death that Jack Flynn, President of Sligo Field Club in 1983 and 1994-1995, suggested we honour the outstanding fieldwalkers of Sligo Field Club; this we do by having a specially designated annual Kitchin-Cahalane memorial lecture.

2 The described enclosures are labelled A1, etc., for Aughris, P1, *etc.*, for Portavaud, L1, *etc.*, for Lackan, C1, *etc.*, for Carrowhubbuck North, and K1, *etc.*, for Kilcummin.

3 O.S. 6" Sligo sheet 12; Recorded Monument Sl.12:2; Grid Ref. 150.336. On some 17th and 18th century maps of Sligo the head is named *Ardrus* (Scale 1776, reproduced in McTernan 1994a, vi; Hogg c. 1786; Grierson 1816, reproduced in McTernan 1994a, 111). The term Aughris Head is used here to refer to the high ground north of the E-W road running through Aughris townland, i.e., about two-thirds of the area of the townland.

4 Part of the east end of Aughris Head is known as "The Ruans".

5 On the southwest there is a further outer ditch for a short length.

6 O.S. 6" Sligo sheet 12; Recorded Monument Sl.12:1; Grid Ref. 1507.3368.

7 Kilcummin has also the remains of at least two series of parallel earthen banks **(Fig. 16)**.

8 *The Griffith Valuation* shows considerable fragmentation of ownership of the 515 acres of this townland (Griffith 1857, 66-68). At that time the immediate lessor was Edward Joshua Cooper of Markree Castle, Collooney, Co. Sligo. Lands at Aughris which were part of the Edward Cooper estate held by C.J. Webber in 1833 were described as being "untitheable, being Abbey lands" (Tithe Applotment Book for Skreen).

9 Michael Gibbons' nine B&W aerial photographs of Aughris, taken in 1989, are now incorporated into the archive of the Record of Monuments and Places, Co. Sligo, at the Archaeological Survey, Dúchas, Dublin.

10 Overall the number of small enclosures is low and to date no side-by-side small enclosures or adjacent small enclosures have been noted at any of the locations.

11 As it seems that Kitchin was only aware of generally rectangular, oval or pear shaped enclosures there is no knowing how many 'square' enclosures were removed at this time. Only a small area of a few fields at the promontory fort end of Aughris is boxed off on the Sligo Field Club copy of OS 6" sheet 12. Within this box twenty-three ovals were pencilled in, more schematically than indicating actual survey, to indicate enclosures, probably in the early 1970s. While Kitchin in his original manuscript (Kitchin 2002) wrote "The overall dimensions of these sites by *the unreliable yardstick of memory* (italics mine, Martin A.T.) varies from a maximum of approximately 3.0m X 2.0m to something substantially less." he apparently did not measure any sites and was thinking mainly of those towards the east end of the distribution.

12 O.S. 6" Sligo sheet 13; Grid Ref. 1585.3336; Recorded Monument Sl.13:82.

13 Kitchin's manuscript refers to 'five or six' sites at Portavaud. The Recorded Monuments Register lists six enclosures. Fieldwalking by the Timoney family located seven enclosures but two of those in the Recorded Monuments list, one to the north of P1 and one to the east of P7, have not been located on the ground. Combined, this should bring the total to at least nine enclosures.

14 O.S. 6" Mayo sheet 8; SMR Ma.8:9; Grid Ref. 1208.3381. Tom Condit informed me of these Kilcummin enclosures in 1991.

15 Gerry Bracken photographed a small triple ditch enclosure, not a promontory fort, here (Condit 1998, 29), well away from the main concentration. This is being severely eroded by a stream. Regrettably this enclosure has been levelled as have some of the fieldbanks in this area. Also the alignment of about ten small boulders visible in the photograph has been pushed into a pile.

16 There is no knowing just how many enclosures were in this field.

17 Sheela Kitchin recalls seeing similar enclosures in the Ardnaglass **(Fig. 1)** area on the north side of Benbulbin, several kilometres inland from the sea (O.S. 6" Sligo sheet 5). Both Pat and Sheela Kitchin told me of these Ardnaglass sites on a number of occasions about 1978, at which stage Pat's eyesight was deteriorating and a site visit seemed impossible. From their verbal description of the location I had it included it in the SMR, Recorded Monument Sl.5:92, where it is listed as 'hut site(s)', with a location at Grid Ref. 1692.3474. In January 1996 she wrote to me as follows "It has been worrying me that I had said these earthworks, similar to the ones at Aughris, were on the slopes of Ben Bulben. They are over the river from Ben Bulben, I suppose more near Ben Wisken. One goes up to the [Arnaglass] reservoir, crosses that river, turn left, cross another river and they are on the slopes beyond that." I brought this sprightly octogenarian to the Ardnaglass area later in 1996 where she directed me to an area of land in Carrownamaddoo, O.S. 6" Sligo sheet 5; Grid Ref. 1707.3478; this area is a kilometre further east than where she had verbally indicated to me in 1978. However two searches of the area described in her letter failed to reveal any earthen enclosures, only a number of stone enclosures of a totally different character. That is not to say the earthen ones are not still there. Regrettably I could not find these sites as their presence, if in fact they are as at the other four sites, far from the seashore has major implications for some of the coast related interpretations discussed herein.

18 1:50,000 Discovery Sheets 24 and 25.

19 The Mayo O.S. 6" sheet 8 indicates that the landing place was at Pollaclogher in the townland of Ballinlena, directly south of Kilcummin, where there has been a coastguard station. From the accounts of the French landing at Kilcummin on 22nd. Aug., 1798, (Stock 1800, quoted by Freyer 1982, passim; Musgrave 1801; O'Reilly 1971, 78; Hayes 1979, 12-28) the soldiers were immediately dispatched in the direction of Killala, leaving no time and no need for them to erect even temporary accommodation in this exposed location. This in practice rules out the possibility of the enclosures having anything to do with the French landing. Westropp (1898, 296) is clear in his mind that the French landed at the seashore near the ancient church at Kilcummin, a good distance to the south of the headland where these enclosures are. Colleran (1982, 88) is clear that the French landed at Kilcummin Strand; Kilcummin head has cliffs on three sides but no strand. Perhaps not unexpectedly in the second centenary year of the French landing there were many who sought to link the enclosures with that historical event.

The reference to "The Year of the Pikes" at Aughris may seem to imply a 1798 connection, but this may simply come from The Leyney people being known by the distinctive name

'The Pikes' (William Kennedy, pers. comm., see also note 27).

Thus, there is no proven link between these enclosures and the French landing at Kilcummin.
20 Aughris is described as 'Several hut sites near coast in four fields', while Portavaud, given in error as 'Portavand' from the 1965 Sligo Field Club list, received no descriptive comment (Raftery 1974, 95).
21 There were salt pans on the shore at Streamstown another 6km farther east (O.S. 6" Sligo sheet 20; Grid Ref. 1635.3299; Recorded Monument Sl.20:255, but we know of no enclosures of this type in that area.
22 Mr. Marcus Ó hEochaidhe was Assistant Inspector of National Monuments, The Office of Public Works, Dublin.
23 The only published illustration of the Slieve Breagh excavations that I am aware of (de Paor 1967, 55) shows an excavated rectangular ditch with rounded corners adjacent to a hut-site of Neolithic date. The scale and the caption are insufficient for reliable comparison.
24 The box tomb of Alexander Black of Ardnaglass at Skreen, Co. Sligo, has a ploughman guiding two horses drawing a plough, with two indicators of grain growing, a stook of corn and a flail, being among the other items indicated (O'Neill 1977, Pl. 91: Mitchell 1990, 107-108; Timoney, M.B., 1992, 29; Somerville 1993, 51). This Ardnaglass is 3 km south-east of Aughris. One line of a poem by Tom Clarke of Dromard that William Kennedy gave me, "Till bullocks are banished away", suggests that at one time tillage, as opposed to cattle, was what the natives of Tireragh preferred. The theme of tillage *v.* cattle was touched on in relation to low population density by Miss Owenson (1807, II, 135) as follows "it being grazing country and of course no hospitality to be found there" and by Fr. Michael McHale, referring to the 'noble tillers of the soil', in a speech at a monster meeting at Dromore West in 1880 (*The Sligo Champion,* 1880, cited by Halloran 1984-1985, 48).
25 Likewise, the same can be said of the hundred or so sites at Goodland, Co. Antrim (*Case et al.* 1969).
26 This suggestion was made in a letter dated 5th. March, 1969, to Finlay Tower Kitchin by Dr. Seán Ó Nualláin, then Archaeological Officer with the Ordnance Survey of Ireland, Dublin.
27 The Leyney people, known by the distinguished name 'The Pikes', were good musicians and generally stayed a week (William Kennedy, pers. comm.; see endnote 19); the Lynne people continued to visit Tireragh after the harvest. Wood-Martin (1892, 328) tells of a man from Tobercurry in south Sligo who had to come to Aughris, ostensibly for the benefit of his health, was followed and had his ears cut off. Maura McDonnell-Garvey, (pers. comm.) tells of her mother, Eileen Talbot, nee Rogers, of Drumacoo, Ballaghaderreen, Co. Roscommon, and others frequently going to Aughris in the last decade of the 19th. century for bathing.
28 Many marriages arose from the match-making between the people of the eastern part of Tireragh and those of Leyney (Maureen Feeney & Patricia Sweeney, pers. comms.).
29 This suggestion, for which I am extremely grateful, was made to me by Mary B. Timoney in Sept. 1996. Subsequently, I found from an outing card written in the late 1970s I had expounded the same idea on a Sligo Field Club outing to Aughris at that time. Incidentally, Sligo Field Club visited Aughris on 27th May 1956 after visiting Carrowculleen cashel and Ardnaglass castle; their visit to Aughris was to see the location of the monastery and that of the battle and also to see the ornithology.
30 Likewise there is no manmade defensive feature at Portavaud or Kilcummin; the Lackan sites are about a kilometre north of Carrowhubbuck North cliff-edge fort.
31 Some fishing takes place off the coast here but in the past there was much more sea activity in these waters, such as the mid-19th. century transport of stone from the rocky Toberpatrick coast to the east of Aughris for the new chapel at Ballina (Lewis ii, 559).
32 This piece of poetry, apparently written by Tom Clarke of Dromard, was given to me by William Kennedy of Farranyharpy.
33 It is most unlikely that this was during the by-election campaign of March and April 1891 (McTernan 1995, 460-466) though when has not been established.
34 See McTernan (1994b, 142-145), for a biography of Dr. J.P. Henry, alias Seaghán P. MacEnrí, who was a cousin of the Boland family at Portroyal, near Portavaud.
35 This name, Eireaball Sionnaigh Racecourse, was given to me independently and spontaneously by John Stephen Kilgallen of Aughris, William Kennedy of Farranyharpy and formerly of Rathglass, Templeboy, and Paddy Kilcullen and Joseph Gilligan of that general area. None could explain the name. Gilligan thought it was a racecourse 'during his father's memory time'.

This reference to a 'sionnach' is not the only curious reference to a fox in Tireragh. The inscription over the door of what I believe to have been a ?towerhouse-type castle at Longford, Beltra, 8km SE of Aughris, reads

"IOHANNIS . HENRICI . VULPISQ .HUGO
FLAVICOMAE . BUEN .   RETIRO .+FLANELY
E.C. ME. F.F.   SCULPSIT 1724"

and in translation (Wood-Martin 1882, 116-117) "The safe retreat of John Henry (Crofton) and his yellow haired Fox. E(dward) C(rofton) caused this to be erected. Hugh Flanely sculpted it 1724". Wood-Martin suggests that the companion's surname was Fox, that 'Hugo Flanely Sculpsit 1724' refers to a renovation of the raised lettering and that it is of much later date than the foregoing; we do not accept this suggestion of Wood-Martin. Ten Years later, Wood-Martin (1892, 1-2) had satisfied himself that 'The Fox' was Alexander Irwin of Tanrego whose wife and children, 'The Cubs', were detained prisoner in a fort at Strandhill, Co. Sligo. I believe this fort to have been the ?moated site at Carrowbunnaun, (Sl.14:70). He also suggests, contradicting himself, that John Henry Crofton had married a Miss Irwin, 'The Fox'.

36 Perhaps this represents a transfer of location from Aughris Head after ownership of the land had become clearly defined. The last race meeting at Dunmoran was in 1930 (William Kennedy, pers. comm.).

REFERENCES

Alcock, Elizabeth, 1992: "Burials and Cemeteries in Scotland" in Edwards and Lane, eds., 1992, 125-129.

Anon., 1943: "Aeridheacht at Aughris" in Bairéad, eag., 60.

Anon., 1995: *Record of Monuments and Places*, Co. Sligo, Dublin, Office of Public Works.

Bairéad, Brian, Eagarthóir, 1943: *Glór Shligigh*, 1893-1943, Sligeach.

Battersby, W.J., 1856: *A History of all the Abbeys, Convents, Churches and other Religious Houses of the Order Particularly of the Hermits of St. Augustin in Ireland*, Dublin, Warren.

Bourke, Edward J., 1994: *Shipwrecks of the Irish Coast*, 1105-1993.

Bradley, Richard, 1992: "The Excavations of an Oval Barrow beside the Abingdon Causewayed Enclosure, Oxford", *Proc. Prehistoric Soc.* 58, 127-142.

Breatnach, Deasúin, 1993: *Chugat an Púca*, Baile Átha Cliath, An Clóchomhar.

Brewster, T.C.M., 1975: "Garton Slack", *Current Archaeology*, 5, 104-116.

Buckley, Victor M., Buckley, Laureen, Mount, Charles, and Ronane, Brian, 1991-1992: "Excavations at a Lintelled Grave, Lacken, Enniscrone, Co. Sligo", *North Mayo Historical J.*, 2, No. 5, 21-24.

Buckley, Victor M., 1998: "Oblong Oddities in County Sligo", *Archaeology Ireland*, 12-2, 40.

Bunn, Michael, 1997: "Splendid Sligo", *The World of Hibernia*, 3:2, 146-166.

Byrne, Francis John, 1972: "Rathmulcagh : An Historical Note", *J. Roy. Soc. Antiq. Ireland*, 102, 73-76.

Byrne, Francis John, 1973: *Irish Kings and High Kings*, London, Batsford.

Canning, Paul, and Dalby, Barry, 1998: *The Sligo Way Map Guide*, Sligo, Sligo County Council.

Case, H.J., Dimbleby, G.W., Mitchell, G.F., Morrison, M.E.S., and Proudfoot, V.B., 1969: "Land Use in Goodland Townland, Co. Antrim, from Neolithic Times Until Today", *J. Roy. Soc. Antiq. Ireland*, 99, 39-53.

Campbell, J.L., 1960: "The Tour of Edward Lhuyd in Ireland in 1699 and 1700", *Celtica*, 5, 218-228.

Colleran, Gabriel, 1982: "The Year of the French", in O'Hara, ed., 88-95.

Condit, Tom, 1997: *Ireland's Archaeology from the Air*, Dublin, Country House.

Condit, Tom, 1998: "Connacht Curiosities", *Archaeology Ireland*, 12-1, 29-30.

Conlan, Patrick 2002: "Irish Dominican Medieval Architecture" in Timoney, ed., 2002.

Cowell, John, 1989: *Sligo, Land of Yeats' Desire, Its History, Literature, Folklore and Landscapes*, Dublin, O'Brien Press.

Dent, John S., 1982: "Cemeteries and Settlement Patterns of the Iron Age on the Yorkshire Wolds", *Proc. Prehistoric Soc.*, 48, 437-457.

de Paor, Liam, and Ó hEochaidhe, Marcus, 1956: "Unusual Group of Earthworks at Slieve Breagh, Co. Meath", *J. Roy. Soc. Antiq. Ireland*, 86, 97-104.

de Paor, Liam, 1967: *Archaeology, An Illustrated Introduction*, London, Penguin.

Dornan, Brian, 2000: *Mayo's Lost Islands, The Inishkeas*, Dublin, Four Courts.

Edwards, Nancy, and Lane, Alan, eds. 1992: *The Early Church in Wales and the West, Recent Work in Early Christian Archaeology, History and Place-Names*, Oxbow Monograph 16, Oxford, Oxbow Books.

FitzPatrick, Elizabeth, and O'Brien, Caimin, 1998: *The Medieval Churches of Co. Offaly*, Dublin, Government of Ireland.

FitzPatrick, Elizabeth, 2001: "The Gathering Place of *Tír Fhiachrach*? Archaeological and Folkloric Investigations at Aughris, Co. Sligo", *Proc. Roy. Irish Acad.*, 101C3, 67-105.

Freyer, Grattan, ed., 1982: *Bishop Stock's 'Narrative' of the Year of the French*, Ballina, Irish Humanities Centre.

Gibbons, Michael, Alcock, Olive, Condit, Tom, Tunney, Mary, and Timoney, Martin A., 1989: *Sites and Monuments Record, Co. Sligo*, Dublin, Office of Public Works.

Gibbons, Michael, Alcock, Olive, Condit, Tom, and Tunney, Mary, 1991: *Sites and Monuments Record, Co. Mayo*, Dublin, Office of Public Works.

Greenwood, Margaret, Connolly, Mary, and Wallis, Geoff, 1999: *Ireland. The Rough Guide*, 5th edition, London, The Rough Guides.

Greer, James, 1924, 1986: *The Windings of The Moy with Skreen and Tireragh*, Dublin, Thom; Reprint 1986, Ballina, Western People.

Grierson 1816: *Map of County Sligo*.

Griffith, Richard, 1857: *General Valuation of Rateable Property in Ireland, County of Sligo, Valuation of Several Tenements in the Union of Dromore West*, Dublin, Thom.

Gwynne, Aubrey, and Hadcock, R. Neville, 1970: *Medieval Religious Houses: Ireland*, Reprint, 1988, Blackrock, Irish Academic Press.

Halloran, Martin, 1984-1985: "Three Noted Castleconnor Men", *North Mayo Historical and Archaeological Society*, 1:3, 45-52.

Harbison, Peter, 1991: *Pilgrimage in Ireland, The Monuments and the People*, London, Barrie & Jenkins.

Hayes, Richard, 1937: *The Last Invasion of Ireland*, Dublin, Gill & McMillian, 2nd Ed. 1979.

Henry, William, 1739: *Hints towards a Natural Topographical History of the Counties Sligoe, Donegal, Fermanagh and Lough Erne by the Rev. William Henry, Martin A., Rector of Killasher in Fermanagh and Chaplain to the Lord Bishop of Kilmore*, National Archives of Ireland, Ms. 2533.

Herring, Peter, "Cornwall Curiosities", *Archaeology*

Ireland, 12-2, 40.

Hogan, Edmund, 1910: *Onomasticon Goedelicum, Locorum et Tribuum Hiberniae et Scotiae, An Index, with Identifications, to Gaelic Names of Places and Tribes*, London, Williams & Norgate.

Hogg, Alexander, c. 1786: *A New and Correct Map of the Province of Connaught, Drawn from the Latest and Best Authorities*, London, Alexander Hogg.

James, Heather, 1992: "Early Medieval Cemeteries in Wales" in Edwards and Lane, eds., 1992, 90-103.

Kitchin, Finlay Tower, 1983: "The Carrowmore Megalithic Cemetery, Co. Sligo", *Proc. Prehistoric Soc.*, 49, 151-175.

Kitchin, Finlay Tower, 2002: "Note on Hut Sites at Aughris" in Timoney, ed., 2002.

Leask, Harold G., 1960: *Irish Churches and Monastic Buildings, III, Medieval Gothic, The Last Phases*, Dundalk, Dundalgen Press W. Tempest.

Lewis, Samuel, 1837: *Topographical Dictionary of Ireland*, London, Lewis.

Mac Aodha, M., 1943: "In Tireragh", in Bairéad, eag., 56.

Mac Giolla Easpaig, Dónall, 1981: *"Noun + Noun Compounds in Irish Place-names"*, *Études Celtiques*, 18, 151-163.

McDonald, Theresa, 1992: *Achill, 5000BC to 1900 A.D., Archaeology, History, Folklore*, np, np.

McDonnell, Thomas, 1976: *The Diocese of Killala from its Institution to the End of the Penal Times*, Killala, Diocese of Killala.

McGuinness, David, 1996: "Edward Lhuyd's Contribution to the Study of Irish Megalithic Tombs", *J. Roy. Soc. Antiquaries Ireland*, 126, 62-85.

McHale, Edward, 1985: *The Parishes in the Diocese of Killala, IV, Tireragh*, Ballina, np.

McHale, Edward, 1990-1991: "More Tireragh Names from the Irish Patent Rolls of James I, 1603-1625", *North Mayo Historical and Archaeological Society*, II-4, 37-46.

McHale, Edward, 1991: *Letters From The Distant Past, Killala Diocese in the Papal Letters and Annates (c. 1200-1500)*, Crossmolina, np.

MacNeill, Maire, 1962: *The Festival of Lughnasa*, Oxford, Oxford University Press.

McTernan, John, 1994a: *Sligo: Sources of Local History, New Edition*, Sligo, Sligo County Library.

McTernan, John, 1994b: *Worthies of Sligo, Profiles of Eminent Sligonians of Other Days*, Sligo, Avena Publications.

McTernan, John, 1995: *Olde Sligo, Aspects of Town and County Over 750 Years*, Sligo, Avena Publications.

Mitchell, Frank, 1990: *The Way That I Followed*, Dublin, Country House.

Moore, Michael J., 1987: *Archaeological Inventory of Co. Meath*, Dublin, Office of Public Works.

Musgrave, Richard, 1801: *Memoirs of the Different Rebellions in Ireland*, Dublin.

Mulligan, Martin, 1943: *Topographical Survey of County Sligo, Parish by Parish*, Irish Tourist Authority, Typescript copy in Sligo County Library Local History Archive, No. 1266.

Munnelly, Jack, 1998: *The French Invasion of Connaught*, np, np.

Murtagh, Ben, 1998: "Recent Discovery in South Kilkenny", *Archaeology Ireland*, 12:3, 5.

Nicholls, Kenneth, 1972-1973: "A List of the Monasteries in Connacht, 1577", *J. Galway Archaeol. Hist. Soc.*, 33, 28-43.

Nimo, Alexander, 1824: *Sixth Report of the Commissioners of the Irish Fisheries for the Year 1824*,

O'Connor, Pat, 1998: *The French are at Killala, An Account of Humbert's Campaign from Kilcummin to Ballinamuck*, np, np.

Ó Muraíle, Nollaig, 2002: "Downing's Description of County Sligo, *c.* 1684" in Timoney, ed., 2002.

O'Neill, Timothy, 1977: *Life and Tradition in Rural Ireland*, London, Dent.

O'Reilly, Gertrude, 1971: *Stories from O'Dowda's Country*, Iniscrone, G. McHale.

O'Rorke, Terence, 1878: *History, Antiquities, and Present State of the Parishes of Ballisodare and Kilvarnet, in the County of Sligo, with Notices of the O'Haras, the Coopers, the Percevals, and other local families*, Dublin, Duffy.

O'Rorke, Terrence, 1889: *The History of Sligo: Town and County*, Dublin, James Duffy. Reprint, Sligo, 1986, Dodd's Antiquarian Books

O'Sullivan, Ann, and Sheehan, John, 1992: "Fionnán Enclosures: Aspects of Traditional Land Use in South Kerry", *J. Kerry Archaeol. Hist. Soc.*, 25, 5-19.

Owenson, Miss, 1807: Patriotic *Sketches of Ireland, Written in Connaught*, London, Phillips.

'Portholanus', 1861-1862: "Antiquarian Notes and Queries", *Ulster J. Archaeol.*, 1st. series, 9, 72.

Raftery, Joyce, 1974: *Preliminary Report on Sites of Archaeological Interest in Co. Sligo*, Dublin, An Foras Forbatha, Limited distribution.

Scale, Bernard, 1776: *Map of County Sligo*.

Skeehan, D. Connor, 1998: "Aughris Head and Promontory Forts", *Archaeology Ireland*, 12:2, 40.

Smith, George, 1984: "Excavations on Goonhilly Downs, The Lizard, 1981", *Cornish Archaeology*, No. 23, 3-48.

Smith, George, 1988: "New radiocarbon dates from Medieval and Bronze Age Monuments on Goonhilly Downs, The Lizard", *Cornish Archaeology*, No. 27, 213-214.

Somerville, Christopher, 1993: *The Road to Roaringwater Bay, A Walk Down the West of Ireland*, London, Harper Collins.

Stead, Ian M., 1985: *Celtic Art in Britain Before the Roman Conquest*, London, British Museum Press; 2nd. ed., 1996.

Stead, Ian M., 1991: *Iron Age Cemeteries in East Yorkshire, Excavations at Burton Flemming, Rudston, Garton-on-the-Woulds and Kirkburn*, English Heritage Archaeological report, No. 22, London, English Heritage / British Museum Press.

Stock, Bishop, 1800: *Bishop Stock's 'Narrative' of the Year of the French: 1798*, 2nd. ed., Dublin, Mercier.

Swords, Liam, 1997: *A Hidden Church, The Diocese of Achonry, 1689-1818*, Blackrock, Columban Press.

Taylor, George, and Skinner, Andrew, 1777, 1783: *Maps of the Roads of Ireland*, 2nd. ed., Dublin, 1783; Reprint, 1969, Shannon, Irish University Press.

Timoney, Mary B., 1992: "The Black Monument", *Living Heritage*, 9, 29.

Timoney, Martin A., ed., 2002: *A Celebration of Sligo, Essays for Sligo Field Club*, Sligo, Sligo Field Club.

Westropp, T.J., 1898: "Proceedings: The Excursions", J. Roy. Soc. Antiq. Ireland, 28, 283-298.

Wood-Martin, W.G., 1882: *The History of Sligo, County and Town, from the Earliest Ages to the Close of the Reign of Queen Elizabeth*, Dublin, Hodges Figgis, Reprint, Sligo, 1990, Dodd's Antiquarian Books.

Wood-Martin, W.G., 1889: *The History of Sligo, County and Town, from the Accession of James I to the Revolution of 1688*, Dublin, Hodges Figgis; Reprint, Sligo, 1990, Dodd's Antiquarian Books.

Wood-Martin, W.G., 1892: *The History of Sligo, County and Town, from the close of the Revolution of 1688 to the Present Time*, Dublin, Hodges Figgis; Reprint, Sligo, 1990, Dodd's Antiquarian Books.

Monuments of Meaning
Role and Symbolism of Passage Tombs in Cúil Irra, Co. Sligo.

Stefan Bergh
National University of Ireland, Galway

ABSTRACT: A megalithic monument was, by its strong physical presence, meant to be seen, read and interpreted. Design, building material, as well as location of a monument, included messages that could be read and understood by the passing Neolithic man. The passage tombs in the Cúil Irra region, Co. Sligo represents a particularly wide range of megalithic monuments, both what concerns construction as well as relation to the local landscape. This indicates that these monuments as well represent a wide range of meanings. This paper discusses some aspects of these meanings.

INTRODUCTION

While passing the hill on his way home, the large cairn on the summit would have been a familiar sight to the Neolithic fisherman. The location, design, size as well as the material of the monument conveyed messages to him, messages which he was able to read and relate to his own life and family.

The modern observer can never understand and relate to the "primary messages" of these monuments in the way the contemporary people did. Nevertheless these monuments convey mean-ings which we in different ways, and to different degrees, find comp-rehensible. Terms which might cross our minds when standing in front of a megalithic monument could be, *e.g.*, physical power, technical skill, greatness, continuity, ritual, mystery, eternity, obsession..... Of course every individual reacts in his or her own way at a visual encounter with a construction of this kind. And so did the individuals in the Neolithic, but in a slightly different way as they did not have the time barrier between themselves and the monument.

This paper aims to shed some light on some general aspects of meaning of these monuments, which could have been valid to the Neolithic fisherman.

The monuments dealt with in this paper are those of the Irish passage tomb tradition (IPTT), and then particularly those built in the Cúil Irra region in Co. Sligo (Fig. 1).

APPROACH

Studies into the rôle and function of megalithic monuments have often centred around their symbolic value. This value has often been seen

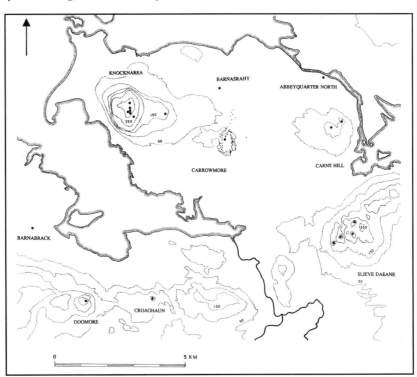

Fig. 1 - Passage tombs within the Cúil Irra region, Co. Sligo.

as high and important, according to the extravagant enterprises that many of them must have involved for the society. As "megalithic monuments" consist of structures of highly different characters, it must however be stressed that they comprise a rather heterogeneous group. From this follows that it is reasonable to assume that the symbolic value have been of different character among different monuments.

A general characteristic is, however, monumentality, which allows a delimitation from earlier, as well as later, burial monuments (Chapman 1981).

Monumentality as a feature of these structures is closely linked to *visibility*, and thereby to the mediation of messages to the world outside. Even though monumentality can be seen as a shared characteristic it varies considerably depending on location, building material and construction. This variation of monumentality is seen as reflecting different rôles of the monuments, and by that conveying different messages to the onlooker.

An important aspect of megalithic monuments is their rôle as symbols of authority. Here their varying levels of complexity are regarded as indicating an increased social complexity (*e.g.,* Sheridan 1986; Whittle 1988). The dead are, in this context, a vital part of the living society as they represent the foundation on which the society is based. Making the dead visible, through the monuments, is a way of giving them a material identity in the present as well as in the future society. Those who are able to demonstrate the greatest concern for the ancestors, *i.e.*, the foundation of the society, by erecting complex or expensive monuments, get the greatest respect in the living society. The ancestors thereby become possible to manipulate, and by this an instrument for groups striving to achieve, keep or enhance a certain position of power.

A different and/or complimentary level of influence can be argued for when the monuments are interpreted in their landscape context (*e.g.*, Bradley 1993; 1998; Scarre 2002; Tilley 1994). The incorporation of the ancestors into the landscape by erecting spectacular monuments meant a both physical and mental alteration of the countryside. Physically the landscape was altered as new and everlasting constructions were added. Mentally the landscape was altered as the monuments became new and earlier unseen places to which people had to relate, or if built in places already vital to the movements and life of the people, their rôle could have been to enhance or alter the meaning of old places.

Nevertheless, the incorporation of the ancestors into the landscape by the building of spectacular, everlasting monuments changed the landscape of the living. The visibility of the monuments became thereby an important means by which it was possible to manipulate people's apprehension of the surrounding landscape, and thereby of their world.

THE IRISH PASSAGE TOMB TRADITION

The Irish passage tomb tradition, being in many ways the most spectacular expression of monument building in Neolithic Ireland, consists of some two hundred and thirty monuments. The majority of the sites are to be found within the four well known clusters at Brú na Bóinne and Sliabh na Caillighe in Co. Meath and at Carrowkeel-Keashcorran and Cúil Irra in Co. Sligo.

One of several characteristic features of the IPPT is the wide variation of constructions, as simple dolmens with rudimentary passages, as well as extraordinary complicated chambers in enormous cairns, both are different aspects within the same tradition of monument-building.

Out of the *c.* two hundred and thirty Irish passage tombs seventy five (30%) are to be found within the area focusing on the Cúil Irra peninsula, just west of Sligo town (Fig. 1). This is thereby by far the largest cluster of passage tombs in Ireland (Bergh 1995). The region is visually dominated by the conspicuous mountain of Knocknarea, the visual impact of which is enhanced by the huge passage tomb cairn of Miosgán Meadhbha on its flat summit. Some eight passage tombs are found on Knocknarea mountain, but only Miosgán Meadhbha seems to have had as substantial cairn.

If Knocknarea, with Miosgán Meadhbha, visually dominates the whole region, Carrowmore at the foot of Knocknarea dominates the region concerning the number of monuments, as this cluster originally consisted of some sixty sites. All but one site at Carrowmore seems to have consisted of boulder circles encircling central dolmens or small cists. These sites were never covered by cairns.

To the east of Carrowmore, overlooking Lough Gill, are two very large cairns on Carns Hill. Both this cairns most likely belong to the IPTT. Outside these three groups, additional passage tombs are found on the southern bank of the Garvogue river, in Abbeyquarter townland, in Barnasrahy north of Carrowmore, in the Ox mountains south of Ballysadare Bay and in Barnabrack just south of Beltra (Bergh 1995).

The large cluster of monuments at Carrowmore, flanked by the passage tombs on Knocknarea mountain to the west and on Carns Hill to the east, forms however the main axis in the ritual landscape defined by the passage tombs in Cúil Irra. This obvious tripartition of the ritual landscape is a feature which also is discernible in the other main passage tombs groups of Brugh na Boinne, Sliabh na Caillighe and Carrowkeel-Keashcorran.

The monument which visually dominates the whole region of Cúil Irra is of course the massive cairn of Miosgán Meadhbha on Knocknarea mountain (Fig. 2). The cairn of Miosgán Meadhbha belongs, together with the two cairns on Carns Hill, to the exclusive group of about ten extraordinary large cairns within IPTT, of which Newgrange, Knowth and Dowth at Brugh na Bóinne are the most well-known examples.

The contrast between these large cairns and the small chambers surrounded be boulder circles at Carrowmore is dramatic, but still they represent ritual activity within the same tradition of monument building. The finds from the relatively speaking small and simple boulder circle monuments at Carrowmore, consisting mainly of stone beads and pendants, bone or antler pins and coarse decorated pottery together with the cremated bones, are by and large identical to those recovered in excavations of more complex monuments such as New Grange and Knowth. Some of the finds made in the large monuments can however be labelled prestige objects according to their quality and character. Besides the obvious similarities in what concerns finds from these two types of monuments, it must also be stressed that they do show similarities in construction, as the basic features of a central chamber enclosed in a circular construction are found in both these extremes. Besides these similarities it is however reasonable to assume that they had totally different significance to the Neolithic observer. When discussing the rôles and meaning of the Irish passage tombs, these two extremes are therefore good points of departure.

It is important to bear in mind that the "small" and "large" monuments dealt with here are extremes within the morphological span of the Irish passage tombs. They thereby expose traits in a more evident way than many of the intermediate monuments, and by doing so, present a more clearcut base for discussion.

By using some of the most evident characteristics of the small monuments, I will, in the following, discuss possible rôles of the small and large monuments. These characteristics can be labelled *complexity, limited labour investment, single burial area and open-ness.*

Fig. 2 - Knocknarea mountain with Miosgán Meadhbha, from the south. Photo Stefan Bergh.

Fig. 3 - Carrowmore No. 7 from the south-west. Photo: Stefan Bergh

An important feature which the small and large monuments have in common, but used in different ways, is the white quartz. The quartz is, in a way, the trademark of the Irish passage tombs and its significance will be discussed in the light of the suggested characteristics of the different monuments.

COMPLEXITY

The relative simplicity of the small monuments is reflected by the chamber of four to six boulders covered by a single roofslab. A boulder circle often forms the outer limit of the monument (Fig. 3). The basic structure of the monuments does not include any complicated constructions or exotic material which would have demanded certain knowledge to copy. There is furthermore no evidence to support the view that the boulder circle monuments originally had covering cairns. This would mean that the different features in the construction were intended to be visible (Bergh 1995, 79ff).

The structure of the large monuments has often been very complicated both concerning the technical structure as well as the planning and performance of the actual building. These monuments reflect technically, artistically and ritually very advanced projects, the accomplishment of which were dependent on specialistskills in many different fields.

It was not only the actual building phase that was complex. Even the means were often complex in the sense that it could include building materials that were not locally available. A well-known example of this occurs at Knowth, in Brugh na Bóinne, where virtual collections of different exotic stones have been set outside the entrances to the two tombs (see Cooney 2000 for discussion on these non-local material).

The relative simplicity of the small monuments reflects a structure based on general knowledge, feasible to undertake by most people in society. The complexity of the large monuments reflects however an achievement requiring very special knowledge and many different skills. It is probable that only a limited group of people had detailed knowledge of, and general view over, these gigantic construction projects.

INVESTED LABOUR

In comparison to other possible labour-intensive activities in the Neolithic, even the building of the relatively small monuments should be seen as a considerable undertaking. Nevertheless it would have been a feasible project for a group of about ten to fifteen individuals during a period of two to four weeks.

To estimate the labour invested in the large monuments is a more complex task. The calculation of actual man-hours involved in projects of such magnitude, often includes to many pitfalls to reach beyond mere speculation. A rather direct measurement of a large part of the labour invested is however the volume of the cairn when such exist. This measurement does not include other aspects of the construction such as the passage and chamber, the gathering of stones used, artistic work, *etc., etc.,* which must be included in calculations which aim to measure the actual time it took to build the monument. Establishing the actual time is however of limited scientific value, and should be treated as a curiosity.

To facilitate a comparison with the small monuments, which *de facto* lack cairns, the volume of hypothetical cairns have been calculated. In this way the relation between a boulder circle at Carrowmore and Miosgán Meadhbha comes to a ratio of 1:150, which expressed in time gives the ratio four weeks as to twelve years! This indicates that the building of Miosgán Meadhbha on Knocknarea required a labour investment 150 times greater than that of a boulder circle at Carrowmore, and this is without taking other parts of the construction such as passage, chamber, decoration, *etc.,* into consideration. A ratio of 1:150 might be hard to imagine, but if expressed in time this represents a ratio of 4 weeks as to 12 years!

The actual building-time of these monuments is both irrelevant and impossible to assess as we have virtually no knowledge of the rules and conventions linked to the erection of these monuments. What is important is however the fact that the small monuments represent undertakings possible to achieve by a limited group of people during a number of weeks. This is in dramatic contrast to the large monuments which most likely reflect projects which affected the whole society for several years.

BURIAL AREA

The extreme contrast between the small and large monuments which is evident when discussing complexity and invested labour, is not always at hand when it comes to the size and complexity of the burial area.

By comparison with the chambers in the small monuments, which rarely have a size exceeding 2m^2, the chambers of Newgrange (16m^2) and Knowth eastern tomb (23m^2) are of course considerably greater. Nevertheless, chamber size in the large monuments does not reflect a direct relation between monuments and chamber size. The chamber of Knowth western tomb has for example an area of only *c.* 2m^2. As has been stressed by Fleming (1973), the "relative effectiveness" of the monument as a burial space decreases with increased size of the exterior. This is especially valid for the large IPTT monuments, and is furthermore emphasised by the fact that a major part of the calculated chamber-area often include the central part of the cruciform chamber, which rarely seems to have been an area used for burials.

In the chambers of the small monuments, the entire chamber was used as a single burial area for a seemingly high number of individuals. The structure of the chamber was mainly directed towards this function and no finds or arrangements indicate that activity other than the actual deposition of burials have taken place in these chambers. The limited size of the chamber would as well not have offered space for additional activity.

In the large monuments this depositing of large amounts of bones does not seem to have been present. The space in the recesses was both at Knowth and Newgrange mainly occupied by the large stone basins. Even if burials have been placed in the basins, they offer a very limited space compared to the whole of the burial chamber.

The burial area in the small monuments indicates that there was no need for a differentiation in death within the burial group. The often very large amount of cremated bones in these small chambers indicates a burial practice in which a majority of the individuals linked to the monument have been buried in the chamber. This might suggest a less complex social milieu wherein the group identity was of prime importance, and thereby maintained in the common burial monument.

The chambers of the large monuments have not been a burial space for a large number of individuals. The formalised tripartition in the cruciform chamber, the occurrence of prestige objects as well as the spatial distribution of art within the tombs (Eogan 1986), point rather towards formalised, symbolic activities linked to the death and the ancestors. Any "ordinary burials" have hardly been performed within these monuments. The deposits of bones that are present in these chambers reflect rather- a ritualised, symbolic behaviour where the deposition only formed a part of a ritual, the main interest of which was beyond the concern of a deceased individual and her final place of rest.

OPENNESS

By the term *openness* I refer to the fact that the burial chamber of the small monuments has been visually accessible, as they were not concealed within a covering cairn. It is reasonably to assume that most of the Carrowmore monuments once had a low supporting cairn reaching to the upper part of the orthostats. The often conical roofslab, consisting of a split boulder, has most likely been visible and thereby formed an important part of the monuments' layout. At some sites the chamber would have been more or less free-standing in the centre of the boulder circle, as has been suggested for the enigmatic site of Carrowmore 27 with its free-standing cruciform chamber (Burenhult 1980).

The important issue here is that the basic construction of the monument would not have been concealed to the naked eye, and thereby made comprehensible to most people in the society. The dead thereby formed a visual feature of the daily life, in contrast to the exclusiveness and mystification signalled by a covering cairn. The distinction between "insiders" and "outsiders" - *i.e.*, between those with access to the monument and with detailed knowledge of it, and those without access and with only limited knowledge - is likely to have been less pronounced in these simple and open monuments. Within the burial group there has been a broad and intimate complicity in the rituals linked to the dead and burial in the megalithic monuments.

The large monuments represent the exact opposite as their size, and by that their strong physical presence, would have appeared to most of society as something almost in-comprehensible. The ultimate expression of this is Miosgán Meadhbha on Knocknarea, the physical presence of which is very strong for a large part of Co. Sligo.

This considerable physical impact that these large monuments had on the local countryside, together with the fact that the inside of the monument was concealed from view, created a relation of power based on concealment of knowledge. The sight of these monu-ments must to a stranger have created amazement as well as estrangement and uncertainty. To the local observer however, within whose socio-religious world this large monument was built, the monument could have held messages of identity, affiliation and security.

The monument was intended to create as strong a physical impact as possible on the local countryside. Visibility was central to its rôle in society. This seems also to have been valid for the entrance areas as these have been enhanced in different ways such as with exotic rocks, standing stones and different types of stone arrangements. These areas have formed strong *foci* which have been important to stress and maintain. Accessibility, however, decreases dramatically at the actual entrance into the monument, as the often narrow and dark passage indicate a strong concealment. From this it follows that three levels of accessibility can be suggested for the large monuments. Firstly, the monument as a physical part of the landscape has been accessible to everybody passing by. Secondly, the entrance area has been accessible to a relatively large, but selected group of individuals. Thirdly, the interior of the monument has been accessible to only a few, selected, individuals.

A strong distinction can here be made between outsiders and insiders, where the later group had access to, knowledge of and control over the interior of the monument and its relation to the rituals performed. The large group of outsiders had however only access to the exterior of the monument and by that very limited knowledge of the secrets of the monument.

QUARTZ

In the small monuments white quartz or sometimes quartzite, is frequently found together with the bone deposits in the chamber. The quartz occur as small pieces measuring 4 to 5 cm, to larger lumps measuring up to 10 to 15 cm. Most of them are angular pieces, and marks from chipping are relatively frequent. It is noteworthy that fragments or larger pieces of worked quartz have been recorded in nearly all excavated monuments at Carrowmore (Wood-Martin 1888; Burenhult 1980; Bergh 1995). An important circumstance is, however, that quartz or other distinctive rock never occur in the actual constructions of the smaller monuments in Cúil Irra. The exterior is always of local rock as the boulder circles consist of different igneous rocks, mainly originating from the Ox Mountains to the south. In all the monuments at Carrowmore there is only one occurrence of limestone used in the boulder circle.

In the large monuments the quartz does not seem to be placed in the chamber to the same extent, but has become a critical ingredient in the exterior of the monument. At a number of monuments there are evidence of quartz playing an active rôle in the exterior, either placed on the face of the cairn or forming separate structures adjacent to the entrance areas (*e.g.*, Newgrange, Knowth, Sliabh na Caillighe T, Carrowkeel C and Miosgán Meadhbha) (O´Kelly 1982; Eogan 1986; Conwell 1873; Bergh 1995). At Miosgán Meadhbha quartz seems to have been included in structures along the perimeter of the cairn.

DISCUSSION

The small monuments can be characterised by *simplicity* (they were meant to be understood and copied), low investment of labour (feasible to "anyone"), *undifferentiated burial area* (linking the individual to the group was the prime focus), and *openness* (a monument without secrets). In an idealised way the small monuments reflect a non-hierarchical ritual context wherein the individuals had a close and active relation to the rituals and monuments of their group. The small monuments show, not just within the dense cluster at Carrowmore in Cúil Irra but within the whole area of distribution, a remarkable uniformity in what concerns labour investment, design and material. This implies burial groups of similar size and character acting within a formalised ritual pattern.

The large monuments can on the other hand be characterised by *complexity* (very complex construction, impossible to copy), *high investment of labour* (extremely labour demanding projects, directed by very influential individuals), *complex burial chambers* (symbolic rather than actual burials), and *concealment* (a monument of secrets, creating a relation of power through knowledge). The large monuments indicate a competitive socio-religious milieu in which the individual was a passive spectator within a highly symbolic ritual action. The rituals as well as the monuments were hard to comprehend to the majority of the people. This increased mystification is also reflected by the way a new dimension of power is added - time. By relating the monuments to certain positions of the sun and or the moon, it was possible to predict recurrent cosmic phenomena, and thereby to control time - the ultimate expression of power.

An interesting aspect of this increased ritualisation, is the use of quartz in the small and large monuments respectively. The frequent occurrence of quartz in the burial deposits implies that it was assigned a certain meaning in relation to the dead. As a source of power, the quartz could have been seen as supplying the power to undertake the journey to the otherworld. As "the stone of light" it could have been the symbol of life, and thereby an assurance of re-birth. No matter how far we stretch our speculations, there is no doubt that quartz is a stone that has been charged with both chemical powers and symbolic meaning.

Against this background and its frequent and very special use in the passage tomb tradition it is evident that this white stone had a certain, and important, significance to the living and the dead, and their relation to the otherworld.

The placing of the quartz together with the burials, and never in the construction in the small monuments, implies a close link between the buried individuals and the power of the white stone. The quartz represents here an act of personal beliefs and personal relations to the meaning of the stone as a link to the otherworld or the gods. The personal aspect of the stone is also underlined by the fact that it only occurs in the interior, and never in the exterior of the monuments. It is thereby never exposed to the outside world in the small monuments.

Within the large monuments the quartz is found either in the construction or in structures located outside the monument. The stone belongs to the exterior of these monuments, and is exposed to the world outside. By this strong external exposure of the quartz, its power is not directed to a buried individual. Instead the power and meaning of the quarts is transformed to the monument as such. The monument becomes the link to the otherworld or the gods. The few initiated in the secrets of the monument, are thereby also in charge of the contact with the gods.

The white quartz is thus transformed from being a symbol of the beliefs of the individual and a medium for individual contact with the otherworld or the gods, into being an active instrument of power used by a few to control, and thereby monopolising, the contacts with the otherworld and the gods.

This distinction between interior and exterior, exemplified by the use of quartz, is also visible on another scale in what concerns the monuments in Cúil Irra. The small monuments at Carrowmore were all confined to a slightly raised area in the lowland and were hardly built to make a visual impact on the landscape. Furthermore the focus of Carrowmore was internally directed towards the centre of the cluster of monuments. This is indicated by the direction of the passages of the tombs as these mostly are orientated towards the centre of the area defined by the monuments. This means that the monuments are turning their back to the world outside, focusing on the interior space of Carrowmore as such. It can be suggested that the originally about sixty monuments at Carrowmore probably represents different family/clan groups, who buried different individuals within the family/clan in their own monument. The monuments would have been family/clan related, and so also the rituals concerning the burials of individuals.

In what concerns visibility there is no prehistoric site in Ireland that visually dominates a whole region in the way that the huge cairn of Miosgán Meadhbha on Knocknarea does (fig. 4). In difference to Carrowmore, this monument is entirely focused on its physical and visual impact (Bergh 2002). Miosgán Meadhbha was not built to be a burial place for any particular person or family/clan, but as a statement of power and authority expressed in this active transformation of the whole landscape. The group behind such as achievement was far from the family/clan represented at the monuments at Carrowmore. We are now seeing a more hierarchical structure which had the power to amalgamate the workforce and planning involving a number of families/clans and their to contribution towards the erection of this ultimate monument.

The interior of Miosgán Meadhbha was concealed, but its exterior was meant to be open to interpretation for anyone that passed by. This was one of its intention in the Neolithic, and its impact is still as strong as it was the day it was completed, some 5,000 years ago.

The two types of monuments discussed constitute the two extremes on the wide morphological scale represented by the Irish passage tombs. Between these two there are many morphologically intermediate monuments, the rôles of which could have been as varied as their design. The suggested rôles of the small and large monuments illustrate however the variety of meaning that these monuments once could have had in their contemporary society.

An earlier version of this paper was published as "Design as Message. Rôle and symbolism of Irish passage tombs" in Casal, A., ed., 1997, O Neolitíco Atlántico e as Orixes do Megalitismo, Santiago de Compostela.

REFERENCES

Barret, J.C., Bradley, R., & Green, M., 1991: *Landscape, monuments and society. The prehistory of Cranborne Chase,* Cambridge.

Bergh, S., 1995: Landscape of the Monuments. A study of the passage tombs in the Cúil Irra region, Co. Sligo, Ireland. *Arkeologiska Undersökningar Skrifter nr 6,* Stockholm.

Bergh, S., 2002: "Knocknarea the ultimate monument: Megaliths and mountains in Neolithic Cúil Irra, north west Ireland", in Scarre, ed., 2002, 139-151.

Bradley, R., 1993: *Altering the Earth,* Society of Antiquaries of Scotland, Edinburgh.

Bradley, R., 1998: *The Significance of Monuments,* London, Routledge.

Burenhult, G., 1980: The Archaeology of Carrowmore, Co. Sligo, Ireland, Excavation Season 1977-79, *Theses and Papers in North-European Archaeology 9,* University of Stockholm.

Conwell, E.A., 1873: *Discovery of the Tomb of Ollamh Fodhla,* Dublin.

Cooney, G., 2000: *Landscapes of Neolithic Ireland,* London, Routledge.

Chapman, R., Kinnes, I., and Randsborg, K., eds., 1981, *The Archaeology of Death,* Cambridge.

Chapman, R.W., 1981: "The emergence of formal disposal areas and the 'problem' of megalithic areas in prehistoric Europe", in Chapman, Kinnes and Randsborg, eds., 1981.

Eogan, G., 1986: *Knowth and the Passage Tombs of Ireland,* London.

Flaming, A., 1973: "Tombs for the living". Man, 8:2, 177-193.

Herity, M., 1974: *The Irish Passage Graves,* Dublin.

O'Kelly, M., 1982: *Newgrange: Archaeology, Art and Legend,* London.

Ó Nualláin, S., 1989: *Survey of the megalithic tombs of Ireland, Vol. V., County Sligo,* Dublin.

Scarre, C., ed., 2002: *Monuments and Landscape in Atlantic Europe,* London, Routledge.

Sheridan, A., 1986: "Megaliths and Megalomania: An account, and interpretation, of the development of passage tombs in Ireland". *J. Irish Archaeology,* 3, 17-29.

Thomas, J., 1991: *Rethinking the Neolithic,* Cambridge.

Tilley, C., 1994: *A Phenomenology of Landscape,* Oxford, Berg.

Whittle, A., 1988: *Problems in Neolithic archaeology,* Cambridge.

Wood-Martin, W.G., 1888: *The Rude Stone Monuments of Ireland (Co. Sligo and the Island of Achill),* Dublin.

Fig. 4 - Knocknarea Mountain with Miosgaun Maedbha, from the east.
Photo: Stefan Bergh.

THE SEARCH FOR AN IRISH PALEOLITHIC: ROSSES POINT REVISITED

Peter C. Woodman
Professor of Archaeology, National University of Ireland, Cork.

ABSTRACT: Since the 1930s the received wisdom in Irish archaeology has led to the complete dismissal of the 'Rosses Point artefacts' as a product of nature. The controversal attribution of a Palaeolithic age to this material would appear to have led to its complete rejection as a product of a human agency. Re-examination of the material has led to the suggestion that some of the 'artefacts' were a product of human activity. There is still no reason to believe that the material is of Palaeolithic age but some consideration should be given to the possibilities that certain pieces were produced in prehistory and the manner in which the personal agendas of the protagonists shaped their interpretations of the site and its artifacts.

INTRODUCTION

In August 1927 J.P.T. Burchell published a note in *Nature*. In this note he claimed to have found a series of limestone artefacts which he felt were produced during the Palaeolithic. Burchell began to find this material while on holidays in Co. Sligo (Burchell normally worked in southern England). The discoveries were announced to the people of Sligo in *The Sligo Champion*, Aug. 27th 1927, a week after their publication in *Nature*. The piece, titled 'Sligo Discoveries - Inhabited 100,000 years ago' was presumably by J.P. Burchell and claims the support of Mr. Smith of the British Museum. As Ireland, in spite of numerous claims by William J. Knowles, (1897; 1914) had no known Palaeolithic this note initiated one of the most acrimonious disputes in Irish archaeology. It was like a supernova exploding across the pages of *Man* and *Nature*. Charlesworth and Macalister (1930) documented 40 papers, pro or contra between August 1927 and May 1929. Like all supernova this Co. Sligo controversy vanished as quickly as it had appeared and in 1936 Whelan, in his *The Palaeolithic Question in Ireland*, did not even refer to the Sligo material. Other authors, notably Movius (1942) and Woodman (1978) were inclined to follow the perceived wisdom that the Co. Sligo material was in one way or another a product of nature. However the rediscovery of some of the material in the stores of the Quaternary section of the British Museum gave the author the opportunity to reassess the so called 'artefacts'.

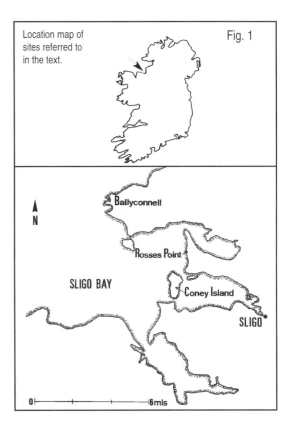

Fig. 1 Location map of sites referred to in the text.

HISTORY OF THE DISPUTE

In 1927 Burchell claimed to have discovered significant evidence of an Irish Palaeolithic at three localities in north Co. Sligo (*Fig. 1*).
They were:

1. Ballyconnell (Sligo 6" O.S. 4; 156.346 & 157.346), where Burchell claimed to have found two 'artefacts' embedded near the base of the boulder clay where it covered the local limestone bedrock.

2. A cave on the northern coast of Coney

Island (Sligo 6" O.S. 8; 161.339), where Palaeolithic artefacts were claimed to have been discovered on the beach adjacent to the cave.

3. The remnants of a 'rock shelter' on the western edge of Rosses Point (Sligo 6" O.S. 8; 162.341), on the northwestern tip of Rosses Lower townland. It was suggested that this was the remnants of a collapsed cave whose presumed back had been filled with a series of large blocks which covered an area which contained over 100 artefacts.

'Under the fallen roof blocks and resting on the limestone floor were discovered over 100 flakes, implements and cores made of limestone together with a quantity of powdered shells, a limited amount of small rolled, beach stones and a few pebbles derived from the 'Boulder clay' (Burchell and Reid Moir, 1928).

It is important to place the dispute over the Sligo Palaeolithic in a broader context. In particular, Burchell was a close confidant of J. Reid Moir who was at this time claiming that he had identified a series of Palaeolithic flint artefacts from in and below the Crag Beds in East Anglia (J. Reid Moir 1927). These he claimed were of much greater antiquity than the usually accepted Palaeolithic assemblages of England. The fact that much of this material was found out of context on beaches adjacent to Quaternary deposits is of crucial importance as Reid Moir claimed to be able to identify these early artefacts from the primitive methods of manufacture. It is therefore not surprising that Bruchell's initial note in *Nature* (Aug. 20, 1927) was followed by a supporting letter from J. Reid Moir on the following page.[1] Thus the Co. Sligo material was being used to underpin a position in a dispute which was centred in East Anglia for which see Clark (1985, 2-7). It is also not surprising that in November 1927 counter arguments were put forward by both a group of senior Irish academics namely Macalister (archaeologist), Charlesworth (geologist), Praeger (naturalist) and Stelfox (zoologist) and by Hazeldine Warren, who also worked on the southern English Lower Palaeolithic and was a consistent opponent of Reid Moir's views on the Cromer Bed artefacts. The substance of the argument advanced by Burchell and Reid Moir was as follows.

The discovery of 'artefacts' in the base of the boulder clay at Ballyconnell convinced Burchell that the limestone artefacts from Sligo had a genuine Palaeolithic antiquity although only two specimens were found at Ballyconnell. As a contrast over one hundred artefacts were claimed to have been discovered at Rosses Point in what was initially claimed to be a collapsed cave. The Rosses Point artefacts were consistently described as being in a comparatively fresh condition.

Explorations at Rosses Point in 1928 by Burchell behind the area where the artefacts were recovered revealed a cliff cut in the limestone which was about 10ft high. Burchell argued that 'This rock bluff, 10ft high, running north and south, would, in our submission, have constituted the east containing wall of the shelter and so have protected its contents from the effects of the ice action from the east', *i.e.*, of glaciation. He also suggested that this shelter had been created before the local boulder clays had been laid down. These boulder clays overlay the limestone. Burchell argued that the degree of marine erosion which was required to create the notch would have eroded away most of the overlying boulder clay if the marine erosion had taken place in the post glacial period.

'Had this erosion taken place in Post Glacial times we submit that the boulderclay face, immediately adjoining this feature to the North, would have been eroded back to a very great extent .... This factor, taken in conjunction with the Archaeological evidence compels us to regard the notch as of Pre Lower Boulder Age'.

Burchell recorded the remnants of the post-glacial raised beach in a notch which had been cut into the bluff at a higher level (Fig. 2).

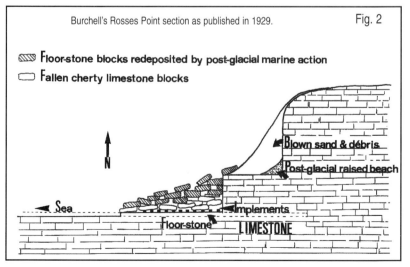

Fig. 2. Burchell's Rosses Point section as published in 1929.

Support for the concept of a rock shelter was initially based on the observation of the existence of another cave on the southern end of Rosses Point and on the existence of the cave at Coney Island with presumed artefacts occurring in the beach (Burchell and Reid Moir 1928). The idea that these caves were ancient was subject to criticism by many others who suggested that the caves were relatively modern and so it is not surprising that in the 1929 monograph the role of the cave was discarded and it was suggested that the Coney Island beach artefacts, including a quartzite core, were derived from the boulder clay - a similar scenario to that for the East Anglia shoreline material.

Burchell claimed that the Rosses Point artefacts were Early Mousterian as they could be best paralleled by the High Lodge material from Suffolk.[2] Until the 1950s it was generally accepted that the High Lodge material represented an early stage of the Mousterian (see Ashton *et. al.*, 1992). Burchell claimed that the major typological characteristic of the Sligo material was that it was a flake industry which lacked an abundance of facetted platforms which would characterise Levallois industries. Therefore it should be considered Mousterian. Essentially the cave artefacts were published in monographs in 1928 and 1929. The authors claimed to have found and identified side scrapers (1928, Pls. 11, 12 and 15) as well as primitive hand axes (1928, Pl. 16 and 17) and choppers (1929, *Fig. 11*).

In summary, Ballyconnell appeared to provide a geological context, Coney Island had an East Anglian parallel and Rosses Point provided an assemblage which could be regarded as Mousterian.

THE COUNTER ARGUMENT

The ideas of Burchell and Reid Moir were not generally well received and as noted earlier, within a few months Irish Quaternary Scientists and Hazeldine Warren had prepared critical replies.

There were several areas of contention raised by the critics.

i. BALLYCONNELL: It was apparent to many who visited the Ballyconnell location, that glacial plucking of the angled limestone bedrock would produce such a large number of angular pieces of limestone, that pseudo artefacts would be expected. Therefore the three pieces from Ballyconnell should be regarded with suspicion.

ii. CONEY ISLAND: The caves referred to by Burchell and Reid Moir in 1928 were generally thought to be of modern marine origin. A cave on the southern face of Rosses Point (Burchell and Reid Moir 1928, Pl. 1) was also felt to be modern.

iii. ROSSES POINT: The argument that there was a cave containing artefacts on the western end of Rosses Point was also subjected to criticism. It is important to remember that ideas were being developed over a two year period and therefore Burchell and Reid Moir were not always consistent with their suggestions. This would have been and still is normal for most workers still in the process of field research. However, even today it is not always clear what they were referring to. It is therefore not altogether surprising that their opponents were able to point to inconsistencies. Instead of a low narrow rock shelter 47 by 9ft. and 3 to 4ft. in height which had survived glacial activity, Jones and Boswell (*Nature*, June 2, 1928) suggested if a cave had existed it had been created by marine erosion. They also noted that 26 of the 36 blocks of limestone which covered the layer containing artefacts were derived from lower limestones which formed the floor of the so called cave. These had probably been derived from further out at present day sea level and were carried up by storms and deposited in their present position on top of the layer containing the so called artifacts.

Initially Macalister expressed scepticism about the human origin of the artefacts and claimed that they were a product of sea action (Macalister *et. al.*, *Nature*, 31st Dec., 1927). However Charlesworth and Macalister in the summary article in *Proceedings of the Royal Irish Academy* (April 1930) quote everyone else's view on this matter but omitted their own suggestion that they were natural - surely a tacit admission that the contention that they were natural was erroneous.

In the same paper Charlesworth and Macalister (1930) list other opinions.

a. C.B. Whelan (*Man*, May 1928) accepted that they are Palaeolithic artefacts.

b. A leading group of British Palaeolithic experts Armstrong, Burkitt, Dewey, Garrod and Smith (*Nature*, January 28, 1928) were satisfied that they are of human workmanship but also note 'This statement is without prejudice to their cultural age'.

c. The Abbé Breuil (*Man*, July 1928) agreed that some pieces could be a product of nature but most were a product of genuine human activity. He did not see any parallel with Mousterian and felt that to determine their age was a geological problem.

d. Sollas (*Man*, July 1929) accepted that they were of human origin.

e. Following on a suggestion initially made by R. J. Welch, Palmer, Jackson and Pierce (*Nature*, March 1928) suggested that the debris was a by-product of stone anchor manufacture. However as Charlesworth and Macalister (1930) noted, R. J. Welch withdrew his suggestion upon inspection of the site. It is unfortunate that Welch, a noted photographer, did not take any photographs at Rosses Point.

What was usually ignored was that a substantial number of what had been claimed as artefacts, *i.e.*, over 100 pieces, had been found in a tiny area of Rosses Point and that no other artefacts were claimed to have been found elsewhere in the Rosses Point area.

Macalister and Charlesworth reinforced their suspicions about the Sligo Mousterian with the dangerous and circumstantial argument that it was unlikely that any evidence of a Palaeolithic occupation could survive in Co. Sligo. They pointed instead to the recent, more believable, finds of human remains in what appeared to be a 'Pleistocene'[3] context at Kilgreany Cave, Co. Waterford (Tratman 1928).

By 1935 Macalister was even more sceptical and again doubted whether the artefacts were of human manufacture.

> 'Other stones are less responsive to the methods of ancient artificers, and the implements made of them would at best be makeshifts, not always to be identified with assurance as products of human manufacture. The tragi-comedy of the alleged implements from Rosses Point, which gave rise to a hot controversy a few years before the publication of this book, is of importance only as illustrating this uncertainty ... . The publication of these implements, though a futility in itself, had the extremely valuable effect of showing that the criteria of human workmanship, upon which their champions had relied, are untrustworthy' (Macalister 1935, 9).

In summary, by 1930 there was a general acceptance that some of the material, in particular from Rosses Point, had been humanly manufactured but there was general agreement that this material could not be accepted as being Palaeolithic unless a more believable geological context was provided. By the 1940s Movius, in his Irish Stone Age, was equally sceptical of the Rosses Point material, admitting to the possible human origin of some flakes, he preferred the stone anchor explanation.

Eventually Irish archaeology was to focus on the negative aspects of the Sligo material in that it was not Palaeolithic. Very little consideration was given to what it actually was. Obviously in the absence of new geological information, the argument could not be advanced and Movius' elucidation of the Kilgreany sequence, showing that the human remains at that site were not Palaeolithic, helped convince many that there was no credible evidence for an Irish Palaeolithic.

REVISITING THE MATERIAL

With the support of the Royal Irish Academy the author was able to examine the collection of Irish artefacts held in the British Museum Quaternary Section stores at Franks House, Orsman Road, London. This examination revealed that a significant sample of Burchell's collection, 26 pieces in all, had been lodged in the British Museum (1927 11-12/1-11 and 1929 12-20/1-15: British Museum Registration Numbers). This contradicted the 1928 monograph which claimed that the material had been lodged in the Ipswich Museum. However Burchell seems to have had a policy of lodging representative artefacts in the British Museum as he also lodged a sample of his Island Magee material there.

The author's re-examination of the material revealed two important points.

1. The material is not in as fresh a condition as had been suggested by many of those who wrote about it in the 1920s. The pieces recovered vary from comparatively fresh to heavily rolled. Therefore the idea of an assemblage being preserved in a cave in relatively pristine conditions is not acceptable and, if a later date than the Palaeolithic is envisaged, is not necessary.

2. There is a variation in the form of the artefacts recovered and it is apparent that the material ranges from a series of natural fragments, both fresh and weathered, through flakes, to pieces which could be argued as showing signs of secondary working.

The 26 pieces in the British Museum included three specimens from Ballyconnell. Two had been found by Burchell and one by Whelan. All were remarkably fresh for pieces recovered from the base of the boulder clay. The two found by

Burchell can only be described as massive. 1929 12-20:1 is over 10cm thick while a piece of limestone (1929: 12-20:5) which is not as clearly struck as is suggested by Burchell *et. al.* (1929:3), has optimistically being described as a hollow scraper yet it is over 6cm in thickness and nearly 25cm in length. Another, a piece of quartzite, was found on the beach at Coney Island (Burchell *et. al.*, 1929:1). This was illustrated as a core.

The remaining 22 pieces are from Rosses Point of which 18 were available for inspection. Of these, six pieces should be described as either naturally fractured pieces of limestone or, perhaps, more importantly both the so-called Mousterian side scrapers (see Fig. 3 which was illustrated by Burchell *et al.* 1929, Fig. 8) and one of the handaxes (see Fig. 4 which was illustrated by Burchell and Reid Moir 1928, Fig. 16) should be described as natural water rolled fragments of limestone. The illustrations are presented together for easy comparison at the end. Two others could be regarded as dubious. The remaining 10 pieces were humanly struck. Usually they had distinctive platforms (Fig. 5) and showed traces of being removed from blocks which had other flakes removed (Fig. 6). They also did not usually resemble the natural flakes from the outer surface of weathered or water rolled blocks. In general these were a series of large flakes which were broader than longer, often more than 10cm in width (Fig. 7). While there were no hand-axes present, two of the pieces showed signs of being trimmed into a regular shape, reminiscent of cleavers, *e.g.*, Fig. 8.

As only 10 of the 18 pieces from Rosses Point were humanly struck and as these were the type specimens which had been published there was always the possibility that they represented the best of the Rosses Point material and that the remainder were natural. It was apparent, therefore, that the British Museum material might not be typical. However, there was a complication in that the material which had been deposited in the Ipswich Museum was not available as an unspecified number of pieces from Ipswich Museum had been sent to Oxford in the early 1960s. Unfortunately the accession registers in Ipswich did not specify which Oxford institution received the Rosses Point material. Conversations with Dr. Derek Roe suggested that the material might have gone to the Pitt-Rivers Museum and eventually a selection of limestone flakes were recovered at the Baden-Powell Laboratory of the Pitt-Rivers Museum at 60 Banbury Road, Oxford. Most of these still retained the Ipswich registration number 1927:98 and individual number.

Unfortunately this again only represented a fraction of the Rosses Point material as a second batch had been donated by Burchell in 1928 to Ipswich Museum. This second batch of artifacts has yet to be recovered. In total 14 flakes were recovered from 60 Banbury Road. Of these 14 pieces, three (1927:13, 14 and 15) were unsatisfactory, being either too incomplete or natural. The remaining 11 pieces show clear signs of human percussion and vary in quality from a specimen marked 1933:217N to water-rolled flakes such as 1927:98:1. An unnumbered flake and 1933:217N are good examples of humanly struck flakes in the Pitt-Rivers collection.

In general the Oxford material contains a higher percentage of struck flakes than the British Museum collection. There is also no pretension towards handaxes or side scrapers but instead there are a number of good flakes present.

These flakes are again of the same type as those in the British Museum collections. From the total material available, *i.e.*, 32 pieces, it is possble state that 21 are clearly the product of human activity. Virtually all the flakes have a maximum dimension of more than 10 cms, in fact a significant number exceed 20 cms.

There is no record that the exploration of the site revealed any small flakes and none were found in any of the surviving assemblages, therefore this assemblage could be described as a massive flake industry.

It is unfortunate that the remaining 50% of the Rosses Point material cannot be located but if the Oxford material is typical then the following observations can be made.

1. BIASES IN PRESENTATION

In order to underpin an argument based on British and Continental parallels, Burchell and Reid Moir were prepared to identify artefacts such as scrapers and handaxes, within the pieces of natural limestone, yet play down the existence of perfectly good struck flakes. The reaction of Macalister, Charlesworth and others was to the Palaeolithic attribution, but they ignored the existence of numerous struck flakes. It is, of course, salutary to remember that this tendency to select the elements which help justify ones own perceptions of a particular assemblage is an inherent danger in all publications of lithics. In other words, do we publish what is representative or those pieces which are either very distinctive or support our own particular agenda? Rosses Point has lessons for us all.

2. CURATORIAL RESPONSIBILITIES

A second lesson of this assemblage is that when a key assemblage is THOUGHT not to be of significance we still have a resonsibility to retain the material for future reconsideration. It is a truism in archaeology to state that no generation has a right to asssume that its interpretations of any assemblage are both complete and infallible yet, today, these responsibilities are expected to take second place to other more immediate pressures in the museum world.

3. THE AGE OF THE ROSSES POINT ASSEMBLAGE

If it therefore became more important to deny the Palaeolithic character of the material, then, the obvious question must be - If not Palaeolithic then what was the Rosses Point material?

During the summers of 1993 and 1994 the author, in the company of Martin A. Timoney of the Sligo Field Club, had the opportunity to visit the three key locations. During these visits attention centred on Rosses Point and, in particular, the cliff face which had been considered as the back of Burchell's suggested cave. Although it was heavily overgrown, it was apparent that it could have been quarried by human agencies, thus the notch cut into the cliff face. It is just possible that this is neither a feature created by a Mid-Holocene marine transgression nor is the cliff face with the limestone blocks entirely modern. Seventy years after the discovery of Rosses Point the area of the rock shelter has altered very little. This would confirm R. J. Welch's feelings that it was not a recent creation, and certainly not from the manufacture of primitive anchors. The idea that this was little more than a modern quarry also suffers from the fact that no unfinished blocks remain. It would be reasonable to presume, therefore, that the activity at Rosses Point had some antiquity but there must some uncertainty as to its actual age.

a. Palaeolithin age?

There is no more reason to believe that the Rosses Point Site and assemblage rather than any other site is Palaeolithic in age. There is no geological evidence and the comparison of certain pieces with Mousterian atrifact types is clearly spurious.

b. Later Mesolithic?

The notch noted by Burchell to be cut into the clifff above the site could be the last trace of the Mid-Holocene Marine Transgression.and it is known that the coastal region of Co. Sligo was subjected to a transgression at or before 5,000 b.p., *e.g.*, as was noted in the Culeenamore area of the Knocknarea penninsula (Burenhult 1984). Therefore the potential for the survival of this location at sea level if the site had been created before before 5,000 b.p. must be questioned. All known Irish Later Mesolithic assemblages used a hard hammer percussion technology to produce large blades and blade-like flakes. While some core tool production took place on certain Later Mesolithic sites there are so far no sites from this period where blade production is entirely absent.

So far there are no known Later Mesolithic axe factory sites though there are numerous polished axes made out of materials other than flint. One possible exception might be the factory site at Fisher street Co. Clare (Knowles 1901). Even here the axes, irrespective of the period of origin, tend to use beach pebbles as blanks for the manufacture of the axes, though Knowles found some blanks which had been chipped in a manner reminiscent of those found at Rosses Point. As noted earlier there is no real evidence of the smaller elements of debitage which might have been expected at an axe manufacturing location but as the site was obviously not in pristine undisturbed state and some of the material was slightly water rolled it is possible that some of the finer elements could have either been washed away or simply not noticed in the excitement.

c. Neolithic in age?

While all the obsevations about the possibility of the site being an axe factory or quarry discusssed earlier can be applied to a suggestion of Neolithic age the possibility that a site of this type would only survive after the Mid-Holocene transgression would increase the prospects of this site being Neolithic or Later.

d. Post-dating the Stone Age?

Very little attention has been given to the possibility that knapping of material such as that found at Rosses Point could continue after the Stone Age and it is possible that quarrying and stone working at Rosses Point to produce large core and/or flake tools for other as yet unidentified purposes had taken place. It may be of significance that occasional similar large flakes of limestone have been recovered from the shores of Lough Gara at the other end of Co. Sligo.

CONCLUSION

At this stage it would be premature to claim that this was an axe factory but it would seem reasonable to presume that at some point in the past quarrying took place at Rosses Point and that some of the residue survived at the foot of the cliff until 1927 but that much of the material has been washed away from this exposed location, just above mean high water mark.

Perhaps some future effort should be put into examining what actually happened at Rosses Point rather than worrying about what did not happen!

Notes

1. Inspite of J. Reid Moir's robust support for Burchell, it is apparent from his correspondance with Burchell (lodged in Ipswich Museum) that he could not be persuaded to visit Co. Sligo in the key 1928-1929 period.

2. Within the Palaeolithic, which is presumed to end with the beginnings of the Holocene/Post-Glacial (10,000 years ago), there are numerous stages which were recognised even in the 1920s. The Middle Palaeolithic whch is best known from a period roughly 100,000 to 35,000 years ago is characterised by two types of assemblages, both based on the production of a series of distinct flake tools. These are

   a. Levalloisian assemblages using the Levallois technique which requires careful preparation of the core before flakes are struck off; thus the diagnostic facetting or flaking of the striking platform.

   b. Mousterian assemblages where a simpler flaking technique is used to produce flakes which are then retouched into one of a series of diagnostic shapes.

3. The geological term Pleistocene was used to distinguish deposits in caves which had accumulated during what was then thought of as the 'Ice Age'. The deposits were usually characterised by the occurrence of either extinct faunas, e.g., Giant Deer, or faunal remains of animals which no longer exist in Ireland, e.g., Reindeer,

CLAUDE BLAKE WHELAN AND ROSSES POINT: *A POSTSCRIPT*

On a recent research visit to the National Museum of Ireland in Dublin and subsequent to the publication of this article in *Antiquity* 72, 562-570, in September 1998, I had the opportunity to examine part of the Claude Blake Whelan collection and I was surprised to note that it contained three large flakes from Rosses Point and one from Ballyconnell.

The flakes from Rosses Point are:

1577 (fig. 11, lower left) which is unusual in that it was struck from the outside of a water smoothed piece of limestone. Therefore unlike many of the other flakes from Rosses Point it lacks flake scars on its dorsal surface. However it retains a striking platform and has a point of percussion. It is slightly weathered.

1578 (fig. 11, lower right) is the smallest of the flakes in the collection. It again retains a striking platform but unlike the previous flake it has a number of flake scars on its dorsal surface.

1579 (fig. 11, upper right) is the least satisfactory specimen in the Whelan collection. It is much thicker, more irregular than the other flakes and is quite weathered. It is also less certain that it was struck.

The flake from Ballyconnell is:

1556 (fig. 11, upper left) is the specimen which Whelan claimed to have found between the upper and lower boulderclays at Ballyconnell. Until now this piece was only known from a cast in the Baden Powell Institute (Pitt Rivers Museum) Oxford. There are several possible flake scars on the dorsal surface and even in a photograph of the bulbar surface (Burchell *et al.* 1929, Plate IV) the fresh whitemark at the point of percussion can be seen. Although this piece initially appears as a potentially convincing humanly manufactured artefact in a Pleistocene context there are certain problems. The piece is remarkably fresh for an artefact in a glacial context and is a single find. Experience has shown that if one searches long enough, occasional pseudo artefacts will be recovered therefore in the absence of an assemblage 1556 must be considered as a pseudo artefact plucked from the local limestone.

DISCUSSION

At one level the identification of this small group of specimens can be seen as one more step in the search for the missing Rosses Point material but it also raises another question. Whelan was one of the first to support the proposition of an Irish Mousterian based on the Rosses Point material (Whelan 1928). However, within five years he had become curiously silent about the site. In his paper to the International Geological Congress in Washington in 1933 (Whelan 1936) "The

Palaeolithic Question In Ireland" he makes no reference to Rosses Point although he did discuss the possible association of human remains and artefacts with Pleistocene faunal remains at Ballynamintra as well as Kilgreaney.

For the rest of his life Whelan was to remain silent about the Sligo Palaeolithic. He was a friend of Burchell and together they identified the Mesolithic sites on Island Magee and at the Warren, Cushendun. He supported his friends and was not usually one to shrink from controversy. Mitchell in his obituary of Whelan (Mitchell 1954) describes a man who was explosive, enthusiastic and generous. He was also fiercely retentive of his beliefs in the spurious Castlereagh industry which he saw as being Tardenoisian (Whelan 1938). He also retained the belief (Whelan 1936) that there was an Aurignacian element surviving in the Irish Mesolithic! Yet in spite of his interest in an Irish Palaeolithic he was never to offer any further opinion on Rosses Point. Even in his Archaeological Bibliographic Notebook (Ulster Museum) there are only the references to his notes in *Man* in 1928 and the Burchell *et al.* 1929 publication.

Perhaps his retention of the four large cumbersome specimens was a silent statement that he believed that "the jury was still out" on the Sligo Mousterian.

Acknowledgements

I thank the staff of the Quaternary Section of the Department of Prehistoric and Roman Antiquities of the British Museum for all their help in retrieving the Rosses Point material which had become scattered to various localities. Similarly I thank the staff of the Baden Powell Laboratory, Pitt Rivers Museum, 60 Banbury Road, Oxford, for their perseverance and vigilance in the search for the elusive Oxford material. Mr. Stephan Plunkett of Ipswich Museum was a fount of information on the East Anglian background. I also thank Ms. Elizabeth Anderson for the drawings of selected artefacts and typing the various drafts. Record photographs were provided by Karen Perkins and Kath Price. I thank Martin A., Mary B. and Martin J. Timoney and Emma Woodman for their hospitality and company during the Sligo fieldwork.

The search for material and the preparation of this paper was made possible through funding provided by the Royal Irish Academy/British Academy Fund, the Royal Irish Academy National Committee for Archaeology Research Fund and the UCC Evening Arts Research Fund.

BIBLIOGRAPHY

Ashton, N., Cook, J., Lewis, S.G., and Rose, J., 1992: *High Lodge: Excavations by G. de G. Sieveking 1962-69 and J. Cook,* London, British Museum Press.

Burchell, J.P.T., 1927: "Discovery of Stone Implements of Lower Palaeolithic Age in Ireland", *Nature* 120, 260-261.

Burchell, J.P.T., 1931: "Early Neanthropic Man and his relation to the Ice age", *Proc.Prehistoric Society of East Anglia,* VI, 253-303.

Burchell, J.P.T., 1934: "Some littoral Sites of Early Post-Glacial Times, located in Northern Ireland", *Proc. Prehistoric Society of East Anglia,* VII, 366-372.

Burchell, J.P.T., and Reid Moir, J., 1928: *The Early Mousterian Implements of Sligo, Ireland,* Ipswich, W.E. Harrison.

Burchell, J.P.T., Reid Moir, J., and Dixon, E.E.L., 1929: "Palaeolithic Man in North West Ireland", *Proc. Prehistoric Society of East Anglia,* Occasional Paper No. 1

Burenhult, Göran, 1984: *The Archaeology of Carrowmore, Environmental Archaeology and the Megalithic Tradition at Carrowmore, Co. Sligo, Ireland,* Theses and Papers in North-European Archaeology, 14, University of Stockholm.

Charlesworth, J.K., and Macalister, R.A.S., 1930: "The Alleged Palaeolithic Implements of Sligo: A Summary", *Proc. Royal Irish Academy,* 39, 18-32.

Clarke, Grahame, 1985: "The Prehistoric Society: From East Anglia to the World", *Proc. Prehistoric Soc.,* 51, 1-13.

Knowles, W.J., 1897: "Survivals from the Palaeolithic Age among Irish Neolithic Implements", *J. Roy. Soc. Antiq. Ireland,* 27, 1-18.

Knowles, W.J., 1901: The 4th report on the prehistoric remains from the sandhills on the coast of Ireland, *Proc. Royal Irish Academy,* 3rd Series, 6, 331-389.

Knowles, W.J., 1914: "The Antiquity of Man in Ireland, being an Account of the Older Series of Irish Flint Implements", *J. Royal Anthropological Institute,* 44, 83-121.

Macalister, R.A.S., 1935: *Ancient Ireland,* London, Metheun.

Mitchell, G.F., 1954: "Obituary for C.B.Whelan", *Ulster J. Archaeology,* 17, 4-6.

Movius, H.L., 1942: *The Irish Stone Age,* Cambridge University Press, Cambridge.

Reid Moir, J., 1927: *The Antiquity of Man in East Anglia,* Cambridge, Cambridge University Press.

Tratman, E.K., 1928: "Excavations at Kilgreany Cave, County Waterford", *Proc. Bristol Speleological Society,* 3, 109-153.

Whelan, C.B., 1928: Ireland in Pleistocene Times, *Man,* 28 (May) 74-76.

Whelan, C.B., 1936: "The Palaeolithic Question in Ireland", in *Report of the XVI International Geological Congress Washington* (1933), 1209-1218.

Whelan, C.B., 1938: "Studies in the significance of the Irish Stone Age: The cultural sequence", *Proc. Royal Irish Academy,* XLIV, 115-136.

Woodman, P.C., 1978: *The Mesolithic in Ireland,* BAR (British Series), No. 58. Oxford.

A CELEBRATION *OF* SLIGO

Fig. 3 - So-called Mousterian side scraper from Rosses Point, British Museum 1929 12-20, 7.

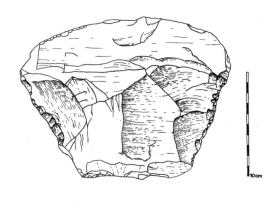

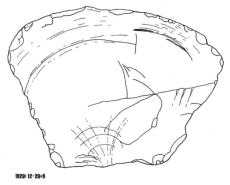

Fig. 6 - Portion of limestone flake retaining flake scars.

Fig. 4 - So-called handaxe from Rosses Point, British Museum 1929 12-20, 13.

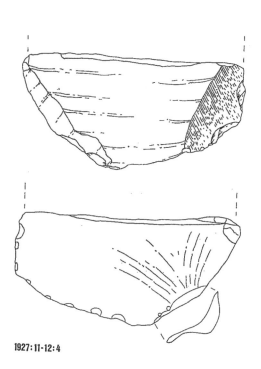

Fig. 5 - Large limestone flake showing clear signs of percussion.

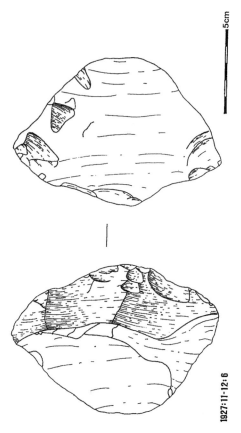

Fig 7 - Large limestone flake showing clear signs of flake scars.

A CELEBRATION OF SLIGO

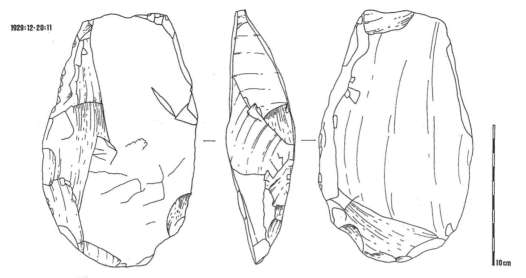

Fig. 8 - Limestone flake which would appear to have been trimmed to a cleaver.

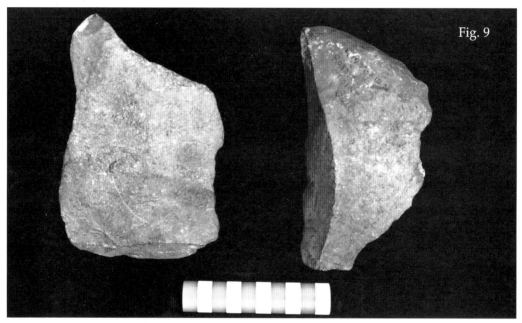

Fig. 9 & 10 Views of both sides of two flakes in the Baden-Powell Laboratory Collection of the Pitt-Rivers Museum at 60, Banbury Road, Oxford.

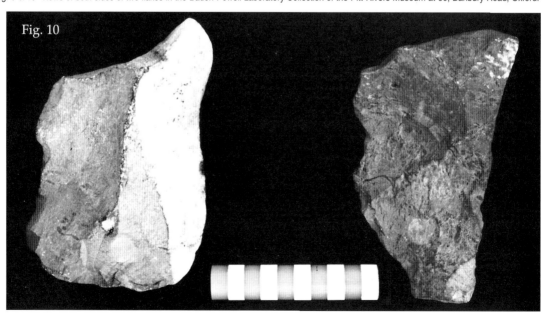

Fig. 11 - Four flakes in the National Museum of Ireland, Dublin. Upper left: flake 1556 from Ballyconnell; Upper right: flake 1579 from Rosses Point; Lower left: flake 1577 from Rosses Point; Lower right: flake 1578 from Rosses Point.
Photo: Copyright National Museum of Ireland.

Carrowmore No. 13, Co. Sligo. Photo: Des Smith, Sligo Field Club Collection.

Carrowmore No. 52, Co. Sligo. Photo: Des Smith, Sligo Field Club Collection.

POLLEN ANALYTICAL INVESTIGATIONS IN THE SLIGO AREA

Hans Göransson,
Ibsberga PL 809, S-260 70 Ljungbyhed, Sweden

ABSTRACT Pollen analytical investigations in the area between the Bricklieve Mountains and Sligo Bay demonstrate that the former rich forests were utilized and manipulated by the the so called "hunter-gatherer". Here and there the broad-leaved trees may have been girdled and burnt. It is suggested that the broad-leaved trees, so to speak, manured and ploughed the soil. Grazing animals were favoured and cultivation of cereals may have taken place already during the Late Mesolithic. From the very beginning of the (conventional) Early Neolithic grazing was of astonishingly great importance (very high values of *Plantago lanceolata*) in the Sligo area. During Middle Neolithic Time cultivation of cereals may have occurred in coppice woods ("wandering arable fields") and probably also on permanent fields. Blanket peat began to form in Bricklieve Mountains at the end of the Neolithic and the beginning of the Bronze Age.

In August 1981, I was invited by Dr Göran Burenhult to the archaeological excavations at Carrowmore, Co. Sligo, to perform samplings for pollen analysis in lakes and bogs. Martin A. Timoney brought Magnus Thelaus and me to Cloverhill Lough to the east of the Carrowmore megalithic cemetery, to Ballygawley Lough in the Collooney Gap of the Ox Mountains and to the Treanscrabbagh Bog in the Bricklieve Mountains. Cores for pollen analysis were taken at all these sites.

Furthermore a piece of the submerged peat, only 9 cm thick but several square metres in area, at Strandhill, was collected by Burenhult. This is only occasionally visible at low-tide. The pollen diagram and the C14-datings from Strandhill turned out to be of great interest. The analysis from Cloverhill Lough, on the other hand, demonstrated that the sedimentation in that lake did not start until *ca.* 300 AD, 1700 years ago. For that reason the diagram from Cloverhill Lough is not discussed in the present paper which concentrates on the Late Mesolithic and Neolithic periods.

THE POLLEN ANALYTICAL METHOD

The pollen analytical method was developed in the 1910s by the Swedish geologist Lennart von Post (von Post 1916). The method works like this. Pollen grains, which are very small, are

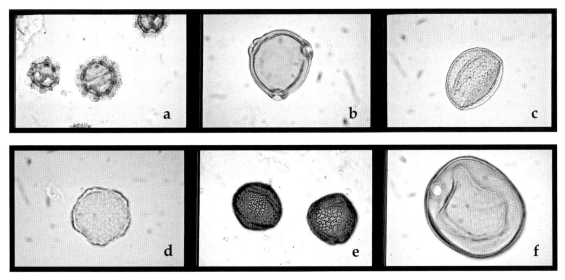

Fig. 1 - Some pollen grains of different genera: a) elm (*Ulmus*), b) oak (*Quercus*), c) birch (*Betula*), d) wheat (*Triticum*), e) ivy (*Hedera*), f) dandelion, (Compositae Liguliflorae). Photo: Thomas Persson.

formed in the stamens of the plants. The mean diameter of a pollen grain from Northern Europe is *ca.* 40 thousandths of a millimetre (= 40μm). The smallest pollen grains, *ca.* 5μm, are developed in the flowers of the forget-me-nots, the largest pollen grains, *ca.* 125μm, are produced by spruces.

The pollen grain is surrounded by a very tough wall called exin. The *exin* is formed of one of the most extraordinarily resistent materials which exists in the organic world. The exin may be boiled in acids and bases for hours without being destroyed. The exin has a characteristic sculpture and structure which make it possible for us to discriminate between different genera and, not seldom, species (fig. 1a- fig.1e). The fern plants produce and spread spores which also have a resistent wall and which can be identified to genera or species.

Pollen grains are produced in immense amounts every spring and summer. Most of the trees are wind-pollinated and will dominate the "pollen rain". Grasses, sedges, plantain species and sorrels are wind-pollinated too, while most of the flowers are insect-pollinated and spread small amounts of pollen. Every year each square metre of the land surface of Ireland is powdered with ca. 300 million pollen grains.

Pollen deposited in lakes and bogs, an environment deficient in oxygen, will be preserved, that is the internal parts of the pollen grain die but the exin survives. Every year the lake sediment and bog peat grow a little and during 10,000 years - from the moment when the final climatic amelioration started - many metres of sediment have been deposited.

Every spring and summer the slowly growing deposits have received immense amounts of pollen from the surrounding vegetation. By taking cores from lakes and bogs we are able to reconstruct an area's vegetational history by studying the fossil pollen and spores in the cores. In *pollen analysis* we identify and count pollen grains from closely lying samples from cores and from that we are able to construct *pollen diagrams*.

Pollen diagrams show the percentage distribution of the *pollen amounts* of different genera and species of trees and herbs from the oldest part of the core up to recent time. The pollen percentage distribution does not correspond directly to the real distribution of the surrounding vegetation as different species produce and spread different amounts of pollen. The relation between pollen and vegetation is a very complex phenomenon which in our days is eagerly studied.

THE C14-METHOD

A very small fraction of all carbon which is a part of the living organisms is radioactive and is named C14. Like other radioactive substances C14 disintegrates at certain rate, the radioactive substance has a fixed half-life. For that reason we can determine the age of old, dead, organic material such as peat, charcoal, etc.

C14-ages are given as C14-years "before present" abbreviated "BP". "Present" is, according to an international agreement, always AD 1950 and the half-life ("$T\frac{1}{2}$") is always 5568±30 years. C14-values of the type just described are named "conventional C14-values".

On the whole, the correspondence between real time and C14-time is good back to the Birth of Christ. During older epochs, C14-ages differ rather considerably from calendar years. By C14-dating of annual rings of trees which are many thousand years old so-called calibration tables can be constructed. With the aid of calibration tables the probable, "real" age of a conventional C14-value can be read off. The "real age" is expressed by the abbreviation "BC" or "AD".

It is very important that we give conventional C14-dates in our pollen diagrams and in our pollen analytical and archaeological texts. Calibrated values may then be stated in the text (BC, AD) which describes the diagram or the archaeological material. Some archaeological papers are difficult to interpret as the authors use calibrated C14-values without mentioning the values (conventional C14-years) from which they performed the calibrations.

THE AIM OF THE POLLEN ANALYTICAL INVESTIGATIONS IN THE SLIGO AREA

The aim of the pollen analytical investigations in the Sligo area was to reconstruct the past vegetation during the time of the megalith builders. This time probably corresponds to that from the later part of the Mesolithic up to the Middle Neolithic, that is from *ca.* 5800 BP to *ca.* 4500 BP (*ca.* 4700 BC to *ca.* 3340 BC) (Bergh 1995).

Before the elm décline level (*ca.* 5150 BP = *ca.* 4000 BC) which happens to correspond with the arrival of Neolithic practises, NW Europe was, according to the older school of archaeology and vegetation history, covered with luxuriant virgin forests of broad-leaved trees which were untouched by man. This view has changed and for more than two decades we accept the view that these forests were manipulated in the Mesolithic (see below).

THE MESOLITHIC FORESTS AND THE HUNTER-GATHERER

All over the forested parts of the world, before the introduction of agriculture, man utilized and transformed the forests for thousands, even tens of thousands, of years in order to favour grazing and browsing wild animals and in order to get better yields of wild edible plants, for instance the aborigines in Australia, the Indians in pre-European North America, *etc.*). Mesolithic Ireland was no exception to that rule. The hunter-gatherer thus did not only live at the coasts, he also utilized the resources of the inland.

FOREST FIRES AND FOREST GROUND FIRES DURING THE MESOLITHIC

In many pollen diagrams from westernmost Ireland in the west to northern Poland and southern Sweden in the east the curve of microscopic charcoal particles larger than 12 μm has high values during the Mesolithic.

When forest fires and forest ground fires take place the charcoal particles rise in the air, above the canopies of the trees, are caught by the wind and brought to lakes and bogs in the same way as tree pollen grains. Naturally, charcoal particles from hearth fires also are transported in the same way. Not infrequently, however, the curve of bracken (*Pteridium*) more or less coincides with that of charcoal dust. Bracken is favoured by forest fires and forest ground fires. Aspen (*Populus*) quickly occupies burnt areas and it grows tall if the environment remains unshaded.

Microscopic charcoal particles, bracken spores and aspen pollen, may thus be named "forest fire indicators" or "forest ground fire indicators" (also other species constitute such fire indicators). Forest fires occurred from Ireland and Great Britain (see, for instance, Edwards 1990, and compilation by Simmons 1994) to Sweden (see below) during most of the Mesolithic; we have similiar evidence from the island of Wolin, in northernmost Poland, during the Late Mesolithic (Latalowa 1992). Thus most of the forests in that very large area were utilised and transformed by the so-called hunter-gatherer (fig. 2).

The Mesolithic "hunter-gatherer" wanted to create a good environment for grazing and browsing game and he wanted to favour hazel and berries of different kinds. By killing trees by ring-barking (girdling) or by setting fire to wood piled around the bases of the trees such an environment was easily produced (Cronon 1984). Big axes were not necessary in this work. This selective burning may have promoted "the edge effect" of the ecosystem (Cronon 1984).

EVIDENCES FOR FOREST FIRES DURING THE MESOLITHIC

Is it really possible that the forests of broad-leaved trees could burn during the Mesolithic? By studying small "kettle holes" on slopes this hypothesis can be tested. As I have only worked in Ireland for a week in 1981 I have had no opportunity to find such a site. In Sweden, however, macroscopic charcoal particles from forest fires from Mesolithic Time have been found in "kettle holes". It is possible to determine such charcoal particles from forest fires to genus or species: the determinations demonstrate that the forests of broad-leaved trees such as oak, lime, hazel, etc., could burn

Fig. 2 - The Atlantic (Mesolithic) forest of broad-leaved trees was here and there transformed by the "hunter-gatherer". The big trees could easily be killed by ring-barking (girdling) or by the use of fire around the bases of the trunks.   Drawing: Hans Göransson.

(see also compilation by Simmons 1994). [In recent time investigations of rather small lakes (Union Wood Lake and Slish Lake) have been performed in the Sligo area (Dodson & Bradshaw 1987). According to the investigators "clearances for pastures" began around 5400 BP in the vicinity of these lakes].

It thus seems to be confirmed that the forests of broad-leaved trees did burn during the Mesolithic. Only dead and dry broad-leaved trees could burn. For that reason it is supposed that the Mesolithic hunter-gatherer killed big trees here and there in the way suggested above. This means that the forests were transformed by man during the Mesolithic in order to favour grazing and browsing wild animals and to create areas where hazel, cherry trees, crab apple trees, wild strawberries and other berries thrived. It may be correct to assume that some of the species mentioned were planted. Thus it may be said the the Mesolithic hunter-gatherer was also a cultivator and that land "was taken" long before Neolithic Time.

MESOLITHIC ACTIVITIES AROUND BALLYGAWLEY LOUGH

Only the Mesolithic part of the Ballygawley Lough diagram is usable as the sedimentation stopped at the end of that period for probably about 1000 years. The pollen rain from the forests during Mesolithic Time was extremely rich and the values of elm and hazel are very high in the diagram (Göransson 1984). The high values for hazel may demonstrate that the forests were rather open as hazel does not thrive in shadow.

The above suggestion is strengthened by the fact, that one pollen grain of ribwort plantain (*Plantago lanceolata*) was found in the core at the latest part of the Mesolithic as were pollen grains of cereal type. Ribwort plantain can not grow in closed forests. The light-demanding heather (*Calluna*) and the fire-favoured bracken (*Pteridium*) have been regularly recorded during the Late Mesolithic. The mean value of microscopic charcoal particles is ca. 10%. We can thus sum up that the Late Mesolithic forests were utilized by the "hunter-gatherer" in the Ballygawley Lough area of the Ox Mountains.

Fig. 4 - The sampling site at Treanscrabbagh, Carrowkeel, in 1981 is at the left edge of the photo. Photo: Martin A. Timoney.

MESOLITHIC ACTIVITIES IN BRICKLIEVE MOUNTAINS

The pollen diagram from Treanscrabbagh, Carrowkeel, in the Bricklieve Mountains starts *ca.* 6000 BP (*ca.* 5000 BC). The values for elm and hazel are still higher than in the Ballygawley Lough diagram, reflecting the good base status of the soils in the Bricklieve Mountains during Mesolithic Time. Before 5800 BP (before 4700 BC), the curve of microscopic charcoal particles rises strongly, reaching a maximum *ca.* 5800 BP. At the same time bracken (*Pteridium*) has a distinct increase (fig. 4).

The presence of pollen of the Umbellifer family (Umbelliferae, today named Apiaceae), *Vicia/Lathyrus*-type, *Geranium* and *Calluna* is probably also an effect of fire; the forests became more open (cf. Berglund 1966). In the Treanscrabbagh diagram published in 1984 forty-two genera and species are found. The present diagram (fig. 4) is simplified with a reduced number of genera and species.

The above discussion means that the trees very likely were girdled and after some years burnt down. In the light environment seedlings grew up. If they were broken or bitten off (say by deer) a coppice wood grew up from the decapitated young plants. The forest got a mosaic structure.

MESOLITHIC ACTIVITIES IN THE STRANDHILL AREA

Offshore at Strandhill is an area of peat, now breaking up. This formerly measured at least 200m by 100m (Personal recollection, Packie Kennedy, Culleenamore, Strandhill). Dr. Patrick Heraghty told me of the off-shore peat at Strandhill and also at Stáid. The pollen diagram from it (Göransson 1984) does not only reflect the presence of shore plant communities but also the forests and some plants of high ground, that is the forests of the resource area of the Carrowmore megalith builders. The oldest part of the peat began to form *ca.* 6000 BP (*ca.* 5000 BC).

The Strandhill diagram shows, that the forests of elm and hazel were very rich in the Carrowmore area during Mesolithic Time. The values of microscopic charcoal particles are higher than 90% in the Mesolithic part of the Strandhill diagram. Pollen of cereal type occur.

It can thus be concluded that the whole Sligo area of today was utilized by man during (at least Late) Mesolithic Time.

THE ELM DECLINE

In all pollen diagrams from Ireland in the west to western Russia in the east we find an almost synchronous and more or less distinct fall of the elm curve at the end of Atlantic Time (Mesolithic Time), at *ca.* 5150 BP (*ca.* 4000 BC). In former days many archaeologists and pollen analysts believed that the elm decline was solely caused by the Early Neolithic farmer. Today we are of the opinion that many interacting physical and biological factors, probably above all the elm disease, caused the reduction of elm cal. 5150 BP (fig. 3). Traditionally the Early Neolithic thus starts at the elm decline level also in Ireland, even if there is no direct connection between the elm decline and the beginning of this archaeological period.

CULTIVATION OF CEREALS DURING THE LATEST PART OF THE MESOLITHIC?

It is a mistake to believe that Neolithic implements were necessary to transform the forests. Man's strongest and most effective tool was fire. Mesolithic know-how and Mesolithic implements were quite sufficient to kill big trees and to create the mosaic structure of the forests which has been described above.

If we are able to interpret the pollen diagrams without looking at them through the glasses of convention we will understand that the forests were transformed over very large areas during the Mesolithic. This is, however, almost impossible to see in conventional diagrams from medium-sized or large basins.

That cereals were cultivated before the elm decline in Ireland is supported by the fact that pollen of cereal type occurs before this level in western Ireland (see, for instance, Lynch 1981; Edwards and Hirons 1984) and also in the Sligo Area (Göransson 1984). In Lismore Fields, a riverine site in Derbyshire, England, Wiltshire and Edwards (1994, 168) found evidence for "both possible pre-agricultural disturbance and subsequent cereal cultivation dating from 6000 BP".

Pollen grains produced by cereals generally are larger than 43μm. Some grass pollen grains which are larger than 37μm have also come from cereals. Cereal type pollen may also have come from some wild grasses such as lyme grass, couches and flote-grass which produce pollen which may be larger than 43μm. It is, however, possible to discriminate between "real" cereal pollen and such ceral-type pollen which has come from the wild grasses mentioned above by, among others, studying the pore with its surrounding "ring" (see fig. 1d).

To be able to find ceral pollen in pre-elm decline deposits it is necessary to study very small holes which were situated in the immediate vicinity of these former "Mesolithic fields" or Mesolithic threshing places. Further it is necessary to count at least 1200, even 2000, pollen grains in each sample. It may take months

Fig. 3 - At the end of Atlantic (Mesolithic) Time the elm curve suddenly falls in the pollen diagrams from Ireland to western Russia. The cause of the reduction of elm is to be sought in a combination of interacting physical and biological factors. After ca. 600-700 years the elm often recovers again. Here we see the Örup elm forest in southernmost Sweden, 22 acres in area. It was suddenly attacked by elm disease in 1979. By 1983 almost 100% of the forest of tall trees was dead. During the first five years of the nineteen nineties the elm disease has spread rapidly in southern Sweden.

When I visited Ireland in 1981 no sick elms were observed. When I returned to Ireland in 1989 most of the elms which I was able to see were sick or dead. Photo of the Örup elm forest in 1981: Hans Göransson.

to find such an ideal site. For the moment we have to content ourselves with the suggestion that cereals probably may have been cultivated in the Sligo Area during Mesolithic time.

That the hunter-gatherer communities in Ireland were pre-adapted to farming and "only required the right contacts and conditions for fully-fledged farming" is also underlined by Cooney (1987-88, 7).

NEOLITHIC ACTIVITIES IN THE BRICKLIEVE MOUNTAINS

The pollen diagrams from Cloverhill Lough and Ballygawley Lough do not span the Neolithic in the Sligo Area. The bog of Treanscrabbagh in the Bricklieve Mountains is situated 24 km SSE of the Carrowmore area. The famous Carrowkeel cemetery is found on the limestone plateau just above it. The bog has earlier been studied by Mitchell (1951) and by Watts (1961).

During my stay in Sligo in 1981 M. A. Timoney, M. Thelaus and I sampled at the side of the high "ombrotrophic" peat wall in the marginal part of the bog (fig. 4). The peat wall was left after peat-cutting and the underlying so called "minerotrophic" peat - a fen or fen-wood peat - had not been removed. Using a 50mm Russian sampler we peformed a boring near the high peat wall and 116 cm of minerotrophic peat was found at this place. "Ombrotrophic" peat is built up of species which do not tolerate ground-water and which are fed only on the water from the precipitation. "Minerotrophic" peat is built up of species which are dependant on ground-water.

At the base of the peat wall, and thus on top of the minerotrophic peat, there was a very big stump of sallow (*Salix*, determination by Thomas Bartholin, Lund) which has been dated to 4010±55 BP (*ca.* 2670 BC) at Lund. Watts (1961, 36) dated a level in Treanscrabbagh where the moss peat with twigs and leaves passes to *Eriophorum* peat to 3120±120 BP. These two dates may at least hint at the time-span during which blanket peat began to form on the limestone hills in that area. Watts suggests that blanket peat began to form shortly before 4000 BP (*loc. cit.*).

The elm decline in the pollen diagram from Treanscrabbagh is found at the level 380 cm (below the top of the ombrotrophic peat). As the pollen diagram of 1981 is of a very local origin, the elm decline is very difficult to observe. Thanks to Mitchell's diagrams from that area (Mitchell 1956 and unpublished - see diagrams in Göransson 1984) it has been possible to fix the exact level of the elm decline in the 1981 diagram. A dating immediately below this level (380-385 cm) gave the C14-age of 5270±60 BP. Thus the elm decline in that area is of the same age as in, for instance, southernmost and southeastern Sweden.

At the elm decline level ribwort plantain (*Plantago lanceolata*) at once expands, reaching astonishingly high values (fig. 5). In our days, winter grazing takes place in, for instance, the Burren hills. In summer the hills are not grazed (Keane 1986) and for that reason the wind-pollinated ribwort plantain may flower in peace and spread enormously high amounts of pollen grains to the surroundings. It can thus not be excluded that winter grazing took place in the

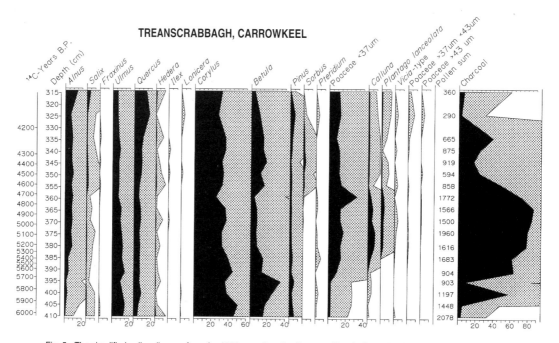

Fig. 5 - The simplified pollen diagram from the 1981-sampling site, Treanscrabbagh, Carrowkeel. Analysis: Hans Göransson. Data-drawing: Thomas Persson.

Bricklieve Mountains already during the Early Neolithic while in summer the livestock may have grazed in the valleys and near the coast (see also de Valera 1979).

The forests were utilized by man already *ca.* 6000 BP (*ca.* 5000 BC) in the Bricklieve Mountains and grazing seems to have taken place at least from *ca.* 5900 BP (*ca.* 4800 BC). The grasses, heather and bracken increase in waves during the Late Mesolithic (Göransson 1984, 166). One may wonder what sort of animals were grazing in that area during Mesolithic Time - perhaps red deer that were half-domesticated?

The grazing goes on in Bricklieve Mountains up to the moment when the hills began to be covered with blanket peat *ca.* 4000 BP (*ca.* 2600 BC). As mentioned, pollen grains of cereal type have been recorded already during the Mesolithic (the curve "Poaceae >37μm <43μm" and the curve "Poaceae >43 μm") (Note: in 1981 the grass family was still named "Gramineae", today it is named "Poaceae"). These curves put together are continuous up to the moment when the blanket peat began to form. The cereals which were cultivated during the Stone Age spread extremely small amounts of pollen grains to the surroundings as the cereal pollen is trapped within the chaffs. This means that even extremely small amounts of pollen of cereals hint at cultivation (and threshing) of cereals.

It may be of interest to observe that the grazing of livestock (disclosed by the *Plantago lanceolata* curve) started ca. 600 years before the megaliths on the hill were built!

NEOLITHIC ACTIVITIES NEAR STRANDHILL

The offshore peat at Strandhill was, according to Magnus Thelaus, formed on land. The undermost dark part of the peat is a sort of a fen peat which probably was formed behind a beach wall. The uppermost light-coloured peat is of dry land origin. It is, indeed, a chance that the peat was built up during the time which we are discussing in the present paper. The elm decline is found in the upper part of the peat. The C14-datings of the undermost dark peat and of the uppermost light peat confirm the pollen analytical results (see fig. 6).

Pine pollen are spread over long distances on the water surface by waves and this accumulates at the shores. Probably huge amounts of pine pollen were thrown up by the waves on the shores of Sligo Bay during the time of the peat formation. For that reason the high amounts of pine pollen in the diagram from Strandhill give us a false picture of the presence of rich pine forests. The pine pollen also "presses down" the percentage values of the other trees and plants in the diagram - the values of elm, etc., are falsely reduced. I beg the reader keep this in mind with the Strandhill diagram.

The high percentages of the goosefoot and the cabbage families reflect the presence of typical shore-bound species. An unknown proportion of the pollen of grasses <37μm was probably delivered by reeds, which constituted a part of the peat-forming plant community.

In spite of the Strandhill peat being formed near the shore of Sligo Bay the diagram does not only reflect the presence of shore plants but also the forests and some plants of high ground, that is the forests of the area which was utilised by the megalith builders of Carrowmore.

The Strandhill diagram discloses that the forests of elm and hazel were very rich in the Carrowmore area between *ca.* 6000 BP (*ca.* 5000 BC) and Early Neolithic Time. The initial fall of the elm curve (which is as difficult to observe in this local diagram as in the local diagram from Treanscrabbagh) is thus found in the uppermost part. At this level the curve of ribwort plantain starts and immediately reaches high values. This is exactly the same picture as we get in the Treanscrabbagh diagram.

The pre-elm decline plantain pollen may also have come from ribwort plantain but the shore bound plantains cannot be totally ruled out. From the very beginning of the Early Neolithic domestic animals grazed in the Sligo area. Pollen

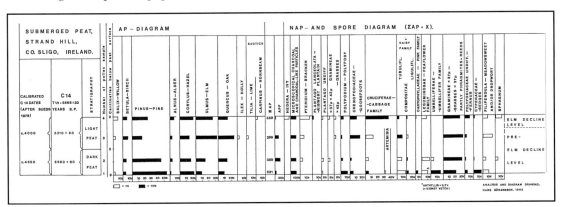

Fig. 6 - The hand-drawn Strandhill diagram. Note that the high values of pine pollen reflect long-distance transport by waves. Analysis and drawing: Hans Göransson.

grains of cereal type have been recorded already in the Mesolithic part of the diagram. We remind ourselves that lyme grass produces pollen of cereal type and that is why we have to be a little cautious when we study the Strandhill cereal type pollen curve (Gramineae >37μm <43μm and Gramineae >43μm).

The curve of microscopic charcoal particles has very high values at all levels in the diagram from Strandhill. The human influence on the forests have been very intense in the Sligo - Carrowmore area already from 6000 BP (from *ca.* 5000 BC). Future studies may demonstrate that these activities started considerably earlier in the Sligo area.

STONE AGE TREES AND THE DRAGON'S HEAD PHENOMENON

It is suggested that the Megalith builders utilized parts of the calcareous soils in the Sligo area for cultivation of cereals. During Late Mesolithic and Early and Middle Neolithic Times the calcareous soils were covered with broad-leaved trees. If an oak or a hazel is cut down in the autumn, winter or early spring the stumps will sprout in the following summer. These sprouts will quickly grow up into "stump-sprout trees". Many such trees will form a "stump-sprout forest" or a "coppice wood".

The growing sprouts will soon become fertile. Stump-sprouts of oaks in my own garden began to flower when they were 13 years old. Hazel gets catkins when the sprouts are two years old. Elm, ash and alder sprout richly after having been cut down. As far as I understand, the growing sprouts of these species will also flower within 10 to 15 years. It should thus be very difficult to observe clearings in forests of the above-mentioned trees - the trees of the Stone Age - by studying pollen diagrams from that epoch. (It is, in the main, because of factors lying beyond man's control that the forests change at the elm decline level.)

Fig. 7 - The dragon's head phenomenon. Drawing: Per Göransson.

When the hero of the fairy-tale cut off the dragon's head, seven new heads grew up immediately from the decapitated monster. In the same way, sprouts thus "immediately" grew up when Stone Age man cut down trees in his forest. I think the term "the dragon's head phenomenon" may be useful when we talk about man and the Stone Age forests (fig. 7). Why should we then be surprised if we find that cultivation of cereals took place at the same time as oak, hazel, etc. flower richly during, especially, the Middle Neolithic?

CULTIVATION OF CEREALS IN COPPICE WOODS

We do not yet know how important cultivation of cereals was compared with grazing during the epoch we are discussing here. Cultivation of cereals nevertheless took place, and we may wonder in which way the Neolithic farmer utlized and manured the soil. Below three models are described.

My model for the cultivation in coppice woods may be summarized as follows. The coppice wood system was introduced to give a secure supply of mineral nutrients and of nitrogen so that continuous cereal growing could be maintained though not on the same field of ground. We have to imagine a system of coppice wood groves of different ages on light soils. These coppice-wood groves were allowed to grow very dense so that the weeds were choked. Every year one coppice-wood grove was cut down by axe and twigs and small stems were burnt . On the slightly burnt and cleared coppice wood areas probably emmer wheat and four-row naked barley were cultivated. The large stems were probably used as fences or for building and fire-wood. Only one harvest was taken on the cleared area. At harvesting time the stump sprouts had already grown. I think that this type of cultivation was accomplished from the first part of Middle Neolithic Time, but that it had its beginnings in the Mesolithic.

The decline of the microscopic charcoal particles during the middle part of the Early Neolithic does not mean a decline in cultivation. The suggested utilization of coppice woods (fig. 8) did not need an extensive use of fire (for details, see Göransson 1984). That cereals were cultivated at the same time as the forests of the broad-leaved trees flowered so richly during the Middle Neolithic is, in my opinion, direct evidence of the presence of coppice woods.

The cleared area was left alone for some deacades, perhaps one or two generations of man. By taking harvests with such a time interval on each small area, the light, calacareous soils could have been utilized for cereal cultivation, theoretically, over thousands of years. Such type of cultivation would give us an unbroken cereal curve such as that found in Carrowkeel - at the same time as the values for broadleaved trees has high values in the diagram (probably hazel produced the best "manure" in the coppice woods, its decaying leaves giving a very rich soil).

We know that cereals were cultivated among the stumps in cut down coppice woods in Siegerland, Germany, at the beginning of the 20th century (Fickeler 1952). Ploughing was done among these stumps by use of an ard, drawn by hand-power or with the help of a cow. It is important that we observe that the soil could be ploughed in such an environment. During Neolithic time a simple form of an ard may have been used. The ard marks were probably rapidly obliterated in the woodland environment.

OTHER MODELS FOR CULTIVATION OF CEREALS DURING NEOLITHIC TIME

It cannot be totally excluded that permanent manured (and also non-manured) fields may have existed during the Neolithic (Troels-Smith 1984; Göransson 1987; 1995; Cooney 1991; and other authors). Ard marks may have been better preserved in such fields than in coppice-wood fields and these marks may sometimes have been "sealed" below megalithic constructions.

In my opinion, wandering arable fields in coppice woods were found at some distance from the habitation sites, while permanent manured fields may have existed in the immediate vicinity of these sites. Very lime-rich soils may have been used for establishing permanent, non-manured fields. This model may be valid for, at least, the Middle Neolithic.

It must be remembered that what we have been discussing above are different models for prehistoric arable systems, models which in the main are built on pollen diagrams. Future detailed pollen diagrams and future investigations of fossil seeds surely will develop these models.

EARLY LAND USE IN COUNTY MAYO

The imposing size of the Neolithic enclosed fields, found below blanket peat, in north-west county Mayo, indicate that they were primarily organized for animal husbandry according to Caulfield (Caulfield 1983, fig. 2). The ard marks at Belderrig may be Neolithic in date (Caulfield 1978, 140). The investigations in north-east Mayo, at the base of the Ox mountains, "point to the possibilty of Neolithic farming with an arable element" (O'Connell 1990).

The possibility that the long fences of Neolithic age in Mayo also enclosed coppice woods of different ages, should perhaps not be totally excluded. So, for instance, the division of the Late Bronze Age cultural landscape into fields or "partitions", which the archaeologist may observe in the field in Denmark and in South Sweden, is a reflection of former bush-fallows (Sjöbeck 1962, 84). Not least bush-fallows of hazel (that is, low-growing coppice woods) of different ages characterized, for instance, the landscape of the island of Öland in the Baltic in prehistoric times. The grass sward was "deep-rooted" with the help of low-growing trees. The arable land was reclaimed in such an environment in Neolithic Time and in the Bronze Age.

(It should be mentioned that Sjöbeck, which I cite above, has had an enormously great influence on Swedish vegetational historians and ethnogeographers. His epoch-making works, about one hundred articles, are all written in Swedish. As far as I know, he is not known in the English speaking world. His first paper appeared in 1927, his last work was published in 1976).

It is thus evident from the above discussion that grazing of livestock and cultivation of cereals was of great importance already from ca. 5150 BP (*ca.* 4000 BC) both in county Sligo and county Mayo.

SUMMARY

The very rich forests of, in particular elm, hazel and oak were the hunter-gatherer's greatest land resourse during Mesolithic Time in the Sligo area. By ring-barking trees and by burning the subsequent dead trees a mosaic forest structure was created. This transformation of the forest was done in order to favour grazing and browsing wild animals and in order to get better yields of wild edible plants.

When domestic animals were introduced during the Early Neolithic the grazing is reflected in the pollen diagrams by astonishingly high values of ribwort plantain (*Plantago lanceolata*) already from 5150 BP (*ca.* 4000 BC). A few pollen grains of ribwort plantain were found in pre-elm decline deposits. Probably the mountains were grazed in winter. It is impossible to say how important cultivation of cereals was during the Neolithic in the Sligo area. The pollen diagram from Carrowkeel shows that cereal cultivation took place during the whole of the Neolithic. Not unlikely cereals were introduced already during Mesolithic Time. From ca. 4500 BP (3400 BC) cultivation in coppice woods may have taken place. Permanent fields may, how-ever, also have existed, already during the Early Neolithic.

During the Stone Age the Sligo area ought to

have been very wealthy with beautiful forests of broad-leaved trees growing on very rich soils. The rivers and the sea were full of fish, the forests full of birds, nuts and berries. It is perhaps no wonder, that so many megalithic tombs were built in that area. The winter-grazed hills became more and more open and about 4000 BP (2600 BC) blanket peat began to form (Göransson 1989); the rich time had come to an end.

Fig. 8 - Drawings of coppice wood groves of different ages during the Middle Neolithic.

1: 20-25 year-old grove just before felling. There are no weeds in the very dense grove. **2**: The grove has been cut down and the ground has been cleared by burning. **3**: One-year-old stump-sprouts and emmer wheat or four-row barley (in August) on the cleared area. A part of a fence, made of coppice wood trunks, is seen. **4**: A two-year-old coppice wood in the previously utilized area. **5**: A four-year-old coppice wood in the same area. Soon the coppice wood will start producing pollen. In the coppice wood landscape the megalithic graves were distinctly seen. DRAWING: Hans Göransson 1981 (redrawn 1985).

Fig. 8

BIBLIOGRAPHY

Bergh, S. 1995: 'Landscape of the Monuments. A study of the passage tombs in the Cúil Irra region, Co. Sligo, Ireland', Arkeologiska undersökningar. Skrifter nr 6. Riksantikvarieämbetet. Stockholm.

Berglund, B. E. 1964: 'Late-Quaternary Vegetation in Eastern Blekinge, South-Eastern Sweden. A Pollen-Analytical Study', *Opera Botanica,* 12:2. Lund.

Burenhult, G., ed. 1984: 'The Archaeology of Carrowmore. Environmental Archaeology and the Megalithic Tradition at Carrowmore, Co Sligo, Ireland', Theses and Papers in North-European Archaeology 14. Stockholm.

Caulfield, S. 1978: 'Neolithic fields: the Irish evidence', in eds. Bowen, H.C. and Fowler, P.J., *Early Land Allotment,* BAR, Brit. Ser. 48, 137-44. Oxford.

Caulfield, S., 1983: 'The Neolithic Settlement of North Connaught', in eds. Reeves-Smyth, T. and Hamond, F., *Landscape Archaeology in Ireland,* BAR British Series 116, 195-215. Oxford.

Cooney, G., 1987/1988: 'Irish Neolithic Settlement and its European Context.', *Irish Archaeol. J.,* IV, 7-11.

Cooney, G., 1991: 'Irish Neolithic Landscapes and Land Use Systems: The Implications of Field Systems', *Rural History,* 2:2, 123-139.

Cronon, W., 1984. *Changes in the Land. Indians, Colonists, and the Ecology of New England,* New York.

de Valera, R., 1979: ed. S. P. Ó Riordáin, *Antiquities of the Irish Countryside,* 5th Edition, 1-28. London.

Dodson, J.R., and Bradshaw, W. H., 1987: 'A history of vegetation and fire, 6,600 B.P. to present, County Sligo, western Ireland', *Boreas,* 16, 113-123.

Edwards, K.J., and Hirons, K.R., 1984: 'Cereal pollen grains in pre-elm decline deposits: implications for the earliest agriculture in Britain and Ireland', *J. Archaeol. Sc.,* 11, 71-80.

Edwards, K.J. 1988: 'The Hunter Gatherer/ Agricultural Transition and the Pollen Record in the British Isles'. In Birks, H.H. *et al.,* eds., *The Cultural Landscape, Past, Present and Future,* 255-266, Cambridge University Press.

Edwards, K.J., 1990: 'Fires and the Scottish Mesolithic', in eds. Vermeersch, P. M. and Van Peer, P. *Contributions to the Mesolithic in Europe,* Leuven University Press, Leuven.

Fickeler, P., 1952: 'Achenbach Söhne Buschhütten', *Festschrift Achenbach Buschhütten,* Siegen.

Göransson, H., 1984: 'Pollen analytical investiga-tions in the Sligo Area', in Burenhult, 1984.

Göransson, H., 1987: 'Neolithic Man and the Forest Environment around Alvastra Pile Dwelling', Theses and Papers in North-European Archaeology, 20, Stockholm. Lund University Press,

Göransson, H., 1989: 'Pollen Analytical Investigations in Treanscrabbagh, Carrowkeel', *The Corran Herald,* No. 17, 11. Ballymote.

Göransson, H., 1995: 'Alvastra Pile Dwelling - Palaeoethnobotanical Studies', Theses and Papers in Archaeology N.S. A6, Stockholm, Lund University Press,

Keane, M., 1986: *The Burren,* The Irish Heritage Series, 30, Dublin.

Latalowa, M., 1992: 'Man and Vegetation in the Pollen Diagrams from Wolin Island (NW Poland)', *Acta Palaeobotanica,* 32 (1). Gdansk.

Lynch, A., 1981: 'Man and Environment in S.W. Ireland', BAR British Series, 85.

Mitchell, G.F., 1951: 'Studies in Irish Quaternary Deposits: No.7', *Proc. Roy. Irish Acad.,* 53B, 111-206. Dublin.

Mitchell, G.F., 1956: 'Post-Boreal Pollen-Diagrams from Irish Raised Bogs. Studies in Irish Quaternary Deposits', No.11, *Proc. Roy. Irish Acad.,* 57B, 185-251, Dublin.

Mitchell, G.F. 1976: 'The Irish Landscape', London.

O'Connell, M. 1990: 'Early Land Use in North-East Mayo - the Palaeoecological Evidence', *Proc. Roy. Irish Acad.,* 90:9, 259-279.

Post, L. von, 1916: 'Skogsträdpollen i sydsvenska torvmosselagerföljder', *Förh. 16. skand. naturforskarmöte 1916,* Kristiania (Oslo).

Post, L. von, 1967: 'Forest tree pollen in South Swedish peat bog deposits', *Pollen et Spores* 9, 375-401, (Translation of von Post 1916).

Sjöbeck, M., 1962: 'Saltängarna vid Öresund och deras historiska förutsättningar', Skånes Natur, *Skånes Naturskyddsförenings Årsskrift,* 77-88.

Troels-Smith, J. 1984: 'Stall-Feeding and Field-Manuring in Switzerland about 6000 Years ago', *Tools & Tillage,* V:1, 13-25, Copenhagen.

Watts, W.A., 1961: 'Post-Atlantic forests in Ireland', *Proc. Linnean Soc.,* 172:1, 33-38. London.

Wiltshire, P.E.J, and Edwards, K.J., 1994: 'Mesolithic, Early Neolithic, and later prehistoric impacts on vegetation at a riverine site in Derbyshire, England', in ed. Chambers, F. M., *Climate Change and Human Impact on the Landscape,* London.

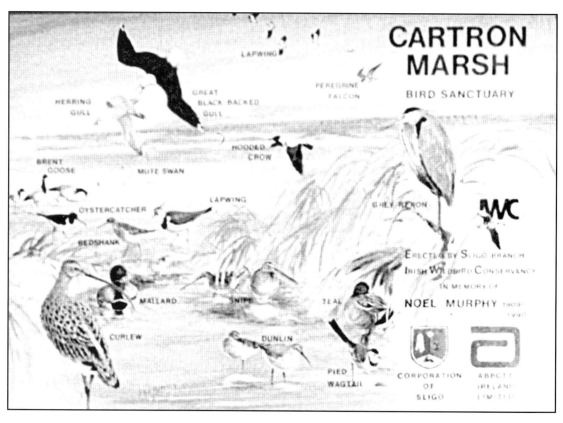

The display board at Cartron, Sligo, painted by Phil Brennan and erected in 1993 to honour the ornithological work of Noel Murphy.

NEW BARROW TYPES IDENTIFIED IN COUNTY SLIGO

*Jean Farrelly and Margaret Keane,
Dúchas - The Heritage Service.*

ABSTRACT: Newly distinguished barrow types identified during a survey of non-megalithic burial mounds in the Barony of Corran, County Sligo, are presented. The form and siting characteristics of enclosure barrows and stepped barrows are discussed and comparative sites described.

INTRODUCTION

In the early 1990s the authors carried out a survey of barrows in the Barony of Corran in the south of Co. Sligo. The starting point for the survey was an examination of the distribution of barrows and cists in the Sites and Monument Record of Co. Sligo (S.M.R.) (Gibbons *et al.,* 1990). There are several distinct concentrations of barrows and cists in the county (fig. 1). The densest group occurs on the Carrowmore Peninsula, in the shadow of the passage tomb cemetery. The Carrowmore group was examined in 1984 by Martin A. Timoney (Timoney 1984) who presented a descriptive survey of the monuments in Burenhult's 1984 book *The Archaeological Excavations at Carrowmore, County Sligo, Ireland*. Other more dispersed spreads of barrows occur in south central Sligo and in the Barony of Corran. There are small clustered groups in Killaraght parish adjacent to Lough Gara and in the parish of Dromard along the western side of Ballisodare Bay. See Alcock and Tunney (2002) for current statistics as regards ring-barrows, bowl barrows and mounds.

THE SURVEY

Our study area, the Barony of Corran, was selected as it allowed for an investigation of monument in a varied landscape of upland and drumlin terrain. From a cursory examination of the distribution of monuments within the barony it became apparent that at least one linear alignment or cemetery of barrows could be observed, extending from Derroon to Rathdooney Beg townlands. The aim of the

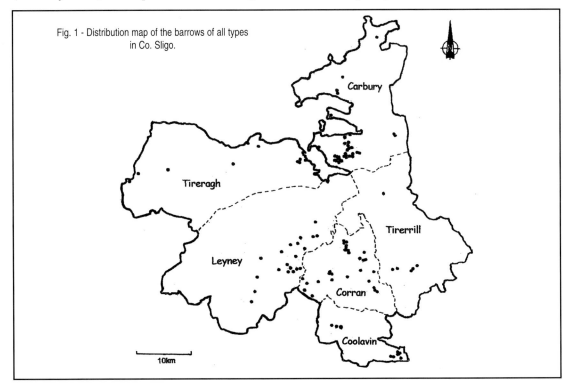

Fig. 1 - Distribution map of the barrows of all types in Co. Sligo.

survey was to identify and classify non-megalithic earthen funerary monuments within the barony. Sites were visited on the basis of their designations on the Ordnance Survey 6" maps and included all small earthen monuments that appeared to be less than 20m in diameter, as well as sites classified by the S.M.R. as being either barrows, mounds or cairns. A description of all monuments was written and each profile recorded.

BARROW BASICS

In Ireland there are three main barrow types, ring-barrows, bowl barrows and mounds.

Ring-barrows consist of a central mound or level area surrounded by an internal fosse and outer bank, sometimes with additional fosses and banks.

Bowl barrows are steep-sided circular mounds with a pudding-bowl shape, composed of earth and stone, with flat or round-topped crests. Some bowl-barrows have encircling fosses.

Mounds consist of a gradually inclining mound which does not conform to the characteristic pudding-bowl profile of the bowl-barrow. These too can be enclosed by a fosse.

Excavations have revealed that these monuments can date from the Neolithic to the Iron Age and are often multi-period.

All the main barrow types were well represented in the study area. However, during the course of the survey it became apparent that not all the barrows identified during fieldwork fit readily into the existing sub-classifications. This paper presents two such barrow types, an *enclosure barrow* and a *stepped barrow*, and suggests that as these barrow types are not confined to Co. Sligo this sub-classification is relevant at a national level.

ENCLOSURE BARROWS FORM

Enclosure barrows are circular sites, usually raised above the surrounding ground level, enclosed by a continuous broad bank. Some have external fosses. The majority appear to be under 20m in diameter, some markedly so.

Nine enclosure barrows have been identified in Corran. These are, with their SMR Sl. numbers as follows:

Aughris	(39:155),	
Cloonagh	(39:156),	
Cloonkeevy	(33:117),	
Deechomade	(39:9),	
Derroon	(33:203),	
Greenan	(40:130, 40:132),	(fig. 2c),
Roscrib East	(33:124),	(fig. 2a),
Spurtown Lower	(39:53),	(fig. 2b).

In some examples the interior slopes downwards from the bank crest to the centre in a continuous slope. In these instances it is impossible to distinguish an internal edge to the bank. Where there is a flat interior, banks tend to be very broad in relation to the area enclosed. This is exemplified at Cloonagh (39:156) where the bank is 5.8m wide, taking up 11.4m of the total 14m site diameter. The smallest example of an enclosure barrow in Corran is at Derroon (33:203) which has an overall diameter of 8m while the largest, Cloonkeevy (33:117), is 27m in overall diameter. External fosses are visible in a few examples. In two examples, Derroon and Deechomade, a break in the bank was observed in the field. The authors excavated the enclosure barrow at Deechomade but found that this reduction of the bank was simply the result of disturbance (Farrelly and Keane 1994, 71).

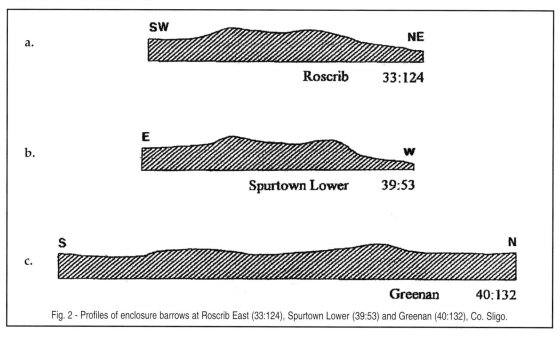

Fig. 2 - Profiles of enclosure barrows at Roscrib East (33:124), Spurtown Lower (39:53) and Greenan (40:132), Co. Sligo.

SITING

With regard to topography sloping ground is the preferred. Several enclosure barrows are situated on drumlin slopes with a range of orientations on NE, NW and S slopes. Other sites are placed on low ridges, all with somewhat restricted views. Cloonkeevy (33:117) is different in that it is located in a low-lying marshy area. Only one site, Greenan (40:132), is in a dominant position. It is on the crest of a drumlin within a discrete barrow alignment.

FUNCTION

Enclosure barrows differ in form, dimension and association from settlement sites such as ringforts or hut sites.

Ringforts are described as *farmsteads which would have enclosed a single farming family and their retainers* (Stout 1997, 32). The small dimensions of most enclosure barrows exclude them from this monument class.

The presence of a continuous bank means that they could not have functioned as hut sites.
However, it is the above factors, together with their close association with other barrows, in cemeteries, which distinguish them from settlement sites and which point to a funerary or ritual function.

In Corran enclosure barrows occur singly or as part of groups of monuments or cemeteries. The barrow cemetery at Greenan consists of a linear arrangement of ring-barrows and enclosure barrows on a drumlin slope. One enclosure barrow (40:132) occupies the crest of the slope, another is located downslope and is conjoined with a ring-barrow (40:130). Another example at Derroon occurs within a linear barrow cemetery, while at Deechomade, an enclosure barrow occupies the same drumlin as a mound and a ring-barrow.

ENCLOSURE BARROWS OUTSIDE CORRAN

Enclosure barrows are not unique to this survey area.

In several County and Barony surveys sites have been included as ringforts which accord more closely in terms of overall dimensions and morphology with enclosure barrows. One example, at Barnane 11, Co. Tipperary, (Stout 1984, 40) is an enclosure 13m in internal diameter, without a clearly defined entrance which has been included within a chapter devoted to ringforts. What is of particular interest in relation to this site is that enclosing rampart with an average width of 6m displays one of the most important characteristics of enclosure barrows - the proportion of the enclosing rampart in contrast to the total diameter of the site. Interestingly in the archaeological survey of West Galway a distinction is made between small enclosures and ringforts, where the former sites are grouped with other unclassified enclosures or earth works (Gosling 1993, 44). At Cabragh, near Crossmolina, Co. Mayo, there is a monument which consists of a broad clearly-defined continuous bank 4.5m in maximum diameter circuiting a flat interior. The internal diameter of this monument is just 7.2m. This is one of several sites in the Crossmolina area which fall below the size-range for ringforts in that district, and which have been classified in the Deel Basin survey as *small enclosures* (Keane 1989, 46).

Several writers have classified similar sites as barrows without grouping them as a distinct class.

As early as 1942, in his survey of antiquities in the Barony of Smallcounty, Co. Limerick, O'Kelly classified several sites, consisting of 'circular low banks', including one in Grange townland, as barrows (1942, 75). Of the seventeen sites included in Timoney's survey of earthen burial sites on the Carrowmore Peninsula (Timoney 1984) the miscellaneous group includes two monuments, Knocknahur North and Carrowmore II, which would fit comfortably in the enclosure barrow category. Timoney (pers. comm.) acepts with this classification of these two barrows. Other authors have included monuments similar to enclosure barrows within the miscellaneous or barrow class without distinguishing the particular characteristics of this monument type (Alcock *et al.* 1999, 13; Lavelle 1991, 68, 69; Lavelle 1994, 4-10; Herity 1984, 129).

EXCAVATION AT DEECHOMADE

As a follow up to the initial survey of the Corran barrows the authors excavated one of the enclosure barrows in the survey area hoping to discover more about the construction and form of these barrows (Farrelly and Keane, 1993, 56; 1994, 71). The site at Deechomade (39:9) is 10.5m by 12m in overall diameter and defined by a 2m wide bank. The interior is circuited by a continuous bank and ditch through which there is no entrance despite the appearance of a break in the bank prior to excavation. A charcoal-rich layer had been deposited in the interior. Unfortunately, excavation revealed that a large modern pit in the interior had cut through the charcoal spread and removed the centre of the site. There was no evidence for burials or token burials in those portions of the site excavated but the dearth of evidence for occupation in the form of post-holes, a hearth, material assemblages, *etc.*, suggests that the monument was not associated with settlement. A radiocarbon date of 2285 +/-35 BP which was calibrated to 400-230

BC but with the old wood effect this becomes 350-30 BC was obtained for charcoal from the base of the bank which places the construction of the enclosure barrow in the Iron Age.

OTHER EXCAVATIONS

A review of published excavations yielded only two possible examples of excavated enclosure barrows.

At Turkhead, Co. Cork, an oval enclosure, 8.5m by 7m, and surrounded by a low earthen bank and outer fosse, was excavated (Danaher 1972, 8-9). No entrance feature was discovered, though part of the site had been disturbed and there were no post-holes and only thin deposits of charcoal in the interior. A function of temporary camping place was tentatively suggested by the excavator but the similarity of the results of excavation to that at Deechomade are striking.

Site A at Feltrim, Co. Dublin, an enclosure 16m in diameter, was described as 'a saucer-shaped hollow' by the excavators (Eogan and Hartnett 1964, 4). In morphology and dimensions the site accords quite well with Deechomade (39:9). The excavators suggested that this site may have functioned as a knapping centre since large quantities of flint and chert artefacts and debris were recovered during the excavation. Although hundreds of sherds of pottery were also recovered from the excavation the authors did not explain the origin of this material or define the site as a centre of pottery production. This material assemblage included both Neolithic pottery and Late Bronze Age coarse ware. There is a general density of flint, chert and pottery in the ploughsoil over Feltrim Hill. As both Neolithic and Late Bronze Age sherds were found together in the excavation it is possible that this material was present in the soil *before* the construction of Site A and that it is not related to the function of the site. Due to the absence of any defined entrance features, post holes or hearth material the site cannot be termed a habitation. There is also an absence of clear evidence for burials so the funerary nature of these monuments must also be queried. However, it is not unusual for barrows to display little or little direct evidence for burial (Daly and Grogan 1993, 58). Some authors have posited that some of these monuments may have functioned as cenotaphs with burial material slight or absent (Daly and Grogan 1993, 60).

STEPPED BARROWS FORM

This barrow type consists of a rounded or flat mound supported on a broader platform base. The lower platform forms a berm or ledge around the upper mound.

A single stepped barrow occurs in Corran. It is located at Kilturra (38:120/1) and consists of a circular stepped-platform, 24.6m N-S and 23.5m E-W in overall diameter (fig. 3). The central platform, 13.4m E-W, is enclosed by a broad berm whose edge is defined by a bank. A holy well (38:120/2) at the river's edge of the barrow is now accompanied by an Early Christian cross-inscribed stone (38:120/03) which was moved from close-by since the late 1890s, a holed stone taken from the river in 1976 following exhortations by Tim Kelly of Sligo Field Club and two 19th century commemorative slabs, one of which is for the Cooke family.

SITING

The stepped barrow is situated directly adjacent to the Black River which is its eastern edge. There are limited views in all directions as the site is situated in flat low-lying ground.

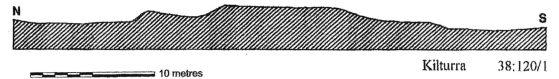

Fig. 3: Profile of barrow at Kilturra (38:120/1), Co. Sligo.

COMPARATIVE SITES

Berms have been identified as components of barrows in a British context, where they are usually associated with ditched bell-barrows and disc-barrows (Megaw and Simpson 1984, 47). In typical British examples berms are on the same level as the external ground level, with a fosse defining the edge of the berm. However, raised berms or terraces have been found on several Irish barrows throughout the country. Examples identified so far are Rathmoon, Co. Wicklow, (Lucas 1960, 84); Longstone Cullen, Co. Tipperary, (O'Dwyer 1959, 72-73), Knockdinnin and Collon, Co. Louth, (Buckley and Sweetman 1991, 44, 48), and Knockmeelmore, Co. Waterford, (Moore 1999, 17) as well as Kilturra. One of the other barrows in Corran, a mound at Knocknawhishoge (39:26) has a low flat ledge or berm, c. 1.8m wide, circuiting the western half of the mound from north to south.

Of the comparative barrows identified perhaps the most informative is that at Rathmoon, Co.

Wicklow. It was described in the 1960s as follows: 'the lower part of the mound, at a height of about 5ft above the field, forms a flat terrace 4 yards wide; the central part rises out of this in a domed-shaped mound' (Lucas 1960, 84). Some years later a levelling operation revealed a short rectangular cist burial under the site which contained the cremated bones of three adult females and two children and a calcinated leaf-shaped flint arrowhead. This places the monument in an Early Bronze Age context (Waddell 1990, 166).

CONCLUSIONS

During the survey of barrows in Corran we have identified two distinct barrow types. These we have termed enclosure barrows and stepped barrows. Although their catagorization had not previously been recognised a literary review has shown that these types exist in the published literature. Our work in Corran highlights the value of detailed field survey and subsequent documentary research. Internal seminars held by the Archaeological Survey of Ireland have recently focused on redefining barrow classifications. Two of the new definitions which emerged are based on the results of our survey of the barrows in Corran. The stepped barrow has been adopted as a site type, as has the enclosure barrow, though the latter has been renamed embanked barrow to emphasise the importance of the defining broad, enclosing bank. It would seem logical that others involved in barrow research will adopt these new sub-classifications.

Fig. 4 - View from west of stepped barrow at Kilturra (38:120/1), Co. Sligo. Photo. Martin A. Timoney c. 1972.

ACKNOWLEDGEMENTS

The field survey was made possible due to funding provided under the auspices of the National Committee for Archaeology of the Royal Irish Academy by the Office of Public Works. We are grateful to all the landowners for their co-operation and to family and friends for their enthusiastic assistance. Most particularly we would like to thank the McHugh family of Deechomade and Agnes and the late Paddy Rogers who made Sligo a second home for us during our fieldwork.

BIBLIOGRAPHY

Alcock, O., de hÓra, K., and Gosling, P., 1999: *Archaeological Inventory of County Galway, Vol. II*, Dublin.
Alcock, O., and Tunney, M., 2002: "Archaeological Survey in Sligo" in Timoney 2002.
Buckley, V.M., and Sweetman, P.D., 1991: *Archaeological Survey of County Louth*, Dublin.
Burenhult, G., ed., 1984: *The Archaeology, of Carrowmore: Environmental Archaeology and the Megalithic Tradition at Carrowmore, Co. Sligo, Ireland*, Theses and Papers in North-European Archaeology, 14, Stockholm.
Danaher, P., 1964: "A prehistoric burial-mound at Ballyeeskeen, Co. Sligo", *J. Roy. Soc. Antiq. Ireland*, 94, 145-158.
Danaher, P., 1972: Turkhead, Hut site in ed. T.G. Delaney, *Excavations 1972*, 8-9.
Daly, A., and Grogan, E., 1993: "Excavations of four barrows in Mitchelstowndown West, Knocklong, County Limerick." Final Report, *Discovery Programme Reports*, 1, 44-60. Dublin.
Eogan, G., and Hartnett, P.J., 1964: "Feltrim Hill, Co. Dublin; A Neolithic and Early Christian Site", *J. Roy. Soc. Antiq. Ireland*, 94, 1-37.
Farrelly, J., and Keane, M., 1993: "Deechomade, Co. Sligo", in ed. Bennett, I., *Excavations 1992*, 56.
Farrelly, J., and Keane, M., 1994: "Deechomade, Co. Sligo", in ed. Bennett, I., *Excavations 1993*, 71.
Gibbons, M., Alcock, O., Condit, T., Tunney, M. and Timoney, M.A., 1990: *Sites and Monuments Record for Co. Sligo*, Dublin, The Office of Public Works.
Gosling, P., 1993: *Archaeological Inventory of County Galway; Volume 1: West Galway*, Dublin.
Herity, M., 1984: "A Survey of the Royal Site of Rathcroghan in Connacht: Prehistoric Monuments", *J. Roy. Soc. Antiq. Ireland*, 114, 125-138.
Keane, M., 1989: *An Archaeological Survey of the Basin of the River Deel, Co. Mayo*, Unpublished M.A. Thesis, University College, Dublin.
Lavelle, D., ed., 1991: *The Face of Aghamore, Mayo*.
Lavelle, D. et al., 1994: *An Archaeological Survey of Ballinrobe and District including Lough Mask and Lough Carra*, Castlebar.
Lavelle, M., 1991: "A recently discovered Barrow Group in Achadh Mór", in ed. Lavelle, 1991, 62-69.
Lucas, A.T., 1960: "Burial Mound at Rathmoon, Co. Wicklow", *J. Roy. Soc. Antiq. Ireland*, 90, 84-88.
Megaw, J.V.S., and Simpson, D.D.A., 1984: *Introduction to British Prehistory*, Leicester, Leicester University Press.
Moore, M., 1999: *Archaeological Inventory of County Waterford*, Dublin.
O'Donovan, P., 1995: *Archaeological Inventory of County Cavan*, Dublin.
O'Dwyer, M., 1959; 1960; 1964: "A Survey of the Earthworks in the District of Old Pallasgrean", *Nth. Munster Antiq.*, 8, 69-78; 8, 111-115; 9, 94-98.
O'Kelly, M.J., 1942: "A Survey of the Antiquities in the Barony of Smallcounty, County Limerick", *Nth. Munster Antiq. J.*, 3, 75-97.
Stout, G., 1984: *Archaeological Survey of the Barony of Ikerrin*, Roscrea.
Stout, M., 1997: *The Irish Ringfort*, Dublin.
Timoney, M., 1984: "Earthen Burial Sites on the Carrowmore Peninsula, Co. Sligo" in Burenhult, G., ed., 1984, 319-325.
Timoney, M. A., ed., 2002: *A Celebration of Sligo*, Sligo, Sligo Field Club.
Timoney, M. B., 1997: "Kilturra Photograph", *The Corran Herald*, 30, 4.
Waddell, J., 1990: *The Bronze Age Burials of Ireland*, Galway.

Food Vessel, Broher, Keash, Co. Sligo. Photo: Des Smith, Sligo Field Club Collection.

THE PROMONTORY FORT, INHUMATION CEMETERY AND SUB-RECTANGULAR ENCLOSURE AT KNOXSPARK, CO. SLIGO.

Charles Mount,
The Heritage Council, Kilkenny

ABSTRACT: Evidence indicates that the site at Knoxspark, Co. Sligo was in use for more than 200 years and may span the Pagan/Early Christian Transition. Some time before 660 to 960 AD the southern end of the low promontory was defended by a wide crescentic ditch and internal bank or wall and counterscarp bank. Within this was found two areas of settlement activity and four possible hut platforms. A considerable cemetery developed on the site and was eventually enclosed by a sub-rectangular wall with west-facing entrance, resembling a small cashel.

INTRODUCTION

In the spring and summer of 1994 excavations were directed by the author on the site at Knoxspark, Co. Sligo, licence No. 94 E 060. The site had been noted by Tom Condit, then of the O.P.W. Sites and Monuments Record, on a Geological Survey of Ireland 1:50,000 aerial photograph and identified as an inland promontory fort and enclosure. Subsequently the site was included in the Sites and Monuments Record for Co. Sligo (Gibbons *et al.* 1989) as No. 20:166. Initially the site was to have been severely affected by the construction of the Collooney to Carraroe by-pass road, with a layby road constructed through the internal sub-rectangular enclosure. The large scale excavation of the interior of the site was attempted and this work took place over a three month period from the 10th. of May to the 29th. of July, 1994. However, as the excavation progressed and the importance of the site was appreciated it became obvious that the site should not be excavated under the constraints of rescue conditions and that a research strategy was more appropriate. Sligo County Council agreed in July 1994 in consultation with the National Monuments and Historical Properties Service, to minimize the impact on the monument and its archaeology by moving the fence-line of the road east, away from the internal rectangular enclosure. This allowed an alteration of the original excavation strategy. Excavation of archaeological features outside (to the west) of the revised road take were postponed and work concentrated on the areas directly affected by the take of the altered road scheme. In the event a number of partly excavated burials were re-covered and an extensive and important area of habitation on the western part of the site was also back-filled. This meant that none of the archaeology to the west of the revised fence-line of the road was in any way archaeologically tested or recorded. The internal sub-rectangular enclosure was subsequently reinstated to its original, pre-excavation form, with the exception of the cairns which were only partly excavated and were not completely reconstructed, the entrance was re-constructed and all areas of the site re-seeded. It is hoped, once the results of the 1994 are published, to return to the site for further research and conservation work on what is undoubtedly one of the largest cemeteries uncovered in Connaught. In the meantime this paper is intended as a preliminary report of the results of the ten weeks excavations with some general comments. The analysis of the site presented is still provisional and may be altered in the light of the evidence from the unexcavated part of the site.

SITING

The site is situated in the townland of Knoxspark, the parish of Ballysadare and the barony of Leyny (Fig. 1); on the six inch Ordnance Survey map Sligo sheet 20, at co-ordinates 559.0mm/222.2mm. The National Grid reference of the site is 16726.32876 (G 672.287). It is on an elongated ridge of limestone till overlying limestone which rises to a height of just 30m above sea level and 4m above the surrounding marsh (Pl. 1). The ridge is situated in a bend of the Ballysadare River, the name given to the combined waters of the Owenmore, Owenbeg and Unshin Rivers, and is

A CELEBRATION OF SLIGO

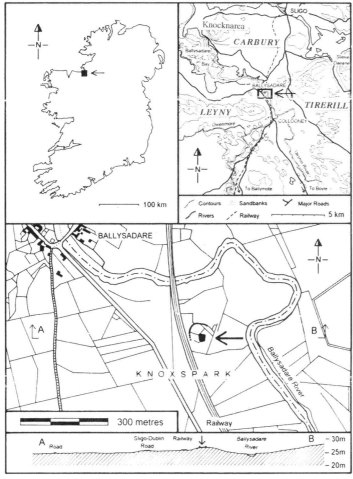

Fig. 1 - Location map.

extensively cultivated in the nineteenth century (see below).

The location of the site invites some comment. Byrne (1973, 233) noted that in the seventh century the Luigni, otherwise known as the Ua hEghra (O'Dowd 1991, 15), and the Gailenga formed a large block, south of the Ox Mountains between the northern Ui Fiachrach to the west and the Uí Briuin to the east. This was an over-kingdom which became the diocese of Achonry in the twelfth century. The territory of the Ua hEghra later became the barony of Leyny, the northern and eastern boundary of which was the Ballysadare River, with the site at Knoxspark on its west bank. On the east bank is the barony of Tirerrill, forming part of the diocese of Elphin, which was controlled by the Uí Ailello until the ninth century and from whose territory it evolved. The competition between the two septs of the Uí Ailello and Ua hEghra in the eight century is well documented in the Annals, corresponding well with radiocarbon dates from the site,

enclosed on three sides by the river and on the fourth by the expanse of a silted marshy lake. The soil of this ridge is a fertile sandy loam brown podzolic/brown earth and was and indicates that control of the river crossings between the two territories would have been important for the security of both groups. In 789 the Uí Ailello defeated the Luigni at Achad

Pl. 1 - View of Knoxspark looking south.

Ablae in the barony of Corrann, south of Knoxspark, and in 790 they were defeated again by the Uí Ailello at Áthrois (the ford of the wood or promontory), which may have been a forested ford across the Ballysadare river, or a ford dominated by a promontory. But just two years later the UÍ Ailello were defeated by the Cairpre and Brie'fne at Ard Maiccrime and disappear from history (Byrne 1973, 249) leaving the Ua hEghra secure in Leyny down to modern times. An important routeway ran from west Ulster through Carbury and across the Ballysadare river near Knoxspark and continued into southern Connaught through the Collooney gap
in the Ox Mountains, with a branch turning westward into UÍ Fiachrach Múaide, the barony of Tireragh (O'Dowd 1991, 2-5). This would have been both an asset and a danger to the Ua hEghra. While it would have allowed them control over the traffic from the northwest and the coast into the interior, this pass was also vital for any power that wished to dominate Connaught. As early as 762 the Luigni were defeated by the Cene'l Cairpri (Byrne 1973, 249), Collooney was the site of a battle in 673 and was plundered in 844, and for the medieval period O'Rorke (1889) noted that the settlement at Ballysadare was taken and burned in 1179, 1188, 1228 and 1235. The promontory fort at Knoxspark was therefore well placed to watch the important

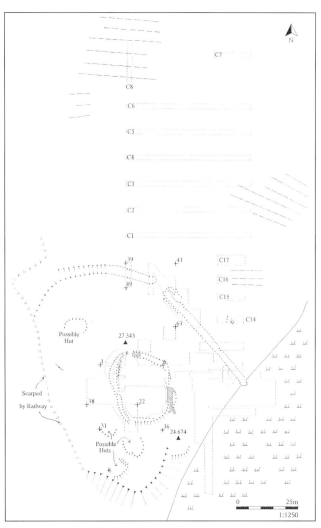

Fig. 3 - Plan of site after excavation with site grid.

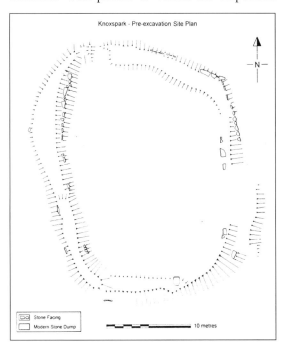

Fig. 2 - Plan of the sub-rectangular enclosure before excavation.

river crossings that allowed access to the territory of the Ua hEghra to the west and could simultaneously control any river traffic from Ballysadare Bay along the Ballysadare River through the Collooney Gap which allows access to Lough Arrow, via the Unshin River, and to Templehouse Lake, via the Owenmore River.

THE EXCAVATION
The Promontory Fort

Examination of air photos indicated the strong possibility that the southern part of the Knoxspark ridge was fortified by a wide ditch with an internal bank and external counterscarp bank. This enclosed an area measuring roughly 64m north to south by 75m from the east, where the bank ran out, to the west of the railway escarpment. In this paper the term promontory fort will be confined to these defences. The ditch was examined in a number of trenches and an extensive area, 12.6m by 4.2m in width, was excavated and a portion of the entrance causeway examined (Fig. 3). The trench through

Pl. 2 - The excavated promontory fort ditch looking east.

Grid Squares 45 and 49 was 10m by 2m. The ditch extended through this cutting in a generally east to west direction and was 4.2m in maximum width at the top and 2.08m in maximum width at the base (Pl. 2). The trench through Grid Squares 45, 46, 50 and 51 uncovered the western terminal of the ditch. It continued at east in a south-eastern direction leaving an uncut causeway 6.5m in width between the two stretches of ditch. At the inner end of this causeway, where the bank terminals were situated (and have yet to be excavated), would have been the entrance gateway. This may have been a substantial structure requiring large post-holes.

To the south-east of the causeway the ditch cut or profile (Context 108) was U-shaped with a sloping outer side and a steeper inner side. It measured $c.1.07$m in width at the base and $c.3.8$m in width at the top widening to $c.5$m in width at the western terminal. Through its entire length it was cut into a layer of grey limestone boulder clay and contained a series of fills. A sample of animal bone from the side of the cut in Grid Square 64 has produced a radiocarbon determination of 1260±40 BP (GrA-2452; 660 to 880 cal AD 2σ). A long section through the ditch was left unexcavated in Grid Squares 64-65 and a section drawn. From top to bottom this consisted of (Context 100a) a layer of grey/brown sandy loam with very few stones which was situated immediately below the sod. Beneath this layer on the external side of the fill was (Context 100b) a gritty yellow brown soil which immediately overlay a dump of large boulders lying on the outer side of the ditch. A lens of yellow clay (Context 101b) was situated over a large boulder in the outer edge of the ditch and overlay (Context 101a) a brown sandy loam which formed a matrix with many stones. This layer contained some iron slag and may have resulted from the bulldozing of the ditch and bank, which the landowner stated had been carried out in 1978. A light brown layer of gravel and clay with sand (Context 102) was noted in the section of the cutting in Grid Squares 45, 46, 50 and 51 below Context 101 but was not present in Grid Squares 64 and 65. This appears to represent an episode of silting.

Below Context 101 was Context 103, a layer of large stones and boulders measuring from 15 to 95cm in a matrix of brown sandy loam with many gaps and air pockets in its lower part. There was considerable root activity throughout this layer. This appears to represent the demolition of the remains of the inner bank and its stone facing which was deposited in the ditch. There is no direct evidence for when this occurred but it may have been in the nineteenth century when the Knoxspark ridge was extensively cultivated. Below this was (Context 104a) a layer of medium brown humus and sand (loam) which was stone free with a few small pebbles under 1cm. This layer was stratified beneath Context 103 and appears to represent a layer of natural silt in the inner side and base of the ditch before the demolition of the inner bank. This context continues into the centre of the ditch as Context 104b, a similar brown coloured humus and sand with many angular stones up to 19cm in length and a quantity of iron slag mixed through it.

The outer edge of the ditch was filled with Context 107, a tumble of limestones up to 18cm in diameter and with larger boulders up to 88cm. The gaps between the stones were filled with a dark brown sandy loam similar to Context 104a. Context 107 appears to represent primary ditch fill, possibly the remains of a counterscarp bank which collapsed into the base of the ditch. It is partly stratified under Contexts 103 and 104b and interfaces with Context 106. The primary silting of the inner side of the base of the ditch (Context 106) consisted of a tan coloured sand and gravel with no humus. A sample of animal bone from Context 106 in Grid Square 57 has produced a radiocarbon determination of 1190±40 BP (GrA-2454; 690 to 960 cal AD 2σ).

The evidence from the aerial photographs (Pers. Comm. Tom Condit) and from the stratigraphy of the ditch indicates that the site defences took the form of an internal and external bank. The quantity of stone in contexts 103 and 107 probably indicates that they are the demolition deposits of two stone-faced banks. This type of construction, an internal and external stone facing with a core of earth and stones, was also used to construct the sub-rectangular enclosure.

THE CEMETERY

Within the area enclosed by the promontory fort was a sub-rectangular enclosure. The interior of the enclosure was covered by Context 1, the sod and top soil, a light brown soil with a small proportion of sand, stony in places with a quantity of medium sized quartz stones. In the central area of the site was a setting of large stones oriented east-west (the east and west cairns). Context 1 sealed Context 2, a light sandy brown soil with many stones from 2 to 30cm. This layer was of considerable depth and was formed through the episodic digging of graves through an earlier occupation horizon. It contained animal bone, iron artifacts and smelting slag. Many nails were recovered in the upper part of this horizon, mainly above the level of the burials. These were in curving linear rather than random arrangements and may mark the decayed walls of structures.

THE EAST CAIRN

The east cairn, situated primarily in Grid Square 17, was 4.5m in diameter east to west by 4.2m north to south and a maximum of 54cm high above the old ground surface (Pl. 3). There was a substantial quantity of stone immediately at east, much of which appeared to have tumbled off the cairn, somewhat reducing its height. The cairn material, Context 20, immediately underlay the topsoil and directly overlay the old ground surface (Context 21) and the old subsoil, (Context 24). Context 20 was a dark brown crumbly humus with inclusions of sand and grit.

Pl. 3 - Section through the south-eastern quadrant of the east cairn showing the old ground surface and the cremation deposit above the further end of the right hand ranging rod.

Within this matrix were a number of large limestone boulders up to 70cm in diameter and flat limestones up to 28cm. From the surface of this deposit (directly underlying the sod) there was cremated bone and small charcoal flecks and nuggets mixed through this matrix (Cremation 1). This material was both above and below (sealed by) the flat stones. The bulk of the cremated bone filled a small depression formed by a number of the limestones. A sample of animal bone from context 20 was submitted for radiocarbon dating and a determination of 1180±40 BP (GrA-2455; 720 to 970 cal AD 2σ) obtained. A number of finds were noted in this context including chert, iron implements (mainly nails and possibly portions of pins), a fragmentary annular bead, a copper tag, flint, and fragments of animal bone. In the north-western part of this matrix, where it covered a linear stone wall, a decorated gold and amber disc was found (No. 94 E 015:588). The Context 21 soil was medium brown with a few stones and charcoal flecks, it contained iron, iron slag and fragments of a possible silver object, a bronze pin, animal bone and a number of seed deposits suggesting the truncated remains of an occupation horizon. Context 24 was a grey/brown gravelly soil sealed by Context 21 filling the interstices between weathered limestones from 2cm to 67cm in diameter. Context 24 contained animal bone and charcoal. There were no inhumation burials either in the old ground or the old subsoil beneath the cairn. This was the only part of the cemetery without inhumations and probably indicates that this feature pre-dates the inhumations. A sample of animal bone was submitted for radiocarbon dating and a determination of 1240±40 BP (GrA-2456; 680-880 cal AD 2σ) obtained. This suggests that the occupation and the cairn are contemporary with the silting of the promontory fort ditch.

THE WEST CAIRN

The west cairn was situated in Grid Squares 15, 16, 21 and 22. It was 3.2m in diameter east to west by 3m north to south and a maximum of 40cm high (Pl. 4). It consisted of Context 31, a cairn of large stones 70cm in diameter with a brown humus mixed into the interstices. This layer contained quartz flakes, animal bone, iron and iron slag. Context 31 sealed Context 32, a layer of dark brown humus with charcoal flecks and burnt daub or clay. This material had fewer stones than Context 31 and contained slag and charcoal. Context 32 contained animal bone, iron implements, iron slag and flint. Context 33 was sealed by Context 32 and was a U-shaped area of

Pl. 4 - Section through the south-western quadrant of the west cairn.

burnt orange clay/daub, oriented north-east to south-west and aligned in the general direction of Context 33 (the possible metal working area). The sides of this feature were orange in colour, the interior was grey. Context 34 was the fill of a curving trench cut (Context 35) and was sealed by Context 33. It was a very dark spread of humus with some charcoal present. Also present was some metal fragments, iron slag and a large amount of burnt bone. There were closely set stones within this context, some of which appeared to have been burned. Context 35 was the cut of the trench containing Context 34 and consisted of a curving trench 1.58m in length, extending from east to west. It was about 45cm in width for much of its length but at 1m from its eastern end it expanded to 90cm in width. This may have been the base of a furnace. It was cut into Context 2 and on its northern side disturbed a possible child burial which has not yet been excavated or numbered. The east and west cairns were linked by a 6m long arrangement of angular stones on the northern side, possibly a wall footing. To the east this walling developed into what appeared to be a tumbled wall which extended to the south-east and partly enclosed the east cairn.

THE INHUMATION BURIALS

To date a minimum of 185 inhumation burials have been noted on the site, but ongoing skeletal analysis will most likely increase this figure. The burials consisted primarily of extended inhumations usually with the heads to the west and the feet to the east with 51 examples (Nos. 1, 2, 4, 5, 6, 7, 8, 9, 10, 11, 17, 18, 19, 20, 21, 23, 27, 30, 32, 38, 40, 41, 42, 43, 44, 45, 46, 47, 50, 53, 54, 55, 56, 57, 58, 59, 64, 65, 66, 70, 73, 74, 75, 77, 80, 87, 89, 90, 91, 93 and 95). Two individuals (Nos. 3 and 49) were extended on their sides. Three burials were crouched (Nos. 31, 34 and 94) and three burials were flexed (Nos. 39, 69 and 76). There were 11 examples of skulls only without any other body parts (Nos. 14, 15, 16, 24, 28, 52, 71, 78, 82, 92 and 73) (bold figures refer to quantities of bone from disturbed or incomplete burials which are called bone assemblages). Eighty-two burials were disturbed (Nos. 12, 13, 51, 67, 68, 79, 81, 83, **1, 2, 3, 4, 5, 6, 7, 8, 9, 10, 11, 12, 13, 14, 15, 15, 17, 18, 19, 20, 21, 22, 23, 24, 25, 26, 27, 29, 30, 31, 32, 33, 34, 35, 36, 37, 38, 39, 40, 41, 42, 43, 44, 45, 46, 48, 49, 51, 52, 54, 55, 56, 57, 58, 59, 60, 61, 62, 63, 64, 65, 66, 67, 68, 69, 70, 71, 72, 74, 75, 76, 79, 80** and **84**) and 13 were disarticulated (Nos. 29, 60, 61, 62, 84, 88, 28, 47, 50, 53, 77, 78 and 85). Twenty burials were only partially excavated and have been left *in situ* (Nos. 25, 26, 33, 35, 36, 37, 48, 63, 72, 85, 86, 97, 98, 99, 100, 101, 102, 103, **82** and **83**). Some of the more interesting burials are described in detail below.

BURIAL 1 (Grid Square 9) an adult inhumation, buried *c.*15cm in depth below the sod, was laid on its back and oriented with the head, the highest part of the body, to the south-west and legs to north-east with its right arm by the chest extending upwards so that the hand was beneath the chin. It was articulated from the skull to the vertebrae, in an extended position, but the legs had become disarticulated and had been placed on to the chest (possibly to make way for Burial No. 2). There was no indication of the right tibia or the lower part of the left tibia and there was no indication of the feet. Most of the vertebrae were also absent. On the right side of the skull, overlying the right hand, was a large limestone which may have been placed into the grave as a protection for the head. The skeleton was generally in poor condition, with the skull broken and considerable disturbance but the lower jaw and back of the skull survived reasonably well. This burial was initially thought to be crouched as both legs were placed up beside the chest. The left arm was missing, although a fragment to the north-east may indicate that the left arm originally extended across the lower body.

BURIAL 4 (Grid Square 9) was an adult male inhumation (associated with Burial 75 and skull 24), buried *c.* 40 to 50cm in depth and laid on its back and oriented with the head to the west and the lower body to the east (Pl. 5). The lower vertebrae were slightly bent to the north so that the pelvis was at a slight angle to the trunk and the right leg curved over towards the left (apparently to avoid a large stone) with the right foot overlying the left. The arms were akimbo (the upper arms extended out from the shoulders with the elbows bent and the lower arms extending back into the pelvis with the hands skeleton was submitted for radiocarbon dating and a determination of 1184±31 BP (UB-3836; 770 to 950 cal AD 2σ) obtained. This places the death of this individual into the late eighth to early tenth centuries.

The right arm of BURIAL 75 was placed directly beneath the arm of Burial 4 indicating that the two individuals were buried at the same time. A socketed iron spearhead (find No. 429) was situated beside the lower vertebrae of Burial 4 and may have originally been in the man's hand (Pl. 6). Burial 75 was $c.75$cm in depth beneath the sod and extended on its back with the trunk to the west and the feet to the east. This burial was in good condition. The head had been removed from the neck and may be represented by the skull Burial 24. The arms were extended by the sides and the right arms touched that of Burial 4. The legs extended from the body in an almost parallel fashion and did not touch.

BURIAL 74 (Grid Square 16) was an adult, buried $c.1.25$m in depth beneath the sod and extended on its back with the head to the south of west, facing north and the feet to the north of east. This burial was not in good condition and the bones were very degraded. The right arm did not survive below the upper part of the humerus but the left extended along the line of the body, was bent at the elbow and the hand extended onto the left pelvis and over the lower stomach. The legs were extended straight out from the body and unusually for this cemetery did not come together but remained almost parallel. The length of the left femur was 0.37m.

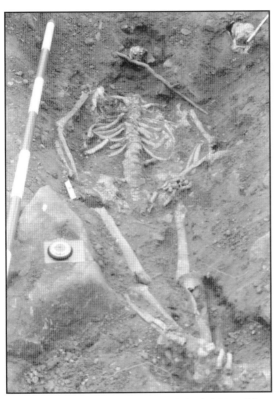

Pl. 5 - View of Burial 4, looking west, with the skull 24, partially uncovered, in the baulk.

lying on each side of the pelvis). Despite the excellent preservation of this skeleton only a small portion of the skull, the chin and some lower teeth, were preserved. This was out of position, 10cm to the north of the neck, and in the light of the decapitation of skull 24 from Burial 75, it is possible that Burial 4 was also decapitated. A portion of the femur of this

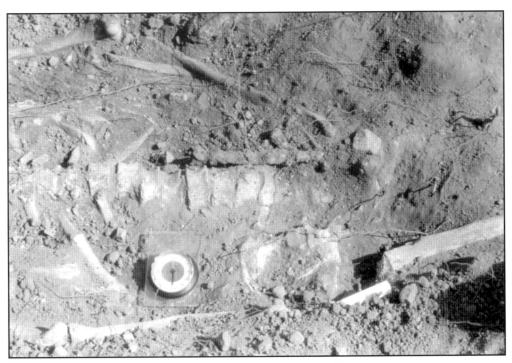

Pl. 6 - The socketed spearhead (find No. 94 E 060:429) *in situ*.

BURIAL 7 (Grid Square 20) was that of a child, buried just a few centimetres immediately underneath the fill (Context 62) of the internal sub-rectangular bank. It was laid on its back with its head to the west but facing north with the chin down on the shoulder. The body extended in a shallow curve to the east. Only the upper body survived, with the left and a fragment of the right humerus and the upper vertebrae and ribs present but the pelvis and legs were missing. It is difficult to tell what the body posture was but it was probably crouched like the nearby Burial 58. This child was buried in the inner southern part of the entrance to the sub-rectangular enclosure. The passage stone which would have been situated directly to the south of this burial was missing (see below) and could indicate that this burial was a later insertion into the entrance-way, probably after it had been blocked. The passage stone might have been removed at this time. However the lower eastern part of the child has been removed and this might have occurred during the construction of the sub-rectangular enclosure and its entrance-way. Burial 7 could also have been disturbed by a subsequent burial, as Burial 27 was disturbed by Burial 58 and the latter burial may have been disturbed by the construction of the sub-rectangular enclosure. The nearby Child Burial 58 is stratified directly underneath one of the structural stones of the enclosure and therefore the enclosure must post-date this burial. It may post-date Burial 7 as well.

Pl. 7 - Multiple grave with Burials 34, 38, 39 and 40.

There were a number of crouched burials including BURIAL 31 (Grid Square 9), an adult, crouched on the right side and at a depth of c.75cm to 1m. This burial was in a poor condition with just the lower half remaining from the lumbar vertebrae and pelvis down. The left foot had not survived. The head would presumably have been oriented to the west or south-west. The right femur measured 0.3m long. This burial would appear to have been cut by BURIAL 28 or any of the nearby bone assemblages. BURIAL 34 (Grid Square 23) was one of a group of four individuals buried together. It was a possible adolescent, buried c.1.25 to 1.5m in depth, crouched on its left side with the upper body oriented to the south-west and the lower body to the north-east (Pl. 7). This individual was intertwined with an extended adult inhumation, Burial 38 and associated with burials 39 and 49. The legs of Burial 34 were extended over those of Burial 38, with the left lower knee forward and leg of Burial 34 extending beneath the right. The right femur measured 0.29m long. The left arm of Burial 34 extended over the upper part of the right femur of Burial 38, was bent at the elbow and extended under the lower part of the femur with the hand near the left femur. The upper portion of the right arm of Burial 34 was present but the lower part was missing as was much of the midriff. The skull of this burial was found not attached to its neck but was placed, on its back, onto the middle arm of the adult. BURIAL 39 (Grid Square 23) was a child buried c. 1.25 to 1.5m in depth and was extended on its back with the upper body oriented towards the south-west and the lower body to the north-east. The burial was well preserved but there was no skull, only a few vertebrae and only the right hand survived. The pelvis and leg bones did survive. This individual was placed onto the left pelvis of the adult. Its right femur extended across the lower femur of the adult (Burial 38) in a flexed posture, with the knee bent and then extended back onto the lower leg, just tucking itself under the knee of Burial 34. This femur measured 0.195m long. The other femur was found, apparently disarticulated, on the northern side of the left femur of the adult. The legs may originally have been crossed.

There were a number of flexed burials including BURIAL 11 (Grid Square 9), an adult, buried c. 50 to 60cm in depth, extended on its back with the head extended to the south-west and the feet to the north-east. The right arm was extended along the body and the hand turned inward and lay over the right pelvis. The left arm is now fragmentary but appears to have been flexed and bent at the elbow, possibly with the hand (which did not survive) extending to the left side of the pelvis. The legs were extended but the right leg was slightly flexed with the heel of the foot extending inwards towards the left leg and the foot lying on its right side. The left leg was nearly straight with the foot lying on its heel in an upright position. This individual appears to have been quite tall with the femur about 50cm in length. The frontal part of the skull and the upper jaw did not survive well but the lower jaw was in good condition. The left foot of this burial overlay Burial 12.

BURIAL 69 (Grid Square 21), an adult, was buried *c.* 75cm in depth and positioned on its back with the head to the west and the flexed legs to the east. This burial was in a poor condition with little remaining of the skull and no teeth surviving. There were no remains of the vertebrae or pelvis. The arms were extended by the sides with the right elbow slightly bent and the lower arm extending in towards the side. The legs were flexed and lying on their left sides with the knees bent and the lower legs extending in parallel. The feet also appear to have been on their left sides. BURIAL 76 (Grid Square 21), an adult, was buried *c.* 20cm in depth and flexed with the head to the west and facing north and the legs extending towards the east (Pl. 8; Mount 1994, 23). This burial was well preserved. The skull was on its side but was propped into a raised position with the jaw extending out of the grave. The individual was on its back with the right arms extending along the side of the body and the hand was placed just beside the right hip. The left arm extended a little out from the body and the elbow was bent at a 45 degree angle with the lower arm and hand extending onto the middle chest. The left leg was extended away from the body on its side and was bent at the knee. The right leg was similarly extended though at a greater angle forming a flexed posture. The lower legs were covered with a number of stones.

BURIAL 80 (Grid Square 23) was an adult, buried c.1m in depth and extended on its back with the head to the west and facing north and the legs extending to the east. This burial was in good condition. The head was somewhat raised and the lower jaw had dropped giving the appearance of "screaming". The upper arms were extended by the sides and were bent at the elbows with the lower arms extending back along the body, overlapping the upper arms, the wrists were bent and the hands were placed onto the chest and were resting on the ribs. The left leg was extended but the right leg was raised with the knee bent in an upward position. The right femur was 0.45m in length. A cattle mandible (No. 94 E 060:677) had been placed into the grave just above the right leg. The unusual posture of this burial suggests that it was either thrown into the grave haphazardly or perhaps buried alive.

BURIAL 45 (Grid Squares 3 and 9) was an adult, buried *c.* 12cm in depth and extended on its back with the head to the north of west and the legs to the south of east. Each ear was covered by a small "pillow stone". The arms were extended closely by the sides with the left and right hands above the pelvis and the feet came together at the ankles. The burial was very well preserved and the left femur was 45cm in length. A fragment of iron slag (No. 94 E 060:496) and flecks of charcoal were found in the fill of this burial.

THE SUB-RECTANGULAR ENCLOSURE

The rectangular enclosure is 23m by 19m and was constructed with its long axis running almost due north-south (Fig. 2). The wall is up to 2.2m in maximum thickness and survives to 95cm in height. It was constructed with an external stone facing or revetment (Context 60) which was composed of spaced uprights and a continuous walling of boulders in places. One of the best preserved sections of this walling was in Grid Square 20 where it consisted of 4 spaced uprights and drystone walling of small boulders and stones which formed a curving section of walling up to 80cm in maximum height (Pl. 9). The internal wall facing (Context 61) consisted in Grid Square 20 of a discontinuous line of medium sized boulders, with three to the north and two to the south. The central section is composed of smaller stones and rubble. The revetment was poorly preserved. On the eastern side of the enclosure in Grid Square 12 the

Pl. 8 - Burial 76.

Pl. 9 - View of the enclosing bank in Grid Square 20 looking east.
The blocked entrance is between the two orthostatic stones to the right of the upright ranging rod.

external facing was a double line of boulders with a single internal revetment wall. These walls retained a bank, Context 62, composed of a matrix of dark brown soil with grit and sand particles mixed throughout. It was retained on the exterior side by Context 60 and loosely on the base of the interior by Context 61 but was mainly piled up. In Grid Square 20 this material contained a substantial number of artefacts and organic remains and was clearly derived from an occupation surface. On the eastern side in Grid Square 12 the bank material was almost sterile.

The exterior side of the wall was covered by an outer wall tumble, Context 63. This was similar to 62 although it was a little lighter in colour. It extended from the top of the bank (Contexts 60 to 62) sloping away for a distance of 1.6m in Grid Square 20. This layer appears to represent tumble from the top of the bank and also possible exterior clearance onto the bank. The inner wall tumble, Context 64, consisted of dark brown soil with grit and sand particles with stones up to 17 cm in diameter. It extended from the bank, making it up to 60 to 70cm in height, sloping c.1m into the interior

The old ground surface, Context 65, was light brown to almost orange in colour. The soil was gritty with sand and gravel and small pebbles and stones. Cut into this layer was Context 67, the cut of the grave for Burial 27. This contained a fill, Context 66. Also cut into it was Context 69, the cut of the grave for Burial 58. This contained a fill, Context 68. As these two graves were cut into the old ground surface and were stratified beneath Contexts 62 and 61 they pre-date the construction of the rectangular enclosure.

The entrance to the enclosure was set asymmetrically in the southern half of the western side in Grid Square 20 (Mount 1994, 22). It was aligned a little to the south of west and consisted of a pair of large orthostatic stones set 72cm apart with their narrow sides east to west forming the western side of the entrance. Behind the northern stone was a second large upright, but there was no corresponding stone on the southern side. The entrance itself was not completely open but was partly blocked, in the manner of a megalithic tomb, by three low jamb-stones. Burial 7 had been placed into the old ground surface in the inner end of the entrance after its construction. At some point in the use of the enclosure the entrance had been completely blocked with soil and stones and was not discernible until the wall was excavated.

Context 22 was the cut of a small pit measuring 80cm north-south by a maximum of 55cm east-west and was 25cm in depth. The pit was situated in Grid Squares 16 and 22 nearly mid-way between the east and west cairns on their southern side. It contained a single layer of fill, Context 22, which was a compact, heavy and cohesive soil, dark grey in colour. The edge was in part defined by a stone layer. The context itself contained few small stones 1cm or less in diameter. Charcoal and cremated bone occurred, particularly in the upper levels of the context. Two iron fragments (Nos. 94 E 060:696 and 94 E 060:758) were found in this context.

Context 8 was the cut of a pit measuring 60cm north-south by 90cm east-west and was 35cm in depth. It was situated in Grid Square 22 just to the south-west of the east cairn. It contained a fill, Context 5, which was medium brown in colour. There were a few small stones present as well as a small amount of cremated and uncremated bone. This pit truncated Burials 19 and 20 and Bone Assemblage 41.

THE CORN-DRYING KILN

An extensive area of 545m² was opened on the eastern side of the promontory fort where the line of the road crossed the line of the ditch and affected part of the site interior. This area consisted entirely of a light brown sandy loam with a fine cultivation soil Context 121, which was 40 to 50cm in depth. This extended from the the exterior side of the sub-rectangular enclosure, across the top of the promontory fort ditch and to the edge of the damp marl which indicated the shore-line of the former lake. Beneath this material was Context 122, an orange to white hard clay, which was very marly in places.

Situated on this cultivation soil in Grid Squares 108 and 109 was a corn-drying kiln. This consisted of a stone structure, Context 124, a series of upright stones which surrounded an area of burnt soil and charcoal. This kiln was aligned with the flue opening to the north-west and the furnace to the south-east. It measured 2.8m in length and the oval furnace area measured 90cm north-south by 1.3m east-west. It contained a very dark compact layer which was very rich in charcoal, Context 125, which also contained a few fragments of burnt bone. There was also a considerable rake out from this kiln, Context 105, a layer of black clay, heavily charcoalized, with some sand and seeds. This extended to the south-east over an area measuring 7.5m north-south by a maximum of 4m east-west through Grid Squares 122, 123, 115 and 116.

DISCUSSION

THE PROMONTORY FORT

At some time before 660 to 960 AD the southern portion of the fertile loamy ridge at Knoxspark was fortified by digging a wide and deep flat-bottomed ditch in an arc across its neck and heaping the spoil into a substantial bank on the internal side. This bank and ditch, with its north-facing entrance, was essentially an inland promontory fort protecting the inhabitants from attack from the north. It enclosed a minimum area of 4800m^2 (0.48ha), but probably originally more as the western side of the ridge was scarped to provide hard fill for the construction of the adjacent railway embankment. This type of enclosure falls into Raftery's (1994, 45-48) Class 3 Hillforts. Other examples are Lurigethan and Knockdhu in Co. Antrim which were upland forts defended by closely spaced banks and ditches. It is comparable in size to the inland promontory forts at Caherconree, Co. Kerry, and Carrighenry, Co. Limerick, which are both less than one hectare in area (*ibid.*, 46-47). While these forts depended upon high altitudes and steep slopes for protection, Caherconree is at 615m, Knoxspark depended upon the protection of a river bend and an extensive marshy lake.

The occupation material noted on the western part of the site and incorporated into the bank of the sub-rectangular enclosure, Context 62, may be related to the occupation horizon, contemporary with the promontory fort, which is stratified beneath the east cairn. Within the defences are also a number of possible oval hut platforms on the western side of the site and the excavations have revealed a large quantity of butchered animal remains, iron tools and nails and vast quantities of iron smelting slag and furnace bottoms. This material does not relate to the cemetery and indicates that this was also an industrial centre. The ocurrence of a possible furnace, Context 35, cutting a burial appears to indicate that industrial activity also continued after the development of the cemetery. The exact dating and nature of the occupation is still speculative and further work will be required before it can be described satisfactorily.

THE CEMETERY

The development of a major cemetery could have ocurred before the site was fortified, when the site ceased to be used as a settlement but while control of the site and the river boundary remained important to the Ua hEghra, or the settlement and cemetery could have been contemporary. It may be significant that a second cemetery has been uncovered in Ballysadare townland, just 270m to the north of the site on the opposite side of the Ballysadare River (1997 Opie). The burial of ancestors at Knoxspark would have secured control of the site for the sept without the need to permanently garrison it. In the eastern part of the cemetery was an oval cairn of boulders. Placed onto this was a cremation deposit associated with a large number of iron nails and a possible iron pin as well as a fragment of a burnt annular bead. Stratified beneath this cairn was a small bronze pin. The occurrence of nails in this deposit may indicate that this individual or individuals were cremated in a wooden coffin. Subsequent burials on the site were inhumed. Crouched, flexed and extended burials with their heads usually to the west but sometimes to the north-west and south-west have been recovered. In the areas of the cemetery which have been excavated to date 185 individuals have been noted and there appear to be over 100 burials remaining in situ in this area. Many of these remains represent just portions of individuals and it appears that disarticulated remains were buried and earlier graves disturbed by later burials.

Children appear to be under-represented in the burial population and were either buried in groups of two or three, or with adults, and in some cases were crouched. One Burial group (burials 34, 38, 39 and 49) consisted of an adult, possibly female, whose head was missing, interred with the remains of three children of which only two had heads. One of the children was crouched and its head was found, not attached to its neck, but lying on the upper arm of the adult. There appear to have been a number of areas of the cemetery which were used for the burial of children. Child Burials 7, 27 and 58 were situated close together in the south-west part of the site beneath the wall of the sub-rectangular enclosure. Child Burials 66, 67 and 68 were close together in the north-west part of the site, possibly associated with Burial 47 and three children were interred with the possible female noted above. It appears to be more than a coincidence that children were buried in groups of three and the significance of these groups will have to be more full explored.

The north-western corner of the cemetery was particularly popular for burial and individuals were placed head to toe and arm to arm, cutting and overlying one another. In the northern part of this area two adult males (Burials 4 and 75) were buried simultaneously with linked arms. One of the men was associated with a socketed spearhead and the other man's head had been cut off and placed separately into the grave. In a number of instances bodies were uncovered without heads, heads were uncovered without bodies and in other examples of severed heads were included with burials. While a proportion of this must be attributed to differential preservation of body parts, evidently the heads were receiving specialised treatment at Knoxspark. Raftery (1994, 185) has written that the head was the for the Iron Age Irish the seat of the soul, the essence of human personality. The heads of defeated enemies were collected and displayed as symbols of power, status and as a source of ritual power. Severed human heads have been found in Iron Age contexts at the King's Stables, Co. Armagh, near Haughey's Fort (Lynn 1977), in Loughnashade, Co. Armagh, near Navan Fort (Warner 1986, 6), at Raffin, Co. Meath, (Newman 1993) and, close to Knoxspark, as secondary depositions in tomb 26 at Carrowmore, Co. Sligo (Bergh 1995, 190-191) and at Knocknashammer, Co. Sligo (Timoney 1987-1988, 77). There are also numerous accounts from the sagas of the severing of heads, later use as totems and their final inclusion in burials (see Hollo 1992, 18-19; Hughes and McDaniel 1990, 56-57). This continuity of Iron Age ritual practices at Knoxspark and the comparative dating of some of the burials (see below) suggests that the cemetery commenced as a pagan burial ground and may pre-date the promontory fort as it is dated at present.

At some time in the use of the cemetery it was enclosed by a sub-rectangular enclosure. This was constructed with an inner and outer facing of boulders and drystone walling and has an orthostatic entrance on the western side. On the western side it was constructed over a number of children's graves, bone from which will provide a post quem radiocarbon date for its construction. Later use of the site appears to have extended into the eighth and ninth centuries as radiocarbon dating and a gold and amber disc indicate. The disk was divided into three panels and was decorated with gold filligree and an amber stud. This may have been part of a penannular brooch similar in type to the Cavan brooch (Pers. comm. Raghnall Ó Floinn) or perhaps part of a reliquary box (Pers. comm. Niamh Whitfield). This elaborate find may indicate the presence on the site of a member of the high nobility, and may have been a deliberate deposition. Presumably by the ninth to tenth centuries the region would have been largely Christianized and the ritual functions of the site were being superceded by St. Fechin's Church at Ballysadare. After this time use of the site appears to have diminished in status and the site at Knoxspark sank into obscurity.

The dating of the burials

Cremation was the classic Iron Age Burial rite and had been common in Ireland since Neolithic times. At Knoxspark the cremation in the east cairn is dated quite late to 680 to 880 cal AD. It is not known how long into the first millenium the use of cremation persisted but at Furness, Co. Kildare, Grogan (1983-1984, 304) uncovered two cremations within a composite stone and earth barrow. A charcoal filled stake hole beneath the centre of the barrow produced a radiocarbon determination in the fifth century AD. O'Brien (1992, 131) has noted that the rite of inhumation was introduced to Ireland from Roman Britain in the first century A.D. A cemetery of crouched inhumations in simple pits was uncovered on Lambay Island, Co. Dublin, in 1927 (Rynne 1976) and the associated Romano-British grave goods place these graves into the second half of the first century A.D. (A.D. 50 to 100). At the Rath of the Synods, Tara, Co. Meath, crouched, extended and cremated burials from a pair of barrows probably dated to the 1st to 2nd centuries A.D (O'Brien 1990, 38). The earliest inhumations at Knoxspark therefore appear to be the crouched and flexed examples which may date to the early centuries A.D.

Extended burials are known in Ireland from the first half of the second century at Bray, Co. Wicklow, (O'Brien. 1992, 132), and early extended burials are known at Tara and Knowth, Co. Meath, and Site B, Carbury Hill, Co. Kildare. The latter site had cremations and then extended inhumations with the heads oriented to the south-west. At Tara an extended inhumation was associated with animal bone and another extended inhumation had the jaw bone of an ox behind the head. This rite provides parallels with Burial 80 at Knoxspark which was also associated with a cattle mandible.

Burials 45 and 55 at Knoxspark were supported by stones on either side of the head. These stones are sometimes referred to as ear muffs. Burial 30 was associated with a pair of cattle teeth which had been placed under the left side of the chin and by the right ear. They are an unusual occurrence in Irish contexts. Nineteen of the 130 burials at Kilshane, Co. Dublin, had ear muffs and O'Brien (1993, 98) has compared this feature to Anglo-Saxon practices which date to the eighth centuries and later.

The cemetery at Knoxspark was dominated by extended burials oriented west to east, with a smaller number of crouched and flexed burials and extended burials with the heads to the south-west and north-west. While the small number of non-extended burials and extended burials oriented other than east to west indicates that this was the overwhelmingly dominant burial posture, it should be noted that later east-west burials would have disturbed earlier burials in other postures and in other orientations and there are 95 disturbed and disarticulated burials recovered to date. For example Burial 10 which was oriented with the head to the north-west and feet to the south-east was disturbed by a later east-west Burial 56, buried at almost right angles to the earlier burial, which removed much of the upper half of the inhumation. Burial 1 which was oriented with the head to the south-west and the feet to the north-east was similarly affected by Burial 2, which had the remains of a bone assemblage running across its feet in a north-west to south-east direction. The variety of positions with crouched, flexed and extended inhumations is enough to indicate this was a multi-period cemetery and the extended use of the site, from perhaps the second or third centuries, would have provided ample time for the earlier crouched and non-east-west burials to be disturbed.

THE SUB-RECTANGULAR ENCLOSURE

There are a number of immediate parallels for this type site. At Knockea, Co. Limerick, O'Kelly (1967, 74-83) completely excavated a similar though much smaller site. The Knockea enclosure was constructed with a low internal and external facing of drystone walling and an earthen core which had been dug from an external fosse (absent at Knoxspark). Knockea measured 8.3m by 8.3m and was oriented with its sides to the cardinal points as at Knoxspark. It also had its entrance on the western side. Knockea enclosed a cemetery with a minimum of sixty-six inhumation burials. Most of these were extended on their backs and oriented east to west with the heads to the west and in one case a burial was crouched. A small number of burials had their heads protected by stones. Analysis of the remains indicated that there were twenty-eight adults and thirty-eight sub-adults.

At Derrynaflan, Co. Tipperary, Ó Floinn (1987, 24-25) excavated a portion of a similar enclosure. It measured 20m by 22m and was constructed with a facing of loose limestone boulders and a rubble fill and a number of rotary quern fragments had been used in its construction. It enclosed a cemetery which contained numerous extended inhumations of adults and children oriented east to west. The Derrynaflan site also produced a large number of iron nails, a whetstone, B-ware amphorae and glazed medieval pottery. At Cloonlaheen, Gurteen, Co. Sligo, (SMR. No. 44:029) is another rectangular enclosure measuring 24m by 21m and oriented north to south. The bank is constructed with an internal and external stone facing and soil core. Like Knoxspark it is situated on the end of a ridge and is enclosed on three sides by a small stream and is also within a large oval ditched enclosure measuring 77m north-south by 160m east-west. The three examples described above are undoubtedly of a site type only now being recognized. These sites appear to have been transitional Iron Age to Early Christian cemeteries which at some time in their use were enclosed. Their importance lies in the fact that they probably fill the chronological gap between the cemeteries of the Late Iron Age, for example, Tara, Knowth and Bettystown, all in Co. Meath, and the emergent sites of the early Christian period, Derrynaflan, Co. Tipperary, Clonmacnois, Co. Offaly, and Ballysadare, Co. Sligo.

ACKNOWLEDGEMENTS

The then landowner, Mr. Brian FitzPatrick gave his permission to excavate. Mr. Seamus O'Toole of Sligo County Council provided practical and material assistance throughout the excavation. Sligo County Council funded the excavation as part of the Collooney to Carraroe bypass. The work was ably supervised by Dr. Kieran O'Conor and during a brief absence by Johann Christiann Corlett. Dr. O'Connor and Mr. Corlett along with James Eogan and others were responsible for much of the planning. Rebecca Sweetman dealt expertly with the burials and was responsible for much of the on site recording and skeletal planning. When Ms. Sweetman had to leave for another project Samantha O'Connor took over and saw the completion of the burial recording. Veronica Tierney, Teresa Bolger, Oliver Hamilton, Ian Russell, Gráine Crowley, Heather Murphy, Thomas Nellany, James Conlon, Joseph Johnston, James Mullen, Eamon Scanlon, John-Joe Gorman, Joseph Tighe, Justin Moore, Séan Cosgrave, Paul Davey, John Clerkin and Patrick McCormack took part in the excavation. Damien Henry and Paul Hampson of Sligo County Council laid out the site grid and established the site datum points and surveyed the two site profiles. Elizabeth O'Brien discussed the burials and artefacts and brought a number of British sites to my attention, Raghnall Ó Floinn discussed the goldwork and the site in general and Niamh Whitfield discussed the gold disc. The radiocarbon dates were produced by the Queen's University of Belfast and the University of Groningen and I thank Gerry McCormick, Jan Lanting and Dr. J. van der Plicht. Figures 1 and 2 were drawn by Joseph Fenwick and the photographs are by the author. To all of these I tender my thanks.

REFERENCES

Bergh, S. 1995: *Landscape of the Monuments: A study of the passage tombs in the Cuil Irra region, Co. Sligo, Ireland.* Stockholm.

Byrne, F.J. 1973: *Irish Kings and High-Kings.* London, Batsford.

Coles, J.M. and Harding, A.F. 1979: *The Bronze Age in Europe.* New York, St. Martin's.

Gibbons, M., Alcock, A., Condit, T. & Murphy, M., and Timoney M.A., 1989: *Sites and Monuments Record. County Sligo.* Dublin, Office of Public Works.

Grogan, E., 1983-84: "Excavation of an Iron Age Burial mound at Furness", *J.Kildare Archaeol., Soc.,* 16, 298-316

Hollo, K., 1992: "The feast of Bricriu and the exile of the sons of Dóel Dermait", *Emania* 10, 18-24.

Hughes, A.J. and McDaniel, E., 1990: "Bryson's translation of the story of Deardre", *Emania* , 7, 54-58.

Lynn, C. 1977: "Trial excavations at the King's Stables, Tray townland, Co. Armagh", *Ulster J. Archaeol.* 40, 42-62.

Mount, C., 1994: "From Knoxspark to Tír na nÓg", *Archaeol. Ireland,* 29, 22-23.

O'Brien, E., 1990: "Iron Age Burial practices in Leinster: continuity and change", *Emania* 7, 37-42.

O'Brien, E., 1992: "Pagan and Christian Burial in Ireland during the first millenium A.D.: continuity and change", in N. Edwards and A. Lane, eds., *The Early Church in Wales and the West.* Oxford, Oxbow Monograph No. 16, 130-137.

O'Brien, E., 1993: "Contacts between Ireland and Anglo-Saxon England in the seventh century", in W. Filmer-Sankey, ed., *Anglo-Saxon Studies in Archaeology and History.* Oxford, Oxford University Committee for Archaeology, 93-102.

O'Dowd, M., 1991: *Power Politics and Land: Early Modern Sligo 1568-1688.* The Institute of Irish Studies, the Queen's University of Belfast.

Ó Floinn, R., 1987: "Derrynaflan, Lurgoe; Monastic Settlement", in I. Bennett, ed., *Excavations 1987,* 24-25, O.I.A.

Opie, H., 1997: "Ballysidare", in I. Bennett, ed., *Excavations 1996,* 96-7.

O'Kelly, M.J., 1967: "Knockea, Co. Limerick", in E. Rynne, ed., *North Munster Studies, Essays in Memory of Mons. Michael Moroney,* 72-101. Limerick, Thomond Archaeological Society.

O'Rorke, T., 1889: *History, Antiquities and Present State of the Parishes of Ballysadare and Kilvarnet, in the County of Sligo.* Dublin, Duffy.

Raftery, B., 1994: *Pagan Celtic Ireland.* London, Thames and Hudson.

Rynne, E., 1976: "The La Tène and Roman finds from Lambay, Co. Dublin: a reassessment", *Proc. Royal Irish Acad.,* 76C, 231-244.

Timoney, M.A., 1987-1988. "Knocknashammer", *J. Irish Archaeology,* IV, 77.

Warner, R.B., 1986: "Preliminary schedules of sites and stray finds in the Navan complex", *Emania,* I, 5-9.

A Curious Inhumation Burial from Dernish Island, Co. Sligo

Victor M. Buckley,[1] Laureen Buckley[2] and Finbar McCormick[3]

ABSTRACT: An extended female inhumation in a slab-lined grave was found in 1992 on Dernish Island, Co. Sligo. Eight roughly circular flat stones formed a mandola-like ring of glory around the skull of the skeleton. This may be a pre-Christian burial of early in the first millennium AD.

INTRODUCTION

Following the report of the finding of an extended inhumation burial on Dernish Island, Co. Sligo, from Mrs. Patricia Curran-Mulligan, Carrowmore, Co. Sligo, in August 1992, Dernish Island was visited as part of the ongoing archaeological survey of Co. Sligo and we met with the owner of the site, Mr. Ron Lenninston. The burial had been found when excavating for a new floor in the outbuilding to Mr. Lenninston's house. It was originally at a depth of only some 25cm. below the surface. The owner carefully removed the contents of the grave and the stones from which the grave was built. The grave has been reconstructed outside of the owner's front door exactly as it was found (Pls. 1 and 2).

SITE LOCATION

The grave was located on Dernish Island, Parish of Ahamlish, Co. Sligo, OS 6" Sheet 2 (58.4cm from W, 3.8cm from S), Nat. Grid. Ref. 16763.35248. Dernish is one of a chain of small islands off the north coast of Co. Sligo. Only 103 acres in size, it rises to a maximum height of just over 100ft above sea level with a largely raised beach shoreline. The island is cut off from the mainland by some 250 metres of water, which shrinks to only a narrow channel twice a day when the tide is out. Although the island supported a population of 220 people at the time of the 1851 Census, Mr. Lenninston was the sole inhabitant in 1992.

The outbuilding under which the grave was located is also shown on the 1836 edition of the OS 6" Sheet.

DESCRIPTION OF GRAVE AND CONTENTS

The grave was orientated N-S and aligned roughly on to the NW tip of Benbulbin Mountain, 6 km to the S. It of the slab-lined type and consisted of 5 capstones with an end stone at N, and with three boulders forming the sides at E and W. It had a maximum length of 1.7m and a maximum width of 1m.

The grave contained an extended inhumation of a female adult, height 157cm, with the head to N. The excellent condition of the remains has allowed a detailed assessment of the lady's lifestyle (see below). Mr. Lenninston gave very precise details of the contents, which he had kept. Interestingly around the head of the skeleton was placed a ring of eight flat stones (Pl. 3), each of which had been chopped around the edges to make them roughly circular in shape. These measure from roughly 6cm in diameter to 15cm in diameter. Each of the eight is of a different type of stone, varying in colour, but apparently of various types of sandstone or grits. These had apparently been arranged around the skull in a ring of glory pattern, roughly resembling a mandola, with the largest pair of stones at ear-level, smallest at jowls and others around the crown of the head. No other grave-goods were found, though in examining the skeletal material from the grave, out of context, a quantity of animal bones was noted. These have been identified by Dr. Finbar McCormick, who suggest that they would fit well with the scenario of the burial cutting into an earlier food midden. The feet bones of a second individual were also found but, again, these were out of context when recognised.

INTERPRETATION

It is unfortunate that the grave was not properly excavated by an archaeologist at the time of discovery. However the type of grave suggests a date of early in the first millennium

THE HUMAN REMAINS AT DERNISH ISLAND, CO. SLIGO

Laureen Buckley

Pl. 2 - End view of the reconstructed grave, Dernish Island, Co. Sligo.
Photo. Patricia Curran-Mulligan, August 1992.

This skeleton was almost complete and in a very good state of preservation. The skull was virtually intact although the facial bones were broken and most of the mandible was missing. The vertebral column consisted of six cervical, twelve thoracic and five lumbar vertebrae.

Both clavicles were complete and both scapulae were almost complete. The humeri were complete and the left radius and ulna were complete apart from their distal ends. Only the proximal end of the right ulna remained. There were only the left third and fifth metacarpals remaining from the hand bones. The manubrium and body of the sternum were complete and there were eleven ribs from the left and twelve from the right present.

The pelvis consisted of the right ilium and ischium and part of the left ilium and fragments of the sacrum.

Both femurs were complete and the left patella was present. The right tibia was complete but the left tibia was broken mid-shaft. The proximal end was missing from the left fibula and the distal end was missing from the right fibula. The tarsal bones consisted of the left calcaneum, left and right talus and first cuneiform, left navicular and second cuneiform. All the metatarsals except for the left fourth and fifth metatarsals were present.

Dentition

The dentition present was as follows.

16 15 14 13 12 11	21 22 23 24 25 26 27 28
48 47 46 45 44 CA	37

AD and the N-S alignment would suggest that this may be a pre-Christian burial. The finding of grave-goods with an inhumation burial is relatively rare and discs of this type in association with a burial is as yet without parallel.

Hopefully at some date in the future a C14 date may add to our knowledge of this hard-working lady who has emerged from Sligo's past. Until then we must be satisfied with an insight into a peculiar burial rite that tells us much about the love and respect that went into her interment, not just in the creation of her tomb, but in the loving crafting of the stone discs and their careful placing around her head in such a decorative manner.

Anomalies:

There was slight crowding in the maxilla with the left canine slightly in front of the premolars. The right first premolar was rotated 45o distally. The lower right third molar had not developed but this is a very common anomaly.

Attrition:

There was a moderate wear on the incisors and slight wear on the premolars. There was a moderate degree of attrition on the molars.

Calculus:

Deposits were not heavy. There were slight deposits on the labial surfaces of the incisors and moderate deposits on the canine.

Enamel Hypoplasia:

Lines of hypoplasia were noted on the incisors and canines and some of the premolars and molars. The episodes occurred between the ages of 2-3 years, 3-4 years and 4--5 years.

Skeletal Pathology

There was a small area of periostitis on the dorsal surface of a rib near the anterior end. The new bone formation appeared to be in the early stages and it was probably caused by a chronic lung infection such as pneumonia.

One of the cervical vertebrae appeared to be congenitally absent. The first thoracic had some features of a cervical vertebrae in that there was a small transverse foramen on the left side only.

There was some arthritis of the posterior joints of the vertebral column. The joints between C4/C5 and C5/C6 were mildly affected. There was also arthritis between the middle and also the lower thoracic vertebrae. Arthritis was severe between the second and third lumbar vertebrae. The fifth lumbar was wedge shaped with the thin end of the wedge to the front. This is the result of a crush fracture of the vertebral body caused by lifting heavy loads. The head of the first metatarsals were mildly arthritic.

Bones from another individual:

There were foot bones from another individual present in this burial. These consisted of the tarsals and metatarsals of a right foot as well as a left calcaneum, talus and navicular.

Summary and Conclusions

The remains are those of an adult female with an estimated stature of 157cm. The teeth were in quite good condition with no caries or periodontal disease but only slight calculus deposits. Molar attrition was moderate, suggesting a fairly coarse diet.

There was indirect evidence of acute infection or nutritional deficiencies in the form of enamel hypoplasia.

There was other direct evidence for infection in the form of periostitis on the dorsal surface of the ribs. This lesion was probably active at time of death and may have spread from a chronic lung infection such as pneumonia or pleurisy.

Pl. 1 - Side view of the reconstructed grave, Dernish Island, Co. Sligo. Length of scale 1 metre. Photo. Patricia Curran-Mulligan, August 1992.

Pl. 3 - Dernish Island, Co. Sligo. Seven of the eight roughly circular flat sandstone or grit stones, 6cm to 15cm in diameter which apparently were arranged around the skull in a ring of glory pattern, with the largest pair of stones at ear-level, smallest at jowls and others around the crown of the head. Photo. Patricia Curran-Mulligan, August 1992.

The vertebral column was affected by a possible crush fracture and a missing vertebrae. The resultant strain on the rest of the vertebral column may have given rise to osteoarthritis of the posterior joints or this may be indicative of a strenuous lifestyle. There was other evidence for osteoarthritis in the first metatarso-phalangeal joints. This joint takes most of the strain during walking.

THE ANIMAL REMAINS AT DERNISH ISLAND, CO. SLIGO

Dr. Finbar McCormick

The animal remains consisted in all of 51 fragments of bone, namely 39 cattle bones, 9 pig, 2 sheep/goat and 1 possible red deer bone. The minimum number of individuals of each species present were 2 cattle, 1 pig, 1 sheep/goat and 1 possible red deer. Preliminary examination showed that some of the bones exhibited signs of chopping and the material would not be out of place in a food midden context and may be part of an earlier midden cut through during the construction of the grave.

1. Dept. of Arts, Heritage, Gaeltacht and the Islands.
2. 32, Ard-RI, Drogheda, Co. Louth.
3. Dept. of Archaeology, The Queen's University, Belfast BT7 INN.

THE IRISH IN WAR AND PEACE, A.D. 400-800

The Sligo Field Club's 50th anniversary inaugural address, 17th February 1995

Etienne Rynne
Department of Archaeology, University College, Galway

A Dhaoine Uaisle!

Fifty years ago, almost to the day, give or take a fortnight, my predecessor as Professor of Archaeology in University College Galway, though at the time still attached to the National Museum of Ireland, gave a lecture in Sligo entitled "Life and Work in Ancient Ireland". The future Professor, Michael V. Duignan, at the time was probably the leading expert on the subject, and as a result of the success of his lecture interest in the archaeology of Sligo and in the past in general blossomed, and shortly afterwards a local field-club was formed. It gives me great pleasure, therefore, to have been flattered and honoured by your invitation to give an updated, fifty-years-on, lecture on the same general subject. In doing my best to oblige, I feel that I am not only acknowledging my predecessor's work but also that of everyone who, during those fifty years, has advanced our knowledge of life and work in ancient Ireland; I include, of course, all those past and present members of the Sligo Field Club who have seen the Club, and interest in Sligo's past, go from strength to strength during that half century. A detailed account of Professor Duignan's lecture was published in *The Sligo Independent*, for the 3rd of February 1945.

It is not my intention to try to repeat the late Professor Duignan's lecture, even with updated material, but rather to approach much of the same subject from a few slightly different aspects. The subject has grown so much since Professor Duignan's lecture, that, unlike him, I will not try to include the whole of the period from about 400 to 1200 A.D., but will concentrate on the first half of that period, from *c.* 400 to 800 A.D., *i.e.*, from approximately the coming of St. Patrick to the advent of the Vikings.

My aim is not so much to present anything radically new or controversial as to present, in outline and in a generally straight forward simple form, a view of the approach to life, secular and ecclesiastical, in war and in peace, of the Irish people during the first few centuries of the Christian era in Ireland, and also to make a few suggestions as to its *raison d'être*, that is, as to why the Irish approach at the time was very different to that elsewhere: an Irish answer to an Irish problem?

It must be understood that to examine the period archaeologically it is necessary to have at least a basic comprehension of the essentially non-archaeological, historical background. This essential background can be found here and there, in bits and pieces, in various books and learned journals, but, to the best of my knowledge, has not been made generally and easily available in any single article which would be readily available to the average reader. It is, therefore, hoped that this present paper may help to redress that position and that it may perhaps prove useful and interesting not only to all the members of the Sligo Field Club but also to members of other Irish archaeological and historical Societies.

* * *

There is one important factor, over-riding in its significance, where Ireland of the period is concerned, and that is that Ireland never came under Roman rule; nor indeed did Angle, Saxon, Jute, Frisian or any other migrating barbarian ever set colonising foot on our shores. This meant that between A.D. 400 and 800, the period between the introduction of Christianity to Ireland and the beginning of the Viking raids, Ireland was what we for better or worse recognise as culturally 'Celtic', pure unadulterated 'Celtic', the only part of the whole world, apart from the Isle of Man and some parts of Highland Scotland, to be able to make this claim. Despite this, however, we should not imagine that Ireland was completely isolated and cut off from the rest of Europe: trade and also other forms of contact with Romanised Britain and Gaul continued, for which there is considerable archaeological evidence.

And what does that imply? Well, it means that life in Ireland, in all its aspects, tended to be somewhat different from that elsewhere. The whole approach of the Celt to life was at odds with that of most of his somewhat Romanised neighbours across the Irish Sea and even more at odds with his contemporaries in the area we generally call "Continental Europe". Socially, politically, linguistically, artistically and economically, the Irish of this period were different from the rest. They did not live in towns, they did not have a centralised government, they did not use money, they did not converse in a Germanic or Latin tongue, and, indeed, even when they became Christian towards the end of the period, they remained very different from their fellow-Christians *thar lear*.

The social and political structure of Ireland at this time is somewhat complicated. The Irish, from one end of the island to the other, spoke the same language, had dress, ornaments and monuments fashioned in the same distinctively Irish style, were governed by the same laws, told the same stories and legends to one another (though perhaps with more emphasis on the Ulster Cycle in the northern half of the country, and on the Fenian Cycle in the southern half of the country), and in general lived in an island which was a cultural unit though with local variations here and there. But this did not correspond to a political entity, as we would nowadays expect from such circumstances.

The primary aggregate of society was the *tuath*, albeit a territorial rather than a political or administrative unit. The term can be roughly translated as the 'tribe' or 'tribal kingdom', but perhaps more accurately as a community. The *tuath*, of which there were at least about 150 of them in the whole country at any given time, consisted of a petty king or ruler, nobles and freemen. These formed what was known as the *fine*, a sort of extended family which could be further broken down into *derb-fine* or 'true-family', the most important being the royal *derb-fine* (i.e., the blood-relations as far as second cousin of the king or ruler of the *tuath*), and the *célí*, or 'clients' or 'vassals'. Each of these petty kings were rulers of a *tuath* of on average about 3,000 people, but had no real powers. They could neither make nor enforce laws, but merely administer them. In time of war, however, they were looked upon as the military leaders of the whole *tuath*. The right to sovereignty was not hereditary but by election - in theory at least - and was confined to members of the royal *derb-fine*. Irish kingship was sacral, and though it did not make the king divine it did give him some priestly functions and, in legend at least, sometimes certain immunities from the evils which might befall the less exalted.

The nobles were the land-owning families of the *tuath*, and also the warriors - druids, poets and some skilled craftsmen also belonged to this class, as did the Christian clergy when Christianity arrived. Ordinary freemen were the farmers and lower grades of craftsmen. At the bottom of the social scale were the unfree 'slaves' and 'bondsmen', though how many slaves (as we nowadays tend to imagine them) were present in early Irish society is open to question.

A number of *tuatha*, joined or allied together, made up a regional kingdom - these would be about the same size as the present ecclesiastical dioceses. A group of these local kingdoms made up an over-kingdom or provincial kingdom, and the Overking was the highest form of kingship known - it was not until the end of the 7th century [in the *Baile Chuind* (Vision of Conn of the Hundred Battles), a pseudo-prophetic list of the High-Kings of Ireland] that the Uí Néill of Tara claimed the High-Kingship of all Ireland; in reality, it was not until several hundred years later that such a claim could be enforced probably firstly with Brian Boru in 1002.

The various *tuatha*, local and provincial kings all had their numerous wars - if one may so term what was seldom more than a glorified battle or two. These kings had no standing army, but when occasion demanded could claim the allegiance of their people or, at least, of those who were high enough in the world to be concerned with such a matter as allegiance. Early Irish warfare was ritualistic and, like a game of chess, usually ended with the death of one or other of the kings involved. Violence may have been fairly commonplace, but was restricted in scope.

The reasons for battle were many, but one of the more usual ones was cattle-raiding. Indeed, one might almost say that cattle-raiding was one of the national sports! Wealth was reckoned by cattle - coinage was unknown in Ireland during this period, and it is often not realised that it was not until about the 16th century that the native Irish began to make any great use of coinage as currency. Cattle, however, were supreme in Ireland - the value of a good bondswoman, for instance, was reckoned as the equivalent of three milch cows. It is no wonder, therefore, that cattle-raiding should be the cause of many minor wars. As an aside to emphasise the importance of cattle to the ancient Irish, I might point out that *Táin*, an old Irish word for cattle, is still used in the saying *"Is fearr an tsláinte ná na táinte"*.

The archaeological evidence bears out the historical evidence for the absence of real warfare in Ireland during this period. The Irish weapons dating from this period are all rather inferior to anything found elsewhere. To begin with, only the sword, spear and javelin seem to have been used - not the battle-axe or the bow-and-arrow. Furthermore, the swords are not only very much shorter than swords elsewhere (by about a third or sometimes more) but they are stiffer, less flexible, and much less viable as really effective weapons. This is less true for the spearheads. For all practical purposes the swords are fundamentally Sub-Roman in type, while the spearheads owe more to Early Iron Age La Tène (or Celtic) prototypes; in both cases they were based on archaic models and were anachronisms. This conservative approach to weaponry, which shows no major development or improvement over these centuries, well illustrates the Irish approach and attitude to serious war in the more generally understood sense of the term. We should not judge these early Irish wars by modern standards. Only very rarely was territorial conquest or dethronement of rival dynasties involved: most consisted of punitive raids to collect unpaid tribute or, as mentioned earlier, were little more serious than ritual cattle-raids, generally associated with inauguration.

Despite the apparently poor-quality weapons, however, the Irish were sufficiently good fighters to make numerous raids on Britain after the fall of the Roman Empire - during the beginning of our period - and were even able to set up small colonies over there: the *Laighin, Déise* and *Uí Liatháin* setting up short-term kingdoms in Wales, and the north Antrim kingdom of Dál Riada conquering most of the Western Isles and setting up a kingdom on the adjacent mainland of Scotland, a kingdom which was later to greatly expand and become the Kingdom of Scotland.

There seems to be some evidence that Christianity had reached Ireland by about A.D. 400, and there is no doubt but that by 431 these communities had become large enough for Pope Celestine to send a bishop - Palladius - to rule them. St. Patrick followed, allegedly in 432, but quite probably as much as thirty years later; the dates from about 461 to 493 nowadays seem more generally acceptable for St. Patrick's mission in Ireland.

Despite the introduction of Christianity, and despite the pious statement that within one year of his arrival St. Patrick had converted the Irish to the Faith, there can be no doubt but that for well over 100 years after St. Patrick large areas of Ireland were still pagan, or Christian in name only. Indeed, some Irish church laws of 6th century date instruct the Christians how to behave towards their pagan neighbours, and in 560 King Diarmait Mac Cearbhaill, the most powerful king in Ireland at the time, celebrated the pagan feast of Tara - only to be cursed by St. Ruadhán and the clergy for so doing! In 561, as a further example, St. Columcille prayed to Christ as "My Druid" when beseeching help in the Battle of Culdreimhne, north of Sligo town. As Caoimhín Ó Danachair, the well-known folklife expert and historian has pointed out:

> *"To the ordinary people there was no conflict or contradiction in this; indeed a trait which characterised Irish Christianity since its first introduction in the fifth century was its sympathy with the native spirit and culture, and its easy tolerance of beliefs and customs which were not directly opposed to faith or morals."*

Paganism lasted on in many forms. The conversion of Ireland to Christianity owed little to the kings - they, after all, stood to loose their semi-divine position. The druids, likewise, would not have been overmuch in favour of their new rivals for the religious following of the masses. It is not surprising, therefore, to find clear traces of paganism lasting well into the centuries following the arrival of Christianity. According to Giraldus Cambrensis, writing in the very late 12th century, there were still people on the west coast of Ireland who had never heard of Christ, and as late as 1256 Pope Alexander IV had to send a letter to Patrick, Bishop of Raphoe, directing him "to use the sword of ecclesiastical censure against lay folk ... of his diocese who still worship idols".

A good example of this residual paganism is apparent in the inauguration of the kings - as late as the end of the twelfth century Giraldus Cambrensis was able to describe the very pagan rituals which even then were still associated with the ceremony of inaugurating a king, and some four centuries later Spenser was able to accurately describe such a ceremony taking place in Ireland. Aed Mac Néill, at the end of the 8th century, was the first king of Tara to be consecrated by the clergy - hence his name "Aedh, the annointed one" - but even this ecclesiastical ceremony was nothing more than a veneer, an optional *extra* to the pagan rites. One might further point out that until the 8th century Irish kings were not buried in Christian monasteries, though later they were buried in Armagh, Clonmacnoise, Clonard, Durrow, and other such important ecclesiastical establishments.

The *rí* or 'king' (Chieftains or tulers might be a more justified translation of rí at the time) presided over his people once a year at the *oenach*, the great annual festival of the *tuath*. The *oenach* was convened for political, social, legal and perhaps commercial purposes. At it the king would confirm the laws adopted by the *tuath*, and law-suits, marriages, games, trade, treaties and, no doubt, tribute or tax payment took place during the *oenach*. The games had a funerary origin and the whole *oenach* was a pagan carry-over into Christian times, essentially a sort of annual renewal of the *tuath*.

During the first half of our period the druids were still powerful, being looked upon as priest, prophet, astrologer, and teacher of the sons of nobles, but by the second half of our period the Church had won out and the druid's rôle had been reduced to that of sorcerer or witch-doctor. Their magic spells were still feared and their power was considered useful in war, but the clergy had taken over many of their functions, notably in regard to religion, teaching, and regulation of the calendar. Just like the druids, too, the clergy also were exempt from military service and from taxes.

Christianity came peacefully, without a military backing to enforce it upon the pagan populace. This meant that the early missionaries tried to fit into the existing system and, *inter alia*, tended to absorb or adapt many of the pagan customs into the new religion. The approach was one of change rather than destruction, which meant the christianisation of pagan monuments, sites and customs rather than their destruction and elimination. Pagan sanctuaries were often taken over and became christian centres, for instance *Ard Macha* (Armagh) itself, or Inishmurray, the fine early monastery sited within the massive circular enclosure of a pagan sanctuary on an island off the coast of Co. Sligo. The pagan Celts everywhere considered springs, sources of water, ponds and suchlike, to be sacred, and these were blessed and thus christianised while generally the pagan customs associated with them were retained - and are often still traditional today; and as a result there are probably more holy wells in Ireland today than anywhere else! The pagan Celts erected pillars and pillar-stones as sacred monuments, and many of these too seem to have been christianised by incising or carving a cross on them - it has even been suggested that the origin of Ireland's famous High Crosses owes much to these christianised pillar-stones. Sites associated with pagan rituals at certain times of the year also were christianised although still retaining many of their associated customs - one has only to think of the climbing of two of Ireland's sacred mountains, Croagh Patrick in Mayo, and Mount Brandon in Kerry, on Garland Sunday or *Domhnach Crom Dubh* (christianised dates for the pagan Festival of *Lughnasa*) not to mention the Garland Sunday festivities at St. Brigit's Well at Liscannor, Co. Clare, and Keash, Aughris and Tobernalt, Co. Sligo to appreciate this. Other pagan feast days have been christianised too, including, of course, *Imbolc*, *Bealtaine* and *Samhain* which in christian terms are St. Brigid's Day, May Day and Hallowe'en respectively. Indeed, the swastika-type St. Brigid's Cross is almost certainly a christianised pagan item associated with *Imbolc* and the beginning of Spring. *En passant* we might point out too the combination of several christianised pagan elements apparent at such sites as St. Brigid's Well at Ballinphull, Cliffoney, Co. Sligo. Marking that holy well is an early cross-inscribed pillar, bearing a swastika, concentric circles and saltire crosses (fig. 2). The well is still visited on her feastday. Many have argued that St. Brigid herself is really a christianised version of a pagan goddess - likewise for Saints Brendan, MacCreihe, Finbarr, Senan, and countless other early Irish saints, all of whom if not direct transformations of pagan gods have assumed their pagan attributes.

When Christianity came it would have come as an episcopal church. However, due to the Irish system of sovereignty and to the rural tribal structure of Irish society there were no fixed sites where diocesan sees could automatically be set up. The dioceses which St. Patrick arranged corresponded more or less to the petty kingdoms, but because of the absence of towns and thus of centralised government this did not really work. By A.D. 500 there were many important monasteries in Britain, and many of the Irish converts to Christianity had studied there. It was soon realised that the monastic system, of an eremitical type ultimately derived from eastern Mediterranean areas such as Egypt and Syria, was more suitable to the peculiarities of the Irish social and political structure, and in or about 490 St. Éanna returned from Britain and is traditionally credited with having founded the first Irish monastery, on the Aran Islands, off the coast of Galway. St. Finian founded Clonard about 510, and soon monasteries were starting up everywhere; by the mid-6th century the monastic system was the eccesiastical system in Ireland.

Irish monasteries were completely self-supporting. They were not only centres of piety and sanctity but also, perhaps more importantly with their introduction of literacy, also centres of learning. They served not only the Irish but also numerous students from England - Bede, not outwardly pro-Irish in his comments about us, tells us that the English students were received kindly, given board and lodgings for nothing, and also supplied with books and a free education.

The monasteries quickly became more important than the dioceses, while the abbots (often elected in much the same manner as the local kings and also often associated with the local royal *derb fine*) became more important than the bishops who had very restricted powers and jurisdiction, though they were accorded primacy of honour in both canon and brehon law. By the mid-6th century, the Irish had taken over the church as a sort of local enterprise, closely associated with the secular life of the local *tuath*. The monastic *familia* had, in fact, become the ecclesiastical equivalent of the *tuath* tribal group, though the clergy shaved their heads and wore tunics to distinguish themselves from their pagan neighbours.

But what of the secular authorities? As they had for generations past, they continued to reside in raths, cashels, promontory forts, and crannogs. Side-by-side with the monastic schools of learning went the schools of native Irish poets and law-makers, some of which schools lasted even into the 17th century, long after the monastic schools had disappeared. One has only to think of the O'Davorens at Cahermacnaughten, Co. Clare, one of the best-known Law Schools in Late Medieval Ireland, sited in a stone cashel apparently of 15th or 16th century date. These native schools preserved the secular tales, laws, history and genealogies of their ancestors, even though it was not until about the 7th century that any of these began to be written down: learning was, until then, as amongst the pagan Celtic druids and *ollamhs*, a question of memory.

The rôle and rights of women in the Ireland of our period are interesting and are worthy of a whole study in themselves. However, suffice it to say that despite the fact that polygamy and concubinage was acceptable and practised, particularly among royalty, so was divorce, and women in ancient Ireland had far more power and rights than in many more recent societies.

And art? The kings had always been the great patrons of the arts and, indeed, continued to be, but when Christianity became widespread and the monasteries began to become important, the Church also became a patron of the arts, particularly during the second half of our period, from about 600 to 800 A.D. This coincided with the high-point of the Church in Ireland, when it not only flourished at home but was also engaged in missionary endeavours abroad, something which introduced new artistic motifs and techniques to fan the dying flames of a late Celtic art, a combination which gave us Ireland's 'Golden Age' exemplified by the Moylough Belt-Shrine, the Tara Brooch, the Ardagh Chalice, the Derrynaflan Hoard, the Books of Durrow and Kells, and the wonderfully carved High Crosses of Ireland.

One authority has put it well when stating that "we stress the fact that Ireland was relatively a prosperous and civilised country during this period, threatened by no external enemies or internal upheavals". The same authority has also pointed out that "golden ages are always likely to be terminated by barbarian invasions", adding that in Ireland's case, when the Viking raids began in 795 A.D., "she had lost the habit of struggle and, when presented by a challenge from outside, was unable to respond to it". And so we must bring to an end our brief and sketchy examination of Ireland in war and peace, between the introduction of Christianity and the advent of the Vikings, with the close of the finest and most glorious chapter in our history, our 'Golden Age'.

TO SUM UP:

Due to historical factors, we Irish have always been more than a little different from the rest of the world, ever since that rest had the misfortune to come under Roman rule. Our wars were perhaps more frequent but were certainly more fun, less destructive and less serious than those elsewhere, while our peace was not without its simple pleasures, always characterised by its own peculiarities, *e.g.*, cattle-raiding, deer-hunting, boar-hunting, horse-racing, hurling, *fidchell* (a form of chess), music on harps, flutes and bag-pipes, and story-telling. The approach of the Irish to life when judged by modern standards might seem somewhat semi-realistic, but is readily explained when we realise that Ireland of the time, between A.D. 400 and 800 - and, indeed, much later - was still Celtic, neither Roman nor Germanic, in outlook.

POSTSCRIPTUM

It should perhaps be pointed out that when this paper was delivered to the Sligo Field Club it was accompanied by many slides illustrating various aspects of the lecture. However, it seems now that the text reads better on its own without requiring such additions.

Acknowledgement:
I am indebted to Bernadette Broderick for typing the text of this lecture.

FURTHER READING

Those who wish to delve deeper and in more detail into the subjects discussed might find some of the following references useful, readable and interesting:

Ludwig Beiler, *Ireland, Harbinger of the Middle Ages*, Oxford 1963.

Francis John Byrne, *Irish Kings and High-Kings*, London 1973.

Liam de Paor, *Ireland and Early Europe*, Dublin 1997.

Liam de Paor, *St. Patrick's World*, Dublin 1993.

Myles Dillon (ed.), *Early Irish Society* (Thomas Davis Lectures), Dublin 1954.

Françoise Henry, *Irish Art in the Early Christian Period (to 800 AD)*, London 1965.

Kathleen Hughes, *The Church in Early Irish Society*, London 1966.

Kathleen Hughes and Ann Hamlin, *The Modern Traveller to the Early Irish Church*, London 1977.

Fergus Kelly, *A Guide to Early Irish Law*, Dublin 1988.

Fergus Kelly, *Early Irish Farming, A Study Based Mainly on the Law-texts of the 7th and 8th Centuries A.D.*, Dublin 1997.

A. T. Lucas, *Cattle in Ancient Ireland*, Kilkenny 1989.

Proinseas MacCana, *Celtic Mythology*, London 1970.

Gearóid Mac Niocaill, *Ireland before the Vikings* (Gill History of Ireland I), Dublin 1972.

Donnchadh Ó Corráin, *Ireland before the Normans* (Gill History of Ireland II), Dublin 1972.

Dáibhí Ó Cróinín, *Early Medieval Ireland, 400-1200*, London 1995.

Caoimhín Ó Danachair, "The Nine Irons", *Festchrift für Robert Wildhaber*, Basel 1973, pp. 471-476.

Etienne Rynne, "The Swastika at Ennis - Symbol of the Resurrection", *North Munster Antiquarian Journal*, 32 (1990), 3-18.

Etienne Rynne, "Dún Aengus and some similar Celtic Ceremonial Centres" in Agnes Bernelle, ed., *Decantations, a Tribute to Maurice Craig*, Dublin, 1992, pp 196-207.

Charles Thomas, *And Shall These Mute Stones Speak? Post-Roman Inscriptions in Western Wales*, Cardiff 1994.

Fig. 1 - The Cashel on Inishmurray, Co. Sligo, from the north. One of two north Sligo monuments indicating a pagan background.

Fig. 2 - St. Bridget's Well at Cliffoney, Co. Sligo. The association of a sacred well with St. Bridget and a swasticka, and visitation ot the site at *Imbolc*, the 1st of February, all indicate a lingering of pagan celtic traditions well into christian times.
W. F. Wakeman drawing after *JRSAI*, XV (1878-1882), 376.

OGAM STONES IN SLIGO AND THEIR CONTEXT

Catherine Swift
Dept. of History, NUI Maynooth

ABSTRACT: Fieldwork by two members of Sligo Field Club has led to the identification of two ogam stones at Corkagh Beg, the first so far identified with certainty in Co. Sligo. This paper discusses these new discoveries in the light of the ogam stones from north Connacht.

In the current national catalogue of Irish ogam stones (Macalister 1945) there are no ogam stones listed for County Sligo. In October 1976, however, Jack Flynn, the newly appointed Chief Agriculture Officer for Sligo and member of Sligo Field Club, learned from Micheal Noone of Beltra, Instructor in Agriculture, of the existence of a cross-marked pillar[1] on a ringfort on Seamus Gilligan's land at Corkagh Beg in the parish of Templeboy, some miles west of Ballisodare, Co. Sligo. Together they examined the stones and accepted the cross pillar as a genuine monument. Soon afterwards Flynn brought archaeologist and member of Sligo Field Club Martin A. Timoney to the site. Timoney remarked in his notebook entry for that site visit on 16th October 1976 that one of the long prostrate pillarstones had five notches on it, but ogam was not suggested, at least not in the notebook. The second stone did not even get a mention. Nagging doubts led to some return visits but it was not until 5th June 1983 that a small group of Sligo Field Club members, Timoney, Flynn, Des Smith, Aodhán O'Higgins and Brían Ó Súilleabháin, properly cleared the stones to a get a good look at them, to do rubbings and to photograph them. The sandstone pillarstone *seemed* to have ten letters, seven, two and one. Brían Ó Súilleabháin suggested that one word *seemed* to be the word ICNAS and, based on this, Aodhán O'Higgins argued that it might be a reference to the father of St Patrick's disciple, Brón mac Icne otherwise known as Bishop Brón of Kilaspugbrone. The second ogam stone at Corkagh Beg was again rejected at this stage as being dubious. Research by Timoney continued for some years, with encouragement including a site visit by Colm Lankford. Other possible Sligo ogam stones, Church Island in Lough Gill and an odd ogam-like addition to a cross-in-circle on a pillarstone at Kilturra, were re-considered. In May 2002, Pat O'Brien of Sligo Field Club drew attention to O'Rorke's citation of a nineteenth-century tradition that ogam characters were said to exist on the buried end of the pillarstone known as *Clogh an Easpuig* on the ecclesiastical site at Killeran, though O'Rorke gives Kilellin, Ballydawley, just north of Ballygawley village, Co. Sligo (O'Rorke II, 247).

Timoney told me of the Corkagh Beg stones in May 2002 after which I visited the stones in the company of Dr. Colmán Etchingham of NUI Maynooth and Timoney was kind enough to send me his records of the stones. In the following paper, the discussion of the Corkagh Beg and Church Island stones draws extensively on Timoney's accumulated research file including exchanges of letters with Siobhán de hÓir of the Royal Society of Antiquaries of Ireland and Professor Próinséas Ní Chatháin of University College, Dublin. My own contribution is to place these monuments within the context of other ogam stones, both the national corpus in general and more specifically those from north Connacht. A list of the north Connacht stones is given in the appendix.

THE OGAM ALPHABET

The Ogam alphabet was the invention of an Irishman at some point during the period of the Roman Empire. It was developed by somebody acquainted with the Latin alphabet and was designed to represent the sounds that were then current in Irish. Our earliest records of this alphabet are to be found on stones, generally 1m to 2m in length with Ogam letters being inscribed along the edges of the monuments. On linguistic criteria, these stones are dated to approximately the fifth to mid-seventh century A.D.

On the stones, the alphabet consisted of

nineteen letters as illustrated in figure 1. Laying the alphabet out in this fashion, makes it fairly clear that the original inventor of the Ogam alphabet produced 4 groups of 5 letters: one to five strokes to the right of the edge, one to five strokes to the left, one to five diagonal strokes crossing the edge and one to five strokes in the centre. It is important to stress, however, that it

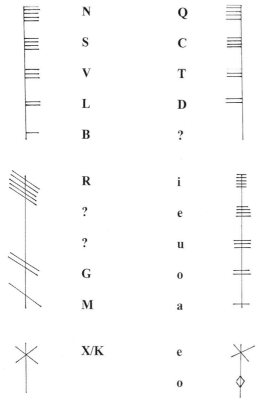

Fig. 1. The Ogam alphabet symbols

is not the *original* Ogam alphabet which we have on the stones but a modification of it. Two symbols do not appear to be used on the stones (McManus 1986, 25): one stroke to the left and four diagonal strokes crossing the edge.[2] Looking at the layout of the alphabet, it seems clear that these letters must once have existed for if the inventor was creating symbols for a mere 18 letters, he would surely not have had symbols of one, two and five diagonal strokes whilst skipping the 4-stroke symbol and, possibly, the 3-stroke figure. In addition, there are additional letters, known as *forfeda*, which do not fit into the scheme of 4 groups of 5, and these *forfeda* had been introduced before the creation of our earliest stones.[3] In the period of the stone carvings, the most common *forfeda* consisted of two diagonal strokes cutting the edge >< which can be either a consonant X (approximately 14 examples) or a vowel (11 examples, confined to Cork and Kerry) (McManus 1991, 79). It seems

logical, therefore, that there is some gap in time between the invention of the alphabet and its appearance on the stones.

The alphabet is used on the stones to carve personal names which invariably are in the genitive case, *i.e.*, belonging to person X. What exactly belonged to the individual is not always specified; there is one category of approximately twenty inscriptions which begin with the word ANM 'name belonging to X'. Another inscription, written in the Latin alphabet rather than Ogam but apparently belonging to the same period, begins LIE or 'stone belonging to X' (McManus 1991, 51). In the cases where no possession is specified, the two alternatives generally canvassed are burial marker or memorial of X or, conceivably, land or territory belonging to X (Plummer 1923).

After the stones ceased to be produced, medieval Irishmen continued to be interested in the Ogam alphabet and further modifications were introduced over time. Versions of the alphabet occur in ninth-century Irish manuscripts now in Berne and in Saint Gall, Switzerland, as well as in the twelfth-century *Book of Leinster* and in the later grammatical tracts *In Lebor Ogaim*, 'The Book of Ogam', and *Auraicept na nÉces*, 'The Scholar's Primer'. In these various manuscript sources, the alphabets all vary, with a number of different symbols being used and different meanings attached to the same symbols. Exactly why medieval Irishmen continued to modify the Ogam alphabet in this way is not absolutely clear but the existence of these many later medieval versions explains why modern scholarship is not consistent in its rendition of the alphabet. (Compare for example, the version of the alphabets published in the Dingle Archaeological Survey (Cuppage 1986, 248) with that published for the neighbouring barony of Iveragh (O'Sullivan & Sheehan 1996, 240)). From the point of view of archaeologists, however, the important thing to note is that these manuscript versions of ogam symbols all differ in certain key respects from the ogam alphabet found on the stones.

THE DATING OF OGAM STONES

Because stone is an inorganic substance, we cannot date it with any of the newly developed scientific dating techniques such as radiocarbon dating or dendrochronology. Thus the only dates which archaeology can provide for ogam stones is through excavating and dating the context in which they are found. The majority of ogam stones, however, were found in the nineteenth century long before the advent of scientific archaeology. Furthermore, when they were found, the vast bulk of the stones were discovered in secondary contexts, where they had been used as building stones and lintels, built into souterrains, ringforts, churches, outhouses and other structures. Of the stones which may have been in their original context when found, seven were found on a sandy knoll, known as Cill Mhic Uíleáin, on the south shore of Smerwick harbour. A sandstorm in the late eighteenth century exposed the stones, in addition to a further possible ogam fragment, a cross-inscribed stone, a number of graves and quantities of bone. The ogams appear to have been set out in a rough semi-circle on top of the mound and there were the ruins of several houses apparently between the mounds and the sea (Cuppage 1986, 250-251). Another stone, which commemorates a priest, was found at the elevated gap between Mount Brandon and Masatiompan, on the Dingle peninsula, apparently buried upright in peat (Macalister 1945, 140-141). Both of these discoveries appear to imply that the stones were erected by a society which had some knowledge of Christianity and this suggestion is strongly supported by the overall distribution of ogam stones. Fionnbarr Moore has shown that the largest category are the one hundred and thirty three stones which come from sixty-five ecclesiastical sites; these can be compared with the one hundred and thirty ogam stones built into forty-five souterrains, fourteen ogams from mounds or small enclosures, seven from stone rows and three from ringforts (Moore 1998, 23). There are also a number of ogam stones which are carved with crosses where the crosses appear contemporary with the carving of the inscription (Swift 2001).

Other stones appear to belong to an earlier burial ritual, most particularly the stone which is located at Island, in Co. Mayo, which currently stands on a low, apparently artificial mound. This may be an Iron Age burial mound or barrow of the type found at Carrowjames in Co. Mayo, Grannagh in Co. Galway, or Rathdooney Beg in Co. Sligo (Raftery 1994, 189; Mount 1998, 21). A recent excavation of a similar barrow on Kiltullagh hill on the Roscommon-Mayo border, has produced two centrally located inhumations with radiocarbon dates, to two standard deviations, from A.D. 410 to 675. No standing stone was found on the Kiltullagh barrow although the excavators concurred with the suggestion, made originally by H.T. Knox in 1913, that a near-by standing stone may once have been located on top of the barrow (Robinson *et al.* 2000). An earlier excavation, around the current location of the standing stone, found an extended inhumation, running east-west from the base of the stone with the head to the west (McCormick *et al*, 1995). This inhumation produced a carbon date, to two standard deviations, of A.D. 406-532.

The Kiltullagh evidence implies that Iron Age ring-barrows may have continued to be used for inhumations as late as the seventh century A.D. and that they were most probably still in use in the period following the adoption of Christianity. If the inhumation excavated by McCormick was intentionally located at the foot of the standing stone, this implies that burials marked by standing stones and located some 4 metres away from a ring barrow, could belong to the fifth century A.D.[4] Thus it is possible that the standing stone, near-by ring barrow and fifth-sixth century inhumations at Kiltullagh, provide a context for the barrow at Island, which has a standing stone, carved with an ogam inscription, currently lying on its surface.

The occurrence of Iron Age and Christian burials on the one site has been found in the excavations at Ballymacaward, in the parish of Kilbarron, in Co. Donegal. Here the primary monument was a cairn, possibly of Bronze Age date, which was subsequently augmented by a level layer of stones, charcoal and cremated bone. This extension appears to date to the second or first century B.C. Five slab-lined graves were then inserted into the monument in the fifth century A.D. whilst other inhumations, in unprotected graves, belonged to the seventh century A.D. (O'Brien 2000, 26-27). These seventh-century graves appear to be Christian for they lay orientated in an east-west direction with their heads to the west. No grave goods were found and at least one appears to have been buried in a shroud (Richards 1999, 174-176).

Sligo, too, has produced a cemetery containing burials of both Iron Age and Christian type, within a promontory fort at Knoxspark in Ballysadare parish. Here two cairns, between 3m and 5m diameter, contained cremation burials and were surrounded by burials in pits. These included some 51 extended inhumations, three crouched and three flexed burials. In most cases, the heads were orientated to the west or south-west. One double burial, of two adult males, apparently buried at the same time, appears to date to between the eighth and tenth centuries A.D. (Mount 1995, 78-79).

Overall, then, the archaeological evidence implies that ogam stones belong to the period of conversion when Christian burial rituals were being practised by some people in Ireland but where they had not been accepted by all (Swift

1997, 27-48). Excavation of cemeteries in the north-west suggest that Iron Age burial sites continued to be used by the Christian population in some instances and this period of overlap would seem to provide the most useful context in which to place the erection of ogam stones. More specific archaeological dating will only come about when an ogam stone is excavated in its original context. In its absence, the only method of dating left is to analyse the language found in the inscriptions. Irish is particularly well suited to this type of analysis in that it changes over time and these changes can be used to differentiate earlier versus later inscriptions.

Without going into excessive detail, the three basic linguistic divisions of the ogam corpus are entitled: pre-apocope, pre-syncope, and post-syncope (Fig. 2). Apocope is the term for the loss of the final syllable of words which is the first major development which we see on the stones. McManus dates its onset to the beginning of the sixth century although it takes some time to be accepted by all carvers. In general, however, pre-

Pre-apocope

COLOMAGNI

Pre-syncope

COLOMANN

Post-syncope

COLMAN

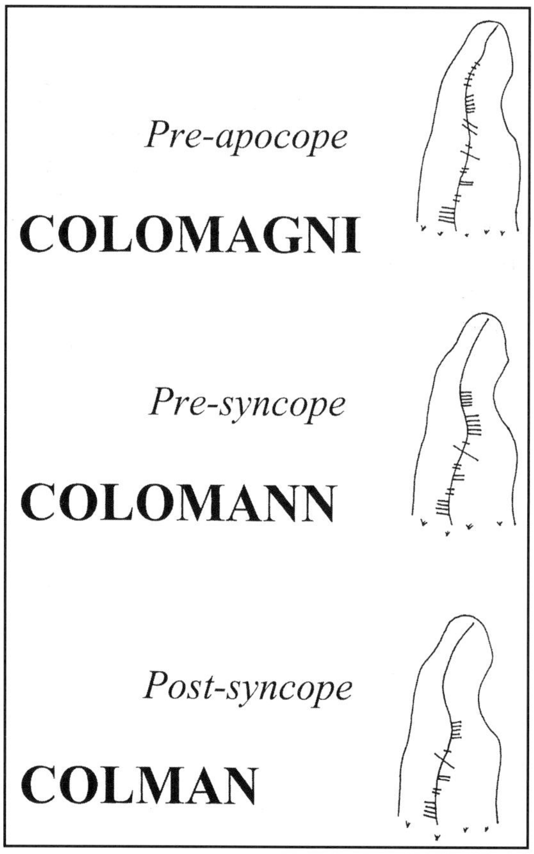

Fig. 2 - The Ogam linguistic sub-phases

apocope stones belong to the fifth century. The second big development is syncope which is the loss of a middle syllable in three-syllable words, a feature which begins around the middle of the sixth century and spreads during the second half of the sixth century. Inscriptions where there is no trace of that middle syllable are termed post-syncope and this is the type of Irish which is revealed in the earliest Irish documents of the seventh century. Thus, in summary, pre-apocope inscriptions tend to belong to the fifth century; pre-syncope inscriptions are likely to be sixth century and post-syncope inscriptions belong to the very late sixth century or early seventh century (McManus 1991, 92-7; Swift 1997, 47-69). This is an abbreviated version of a more complex process and there are complications. There is some evidence, for example, that the fifth-century style was seen as the convention which should always be used on the stones, even when the language had moved on and developed later forms. The dating of apocope and syncope involves juggling probabilities rather than precise facts and as a method, linguistic analysis cannot provide precise dates for specific stones. In the absence of archaeological data, however, this type of relative linguistic categorisation provides us with the best dating method currently available.

THE CORKAGH BEG OGAM STONES

The site of Corkagh Beg consists of an area of raised ground, possibly a raised ringfort, and a standing cross-pillar on which a Latin-style cross is carved on the western face, in the lower section of the pillar. Some fifty metres to the east are three prostrate stones which are currently embedded in the topsoil and two of these are inscribed with ogam inscriptions.

Stone 1 (figs. 3 - 6) is a rectangular stone, squared off at one end and tapering somewhat at the other. It is 1.93m in length, 0.43m wide at the squared off end and 0.32m at the other end. At the moment approximately 0.12m of the stone's depth is exposed but its current position is not original. The inscription is found on the western face, on the upper edge of the stone, beginning 0.65m from the narrower end.

Fig. 3. Corkagh Beg Ogam Stone No. 1, from the narrow end.
Photo: Martin A. Timoney

The first four letters of the inscription are very clear and reading up the stone, from narrow to wide end, they read as follows:

M (a long diagonal stroke running across the line of the edge)

A (a tear-drop shaped notch on the upper edge)

C (four strokes running down the western face)

I (four clear notches along the edge with a probable fifth which has been damaged by flaking stone).

Separated by a small gap from these letters are two strokes running down the western face, shortened at the lower end by the missing flake. If complete, this would be a D; if strokes were

Fig. 4 - Corkagh Beg Ogam Stone No. 1, from the broad end. Photo: Martin A. Timoney

missing, it could be a T, C or Q. The strokes are very worn and in 2002 we could only see two definite examples. This was also the view at the time the stone was raised in 1983, as suggested by photographs and rubbings in Timoney's research file. In Timoney's notebook of June 1983, however, he recorded a four-stroke letter C.

Fig. 5. The central part of the inscription on Corkagh Beg Ogam Stone No. 1. Photo: Martin A. Timoney

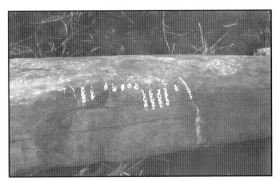

Fig. 6 - The central part of the inscription on Corkagh Beg Ogam Stone No. 1. Photo: Martin A. Timoney.

Timoney (pers. comm.) says that none of the people present in 1983 had any proper knowledge of ogam so contradictions between readings were inevitable; their next task after being certain that there was ogam at Corkagh Beg was to find someone who knew ogam and could read the inscription properly.

The section of the stone, from the letter M to the D/C was approximately 0.20 m. long. There was then a gap of approximately 0.35m followed by a single faint vowel notch (A) and two strokes running up from the edge, a putative L. Again these strokes were too shallow and worn to be positive about their identification. We saw nothing more in our visit of May 2002 and it appears that nothing more was visible at the time of the 1983 rubbing in the research file which amalgamated these two letters (AL) into a three-stroke letter V. Timoney's 1983 notebook, in contrast, records these letters as a single central stroke letter A, followed by a four-stroke letter S. The 1983 notebook reading also depicts a gap followed by a two diagonal stroke letter G and what they read as a single stroke to the left. Neither of these letters were seen by ourselves in 2002 nor in the 1983 rubbing. The single stroke to the left appears particularly doubtful as no example of this symbol is known on the stones (see above) and it seems more likely that, if this stroke exists, it is a remnant of a two, three, four or five stroke symbol to the left (D, T, C or Q). Finally, both the 1983 rubbing and Timoney's notebook records a further sequence of five vowel strokes (= I) at the top of the stone and a photograph was taken of chalk marks depicting this letter at the time.

We thus have three readings:

1983 notebook:	MACI C.... AS.....G.... I
1983 rubbing:	MACI D....V....I
2002 reading:	MACI D....AL...

It has to be said that the initial word MACI is quite clear and has been read as such by ourselves, by the earlier investigators and by Professor Próinséas Ní Chatháin of the

Department of Old Irish (who was shown unchalked photographs by Martin A. Timoney from 1983). The other strokes are all debatable and the rubbing of the stone from 1983 has not clarified matters. Because of the attractiveness of the possible association with Bishop Brón, it is worth noting that no reader of the stone has found clear evidence in favour of ICNAS. The 1983 notebook reading comes closest but not only does it show no sign of the N; its reading of both the C and the AS requires us to insert strokes which were not visible to others who have examined the stone.

STONE 2 (fig. 7 - 8), lying immediately to the east of stone 1, is approximately 1.90m in length. It is 0.30m wide at its northern end and some 0.28m at the southern end. The stone is not in an original position. A small piece, roughly 0.08m by 0.05m, is missing from the southern end. The only clear part of the inscription is found on the eastern edge, 0.60m from the southern end and approximately 1m from the north. (If the inscription follows the normal arrangement of ogam stones, it should be running from the bottom of the stone and counter-clockwise around the top as it faces the reader; the reading should therefore be from what is now the northern end.) It consists of seven clear strokes running down the eastern face; the exact length of these was difficult to determine owing to a pronounced horizontal crack, 1cm to 2cm, which cut through them. The Sligo Field Club felt these letters were dubious while in 2002, we read them as a possible two-stroke letter D, followed by a five stroke letter Q. We also thought we could detect a single possible vowel stroke with the resultant reading being A...DQ. Removing lichen from the rest of the face we came across other possible individual strokes along its length but nothing which was indisputably a letter.

The only dating evidence for either of these stones is the linguistic analysis of the word MACI on the first stone. This is the genitive case of the word for 'son', the word which later became Old Irish *maicc*. In its earliest possible form, the word was spelt MAQ(Q)I with a letter Q but during the early period of erection of ogam stones, the sound Q /k^w/ fell together with the sound C /k/ in Irish so that both symbols could be used to designate the one sound. This development takes place prior to the onset of apocope and is thought to belong to the later fifth century (Jackson 1953, 139-143; Wright & Jackson 1968, 299; McManus 1991, 77; Swift 1997, 54-55). This means that the Corkagh Beg stone must, therefore, post-date this development.

At first sight, the existence of the final I in MACI suggests that the Corkagh Beg ogam stone can be closely dated, belonging to the period after the falling together of Q and C and prior to the onset of apocope when the I would have been lost. Unfortunately this is not necessarily the case. This word for 'son' is the most common word in the entire ogam corpus and perhaps, because of this, carvers of ogam inscriptions often keep the older spelling even where the rest of the inscription shows that apocope has taken place in the spoken language (McManus 1991, 81-83). This practice had largely died out by the time of the post-syncope inscriptions of the seventh century when MACI had generally become MAC or MAQ.[5] On the other hand, if the final letter of the inscription is I as suggested by the 1983 notebook, the 1983 rubbing in the research file and the photographs taken in the 1980s, this would appear to imply that whatever the second name was, it too shows pre-apocope spelling. Overall, therefore, the

Fig. 7. Corkagh Beg Ogam Stone No. 2.   Photo Martin A. Timoney.

Fig. 8.   The inscription on Corkagh Beg Ogam Stone No. 2.
Photo: Martin A. Timoney.

Corkagh Beg MACI stone seems to belong to the later fifth century or the sixth century and is more likely to have been erected in the earlier part of that time-scale.

From its position on the stone, it appears that the MACI stands at the beginning of the inscription. This implies that in this case the word *'mac'* is not functioning here as the word for son but as the beginning of a personal name. There is a category of Irish personal names which are compounds: the first word being *mac* and the second being a divine name, the name of a tree or a word associated with trade. In these names, mac probably had the meaning of devotee or the like. Examples are names such as *Mac-Erce* 'devotee of the divinity Erc', *Mac-Cuilinn* 'devotee of the holly tree' or *Mac-Táil* 'devotee of the adze' (McManus 1991, 108-109). It seems probable that the Corkagh Beg inscription commemorates a name such as this.

OTHER NORTH CONNACHT OGAM STONES

The Corkagh Beg ogam stones belong to a small group of ogam stones which is isolated from the main bulk of ogam stones in the south-west of Ireland in the counties of Cork, Kerry and Waterford (Fig. 9). This north Connacht group are found in Mayo (nine possible examples of which two seem dubious), Leitrim (one example) and Roscommon (three examples), as well Sligo (two Corkagh Beg stones and a doubtful example from Church Island; see catalogue entry below). Of these, three have clear ecclesiastical associations while two other possible candidates also have ecclesiastical connections: Cloonmorris in Leitrim, found on a church site; Kilmannin, built into a church building and Kilgarvan, also found on a church site. One of the dubious Mayo examples, Dooghmakeon, is said to be carved along the edge of a standing stone bearing a large Maltese cross on the flat face. Having examined the stone, however, I could find no traces of the inscription and Macalister indicates that he was doubtful about it. The Church Island stone is built into the inside of the doorway of a ruined medieval church.

Four of these ogam stones have been found as isolated field monuments while a fifth, at Drummin in Co. Roscommon, is part of a two stone-row. Two, at Rathcroghan, were built into a dry-stone entranceway to the cave of Crúachan and a third, at Rusheens East, was found lying on a dwarf wall, surrounding a holy well. One, discussed already above, at Island in Bekan parish, now lies prostrate on what appears to be an Iron Age barrow.

There are two distinct sizes of ogam stones involved: nine are 2m or smaller whilst two others are 2.80m and 3.30m in height, respectively. It is probably significant that these larger stones are both found as isolated field monuments. They may represent re-used prehistoric standing stones or, perhaps, stones which had a different function from the smaller examples.

Judging by the inscriptions, the ogams of this north Connacht group were erected throughout the period these stone monuments were being produced. Five inscriptions are pre-apocope or probably fifth-century in date, including the Island stone on its barrow, the new stone from the medieval church at Kilgarvan, Rusheens East and the two inscriptions from the cave at Rathcroghan. A sixth, from Drummin in Co. Roscommon, looks to be late fifth century in that it has lost what would have been the final S (*CUNOVATOS > CUNOVATO)[6]; this is a development which occurs immediately prior to the onset of apocope (McManus 1991, 93, 176). The site of Tullaghaun has produced what looks to be a defective pre-apocope inscription; it now reads QASIGN[I] MAQ... Although there is no trace of the final I of QASIGNI today, there is a gap of the right size and it seems likely that this is also a pre-apocope inscription. These seven inscriptions of early type are concentrated in the south-eastern sub-group amongst the north Connacht stones, from the neighbouring baronies of Costello, Co. Mayo, and Castlereagh, Co. Roscommon. The exception is Kilgarvan, immediately to the east of Ballina, Co. Mayo.

The stone from Cloonmorris, in Leitrim may belong to the intermediate pre-syncope phase (approximately sixth century) for it still has the medial vowel U in QENUVEN. Careful study of the stone by Mac Neill at the time of its discovery, however, makes it clear that the edge of the stone had flaked away immediately below the N (Mac Neill 1909a, 134) so it is possible that the original inscription had more letters, indicating a pre-apocope origin. In favour of this suggestion is the fact that the initial element in the name QENU - correctly uses Q rather than the later C which replaced it. The modern Irish equivalent is *ceann* 'head' but it is known that it originally would have been spelt *qen- paralleling the P-Celtic *penn* in Welsh (McManus 1991, 121). On the other hand, the medial U reflects the gradual weakening of this sound prior to its loss in syncope (it would originally have been an A) and this might suggest a slightly later date (McManus 1991, 117-118).

The stone from Kilmannin has both LUGADDON and LUGUDEC with no final ending. Both words are post-apocope but both retain their medial vowel, implying a pre-syncope date. In fact, LUGADDON with its medial A never lost its medial vowel, becoming *Lugáed* in the nominative and *Lugedon* in the genitive, so this particular word is not useful for dating purposes (McManus 1991, 117). Given its association with the pre-syncope LUGUDEC, however, it seems likely that this inscription belongs to the sixth century.

A third stone from Aghaleague, with the word MAQ-ACTO has two examples of the post-apocope spelling MAQ. The associated word ACTO is likely to be a u-stem noun with a genitive ending in a long 'O'; in the case of words ending in a long 'O', the final 'O' was not lost in the process of apocope (McManus 1991, 116). On the whole, it seems likely that this stone is later sixth or early seventh century in date.

There are two other late stones (late sixth or early seventh-century), each enigmatic in their own way. Corrower has an inscription ..Q CERAN on the left hand side while the second part of the inscription, on the right-hand side reads AVI ATHECETAIMIN. This last is a phrase which has been translated tentatively by Patrick Sims-Williams as 'descendant of the original rent-payers'. (Sims-Williams 1992, 50) and he would date this inscription to the very end of the ogam period, possibly as late as A.D. 700. The second late stone is the famous stone from Breastagh, in the parish of Templemurry. This too has two inscriptions but only the second is comprehensible. It reads MAQ CORRBRI MAQ AMMLLO..TT.. Here, in addition to the shortened form MAQ, the medial vowel in CORRBRI has been dropped making this a clear example of a post-syncope inscription.

Of these later stones, only the Kilmannin inscription belongs to the south-eastern sub-group in east Mayo and Roscommon. The others come from three parishes in northern Mayo: Lackan, Templemurray and Attymass while the somewhat ambiguous stone at Cloonmorris forms an outlier in the parish of Mohill in south Leitrim. It is also worth noting that these later stones are the larger of these north Connacht stones, being 2m (Aghaleague), 2.80m high (Corrower) and 3.30m high (Breastagh) respectively. The exception here again is the Cloonmorris stone which, as discussed above, is not definitely a post-apocope inscription. It is possible that these later inscriptions were thus deliberately designed to have a more monumental function than the earlier stones; that they had less of an individual grave-marker and more of a territorial boundary function. This seems particularly plausible in the case of the Breastagh stone for Eoin Mac Neill has suggested that the final name is an earlier version of the personal name *Amlongaid*, the name used of the ruling dynasty of this area in the later seventh century, who gave their name to the barony of Tirawley (Mac Neill 1909, 332).

In terms of formulae used, six of the north Connacht inscriptions use the X MAQ[I] Y formula or 'belonging to X son of Y'. This is the most common formula on ogam stones, occurring on approximately sixty-one inscriptions in Macalister's corpus. As in the national corpus of ogam stones as a whole, this formula is used in inscriptions of all periods from the north Connacht area.

There are also two north Connacht examples of single names occurring on their own: DOTAGNI in Kilgarvan and CUNOVATO in Drummin. There are some 29 examples of these single-name inscriptions in the national corpus and their dating appears confined to the period before syncope. In other words, this fashion of single names without mentioning the father or other ancestors is a feature of the fifth and sixth-century stones. In terms of location, the two stones with this formula in north Connacht come from an early ecclesiastical site and from a two-stone row.

A third formula occurs at Island where the inscription reads X AVI Y with *avi* being the earlier form of the word *Uí* or descendant, a word which is used to describe the ruling dynasty (So, for example, you have the Uí Néill kings of Tara, descendants of Níall Noígiallach or Niall of the Nine Hostages). This is one of the rarer ogam formulae, occurring only twelve times in Macalister's corpus and, like the single names, it appears to belong to the earlier period of ogam-stone production (McManus 1991, 52, 79-80). The stone from the Island barrow, therefore, which reads CUNALEGI AVI QUNACANOS, commemorates a member of a local ruling dynasty in the fifth century.

There is no unambiguous example of a fourth formula involving the use of the word MUCOI, later *moccu*, a word which has often been translated as tribe or community (Mac Neill 1907; Charles-Edwards 2000, 96-100). It is possible, however, that the unfinished word MU.... on one of the stones from Rathcroghan and the odd MO...CQU from Kilmannin may have originally represented forms of this word.

Finally, one should note that there are two, possibly three, examples of the *Mac-* names in the north Connacht group, apart from the probable example at Corkagh Beg. Of the two clear examples, the first is Aghaleague where the initial name is MAQ-ACTO while the second, at

Breastagh, is MAQ-CORRBRI. The third and less clear-cut example is perhaps the most interesting in that it appears to be (MA)Q CERAN 'devotee of Cíarán' from the site of Corrower in Attymass. It seems probable that this is a reference to St Cíarán of Clonmacnoise for Bishop Tírechán, writing of early churches in north Connacht in the later seventh century A.D., makes it clear that the community of Clonmacnoise held land in south Sligo and surrounding areas at that period (Bieler 1979, 143). All three of these MAQ(I)-names, unlike the Corkagh Beg example, show the post-apocope spelling MAQ rather than the earlier MACI.

CONCLUSIONS

The Corkagh Beg stones represent an important addition to the national corpus of Irish ogams for up until now, only the extremely doubtful example of Church Island had been found in Sligo. (The other two possibilities, from Kilturra and Killeran are even less convincing.) Corkagh Beg's location, in the parish of Templeboy, north of Skreen church, represents an easterly extension of the small group of stones already known from the hinterland of the Moy estuary. The close proximity of the Corkagh Beg stones with a cross-carved pillar also coincides with the ecclesiastical associations of three north Connacht stones: from Kilgarvan near Ballina and (further south) from Cloonmorris and Kilmannin churches.

Examination of the Corkagh Beg stones produced only one readable word: MACI although there are traces of other letters to be seen. The position of MACI at the beginning of the inscription makes it likely that here this word is being used in the sense of devotee rather than son but in the absence of the rest of the inscription, we cannot be sure of what or of whom the dead man was a devotee. The spelling of the word implies that this stone was carved in the later fifth or sixth centuries A.D.

In terms of size, the Corkagh Beg stones are on the large size for north Connacht stones, being between 1.90m and 1.93m in height. This is similar to the stone at Tullaghaun in the parish of Annagh but contrasts with the seven of the north Connacht stones which are under 1.50m in height. The tallest of these north Connacht examples are Breastagh at 3.30m high and Corrower at 2.80m. It must be remembered of course, that the Corkagh Beg stones would originally have been standing upright and thus they would have appeared somewhat shorter. In the case of the MACI stone where the inscription begins some 0.6m from the base of the stone, the part of the stone standing above ground level may only have been 1.3m high. Given the extremely patchy evidence for stone no.2, we cannot tell how much of it was buried but the surviving letters are 1m from the base.

A date of late fifth or sixth century A.D. for at least one of the Corkagh Beg stones coincides with that of the majority of the north Connacht stones. Five of these are definitely pre-apocope or fifth-century in date; two more are probably pre-apocope and one is possibly so. These early stones tend to be found in the south-eastern sub-group of north Connacht stones, in east Mayo and Roscommon while a further possible example was located at Cloonmorris in Mohill. In addition, at least one pre-apocope stone is found near Ballina. This last stone, on the northern edge of the distribution of earlier, pre-apocope ogams from Connacht, is found on an ecclesiastical site which makes the association of the Corkagh Beg stones with a cross-carved pillar more significant. On the basis of our information to date, it is possible to speculate that Kilgarvan and Corkagh Beg may have been erected by Christian communities of the later fifth or sixth centuries A.D. Given the clear evidence that burial places such as Ballymacaward and Knoxspark continued in use from the prehistoric into the Christian period, however, this cannot be stated conclusively for it is possible that these sites only acquired Christian significance after the ogam stones were erected.

Of the early stones in the east Mayo and Roscommon group, the majority are found either in re-used contexts or as isolated field monuments but the stone from Island is found on what appears, from field survey, to be a prehistoric barrow. Its inscription makes it clear that it commemorated a man belonging to the local ruling dynasty. A second early inscription, from Drummin, appears on a two-stone row and this is a type of monument which is also found with inscriptions of early date at Rathglass in Carlow and Cotts, in Co. Wexford. Such two-stone rows may, therefore, also be Iron Age monuments on occasion although it is normally thought that stone rows are a Bronze Age phenomenon (Ó Nualláin 1988). Given these associations with monuments of prehistoric style, there is no strong evidence to associate the majority of the early east Mayo and Roscommon ogams with Christianity. On the other hand, the rather later inscription from Kilmannin, belonging to the transitional pre-syncope phase, was found built into a church while the possible pre-apocope stone from Cloonmorris, in south Leitrim, was found in a churchyard. This might

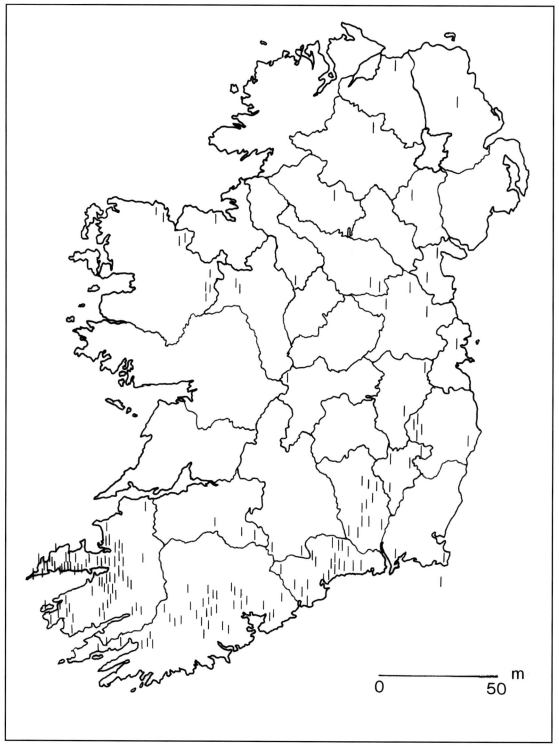

Fig. 9. Confirmed ogam sites in Ireland

imply that the custom of erecting ogam stones was introduced into the Castlereagh/Costello area when the prevailing burial mode was still a non-Christian one and it was only subsequently that ogam stones began to be erected on what became Christian sites. One could speculate, therefore, that within the broad time-frame of late fifth to sixth centuries, the Castlereagh/Costello stones are slightly earlier than the pre-apocope stones further north at Kilgarvan and Corkagh Beg.

As already mentioned, the latest stones from north Connacht appear to be taller than the average and may have had a different function from the earlier inscriptions. It is noteworthy that in at least two cases, at Corrower and Breastagh, there are difficulties in reading parts of the inscription and that they do not appear to use the stock formulae which are the norm in the national corpus as a whole. One of the stones, at

Breastagh, may have an early version of the name *Amlongaid*, the name of the ruling dynasty which gave its name to the barony of Tirawley and this would support the theory that, in this case, we are looking at a stone which functioned as a territorial marker rather than as a simple memorial of a burial.

It must be said that the foregoing analysis is based entirely on the north Connacht stones as they are currently known. The discovery of the Corkagh Beg stones, like Gerry Cribbin's recent discovery of the stone from Kilgarvan, makes it clear that there is every possibility that more ogam stones may be found in north Connacht in the future. Some may be found through development whilst others, as in these two cases, will be found through local fieldwork. The national corpus of ogam stones was created through the enthusiasm and interest of those who found the stones on their own land and contacted the authorities; it is still the case that this is the most likely method by which our knowledge of ogam stones and their function in early Irish society will grow. In addition, it is crucial that, when such discoveries are made, subsequent interpretations concentrate on the local context in which the stones are found. No national movement or cultural change happens in the same way and at the same time throughout the country. Dealing with archaeological material on a national level alone means that inevitably one is constructing generalisations about our archaeological past and it is necessary that we move beyond this to create local histories for every part of the country. It is in this context that I offer the foregoing paper as my contribution to the valuable work of the Sligo Field Club.

APPENDIX

Ogam Stones in Leitrim, Mayo, Roscommon and Sligo

Cloonmorris, parish of Mohill, Co. Leitrim; Le.037:004; Grid Ref. 20832.28526. Found marking a modern grave in front of a ruined medieval church. It is approximately 0.85m long. On the right-hand angle it reads (from the top down) as QENUVEN; on the left-hand at the bottom, there is a G, followed by a fracture and following T so that it now reads: G..T...............QENUVEN (Macalister 1945, No .2).

Island, Bekan parish, Co. Mayo; Ma.093:03801; Grid Ref. 14733.28070. Now lying on an barrow. It is approximately 1.58m long with an inscription running from bottom left around top and down right. It reads CUNALEGI AVI QUNACANOS (Macalister 1945, No. 3).

Kilmannin, Bekan, Co. Mayo; Ma.093:1045; Grid Ref. 14960.28062. Found built into the wall of an old church but now in the National Museum of Ireland. Macalister gives the townland as Kilmannia whereas it should be Kilmannin. It is approximately 1.20m long with an inscription on all four sides, consisting of two pairs, each running from bottom left, across top, and down the right hand side as they face the reader. The first pair reads LUGADDON MAQI LUGUDEC; the second inscription is less clear but has been read as DDISI MO...CQU S...EL (Macalister 1945, No.4; McManus 1991, 65).

Rusheens East, Kilmovee, Co. Mayo; Ma. 073:012; Grid Ref. 15567.29428. Found on wall surrounding a holy well and currently standing in a field, some hundreds of metres from the ruins of Kilmovee church. Macalister gives the townland as Rusheens East whereas it should be Rusheens West. It is approximately 1.20m high with inscription running up the left-hand side. It reads ALATTOS MAQI BR (Macalister 1945, No. 5).

Tullaghaun, Annagh, Co. Mayo; Ma.103:022; Grid Ref. 15402.27539. Found in a field. Macalister gives the townland as Tullaghaun whereas it should be Ballybeg. It stands some 1.95m with the inscription running up the left-hand side. It reads QASIGN[I] MAQ..; the final I of the first word being indicated only by a gap with none of the vowel strokes surviving (Macalister 1945, No. 6).

Corrower, Attymass, Co. Mayo; Ma.040:048; Grid Ref. 12946.31420. Found in a field. It stands some 2.80m high, inscribed on both angles of the north-west face, each running from bottom to top. (This type of arrangement, while not the normal one, is found elsewhere). On the left-hand side, it reads ....Q CERAN; on the right hand side, ..I AthECETAIMIN with the *th* being Macalister's interpretation of an anomalous symbol (Macalister 1945, No. 7).

Dooghmakeon, Kilgeever, Co. Mayo; Ma. 095:02302; Grid Ref. 07514.27845. A slab with Maltese cross found in the sandhills, some 1.30m in height. Macalister found it impossible to be certain that this was a real inscription; having examined the stone on two occasions, I would agree that it is a very dubious example (Macalister 1945, No. 8).

Aghaleague, Lackan, Co. Mayo; Ma.014:101; Grid Ref. 11323.33512. Found in a field. It stands 2m high and the inscription is very battered. Macalister read it as MAQ-ACTO MAQ GAR... (Macalister 1945, No. 9).

Breastagh, Templemurry, Co. Mayo; Ma.015:01801; Grid Ref. 11834.33380. Found prostrate in a field. It stands nearly 3.30m high with the inscription carved on two angles). The left-hand side inscription was read by Macalister as L[E]GG ....SD......LE\\\GESCAD with \\\ being the three diagonal stroke symbol discussed above. The right-hand inscription reads MAQ CORRBRI MAQ AMMLLO..TT, with the missing letter being a second possible example of the three diagonal stroke symbol (Macalister 1945, No. 10; McManus 1986, 22-23).

Kilgarvan, Kilgarvan parish, Mayo; Ma.040:031; Grid Ref. 13280.31611. This is a new discovery made by Gerry Cribbin in 2000 on the early ecclesiastical site of Kilgarvan. The stone is 1.40m in length with the inscription reading up the left-hand side and it reads DOTAGNI (Moore 2001).

Drummin, Kilcorkey parish, Roscommon; Ro.015:05102; Grid Ref. 17572.28727. Standing in a field. Two stones, some 1.50m apart, each standing approximately one metre tall. On one is an inscription reading CUNOVATO (Macalister 1945, No. 11).

Rathcroghan, parish of Ogulla, Roscommon; Ro.022:05830; Grid Ref. 17959.28312. Two inscriptions on lintel stones, acting as entrance porch to the natural rock-fissure known as the *Oweynagcat,* the Cave of Crúachan in Glenballythomas townland. The ends of both are hidden so dimensions can not be established. One inscription, arranged in two lines, each running bottom to top, reads VRAICCI MAQI MEDVVI; the second inscription, in a single line, reads QREGAS MU...... (Macalister 1945, Nos. 12, 13).

Church Island, parish of Calry, Co. Sligo; Sl.15:09601; Grid Ref. 17483.33393. This is recorded as two or three letters by Sir Samuel Ferguson in 1887 and in more detail by Tadhg Kilgannon in 1926 (Kilgannon 1926, 179). The stone in question is some 0.45m by 0.24m by 0.12m with eight vertical ogam-like characters inscribed across the flat of the stone rather than along the edge. There is no stem line. This arrangement of ogam characters is also found on later ogam stones such as Maumanorig on the Dingle peninsula (Cuppage 1986, 333) but it is relatively rare. The Church Island stone is built into the inner right side of an entrance door of the church. A cast was made of it in the nineteenth century by Col. W.G. Wood-Martin, the Sligo historian, and submitted to Sir R., *recte* Samuel, Fergusson, who pronounced it to be ogam characters. A group of six Sligo Field Club people, by their own admission none of them experts in ogam, who examined it on 28th August 2002 were not in the least convinced that it is ogam.

Corkagh Beg, parish of Templeboy, Co. Sligo; Sl.13:10802 & Sl.13:10803; Grid Ref. 15174.33482. Found in 1976 by Jack Flynn of Sligo Field Club but not accepted as ogam until June 1983; detailed above.

Footnotes:

1. The cross pillar is on the platform earthwork; while the two ogham stones lie to the east. There was a bullaun stone at the adjacent house to the north, but that has disappeared since the house was demolished before March 1984.

2. A third symbol, consisting of three diagonal strokes crossing the edge, occurs only on two stones and it may be being used of different sounds on each of them (McManus 1986, 19-23; Sims-Williams 1993, 146-7). The earlier of the two stones is no longer extant while the reading of the second is controversial (Macalister 1945, 289; McManus 1986, 22-3). It is for this reason, I have left the symbol of three diagonal strokes out of the discussion.

3. In the following discussion, only the stones found within Ireland are considered. A representation, thought to mean the letter 'p', may occur on the stone from Valencia Island and is also found on two stones from Wales (Sims-Williams 1992, 39). Other supplementary characters were identified by Macalister but these have been subsequently classified as doubtful (McManus 1991, 79).

4. The argument that the standing stone may originally have been located on the barrow rather than in association with the burial excavated by McCormick *et al* in 1994, appears based on a) Knox's suggestion and b) the discovery of fragments of sandstone in the central depression of the barrow. The standing stone is also of sandstone, a stone not local to the hilltop itself but found 3 km away. The excavators in 1994, some of whom also took part in the excavation published in 2000, did not find Knox's suggestion convincing (McCormick *et al.* 1995, 95).

5. The relevant stones are those with MACI (CIIC Nos. 76, 94, 121, 137, 187, 235, 267); MAC (CIIC Nos. 83, 90, 127, 256); MAQ (CIIC Nos. 7, 9, 10, 55, 112, 145, 219, 220, 233, 248, 364, 409, 506).

6. *indicates a form that is not attested but has been reconstructed by historical linguists.

BIBLIOGRAPHY

Bieler, Ludwig, 1979: *The Patrician Texts in the Book of Armagh*, Dublin.

Charles-Edwards, Thomas, 2000: *Early Christian Ireland*, Cambridge.

Cuppage, Judith, 1986: *Archaeological Survey of the Dingle Peninsula: Suirbhé Seandálaíochta Chorca Dhuibhne*, Ballyferriter.

Ferguson, Sir Samuel, 1887: *Ogham Inscriptions in Ireland, Wales and Scotland*, Edinburgh.

Jackson, Kenneth, 1974: *Language and History in Early Britain*, Edinburgh.

Kilgannon, Tadhg, 1926: *Sligo and its Surroundings*, Sligo.

Macalister, R.A.S., 1945: *Corpus Inscriptionum Insularum Celticarum*, Dublin.

Mac Neill, Eóin, 1907: "Mocu, Maccu", *Ériu*, 3, 42-49.

Mac Neill, Eóin, 1909: "Notes on the Distribution, Distory, Grammar and Import of the Irish Ogham Inscriptions", *Proceedings of the Royal Irish Academy*, 27C, 329-370.

Mac Neill, Eóin, 1909: "Ogham Inscription at Cloonmorris, County Leitrim", *Journal of the Royal Societies of Ireland*, 39, 132-136.

McCormick, Finbar, 1995: "A Pagan-Christian Transitional Burial at Kiltullagh", *Emania*, 13, 89-98.

McManus, Damien, 1986: "Ogam: Archaizing, Orthography and the Authenticity of the Manuscript Key to the Alphabet", *Ériu*, 37, 1-31.

McManus, Damien, 1991: *A Guide to Ogam*, Maynooth.

Moore, Fionnbarr, 1998: "Munster Ogham Stones: Siting, Context and Function" in *Early Medieval Munster: Archaeology, History and Society*, ed. by M.A. Monk & J. Sheehan, Cork, 23-32.

Moore, Fionnbarr, 2001: "Ogham Discovery in Mayo", *Archaeology Ireland*, 15.1, 33.

Mount, Charles, 1995: "Knoxspark" in *Excavations* 1994, ed. I. Bennett (1995), 78-79.

Mount, Charles, 1998: "Ritual, Landscape and Continuity in Prehistoric County Sligo", *Archaeology Ireland*, 12.3, 18-21.

Mount, Charles, 2002: "The Promontory Fort, Inhumation Cemetery and Sub-Rectangular Enclosure at Knoxspark, Co. Sligo" in Timoney, ed., 2002.

O'Brien, Elizabeth, 2000: "Ballymacaward" in *Excavations 1998*, ed., I. Bennett (2000), 26-27.

Ó Nualláin, Seán. 1988: "Stone Rows in the south of Ireland", Proceedings of the Royal Irish Academy, 88C, 179-256.

O'Rorke, Terrence, 1889: *The History of Sligo: Town and County*, 2 Vols. Dublin, James Duffy, Reprint, 1986, Sligo, Dodd's Antiquarian Books.

O'Sullivan, Anne & Sheehan, John, 1996: *The Iveragh Peninsula: an Archaeological Survey of south Kerry: Suirbhé Seandálaíochta Uibh Ráthaigh*, Cork.

Plummer, Charles, 1923: "On the Meaning of Ogam Stones", *Revue Celtique*, 40, 387-390.

Raftery, Barry, 1994: *Pagan Celtic Ireland: the Enigma of the Irish Iron Age*, London.

Richards, Julian, 1999: *Meet the Ancestors*, London.

Robinson, M.E. *et al.*, 2000: "Early Christian Inhumations on Kiltullagh Hill, Co. Roscommon", *Emania*, 18, 65-73.

Sims-Williams, Patrick, 1992: "The Additional Letters of the Ogam Alphabet", *Cambridge Medieval Celtic Studies*, 23, 29-75.

Swift, Catherine, 1997: *Ogam Stones and the Earliest Irish Christians*, Maynooth.

Swift, Catherine, 2001: "Irish Monumental Sculpture: the Dating Evidence Provided by Linguistic Forms" *in Pattern and Purpose in Insular Art*, ed. by M. Redknap et al., Oxford, 49-60.

Timoney, Martin A., ed., 2002: *A Celebration of Sligo*, Sligo.

Wright, R.P. & Jackson, Kenneth, 1968: "A Late Inscription from Wroxeter", *The Antiquaries Journal*, 48, 296-300.

Cashelore, Ballintogher, Co. Sligo. Photo: Dúchas - The Heritage Service.

Some Sligo Stones

a.

b.

d.

a. Stone with pre-historic art from Mrs. Chambers' School at Cloverhill, Co. Sligo, now in Sligo Museum
b. Early Christian slab from Keelty, Co. Sligo; recovered from the Dusseldorf area of Germany thanks to the dilligence of several Sligo Field Club members
c. Two matching sections of shaft of a major high cross exposed within the Church of Ireland church at Drumcliffe, Co. Sligo
d. "The Elinora Butler Countess of Desmond Stone", found at the Denney's Bacon Factory site, Quay St., Sligo.

CARROWNTEMPLE, CO. SLIGO: A REVIEW

Martin A. Timoney
Keash, Co. Sligo.

ABSTRACT: Some further information on diverse aspects of Carrowntemple, Co. Sligo, particularly some of the highly decorated and unusual Early Christian slabs are commented on. One of these slabs, No. 4, is the Logo of Sligo Field Club.

INTRODUCTION

The initial publication of the early monastery at Carrowntemple[1], south of Gurteen, and close to where Cos. Sligo, Roscommon and Mayo come together, was by Dr. Patrick F. Wallace[2] and Martin A. Timoney. The essentials of this site are as follows.

There are indications of concentric enclosures of 0.4 ha. (1 acre) and 6 ha. (15 acres). At the centre is the old graveyard with the remains of a now featureless plain medieval parish church[3], probably on the site of earlier wooden and stone churches. Two souterrains to the west would have served for storage and refuge.

Five sandstone Early Christian grave slabs were discovered in the late 1960s, perhaps initially by the late D. Leo Swan. Joseph Sweeney, N.T., of Gurteen showed them to Dr. Patrick F. Wallace in 1973 and by the end of 1977 ten had been discovered. Four more were discovered during a clean-up of the graveyard by Sligo County Council late in 1986. These fourteen slabs were found within the old graveyard, mainly to the south and east of the church[3]. They were published by Wallace and Timoney in the 1987 volume of essays (Rynne 1987b) to honour Helen M. Roe who described the find as "the most important find of the Early Christian period of the previous fifty years". County-wide field-work by the writer has shown that these slabs are much more elaborate than those of any other Co. Sligo site of the period with the exception of those on Inishmurray which are of a rich style of their own.

REMOVAL OF SLABS

The saga of the Carrowntemple slabs could take up several pages. Suffice it to say that in August or September 1984 five of the highly decorated slabs, Nos. 3, 4, 6, 8 and 10, were removed from the graveyard without state approval[4]. They were recovered by Wallace and Timoney in July 1986. John Armstrong in The Irish Times of 28th September 1986 announced the recovery. The story was widely covered by the Irish media at the time of the recovery, in 1988 when Sligo County Council took the matter to the courts and again in 1992 when the replica slabs (Figs. 1 and 4) were erected[5].

The five recovered slabs and the inscribed slab fragment are in the National Museum of Ireland in Dublin[6], where two, Nos. 3 and 10, are on display in The Treasury (Wallace 2000, 47). All but one of the remaining slabs were taken for safety reasons into care by Sligo County Council in December 1986. Four, Nos. 2, 5, 11 and 12, are at present on display in Sligo County Museum in Stephen St., Sligo[7].

Fig. 1 - The replica slabs erected at Carrowntemple by Sligo County Council in 1992. Photo Martin A. Timoney.

REPLICA SLABS

In Summer 1992 Sligo County Council erected replicas at Carrowntemple of twelve of the slabs (Figs. 1 and 4). The exceptions are No. 7, which was concealed on site in 1977, and No. 13, the fragment of an inscribed slab which was omitted as it was so incomplete. These were made by Cillian Rogers of Dromore West, Co. Sligo (Timoney 1992,10). Eleven of these are fixed against the reconstructed wall of the old graveyard. At the end of the reconstructed wall the double-sided No. 10 was set erect, as it originally would have been. The idea for this project came from the National Monuments Advisory Committee of Sligo County Council and the work was funded by The Heritage Council. The writer provided the text for the information plaque. This article derives from that text to which published material, more recent research and an explanation of the Sligo Field Club logo have been added.

COMPARABLES TO THE FRET ON NO. 8

Carrowntemple No. 8 (Fig. 2; Wallace and Timoney 1987, 52, No. 8, Illus. 2:12 and 2:13) is an almost square slab, 74cm by 73cm, and is 5cm thick. The framed square design, 43cm by 43cm, consists of a 3.5cm wide continuous band taking successive right-angled turns to form a symmetric fret or maze pattern. There is a plain 16.5cm by 12.5cm rectangle inside this pattern.

Two comparable pieces for this unusual slab have come to the writer's attention.

There is a basically similar fret design on a stone believed to have been a cross-base that was re-used as a font (Allen 1899, opp. p. 40, top; Bond 1908, 100, lower; Hughes 1920, figs. 15-17). This is now at Penmon Priory on Anglesey,

Fig. 2 - Carrowntemple No. 8, the symmetric fret or maze pattern.
Rubbing: Martin A. Timoney.

Wales, but was found in a stone-mason's yard in nearby Beaumaris in the 19th century. This stone is c. 68cm wide and 50cm high.

The fret frames two triquetra knots below one or two loose pieces of fret. The corners of the design were differently executed and the overall effect has an unfinished look about it. Despite its odd corners this design of a fret surrounding a central space is similar to the design of a continuous plain fret around the square on Carrowntemple No. 8. Could the Carrowntemple slab have had a painted design at the centre?

The second comparable fret is on the side of the base of a small, 34cm wide by 25cm high, steep-sided cross base from Ballynaguilkee Lower, Ballynamult, Co. Waterford (Harbison, 1992, Vol. 2, figs. 57 - 60; 1993, 6, fig. 1, end panel in left reconstruction[8]). Harbison (1993, 19) dates this cross-base to the mid-9th century. Unfortunately it is no longer to be seen at Ballinaguilkee Lower[9].

COMPARABLES TO THE SOCKET-STONE

Half of a cylindrical socket-stone or slab base was also found at Carrowntemple. This was presumably to hold erect the double-sided slab No. 10. In comparison Wallace and Timoney (1987, 58) cited other instances of socket-stones at Glendalough and Inish Cealtra. Marshall and Rourke (2000b, 157-158, fig. 120) illustrate a plinth stone for a cross pillar on Ardoileán, otherwise High Island, Co. Galway, and how it would have been used.

SHRINE OF THE FOUNDER SAINT

There has been considerable debate on the shrines of stone and metal from this period in recent decades (Thomas 1971, Chapter 5; 1983; Herity 1987; 1993a; 1993b; Harbison 1991, Chapters 11 and 12; Ryan 1989; Ó Floinn 1994; 2002, 191).

Stone slabs were used for Early Christian shrines, variously called slab-shrines, tomb-shrines or box-shrines, of different forms[10]. Some of the debate, which is what concerns us here, has centred on the use of decorated slabs being from such shrines.

Herity (1987) interpreted George Petrie's 1820 description (Petrie 1845, 425) of slabs at St. Fechin's Ardoileán, Co. Galway, as having formed a box-like tomb-shrine of the founding saint. However, the excavations on Ardoileán by Scally (Scally 1999; Marshall and Rourke 2000b, 102, 115-116) do not confirm Herity's interpretation of what was at Ardoileán.

Following from Ardoileán Herity (1993a, 1993b, 191 and fig. 23.4) makes the plausible suggestion that a combination of four of the Carrowntemple slabs, Nos. 2, 3, 4 and 8, could have been used to form a shrine of about the 7th century, with presumably Nos. 2 and 3 for the sides and Nos. 4 and 8 for the ends[11]. In support of this idea Herity points out that two of the slabs, Nos. 2 and 3 (Figs. 3 and 4), have circular designs similar to the roundels on metalwork house-shaped shrines.

Fig. 3 - Carrowntemple No. 8, the symmetric fret or maze pattern. Rubbing: Martin A. Timoney.

Some may seek to refute Herity's suggestion on the basis that the Carrowntemple slabs are not grooved for insertion into corner posts and that we do not have corner posts at Carrowntemple. Sufficient length exists below the designs on the slabs in question for them to form a stable box-shrine without use of corner posts; the slabs could simply have been inserted into the

Fig. 4 - Replica by Cillian Rogers of Carrowntemple No. 3, Triskele with knots. Photo: Martin A. Timoney.

ground[12]. Anker and Andersson (1970, Pl. 97 and 191) illustrate such a box made of four highly decorated stones of 8th century date from Buttle Änge, now in Gotlands Fornsal in Visby (Fig. 5). As each of the stones have arched tops it is difficult to see how the structure may have been roofed. Neither Herity nor I make suggestion as

Fig. 5 - The 8th century date box made of four highly decorated stones with arched tops from Buttle Änge, now in Gotlands Fornsal in Visby. After Andersson 1968.

to how the Carrowntemple structure may have been roofed. Perhaps these tomb-shrines were open on top. None of the Carrowntemple slabs seem suitable for use as a lid[13]. Perhaps we should consider if in fact there could have been two shrines as eight of the slabs have that distinctive rectangular format; there were two founding brothers whose names are not remembered (Wallace and Timoney 1987, 44, citing OSL).

Stone tomb-shrines of the A-roofed type are to be found at Temple Cronan in the Burren, Co. Clare, (Ó Floinn 1994, Pl. 8; Thomas 1971, Pl. VII), and at several sites in Co. Kerry, Beginish, Kilabuonia, Illaunloghan, Kilreelig, and Killoluaig, (Henry 1957, Pls. XXXIX-XL; Thomas 1971, Chapter 5). Dennehy (2001, 22) provides an excellent photograph of Killoluaig. The A-shaped Shrine of St. Manachan at Lemanaghan, Co. Offaly, (Ó Floinn 1994, Photo 13) is an early 12th century manifestation in metal of the A-shaped stone shrines; Thomas (1971, 165) suggests that it may be a replica of a late 7th or early 8th century wooden shrine.

Could it be that slabs Nos. 2 and 3 formed an A-roofed structure that once stood at Carrowntemple? If so should we be looking for triangular end pieces? Certainly suitable stone exists hereabouts for such a shape but it is possible that wooden ends were used[14]. As the slabs were found scattered about the old graveyard this arrangement and that of a rectangular format (see above) is purely speculative.

We do seem to have stone shrines where the slabs are decorated other than at Carrowntemple. Herity (1993b, 191) points to decorated slabs of square outline at St. Berrihert's, Tullylease, Co. Cork, and St. Caimín's, Inishcealtra, Co. Clare, which he suggests may have been parts of box-shrines. Herity (1993b, 191) also points to a stone roundel from Gallen, Co. Offaly, which he suggests may have been part of a tomb-shrine. Herity (1990, 215-221 and figs. 5 and 6) has broken up this very complex design. It has the angular turn of the interlace seen in the central roundel on fol. 192v of the Book of Durrow. This is directly comparable to the design on slab No. 3 at Carrowntemple (see below).

Stone corner-posts for shrines have been mentioned by Thomas (1971; 1983) and Herity (1993b, 191-193). No suitable pieces for stone corner posts[15] are to be seen at Carrowntemple. Might there not have been wooden posts?

Herity, Kelly and Mattenberger (1997, 118-120) include thirteen of the fourteen Carrowntemple slabs in their list of Early Christian cross slabs of the northwest of Ireland[16].

The writer has seen a broken slab at Maughold, Isle of Man, which has a similiar ear-like ridge.

Veelenturf (2001, 213-214), draws attention to the comparability of the interconnected spirals on No. 3 with similar compositions on several high crosses. However, his attributing an eschatological meaning, the doctrine of death, judgement, destiny, heaven and hell (2001, 212-217), requires, as he himself admits, considerable further study.

USE OF CARROWNTEMPLE DESIGNS

Several of the Carrowntemple designs have been used in recent years.

SLIGO FIELD CLUB LOGO

The Sligo Field Club logo (Fig. 6) is the design of Carrowntemple No. 4, "Double-band ellipses and circle" (Fig. 7; Wallace and Timoney 1987, 50, No. 4, Illus. 2:7 and 2:8). This rectangular sandstone slab measures 97cm by 70cm and is 6cm thick. The framed design is a cross, in saltire position, made up of two elliptical double bands intertwined at right-angles to one another and having a double band circle woven through the elliptical bands. This design is known as a Duplex or Solomon's Knot.

This logo was decided on, at the author's suggestion, by Sligo Field Club in the Autumn of 1991. The design of intertwined bands may be seen as representing the intertwined disciplines

Fig. 6 - The Sligo Field Club logo. Computer image by Maghnus O'Brien from rubbing by Martin A. Timoney of Carrowntemple No. 4.

of interest to Sligo Field Club members, archaeology, history, folklore, folklife, nature including natural history, botany, ornithology, geology, industrial, architectural and engineering history, fine arts, the quality of the environment and planning.

About 1992 Martina Gillen of The Cat and The Moon, Sligo, was asked by Sligo Field Club to make up the design in silver and this has been on sale since, as lapel pins and tie pins.

Fig. 7 - Carrowntemple No. 4, Double-band ellipses and circle.
Photo: Martin A. Timoney.

The logo is, as is appropriate, on the spine and as a ghost image on the back cover of this book and also is being used on a car-sticker to promote Sligo Field Club with the wording "Celebrate Sligo with Sligo Field Club" having two ideas.

THE CORRAN HERALD

The cover design of the Ballymote Heritage Group's The Corran Herald[17] is by Brenda Friel. She independently chose Carrowntemple No. 4 as the centre piece; some of the unusual boxed cross elements of Carrowntemple No. 9 and a bird from the Book of Kells are included.

EUROVISION 1988

The figured side of No. 10 (Fig. 8) was shown in the introduction to Eurovision 1988 (Timoney 1988).

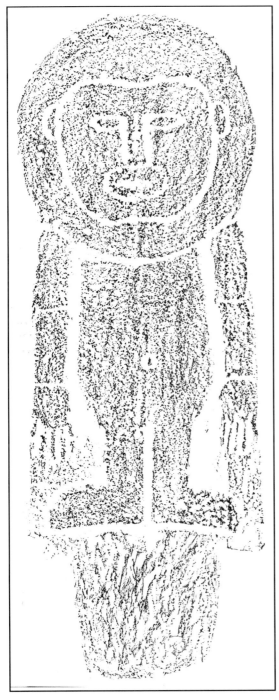

Fig. 8 - The figured side of Carrowntemple No. 10.
Rubbing: Martin A. Timoney.

ON PAPER[18]

It was used to great effect as the illustration on the front of the dust jacket of the 1987 volume of essays to honour Helen M. Roe (Rynne, ed. 1987b).

DATING

Rynne (1987a, 89) clearly tabulated his dating, given roughly in generations, of the major art objects of this period. Wallace and Timoney (1987) gave a date close to that of the Book of Durrow, c. 650-670, because of close comparison of the angular turn of the interlace on slab No. 2 with that in the central roundel on fol. 192v (e.g., Meehan, 1996, 64). Herity accepted this dating. Henderson, in a review rather than in an analysis (1989, 73), suggested a date of c. 800 because of her comparison of the design on slab No. 3 with Book of Kells fol. 33, top right terminal of the cross, both designs having triple spirals linked by interlaced knots. In a recent communication she referred to the constant reworking of the designs at this period. Kilbride-Jones (1987, 13) argues for a seventh, rather than an eighth, century date and refers to comparable quality English pieces such as hanging bowls, the Hitchen disk and the Willoughton print pattern.

The Moylough belt-shrine (Duignan 1951; O'Kelly 1964; Ryan 1989, 58-59; Ó Floinn 2002, 176, 183, 195) was found in 1943 in a bog only eight kilometres to the west of Carrowntemple. Medallions 1 and 2 on it (O'Kelly 1964, Pls. 11 and 17) and the square silver ornament of the buckle (O'Kelly, Pl. 19a) are out of the same mind-set that produced Carrowntemple slabs Nos. 2 and 3. Is it too much to suggest that these two slabs are from the same artistic workshop as the Moylough belt-shine? Could it be that the Moylough belt-shrine is from a workshop at Carrowntemple? I know of no other monastic site hereabouts that is a suitable candidate for the home of the Moylough belt-shrine[19]. The artwork of the rectangular silver panels on the Moylough belt-shrine, those with eight knops, curves and spirals, (O'Kelly 1964, Pls. 20a, 21 and 22; Ó Floinn 2002, 195) bears quite a strong resemblance, as Harbison (1993, 4-6) has pointed out, to the artwork on the front of the Cashel cross base[20] (Harbison 1993, Pls. Ib and II).

The technique of the design being formed by broad bands, as opposed to the groove, is found on six of the Carrowntemple slabs, Nos. 3, 4, 5, 6. 8 and 11. The feeling is that these slabs are broadly contemporary. Several of the design are closely related. No. 3 has a design that is a more in use in Christian contexts than the Pagan La Tène art on No. 2. The dating of comparables, the Book of Durrow, *c.* 650, and the Moylough belt-shrine of pre-700, is applicable to many of the Carrowntemple slabs. Harbison's dating of the Ballinaguilkee Lower cross base to around the mid-9th century would expand the time span for these.

The slab rough-out, No. 14, has two short lines at right angles, the initial corner of a design. This initial work indicates that the decoration was done on the site, not at the quarry. The quarry for these slabs has not been identified but geologically the stone is local, particularly in the Curlew Hills to the south.

REVIEW

Bourke in his review of the Helen Roe volume wondered (1987, 77) if the enigmatic ridges on No. 10 (Fig. 9) are zoomorphic. Re-examination does not confirm this.

The numbering error noted by Bourke (1987, 77) regarding the frame and base lines can be clarified and added to now that all of the slabs are out of the ground. Nos. 2, 3 and 4 have frame lines outside the main design. The design of No. 5 is in a slightly sunken rectangular panel and the design of No. 8 is rectangular and so in a sense both have 'frame lines'. Nos. 2, 3, 4, 6 and 8, and perhaps 5, have base lines.

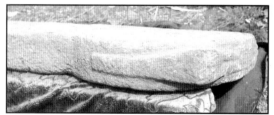

Fig. 9 - The ear-like ridges on the top of Carrowntemple No. 10. Photo: Martin A. Timoney.

CONCLUSION

Carrowntemple monastic site (Fig. 10) has artistic links rooted back in Pagan La Tène art but very clearly cognisant of major Early Christian art pieces, The Book of Durrow and the Moylough Belt-Shrine, and distant links to sculpture at Gallen, Co. Offaly, Ballinaguilkee Lower, Co. Waterford, and Penmon, Anglesey. It may even have had its own special decorated tomb-shrine(s) of the founder(s), though the shape of the tomb-shrine(s) is uncertain. Its art has been brought into use in recent years and for Sligo Field Club members, whose logo it is, it should be a place of special pride, perhaps a place of an annual pilgrimage-outing. Certainly Carrowntemple was a high status site in Early Christian times, and that is something that has not yet been fully appreciated.

Fig. 10 - Carrowntemple monastic site from south. Photo D. Leo Swan.Carrowntemple monastic site from south. Photo: D. Leo Swan.

ACKNOWLEDGEMENTS:

I thank Joe Sweeney, Dr. Patrick F. Wallace, Prof. Etienne Rynne, Siobhán de hÓir, Prof. Frances Lynch, Brendan Byrne, Frank Burke, Margaret McBrien, Mary B. Timoney, Peter McGrath, Ann Thompson, Evelyn Sweeney, Prof. Roger Stalley and Raghnall Ó Floinn for various pieces of information and help as regards Carrowntemple.

Footnotes:

1. Carrowntemple, pronounced somewhat as if Carro-'n-teampuill, is incorrectly given as Carrentemple on one signpost.

2. Dr. Patrick F. Wallace, now Director of the National Museum of Ireland, was then excavating an Early Bronze Age ring-cairn at Shroove, Monasteraden, Co. Sligo, that had been saved by Michael Garvey of Ballaghaderreen, Co. Roscommon. Sweeney's stringent efforts to interest a Dept. of Education official in them came to naught.

3. Besides the Early Christian slabs the only recorded finds from Carrowntemple are several pieces of metal slag, including a furnace base, a rounded ?pounding stone and a now-broken sandstone quern stone of which only about two-thirds survive in two parts; these are now in the National Museum of Ireland.

4. Four simple but large sandstone cross-slabs (Fig. 11) from the nearby graveyard at Knockmore, alias Mount Irvine, are also missing since about 1984. Despite much inquiry we have not found where they are now. Some serious errors crept in at the initial printing of the publication of these slabs but only some of these faulty copies were distributed (Timoney 1997). A corrected printing, most easily identifiable by the fact that the drawings of the slabs are numbered, was added within days to the undistributed copies; some copies have both printings.

5. *Irish Times* 23 Aug.1983; 27 Sept. 1986; 29 Sept. 1986; 30 Sept. 1986; Nov. 1986; 26 Feb. 1987; 11 Feb. 1989; 10 Nov. 1992. *Irish Independent* 29 Sept. 1986; 30 Sept. 1986; 16 Dec. 1986; 26 Feb. 1987. *Sligo Champion* 3 Oct. 1986; 6 March 1987. *Roscommon Herald* 6 March 1987. *Leitrim Observer* 7 March 1987.

6. Registration Numbers, Irish Antiquities Loan 1986: 2-6.

7. One by-product of the Carrowntemple saga was the active realisation by Sligo County Council that there could have been a major cultural loss to the county and that the county needs a much enlarged and better staffed museum than what we have at present in Stephen St., Sligo. A Museum for Sligo is badly needed; we should be concerned to keep our heritage in Sligo and not have it taken from these shores. Following the court case the writer provided a detailed submission to Brendan Byrne, then Sligo County Secretary, on ideas, sources of material, etc., and the security and continuity requirements for a County Sligo Museum. The idea of a museum may only now be bearing fruit. The author would again suggest that toys, the most obvious but yet generally unused way to get children of all ages into a museum, should be a major element of the local museum.

8. Professor Etienne Rynne has pointed out to me that the reconstruction drawing is incorrect. In the left drawing the end with the fret surrounding the square should be left of, not right of, the panel with the interlace. The two drawings should have been similarly aligned.

9. Moore (1999, 167, No. 1323) gives the inventory entry for this site. The earthen enclosure here has been seriously altered to say the least. Searches for the cross-base in 2001 and 2002, one with the aid of a local man, Peter McGrath, who believes that it was put against the field wall over forty years ago, failed to find the piece.

10. Herity (1993b, fig. 23:1) mapped about fifty sites for the tomb-shrines of the founder saint whose form assumes different aspects at different times. Presumably Teach Molaise is the tomb-shrine of the founder saint mapped for Inishmurray.

11. Slab No. 3 is shown upside down in fig. 23.4.

12. Thomas (1971, 155-156) doubts the presence of grooved corner-posts on Orkney and Shetland, at least at this early period, having anything to do with west coast Scottish Christianity or the Irish church.

13. Nos. 1, 7, 9, 10 and 14 are not suitable as parts of a tomb-shrine; No. 13 is too fragmentary to judge.

14. The display stand for the slabs in Sligo Museum is in the shape of the roof of a house and Slab No. 2 rests fittingly against one side.

15. There is one Sligo site which does have pillars with a slot in the top. Derryleghan (Sl.5:61), below Benwiskin in north Sligo, is a sub-circular enclosure with the base courses of a small building within its NE quadrant. The rectangular building is marked on the OS map as "Church in Ruins". It measures 5.45m by 3.55m internally, a ratio of 1:1.54 or close on 2:3. The walls are about 1.60m in width and the entrance is in the west end. There are scores of stones strewn around this enclosure, particularly around the building. The author deposited a very simple small cross slab found at this building and some metal slag from the NW side of the enclosure in the National Museum of Ireland.

Here the writer has discovered five pillars, the longest is 1.10m above ground, each of which has an L-shaped slot in the top. The better made of these slots are 12cm by 7cm by 5cm deep. The longer side of the L is sloped while that opposite is undercut. These pillars look as if they were to hold a sloping slab, no more than 6cm in thickness in place, the shape of the slots providing extra stability. These pillars are presumably the corner supports for the roof of a shrine or tomb-shrine. Today three pillars are at the internal corners of the foundations of the structure while the other two are outside the SE corner. It is not certain if any of these stones are in their original positions. One pillar is damaged which may explain the presence of a fifth pillar. Could these slots have held the sloping roof of an A-roofed shrine?

Derryleghan, like Carrowntemple, is situated in good land close to areas of bogland.

16. No. 13, the fragment with the inscription is omitted and not all of the Carrowntemple slabs have crosses.

17. *The Corran Herald,* Volume 29 (1996) to the current Volume 35 (2002-2003); some late ogham, or ogam, from the Book of Ballymote was used in the earlier cover design.

18. Patrick F. O'Donovan, archaeologist, has used the design of No. 3 on his headed paper.

19. Duignan (1951, 89) refers to a quatrain in a number of early texts which mention the girdle of St. MoBhí. Could this St. MoBhí be of Kilmovee, Co. Mayo, 16 km S of Moylough and 10 km SW of Carrowntemple? Could the Moylough Belt-Shrine be that of St. MoBhí? Whatever the date of the belt-shrine, 7th, 8th and 9th centuries have been suggested, the Saint whose belt it contains must be earlier than the shrine.

20. Ann Thompson of The Rock of Cashel Visitor Centre informs me that this Cashel cross base is now at the Dúchas Depot in Kilkenny.

REFERENCES

Allen, J. Romilly, 1899: "Early Christian Art in Wales", *Archaeologia Cambrensis,* 5th Series, Vol. 16, 1-69.

Andersson, Aron, 1968: *L'Art Scandinave*, Paris, Zodiaque La Nuit Des Temps.

Anker, Peter, and Andersson, Aron, 1970: *The Art of Scandinavia*, Vol. I, London, Paul Hamlyn.

Bond, Francis, 1908: *Fonts and Font Covers,* London.

Bourke, Cormac, 1987: Review of Rynne, ed., 1987, *Archaeology Ireland,* 1:2, 77-78.

Dennehy, Emer, 2001: "Children' Burial-Ground", *Archaeology Ireland,* 15:1, 20-23.

Duignan, Michael, 1951: "The Moylough (Co. Sligo) and Other Irish Belt-Reliquaries", J. Galway Arch. Hist. Soc., XXIV, 83-94.

Harbison, Peter, 1991: *Pilgrimage in Ireland, The Monuments and the People*, London, Barrie & Jenkins.

Harbison, Peter, 1992: *The High Crosses of Ireland, An Iconographical and Photographic Survey*, 3 Vols., Bonn, Rudolf Habelt.

Harbison, Peter, 1993: "A High Cross Base from The Rock of Cashel and a Historical Reconsideration of the 'Ahenny Group' of Crosses", *Proc. Roy. Irish Acad.,* 93C1, 1-20.

Henderson, Isabel, 1989: "Françoise Henry and Helen

Roe: Fifty-Five Years' Work on Irish Art and Archaeology", *Cambridge Medieval Celtic Studies*, No. 17, Summer 1989, 69-74.

Henry, Françoise, 1957: "Early Monasteries, Beehive Huts, and Dry-Stone Houses in the Neighbourhood of Caherciveen and Waterville, Co. Kerry", *Proc. Roy. Irish Acad.*, 58C3, 45-166, Pls. I-XLIII.

Herity, Michael, 1987: "The Ornamented Tomb of the Saint at Ardoileán, Co. Galway" in Ryan, ed., 1987, 141-143.

Herity, Michael, 1993a: "Les Premiers Ermitages et Monastères en Irlande, 400-700", *Cahiers de Civilisation Médiévale*, X-XII Siecles, 36:3, 219-261.

Herity, Michael, 1993b: "The Forms of the Tomb-Shrine of the Founder Saint in Ireland" in Spearman and Higgitt 1993, 188-195.

Herity, Michael, 1990: "Carpet Pages and *Chi-Rhos*: Some Depictions in Irish Early Christian Manuscripts and Stone Carvings", Celtica, 21, 208-222.

Herity, Michael, Kelly, Dorothy, and Mattenberger, Ursula, 1997: " List of Early Christian Cross Slabs in Seven North-Western Counties", *J. Roy. Soc. Antiq. Ireland*, 107, 80-124.

Hughes, H. Harold, 1920: "Early Christian Decorative Art in Anglesey", *Archaeologia Cambrensis*, 6th Series, XX, 1-30.

Kilbride-Jones, Howard E., 1987: "Giving Credit Where Credit is Due – A Review Article", *N. Munster Antiq. J.*, 29, 12-15.

Marshall, Jenny White, and Rourke, Grellan D., 2000: *High Island, An Irish Monastery in the Atlantic*, Dublin, Town House and Country House.

Meehan, Bernard, 1996: *The Book of Durrow, A Medieval Masterpiece of Trinity College Dublin*, Dublin, Town House.

Moore, Michael, 1999: *Archaeological Inventory of County Waterford*, Dublin, The Stationery Office.

O'Connor, Anne, and Clarke, D.V., 1983: *From The Stone Age to The 'Forty Five, Studies Presented to R.B.K. Stevenson*, Edinburgh, Donald.

Ó Floinn, Raghnall, 1994: *Irish Shrines & Reliquaries of the Middle Ages*, Dublin, Country House / National Museum of Ireland.

Ó Floinn, Raghnall, 2002: "Beginnings, Early Medieval Ireland, AD 500-850" in Wallace and Ó Floinn 2002, 171-212.

O'Kelly, Michael J., 1964: "The Belt-Shrine from Moylough, Co. Sligo", *J. Roy. Soc. Antiq. Ireland*, 94, 149-188, Pls. 8-32.

Petrie, George, 1845: *The Ecclesiastical Architecture of Ireland Anterior to the Norman Invasion*, Second Edition (1971 Reprint, Shannon, Irish University Press).

Ryan, Michael, ed., 1987: *Ireland and Insular Art*, A.D. 500-1200, Dublin, Royal Irish Academy.

Redknap, Mark, Edwards, nancy, Youngs, Susan, Lane, Alan, and Knight, Jeremy, 2001: *Pattern and Purpose in Insular Art*, Oxford, Oxbow.

Ryan, Michael, 1989: "Church Metalwork in the Eighth and Ninth Centuries" in Youngs 1989, 125-169.

Rynne, Etienne, 1987a: "The Date of the Ardagh Chalice" in Ryan 1987, 85-89.

Rynne, Etienne, ed., 1987b: *Figures From The Past, Studies on Figurative Art in Christian Ireland, in Honour of Helen M. Roe*, Dunlaoighre, Glendale Press for Royal Society of Antiquaries of Ireland.

Scally, Georgina, 1999: "The Early Monastery of High Island", *Archaeology Ireland*, 13:1, 24-28.

Spearman, R. Michael, and Higgitt, John, 1993: *The Age of Migrating Ideas, Early Medieval Art in Northern Britain and Ireland*, Edinburgh, National Museums of Scotland.

Thomas, Charles, 1983: "The Double Shrine 'A' from St. Ninian's Isle, Shetland" in O'Connor and Clarke 1983, 285-292.

Thomas, Charles, 1971: *The Early Christian Archaeology of North Britain*, London, Oxford University Press.

Timoney, Martin A., 1988: "A Carrowntemple Slab On Eurovision 1988", *The Corran Herald*, 15, 1988, 1-2.

Timoney, Martin A., 1992: "The Replica Grave Slabs At Carrowntemple, Co. Sligo", *Echoes Of Ballaghaderreen*, 1992, 10.

Timoney, Martin A., 1993: "Replica Slabs Erected in Carrowntemple, Co. Sligo", *Excavations* 1992, 1993, 64.

Timoney, Martin A., 1997: "Where are they now, the Knockmore Early Christian Slabs", *The Corran Herald*,. 30, 3-4.

Veelenturf, Kees, 2001: "Apocalyptic Elements in Irish High Cross Iconography?" in Redknap *et al.*, eds., 209-219.

Wallace, Patrick F., 2000: *A Guide to the National Museum of Ireland*, Dublin, Town House / National Museum of Ireland.

Wallace, Patrick F., and Ó Floinn, Raghnall, eds., 2002: *Treasures of the National Museum of Ireland, Irish Antiquities*, Dublin, Gill and Macmillan.

Wallace, Patrick F. and Timoney, Martin A., 1987: "Carrowntemple, Co. Sligo, and its Inscribed Slabs", in Rynne, ed., 1987, 43-61.

Youngs, Susan, ed., 1989: *'The Work of Angels', Masterpieces of Celtic Metalwork, 6th - 9th Centuries AD*, London, British Museum.

Three of the missing Knockmore slabs.

St. Feichin's, Ballisodare, Co. Sligo: Discoveries and Rediscoveries

Mary B. Timoney
Keash, Co. Sligo.

ABSTRACT: Some of the Romanesque and medieval carved architectural pieces, a Romanesque font and a late medieval graveslab found in 1995 in the graveyard at St. Feichin's Church, Kilboglashy, Ballisodare, Co. Sligo, are brought to notice as is some rediscovered historical information about the site. A suggested reconstruction of both the Romanesque east window of the church and its Medieval successor are given.

"At the spot where the River tumbles into the Strand on its South side, are the Ruins of a Curious old Abbey; and just by it the Ruins of the Parish Church. It is not easy to find anywhere a situation so well adapted for Religious Adoration, or Retirement; the natural Solitude of the place, the Dreary Glinn beneath, The murmuring of the Sea, the Grand Cataracts of the River, its Eternal Roaring; and the whole prospect around conspiring to raise in the mind a solemn Awe and Reverence."

(Henry 1739, 355).

INTRODUCTION

In 1885 Wakeman (1885, 43-54) gave a detailed description and drawings of St. Feichin's Church at Kilboglashy, Ballisodare, Co. Sligo. Since then there have been new discoveries and rediscoveries of several points of interest scattered in publications, some of them quite obscure. These are drawn together into a further record of this important site, a site long overdue for being taken into full state care.

LOCATION

Ballisodare Early Christian monastic site (O'Rorke 1878, 1-23)[1] is situated in Kilboglashy townland on west bank at the mouth of the Ballisodare River (See Moriarty 2002), the united waters of The Owenmore, The Owenbeg and The Unsion. It has been an important bridging point on the land route linking north Connacht and south Donegal for centuries and is not far west from Ballinadrehid, another famous bridging point. Ballinadrehid, known in earlier times as Droichead Mharta, was the scene of many battles. Warner (1976, 277, fig. 3) indicates a route from Donegal into Connacht passing through these places. Allegedly the first stone and mortar bridge in the country was built at Ballisodare in 1360 or 1361 by Cathal O'Connor (O'Rorke 1878, 2 & 11; Wood-Martin 1882, 229) and another bridge was finished here in 1586, this one by Donnell, alias Sir Donald O'Connor, alias O'Connor Sligo (O'Rorke 1878, 12).

FIELD BANKS

There are indications in the surrounding field systems of a circular enclosure centred on St. Feichin's Church. Much of the land adjacent to the graveyard had field banks, apparently associated with the Early Christian Monastery; regrettably the area to the south of the graveyard was bulldozed in the late 1980s[2]. The field directly to the west of the graveyard still has foundations of houses in it and to the north there is a ringfort.

GRAVEYARD

The oldest section of St. Feichin's graveyard is on the high ground surrounding the church (Grose 1791, Pl. 93). The second part is to the south and dates to 1883 or soon after (Rountree 1988, 114). The third part is to the east of both of these and dates to the earlier years of the 20th century.

HISTORY

St. Columbkille met the clerics of the neighbouring areas and a large number of people at an assembly at Ballisodare in 575 (Wood-Martin 1882, 142; O'Rorke 1878, 2), or 585 (O'Rorke 1878, 2) or 590 (Petrie 1845, 322) which suggests it was a place of importance at that early date. Its founder[3] was St. Feichin (Thunder 1888; Coyle 1915; Morris 1928; Gunning n.d.), a

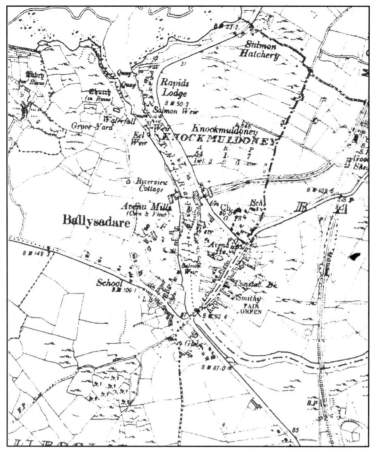

O.S. Map of Ballisadare, Co. Sligo, Ordnance Survey permit no. 6785

native of Billa, west of Collooney (O'Rorke 1878, 427). This founding was before 665 or 668 (Gwynn and Hadcock 1970, 160).

St. Feichin's Church was important enough for the Berminghams to plunder it in 1261 and on that occasion Cathal O'Hara and five of his men were slain within the church (O'Rorke 1878, 7-8). Soon after, Sefin Bermingham was slain by Donal O'Hara despite wearing for protection the Bell, or Bellcover, of St. Feichin which he had earlier stolen (O'Rorke 1878, 7-8; Wood-Martin 1882, 199).

The Early Iron Age and Early Christian promontory fort and cemetery at Knoxspark, one km to the southeast, continued to be used after St. Feichin founded his church in the 7th century (Mount 1994; 2002).

Three hundred metres to the west of the graveyard at the sea shore level are the remains of the Augustinian Canons Abbey[4] (Grose 1791, I, 51-52; O'Rorke 1878, 23-24 with fig.; O'Rorke 1889, ii, 333; Gwynn and Hadcock 1970, 153; Healy and Ryan 1982). Sadly it is surrounded by the waste of a long existing quarry (O'Rorke 1878, 24; Buckley 1992, 11) and a current concrete products works, though at O'Rorke's time (1878, 24) the build-up was "more than twenty feet deep". The inquisition taken in 1587 mentions "a cemetery in a state of ruin". Are we to assume that the graveyard around the St. Feichin's Church is what is being referred to here, and if so has it continued in use from when it began as a graveyard presumably in Early Christian times to the present? O'Rorke (1878, 16-19) gives an inventory of property based on this inquisition and the lease of 1588 to Bryan Fitzwilliams which mentions these lands and buildings. Later Fitzwilliams assigned it to Edward Crofton (Grose 1791, 51).

RESOURCES

Ballisodare's location was economically boosted by the waterpower of the falls (Bunn 1997, 154-155), the fish from the river and the sea (Went 1969; Moriarty 2002), and salt from the sea to the west of Ballisodare where there were salt pans of more recent date at Streamstown (Rountree 1988, 145). Just outside the northeast wall of the original graveyard there is a midden, mainly of oyster shells. Oyster shell was also to be seen on the graveyard surface after the clean up scheme in 1995.

Lead, zinc and silver were mined adjacent to the Augustinian Canons Abbey (McTernan 1998, 571-575) three hundred metres west of St. Feichin's Church. Here there are mine shafts of two phases. The smaller ones, known as The Monks' Tunnels, are of an earlier age than those of the 18th (Young 1776, 238; Ní Chinnéide, 1976, 65) and 19th (Kilroe 1885, 30) centuries and may be Medieval or even Early Christian in date. In a lease of 1588 to Bryan Fitzwilliams "all manners of mines and minerals" were included (O'Rourke 1878, 18). In the mid 18th century Charles O'Hara initiated mining at Abbeytown and Lugawarry (McTernan 1998, 571), although Wood-Martin (1892, 260) records that the lead mines proved unremunerative in 1778. In 1786 Sir Edward Crofton of Mote exhibited a rich lump of lead ore from the Ballisodare mines at the Royal Exchange in Dublin as "an effort to encourage mining in Ireland" (McTernan 1998, 571). Robert J. Kirwan, founder member and first Chairman of Sligo Antiquarian Society and Sligo Field Club, took a private interest for three

Fig. 1 - Antiquarian drawing of St. Feichin's by Bigari 1779, engraved 1791 by Cocking.

years in the Ballisodare Abbeytown mines with two partners about 1917. The antiquity of use of these resources has not been fully established.

The port of Ballisodare was capable c. 1791 of taking ships up to at least 60 tons (Ní Chinnéide, 1976, 65). Cooper (1794, 159) commented on the "badness of its harbour" in 1794. Manning (1847, 4) reported that Ballisodare was navigable at Spring tides up to the quay of Ballisodare for vessels of from 100 to 150 tons, drawing 7 to 11 ft. of water. Henry (1739, 355) wrote of Ballisodare Bay " I have heard that this opening afforded formerly an Harbour for large Ships But the Sand Banks continually agitated by the rapid Flux and Reflux of the Sea, into and from this Extended Strand, have so choaked it up that it is scarce safe for large Boats." In 1822 Ballysadare Bay is referred to as Ardnaglass Bay and Ballysadare is given as being on Ardnaglass Harbour (*Edinburgh Gazetteer*, 1822, Vol. 1, 237, 356). A quay is marked on the 1837 1st OS map as being on the east bank of the mouth of the river.

BUILDINGS

At least four buildings stood here (O'Rorke 1878, 22-23).
St. Feichin's Church (O'Rorke 1878, 20-22; Wakeman 1885, 43-54) stands in good condition at the highest point of the graveyard. It shows building work of more than one period, perhaps even of the earliest period (O'Rorke 1878, 4).
The much-mutilated walls of another building stand near the access lane on the south side of the graveyard. There are no datable features remaining. Possible foundations of a third building exist between these.

Outside the graveyard wall on the north side are the ruins of yet another building.

Neither of these three other buildings retain features that would date them or indicate their function. The makeup of the walls of the St. Feichin's Church shows much alteration and repair (O'Rorke 1878, 22; Wakeman 1885, 45).

Wakeman (1885, 43-54) gives a detailed description and drawings of St. Feichin's Church. Today the general appearance of the building is no worse than it was then but the carving details have suffered from weathering. The fill of the head of the doorway[5] is still intact. The 1943 Irish Tourist Authority Survey quoted below in Appendix 1 claims that these buildings were "vaulted with stone", evidence for which is not otherwise forthcoming.

ANTIQUARIAN DRAWINGS OF St. FEICHIN'S CHURCH

St. Feichin's Church has been recorded in at least four antiquarian drawings. The earliest known drawing of St. Feichin's (Fig. 1) is that by Angelo Maria Bigari[6] (National Library of Ireland, 2111 TX(2) 46), probably on 28th. June 1779 (see also Harbison 2002, 18,36,71-75). This was engraved in 1791 by Thomas Cocking[7] (Grose 1791, I, Pl. 93; 51-52; McTernan 1995, 108). James Saunders painted St. Feichin's, possibly on 1st May 1793. That painting was drawn by J.C., "J.C. Delin", probably Joseph Cooper,[8] (Cooper 1794, Pl. opp. 159) and engraved by Clayton in 1794. Harbison 2002, 18,36,71-75)

St. Feichin's was painted by J.S. Cooper, after Angelo Bigary, in April 1794 (National Library, 2122 TX (2) 46; Harbison 2000, 281).

On 24th October, 1878, William Frederick Wakeman drew St. Feichin's. The original is in the Cooper Drawings in Sligo County Library Local Studies Archive, 450(A)1, and it is reproduced in the Sligo Co. Co. Annual Report 1994, page 12.

RECENT ARCHAEOLOGICAL DISCOVERIES

During 1995 and 1996 a Foras Áiseanna Saothair (FÁS) funded graveyard clean up scheme sponsored by Ballisodare Community Council several architectural pieces, a Romanesque font and a medieval grave slab were revealed at different locations within the graveyard. Not all these architectural pieces are explainable within the context of the surviving buildings. Some of those that are, are now described and hopefully put in their proper context.

THE WINDOW HOOD FRAGMENT

In March 1995 the right end portion of a sandstone Romanesque window hood (Fig. 2) was found being used as a gravemarker in the south extension of the graveyard. It measures 42cm long, 38cm wide at the top and 27cm wide at the base and is 17cm in depth. The bottom end of it is finished in two planes. The radius of the curvature is about 39cm. Six units of nail head design (Leask 1966, Fig. 75) are carved between two grooves along the edge of it. There is a coiled scroll-ending to the front of it. This piece has been deposited in the National Museum of Ireland (NMI IA registration pending. The file number for the Ballisodare finds is IA/95/2000).

THE VOUSOIR

The sandstone vousoir measures 77cm by 34cm and 14cm to 23cm in thickness. The radius of the inner curvature is about 33.5cm. It would have served best positioned just above the springing. It was found south of the church and is now within the church.

THE ROUND WINDOW HEAD

The sandstone window head measures 61cm by 37cm and 18cm to 26cm in thickness. It was the top stone of a single-light opening 21cm in width. It was found southeast of the church in the southern extension of the graveyard near the late 19th century Clarence vault and is now within the church.

THE STONE HEAD

A sandstone corbel head (Fig. 3) was discovered lying on the ground surface to the west of St. Feichin's Church in February 1995. It is in good condition and is less weathered than the heads around the doorway of the St. Feichin's Church. It measures 32.5cm in depth and approximately 7cm in height. It widens from 4cm behind the head to 6cm at the back. There are indications of a crown or a head-dress on it. The left side of the head is chipped and is badly weathered. The eyes are positioned more than half-way down the face with the left eye lower than the right. The eyes slant downwards. The mouth is down-turned. The nose has been chipped. There is indication of a right ear but the left side is more weathered and no trace of an ear survives here. The head has been deposited in the National Museum of Ireland (NMI IA registration pending).

THE BAPTISMAL FONT

Half of a hemispherical sandstone baptismal font (Fig. 4) was discovered close to the south

Fig. 2 - The right end portion of a sandstone Romanesque window hood, Ballisodare, Co. Sligo. Photo Mary B. Timoney

Fig. 3 - A sandstone corbel head, Ballisodare, Co. Sligo. Photo Mary B. Timoney

Fig.4 - Half of a hemispherical sandstone baptismal font, Ballisodare, Co. Sligo. Photo Mary B. Timoney

wall of the St. Feichin's Church in February 1995. When complete it would have measured 60cm in diameter and 22cm high. The cylindrical hole, 11cm in diameter, was not cut cleanly through the base. The rim of 4cm stands vertically around a gently sloping basin which has a maximum depth of 10cm and a diameter of 52cm. There is a cushion ring 5cm thick along the base.

The decoration on the underside of the font is 53cm long. It consists of a series of ten slightly differing leaves rising from the cushion ring. The leaves are 8 to 9cm tall and stand no more than 5mm above the curved surface of the font. There is only one pair of nearly symmetrical leaves among the ten leaves depicted. The font has been deposited in the National Museum of Ireland (NMI IA registration pending).

THE MEDIEVAL WINDOW SILL

A limestone windowsill (Fig. 5) was noted in 1995 outside the east window of St. Feichin's Church. It is now on the ground inside the doorway of St. Feichin's Church. It measures 98cm by 23cm by 17cm high. Two sloping opening bases, each 16.5cm wide, indicate that it was from a two-light window. Two grooves at the ends of the stone still contain iron stability straps. The stone is interpreted here as the base-stone of the medieval two-light east window of St. Feichin's Church that was noted by O'Rorke (1878, 21, footnote) as being then in situ.

Fig. 5 - A limestone windowsill, Ballisodare, Co. Sligo. Photo Mary B. Timoney

THE MEDIEVAL WINDOW HEAD

A left medieval window head (Fig. 6) is now used as a coping stone on the roadside wall. It measures 46cm by 30cm by 17cm thick. There is an off-centre cusped ogee headed opening with poorly proportioned trefoil in each of the spandrels.

THE MEDIEVAL GRAVESLAB

A decorated Medieval graveslab (Fig. 7) was discovered south-east of St. Feichin's Church and has been taken into care by Sligo County Council in its Sligo Jail depot. The trapezoidal limestone slab now measures 1.88m long, the

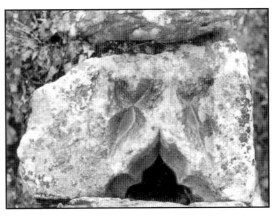

Fig. 6 - A left medieval window head as a coping stone on the roadside wall, Ballisodare, Co. Sligo. Photo Mary B. Timoney

end portion having been broken off in antiquity. It tapers from 41cm wide at the top to 35cm at the bottom and is 14cm thick. The sides of the stone are dressed. There are traces of a moulding along the top edges of the sides of the stone.

It is decorated with a pair of rampant animals, a medieval sword of Hiberno-Scottish type and foliage. The facing animals are possibly a lion and a dragon. The tail of the dragon extends to form three units of foliage surrounded by tendrils. The lion's tail forms a single unit of foliage. The foliage has double incised lines along the edges.

The sword has a wheel pommel with a tang, downward sloping crossguard or quillons and a short langet.

Regrettably there is no inscription on the stone[9], and late medieval and post-medieval records for Co. Sligo are notoriously scarce.

DISCUSSION

THE FONT

On August 5th 1879 W.F. Wakeman drew a font at Aghanagh, Co. Sligo for Colonel Edward Cooper (Wakeman 1883, 120) Sligo County Library Local Studies Archive, 450(A)1. It was a

A CELEBRATION OF SLIGO

Fig. 7 - A decorated Medieval graveslab, Ballisodare, Co. Sligo.
Photo Mary B. Timoney

badly damaged plain hemispherical font with a central hole. Wakeman gives the diameter to be 2 feet 6 inches. It was not to be seen in recent times[10]. Though there is no evidence in Wakeman's drawing to date this font it could well be Romanesque, given the presence of the Romanesque three-order doorway in the north wall of Aghanagh church[11]. The geographically nearest example of a Romanesque font is at Ballintubber Abbey, Co. Mayo[12] where the circular font has four moulded supporters.

Pike, in her all-Ireland work on ninety-two medieval fonts and stoups, records only two round fonts. The first (Pike 1989, 33) is from Errigal Keerogue amd is now at the nearby St. Mathew's Church of Ireland, Ballynasaggart, Co. Tyrone. It has fleur-de-lis decoration. The other (Pike 1989, 33-34) is said to be from St. Cronan's Abbey and is now at St. Columbkille's R.C. church, Swords, Co. Dublin. It has continuous vine and grape decoration. Both of these appear, from the miniscule drawings, to be Romanesque. Leaves of the type on the font do not appear on any of the visible pieces of Romanesque carvings in Ballisodare or elsewhere in Co. Sligo. Dr. Elizabeth FitzPatrick, in a letter to the author dated 19/2/1999, writes "I thought from the photo that some of the motifs looked a bit more like palmette or anthemion than acanthus. Its simplicity, i.e., not enriched, might suggest a reasonably early date- mid 12th century." Acanthus and palmette leaves frequently occur at Boyle Abbey, Co. Roscommon, (Stalley 1971, Pls. 52-53; Stalley 1987, Pls. 191-195, 197-198; Kalkreuter 2001, figs. 23, 24 & 31), Ballintubber, Co. Mayo, and Corcomroe, Co. Clare (Stalley 1987, Pl. 204; Kalkreuter 2001, fig. 84), all sites that were of The School of the West, (Stalley 1973; Kalkreuter 2001).

This Ballisodare font would have been supported on a pedestal such as that from Newtown Early, Co. Kilkenny, (Harte 1987, 408-409). That sandstone hexagonal pedestal is most likely to be Romanesque.

This font emphasises Ballisodare's status in Romanesque times and it should not be seen as just an outlier in the distribution of Romanesque architectural sculpture (de Paor 1967).

THE HEAD

The corbelled head is probably of Romanesque date. The type of sandstone is similar to that of the heads of the Romanesque doorway. The two corbel heads on either side of the Romanesque doorway of St. Feichin's Church and the heads around it[13] are too weathered for comparison and reference to Wakeman's original drawings (1883; 1885) does not help. This head could have adorned the original Romanesque east window together with a hood moulding of which we have but one stone.

THE EAST WINDOWS OF ST. FEICHIN'S CHURCH

The medieval east window of St. Feichin's Church had collapsed by the time of Bigari 1791 (Grose 1791, Pl. 93; Cooper 1794). O'Rorke (1878, 21) saw evidence for a two-light window and a mullion and the sill stone was still in situ at that time. The north side of the window opening is intact for a height of close on 4 metres and consists of sandstone blocks forming the side of a widely splayed opening. The south side has collapsed to almost a metre back from the splay, though a few stones at the base indicate the splay. The splay widens from 65cm at the outside to 1.75m at the inside. From the above-described pieces and the remaining masonry of the east gable it is possible to suggest a format of both the Romanesque east window of the church and its Medieval successor.

THE ROMANESQUE EAST WINDOW

Three of the stones, the hood, the vousoir and the round window head, together with the sandstone masonry of the sides of the window could suggest a reconstruction of a Romanesque two-light east window with a hood moulding on the outside, with at least one stone head further adorning it.

There is no other hood fragment visible at Ballisodare today. Neither of the ruinous buildings have any window from which it could have come. Cooper's 1794 drawing of Ballisodare shows that the building south of St. Feichin's near the lane had only a small opening in its east gable and none in its west gable. The side windows of the St. Feichin's Church are all intact so the hood fragment could not have come from either of those windows.

Similar nail-head ornament appears on the capital of a pillar in Cashel Cathedral and on a capital in the choir of Christchurch Cathedral in Dublin (Champneys 1910, 162, 166). The decorative coil on the hood moulding is similar to one in Boyle Abbey on the capital in the nave decorated with dogs and cocks tussling over prey and dated to c.1215-1220 (Stalley 1987, Pl. 193; Kalkreuter 2001, fig. 27) and to coils on capitals in the choir of Ballintubber Abbey, Co. Mayo (Stalley 1971, Pls. 55-56; Kalkreuter 2001, fig. 86).

THE MEDIEVAL WINDOW

While allowing for the possibility that the ogee headed stone could have come from the Augustinian Abbey sufficient other evidence suggests that it is from the Medieval east window of St. Feichin's Church which had collapsed by the time Bigari drew it in 1779. The two-light limestone sill, which fits the appropriate space opening in the east wall and was still in position in 1878 (O'Rorke 1878, 21, footnote) matches the ogee headed stone in the roadside wall. Thus, the evidence suggests that a Medieval two-light cusped ogee headed window decorated with trefoils in the spandrels replaced the Romanesque window[14].

Similar Medieval two-light cusped ogee headed windows of the period in Co. Sligo include that at the old church of Collooney (O'Rorke 1878, 526; Wakeman 1883, Drawing No. 95), now within what was McMahon's Timber Yard, that in the south transept of Court Abbey (Grose 1791, Pls. 96) and those in the tower of Benada Abbey (Grose 1791, Pls. 94-95) to mention a few.

THE MEDIEVAL GRAVESLAB

The Ballisodare slab is of a style found in late Medieval Ireland and Scotland.

Medieval slabs are rare in Co. Sligo, being found only here (one slab and a fragment of a slab) and at Sligo Abbey[15]. Bradley and Dunne (1987) list nine Medieval cross-slabs and eight Medieval grave-slabs at Sligo Abbey. They illustrate two slabs, both of which are fragmentary and worn, which have swords. Grave slab No. 1 of ?13th or 14th century date (1987, fig. 8, top left) has the hilt of a sword on the left side, an incised band for the shaft of a cross, and the top has an elaborate foliage pattern. The sword has slightly down-facing crossguard but no langet. Cross slab No. 3, of 13th/14th century date, (1987, fig. 8, bottom left) has what appears to be the hilt of a sword. In the late 1970s Martin A. Timoney saw a very small fragment of a slab with the blade of a sword cut on it in Sligo Abbey during restoration work by the then Office of Public Works but does not know of its present whereabouts.

Three other medieval slabs in Sligo Abbey have animals on them. These animals have little similarity to the ones at Ballisodare. The style of the foliage on the Ballisodare slab is akin to that of cross slabs Nos. 1 and 4 in Sligo Abbey (Bradley and Dunne 1987, Figs. 6, left, and 7, right) of the ?13th/14th centuries (Bradley and Dunne 1987, 42-43).

The Medieval slab made by Fergus mak Allan for Magnus Mac Orristin, known as the 'Magnus and Fergus' slab, at Clonca, Co. Donegal, has a somewhat similar sword on it (Lacey 1983, 255, Pl. 32). Although it does not have a ring pommel, the crossguard is similar and it has a langet. The slab also has a cross, foliage, a hurley-like playing stick and ball, and an inscription on it. The foliage is very different to that on the Ballisodare slab. None of the swords depicted on the Co. Down grave-slabs (Anon. 1966) are closely comparable to that on the Ballisodare slab. Many of the Late Medieval Scottish grave-slabs with swords depicted (Steer and Bannerman 1977) initially look similar to that at Ballisodare but on closer inspection show minor to considerable variations. The swords depicted on slabs at Oronsay (Steer and Bannerman 1977, 168, No. 6, Pl. 26) seem closest to the one at Ballisodare.

Close dating of the Ballisodare slab is not possible since we can not be sure if the sword depicted is that of the deceased or a family heirloom (Steer and Bannerman 1977, 167). However, the sword is closest to Halpin's Group 2 swords (1986, 195-207) such as those at Ballinakill, Co. Galway, Strade, Co. Mayo, and the Dominican Abbey, Roscommon.

Hunt dates the sword of Liam Garmh Burke at Ballinakill, Co. Galway, (Hunt 1974, ii, Pl. 169; Halpin 1986, Pl. IVa), to the first quarter of the sixteenth century though Halpin (1986, 205-206) thinks this is slightly too late. The sword in the hand of St. Paul at Strade, Co. Mayo, (Hunt 1974, ii, Pls. 253 and 255; Halpin 1986, Pl. Va), belongs to the second half of the fifteenth century. The swords in the hands of seven gallogliagh in the Dominican Abbey at Roscommon (Hunt 1974, ii, Pls. 250-251) are of the second half of the fifteenth century. Halpin (1986, 207) feels that these swords are of a Scottish trend. However, Halpin has personally expressed to the author the opinion, based on seeing a photograph only, that the sword on the Ballisodare slab is fifteenth century or first decade of the sixteenth century in date. This gives a terminus post quem for the slab. See Rynne (1983-1984, 19) for a general dating of this type of sword to *c*. 1450 to 1525 AD.

CONCLUSION

The quality of these Romanesque pieces of sculpture at Ballisodare further emphasise the importance of Ballisodare in this period. The late Medieval grave slab indicate the continued importance of the location as a place to be buried in during the Later Middle Ages.

ACKNOWLEDGEMENTS

I am indebted to many people for help with this article. Jim Ganley, Michael Scanlon, Padraig Corcoran, Liam Duignan, Ossy Finan, Gerry Gethins, Declan Brown, James Lee and Vincent Malee, members of the Ballisodare Foras Áiseanna Saothair funded clean up scheme of St. Feichin's graveyard. Sylvester Mulligan of Sligo County Council afforded easy access to the Medieval slab which is in Sligo Co. Co. storage depot. Hazel Gardiner, Prof. Roger Stalley, Prof. Etienne Rynne, John Bradley, Margaret Keane, Dr. Andrew Halpin, Dr. Peter Harbison, Dr. Elizabeth FitzPatrick, Dr. Rhoda Kavanagh and Dr. Dorothy Kelly commented on the various stones described above. Colette O'Daly of the National Library of Ireland gave the reference to R. Austin Cooper's *Butterhill and Beyond;* Dr. Niamh Whitfield, London, Prof. John Waddell and Eamon Cody assisted in proving that there is no Lhuyd drawing of the Ballisodare medieval slab. To these I offer my sincerest thanks. This article would never have been completed without the encouragement and help of Martin A. Timoney.

I acknowledge the permission of the National Archives of Ireland to quote from William Henry's 1739 manuscript (NAI MS 2533).

APPENDIX I
Irish Tourist Authority Survey, 1943
BALLYSADARE OLD CHURCH

Kilboglashy O.S. Sligo 20/7/S.W.
Church 48.8/30.

Situated in the townland of Kilboglashy, about 1 mile from Ballysadare Village and stated to have been built by Saint Feichin in the seventh century. The ruin is an oblong quadrangular structure, seventy feet in length, and thirty-three in breadth. The entrance is on the S. side, at a distance of eighteen feet from western gable; the height of the doorway is nine feet six inches from sill to apex of arch, and the breadth five feet ten inches from the outside face of the wall, but contracted by jambs to four feet on the inside; the head of the door consists of a double Norman arch, filled in with masonry, and is three feet three from line of springing to apex of lower arch, and three feet eleven from the same line to the apex of the higher; eleven carved human heads project, in bold relief, from lower arch, and there are two more, one at each side of the springing, making in all thirteen, and representing, in all likelihood, Our Lord and the Twelve Apostles. There are three windows, one in eastern gable and two in southern side wall; the latter are lancet, each four feet nine inches high from sill to soffit of arch, and seven inches wide on outside of wall, but splayed to four feet ten inches on inside; the eastern window seems also to have been of the lancet kind, but owing to a part of the gable having fallen, one cannot be now sure of its dimensions.

The remains of two other houses, stand on the cemetery plot, along with the church, one on each side of it, but distant about twenty feet. The three buildings lie in an easterly direction, and are nearly parallel, but the church is further east than the others, its western gable being nearly on a line with the eastern gables of the other two. The dimensions of the southern house are fifty-two feet long, and twenty-three wide, measured externally. The northern structure is, internally, thirty-three feet long, and fourteen wide. Both these buildings were vaulted with stone, and contained each two apartments - one in the basement, and the other a croft, between vault and roof. The northern house was singularly well lighted for so old a building, having three opens for the upper floor, two in side wells (opposite one another), and two for the basement - one in western gable, and one in northern side wall. It is likely that these houses were the refectory, and Abbot's house.

The burial ground is still used. Not under care of Office of Public Works. Free right of way to public.

EB

1. Recorded Monument Sl.20:109. The church in the graveyard is herein called St. Feichin's Church, even though it incorporates masonry of several periods, none of which may be as old as the time of St. Feichin. The locally applied term Abbey would be both wrong and confusing since the Augustinian Canons Abbey to the west is an abbey.

2. These are recorded on photographs ASX 62 to ASX 65 of 1967 and BGM 31 and BGM 32 of 1971 taken by Dr. J.K. St. Joseph for The Cambridge University Committee for Aerial Photography. The lines of some of these walls are still to be seen under favourable lighting conditions.

Some antler and querns from the fields south-east of the graveyard, where bones, oyster and cockle were also noted, were deposited in the National Museum of Ireland in 1970 by Mr. Joseph McMullen.

3. Five other sites, Billa, Drumrat and Kilnamangh, Co. Sligo, Fore, Co. Westmeath, and Omey, Co. Galway, are also attributed to St. Feichin.

4. Recorded Monument Sl.20:108.

5. As the curved top space of the doorway is filled with several stones, as opposed to a single stone, Rynne (1987, 4-5) does not consider it to be a true tympanum.

6. Angelo Maria Bigari, an architect and theatrical scene painter from Bologna, together with Gabriel Beranger, recorded many antiquities in Connacht under the patronage of in 1779 (Harbison 2002).

7. Several of Thomas Cocking's engravings are in Grose's Antiquities of Ireland.

8. "An Account of the Abbey of Ballyfadare: - With a Beautiful Engraving" (C(ooper) 1794, 159-160) is initialled J.C., the view of the church, made on 1st. May 1793 is credited 'J.C. delin' and the engraving of it is credited 'Clayton Sculp'. The J.C. has not been positively been identified but most likely it was Joseph Cooper. Of the seven in the Tabula Gratulatoria that have the initials J.C. one is Joseph Cooper.

9. When this slab was shown on the occasion of the Royal Society of Antiquaries of Ireland Summer outing to Sligo which included a visit to Ballisodare in 1995, among other places, Dr. Rhoda Kavanagh and Dr. Dorothy Kelly of UCD informed us that there was a drawing of it by Edward Lhuyd. Despite much searching the drawing has not been traced. It is not in the Lhuyd material in The British Library, Stowe Ms. 1024, nor in the Manuscripts Room at Trinity College, Dublin. At this stage it appears that there is no Lhuyd drawing of the Ballisodare medieval slab. Edward Lhuyd was in Sligo in 1700 (Campbell 1960; McGuinness 1996).

A small fragment of another dressed but undecorated slab was found in 1995 alongside the first by Margaret Keane, Dúchas, Dublin.

10. It was not revealed during the 1995-1996 clean up of Aghanagh graveyard.

11. There is a broken rectangular medieval font at Sligo Abbey (Bradley and Dunne 1987, 49).

12. Hazel Gardiner, pers. comm.

In December 2001 Teeling Community Response published *Collooney: From Medieval to Modern Times*, written by FÁS Trainees at Collooney. A tiny photo of a 'holy water stoup', more accurately a font, that used to be at Cloonamahon is illustrated on p. 20. The Passionist Community have left Cloonamahon and the font is not now at Cloonamahon nor with the Passionist Community; in fact it may have been taken to Romania with the church furniture. The dimensions scaled off the photograph are about 42cm in diameter and 26cm high. Mrs. Carmel Wims of Cloonamahon has kindly provided an original print of the photo and from it we judge this to be an undecorated cylindrical font. Mr. James McGarry, LLB, of Collooney says that this font was associated with the Bishop John O'Hart of Cloonamahon of Penal Times. We do not know if this association was secondary to an existing font.

There is an undated but similar font, Sl.19:193, 50cm in diameter and 30cm high with a 28cm diameter and 16cm deep well, adjacent to The Abbey Field at Ballinlig, Beltra, Co. Sligo. The rim is scalloped. The Abbey Field, pronounced 'Aabee', Sl.19:4301, is a moated site, curiously depicted on Larkin's 1819 Map of Sligo as a fort with corner bastions.

In addition to these sites with fonts the RMP includes seven other sites with fonts. Four of these, Ballinalig, Sl.19:4302, Rathglass, Sl.22:14, Stoneparks, Sl.33:115, and Battlefield, Sl.39:132, are stoups. Churchill font, Sl.32:195, is only known by tradition and Kilross, Sl.21:5501 and Sl.21:5501, are listed as "font site".

13. Zarnecki and Henry (1957-1958) include Ballisodare in a list of places having Romanesque arches decorated with human and animal heads but do not comment specifically on the Ballisodare heads. They argue that human and animal heads in arches seen by pilgrims on route to Saint Iago de Compostella or Rome were the inspiration for the Irish series.

14. Set vertically at the foot of a grave to the SE of the church is a piece of limestone window tracery. It measures 19cm thick, 40cm wide and 34cm of it is above ground. The openings have a medial groove. From what can be seen of this piece there is no building that it could have come from at this location. The Cooper drawing of March 1794 shows that the building near the road had only a small opening in its east gable and none in its west gable. This leaves us with the probability that the tracery piece came from the east window of the adjacent, sadly neglected and almost buried Augustinian Canons Abbey. There should be several traceried window pieces in and under the spoil there.

15. The 17th. century monument in St. John's Cathedral, Sligo, to Roger (d. 1637) and Maria Jones (O'Rorke 1889, i, 303; Wood-Martin 1889, 24) displays Roger and Maria Jones with their coat of arms and crest.

REFERENCES

MANUSCRIPT:

Henry, William, 1739: *Hints towards a Natural Topographical History of the Counties Sligoe, Donegal, Fermanagh and Lough Erne by the Rev. William Henry, M.A., Rector of Killasher in Fermanagh and Chaplain to the Lord Bishop of Kilmore*, National Archives of Ireland, Ms. 2533.

PUBLICATIONS

Anon 1966: *An Archaeological Survey of County Down*, Belfast, HMSO.

Anon 1995: *Record of Monuments and Places, Co. Sligo*, Dublin, Office of Public Works, Limited Distribution.

Bradley, John, and Dunne, Noel, 1987: *Urban Archaeological Survey, Part XXI, County Sligo*. Dublin, Office of Public Works. Limited distribution.

Buckley, Victor, 1992: "Ballisodare, Co. Sligo, The Case of the Underground Abbey", *IAPA Newsletter*, No. 15, 11.

Bunn, Michael, 1997: "Splendid Sligo", *The World of Hibernia*, 3:2, 146-166.

Campbell, J.L., 1960: "The Tour of Edward Lhuyd in Ireland in 1699 and 1700", *Celtica*, 5, 218-228.

Champneys, Arthur, 1910: *Irish Ecclesiastical Architecture with some Notice of Similar or Related Work in England, Scotland and Elsewhere*, London, Bell, Dublin, Hodges Figgis & Co.

C(?ooper), J(?oseph)., 1794: "An Account of the Abbey of Ballyfadare: - With a Beautiful Engraving", *Anthologia Hibernica*, III, 159-160.

Cooper, R. Austin, 1991: *Butterhill and Beyond*, Cooper, Hurst Reading.

Coyle, J. B., 1915: *The Life of St. Feichin of Fore, The Apostle of Connemara*, Dublin.

Edinburgh Gazetteer 1822: *The Edinburgh Gazetteer or Geographical Dictionary . . . of the World*, 1822, Edinburgh, Archibald Constable,

Elmes, Rosalind M., and Hewson, Michael, 1975: *Catalogue of Irish Topographical Prints and Original Drawings*, Dublin, Malton Press for National Library Society.

Gibbons, Michael, Alcock, Olive, Condit, Tom, Tunney, Mary, and Timoney, Martin A., 1989: *Sites and Monuments Record County Sligo*, Dublin, Office of Public Works, Limited Distribution.

Grose, Francis, 1791: *The Antiquities of Ireland*, Vol. 1., London, Hooper.

Gunning, John P., n.d.: *Saint Feichin: His Life and Times*, Dublin.

Gwynn, Aubrey, and Hadcock, R. Neville, 1970: *Medieval Religious Houses: Ireland*. Reprint, 1988, Blackrock, Irish Academic Press.

Halpin, Andrew, 1986: "Irish Medieval Swords", *Proc. Roy. Irish Acad.*, 86C5, 183-230.

Harbison, Peter, 2000: *Cooper's Ireland, Drawings and Notes from an Eighteenth-Century Gentleman*, Dublin, O'Brien.

Harbison, Peter, 2002: "The Antiquities of Sligo in 1779 as seen by Lewis Irwin of Tanrego House" in Timoney 2002.

Harbison, Peter, 2002: *'Our Treasure of Antiquities', Beranger and Bigari's Antiquarian Sketching Tour of Connacht in 1779*, Dublin Wordwell/NLI.

Harte, Rita, 1987: "Tombstones at Newtown Early", *Old Kilkenny Review*, 3:4, 408-417.

Healy, P., and Ryan, N., 1982: *Report on the Present Condition of St. Feichin's Abbey, Ballysadare*, Dublin, An Foras Forbatha. Limited distribution.

Hunt, John, 1974: *Irish Medieval Figure Sculpture, 1200-1600, A Study of Irish Tombs with Notes on Costume and Armour*, Dublin and London.

Kalkreuter, Britta, 2001: *Boyle Abbey and The School of The West*, Bray, Wordwell.

Kilroe, James R., 1885: *Explanatory Memoir to Accompany Sheet 55 of the Maps of the Geological Survey of Ireland, Comprising Portions of the Counties of Sligo and Leitrim*, Dublin and London.

Leask, Harold G., 1966: *Irish Churches and Monastic Buildings, II, Gothic Architecture to A.D. 1400*, Dundalk, Tempest.

McDermott, Connor V., Long, C.B., and Harney, S.J., with Contributions by K. Claringbold, D. Daly, R. Meehan and G. Stanley, 1996: *A Geological Description of Sligo, Leitrim, and Adjoining Parts of Cavan, Fermanagh, Mayo and Roscommon, to Accompany the Bedrock Geology 1:100,000 Scale Map Series, Sheet 7, Sligo- Leitrim*, Dublin, Geological Survey of Ireland.

McGuinness, David, 1996: "Edward Lhuyd's Contribution to the Study of Irish Megalithic Tombs", *J. Roy. Soc. Antiquaries Irel.*, 126, 62-85.

McTernan, John C., 1995: *Olde Sligoe, Aspects of Town and County over 750 Years*, Sligo, Avena.

McTernan 1995: "18th Century Sligo", in McTernan 1995, 100-110.

McTernan, John C., 1998: *In Sligo Long Ago, Aspects of Town and County Over Two Centuries*, Sligo, Avena.

McTernan 1998: "Mining at Abbeytown", in McTernan 1998, 571-575.

McTernan 1998: "Mills and Milling" in McTernan 1998, 346-386.

Manning, Robert, 1847: *Report to the Commissioners Appointed under Acts on the Drainage and Improvement of the Lands in the Breeoge District, Co. Sligo*, Dublin, Thom.

Morris, Henry, 1928: "St. Feichin", *The Roscommon Herald*, 2nd June 1928.

Mount, Charles, 1994: "'From Knoxspark to Tír na nÓg'", *Archaeology Ireland*, 8:3, 22-23.

Mount, Charles, 2002: "The Promontory Fort, Inhumation Cemetery and Sub-Rectangular Enclosure at Knoxspark, Co. Sligo" in Timoney, ed., 2002.

Moriarty, Chris, 2002: "Eels and Eel Fishing in County Sligo", in Timoney, ed., 2002.

Ní Chinnéide, Síle, 1976: "A Frenchman's Tour of Connacht in 1791", *J. Galway Archae. Hist. Soc.*, 35, 52-66.

O'Rorke, Terrence, 1878: *History, Antiquities, and Present*

State of the Parishes of Ballysadare and Kilvarnet, in the County of Sligo; with Notices of the O'Haras, The Coopers, The Percevals, and other local Families, Dublin, Duffy.

O'Rorke, Terrence, 1889: *The History of Sligo: Town and County,* 2 Vols. Dublin, James Duffy, Reprint, 1986, Sligo, Dodd's Antiquarian Books.

Petrie, George, 1845: *The Ecclesiastical Architecture of Ireland Anterior to the Anglo-Norman Invasion, An Essay on the Origin and Uses of The Round Towers of Ireland,* 2nd. ed., Dublin.

Pike, H.K. Joan, 1989: *Medieval Fonts of Ireland,* Typescript in Royal Society of Antiquaries of Ireland, Merrion Sq., Dublin 2. (See *Old Kilkenny Review,* 4:1, (1989), 582).

Rountree, Mary, ed., 1988: *Ballisodare, (1800-1987), A Local History Study,* Sligo, Blackwood.

Rynne, Etienne, 1983-1984: "Military and Civilian Swords from The Corrib River", *J. Galway Archaeological and Historical Society,* 39, 5-26.

Rynne, Etienne, 1987: "Evidence for a Tympanum at Aghadoe, Co. Kerry", *North Munster Antiq. J.,* 29, 3-6.

Sligo County Council: *Sligo County Council Annual Report and Accounts 1994,* Sligo, Sligo County Council.

Stalley, Roger, 1971: *Architecture and Sculpture in Ireland, 1150-1350,* Dublin, Gill and Macmillan & Browne & Nolan.

Stalley, Roger, 1973: "A Romanesque Sculptor in Connaught", *Country Life,* (21st. June, 1973), 1826-1830.

Stalley, Roger, 1987: *The Cistercian Monasteries of Ireland,* London and New Haven, Yale University Press.

Steer, K.A., and Bannerman, J.W., 1977: *Late Medieval Monumental Sculpture in the West Highlands,* Edinburgh, RCAHMS.

Stone, Lawrence, 1955: *Sculpture in Britain in the Middle Ages,* London, Penguin.

Swords, Liam, 1997: *A Hidden Church, The Diocese of Achonry, 1689-1818,* Blackrock, Columban Press.

Thunder, John M., 1888: "Saint Feichin of Fore", *Irish Ecclesiastical Record,* Third Series, IX, 437-441.

Timoney, Martin A., ed., 2002: *A Celebration of Sligo,* Sligo, Sligo Field Club.

Wakeman, William F., 1883: "Ballysadare", Dublin Saturday Magazine, 2:25, 25-26.

Wakeman, William F., 1883: *Drawings of Antiquities on the County of Sligo. By W.F. Wakeman, M.R.H.A.I., made in the years 1878, 1879, 1880, 1881, 1882 for Colonel E.H. Cooper, Markree Castle.* Bound London 1883. Originals are housed in County Sligo Library Local Studies Archive, 450(A)1.

Wakeman, W.F., 1885: "Architectural Peculiarities of Some Ancient Churches in County Sligo", *J. Roy. Soc. Antiq. Ireland,* 17, 43-54.

Warner, Richard B., 1976: "Some Observations on the Context and Importation of Exotic Material in Ireland, from the First Century BC to the Second Century AD", *Proc. Roy. Irish Academy,* 76c, 267-292.

Went, Arthur, E.J., 1969: "Historical Notes on the Fisheries of the Two County Sligo Rivers", *J. Roy. Soc. Antiq. Ireland,* 99, 55-61.

Wood-Martin, W.G., 1882: *The History of Sligo, County and Town, from the Earliest Ages to the Close of the Reign of Queen Elizabeth,* Dublin, Reprint, 1990, Sligo, Dodd's Antiquarian Books.

Wood-Martin, W.G., 1892: *The History of Sligo, County and Town, from the close of the Revolution of 1688 to the Present Time,* Dublin, Hodges Figgis; Reprint, 1990, Sligo, Dodd's Antiquarian Books.

Young, Arthur, 1780: *A Tour in Ireland with General Observations on the Present State of that Kingdom: Made in The Years 1776, 1777, and 1778, Brought down to the End of 1779,* London. Reprint 1970: Shannon, Irish University Press, Introduction by J.B. Ruane.

Zarnecki, George, and Henry, Françoise, 1957-1958: "Romanesque Arches Decorated with Human and Animal Heads", *J. British Archaeol. Assoc.,* 20-21; reproduced in *Studies in Romanesque Sculpture,* 1979, London, Dorian Press.

Fig. 8 - Recumbent slab, possibly to a miner, at Ballisodare, Co. Sligo. Photo: Mary B. Timoney.

SLIGO ANTIQUARIAN SOCIETY AT DEERPARK, MAY 1945

See Timoney and Heraughty, page 278.

Photo: Tony Toher

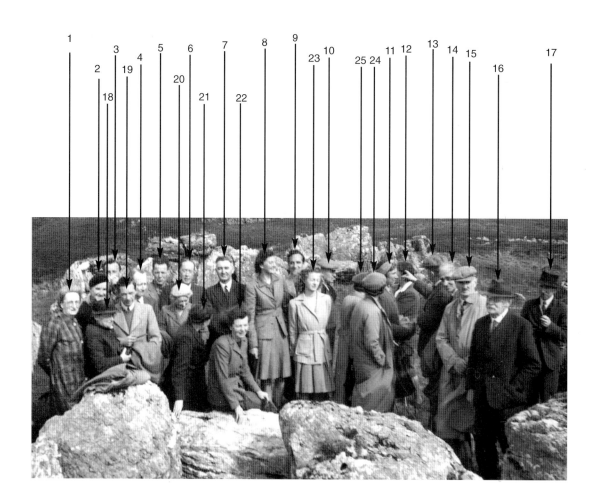

A Romanesque Sculpture found at Carrowculleen, Skreen, Co. Sligo

Martin A. Timoney
Keash, Co. Sligo

ABSTRACT: A carved sandstone bearing a figure, with a short sword held in both hands across his lap, seated on a throne in an arched niche, between a lion and an eagle, found in June 1984 at Carrowculleen, Co. Sligo, is described. The seated figure is very similar to the Lewis and Cluny chessmen kings of the Scandinavian Romanesque of the second-half of the 12th century. There are some Irish and mainland European *comporanda* for the lion and the eagle but these are not very convincing. Despite claims that the piece is modern the piece looks to be 12th century. No single entity provides inspiration for the complete sculpture which overall stands apart from the Hiberno-Romanesque.

My Self: The consecrated blade upon my knees
Is Sato's ancient blade, still as it was
Still razor keen, still like a looking glass
Unspotted by the centuries;

W.B. Yeats, *A Dialogue of Self and Soul*
From *The Winding Stair and Other Poems*, 1933[1]

DISCOVERY

Sligo Field Club has a long tradition of fieldwalking and assisting genuinely motivated students of the archaeology of Sligo. Thus, on Thursday 28th June 1984, three of its members, Martin A. Timoney, Mary B. Murphy (now Timoney) and Jack Flynn, took Swedish archaeologists Stefan and Margareta Bergh to visit, among other sites, the cashel and souterrain on The Red Hill, Skreen, some fifteen kilometres west of Ballisodare, Co. Sligo.

We approached the hill from the south, up a laneway past an apparently abandoned farmhouse and its roofless predecessor, noting a pillar with a possible small cross cut on it standing outside the door, and proceeded to the cashel. As we returned past the farmhouse I decided to re-examine the possible carved cross on the pillar again. Eventually I ruled it as being modern and not of archaeological interest. Meanwhile, the others looked for further stones of interest. One, Jack Flynn, was successful and that beyond his wildest dreams[2]. He found a carved sandstone sculpture (Fig. 1) bearing a figure, with a short sword held in both hands across its lap, seated on a throne in an arched niche, between a lion and an eagle. On a return visit some days later we met the occupants of the dwelling house, George Williams and Ann Presley.

REMOVAL

Following the discovery of the sculptured stone many archaeological colleagues were consulted and, following on their advice, extensive library, museum and site research was undertaken. The stone was removed from the wall by a man from Leekfield, Skreen, and brought to Sligo Library before August 1988 for an opinion but such could not be provided by those present. After it was returned to Carrowculleen it was lying on the ground outside the house for a while in 1988 with the carved face upwards where there were cattle. At the completion of the Supreme Court hearing in the action referred to as McGarry and others at the Relation of the Attorney General *v.* Sligo County Council, popularly known as the Carrowmore Dump Case, I went to the National Museum of Ireland. There, following discussions with Dr. Michael Ryan and Mr. Eamon P. Kelly, National Museum of Ireland, and with authorisation from the National Museum of Ireland and the Office of Public Works and assisted by John Corcoran, Office of Public Works Depot, Dromahaire, Co. Leitrim, it was taken to Keash on 18th Nov., 1988, and finally to National Museum of Ireland care in 1989. Following a visit to George Williams and Ann Presley at Carrowculleen, by Dr. Michael Ryan and the author in July 1990, it was acquired by The National Museum of Ireland in 1990. Its NMI registration number is 1990:129.

Fig. 1 - Romanesque sculpture in the wall of the house at Carrowculleen, Co. Sligo. Photo 1984 Martin A. Timoney.

FINDPLACE

The findplace is in the Townland of Carrowculleen, Parish of Skreen, Barony of Tireragh, County of Sligo[3]. Carrowculleen is on the south side of The Red Hill of Skreen, known as *Cnoc na Maoile*, alias Knocknamaoile, and Knocknadrooa, the Hill of the Druids (Wood-Martin 1895, 81; Harbison this volume; Ó Muraile this volume; Reeves 1857, LXII), and at the north end of The Lady's Brae, a north-south gap through the Ox Mts.

The sculpture was an integral part, and not an insert, of the north-facing front of the roofless house (Fig. 2). It was the second stone down from the top of the front wall at the east gable

Fig. 2 - The house at Carrowculleen, Co. Sligo, where the Romanesque sculpture was positioned.
Photo 2001 Martin A. Timoney.

end. The base of the stone was 176cm above ground level. The roofless eastern house where the stone was found is indicated on the 1837 O.S. 6" map, so it probably was a dwelling then, but the currently occupied adjoining western house is not on the map. Larkin's 1819 *Map of Sligo* suggests that the lane up to these house continued on as the through road here. The 1837 O.S. 6" map indicates far less fields then than were present until about 1990 when considerable amalgamation of fields to the east of the house took place. Even by grasping at straws it is not possible to find in the field-fence pattern any indication of a circular or other enclosure of an Early Christian monastic site. Neither is there any indication of any medieval building hereabouts nor is there any historical record or folk memory that would shed light on the presence of the stone here, hence 'found at' instead of 'from' in the title of this article. There is no lost historically-attested monastic site hereabouts. The Early Christian monastic site of Skreen, alias *Scrín Adomnán*[4], is three kilometres over the hill to the north.

GEOLOGICAL IDENTIFICATION

Dr. Richard Thorn, currently Director, Institute of Technology, Sligo, examined the stone when it was here at Keash and classified the stone as

Lower Carboniferous Sandstone with white quartz. Five major geological layers of varying thickness can clearly be seen in the right side of the stone. There are many pieces of white quartz visible in this sculpture, *e.g.*, in the right column, on the left side of the seat, over the left capital and in the central figure's right arm. There is a 6cm diameter lump of quartz in the back of the stone. The sculptor may not have expected the quartz so close to the surface and only ran into difficulty as he cut into the stone.

This stone type is found in a band running along the east side of The Red Hill of Skreen (pers. comm. The late Connor McDermott of The Geological Survey of Ireland). The petrology of the stone is similar to that of many loose stones in the fieldwalls of the Carrowculleen area. Several other stones of the same geology in the wall of the house or the intervening garden wall. It is also to be found in a narrow belt running along the south side of the Ox Mts. from Cloonacool to Ballintogher from where it could have been transported across the Ox Mts. by ice. See McDermott, Long and Harney (1996) for the complicated geological pattern of this part of Co. Sligo.

Dr. Nigel Monaghan and Dr. Ivor Harkin of the National Museum of Ireland have examined the relief from a geological point of view. They commented as follows

"In addition to the information supplied by Dr. Richard Thorn (above) the stone should be identified as a quartz conglomerate. This would not be the ideal material on which to carve or sculpt as it has bands of quartz pebbles in a sand mix. Geologically the stone is an example of material deposited after a flash flood or in proximal region of a high energy water system. The information on local geology supplied by Connor McDermott does not need further additions."

While there is a difference of geological terminology used there is agreement between the specialists as to the nature of the stone.

All surfaces of the stone display a matured weathered state. There is no appreciable difference between the faces of the stone which would allow the carving to be of a vintage between 1977, when Williams and Presley bought the house, and 1984, when Flynn found the sculpture. See Appendix I for more on this aspect of the discussion. The damage of about 1988 shows a fresh and different surface to the carved surface.

Despite the use of sandstone with quartz inclusions the carving is very detailed. Sandstone with pieces of white quartz is to be found in the vicinity of Carrowculleen stratified along the base of the Ox Mts. and also along the east side of The Red Hill of Skreen, adjacent to Carrowculleen. Thus the stone is most likely to be of local origin and, likewise, the sculpture. There is no need for the stone, in a raw or a carved state, to have been imported from outside the Skreen area.

Reeves (1857, 318) mentions the Adomnán records that the reliquary of Colmcille contained among other things a white pebble which was used a charm among the Picts. Perhaps this is the explanation of why the sculptor chose so difficult a piece of stone, with white quartz inclusions though he may not have expected so many in the layers so high up in the stone.

DESCRIPTION

The stone (Figs. 1, 3-8) measures 43cm to 56cm in width, 39cm to 42cm in height and 16cm to 20cm in thickness. The top, left and bottom edges of the stone seem to be contemporary with the carving but the right edge has suffered two major breaks in antiquity, at least before it was inserted in the house wall; these have resulted in part of the eagle, and perhaps much more, being lost. If the composition was just of three main elements and was symmetrical then no more than 6cm has been lost, *i.e.*, the stone would have been 60cm to 62cm wide. Alternatively a frieze to accommodate a possible maximum of seven elements (see below under 'Identification of the Seated Figure'), though not necessarily on one stone, would require a length of 150cm.

The geological layering of the stone has resulted in loss of detail of the upper head of the figure. The surface of the stone is well weathered and has decayed in places though, except for some areas of recent damage, the rest of it seems intact. There are what appear to be tool marks to be seen on the figure's left arm and dress. In other places the surface of the stone shows evidence of having been covered, at least in part, by a black substance and by colouring (see below under 'Surface Dressing'). These are best seen in six photos taken by the late Desmond Smith of Sligo Field Club in 1984 on our second visit to the findplace. There has been some surface damage, rather than weathering, done to the stone in antiquity, *e.g.*, the hindquarters of the lion, the area below it, the eagle's tail and the person's beard. There has been also some modern damage to the surface of the stone since we first saw it in the wall, *e.g.*, to the nose and to both hands, to the front leg of the lion and most regrettably to the sword pommel. Some of this could have been accidental while

Fig. 3 - The seated figure in the alcove, Carrowculleen, Co. Sligo. Photo 1984 Martin A. Timoney.

some could have been someone desirous of improving its condition. There has been damage to the body of the seated figure and the area to its left since the stone was removed from the wall in 1988. This is in the form of discolouration, perhaps from animal excretion. There is some mortar adhering to the left side of the stone; this mortar is the same as the rendering on the walls of the house.

The sculpture of the stone may be described in ten elements, *viz.*, the 'architectural' niche with its columns and arch, the throne, the seated figure, the sword, the lion, below the lion, above the lion, the eagle, below the eagle and above the eagle.

THE CENTRAL SECTION
THE ARCHITECTURAL ELEMENT

The 2.3cm deep arched niche (Fig. 3) in a sedilia like-format, is 38.5cm high by 17.5cm wide. It has dissimilar columns (Figs. 3, 5-8), 3.5cm in diameter. The twisted columns rise from the throne bench and not the ground. The columns are not quite cylindrical but present three somewhat flat surfaces and have unevenly spaced slanting scorings giving the appearance of spiral decoration. In both cases the scorings are 'bottom left to top right'. The left column has one to three vertical grooves down the top of half of it while there is one vertical groove on the right column; these do not follow the geological structure of the stone.

The left column is topped by a cubic capital with chamfered edges. There are five drilled holes arranged in two rows, three above and two below, though there may have been three below. There are arcs around the bottom ones which look like foliage. Below this capital is a short section of the column marked off by a groove. There is a shallow drilled hole in either side of this section.

The right capital is a somewhat similar cubic capital. There are eight less-well drilled and less-well arranged holes in it which may have been foliage. As on the left, between this capital and the column a section of the column marked off by a groove. This is much smaller than that on the left.

The inner two orders of the multy-order segmental arch spring, not from, but between the capitals. The soffit is moulded. The outer two orders continue as a double architrave across the front of the stone. The lower groove of the architrave is continued down the left side of the stone for 5cm, suggesting that this was the limit of the carving on the left side.

There are some small vertical lines above the left capital. The flat area over the right column is blank.

THE THRONE

Within an arched niche the figure sits on a throne (Figs. 1, 3, 8). Very little of the seat is to be seen because of the broad seated figure. Above the shoulders of the figure are the raised rectangular pommels of the throne and there is a scored line joining them indicating the top of the chair. The left pommel is damaged.

There are 5cm extensions of the seat of the throne to either side. Towards the end of the right one there is a slightly raised disk, perhaps with faint radial lines. There appears to be an indistinct linear design, perhaps foliage, towards the end of the left one which has a moulded finish; there is a piece of quartz here which made the carving difficult. There are no indications of animal ends to either the seat or the pommels of the chair. There may be a semi-circle with three pendant triangles beneath the left extension of the seat.

The columns above and below the seat of the throne are not aligned. Below the seat the left column is not in line with that above, while the column on the right is not quite out of line; it has faint scorings going somewhat differently to those above the seat.

Fig. 4 - Detail showing the sword, Carrowculleen, Co. Sligo. Photo 1984 Martin A. Timoney.

THE SEATED FIGURE

The seated figure (Figs. 1, 3, 8) is shown in greater relief than the lion and the eagle. He is seated with his head upright. The mouth is shown as an incised groove above which a wide moustache is shown. There is a substantial 'rectangular' beard and a complete substantial nose, damaged since it was first seen in the wall. Both of the deep set eyes are also damaged, one since first seen in 1984, and they have drilled holes, perhaps for adding studs. The left ear is large and protruding but that on the right seems to be covered in long locks of hair or was never crisply carved. The face is long and drawn. Some evidence for ridged hair survives on the head but, due to the geological layering of the stone, it is not possible to say if it came onto the forehead.

The figure has a deeply scored halo formed by several concentric arcs, one ridge around the top of the head breaking into two down the sides. There is no evidence on the halo for a cross or a crown.

The figure is robed with a ?single-piece round-necked garment with a collar band that reaches to the feet. Up-curving arcs on the chest and at the shoulders indicate cloth folds. There are substantial folds above the cuffs on both downward sloped forward reaching arms.

With a great deal of faith one might recognise a scored line crossing a small circle on his left chest; one hesitates to say this represents a brooch, it may be a reflection of work around a piece of quartz.

The feet, which are damaged, are set straight forward flat on the ground. The legs are at an angle with the figure's left knee, which has been damaged in antiquity, higher than the other. The garment passes across both legs, sagging between them. The tubular folds of the garment are shown parallel to the legs even though his right leg is well slanted. One of the folds is much more substantial than the others. This stylised tubular drapery gives the appearance of stiff shin guards. The garment curls over the feet. It is not clear if there is anything under the feet.

THE SWORD

The seated figure holds a double-edged sword (Fig. 4). The short sword is 19cm long, and has a blade 2.5cm wide and 1cm thick. The straight guard is 4cm by 0.6cm and is 2.3cm from the pommel which measures 2.8cm by 1.5cm. It has a round-bottomed fuller's groove and a round tipped blade.

It is held across his knees with the fingers of both hands placed downwards across the sword. His right hand is placed between the guard and the pommel and his left hand near the tip of the blade. Most regrettably, for archaeological comparison reasons, the pommel has suffered recent damage. It has three simple lobes, the centre one being larger than the others.

THE LION

The lion (Figs. 5, 8) is on the figure's left. It is standing with its head turned backwards and thus looking away from the seated figure. Only its two right legs are carved and the feet are no longer distinguishable. The foreleg hip joint is marked by two concentric shapes and the point for their centre is evident.

The front two-thirds of the lion's body and its neck are covered with pendant triangles, suggestive of feathers, above scored lines. There is a small curving piece behind the front leg hanging down which does not look like a down-turned wing. This lion does not have wings.

The lion's tail emerges from below its proper anatomical position and rises with a flourish over its rump; the hairs of its end are individually indicated.

Holes of varying sizes are drilled into the lion's

Fig. 5 - The lion with foliage above, Carrowculleen, Co. Sligo.
Photo 1989 Martin A. Timoney.

head. The hole in the eyeball is surrounded by an oval groove. There is one hole for an ear and another for a nostril. Holes above and below the tongue form teeth and give the feeling of ferocity.

The lion's massive curved and grooved tongue emanates from its open mouth, runs along its back and passes under its chin and behind its neck to rise up by the back of its back-turned head. The end of the tongue widens and its end seems to get entangled in foliage. There is a drilled hole at either side of the end of the tongue.

Above the lion there is foliage (Figs. 1, 5, 8) of varying quality of depiction or survival. At either side the stem of the left piece of foliage there are tightly curved ridges, emanating from drilled holes, that on the right merging with the stem. There is space below the lion is now indistinct or insufficient for identification. With the eye of speculation possible ovals and arcs can be suggested. Whatever was there appears to be an upturned animal.

THE EAGLE

The right side of the stone has suffered from two breaks in antiquity. There is no indication of an original edge or frame at the right extremity. However, the eagle (Fig. 6, 8), shown in a vertical stretched upright pose, is complete except for the end of its beak and the end of one wing. The eagle faces away from the seated figure. It appears to be standing on a perch at the level of the seat with its damaged tail feathers fanning out and concealing all below. The ends of the feathers are not distinct. Only a few feathers are indicated on the bird's body. Two grooves give the appearance of a neck-band and some scorings above this suggest feathers. The head is held high, almost in a startled rather than proud posture. Its beak is closed. Its eye is shown by a low boss surrounded by two concentric ovals. Its left wing points outward in a posture as if indicating something of importance. Under the eagle's pointing wing the stone has not been fully cut back.

There is nothing carved either above or below the eagle.

Fig. 6 - The eagle, Carrowculleen, Co. Sligo.
Photo 1989 Martin A. Timoney.

Fig. 7 - The black substance adhering to parts of the carved surface of the sculpture, Carrowculleen, Co. Sligo.
Photo 1984 Des Smith.

SURFACE APPEARANCE

There was colouring and a black substance, all of unknown date, surviving on parts of the background and on some sculpted details of the stone when we first saw it. Some of that is no longer there but their maximum presence is now set out.

There are or were traces of several colours on parts of the carving, mostly on the lion and on the halo.

There was blue-green on the foliage, under the arch, to the right of the eagle's neck, both sides of halo and on it, and between the lion's legs.

There is yellow/orange on the lion's tail, head, body and front leg, all suggestive of a golden lion, and also in groove of the halo and under the arch. There is cream colouring on the lion's body and white on its rump.

There was some green in the top left corner of stone. There was some yellow coming through the blue on one point of the halo.

When the stone was in the wall and was damp there were traces of red and green colouring, as opposed to lichen, on it. There were greater extents of the other colours visible also.

There is black substance adhering to parts of the carved surface (Fig. 8); one can see brush lines on some pieces of it. The substance fills the grooves of the eagle's head and tail, the figure's left neck, right knee and grooves on his chest, the lion's neck, at the sword guard and in some of the drilled holes of the left capital. There are spreads of the substance on the eagle's body, either side of its neck and under the arch. One gets the impression that the substance covered all of the stone at one time and that it now survives only in the deepest carving but one can not be certain of this.

There is no colouring over the black substance and without a microscopic examination we do not know if there is colouring under the black.

One wonders if the black substance was put on the stone to keep plaster from adhering to the carving at a time when it was being concealed[5].

GENERAL DISCUSSION

This Carrowculleen sculpture is very problematic. The Carrowculleen sculpture's original function is uncertain, the pre-1984 story of the stone is lost in the mists of time, its recent history is lost and a touch of mystery is added by claims of it being modern (see Appendix I), its medieval provenance is unknown, the subject is unclear, the carving overall has no obvious *comporanda* in Hiberno-Romanesque and the stone itself must have been very difficult to carve because of the pieces of quartz.

There is nothing comparable in Early Christian sculpture nor in Gothic nor later sculpture. As one progresses through the *corpora* of Early Christian, Romanesque and Gothic sculpture it is only when in the Romanesque that one gets the feeling that one is looking in the right place. Even then this piece stands apart from the Irish material, but even more problematic is the fact that there is no substantial body of Romanesque sculpture in the northwest of Ireland; Tuam, Clonmacnois, Clonfert, Devenish and Kilmore are the nearest prolific sites but that Romanesque is not the same style or feeling.

Research has been even more hampered than usual by the lack of a true locational context, its findspot being totally devoid of any ecclesiastical connotation.

It has been acquired by the National Museum of Ireland from George Williams and Ann Presley. Hopefully someone will see it in the National Museum of Ireland and will come up with answers or perhaps this publication will have the required success that piece-meal publicity since 1984 has failed to achieve.

Since Jack Flynn found the stone in June 1984 the advice of many experts in Ireland, Britain and beyond was sought. Photographs of the stone were widely circulated and suggested avenues of research were followed. The reaction of most was "Well, amazing, mm, Romanesque, about 1150, or later", followed by "Have you shown this to . . ?" Well, I have, and so the process has gone on, with limited success. Following the frequent exhortation many years ago of my physics teacher, Fr. Thomas Fannin, "All knowledge is to be found in books; only problem is 'Which one?'" advice was followed up on. France, Italy, Spain and Portugal were suggested as the most likely sources for similar sculpture. Scores of books in the National Library of Ireland, the Royal Irish Academy, the Royal Society of Antiquaries of Ireland and the Society of Antiquaries in London Libraries and those of some of those credited at the end were consulted, and one must admit to having turned many a bookshop into a research library. Sculpture on scores of sites and in

Fig. 8 - Areas of damage to head, hands and sword, Carrowculleen, Co. Sligo. Photo 1989 Martin A. Timoney.

museums in Dublin, London, Copenhagen, Stockholm, Budapest and Paris have been examined.

The writer concedes that he is not as well versed in the finer points of art history and appreciation of details of sculpture as he would wish, nor in the required sculptural vocabulary either. However, he feels that it is worth putting on record a description and the possible *comporanda* that he has come across or been guided to since May 1984 deriving from the assistance of so many willing colleagues and experts.

The writer does this in the hope that it can be the foundation for greater and much more expert research which will put this piece of Romanesque sculpture in context.

SCULPTURAL CONTEXT OF THE STONE

The possibility of a 17th, 18th or 19th century date has been raised for the Carrowculleen relief, with unjustifiable attempts to link it with the Guilfoyle family of Carrowculleen House in the adjacent townland of Lecarrow. For the relief to be of these more recent centuries, and since the stone is local and therefore not an import, a sculptor with subtle knowledgeable of the European Romanesque in this part of Ireland during the last few centuries would be needed. Fieldwork by Mary B. Timoney for a Masters in Arts Thesis on Sligo and north Mayo box-tombs, 1780 to 1850, involved searching every potential location of any sculpture, be it graveyard, church, castle or big house, for sculpture of all periods. There is nothing that matches the Carrowculleen relief in any sense at that time in this area.

IRISH & SLIGO ROMANESQUE

Irish Romanesque is a wonderful combination of decorative geometric and representational art. Carrowculleen lacks decorative geometric art, and is instead a piece of symbolic representational art. While the Carrowculleen sculpture is Romanesque and some elements have Irish *comporanda* the Carrowculleen stone stands apart from Irish Romanesque. The Irish examples are not very satisfactory. The Romanesque of Sligo, a list of which is provided below in an Appendix III, is much more mundane, to say the least. The best 12th century sculpture in the north-west is at Boyle Cistercian Abbey (Stalley 1973; Kalkreuter 2001). Some Irish and foreign Romanesque *comporanda* are now examined[6].

THE SEATED FIGURE WITH A SWORD

There are a few, somewhat strained, Irish examples of a seated figure with a sword across the lap.

On the side of late 11th century Shrine of the Stowe Missal* there is a bearded figure holding a sword across his lap (Mahr 1932, Pl. 67, lower; Henry 1970, 29; M de Paor 1977, 184-185; Ryan 1983, 66; Wallace 2002, 253). The depiction is more of a figure almost painfully attempting to sit down than one actually seated. He is flanked by pairs of dog-like animals.

Less close is the cleric seated between two standing figures depicted on a tympanum at Glendalough*, Co. Wicklow (Petrie 1845, 251).

There is a seated crowned Virgin holding the Divine Son on her lap in the southern bow of the programme of iconography at Ardmore*, Co. Waterford (Harbison, 1995, fig. 9; 1999, Pl. 218). While the content of this image is different the seat and seating arrangement are very similar to Carrowculleen.

In the ?8th to 9th century Garland of Howth*, alias Codex Usserianus Secundus, T.C.D. A.4.6(56), the right panel on the opening page to St. Mathew shows a seated figure holding a short sword upwards across his right shoulder in one hand and a closed book in the other (Cochrane 1893, 407, Fig. 22; Alexander 1978, Pl. 274).

In the ?9th or 10th century Irish-style book Book of Deer, Cambridge University Library MS Ii.6.32, f. 4v, a staring bearded St. Mathew has a short sword held at waist level and down between his legs (Alexander 1978, 87, No. 72; Hughes 1980, 22-37, Pl. 3; Ohlgren 1986, 63 and Pl. 2). Hughes (1980, 37) thinks that this was written in "some provincial scriptorium, quite possibly in Scotland". The sword of both of these is not unlike that at Carrowculleen.

On the left side of the Romanesque east window of c. 1184 within the Church of Ireland Cathedral at Tuam*, Co. Galway, is a strange and unidentified standing figure holding a short sword across its lap (Stalley 1987, Pl. 8).

A single queen* from a chess set was found in 1817 in a bog in Co. Meath (Joyce 1913, 479, fig. 338; Liddell 1937, 133, Ó Floinn, 1983, 189; 2002, 261, 268, 282). This has an exact parallel in the Lewis set[7].

The Breac Maodhóg* or Breac Maedóic shrine, of the O'Reilley of Breifne, (Henry 1970, Pls. 34-37; Harbison, 1999, Pls. 191-193; Mahr 1932, Pls. 60-61 figures; Wallace 2000, 59, Pl. 53; 2002, 234, 254) of about 1100 AD from Drumlane, Co. Cavan, has a number of attached plates with figures. The feeling of the pose of the heads of some of these figures is not unlike that of the Carrowculleen figure. The beard of the second figure from the left on the bottom row is close to that of the Carrowculleen figure. Also comparable is the sitting harper on the end of the shrine (Mahr 1932, Pl. 62:1a; Henry 1970, Pl.31; Stalley 1977, 191, fig. 39).

The 46 cm high sandstone baptismal font pedestal from Newtown Early*, Co. Kilkenny, (Harte 1987, 408) shows three seated male figures, each with the right hand raised in blessing; one holds a book in the left hand. The depiction of the figures, particularly of the clothes from the waist down, is not unlike that at Carrowculleen. The date of this pedestal is surely Romanesque rather than Medieval.

FOREIGN *COMPORANDA*

While the Irish *comporanda* for the seated figure with the sword are poor and strained some foreign ones[8] are much better.

The closest ones for the seated figure clearly are the kings in the sets of ?ivory chessmen found at Uig on the Isle of Lewis*, Outer Hebrides, Scotland, in 1831[9]. There are eight kings from this find, now housed in the National Museum of Scotland in Edinburgh or in the British Museum in London. While the depictions of the seated kings vary in detail they all have the same seated posture and all hold the short sword across the lap in the same way (Fig. 9). The scabbards are variously decorated. They wear a ?single-piece garment that shows several folds from the knees down. Some of the kings are bearded. The generally accepted date

Fig. 9 - One of the chessman kings, H.NS.19, from Lewis, Outer Hebrides, Scotland. © The Trustees of the National Museums of Scotland.

Fig. 10 - Herod in a carving of the Massacre of the Innocents at the reconstructed west door, Vor Frue kirke, Aalborg, Denmark. Photo 1985 Martin A. Timoney.

for these pieces is that they belong to "the milieu of Scandinavian Romanesque art of the twelfth century" (Stratford 1997, 47) though occasionally fine-tuned to the mid-12th (*e.g.*, Zarnecki 1984, 211, 227). There is debate as to the origin of these pieces, some arguing that they are of British manufacture, be that East Anglia or The Hebrides, while others see them as being of Scandinavian origin (Taylor 1978, 11-15).[10] Of all the eight Lewis kings the short sword of No. 187 in Goldschmidt's 1926 listing is closest to the Carrowculleen sword. However, if one allows for painted decoration of the scabbard then all but one, No. 182, would be comparable. Recent studies of these pieces (Stratford in Roesdahl and Wilson 1992, 391; Stratford 1997; Williams 2000, 19-22) indicate that the sets characterise a

Fig. 11 - Seated chess king from Trondheim, Norway, with what appears to be a sword held across the lap. After Ringstad 1996.

A CELEBRATION *OF* SLIGO

medieval Nordic army associated with a royal court, use a Viking "Berserker" in place of a castle, and that they are from Trondheim, the medieval capital of Norway, whose rulers were overlords of the Isle of Lewis from 1098 to 1266[11]

The next closest parallel which we have seen for the seated figure is Herod as depicted in a carving of the Massacre of the Innocents story now set in the wall near the west door of the reconstructed Vor Frue kirke, Aalborg*, Denmark (Fig. 10; Andersson 1968, 63, Pl. 57; Olesen 1978, 19), built between 1125 and 1150 according to Andersson, though the Herod is not very clearly dated within the 12th century. Here Herod is shown with the short sword across his lap, but held as one might expect with a more determined grip, being bent on a reign of terror!

Liddell (1937, plate after p. 18) and Stratford (1997, 46) illustrate a Scandinavian sub-Lewis walrus-ivory seated king now in the Louvre in Paris. The short sword held in his right hand across his lap is partly pulled from its scabbard while his left hand holds his very long beard. Stratford (1997, 46) gives a date of about 1200 for this.

Ringstad (1996, 113, fig. 15) illustrates (Fig. 11) a seated chess king with what appears, in a very unclear drawing, to be a sword held across the lap from Trondheim, Norway.

Dixon (1976, 74, lower; the photo is printed in reverse) illustrates a metal plate from the helmet of Agilulf, King of the Lombards (590-615). The central figure of this 7th century north-Italian piece holds a sword flat on his left knee while his right hand is held in blessing, the only instance of such a combination we have noted.

There is a seated figure with a similar short sword held down by his right side on the Nunburnholm cross-shaft (Collingwood 1927, fig. 152; Pattison 1973, Pl. XIa). This is dated to the late 9th or early 10th century.

David I and Malcolm IV, King of Scotland, are shown on a Charter (Boase 1953, 154 & Pl. 50a; Sharratt and Sharratt 1985, p. 371 & colour plate; Nicholls 1999, 23) granted to Kelso Cistercian Abbey in 1159 by Malcolm IV, King of Scotland. The youthful Malcolm is shown with his legs crossed and the long sword lying on his knees in a fashion akin to that at Carrowculleen. It differs also in that the sword is held in one hand only, the left one.

There are at least two seated figures with a sword of a different type across the lap in the early 12th century Bible of St. Etienne Harding (Dimer, 1971-1974: Pls. 141, 143).

There are two Scandinavian whalebone chessmen* on display in the Musée de Cluny,

Fig. 12. Seated chess king, Musée de Cluny (Cluny No. 11285) Paris, with sword held across the lap. After Sandron 1993. Photo Courtesy and © Musée de Cluny.

Paris (Cluny Nos. 11285 & 11286). The king (Fig. 12; Liddell 1937, 148, pl. opp. p. 31, middle row, right; Sandron 1993, 136; Huchard, Antoine, Lagabrielle and Le Pogam 1996, 121, fig. 153) holds a short sword in his right hand across his lap, with his hands gently down on the sword. To the right of the Cluny king a figure throws an enemy to the ground while to his left a man plays the bagpipes! Two soldiers appear to be on guard behind the throne. Liddell (1937, 148) gives the date as "probably 16th century" but the museum display card and Sandron (1993, 136) give the date as early 14th century[12].

Could this positioning of the sword, around which so much of my argument has revolved, be caused by nothing more than the carver's desire not to have projecting pieces that might snap off in carving or in playing? See Taylor (1978, 7) for comment on the lack of breakable protrusions on the pieces other than the kings in the sets.

THE LION AND THE EAGLE

This discussion has so far concentrated on the distinctive element of the sculpture, the seated figure with the sword. The two creatures, the lion and the eagle, are left for others to scrutinise in greater detail, but some comments are now included indicating that the sculpture overall fits into the Romanesque of Europe.

The lion is a frequently depicted animal in Irish Romanesque. Quite often it is as a mask only but those are not considered as our lion is in side view. There are lions in bold relief at Killeshin*, Freshford*, Liathmore, and Cormac's Chapel*. The geographically nearest lion to Carrowculleen is that on the east face of the high cross at Drumcliff*, Co. Sligo (Harbison 1992, No. 79, Pls. 213 and 218). Its date is debated, 9th century and not earlier than the 11th century (Harbison 1992, 374-375) being suggested.

There are three lions on the south face of a pillar, probably a high cross shaft, at Clonmacnois*, Co. Offaly, (Harbison 1992, No. 58, fig. 166). While there are differences the curl of the tails, the long legs and the backward-looking heads have a feeling somewhat reminiscent of the Carrowculleen lion.

The middle quadruped in the upper panel on the north face of the North Cross* at Clonmacnois (Harbison 1992, No. 55, p. 54) is a lion which is similar to the Maeshowe lion mentioned below. "The models for these date to within the first three or even four decades of the 9th century" (Harbison 1992, 379), three centuries before our period, but are mentioned for their similarity.

There is a humorous looking lion at the foot of the outer order of the Romanesque doorway at Killeshin* (Crawford and Leask 1925).

There are facing lions amidst foliage on the back of at least one of the Lewis Queen's thrones (Taylor 1978, Pl. 6b; Stratford 1997, 17, Pl. 17, left).

The backward-facing lion at Carrowculleen finds a parallel in the 8cm by 6.5cm lion scratched on the face of the north-eastern buttress of the passage tomb at Maeshowe, Orkney, Scotland. (*JRSAI*, Vol. 29, 284; Mackay Mackenzie 1936-1937, Fig. 1; RCAHMS 1946, No. 886, 313, Pl. 72; O'Meadhra 1987, fig. 65). It is quite similar in that each shows a vibrant lion with scales above and lines below on body. It may belong to the beginning of 12th century or as O'Meadhra (1987, 91-92) suggests, to the mid-12th century, having been cut by a passer-by en route home from a Jerusalem crusade.

In November 1987 Prof. George Zarnecki, London, wrote a very informative letter to me following examination of my notes and photos of the stone. It is quoted in part below with more below again where appropriate.

"I am afraid I have no easy answers to your questions, for the relief is most unusual.
I agree with your dating. There can be no doubt that it is 12th century.
You assume that the lion and the eagle are two of the symbols of the Evangelists. Perhaps. There are only two symbols on a tympanum at Aston, Herefordshire (Keyser, *A List of Norman Tympana and Lintels,* London 1927, fig. 105), John and Luke, and Fownhope, Herefordshire, (Keyser, *op. cit.,* Fig. 89), so there are precedents. But I confess that I have never seen symbol of St. Mark feeding on foliage. Your lion is not a symbol of St. Mark. The "spagetti" foliage above your beast is very similar to that on the tympanum at Moccas, not the one in Keyser (*op. cit.* Fig. 42) but over

the north doorway, which Keyser (p. 36) describes as "A lion amidst interlacing foliage". This is illustrated in my Ph. D. thesis, Pl. 80c (in Courtauld Institute). In conclusion on this: the lion is not a symbol of St. Mark but a conventional Romanesque animal "amidst foliage". The lion has a characteristic spiral form of hips (of Viking derivation) – see the Sarachophagus from Old St. Paul's, London, London Museum No. 4075, in *English Romanesque Art 1066-1200* Exhibition, London, 1984, No. 95.

My initial impression is that the relief is possibly English but the form of the capitals makes me hesitate."

Carved foliage is common at this period. There is foliage above the lion at Lathbury, Buckinghamshire (Zarnecki, Holt and Holland 1984, 63 and 154). There are facing lions amidst foliage on the back of at least one of the Lewis Queen's thrones (Taylor 1978, Pl. 6b; Stratford 1997, 17, Pl. 17, left).

The angle of the eagle's head is considered to be Irish in style. The eagle is not unlike the eagle of the early 9th century on fol. 32v of the Book of Armagh (de Paor 1977, Pl. 43) and to the much more elaborate eagle of *c*. 800 AD in the Book of Kells, folio 27v, (Ryan 1983, 10 and inside back cover). The shaping of the eye and the curve of the mouth is very similar to that of the lion in the Corpus Christi College, Oxford, Gospels, Ms. 122 (Harbison 1999, Pl. 168) dated to 'perhaps after 1140'.

INTERPRETATION
IDENTIFICATION OF THE SEATED FIGURE

The problem of identifying the theme depicted on this stone has not been resolved and not being sure how much more there was makes identification of what we have most problematical. There is a feeling of benevolent dominance, of a caring righteous father figure or ruler in this seated figure. Two lines of argument are possible, one religious and one secular.

If there were only three elements to the frieze then the seated figure could be God seated between the Lion of St. Mark and the Eagle of St. John, but Prof. George Zarnecki thinks otherwise.

What then of the other two evangelists, the Man for St. Matthew and the Ox for St. Luke? Perhaps they were never included. But could these be depicted to the right, perhaps on other stones. The left edge of the stone is an original end. This would preclude our figure from being Christ, who should surely have to be centrally positioned. In this arrangement the stone would be the left end of a five or a seven evangelist/person frieze. This would cause problems of identification of the seated figure, suggesting that the central figure we now see could not be God, and that we would then be looking for an even more stately central figure, but then we do not have the other parts of the either. It is possible that a long-enough section of this sandstone could be found locally.

Could this be part of a multi-stone frieze, with other stones to the left and right, with figures and creatures? This could mean a long frieze to accommodate five or seven elements, perhaps up to 150cm long, though not necessarily of one stone. Combinations of Evangelists and Persons such as [E P E] P [E P E] or E] [E P E] [E could be possible. A complex Romanesque programme of iconography is to be seen in the west wall of the Cathedral at Ardmore, Co. Waterford. However, if the lion and the eagle are not religious symbols then the need for finding the other two 'evangelists' and the search for a long frieze of up to seven elements and where such could have been becomes redundant.

Who then could the male seated figure be? Several copiously illustrated volumes of religious themes such as Schiller's *Iconography of Christian Art*, Farrar's *Life of Christ as Represented in Art* (1896), Smith and Cheetham's *Dictionary of Christian Antiquities*, Saint Laurent's *Guide de L'Art Chretien* (1874) and Harbison's *High Crosses of Ireland* (1992) all are devoid of precise *comporanda*. One is therefore left wondering if this figure is in fact Christ at all.

Male personages have been suggested and these together with those listed by Hall (1994, 88; 1996, 294-295) as having a sword as at least one of their attributes include David, Solomon, Paul (as at Holme-on-the-Wolds) but the Carrowculleen Paul is not bald, Saint Iago de Compostella despite the lack of a shell, Martin of Tours despite the lack of a cloak, Daniel on the basis of being between two living things, a different theme recently discussed by Lucas (1987), Colmcille, Adomnán and even a local "Regal Saint". Martin Blindheim suggested a royal saint between symbols of might and force and a date of about 1150. The epithet *nia*, for champion, hero, prize fighter or warrior, was used in relation to Columba, and maybe the sword here is symbolic of such ability.

On the other hand the eagle faces away from the seated figure, and one is left wondering if it is facing towards a central figure to its right? Its left wing points forward as if indicating something of importance, a lost centrally-positioned major figure?, but what then of the lion which is also facing away from the central figure? Is it a case of both the lion and the eagle being overpowered by the splendour of the central figure who has then to be God? Perhaps the lion symbolises the human nature of Christ and the eagle the divine nature. At Fownhope, Herefordshire, there is a carving of a Madonna and Child flanked by a lion and an eagle (Zarnecki, Holt and Holland 1984, 64 and 178); Stalley (pers. comm.) says the lion and eagle there do not have an obvious religious function.

Prof. George Zarnecki's thoughts of November 1987 are as follows.

> "Subject? The figure has a nimbus, so your belief that it is Christ is a possibility but not certainty. It is not a cruciform nimbus. Christ with a sword? In the vision of St. John, Christ is shown with a sword emerging from His mouth (see Émile Mâle, *Religious Art in France, The Twelfth Century,* Princeton, 1978, pp. 15 ff.). But your figure looks more like Solomon (see Pierpont Morgan Ms. 43, Huntingfield Psalter) on the Beatus viv page, though there he holds the sword upright.
> As for the subject – it is obviously influenced by images of Christ, but it is not Christ but a ruler, perhaps a saintly (nimbus!) ruler. Any candidates in Ireland?"

RELIGIOUS *COMPORANDA*

The Bible, particularly the Book of Revelations, has many references to swords but frequently these describe the sword as coming out of the mouth of God; there are many depictions of such biblical references. This Carrowculleen sculpture is not a depiction of the Sword, the Sword of Truth, coming out of the Mouth of God as frequently mentioned in the Bible (e.g., Rev. 1:16, 2;16, 19:21; Hosea 6:5; Isaiah 49:2) and depicted, e.g., on a 12th century tympanum in the church at La Lande-de-Cubzac in Gironde (Mâle 1922, fig. 7) and in the vision of St. Jean in the 12th century Manuscrit de l'Apocalypse de Beatus in the Bibliothèque National in Paris (Mâle 1922, fig. 8).

The halo and an interpretation of the lion and the eagle being symbols of the evangelists argues for the central figure being a religious figure, maybe even Christ. One might expect a cross but there is no evidence for a cross; one could have been painted on.

Except for the halo on the central figure there is nothing unequivocally religious about this piece. The lion lacks wings and a halo and the eagle lacks a book and a halo, attributes one would expect with symbols of the evangelists. Can we then take the lion and the eagle as representing two Evangelists at all? This possible religious attribution is further discussed below under function.

The late Helen M. Roe, an expert on medieval Irish sculpture, regarded the stone as being too important and of too great a quality for it to be Herod. She thought Herod would be depicted more in caricature than here, but then at Aalborg he is well carved in a quite similar manner. However, the presence of a halo certainly rules Herod out.

SECULAR *COMPORANDA*

Can we take the Lewis, Cluny and Louvre examples to imply that the Carrowculleen figure is a king, but not Christ? Could the lion simply be a symbol of nobility and the eagle one of swiftness see above? Should we look at the lion and the eagle as kings of their respective animal and bird kingdoms?, and if so what of the central figure?

If we leave aside the belief that the piece is a religious depiction and consider it to be secular, *i.e.,* of a local of even provincial ruler. The presence of a halo could indicate that the figure was in life a good and saintly person. Despite the damage to the eyes there is a feeling of the benevolent dominance of a caring righteous father figure or stately ruler, a King in Judgement or a King in a Decision Making pose, 'a heroic and saintly figure, the precise identity of whom remains unknown' to quote Stalley. The closest *comporanda* of the period, the Lewis chessmen, are secular as opposed to religious. There are lions on the back of the throne of at least one Lewis queen. If the sculptor saw a full set he chose the secular king as opposed to the religious bishop as the model.

THE 'ARCHITECTURAL' ARCH

Miniature arches are known from the Romanesque. There is a small arched carving (Eygun 1970, 85) with the Holy Women at the Tomb at the Romanesque church at Chadenac, France, and a less elaborate miniature arch at Chauvigny, France, has St. Peter within (Dursel 1975, Pl. 66). The programme of iconography at Ardmore, Co. Waterford (Harbison, 1995, fig. 9; 1999, Pl. 218) has many simple arches with figures within them and arches with heads form the pediment at Clonfert, Co. Galway (Harbison 1999, Pl. 225).

The Virgin and Child at the Benedictine (Cluniac) Priory of Sainte-Marie de Donzy-le-Pré, Nièvre, France, of *c.* 1130 (Evans 1948, Pl. 43a) seated in a splendid baldacino on a tympanum which has differently carved columns, one twisted and the other herringbone. The arrangement of the arch is very similar to that at La Vielle Major, Alte-Kathedrale, in Marseille, Bouches-du-Rhone, (Rupprecht 1975, Pls. 246-247) where the arch falls short of resting on the columns; symbols of the evangelists are positioned over the columns.

Liddell (1937, plate after p. 18) illustrates medieval ivory chess pieces, formerly in the Abbey of St. Denis, where the Kings and Queens are within very fine decorative miniature arches. There are twisted columns at Cashel, Co. Tipperary, and perhaps at Cloonkeen, Co. Limerick, and they are well known abroad, *e.g.*, Durham.

INSPIRATION FOR THE SCULPTURE

How did this Carrowculleen sculpture come into existence? The idea of the scene of the Carrowculleen sculpture could have come from a coin, manuscript, tapestry, ivory[13], wooden model, seal, chess piece or pattern book; see Zarnecki (1984) for the range of materials and objects in circulation at this period. Curiously the stonework in the Zarnecki catalogue is not productive of thought while those in other materials have been more so. The feeling is that the inspiration for this overall carving lies in detailed manuscripts or ivories. The arch could have derived from a painted one, such as one in the Winchester Bible of 1160-1180 (Zarnecki, Holt and Holland 1984, Pl. 65, p. 57). The sculpture is different to Hiberno-Romanesque and it may have been done here by a foreign sculptor. Taylor (1978, 13) proposes such a scenario for doorways at Ely. There is a difficulty in that, while different sources may be plausible for the three main parts of the design, no one source fits all three.

The inspiration for the central seated figure is surely a chess piece of the Lewis workshop. Is it possible that the idea of the seated figure reached Ireland via a Lewis workshop piece. Joyce (1913, II, 477-481) indicates that chess playing was widespread in ancient Ireland, so pieces could have been frequently seen. But then chess was widely played throughout Europe and beyond, mainly by the aristocratic laity. But only a few known from Ireland.

Williams (2000, 23-24) illustrates some of the Charlemagne Chessmen in the Bibliothèque Nationale in Paris and points out that these 11th century southern Italian made pieces have their inspiration coming from the two ends of Europe, Byzantium and the Nordic world; they are believed to record a real conflict.

Perhaps the idea of the seated figure with the sword across the lap has a meaning that we no longer appreciate. As it is so similar to the Lewis kings perhaps the sculptor saw such a chessman. There is no reason why that could not have been here in Skreen, considering the mobility of such chess pieces and the closeness of that part of the design. It is also quite possible that a pilgrim from Skreen could have gone abroad and picked up the idea or even a chess piece. Harbison (1991) details pilgrimages through the ages and Stalley (1988, 397-420) has discussed the pilgrimage to Saintiago de Compostella; pilgrimages were just one form of people, and ideas, on the move. Furthermore, three Sligo monastic sites, Inishmurray, Drumcliff and Skreen, had close connections with Iona, an island at one end of the Hebrides while Lewis is at the other.

Have we here a combination of local stone and foreign ideas, implying a foreign sculptor or one in a foreign frame of mind, sculpting a difficult piece of stone, even though there is good consistent sandstone to be found locally?

WHAT IS THIS SCULPTURE FROM?

The lack of a known location leaves us with the problem of what the function of this piece was and this is compounded by not knowing just how much more there was. If the piece had a religious function it could have been a door lintel though the underside makes this seem unlikely, part of a tympanum, an altar frontal or part of a programme or frieze of iconography. Highly decorated door lintels exist at Carndonagh, Maghera, Clonca, all in Co. Donegal, and Dunshaughlin, Co. Meath (Harbison 1995, 271-280). There is no evidence that this stone was a mandorla.

As for a tympanum Ballisodare is the only nearby site with any decent Romanesque sculpture that could have had a tympanum (Wakeman 1885, 52). There is uncertainty about the date of the material above the lintel there and early drawings (Timoney, M.B., 2002) are not detailed enough to tell us unequivocally if it was always as it is now. The writer placed a full size photocopy of the design above the lintel but was not satisfied that it was a proper arrangement. I do not believe that the Carrowculleen sculpture is from Ballisodare even though sandstone with quartz is used there, though the grains there are not as large as the grains at Carrowculleen.

If the piece is of a secular, rather than a religious, background then its function should be separately considered. Again we are hampered by the lack of a true locational context and that we do not know how much more there was. On the other hand it could be a symbolic or decorative sculpture from a secular masonry building or a bridge[14].

Stalley's (2002) article on the Romanesque wall painting at Cashel brings out the significant association of wealth, power and patronage with the arts at that time in the rich fertile area of east Munster. Similarly, but not to such a great extent, Carrowculleen is close to some of the best land in Co. Sligo, the Barony of Tireragh[15]. How much of our history is lost because of the lack of early records of this part of Ireland?

POSSIBLE ORIGINAL LOCATIONS

There is no indication of an Early Christian monastic enclosure or feature of any sort on the ground nor on any O.S. map of Carrowculleen, nor is there a lost historically-attested monastic site hereabouts. Neither is there any indication of any appropriate medieval building hereabouts nor is there any historical or folk memory that would shed light on the presence of the stone here. The sculpture had to have been brought from elsewhere, but as the stone is local it need not have been brought from afar.

Since there is nothing of a monastic nature at Carrowculleen, Sl.19:180, the temptation is for to suggest the nearest Early Christian monastic sites, Skreen, Sl.19:7, *alias Scrín Adomnán*, three kilometres over the hill to the north, and Corkagh Beg, Sl.12:25, six kilometres to the north-west. However there is no evidence for the <u>sculptured</u> use of similar stone at either Skreen or Corkagh Beg (M.B. Timoney pers. comm.). There is only one piece of this type of sandstone, in the north-east quoin, to be seen in Skreen medieval church. The medieval church at Skreen had inner lining walls added sometime in the early eighteenth century by the Protestant church authorities. A porch was then added to the west gable and perhaps then the original western doorway was altered; the form of the original doorway is unrecognisable today due to collapse and ivy. Could the Carrowculleen sculpture have come from this doorway or from one of the supposed seven churches which Thomas O'Connor records the tradition of at Skreen in *The Ordnance Survey Letters* in 1836?[16] Unfortunately O'Connor does not state the positions of the five churches still remembered at that time and we therefore do not know if they were all at the one site or distributed throughout the parish. [17]

As indicated elsewhere in this volume (Timoney, M.A., 2002, Appendix II) we know of no remains of the Augustinian foundation on Aughris, 8km to the north-west. Perhaps we should be looking towards the sites of incoming Cistercians in the mid-12th century. Before settling at Boyle that the Cistercian community was at Grellachdinach in 1148, then at Drumconaid *alias* Drumcunny and then at Bun Finni *alias* Buninna near Beltra before finally settling at Boyle in 1161 (Gwynn & Hadcock 1970, 128; Carville 1990, 49) [18].

DATE

Two possibilities as to the date of this sculpture have been proposed. One is that the work is a modern creation, perhaps of 1983 vintage. Argument against this are set out in Appendix I. The alternative is that the sculpture is 12th century and that has been the thrust of this research.

Taylor (1978, 14) argues for a date between 1135 and 1170 for the Lewis chessmen but because of the way the bishop's mitres are set on the heads, points front and back, suggests to him a date no earlier than 1150 (1978, 15).

The tubular drapery here is stylised, not yet the free flowing Gothic.

From the above cited examples it would seem that the closest *comporanda* for the seated figure are to be found, not 'towards Rome' in France or Italy nor 'towards Santiago de Compostella' in France or Spain, but, painful as it might seem to some, it is northwards and north-eastwards, in Scandinavia and its world, particularly Denmark and Norway, that *comporanda* for the distinctive seated figure are to be found. The geological assessments of the stone leave no doubt that it is from the local area. The assessment of the surface condition by Pavía and Bolton (Appendix II) is that the sculpture is ancient. The sculpture is Romanesque, which in Ireland is from 1130 to 1200, but from the *comporanda* cited above the date for Carrowculleen is probably later in this time-span, in the second half of the 12th century, and close to that of the Lewis chessmen.

ACKNOWLEDGEMENTS

Many friends, colleagues and 'friends I never have met' have had input into the research for this article and their help I now acknowledge.

Jack Flynn found the sculpture and the reference to Sato's sword, Prof. Roger Stalley arranged access to the Trinity College Art History Library, made many constructive comments and provided a draft copy of the entry for the *Corpus of Romanesque Sculpture in Britain and Ireland*, Prof. Etienne Rynne suggested Lewis, Raghnall Ó Floinn suggested Aalborg, The Garland of Howth and Book of Deer, Prof. Prof. George Zarnecki helped with English comparisons, Dr. Michael Ryan suggested Breac Maodhóg and we jointly interviewed George Williams and Ann Presley at Carrowculleen in 1989 and has been very supportive throughout, Con Manning suggested Maeshowe, Conor Newman suggested Glendalough, Ian Fisher suggested the Kelso Charter, Dr. Peter Harbison wrote me many discursive letters; Helen Roe, Shiobhán de hÓir, Dr. Neil Stratford and Miriam Clyne were very helpful.

In addition the following were helpful.

In Sligo: John Corcoran, David Johnston, Kieran and Margaret Kennedy, Petie Diamond, John McTernan, Desmond Smith, Aodhán O'Higgins, Yvonne Perceval, Mary B. Timoney, Brendan and Yvonne Kilcullen.

In Dublin: John Bradley, John Foley, Tom Condit, Liam de Paor, Dr. Raymond Gillespie, Heather King, Elizabeth Kirwan, Eamon P. Kelly, Dr. Andrew Halpin, Susan McNab, Victor Buckley, Paul Mullarkey, David Sweetman, Denise Sheehan, Prof. George Sevastopulo.

In Ireland: Cormac Bourke, Sr. Mary Devine, Elizabeth FitzPatrick, Bishop Thomas Flynn, Dr. Raymond Gillespie, Daniel Kinnahin, Fr. Michael Murphy, Dr. Brian Scott, Frank Tivnan, Eithne Verling, Aidan Walsh, Heinrick Härke, Michael Gibbons, Olive Alcock, Caroline Duignan.

In England: Prof. Rosemary Cramp, Peter Draper, Hazel Gardiner, Dr. Ron Baxter, Dr. Ian Kinnes, Jim Lang, Dr. David Tomlin, Sir David Wilson.

In Scotland: Dr. Allison Sheridan, Helen Nicoll.

In France: Jean-Christophe Ton-That.

In Sweden: Dr. Stefan & Margaretha Bergh, Henry Bengston, Prof. Patrik Reuterswärd, Jan Svanberg, Dr. Uaininn O'Meadhra.

In Norway: Prof. Martin Blenheim.

In Denmark: Anna-Maria Gebaur, Poul Otto Nielsen.

In Holland: Elizabeth de Jong, Prof. Elizabeth den Hartog.

The archaeological and library staff of the National Museum of Ireland, the Royal Society of Antiquaries of Ireland, Trinity College Library, the Royal Irish Academy, the Victoria and Albert Museum, the British Museum and the Society of Antiquaries in London.

To all these, and any others who have been inadvertently omitted, I offer my sincerest thanks. Hopefully this article goes some way towards recognising their individual efforts.

I thank Michael Yeats for permission to quote from W.B. Yeats, *A Dialogue of Self and Soul* from *The Winding Stair and Other Poems*, 1933.

Hopefully the sculpture being no longer 'Unspotted' will, in the fullness of time, find its proper place in the story of sculpture.

APPENDIX I

CLAIMS THAT THE CARROWCULLEEN RELIEF IS MODERN

There have been claims, by a neighbour in 1992 and by Ann Presley in 2001, that George Williams had carved the Carrowculleen relief. This had to have been sometime between 1977 and 1984. Ann Presley & George Williams came to Carrowculleen in 1977 via Galway from the Isle of Wight and Glastonbury in England; we first saw the relief in 1984. The year 1983 was suggested for the sculpture by a neighbour at which time George Williams, 1913-2000, was 70 years old. This claim should be set against the following facts.

The Carrowculleen relief was first seen by Martin A. Timoney, Mary B. Murphy (now Timoney), Jack Flynn, and Stefan and Margareta Bergh on Thursday 28th June 1984. Some days later in early July 1984 we, Flynn, Timoney, Murphy and the late Des Smith went to Carrowculleen to properly record the relief about which we had no doubts as to its antiquity and authenticity. Here we met Ann Presley and George Williams for the first time. They were quite excited at the prospect of 'experts' coming to tell them of the art history of the stone in their wall. The discussion revolved around the relief being ancient. Either the first or the second volume of Françoise Henry's trilogy on Early Christian Art was produced by Ann Presley where she pointed to some 'comparable' illustrations. Having had some time to consider the relief I told her that it was the third, or Romanesque, volume we needed.

The relief was found to have been taken out of the wall sometime prior to September 1988. It was deposited in the National Museum of Ireland in Dublin in 1989. Despite a number of visits to Carrowculleen it was not until July 1990 that I found anyone to be at home. On the next day Dr. Michael Ryan, Keeper, Irish Antiquities Division of the National Museum of Ireland, and I visited Ann Presley and George Williams at Carrowculleen. Dr. Ryan pointed out that the relief was an archaeological object within the meaning of the National Monuments Acts and this was accepted by George Williams. The question of the origin of the relief was raised with Ann Presley and George Williams but they had "no useful information on that matter" and said that "it must have been built into the wall when they bought the property in 1977". George Williams talked about "traces of <u>original</u> pigment on the stone". George Williams did not claim that he had carved the relief.

I went to Ann Presley at Carrowculleen in 1998 to ask about the relief. George Williams was at this time confined to bed but Ann Presley said George Williams knew nothing of the relief and she did not make any claim then as to it being modern. There were no claims that George Williams had carved the relief.

During my lecture in Beltra Hall in May 2001, which Martin Wilson had arranged, I talked of the relief and of it being Romanesque. Ann Presley was in the audience but did not make any claim then as to it being modern.

At no stage did George Williams claim to have carved the stone.

If the sculpture was modern there was no need for it to be removed from the wall by a neighbour, perhaps without the house owner's permission, and brought for identification to Sligo Library about August 1988.

I have tried to find someone who might have seen this sculpture in position a quarter of a century ago but there does not seem to be anybody alive now who worked land hereabouts then; the late P. Kilcullen, the former resident, was not married.

Ann Presley & George Williams went to Pat Kitchin, former Vice President of Sligo Field Club, and his wife Sheila at Ballisodare about 1981 but the sculpture was not mentioned at all; perhaps it was not even exposed at all at this stage?

Other work by George Williams that I have seen is nothing more than basic, of a totally different character and lesser quality than that of this stone. These works include simple 'megalithic art' of 1984 vintage on an elongated sea-rolled boulder; the flat slab and the pillar with a faint cross, now marking his grave in Skreen R. C. cemetery, which were at the Carrowculleen house in the 1980s may have been introduced to the area. The pillar bears the following "George Fent Williams, 1913-2000", a finely tooled small hedgehog and "A.G.". The latter is not the recent sculptor's initials as that was Petie Diamond of Sheeanmore.

If George Williams was capable of carving this stone he would have had, not just a national, but, an international reputation as a sculptor, and would have commanded substantial fees for his work.

There are a number of other points to be kept in mind as well.

When we first saw the stone in 1984 geological weathering was quite evident, much more so than a year facing the Atlantic winds could have produced, or even seven if carved in 1977. Most telling is that there is no appreciable difference in the surface condition of the stone all around, carved or not, whereas modern surface alterations caused by modern damage show a distinctively fresher surface than when we first saw the stone in 1984. Other stones in the wall are similarly well weathered. See the Appendix by Pavía and Bolton on the surface condition of the Carrowculleen relief.

Why did George Williams use a broken sandstone, peppered with so much quartz, when there are many more conveniently positioned suitable stones of similar geology in the buildings and fieldwalls hereabouts? If the sculpture is modern why are there traces of several different paints and a tar-like substance on its surface? The relief was so rigidly secure in the wall that all us who saw it in 1984 doubt if it could have been carved in the wall.

The Irish Antiquities Division of the National Museum of Ireland has purchased the relief. Several archaeologists and art historians have seen the relief, or photographs of it.

If Ann Presley is correct in her assertion that George Williams spent time working at the stone then what was he doing there if he was not carving it? How come the sculpture was not revealed until between 1977 and 1984? Perhaps there is one answer to these two questions. There is a black substance adhering to parts of the deepest carved surface and one gets the impression that it covered all of the stone at one time. Was the black stuff a substance put on the stone to keep plaster from adhering to the carving at a time when the relief was being concealed? Could George Williams have simply been picking away this black substance[19] to reveal the sculpture beneath?

APPENDIX II

THE SURFACE CONDITION OF THE CARROWCULLEEN RELIEF

Sara Pavía and Jason Bolton
Faculty of the Built Environment
Dublin Institute of Technology

The aim of this assessment was to determine whether the surface of the Carrowculleen sculpture was carved relatively recently or at some point in antiquity. The assessment was based on examining the weathering forms and patina visible on the stone surface.

The Carrowculleen sculpture was carved from a medium-grained, beige to light brown sandstone containing conglomerate levels of quartz pebbles. The sandstone currently shows marked fractures along the sedimentary bedding to the uncarved surface of the sculpture. This sandstone displays a number of weathering features which may give an indication of the amount of time likely to produce this surface appearance.

The carved surface is intensely weathered showing a weathering patina, including organic remains, mineral dust, lime, paint and a non-identified black pasty substance. The surface is also colonised by lichen, algae and moss.

Stone weathering is typically selective and develops naturally when a stone is exposed outdoors. The weathering noted in the Carrowculleen sculpture is selective. For example, some of the quartz pebbles in the sandstone appear fractured. However, none of these quartz pebbles show biological colonisation and the weathering patina is mostly absent. The lichen and moss colonisation is also selective and is determined by local variations of the sandstone composition as well as surface porosity and roughness. For example, there is a significant development of lichen filling a depression in the carved surface of the stone underneath the sword. This lichen appears dehydrated with shrinkage fractures indicating that this may be an old coating.

It is unlikely that the sandstone was artificially coated with an ageing patina as this would have not been selective. Artificial patinas would show even textures of initial application and local traces of later alteration(s) to show artificial ageing or "antiqueing". Other features of the sandstone surface, including roughness and porosity, suggest that this stone surface has been exposed for a very long time period. The selective patina recorded "would have also required a long exposure.

It is our opinion that that this carved sandstone is not a modern carving but an historical sculpture. Romanesque sculpture and archaeological stone artefacts that have not been cleaned, when located in rural atmospheres, usually show weathering patinas and surfaces with similar features to that of the Carrowculleen sculpture.

APPENDIX III

SITES IN CO. SLIGO WITH ROMANESQUE ARCHITECTURE OR SCULPTURE

Martin A. Timoney and Mary B. Timoney

Romanesque architectural pieces or sculpture are known from the following Sligo sites.

Aghanagh: Sl.40:171. Plain round-headed doorway: Wakeman 1885

Ballisodare: Sl.20:109. Window, doorway, quoins, font; Wakeman 1885; Timoney, M.B., 2002.

Carrowculleen: Sl.19:180. Relief, this article.

Church Hill: Sl.32:195. Arcading with pellet ornament on a re-used stone in a south window.

Corcoran's Acres: Sl.12:25. A few columns and a possible capital now buried.

Drumcliff: Sl.8:84. High Cross, if 12th century; See Harbison (1992, I, 70-74, 373-375).

Keeloges: Sl.6:8. Plain round head of a window, now buried.

Killaspugbrone: Sl.13:2. Plain round-headed doorway; Wakeman 1885

Killoran North: Sl.25:112. Moulded stone in west jamb of south doorway and in window to the west.

Oliver Davies suggested two others (copy of his notes in Sites and Monuments Record.

Ballintemple: Sl.7:14. Oliver Davies noted 'probably Hiberno-Romanesque'; not proven.

Creeveymore: Sl.2:7. Oliver Davies noted '?Hiberno-Romanesque'; not proven.

Notes

1. Despite W.B. Yeats' almost prophetic words on Sato's sword, written in 1927, are to the Carrowculleen sculpture they relate to the 550-year old sword that Yeats received as a present from a Japanese man in Portland, Oregon. It is quoted here courtesy of Senator Michael Yeats.

2. My unprintable initial remark to Jack Flynn when he pointed it out to me led to the stone immediately acquiring the name "The Pink Stone".

3. Co. Sligo 6-inch O.S. sheet 19, 2.7cm from West, 36.3cm from South; Grid Reference 15190.33036; Recorded Monuments and Places Sl.19:180, with the cautious title "architectural fragment". There is no known link with Carrowculleen House, to the east in Lecarrow townland, which was bought in 18th century by the Guilfoyle, *alias* Gilfoyle, family.

In July 1954, only weeks after the Revival of Sligo Field Club, our Society visited the cashel and souterrain on Mr. Kilgallon's land on the top of Carrowculleen Hill, i.e., The Red Hill of Skreen, before going on to Ardnaglass castle and Aughris head. There is no mention of the Romanesque sculpture in the Sligo Field Club files for this or any other occasion.

4. Skreen is *Scrín Adamnán*; Adamnán being abbot of Iona from 680 until his death in 720. The shrine in question was a collection of twenty-six articles assembled in the late 7th century by Adomnán (Gwynne 1914; 1915). It must have been a quite sizeable shrine to hold all these relics. Despite this it passed back and forth between Ireland and Scotland until at least the early 12th century when it is mentioned in a

poem in B. Mus. MS Harleian 5280, f. 27, after which we have no further record of its existence. The poem about the shrine is of 11th or early 12th century date and is indicative of continued connections with Scotland down to that time. The shrine had a relic of St. Paul, one of the suggested candidates for the Carrowculleen figure, but there was no sword in the shrine.

In "Notes on Ancient Skreen by J. M.", perhaps J. Mulligan, in *The Sligo Champion* of Sept. 18th 1926, page 2, the author writes "In a garden adjacent to the burial ground, there is a slab or stone which is three feet ten inches long [117cm], nearly two feet seven inches wide [79cm] and ten inches high [26cm] having a rectangular cavity in the centre measuring fifteen inches long [38cm], eight wide [20cm] and five inches in height [13cm]. This stone is supposed to be the altar used by St. Adamnan and as an altar also means a shrine it is more likely that it was from this altar that the parish got its present name." There is strong local tradition of this stone, and of a reputedly j-shaped stone to perhaps fit into it, being at the farmyard to the east of the graveyard.

5. There is a cast of monarch's heads at a house in south Sligo which was concealed during troubled times by the application of pebble dash.

6. The writer has examined the actual items, as opposed to illustrations, marked by an *.

7. Ó Floinn (1983, 189) mentions that only two other figures are known from the same workshop as the Lewis chessmen. One of these, a knight, is from Grägard on Öland, Sweden. The other, a warder, is an unprovenanced piece in the Bargello in Florence, but we unfortunately do not know how or when that piece reached Italy at the other end of Europe.

Nine other carvings in wood, stone and ivory which form a group of sculptures around the Lewis chessmen are mentioned by Taylor (1978, 11) who states that they are of the same Scandinavian artistic *milieu* (1978, 13).

This Meath piece seems to be the only ivory chessman found in Ireland. Liddell (1937, 133) mentions another ivory chessman in Dublin, and ascribes it to the R. Bale Collection. He describes it as follows "It measures 2" high and $1/2$" wide. Irish 12th century. A bear is devouring a crouching male figure covered with a cowl and holding in his right hand what is apparently one of the square handbells used in the early Irish church. A cast is in the Victoria & Albert Museum." Raghnall Ó Floinn has located this piece in the National Museum of Ireland. It is a non-Irish late-medieval, possibly 16th century, piece that came into the Royal Irish Academy collection before 1864 from the Murray collection from Mullingar, Co. Westmeath. Its registration number is R.2531 and it also had an Art and Industry number, 15-1921.

8. Of 1907 vintage is the sculpture by H.P. Pedersen-Dan of the sleeping Holgar Danske at Kronberg Castle, Helsingor (Elsinore), Denmark. His long sword is laid across his lap with his arms folded across it and his shield rests against his seat.

9. There would have been four full sets of chessmen originally, the stock in trade of a merchant (Taylor 1978, 15); forty-five pawns, one knight and two rooks are missing. Williams (2000, 13, 19, and particularly 20) gives wonderful photos of these most endearing pieces.

10. There may be significance in the way the sword is held. Youngs (1989, 142, fig. 134) and Finlay (1979, after p. 160) illustrate an angel from an 8th - 9th century Irish mount found in a woman's grave at Rise Farm, Oppdal, S. Trondelag, Norway. This angel, in a semi-seated pose, holds a short sword diagonally down across its body. On a French Gothic ivory ?chess piece in the Victoria and Albert Museum in London it is shown from right shoulder to left toe, with the scabbarded blade between the legs (Picard 1924, Pl. CCXI, No. 1255) and in the Cistercian Heda Kyrka*, Alvastra, Sweden, the second half of the 12th century seated figure, perhaps Samson because of his long hair, has his left leg wrapped around the scabbarded sword (Andersson, 1968, 123, Pl. 78).

11. See Long (1975) for the history and a report on excavations of medieval Trondheim, and specifically (1975, 21-22, 23) for finds of bone and horn.

12. Perhaps Liddell (1937, 148) intended XIV Century, not XVI Century, and this error was copied from the text into the photo caption (Plate opposite p. 31) as "probably sixteenth century". Huchard, Antoine, Lagabrielle, and Le Pogam (1996, 121, fig. 153, front left) illustrate the second Cluny* chess piece, a rook or horn-blower. Sandron (1993, 136) points out that the Cluny seated king and horn-blower are matching pieces. The two Cluny pieces came together into that museum from the Charles Stein Donation in 1885. Stratford illustrates (1997, p. 46, fig. 58) an identical horn-blower, though the horn has been broken off, in the British Museum in London. That piece was apparently acquired in the 1850s, indirectly through J. Webb, from the Copenhagen collection of Col. Somers (Stratford 1997, 59, note 50 and copy of British Museum record courtesy of Prof. Stratford). The later record also refers to a comparable chess piece in the

Kunstindustrimuset in Oslo, OK 10876, to a piece in The Walters Art Gallery, Baltimore (found in Puddle Dock, London) and to a piece sold at Sotheby's London (16/5/1968, Lot 48; exhibeted Victoria and Albert Museum, "Growth of London Exhibition", 17th July – 30th August, 1964, No. C41). These pieces are of the same workshop and possibly even of the same set. One is tempted to think that these pieces date close to the Lewis chessmen. Stratford (1997, 59, note 50) disagrees. He says that the Scandinavian piece in the British Museum "may date from the later 14th century" but while continuing a theme of a seated king with a sword across the lap into later centuries it has nothing to do with the Lewis hoard.

13. An early 12th century ivory crosier crook found at Aghadoe, Co. Kerry, has been in Stockholm Museum since about 1922 (Henry 1970, 114, fig. 9, Pl. 85).

14. There is a tantalizing reference in Skene's edition of Reeves *Adomnán,* clxv, to a bridge, *Drehid Awnan,* over a stream from The Well of Skreen to the Atlantic, a distance of less than three kilometres. The bridge is no longer locally recalled. There is no bridge over the stream at Skreen itself. That over the main road in Masreagh is now a deeply covered concrete pipe. There is a probably 18th of 19th century round arched bridge where the sea road crosses the stream in Toberawnaun. We could find no indication of stepping stones, as indicated on OS 13, some fields upstream of this. The 1849 maps for the drainage of several adjacent townlands up from Dunmoran, SLLSA #1079, do not name any of the features on the stream from Skreen to the sea at Dunmoran. In "Notes on Ancient Skreen by J. M.", perhaps J. Mulligan, in *The Sligo Champion* of Sept. 25th 1926, page 2, the author relates that convenient to the well at Toberawnaun "lies the great lec or stane which at one time spanned the river Dunmoran, and was known as *Droichead Aionan,* or the bridge of Adamnan. This stone now lies in parts at the bottom of the river." This writer has not found the parts of this stone.

15. Tirereagh was known in the early 18th century as 'The Granary for the Counties of Leitrim and Fermanagh' with 'a considerable store still left for exportation, sometimes 30,000 barrels of barley are exported from the port of Sligo in one year' (Henry 1739, 349).

16. Two matching sections of the shaft of a substantial high cross (Timoney 1999; 1999-2000) were incorporated into the masonry of Drumcliffe Church of Ireland church about 1811 when the present building was being erected. Are we seeing here a pattern of Early Christian or Romanesque sculpture being spirited out of sight by the Church of Ireland?

17. One wild suggestion is that the sculpture could have come from a church or building adjacent to Lough Achree, a few hundred metres to the south of Carrowculleen. The basis for this notion is that there was an earthquake here in 1490 and as a result bog may have slid across a valley blocking it to form a lake; either a church or building could be concealed by the bog or be beneath the waters of the lake! The isolated location here is no worse than that of Oughtmama, Co. Clare.

18. Sl.19:43 in the adjacent townland of Ballinlig is a moated site, known as The Abbey Field, pronounced 'Aabee', but curiously depicted on Larkin's 1819 *Map of Sligo* as a fort with corner bastions. There is a holywater stoup in a lane wall here and a baptismal font, 50cm in diameter by 30cm high with a 16cm deep sub-cylindrical basin 28cm in diameter, at an adjacent house to the west. See O'Rorke (1889, II, 398) for Archdall quoting Bishop Pococke as regards an abbey at Ballinley, now Ballinleg, near Buninna.

19. Contrast Figs. 1, 3, 4 and 7 of 1984 with Figs. 5, 6 and 8 of 1989.

REFERENCES

Alexander, Jonathan J.G., 1978: *Insular Manuscripts 6th to 9th Century, A Survey of Manuscripts Illuminated in the British Isles, Vol. 1,* London, Millar.

Andersson, Aron, 1968: *L'Art Scandinave,* Paris, Zodiaque La Nuit Des Temps.

Anker, Peter, and Andersson, Aron, 1970: *The Art of Scandinavia,* Vol. I, London, Paul Hamlyn.

Anon, 1982: *Angels, Nobles & Unicorns, Art and Patronage in Medieval Scotland,* Edinburgh, National Museum of Scotland.

Boase, T.S.R., 1953: *English Art, 1100-1216,* Oxford, Clarendon Press.

Bourke, Cormac, 1995: *From The Isles of The North, Early Medieval Art in Ireland and Britain,* Belfast, HMSO.

Bourke, Cormac, 1999: "Northern Flames, Remembering Columba & Adomnán", *History Ireland,* 7:3, 13-16.

Bradley, John, 1988: *Settlement and Society in Medieval Ireland, Studies Presented to F.X. Martin,* o.s.a., Kilkenny, Boethius.

Cochrane, Robert, 1893: "Notes on the Ecclesiastical Antiquities in the Parish of Howth, County of Dublin", *J. Roy. Soc. Antiq. Ireland,* 23, 386-407.

Collingwood, W.G., 1927: *Northumbrian Crosses of Pre-Norman Age,* London, Faber & Guyer.

Cone, Polly, 1977: *Treasures of Early Irish Art, 1500B.C. to 1500A.D.,* New York, Metropolitan Museum of Art.

Crawford, Henry S., and Leask, Harold, G., 1925: "Killeshin Church and its Romanesque Ornament", *J. Roy. Soc. Antiq. Ireland,* 55, 83-94.

de Paor, Liam, 1977: "The Christian Triumph: The Golden Age" in Cone, 1977, 93-143.

de Paor, Maire, 1977: "The Viking Impact" in Cone, 1977, 144-186.

Dimier, M-A, 1971-1974: *L'Art Cistercien*, 2 Vols., Paris, Zodiaque La Nuit Des Temps.

Dixon, Philip, 1976: *Barbarian Europe*, Oxford, Elsevier-Phaidon.

Dursel, Raymond, 1975: *Haut-Poitou Roman*, Paris, Zodiaque La Nuit Des Temps

Erlande-Brandenburg, Alain, Le Pogam, Pierre-Yves, and Sandron, Danny, 1993: *Musée National du Moyen Age, Thermes de Cluny, Guide to the Collections*, Paris, Réunion des Musées Nationaux.

Evans, Joan, 1948: *Art in Medieval France, 987-1498*, Oxford, Cumberlege.

Eygun, Francois, 1970: *Saintonge Romane*, Paris, Zodiaque La Nuit Des Temps.

Farrar, Frederick W., 1896: *The Life of Christ as Represented in Art*, London.

Finlay, Ian, 1979: *Columba*, London, Gollancz.

Goldschmidt, Adolf, 1926: *Die Elfenbeinskulpturen aus der Romanischen Zeit*, Vol. 4, Berlin.

Gwynne, Lucius, 1914: "The Reliquary of Adomhnán", *Irish Ecclesiastical Record* 1914, 457-462.

Gwynne, Lucius, 1915: "The Reliquary of Adomhnán", *Archivium Hibernicum*, No. 4, 199-214.

Gwynn, Aubrey, and Hadcock, R. Neville, 1970: *Medieval Religious Houses: Ireland*, Reprint, 1988, Blackrock, Irish Academic Press.

Hall, James, 1994: *Illustrated Dictionary of Symbols in Eastern and Western Art*, London, Murray.

Hall, James, 1996: *Dictionary of Subjects and Symbols in Art*, London, Murray.

Harbison, Peter, 1991: *Pilgrimage in Ireland, The Monuments and the People*, London, Barrie and Jenkins.

Harbison, Peter, 1992: *The High Crosses of Ireland, An Iconographical and Photographic Survey*, 3 Vols., Bonn, Rudolf Habelt.

Harbison, Peter, 1995: "The Biblical Iconography of Irish Romanesque Architectural Sculpture", in Bourke 1995, 271-280.

Harbison, Peter, 1999: *The Golden Age of Irish Art, the Medieval Achievement, 600-1200*, London, Thames and Hudson.

Harte, Rita, 1987: "Tombstones at Newtown Early", *Old Kilkenny Review*, 3:4, 408-417.

Henry, Françoise, 1970: *Irish Art in the Romanesque Period (1020-1170)*, London, Methuen.

Henry, William, 1739: *Hints towards a Natural Topographical History of the Counties Sligoe, Donegal, Fermanagh and Lough Erne by the Rev. William Henry, M.A., Rector of Killasher in Fermanagh and Chaplain to the Lord Bishop of Kilmore*, National Archives of Ireland, Ms. 2533.

Huchard, Viviane, Antoine, Elisabeth, Lagabrielle, Sophie, and Le Pogam, Pierre-Yves, 1996: *The Musée National du Moyen Age, Thermes de Cluny*, Paris, Réunion des Musées Nationaux.

Hughes, Kathleen, 1980: *Celtic Britain in the Early Middle Ages*, (Studies in Scottish and Welsh Sources), Studies in Celtic History, Vol. 2.

Hunt, John, 1974: *Irish Medieval Figure Sculpture, 1200-1600, A Study of Irish Tombs with Notes on Costume and Armour*, Dublin and London, Irish University Press & Sotheby Park Bernett.

Joyce, P.W., 1913: *A Social History of Ancient Ireland*, 2 vols., Dublin and Belfast, Phoenix.

Kalkreuter, Britta, 2001: *Boyle Abbey and The School of The West*, Bray, Wordwell.

Kilroe, James R., 1885: *Explanatory Memoir to Accompany Sheet 55 of the Maps of the Geological Survey of Ireland, Comprising Portions of the Counties of Sligo and Leitrim*, Dublin and London.

Liddell, Donald M., 1937: *Chessmen*, New York, Harcourt Brace.

Long, Clifford D., 1975: "Excavations in the Medieval City of Trondheim, Norway", *Medieval Archaeology*, 19, 1-32.

Lucas, A.T., 1987: "'In the Middle of Two Living Things': Daniel or Christ?", in Rynne, ed. 1987b, 92-97.

Mackay Mackenzie, W., 1936-1937: "The Dragonesque Figure in Maeshow, Orkney, *Proc. Soc. Antiq. Scotland*, 51, 157-173.

Mahr, Adolph, 1932: *Christian Art in Ancient Ireland*, Vol. 1, Dublin, Stationery Office.

Mâle, Émile, 1922: *L'Art Religieux du XIIe Siècle en France*, Paris.

Mâle, Émile, 1978: *Religious Art in France, The Twelfth Century*, Princeton.

McDermott, Connor V., Long, C.B., and Harney, S.J., with Contributions by K. Claringbold, D. Daly, R. Meehan and G. Stanley, 1996: *A Geological Description of Sligo, Leitrim, and Adjoining Parts of Cavan, Fermanagh, Mayo and Roscommon, to Accompany the Bedrock Geology 1:100,000 Scale Map Series, Sheet 7, Sligo- Leitrim*, Dublin, Geological Survey of Ireland.

Nicholls, Kenneth, 1999: "Celtic Contrasts, Ireland & Scotland", *History Ireland*, 7:3, 22-26.

Ó Floinn, Raghnall, 1983: "Ivory Chessman" in Ryan, ed, 1983, 189.

Ó Floinn, Raghnall, 2002: "Later Medieval Ireland, AD 1150-1550" in Wallace and Ó Floinn, 2002, 257-300.

Ohlgren, Thomas H., 1986: *Insular and Anglo-Saxon Illuminated Manuscripts, An Iconographic Catalogue, c. A.D. 625 to 1100*, New York & London, Garland.

Olesen, Svend B., 1978: *Vor Frue Kirke i Aalborg*, Historisk Samfund for Himmerland og Kjær Herred.

O'Meadhra, Uainínn, 1987: *Early Christian, Viking and Romanesque Art Motif-Pieces from Ireland, Vol. 2, A Discussion on Aspects of Find-context and Function*, Theses and Papers in North-European Archaeology, 17, Stockholm, Almquist & Wiksell.

Pattison, Ian R., 1973: "The Nunburnholm Cross and Anglo-Danish Sculpture in York", *Archaeolologia*, 104, 209-234.

Petrie, George, 1845: *The Ecclesiastical Architecture of Ireland Anterior to the Anglo-Norman Invasion, An Essay on the Origin and Uses of The Round Towers of Ireland*, 2nd ed., Dublin; Reprint Shannon, Irish University Press.

Picard, Auguste, ed., 1924: *Les Ivories Gothiques Français, au Raymond Koechlin*

RCAHMS 1946: *Royal Commission on the Ancient Monuments of Scotland, Twelfth Report with an Inventory of Monuments of Orkney & Shetland, Vol. II, Inventory of Orkney*, No. 886, 313, Pl. 72

Reeves, William, ed., 1857: *The Life of St. Columba, Founder of Hy*; written by Adamnán Abbot of Hy, Skene's 1874 Edition (*The Historians of Scotland VI*).

Ringstad, Bjorn, 1996: "En underlig steinfigur fra Tornes I Romsdal", *Viking,* 59, 101-118.

Robb, David M., 1973: *The Art of the Illuminated Manuscript,* Cranbury.

Roesdahl, Else, and Wilson, David M., 1992: *From Viking to Crusader, The Scandinavians and Europe 800-1200,* Copenhagen, Nordic Council of Ministers.

Rupprecht, B., 1975: *Romanische Skulptur in Frankreich,* Munich.

Ryan, Michael, ed., 1983: *Treasures Of Ireland, Irish Art, 3000B.C.-1500 A.D.,* Dublin, Royal Irish Academy.

Rynne, Etienne, 1987: "Evidence for a Tympanum at Aghadoe, Co. Kerry", *North Munster Antiq.* J., 29, 3-6.

Rynne, Etienne, ed. 1987b: *Figures from the Past, Studies on Figurative Art in Christian Ireland, in Honour of Helen M. Roe,* Dun Laoighre, Glendale for Royal Society of Antiquaries of Ireland.

Saint Laurent, Le Comte de Grimoaürd de, 1874: *Guide de L'Art Chretien,* Paris.

Sandron, Danny, 1993: "Sculpture" in Erlande-Brandenburg, Le Pogam and Sandron, 1993, 109-157.

Schiller, Gertrud, Iconography of Christian Art, translated by Janet Seligman, 2 Vols., London.

Sköld, Axel, n.d. (pre 1985): *Heda Kyrka,* (leaflet).

Sharratt, France, and Sharratt, Peter, 1985: *Ecosse Romane,* Paris, Zodiaque La Nuit Des Temps

Smith and Cheetham: *Dictionary of Christian Antiquities.*

Stalley, Roger, 1971: *Architecture and Sculpture in Ireland, 1150-1350,* Dublin, Gill and Macmillan & Browne & Nolan.

Stalley, Roger, 1973: "A Romanesque Sculptor in Connaught", *Country Life,* 21st. June, 1973, 1826-1830.

Stalley, Roger, 1977: "Irish Art in the Romanesque and Gothic Periods", in Cone ed., 1977.

Stalley, Roger, 1987: *The Cistercian Monasteries of Ireland,* London and New Haven, Yale.

Stalley, Roger, 1988: "Sailing to Saintiago: Medieval Pilgrimage to Saintiago de Compostella and its Artistic Influence in Ireland", in Bradley 1988, 397-420.

Stalley, Roger, 2002: "Solving a Mystery at Cashel, The Romanesque Painting in Cormack's Chapel", *Irish Arts Review,* 18, 25-29.

Stone, Lawrence, 1955: *Sculpture in Britain in the Middle Ages,* London, Penguin.

Stratford, Neil, 1997: *The Lewis Chessmen* and the Enigma of the Hoard, London, British Museum.

Taylor, Michael, 1978: *The Lewis Chessmen,* London, British Museum.

Timoney, Martin A., 1999: "Substantial Archaeological Discovery in Drumcliffe, Co. Sligo", *The Church of Ireland Gazette,* 23rd July, 1999, 8-9.

Timoney, Martin A., 1999-2000: "Recently Discovered High Cross at Drumcliff, Co. Sligo", *The Corran Herald,* 32, 41-43.

Timoney, Martin A., 2002: "Aughris, Portavaud, Lackan and Kilcummin" in Timoney ed. 2002.

Timoney, Martin A., ed., 2002: *A Celebration of Sligo, First Essays for Sligo Field Club,* Sligo, Sligo Field Club.

Timoney, Mary B., 2002: "St. Feichin's, Ballisodare, Co. Sligo: Discoveries and Rediscoveries", in Timoney, ed., 2002.

Wakeman, W.F., 1885: "Architectural Peculiarities of Some Ancient Churches in County Sligo", *J. Roy. Soc. Antiq. Ireland,* 17, 43-54.

Wallace, Patrick F., 2000: *A Guide to the National Museum of Ireland,* Dublin, Town House.

Wallace, Patrick F., 2002: "Viking Age Ireland, AD 850-1150" in Wallace and Ó Floinn 2002, 213-256.

Wallace, Patrick F., and Ó Floinn, Raghnall, eds., 2002: *Treasures of the National Museum of Ireland, Irish Antiquities,* Dublin, Gill and Macmillan.

Williams, Gareth, 2000: Master Pieces, *The Story of Chess: the Pieces, Players and Passion of 1,000 Years,* London, Apple.

Wood-Martin, W.G., 1882: *The History of Sligo, County and Town, from the Earliest Ages to the Close of the Reign of Queen Elizabeth,* Dublin, Reprint, 1990, Sligo, Dodd's Antiquarian Books.

Wood-Martin, W.G., 1892: *The History of Sligo, County and Town, from the close of the Revolution of 1688 to the Present Time,* Dublin, Hodges Figgis; Reprint, 1990, Sligo, Dodd's Antiquarian Books.

Wood-Martin, William Gregory, 1895: *Pagan Ireland, An Archaeological Sketch, A Handbook of Pre-Christian Antiquities,* London, Longman Green.

Youngs, Susan, ed., 1989: *'The Work of Angels',* Masterpieces of Celtic Metalwork, 6th - 9th Centuries AD, London, British Museum.

Zarnecki, George, Holt, Janet, and Holland, Tristram, eds., 1984: *English Romanesque Art, 1066-1200,* London, Weidenfeld & Nicolson.

SLIGO CASTLE

Kieran Denis O'Conor
National Univrsity of Ireland, Galway

ABSTRACT: The purpose of this paper is to discuss the history and morphology of Sligo Castle from the date of its erection in 1245 until the time it fell into the control of the Gaelic Irish in the middle years of the 14th century.

THE EARLY HISTORY OF THE CASTLE.

Scholars interested in the dating and phasing of the many standing castles throughout Ireland generally suffer from a lack of surviving historical references to these structures. This makes it difficult to date the erection and subsequent rebuilding of many Irish castles. It must always be remembered that the in-depth architectural analysis of any given castle will only allow an approximate date for its construction (Leask 1944, 1-2). However, the situation is the opposite regarding Sligo Castle. Today there are no visible standing remains of the castle. Yet our knowledge of Sligo Castle from contemporary historical sources is quite impressive, especially as it was never a royal castle. This was partly due to its location on the Connacht/Ulster border. Many of the surviving medieval Gaelic annals were compiled in this region. Obviously they tended to be concerned more with local events and places rather than faraway ones. It is also fortuitous that Sligo Castle was held during this early period by the Geraldines and later the de Burghs. These families were amongst the most powerful in medieval Ireland. Their affairs were clearly of major concern to their contemporaries and hence were recorded by clerks. Lastly, the Fitzgeralds have remained an important Irish family down to the 20th century and this has meant that certain medieval economic documents relating to their possessions, including Sligo, have survived intact until the present day (Barry 1987, 5). These are the reasons as to why quite a number of historical references exist to Sligo Castle throughout the medieval period. It is a pity that these numerous references cannot be matched today by the standing remains of a castle. As noted, the situation is usually the reverse in Ireland - a fine masonry castle with few contemporary references to it.

Sligo Castle was first built in 1245 by the then justiciar Maurice Fitzgerald with the help of Felim O'Conor. Cut-stone and lime appears to have been taken from the nearby Trinity Hospital, which was then being built, and used in the construction of the castle (A.U.; A.Cl.; A.C.; A.F.M.). The hostages of Tir Conaill were placed in Sligo Castle for safekeeping in 1246 (A.C.). O'Donnell of Tir Conaill attacked Sligo in November 1249 (A.C.). He burned the nascent Anglo-Norman town but was unable to capture the castle. The castle garrison then proceeded to hang the above-mentioned hostages in front of the besieging forces (A.C.). Sligo is next mentioned in 1249 (A.C.). In 1265 the castle, along with some other Anglo-Norman fortifications, was taken and pulled down (do scailed) by Aedh O'Conor, King of Connacht (A.C.; A.F.M.). In 1269 Sligo Castle was rebuilt by the Fitzgeralds (A.C.). It was again captured by Aedh O'Conor in 1271 (A.U.; A.Cl.; A.F.M.). In 1294 it was levelled by another Aedh O'Conor, King of Connacht, apparently at the behest of Richard de Burgh, Earl of Ulster and Lord of Connacht, who was at war with the Geraldines (A.L.C.; Orpen 1911-1920, iv, 116-117). John Fitz Thomas Fitzgerald handed over Sligo Castle and other possessions in Connacht to Richard de Burgh in 1299, as part of a peace agreement between the two men (Orpen 1911-1920, iv, 119; Lydon 1987b, 188-189). In 1310 Richard de Burgh rebuilt Sligo Castle (A.Cl.; A.C.). It was also taken temporarily by Rory O'Conor later in the same year (Orpen 1911-1920, iv, 172). Direct historical references to Sligo Castle do not occur for about another four decades. It would appear that the Sligo branch of the O'Conor family seized control of Sligo Castle in the mid 14th century (O'Dowd 1991, 16). The next actual reference to the castle comes in 1362 when Cathal O'Conor of Sligo dies peacefully in it. It was clearly his castle at this date (Wood-Martin 1882,

229). Donnell O'Conor of Sligo held the castle in 1371, dying there in 1395 (A.U.; A.C.; A.Cl.; A.F.M.).

Sligo Castle was to remain in the hands of the O'Conors of Sligo well into the 16th century, although it was continually under military pressure from the O'Donnells for much of this time. During most of the 16th century and into the next, the castle changed hands on a number of occasions between the O'Conors of Sligo, the O'Donnells and the English (Wood-Martin 1882, 235-373; O'Rorke 1889, 105-145; Bradley and Dunne 1987, 32-34; O'Dowd 1991, 16-44).

Certain points raised about Sligo Castle from the surviving historical references will now be discussed.

WHY WAS SLIGO CASTLE ERECTED BY MAURICE FITZGERALD IN 1245?

Richard de Burgh, first Lord of Connacht, was granted most of this province in 1227. However, this royal grant only really became effective after his 1235 campaign in Connacht. Following this date, de Burgh began the subinfeudination of the region, rewarding both his own vassals and other magnates who had helped him in his conquest there. Specifically, he granted Hugh de Lacy, Earl of Ulster, five cantreds in north Connacht as part of this process. This particular grant comprised most of the present county of Sligo, as well as part of modern Mayo. Yet de Lacy was more occupied with his lands in Ulster and, therefore, he immediately made over most of his new fief to other men. Specifically, he granted the cantred of Carbury-Drumcliff and the northern half of the cantred of Leyney (which included the Ballysadare area) to Maurice Fitzgerald (Orpen 1911-1920, iii, 193-195; Lydon 1987a, 165; O'Dowd 1991, 13-14). This grant of Carbury-Drumcliff and northern Leyney was the nucleus of the Fitzgerald manor of Sligo. It might be added that Maurice soon obtained the other half of Leyney from its original grantee. His son, another Maurice, gained control of the cantred of Corran by marriage to one of the de Prendergasts in the late 1250s (Orpen 1911-1920, iii, 198-199; O'Dowd 1991, 14). This all meant that the Fitzgeralds controlled about half the present county of Sligo by c. 1260.

The erection of Sligo Castle in 1245 by Maurice Fitzgerald must be seen partly in the context of these land grants. The castle was primarily built to act as the caput or centre of this large new fief. Maurice could control and administer his estates in Sligo from this secure, well-defended base. The very erection of the castle was a statement by him that his lordship over the area was to be permanent. Its existence meant that the native Irish lords of the region would find him difficult to oust from his new position.

Sligo was clearly an ideal place for an administrative and military centre on Fitzgerald's new lands. The castle was erected overlooking a ford and bridge on a well-known medieval routeway linking north Connacht to western Ulster (Fitzpatrick 1927, 83; O'Dowd 1991, 4; 1994, 143). It also had the added advantage of having a coastal location. Sligo Castle's relatively central position within the original Fitzgerald fief of Carbury-Drumcliff, along a north-south routeway, would have allowed Maurice easy access to his new lands. This would have made their administration, economic development and military control far easier to achieve. Furthermore, at a purely local level in the context of Sligo's excellent geographical position and the implications of this for trade, a 13th-century lord like Maurice Fitzgerald would have fully realised that the security offered by the castle would have encouraged artisans and merchants from other parts of Anglo-Norman Ireland to settle in Sligo. Therefore, the foundation of Sligo Castle in 1245 plays an essential part in the development of Sligo as a town and economic centre.

Yet there was another reason as to why Sligo Castle was built in 1245. Hugh de Lacy, as Earl of Ulster, granted Maurice Fitzgerald the land of Tir Conaill (most of modern Donegal) in the late 1230s, apparently in 1238. This was purely a speculative grant and Maurice himself was supposed to make it effective by military action (Orpen 1911-1920, iii, 257-8; Otway-Ruthven 1980, 100). As noted above, Sligo Castle was located on a north/south routeway linking northern Connacht to western Ulster. Overall it was an ideal base from which to attack modern Donegal by land and sea. Both Maurice Fitzgerald and his son did precisely this during the 1240s and 1250s. Therefore, Sligo Castle was also erected in 1245 to act as a secure, well-defended centre from which Donegal could be conquered and brought under Geraldine domination. In the long term it was intended to act as the capital of a massive lordship stretching from north Donegal to south Sligo. However, this was not to be the case as Gofraid O'Donnell's victory at Credran Cille in 1257 ended Geraldine hopes of conquering Tir Conaill (Lydon 1987c, 247). This failed Geraldine attempt on Tir Conaill emphasises the fact that many Anglo-Norman land-grants were purely speculative, often granted prior to the actual conquest of any given area. It is also a reminder that even before the main Gaelic revival of the

14th century, Irish armies could halt Anglo-Norman encroachment by direct military action.

The very earliest reference to Sligo Castle also allows some insight into the length of time it took to build militarily defensible castles.

It is generally held that castle-building in stone was a complex, costly and lengthy undertaking for any medieval lord - taking a number of years to complete (Brown 1976, 157-171; Sweetman 1995, 12). For example, Dublin Castle seems to have taken about two decades to erect fully (Lynch and Manning 1990, 65). It is certainly clear that masonry castles were the most expensive buildings of their day to construct. Yet the historical evidence for the construction of Sligo Castle in 1245 suggests something different to this view. As noted above, the O'Donnells launched what appears to have been a fearsome attack on the town of Sligo and its castle in November 1246. The town was overrun by the Irish but the castle itself held out against this onslaught. Its garrison even felt confident enough to hang captive hostages, kinsmen of the besiegers, from the battlements of the castle. This suggests that a strong, militarily effective, castle, which had been started at some stage in 1245, existed at Sligo by late 1246. Indeed the placing of the unfortunate hostages of Tir Conaill in the castle early in 1246, suggests it was even then a place of strength. This overall evidence from Sligo suggests it took mere months to erect a masonry castle there, strong enough to successfully hold out against the forces of a powerful Gaelic king.

Furthermore, the documentary sources allow some insight into the processes behind this rapid construction of the 1245 castle of Sligo. In 1242 Maurice Fitzgerald had founded a hospital at Sligo in honour of the Trinity (A.C.). He clearly cut down on time and costs in building Sligo Castle by ruthlessly requisitioning available building-stone and lime from this adjacent hospital and using this material in his own fortification. This availability of cut-stone at Sligo must have been one of the reasons why the castle was erected so quickly. It meant that stone did not have to be quarried, dressed and then carted to Sligo from outside or at least not to the same extent as for many other castles. Obviously much skilled and unskilled labour was needed to build a masonry castle. Presumably this was not only provided by Maurice Fitzgerald's own men but also by the arguably sizeable population living in Sligo by 1245. Certainly the 1236 reference to women being captured here by a raiding party suggests a relatively large Irish settlement at Sligo by this date (A.U.). Obviously his requisitioning of building materials from Trinity Hospital surely meant that construction of this particular building could not continue. Perhaps Maurice also took the masons and labourers from this project for work on his own castle. Therefore, the available evidence is that a sizeable proportion of the skilled and unskilled workers needed to build Sligo Castle was there before Maurice Fitzgerald started work on this fortress. The time-consuming job of gathering workmen from outside Sligo for work on the castle there does not seem to have been needed to any great degree. This all shows that the human and material resources needed for Fitzgerald's castle seem to have been largely in place at Sligo before construction began on it. The implication for castle-studies in general from Sligo is that where conditions were right, militarily-effective, masonry castles could be erected in a matter of months. It also indicates that the administrative abilities of a ruthless and ambitious medieval lord like Maurice Fitzgerald to quickly complete a project, such as the erection of a castle, should never be underestimated.

WHY WAS SLIGO CASTLE REBUILT BY RICHARD DE BURGH IN 1310?

The rebuilding of Sligo Castle in 1310 by Richard de Burgh, Earl of Ulster and Lord of Connacht, known as the 'Red Earl', was part of a wider campaign of castle-building by him throughout north-west Ireland in the first decade of the 14th century. The large masonry castles of Ballymote, Co. Sligo, and Greencastle, Co. Donegal, were begun by de Burgh in 1300 and 1305 respectively (A.U.; A.L.C.; A.Cl.; A.F.M.). It would appear that Ballintober Castle, Co. Roscommon, was erected by him at about this time too (Orpen 1911-1920, iii, 204-205; iv, 148; Claffey 1974-1975, 218-221; Rae 1987, 756; O'Conor 1993, 226-227). The construction of these four masonry castles must have represented a huge investment of resources for de Burgh. By *c.* 1300 he controlled approximately half of Ireland as Earl of Ulster and Lord of Connacht, with numerous Gaelic kings and Anglo-Norman lords acknowledging they held their territories of him (Orpen 1911-1920, iv, 157-158). Monies from this large hegemony would have helped pay the huge costs incurred in the erection or complete rebuilding of these castles. Yet de Burgh had also made massive profits campaigning in Scotland for Edward I during the 1290s and the first years of the 14th century (Lydon 1987b, 198, 200). These extra resources must have greatly aided de Burgh's ability to carry out these castle-works in north-west Ireland. Indeed, their availability must have helped de Burgh make the decision to build these castles in the first place.

What were the political and military reasons behind the erection of these new castles and the rebuilding of Sligo Castle? It is held that the construction or refortification of these fortresses was part of Richard de Burgh's plan to further consolidate his authority over the often troublesome Gaelic lords of western Ireland and to bring their lands under closer control, as well as to protect his own direct possessions from Irish attack (Orpen 1911-1920, iv, 119; McNeill 1980, 31-32, 73; Watt 1987, 354). The view that these castles were erected to control the Gaelic Irish or to place their lands under more direct Anglo-Norman hegemony is still valid to a degree. Ballintober Castle was clearly in an excellent geographical position from which to militarily overawe the turbulent O'Conor kings of Connacht (Orpen 1911-1920, iii, 205). Ballymote Castle seems to have been erected in 1300 partly to protect the southern flanks of the manor of Sligo, in de Burgh hands since 1298, from Irish attack (Orpen 1911-1920, iv, 119). Greencastle was begun in 1305 as part of the latter's plan to bring the whole northern coast of Ulster under his direct control (McNeill 1980, 31-32, 73). The O'Donnells of Tir Conaill seem to have continuously refused to acknowledge that they held their territories of de Burgh as Earl of Ulster (Orpen 1911-1920, iv, 158). Perhaps the refortification of Sligo Castle in 1310 and the building of Greencastle was partly due to a desire on de Burgh's part to bring Tir Conaill to submission. As noted above, Sligo Castle was in an excellent position to attack the area of modern Donegal by both land and sea.

However, it was never just a simple question of Gaedheal against Gaill in medieval Ireland. Disputes between the Anglo-Normans themselves were numerous. Nor should Richard de Burgh be seen as a man deeply hostile to Gaelic Ireland. It is true he was a great Anglo-Norman magnate, heavily involved in the political events of the day in both Ireland and Britain. Yet he was also a patron of Irish bards and spoke Irish fluently. Many of his most important allies and vassals were Gaelic lords who would have provided him with troops for his campaigns. In all he emerges from history as a man at home in both the Gaelic and Anglo-Norman worlds (Watt 1987, 353-354).

It must be remembered that Richard de Burgh's main trouble in north Connacht during the last years of the 13th century had been with John fitz Thomas Fitzgerald, the heir of Maurice fitz Maurice Fitzgerald. The origins of this feud between the Geraldines and the de Burghs can be traced back to the 1260s at least. The actual dispute in the 1290s seems to have been caused by the de Burgh's claim for direct overlordship over the manor of Sligo as Lord of Connacht. John fitz Thomas appears to have tried to resist this claim in turn, hoping to hold Sligo directly of the king. The affair broke out into open war between the two factions in late 1294 and early 1295. The justiciar then arranged a truce between the two magnates. Eventually, in 1298, an agreement was reached between them. John fitz Thomas agreed to surrender his lands in Connacht and Ulster, which included the manor and castle of Sligo, to Richard de Burgh in exchange for lands elsewhere in Ireland. In 1299 the manor and castle of Sligo officially came into de Burgh's hands (Orpen 1911-1920, iv, 116-119; Lydon 1987b, 187-188; O'Dowd 1991, 14). However, both de Burgh and John fitz Thomas were to remain deeply suspicious of one another for many years after this agreement (Lydon 1987b, 188). Therefore, it could be argued that the de Burgh refortification of Sligo Castle, as well as his erection of Ballymote Castle, was as much part of a desire to consolidate his authority over the Fitzgerald's Anglo-Norman ex-tenants as it was to keep the Gaelic lords of the region in check. The construction of these two fortifications meant that de Burgh's enemies, be they Anglo-Norman or Gaelic, would have found it difficult to break his hold on his newly acquired manor of Sligo.

THE LOCATION OF SLIGO CASTLE WITHIN THE MEDIEVAL TOWN.

One important question for future excavation, urban renewal and development in Sligo is where was the castle located within the medieval town? As noted, there are no known standing remains of the castle, nor are there any 18th or 19th drawings of it to quickly answer this question, but there are other means of deducing where it was sited originally. Leaving aside late medieval tower houses erected by merchants, one writer has argued that two distinct castles were built in Sligo during the medieval period (McTernan 1995, 19-21). Based on evidence from the Ordnance Survey's 1837 plan of Sligo which marks the sites of two castles within the town, it has been argued that the Fitzgerald/de Burgh castle was located somewhere at the junction of Abbey Street and Teeling Street, close to the Dominican Priory (McTernan 1995, 19-21). It is postulated that the O'Conors of Sligo took over this castle in the 14th century, eventually deserting it and building a new castle in the

Fig. 1 - Thomas Phillips' *Prospect of Sligo*, 1685, The Town of Sligo.

general area of Quay Street near the present Town Hall (McTernan 1995, 19-21). The placing of a large Anglo-Norman castle in the Teeling/Abbey Street area is unlikely at a purely military level. Maurice Fitzgerald founded the Dominican Priory, which still stands today, in this part of the town in either 1252 or 1253 (A.C.; A.F.M.). No medieval lord, trained in the arts of war, would have placed a large masonry abbey so close to his castle, as it would have provided shelter for a besieging force. Thus, military logic would suggest that the castle was located well away from the priory. This is the situation elsewhere in Europe. Furthermore, as was noted above, there are a large amount of historical references to Sligo Castle throughout its usage. There is no historical evidence to suggest that the O'Conors of Sligo built a completely new castle away from the site of the original Anglo-Norman fortress. The implication from the evidence in historical sources is that there was only one Sligo Castle during the medieval period. The castle site marked on the 1837 plan of Sligo in the Abbey Street/Teeling Street area seems to have been an urban tower-house (Wood-Martin 1889, ii, 38; Bradley and Dunne 1987, 28-29).

The castle-site marked on the 1837 map in the vicinity of the present Town Hall is held by most writers to be Sligo Castle (OSL, Sligo; Bradley & Dunne 1987, 34-35; O'Dowd 1991, 153). Certainly this is the most logical place for a castle within the medieval town, being on slightly rising ground just above an important ford and bridge on the Garvogue River. Furthermore, its closeness to the sea at this point is also important, as in the event of a siege, the castle could have been reprovisioned easily by water. Therefore, for related military, geographical and cartographic reasons, the Quay Street/Town Hall area is the most likely location for Sligo Castle.

However, the most convincing piece of evidence in this regard comes from Thomas Phillips's 1685 Prospect of Sligo (Pls. 1 and 2; Gunning and Feehily 1996, 24-25), preserved in the National Library of Ireland, apparently drawn from somewhere to the south of the present town, probably from the high ground in the townland of Knocknaganny through which the road from the south passed at this time into Sligo (Taylor and Skinner 1778, 65). It will be shown below that the large fortified structure seen in the depiction represents the remains of Sligo Castle. This depiction indicates that this fortress, apparently a large keepless castle of medieval date, occurs somewhere in the vicinity of Quay Street, well away from the Dominican Priory (Pl. I; Bradley & Dunne 1987, 34-35).

One last point needs to be discussed concerning the location of Sligo Castle. At some stage, in either the 1640s or 1650s, a new artillery fortification, called the Stone Fort, as opposed to the Green Fort which is of earth, was erected in Sligo (O'Rorke 1889, I, 188-189; Bradley and Dunne 1987, 34-35; Kerrigan 1995, 98). It has been stated that this Stone Fort was built exactly on the site of Sligo Castle (OSL, Sligo, MS 20, typescript 82; Bradley and Dunne 1987, 34-35). However, the overall evidence suggests a somewhat different picture. A description of the

Stone Fort in 1666 shows it to have been rather a small fortification (O'Rorke 1889, I, 190-191; Kerrigan 1995, 107). There is absolutely no mention of it being located in the medieval castle. In October 1689, during the Williamite War, a band of Huguenots, said to be 400-strong, took refuge in Sligo Castle upon the approach of a Jacobite force. However, they found the castle to be completely untenable and had to take over the adjacent Stone Fort (O'Rorke 1889, I, 215-216; Wauchope 1992, 84; McTernan 1995, 79). The overall implication from this evidence is that Sligo Castle and the Stone Fort were separate structures, albeit extremely close to one another in geographical location.

It is also unclear as to why Sligo Castle, as depicted in the 1685 Prospect of Sligo, is not shown on Lutterel's 1689 Plan of the Town and Fortifications of Sligo. Only the Stone Fort is indicated on this plan in this part of the town (Wood-Martin 1889, opp. 134). Lutterel's decision to omit the castle from his plan may be due to the fact that, like the Huguenots in October 1689, he also saw it as being of no military significance.

THE MORPHOLOGY OF SLIGO CASTLE. GENERAL.

Today there are no visible standing remains of Sligo Castle. Yet some statement can be made about its morphology.

Some basic points about the castle can be gleaned from documentary sources. The 1245 reference to the erection of the castle shows that it was apparently built in masonry from the beginning (A.U,; A.Cl,; A.C.; A.F.M). There seems to have been no primary earthwork castle here - mortared stone was used in its defences from the start. Furthermore, Sir Henry Sidney was clearly impressed by the defences of Sligo Castle in the late 16th century (Caulfield 1870-1871, 22-23). These historical references suggest that Sligo Castle was a strong, well-defended, masonry castle throughout the medieval period.

However, as noted, the main evidence for what the castle looked like in the medieval period comes from a late 17th century Prospect of Sligo depicted by Thomas Phillips. His 1685 depiction shows a large edifice located on the western side of the town (Pls. 1 and 2; Gunning and Feehily 1996, 24-25. The full Phillips prospect of Sligo is best seen in D.G.H, G&F.). This masonry structure represents the remains of Sligo Castle at that date. It shows that the castle consisted of a square or rectangular crenellated stone-walled enclosure, apparently aligned north-west/south-east, with a large tower at each of its four angles. There is no sign in the depiction of a dominating keep within the enceinte of the castle, capable of independent defence if the rest of the fortress had fallen. This indicates that Sligo was a type of castle known as a 'keepless castle'. At such fortresses, the defences were concentrated purely on the curtain walls and angle-towers of the castle. However, there is no indication from the depiction that Sligo Castle ever had a twin-towered gatehouse. Most other keepless castles in Ireland were provided with such gatehouses, allowing not only extra mural defence but also fine accommodation. The entry to Sligo Castle must have been by some simple gateway in one

Fig. 2 - Thomas Phillips' *Prospect of Sligo*, 1685, The Castle.

of its curtain walls, possibly along its south-eastern wall facing the town. Furthermore, this lack of a keep or large gatehouse at Sligo Castle must suggest that rooms within its angle-towers were used for domestic and administrative purposes too. Presumably other buildings, such as a kitchen and a hall, were located in the courtyard of the castle.

The four angle-towers, which are the most distinctive feature to be gleaned from the 1685 depiction of Sligo Castle, seem to have projected out from the curtain walls of the castle. On analogy with elsewhere, it can be presumed that these towers were looped for archery at a number of different levels. These arrowslits in the angle-towers would have allowed archers or crossbowmen to control the base of the castle's curtain walls in times of attack without over-exposing themselves to danger. The forms of these angle-towers are also interesting. Two of the towers are clearly polygonal. If it is accepted that the castle is aligned north-west/south-east, these two towers occur on the western and northern angles of the fortress. The other two angle-towers, on the eastern and southern sides of the castle, are shown as being either square or rectangular. They are depicted as rising above the curtain walls. At least three of the towers seem to have been up to three-storeys in height.

WHAT IS THE ARCHITECTURAL DATE OF THE CASTLE DEPICTED IN PHILLIPS'S 1685 PROSPECT OF SLIGO?

Phillips's 1685 Prospect of Sligo was drawn from too great a distance from Sligo Castle for specific architectural details, such as window types or arrowslits, to be depicted. Only the general outline of the castle can be seen. However, despite these limitations, can a date be argued for the erection of the castle as seen in the Prospect of Sligo? Is the castle as seen in the depiction the stronghold erected by Maurice Fitzgerald in 1245 or is it architecturally later in style?

As noted above, the edifice depicted appears to be a quadrilateral keepless castle of medieval date, with projecting angle-towers at each of its four corners. Most Irish castles of the late 13th and very early 14th century are of the keepless type. However, a few keepless castles were built well before 1250 A.D. The keepless castles of Dublin, Kilkenny and Limerick were all begun in the first years of the 13th century (Leask 1944, 53-57, 67; Sweetman 1995, 12-13). The situation is similar to this in England and Wales too (King 1988, 78). The defensive principle of projecting angle-towers enfilading the base of castle walls had been generally adopted in castle design during the very first years of the 13th century (King 1988, 77-78). Therefore, in theory, the keepless castle seen in the 1685 depiction could have been erected by Maurice Fitzgerald in 1245.

However, there are elements within the architecture of the castle seen in the 1685 Prospect of Sligo that suggest that it is later than 1245. As noted, the refortification of Sligo Castle in 1310 by Richard de Burgh was just part of a wider programme of castle-building by him throughout north-west Ireland in the first years of the 14th century. Ballymote, Ballintober and Greencastle were all begun by him at this time. What architectural features are common to all three castles and how do they compare to Sligo Castle as seen in the 1685 Prospect of Sligo? Ballintober and Ballymote castles are keepless, having the same general quadrilateral plan that Sligo Castle has in Phillips's depiction of it. It might be added that Greencastle, whose design is dictated by the natural platform upon which it is sited, has no true keep either. Ballintober and Greencastle use large, projecting, polygonal towers in their defences. Greencastle also has a gate-house whose two towers are also polygonal in shape.

The normal shape of castle towers was round in plan since the first years of the 13th century (King 1988, 77, 92-93, 121). Polygonal towers were rare before the late 13th century and even then were not that common (King 1988, 121). Therefore, the occurence of polygonal towers at both Ballintober and Greencastle can be seen as relatively unusual. The evidence from both these sites suggests that the use of polygonal towers in the defences of castles was a distinctive feature of de Burgh work in north-west Ireland at the very beginning of the 14th century. This point is important as it was noted above that both the northern and western angle-towers seen in the 1685 depiction of Sligo Castle were polygonal in plan. On analogy with Ballintober and Greencastle, it would seem that these two towers at Sligo were part of Richard de Burgh's refortification of the castle there in 1310.

It has been suggested that the use of polygonal towers at Greencastle, amongst other features, was heavily influenced by Edward I's great castle at Caernarvon, Wales, begun in 1283 (Waterman 1958, 85; McNeill 1980, 75-76). Much the same could be said for both Ballintober and Sligo Castles. It might also be added that Richard de Burgh's massive gatehouse at Ballymote, with its ample provisions for sumptuous accommodation, must surely be compared to the Edwardian gatehouse at Harlech, Wales. Indeed the gatehouse at

Greencastle has been compared to the gatehouses at both Harlech and Caernarvon (McNeill 1980, 74-76). Therefore, Richard de Burgh's work at Ballymote, Ballintober and Greencastle, as well as his refortification of Sligo Castle in 1310, appears to have been heavily influenced by Edward I's massive castle building programme in north Wales in the last years of the 13th century.

The 1685 depiction also shows that the southern and eastern angle-towers, at Sligo were square or, more probably rectangular in shape. As already stated, the overwhelming majority of mural towers in castles were round or half-round in plan from *c*. 1200 onwards. Large square or rectangular flanking towers are rarely seen on castles of 13th century date. This seems to have been because such towers were regarded as more susceptible to undermining in comparison to round ones. Therefore, it would appear that these two angle-towers at Sligo were not the work of Maurice Fitzgerald in the 1240s. Such towers would be highly unlikely in a 13th century context.

As noted above, the vital function of a projecting mural tower was to allow the castle's defenders to cover the exposed bases of the curtain walls from them. Another important military function of a tower was to act as a strongpoint if the wallwalk of the adjacent curtain wall had been taken by the enemy. A normal mural tower rose above the curtain walls of a castle and this allowed its defenders to dominate the latter if the attacking force gained a foothold on the walls. Brown (1979, 97) has argued that the actual shape of the tower mattered little so long as it could fulfill these essential functions of defence. This is important, as rectangular and square mural towers became popular again in castles built in the 14th century, after c. 1310, especially in the north of England (Brown 1976, 97; King 1988, 122). Dunstanburgh Castle, Northumberland, begun by Thomas of Lancaster in early 1313, is regarded as an early example of this new trend. Both square and rectangular mural towers are seen along its curtains (Summerson 1993, 3-27). Ballymoon Castle, Co. Carlow, has been dated generally to the early 14th century due to its use of 'Caernarvon' arches and late loops (Sweetman 1995, 24). This quadrangular castle also has rectangular and square towers offering some degree of flanking defence to its curtains. It must be presumed that Ballymoon is a reflection in Ireland of this trend towards straight-faced mural towers seen in English castles built after c. 1310. Perhaps this latter date should be seen as the earliest date for the construction of Ballymoon. Its use of Caernarvon arches suggests that it should not be dated later than c. 1330, as this form of arch is seen as early 14th century in date in Ireland (Leask 1944, 24).

Given the evidence from both England and Ireland, it would seem that the square or rectangular angle-towers visible in the 1685 depiction of Sligo Castle were built in the 14th century or later. As noted, Sligo Castle was taken over by the O'Conors of Sligo around the middle of the 14th century. Is it possible that it was this family who built these two towers after *c* 1350? This is unlikely as it is becoming clear from excavation and survey that Gaelic lords did little in terms of actually adding substantial new defences to captured Anglo-Norman castles. They just occasionally repaired already existing defences at these places (O'Conor 1992, 10; 1993, 231-236). Therefore, it is much more likely that these two mural towers were in fact erected as part of the rebuilding of Sligo Castle begun in 1310 by Richard de Burgh. His use of two square or rectangular flanking towers on the corners of the castle facing the town shows that not only were his masons completely in touch with new architectural trends in English castle building, but that they were developing the new style themselves. This is precisely what to expect from men working for a powerful magnate like de Burgh and it shows that no lapse of time is needed for new architectural ideas to come from England to Ireland.

One other statement needs to be made about the architecture of Sligo Castle as seen in the 1685 Prospect of Sligo. The most impressive feature of Ballymote Castle would have been its massive four-storeyed twin-towered gatehouse (Sweetman 1985-1986, 114). The size of the gatehouse here, with its garderobes and fireplaces, suggests that it was provided with suites of rooms designed for the accommodation of the Earl, his family and retainers. Furthermore, excavation has revealed that the walls of this gatehouse were built with a double-facing, thus making them more difficult to breach (Sweetman 1985-1986, 121, 123; 1995, 16). At Greencastle the private accommodation of the Earl and his guests was also located in the impressive twin-towered gatehouse there (McNeill 1980, 74-76; Mallory and McNeill 1991, 258). These great gatehouses at both Ballymote and Greencastle clearly illustrate how these structures had taken on both the domestic and military functions of earlier keeps. Yet the gatehouse at Ballintober seems to have been rather small and insignificant. Accommodation for the Earl and his constable here seem to have been placed in the south-western and north-western angle-towers instead (the latter tower was largely rebuilt around 1600). The south-western angle-tower at Ballintober has a smaller contemporary rectangular tower attached to it. This is similar to the layout of the north-eastern tower at Greencastle, which also has a small contemporary rectangular tower built onto it. This tower also had a suite of rooms designed for lordly accommodation within it (McNeill 1980, 73-74). It has been suggested that this tower was designed to house the constable of the castle (Mallory and McNeill 1991, 258). As noted, no gatehouse is to be seen in the 1685 depiction of Sligo Castle and it must be presumed that all the upper floors of the corner towers here provided varying standards of living accommodation for the garrison. Yet in what part of the structure were there rooms set aside for the private use of de Burgh, when resident, and his officers, such as his constable who would have ordinarily inhabited the castle? The 1685 depiction goes some way to answering this question. It shows that the northern corner tower at Sligo was by far the largest, and is almost keep-like in its appearance. Its size must suggest that this is where the most luxurious accommodation was located. The placing of the best accommodation at Sligo and Ballintober in large polygonal corner towers, as opposed to within a gatehouse, is very reminiscent of the Eagle Tower at Caernarvon. Again this shows that there is a strong Edwardian influence in the castles built by Richard de Burgh throughout north-west Ireland in the first years of the 14th century. Therefore, the overall evidence suggests that the castle in the 1685 depiction of Sligo town is largely the work of Richard de Burgh begun in 1310. John Maiben Gilmartin, Lecturer in the History of Art, Dublin, in a letter to Martin A. Timoney in Nov. 2001, writes of an ancestor of his in relation to Sligo Castle as follows. "Within it (Sligo Castle) in a chamber Andrew Maiben used to conduct his prayer meetings". This would have been *c.* 1775-1800. So part of it must have been tolerably habitable up to the last decades of the 18th century."

CONCLUSION

Sligo Castle was erected in 1245 by Maurice Fitzgerald to act as the caput of his new lands in modern Co. Sligo and to function as a military base from which to attack, conquer and control modern Donegal. The indications are that this 1245 castle was erected rapidly. The evidence shows that masonry castles could be built in a matter of months rather than years, given the right circumstances and direction. Richard de Burgh's refortification of Sligo Castle in 1310 was part of a wider campaign of castle-building by him throughout north-west Ireland in the very first years of the 14th century. This was part of a desire to further his control over the region and its often troublesome inhabitants, be they Gaelic lords or Anglo-Norman ex-tenants of his enemy John fitz Thomas Fitzgerald.

It was argued that the castle seen in Thomas Phillips's 1685 Prospect of Sligo was ultimately the work of Richard de Burgh. His refortification, begun in 1310, seems to have amounted to an almost complete rebuilding of the castle. Yet it must also be presumed that this 1310 rebuilding incorporated parts of the 1245 castle. However, Phillips's Prospect of Sligo was drawn from too great a distance for any chronological interpretation and is just not detailed enough for this type of analysis.

Sligo Castle was located in the Wine Street - Quay Street - Town Hall area and any future excavation in this part of Sligo should take cognizance of this point. It must also be remembered that Sligo Castle the was centre of local administration in the region throughout the medieval period. Sligo's Town Hall continues that tradition from the same general location today.

ACKNOWLEDGEMENTS

I thank the National Library of Ireland for their permission to produce Thomas Phillips's 1685 Prospect of Sligo (Pls. 1 and 2). I thank Mary B. Timoney, Martin A. Timoney, Conleth Manning, Karena Morton and David Sweetman for their comments on the text and Karena for also typing the text.

REFERENCES

MEDIEVAL

Barry, T.B. 1987: *The Archaeology of Mediaeval Ireland,* London & New York.

Bradley, J. & Dunne, N. 1987: *Urban Archaeological Survey - County Sligo* (limited distribution), Office of Public Works, Dublin.

Brown, R.A. 1976: *English Castles,* 3rd. ed., London.

Caulfield, R. 1870-1871: 'Note on an attack on a crannog near Omagh', J. Roy. Soc. Antiq. Ireland, 11, 15-25.

Claffey, J.A. 1972-1973: 'Ballintubber Castle, Co. Roscommon', J. Old Athlone Soc., 1(3), 143-147.

Claffey, J.A. 1974-1975: 'Ballintubber Castle, Co. Roscommon', J. Old Athlone Soc., 1(4), 218-221

Cosgrove, A., ed. 1987: *A New History of Ireland,* II, Medieval Ireland, Vol. II, 1169-1534, Oxford.

Fitzpatrick, J.E. 1927: 'Ballymote Castle', J. Roy. Soc. Antiq. Ireland, 57, 81-99.

Freeman, A.M., ed. 1944: *The Annals of Connacht*, Dublin.

Gunning, Paul, and Feehily, Padraig, 1996: *Down Gallows Hill, An Illustrated History of Sligo from 1245 to 1995*, Sligo Heritage Group, Sligo

Hennessey, W.M., ed. 1871: *The Annals of Loch Ce*, 2 Vols., Dublin.

Hennessey, W.M., ed. 1887-1901: *The Annals of Ulster*, 4 Vols., Dublin.

King, D.J.C. 1988: *The Castle in England and Wales*, London & Sydney.

Lacy, B. 1983: *Archaeological Survey of County Donegal*, Donegal.

Leask, H.G. 1944: *Irish Castles and Castleated Houses*, 2nd. ed., Dundalk.

Lydon, J.F. 1987a: 'The Expansion and Consolidation of the Colony, 1215-54', in Cosgrove 1987, 156-178.

Lydon, J.F. 1987b: 'The Years in Crisis, 1254-1315', in Cosgrove 1987, 179-204.

Lydon, J.F. 1987c: 'A Land of War', in Cosgrove 1987, 240-274.

Lynch, A. & Manning, C. 1990: 'Dublin Castle - The Archaeological Project', Archaeol. Ireland, 4(2), 65-68.

Mallory, J. & McNeill, T. 1991: *The Archaeology of Ulster*, Belfast.

McCarthy, B., ed. 1887-1901: *The Annals of Ulster*, 4 Vols., Dublin.

McNeill, T. 1980: *Anglo-Norman Ulster*, Edinburgh.

MacNiocaill, G., ed. 1964: *The Red Book of the Earl of Kildare*, Dublin.

McTernan, J. 1995: *Olde Sligoe: Aspects of Sligo Town and County over 750 Years*, Sligo.

Murphy, D., ed. 1896: *The Annals of Clonmacnoise*, Dublin.

O'Conor, K.D. 1992: 'Irish Earthwork Castles', Fortress, 12, 3-12.

O'Conor, K.D. 1993: *The Earthwork Castles of Medieval Leinster*, unpublished Ph. D. Thesis, University of Wales, Cardiff,

O'Dowd, M. 1991: *Power, Politics and Land: Early Modern Sligo, 1568-1688*, Belfast.

O'Dowd, M. 1994: 'Sligo', in Simms and Andrews, 1994, 142-153.

O'Donovan, J. *Ordnance Survey Letters*, Sligo. 1836-1837.

O'Donovan, J., ed. 1848-1851: *The Annals of the Four Masters*, 7 Vols., Dublin.

O'Rorke, T. 1889: *The History of Sligo, Town and County*, 2 Vols., Dublin.

Orpen, G.H. 1911-1920: *Ireland Under the Normans, 1169 - 1333*, 4 Vols., Oxford.

Otway-Ruthven, A.J. 1980: *A History of Medieval Ireland*, 2nd. ed., London.

Philips, T. 1685: *Prospect of Sligo*, National Library of Ireland, MS 3137, No. 35.

Rae, E.C. 1987: 'Architecture and Sculpture, 1169 - 1603', in Cosgrove 1987, 737-777.

Simms, A. & Andrews, J.H. 1994: *Irish Country Towns*, Dublin.

Summerson, H. 1993: *Dunstanburgh Castle*, English Heritage, London.

Sweetman, P.D. 1985-1986: 'Archaeological Excavations at Ballymote Castle, Co. Sligo', J. Galway Archaeol. Hist. Soc., 40, 114-124.

Sweetman, P.D. 1995: *Irish Castles and Fortified Houses*, Dublin.

Taylor, G. & Skinner, A. 1783: *Maps of the Roads of Ireland*, 2nd.ed., Dublin.

Waterman, D.M. 1958: 'Greencastle, Co. Donegal', Ulster J. Archaeol., 21, 74-88.

Watt, J.A. 1987: 'The Anglo-Irish Colony under Strain, 1327-99', in Cosgrove 1987, 352-396.

Wauchope, Piers, 1992, *Patrick Sarsfield and the Williamite War*, Irish Academic Press, Dublin.

Wood-Martin, W.G. 1882: *History of Sligo, County and Town, from the Earliest Ages to the Close of the Reign of Queen Elizabeth*, Dublin.

Wood-Martin, W.G. 1889: *History of Sligo, County and Town, from the Accession of James I to the Revolution of 1688*, Dublin.

Archaeological Excavation at Sligo Town Hall Gate Lodge, June 2002

Eóin Halpin
Archaeological Development Services, Dublin and Belfast

ABSTRACT: Recent archaeological testing (Halpin 2002, 310) and a follow-up excavation in May June 2002, both undertaken in advance of the refurbishment of the Town Hall Gate Lodge of 1876 in Quay Street in Sligo, uncovered tantalizing evidence for previous building in the area.

The medieval urban survey by Bradley and Dunne suggests that the Gate Lodge and adjacent Town Hall may have been constructed on the site of Sligo Castle. Archaeological investigations of the proposed extension to the Gate Lodge, located to the south of the Town Hall, revealed quite convincing evidence for an earlier building or buildings, almost certainly the mid-17th century Cromwellian Ordnance Fort and possibly the 13th century castle. Examination of the documentary sources revealed details of a plan made in 1825 in the Public Record Office, London of the 17th century fort (Public Record Office, London, MSQ 520(m) BP/1478; copy in SLLSA #987), the southern end of which consists of two rectangular parallel rooms, the northern one noted as a 'Store', with the room to the south annotated as 'Store in possession of Mr. Coghran Merchant'. Interestingly the width of both rooms are recorded, with the southern store measuring 10ft while that to the north measures 19ft, equating to roughly 3m and 5.5m respectively. The results from the archaeological testing showed that the gap between the two walls uncovered was slightly over 5m, suggesting that it is the northern store room of the castle which was uncovered. The thinner room would appear to have been preserved in the building to the south housing Henry Lyons complex of shops.

It would be expected that if both walls were interior divisions within the fort that they would be of similar dimensions. However, the southern example was over twice the width of the northern, 1.2m and 0.4m respectively. This leads to the possibility that that the more massive southern example may be the southern wall of the earlier 13th century Sligo Castle. This wall was founded on natural glacial subsoil and, where ground conditions warranted it, a flat stone plinth. In contrast, the narrower wall to the north was found on made ground which

The more massive wall found behind the Town Hall Gate Lodge.

overlay the plinth and therefore securely post-dates it.

Although no direct dating evidence was recovered associated with the possible castle wall, it is demonstrably earlier than the 17th century fort wall and would seem to be much too massive by comparison to be another interior wall of the later fort. It is reasonable to interpret the two walls as parts of different buildings, the substantial 13th century castle wall being re-used as a foundation of an interior wall of the 17th century fort.

The ground towards the northern end of the excavation area was severely disturbed by the construction of the basements associated with the later Town Hall. Such was the scale and extent of the excavations associated with the construction in 1864 of the Town Hall to the design of William Hague, that it is likely that it is only at this southern end of the area, that further evidence of the earlier castle will survive.

June 2002

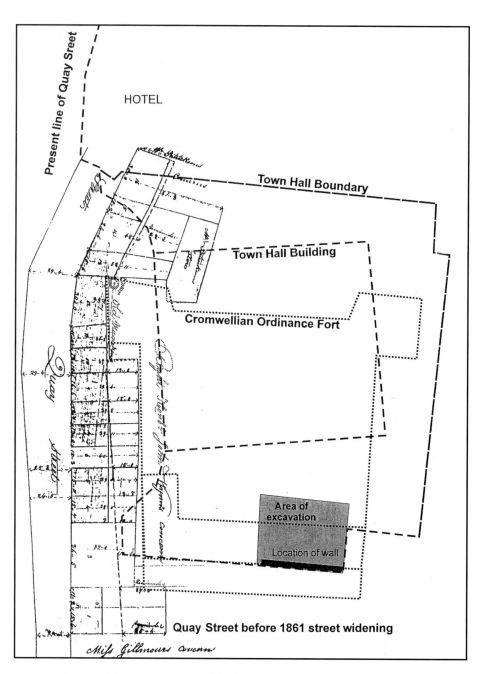

Sequence of developments at Town Hall Gate Lodge Sligo. Wall uncovered during excavations.
Cromwellian Fort, Quay Street in 1881 and Modern Quay Street and Sligo Town Hall.

SLIGO'S DE BURGO CASTLE OF 1310: AN ADDENDUM

Patrick E. O'Brien and Martin A. Timoney
Sligo Field Club

ABSTRACT: An assesment of the extent of Sligo castle of 1310.

A reading of the foregoing study by O'Conor, the excavations in May 2002 by Halpin to the rear of the Gate Lodge on the south side of Sligo Town Hall and an analysis of the only known graphic record of a castle in the Town Hall area, Thomas Phillips' *Prospect of Sligo* of 1685, provide us with an opportunity to offer a detailing and a positioning of Richard de Burgh's Sligo Castle of 1310 and to position Sligo's Stone Fort in relation to that castle[1].

O'Conor (2002) has suggested that de Burgh's castle was located close to the Old Bridge across the Garvoge. Its design was influenced by the castles of Edward I, built under the direction of Master James of St. George. A study of Thomas Phillips' *Prospect* shows a massive structure on high ground, overlooking the harbour, the river-crossings and the developing seventeenth century town. On the south-east is a three-story hall-type building with battlements. Centrally positioned along the south facing defensive wall is a possible single-block gate-tower. On the south-west corner is a polygonal tower and on the northern extremity a visually massive polygonal tower dominating all other structures. These buildings are connected by battlemented defensive walls. We can only speculate about the wall connecting the northern polygonal tower with the south-eastern hall-type building as it is concealed by the latter. All the buildings, as far as we can see them, fit comfortably into the style of de Burgh castles but Phillips' *Prospect*, which is of a time 375 years after the castle was built, could include buildings and alterations subsequent to de Burgo's 1310 work. These buildings may also have incorporated some remnants of the earlier FitzGerald castle, if, indeed, FitzGerald's castle stood at this location.

de Burgh's other Connacht castles are symmetrical, being either approximately square or rectangular. Sligo Castle differs in that the *Prospect* portrays Sligo as being an irregularly shaped enclosure, more akin to that of Greencastle, Co. Donegal, and further afield, Caernarvon, in north-west Wales, which was designed by Master James of St. George. Sligo Castle, in Phillips' *Prospect* also lacks a twin-towered gate.

O'Conor refers to castles associated with de Burgh and Edward I. The approximate outer dimensions of the relevant ones are – Ballintober, 85m by 77m, Ballymote, 50m by 59m, Roscommon, 70m by 58m and Greencastle, 83m by 33m. The irregularly-shaped Caernarvon, as a major statement of power in Wales, was proportionately larger at 171m by 64m (Sweetman 1999, 98, 102, 104; Salter 1993, 9).

What were the dimensions of Sligo Castle in Phillips' *Prospect*? These can be deduced by observation of the *Prospect* and evidence from Registry of Deeds records of the early eighteenth century. Phillips shows houses and tenements, possibly five or six, south of the castle and, possibly, some distance from it. John's Lane, now John St., Bridge St., now O'Connell St., and possibly Wine St. were then in existence; the houses on those streets may be those depicted by Phillips. A review of the dimensional details in an early eighteenth century deed of Sligo town properties suggests that an average frontage of some tenements recorded was sixteen to nineteen metres approximately (Registry of Deeds, 47-536-31777). Assuming that the five or six houses south of the castle reflected these dimensions - regardless of perspective - the overall length of the south facing structures of the castle can be deduced to be between 80 and 114 metres.

An additional exercise, which entailed the measurement of 1) the profile of the castle in Phillips' *Prospect* as a proportion of the distance between his eastern end of the castle and the western end of his St. John's church in the west and 2) from a viewing point on the Circular Road on the 1837 O.S. map of the vicinity of Sligo town, the distance of a line along the assumed south wall of Sligo castle bounded on the east by

Fig. 1-Sligo Castle in Thomas Phillips' *Prospect of Sligo*, 1685.

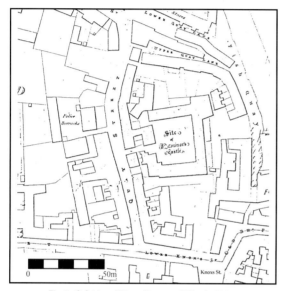

Fig. 2- O.S Map of Quay St. area of Sligo in 1837
Scale: 5ft.:1 mile

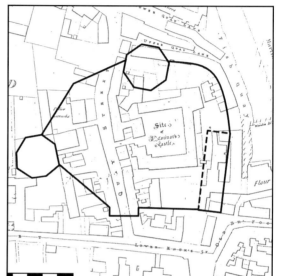

Fig. 3 - O.S Map of Quay St. area of Sligo in 1837 with suggested plan of Sligo Castle based on Phillips.

the assumed east end of Sligo castle and on the west by a line through the west end of St. John's church, provides us with a corroborating south wall dimension of *c.* 100 metres (O.S Sligo 1837, sheet 14 at a scale of 6 inches: 1 mile)

Analysis below will indicate that the depth from south facing curtain wall to the back tower may have extended to 100 metres. This suggests an enormous castle with a total perimeter wall length of *c.* 350 metres.

It is revealing that although the Stone Fort had existed since the 1650s, it was not depicted in 1685 by Thomas Phillips, the superb military engineer and military artist. His chosen viewing position was a high-point on present-day Circular Road in Knocknaganny townland to the east of Gallows Hill. If it were visible from there, Phillips, who was commissioned to chart the defences of Irish ports and had a reputation for exactness, would most certainly have recorded it (Ross 1976, 552-553). The Stone Fort was a substantial building, measuring approximately 54m x 55m overall as indicated on the *Plan of Ordnance Land at Sligo 1825*. Were the Stone Fort to have been visible from some other location Phillips would have been bound to have recorded it from that location. It may not have been high enough to be visible to Phillips from an outside location.

Was the Stone Fort within the larger castle and, thus, not visible? During the 1690 siege, the Huguenot defenders[2] of Sligo Castle retreated, to the Stone Fort for greater security, the old castle being less defendable (Wood-Martin 1880, 118-122; Wauchope 1992, passim.); the structures were close to one another. The 1689 map of Sligo shows that the Stone Fort was a bastion-type defense. Curiously this sole 17th century map of Sligo town does not record a castle at the site (Wood-Martin 1889, opp. 134), perhaps because the castle may have been defensively redundant by then. Or, was the older castle being dismantled, possibly for use in the retrenchments (Wood-Martin 1889, 116-117; Kerrigan 1995, 122) of Sir Henry Luttrell? In the second siege of Sligo in 1691, with Jacobite forces entrenched at the Green Fort, the Stone Fort played no strategic part in hostilities (Wood-Martin 1882, 133-138; O'Rorke 1889, I, 219-221). Was it less defendable because the surrounding old castle provided close quarter shelter for attacking forces?[3]

The O.S. map of 1837 and new archaeological excavation evidence show that the Stone Fort was largely located within the Town Hall complex and stretching some three metres south into the modern Henry Lyons and Co. premises on the east side of Quay St. (O.S. Sligo, 1838, = M4 in SLLSA[4]; O.S. Sligo 1876, sheet 12 at a scale of 10ft.:Mile,). Accepting the proposed dimensions of de Burgh's castle and the known dimensions of the Stone Fort, it is most unlikely that both could have existed side by side on an east-west axis[5]. No substantial defensive works are visible to the east or west of the Sligo Castle in Phillips' *Prospect* and the 1824 map clearly places the Stone Fort on the Town Hall location on the east side of Quay St. The Stone Fort would show in Phillips' *Prospect* if it were south of the castle. The current Wine St. reflects the evolution of a streetscape south of the medieval castle at a distance which allows for a moat and bank. This is assuming the proposed and given depths of both Castle and Stone Fort and the archaeological evidence of a wall of the Stone Fort found by Halpin just north of an earlier and more substantial castle wall. Both structures could not have fitted on the landscape as separately located structures on a north-south axis. The 1824 drawing shows that the Stone Fort was on the Town Hall site, not north of it.

One can propose that the Stone Fort was not visible in the 1685 depiction because it was erected within the de Burgh Castle complex. It would seem that part of the south facing wall of de Burgh's Sligo Castle was situated and passed through the present Henry Lyons building.

The Stone Fort, in the control of State Ordnance, is not recorded in the Strafford Estate Rentals of 1682 (Strafford 1682, 13). Deeds of 1708 and 1734 record a property described as 'the fort in New Street . . . then or late in the tenure of Humphrey Booth' (Registry of Deeds, 1-331-209 and 76-392-55021). New Street, a lane between Upper Quay Lane and Lower Quay Lane was situated north of the Town Hall complex and thus north of the Stone Fort. Was this 'fort in New Street' a northern outer bastion of the Stone Fort or the last remains of the earlier de Burgh polygonal tower? A theory on the morphology of Quay Street may support the latter idea.

Phillips' *Prospect* shows a possible gate-tower on the south wall and a tower to the north near the quay. The castle would not have been cut off from its maritime access route. It may have had a water-gate to the quays. It would have been close to the north tower for defensive purposes. To control access to the quays from the town, a straight-through route across the castle ward from gate-tower to water-gate would have been a logical development. The erection of the Stone Fort on the high ground may have impinged on this through-route at the north end of the present Town Hall following which Quay Street may have been re-directed into the angular shape that we have today. Thus, assuming that the south castle wall passed through the mid-line of the Henry Lyons building and that the north tower stood above the quay, we suggest that the castle may have been approaching one hundred metres in depth on a north-south axis.

Where were the possible boundary lines of the castle? A study of Phillips' *Prospect* shows that it was positioned on an approximate WNW-ESE axis. Assuming a south-east corner within the Henry Lyons / GPO complex at the south end of Quay St., as the wall found by Halpin suggests, at sufficient distance north of the present Wine St. to allow for a defensive moat and bank, the south wall extended 80 to 114 metres on this WNW-ESE axis, through a gate-tower on the line of Quay St., to a polygonal tower at its west end. Enigmatically, at 120 metres distant from the assumed south-east corner a possible vestige of a polygonal boundary line is recorded on mid-19th century O.S. maps in an otherwise regularly bounded series of properties. This is north of No. 4, The Bohemian Bar, on the north side of Wine St., and west of Nos. 15-16, The Chamber of Commerce, on Quay St. opposite the Town Hall. The west wall may have extended north from this tower through the VEC site on the west side of Quay St, to the massive north tower at the west end of Upper Quay Lane and Lower Quay Lane; *i.e.*, to the 'fort on New Street', and possibly reflected in a bastion or tower shape building recorded on the 1837 OS town map (O.S. Sligo, 1838, = M4 in SLLSA). From there, it may have followed a curvilinear route along the high escarpment, skirting the eastern side of the site on which the Stone Fort and the Town Hall were later to be built, to the hall-type building on the south-east corner of the castle. The route of Upper Quay Lane curving eastwards into Fish Quay may represent an early development of cabins outside and in the shelter of this walled escarpment. Likewise, the entrance from Lower Knox's St., to Fish Quay may reflect a riverside access route to this area.

In the end, where was and what was the shape of de Burgh's Sligo Castle of 1310? We have the records of the Annals, Phillips' *Prospect of Sligo* of

1685, Wood-Martin's record[6], O'Conor's analysis, some fragments of early eighteenth century evidence, the tantalizing evidence of a short length of a substantial medieval wall on the Gate Lodge site and much surmise. Only further excavations will confirm or deny such surmise!

Notes

1. This addendum began with an analysis by Timoney of the cartographic evidence from the early 19th century O.S. maps of Sligo and analysis of documentary evidence, mainly in the Registry of Deeds, by O'Brien. It has been commented on by John J. Flynn and Dr. Kieran D. O'Conor. Phillips' *Prospect*, so pivotal in all this discussion was first shown at Sligo Field Club lecture by Dr. John A. Claffey in 1978. An attempted reconstruction of the perimeter layout, based on Phillips' *Prospect* and the OS maps, is included.

2. These 400 Huguenots were the Grenadier Company of La Mellonére's regiment, one of three infantry regiments raised from exiled French Protestants who accompanied Schomberg's expedition to Ireland in August 1689. They were commanded by Capt. Sauveur. (pers. comm. Dr Harman Murtagh).

3. William Henry, in his *Hints towards a Natural Topographical History of the Counties Sligoe, . . .* National Archives of Ireland, Ms. 2533, does not refer to the Castle in 1739. *The Edinburgh Gazetteer or Geographical Dictionary . . . of the World*, published by Archibald Constable in 1822, suggests (Vol. 5, 647) that at least some of the castle survived as late as 1822, - "This town owes its origins to a castle and an abbey erected here by Maurice Fitzgerald . . . this castle was destroyed; but was again rebuilt in 1310. Its ruins now evidence its former splendour". The source of this information is not known and it could be that walls of the Stone Fort are what are being referred to. Regrettably these two historical sources do not provide comfortably secure information and can not be relied on.

4. SLLSA = Sligo Library Local Studies Archive.

5. Halpin (2002) located what is convincingly a wall of medieval proportions, most likely of the 1310 castle. The ground to the east of here drops dramatically before flattening out to the Garvogue River's edge. As far as we can ascertain from local knowledge of the area behind Sligo Post Office, provided by Briga Murphy, Aidan Mannion and Tony Toher, there have not been major changes in the topography here. Late 19th and early 20th century ground photographs, maps and aerial photographs combine to indicate that the ground level east of The Town Hall was always roughly at its present level. Engineering works for the Buttermarket development, on the west side of Quay St., encountered stiff resistance below the surface in the form of heavy densely compacted clay of more tenacious durability than rock. From this we are confident that the castle could not have extended further east than the Town Hall but stood dramatically on high ground overlooking the river where it becomes tidal. Dr. Harman Murtagh provided the reference to Ross (1976).

6. The frequently published drawing of The Siege of the Green Fort (*e.g.*, Wood-Martin 1882, Frontispiece; Gunning and Feehily 1995, 26) is not of Sligo at all but was taken by A. Schoonebeek in 1689 from a drawing of the Siege of Bonn by J. Tangena of Lyden (O'Neill 1966). Apparently variations of this drawing has been used to illustrate many sieges throughout Europe.

SOURCES

MANUSCRIPT

Strafford Ms.: Rental of the estate of the Earl of Strafford, 1682, (Microfilm copy SLLSA #571)

PUBLISHED

Halpin, Eóin, 2002: "Archaeological excavations at Sligo Town Hall Gate Lodge", in Timoney, ed., 2002.

Kerrigan, Paul M., 1995: *Castles and Fortifications in Ireland, 1485-1945*, Cork, Collins.

O'Neill, T.P., 1966: "Dutch Engraving of the Williamite Wars 1689", *Irish Book*, 1:3, 1-4.

O'Rorke, Terrence, 1889: *The History of Sligo: Town and County*, Dublin, James Duffy, Reprint, Sligo, 1986, Dodd's Antiquarian Books.

Salter, M., 1993: *Castles and Stronghouses of Ireland*, Malvern, Folly.

Sweetman, David, 2002: *The Medieval Castles of Ireland*, Cork, Collins.

Ross, Ruth Isabel, 1976: "Phillips's Pleasing Prospects, A Seaman Artist in Ireland", *Country Life*, March 4 1976, 552-553.

Timoney, Martin. A., 2002: *A Celebration of Sligo, First Essays for Sligo Field Club*, Sligo, Sligo Field Club.

Wauchope, Piers, 1992: *Patrick Sarsfield and the Williamite War*, Dublin, Irish Academic Press.

Wood-Martin, W.G., 1880: *Sligo and the Enniskilleners from 1688 to 1691*, Dublin.

Wood-Martin, W.G., 1882: *The History of Sligo, County and Town, from the Earliest Ages to the Close of the Reign of Queen Elizabeth*, Dublin, Reprint, Sligo, 1990, Dodd's Antiquarian Books.

Wood-Martin, W.G., 1889: *The History of Sligo, County and Town, from the Accession of James I to the Revolution of 1688*, Dublin, Hodges Figgis; Reprint, Sligo, 1990, Dodd's Antiquarian Books.

ARCHAEOLOGICAL SITE ASSESSMENTS, 1993-1994, ROCKWOOD PARADE, SLIGO

Eoin Halpin Archaeological Development Services, Dublin and Belfast

ABSTRACT: The archaeological site testing in 1993 and 1994 of ten sites in the Rockwood Parade Recommended Action Plan area in Sligo town revealed that the area on the south side of the river was reclaimed, probably in the early years of the 17th century, and was quickly developed. Tobergal Lane dates to this period; however, Water Lane may have been the course of an old stream.

HISTORICAL BACKGROUND

Located on a strategic fording point of the Garvoge River between the sea to the west and Lough Gill to the east, the town of Sligo dates back to the Early Middle Ages. There is some evidence for prehistoric man in the area (Bradley and Dunne 1987; Bergh, 1995). The first documentary evidence, which records that a bridge was established across the river, dates to sometime before 1188. Under Maurice Fitzgerald of the Kildare Geraldines a hospital (1242), a castle (1245; (O'Conor this volume)), town defences (1246) and an abbey (1252) were constructed. In 1293 the castle was given to John Fitz-Thomas. Richard de Burgh built a castle in the town in 1310 (O'Conor this volume). The town was created a borough in 1612.

Thomas O'Connor (Ordnance Survey Letters 1836, 191-203 in Ms., 77-82 in typescript), Wood-Martin (1889; 1892), Kilgannon (1926, 99-111), O'Dowd (1991, 149-164), Bradley and Dunne (1987, 15-29), Gallagher (1987) and McTernan (1988; 1994) and the Rockwood Parade Recommended Action Plan (1992, 4) record and/or analyse the development of the town down the centuries. From these it is reasonable to expect that remains of this early town of Sligo still exist beneath the present town. The precise location of this early town still eludes us but the area on the south side of The Garvogue River between the Abbey and the supposed site of the castle of 1310 somewhere in the vicinity of The Town Hall seemed most likely.

In 1992 at the request of Sligo Corporation The National Building Agency in the person of Mr. Derry O'Connell, architect with the National Building Agency, drew up the *Rockwood Parade Recommended Action Plan*, hereinafter *RPRAP*, as an overall redevelopment plan for the inner city area. See O'Connell (1995, 171) for a summary of *RPRAP* from a planning and development point of view.

The area in question along the south side of The Garvogue River is between Lower Knox St., O'Connell St., Grattan St. the lower northern end of Market St., Castle St., Thomas St. and Rockwood Parade. Two lanes cross this area. Tobergal Lane joins the middle of O'Connell St. eastwards to the bend in Rockwood Parade. Water Lane joins the west end of Castle St. northwards to Rockwood Parade.

The legal need for archaeological site testing was indicated in the RPRAP. Martin A. Timoney, as Hon. Secretary of Sligo Field Club, pointed out in communications to Sligo Corporation and to the Office of Public Works the substantial body of information, referred to above, indicating that this area was one of potential archaeological deposits and that site testing was a legal requirement. In 1993 and 1994, in compliance with statutory controls on development within an archaeological area, Archaeological Development Services were requested by the individual developers to do the archaeological site testing. The archaeological excavation licence numbers are 93E0118, 93E0162, 94E047 and 94E135 and summary accounts by the writer have appeared in print (Halpin 1994; 1995). Many standing buildings were photographically recorded by Martin A. Timoney and James McHugh before and during demolition.

Ten sites were investigated. For each the Site number, *Rockwood Parade Recommended Action Plan* number, topographical location and the name of the developer who initially applied for the planning permission is given herein Table 1. At each descriptive entry they are given in a shorter form.

Site No.	RPRAP No.	Location	Developer
Site 1:	*RPRAP* 30	O'Connell Street to Rockwood Parade,	James Callery, Westward (Sligo) Ltd.
Site 2:	*RPRAP* 28	Rockwood Parade, Youth Centre,	The Bishop of Elphin.
Site 3:	*RPRAP* 25B	Tobergal Lane & Rockwood Parade,	Kilcawley & The National Building Agency.
Site 4:	*RPRAP* 16	Tobergal Lane & Rockwood Parade,	Mr. Leslie Bagnell.
Site 5:	*RPRAP* 21A	Tobergal Lane,	Mr. Peter Martin.
Site 6:	*RPRAP* 26	Tobergal Lane,	Moffitt of Sligo.
Site 7:	*RPRAP* 23	Tobergal Lane,	Carraig Donn Sales Ltd.
Site 8:	*RPRAP* 9 & 14,	Blackwood's Yard, Rockwood Parade & Water Lane, Rippon	Seamus O'Dowd & Mark Francis Calliendo
Site 9:	*RPRAP* 25A	Tobergal Lane,	
Site 10:		Junction of Tobergal Lane and Rockwood Parade.	

Table 1

SITE 1:

RPRAP 30

O'Connell St. to Rockwood.   **Callery**

The site of No. 30 O'Connell Street runs west to east, from O'Connell Street to the river (Figs. 1 & 2). Bradley & Dunne (1987, fig. 2) noted that this site was one of the few, recorded on early documents, which extended this full distance. The pre-development archaeological testing took the form of the detailed recording of five of the previously hand dug engineering test pits which had been monitored by Martin A. Timoney, the excavation of one further shallow pit and the examination of two long machine dug trenches. In each case, with one exception, excavation was down to bedrock.

The findings revealed that at the O'Connell Street end, bedrock was a mere 0.8m below modern ground surface and, due to later disturbance, only 0.35m of archaeology survived *in situ*. No finds dated to earlier than circa 1600 were recovered, even from primary deposits. The base of the pit nearest O'Connell St. revealed the uneven line of limestone bedrock. This uneven surface was levelled off with a mixture of naturally occurring weathered bedrock and grey silt clay. Over this, lay a 10cm thick deposit of dark grey-black charcoal flecked silt clay with some shell and small pieces of animal bone.

One small fragment of a clay pipe stem was recovered from this deposit. This layer was topped with a 0.5cm thick layer of compacted clay and sand, apparently representing a floor surface, over which lay a second deposit of dark grey silt clay, once again with clay pipe fragments but also small fragments of glass bottle. The remains of a recent red-brick wall was laid directly on this deposit before it was levelled and became the foundation for the most recent concrete floor in the building.

At a distance of 7m from the present frontage, a substantial cross-wall was uncovered, keyed into the original wall

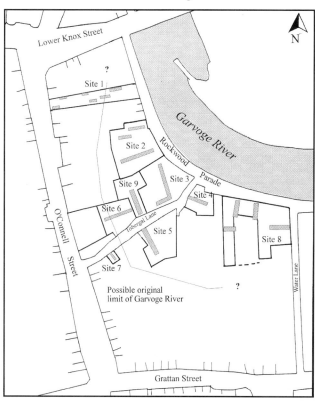

Fig.1 - Location of the sites and test trenches

which formed the northern limit of the plot. This wall and plinth contained six courses and survived to a height of 1m above bedrock, with the plinth standing 10cm proud of the wall face and 20cm high, suggesting a possible floor level. The wall over the plinth was 60cm thick and consisted of angular, roughly hewn, blocks on average 25cm thick and was bonded with a light-grey, gritty, mortar. It was interesting to note that the northern wall was also supported by a plinth at the same level as that noted under the cross-wall.

Examination of the boundary wall on the north side some 15m to the east revealed that it also was founded on bedrock, but contained no evidence for a plinth. However, there was reasonably clear evidence for the foundation trench for this wall, which cut through some 6cm of unstratified, highly organic, soils. These soils were not noted to the west of the previously described cross-wall.

Some meters to the east and south a shallow pit was excavated to examine the possible junction of two substantial walls which survived above ground. Here, beneath the clearly modern red brick wall, a more substantial wall of rough hewn angular blocks was noted, similar to that seen on the north side of the plot. In this case the wall was noted to run through from west to east, with a cross-wall joining at right angles.

Two trenches were machine excavated further to the east, the first revealed evidence for the continuation of the east-west wall noted in the adjacent cutting. However, later disturbance truncated this wall and it was not noted at the eastern end of the trench. On the north side of this cutting the remains of a stone lined culvert was revealed, the southern edge of which was truncated by later disturbance. The side walls stood a maximum of 75cm above bedrock and was traceable over a distance of 3.60m At least one of the covering lintels survived *in situ* at the eastern end, while a return to the north, at the west end, suggests a possible junction with another culvert joining from that side.

The final trench was along the line of the northern boundary wall towards the east end of the site. Here a 6m long trench was dug, once again to bedrock, and uncovered evidence for a third cross wall of similar type to those already seen. These two walls were both founded on bedrock, which was some 2m below the present ground level.

The soils noted during excavation fell into two main types, firstly the compacted light grey and grey soils found to the west of the westernmost cross-wall. It is likely that these represent the remains of occupation layers and the fact that no finds dating to earlier than 1600 were recovered is significant. Secondly, the very deep, highly organic, unstratified, dark grey and black soils of the site found towards the eastern end of the area. As mentioned above, no finds were recovered from these soils which could be dated to earlier than the 17th century. Indeed the lack of finds and the depth of soil without any appreciable stratification strongly suggests that these soils are akin to those noted in other urban excavations where they are interpreted as soils introduced into city garden plots.

The nature of the deposits was such that it was not possible to detect the trenches cut for the large active sewer-pipe which crossed the site nor for the modern timbers at base of deposits at the SE of the site.

At the very east extremity of the site a fine millstone was discovered.

SITE 2.

RPRAP 28
Rockwood Parade **Bishop of Elphin**

Three trial trenches (Figs. 1 & 4) were machine excavated down to bedrock in the proposed development area. Nothing of archaeological significance was noted in the two northern examples save only for an area of very disturbed ground at the extreme eastern end of Trench 1, recognised by the large quantity of loose angular and sub-angular boulders which had been dumped there. The bedrock was noted to slope from some 2.2m below ground level (BGL) at the W end of Trench 2 down to 2.4m BGL at the E end of Trench 1. A large 'live' sewer-pipe, encased in concrete, was uncovered 4m from the W end of Trench 2.

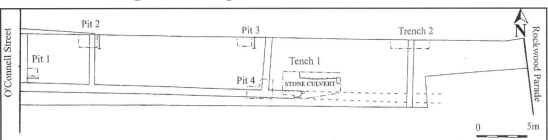

Fig. 2 - Plan of cuttings in Site 1, 30 O'Connell Street, Sligo

The soil profile revealed in these two cuttings consisted of smooth shelving bedrock, overlain by some 0.3m of blue grey riverine silts and muds, over which lay a brown organic deposit of twigs, leaves and grasses. These in turn were covered by up to 1.8m of redeposited soils which contained a wide variety of ecofacts and artifacts, ranging from sea shells and animal bones to clay pipes and roof tiles. The upper 0.4m consisted of modern rubble and concrete flooring.

A number of interesting features were noted in Trench 3 to the S of the area. However, generally speaking, the soil profile was the same as was noted in the other two trenches. Bedrock lay at between 2.1m and 2.4m BGL. Riverine silts and muds were covered by redeposited soils which were in turn covered by modern rubble and concrete. Evidence for an early plot division was noted in the form of a 0.6m wide wall which ran perpendicular to the western edge of the development area. The wall consisted of angular, roughly hewn blocks on average 0.25m thick and bonded with a light-grey, gritty, mortar. The wall was founded on the bedrock with the foundation trench cut into the redeposited soils.

Also cut into the redeposited soils were two timber lined pits. The western example consisted of a wooden box apparently rectangular measuring some 3m E-W and respecting the E-W line of the early wall. The E and N walls of the box, as well as the floor, were revealed during the trenching. The box was set in a clay lined pit presumably to make it water tight. The primary deposits within the box consisted of bark and wood chippings and other organic matter. Bark chippings are an important element in the tanning process. The other pit lay some 10m to the E of the first and consisted of the slight remains of bark chippings and the outline of the clay lining. No wood was noted in his case. Two further features were uncovered in this trench, firstly a stone drain was noted at the extreme E end of the trench and secondly the line of the sewer, first seen in Trench 2, cut through the early wall at the western end of this cutting.

SITE 3:

RPRAP 25B
Tobergal Lane & Rockwood Parade
Kilcawley & NBA

The site of 25B Tobergal Lane (Fig 1) lies immediately to the southeast of Rockwood Parade where the River Garvoge turns northwards. The site is bounded to the south by Tobergal Lane and to the west and north by buildings. The area thus defined measures approximately 22m east west by, at most, 30m transversely. Testing took the form of a 21m long machine cut trench running NW to SE, with an additional 6m trench running south from its east end. Previously engineering test pits here had been archaeologically monitored by Martin A. Timoney as the first archaeological involvement in the entire Rockwood Parade development.

The results showed that the majority of the archaeology consisted of redeposited material. These deposits took two distinct forms, the first consisted of up to 1.5m in depth of grey or dark grey silt clays with shell, wood and charcoal inclusions. However, towards the western end of the site, in an area which may have once been particularly marshy or prone to flooding, a large quantity of stones and boulders were used to make up the ground. As a possible aid to drainage in this area, a wooden culvert was laid running south to north towards the river. It consisted of dressed timbers forming an enclosed drain 75cm square. The base timbers, which were set running along the line of the

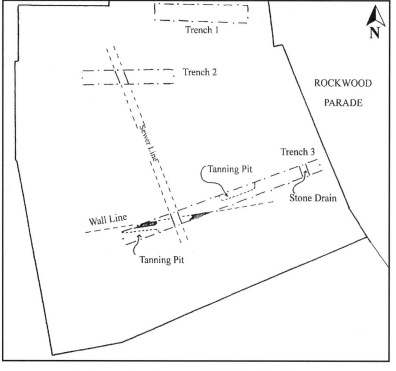

Fig.3 - Location of trenches in Site 2, the Youth Centre

drain, supported the floor of the structure. The sides consisted of thin planks, on average 10cm wide and 1cm thick, with grooves cut along top and bottom housing the floor and roof timbers. The roof had collapsed at the time of investigation. Some of these timbers had been previously used.

Some 5m to the east, a wall was revealed, probably contemporary with the drain, in that the foundation trench for the wall and the trench cut to house the drain were cut down from the same level. This wall measured 6cm thick and consisted of yellow sandstone blocks bonded with a grey gritty mortar. The foundations rested on the surface of the stone land fill deposit. The line of this wall appears to coincide neatly with the projected line of the northern return of the wall on the north side of the open shed and the remains of a wall marked by the line of some projecting stones on the inside face of the northern boundary wall. In section, the area to the west side of the wall consists of rubble while to the east, in the 9m between this wall and the next, a cobbled yard was noted. The second wall is probably quite recent in date and is likely to be a continuation of the west wall of the shed built against the west side of Tobergal Lane. The remains of a stone filled drain was noted beneath the foundation of this wall.

The east end of the long trench and the short southern return stayed dry long enough to allow for a detailed examination of the 1.5m of land fill. The basal 10cm, which rests directly on bedrock, consists of a mixture of sands, silts and weathered bedrock. Immediately above this is a layer of brown organic material, consisting of small twigs, leaves, matted grasses and roots. The layer is of variable thickness but averages some 2cm. On this layer lies the 1.5m thick deposit of grey or dark grey silt clays which contain isolated fragments of shell, some animal bone, small pieces of timbers, some of which appear to have been worked, and some small pieces of leather. However despite extended periods of searching only objects of post-medieval date were recovered. In general the land fill deposit is lighter in colour and more compacted close to the surface than at the base, the explanation for this is likely to be natural in that the lower layers are likely to be permanently saturated being under the water level of the River Garvoge.

The remains of two large, stone filled, wooden boxes, used as early foundation pads for subsequent buildings, were found north of the centre of the site.

SITE 4:
RPRAP 16
Tobergal Lane & Rockwood Parade   Bagnell

The site to the rear of 8-9 Grattan Street (Fig 1) presently takes the form of a dog-leg with access to the northern end gained from the west via Tobergal Lane. A 16m long trench was machine excavated down to bedrock, with a 2.5m gap left to allow for a live sewage main. The bedrock sloped upwards from east, 2.0m BGL, to west, 1.6m BGL. The lowest layer was a continuous 10cm thick layer of slits and sands with small fragments of weathered bedrock. Over this lay a layer of brown highly organic soil, consisting of small twigs, leaves, matted grasses and roots. The layer was of variable thickness but averaged some 20cm. On this layer lay a thick deposit of grey or dark grey silt clays which contained isolated fragments of shell, some animal bone and small pieces of timbers. This deposit measured 1.3m deep to the east but was only 9cm deep towards the west end.

The foundation trench to a wall was dug through this layer. The roughly built foundations rested directly on bedrock with the fair face starting at some 80cm above this level. The wall measured 60cm wide with no clear plinth, although the founds were wider that the wall proper. The wall was built of roughly hewn stone blocks bonded with a gritty grey mortar. Examination of the upstanding walls in the area reveal that this wall is most probably a continuation of the main west boundary wall of the plot.

Two other possible walls were noted during trenching, both of which were located towards the east end of the site. It was noted that neither of these two walls continued through to the north side of the cutting and neither were founded on the bedrock, although the westernmost example had a markedly deeper foundation trench. It is possible that these two walls form the corner of a building which has been removed above ground. This does not explain why one of the foundation trenches should be so markedly different to the other. Another explanation may be that the wall with the deeper foundation is in fact an original plot wall running north-south. The width of the plot as it stands now is some 10m, measured from the newly discovered wall, eastwards, to the line of the modern upstanding building. Interestingly the wall in question bisects the plot into two equal strips 5m wide, exactly the width of the plot noted in No. 30 O'Connell Street. There are two main problems with this hypothesis, the first is that the wall does not continue across the cutting and secondly, although the foundation trench is deep it did not appear, at least in section, to be found on bedrock, a feature of all the early plot walls thus far encountered. The upper 60cm of the section consisted of a mixture of rubble and hard core over which a concrete floor had been laid.

The plot probably post-dates 1600 with the majority of the site consisting of redeposited, unstratified, soils.

SITE 5:

RPRAP 21A
Tobergal Lane   **Martin**

This site (Fig 1) ran south from Tobergal Lane. An 11m long trench was machine excavated down to bedrock. Water quickly flowed into the base of the trench and so a 1m cross baulk was left in order to achieve a dry section from ground level to bedrock. The bedrock was a constant 2m BGL. It was immediately overlain by a 15cm deep deposit of silt and sands with fragments of weathered bedrock. Above this was a 20cm thick layer of brown highly organic soil containing twigs, matted grasses and leaves. Over this and extending to within 6cm of the surface was a layer of grey or dark grey silt clays which contained isolated fragments of shell, some animal bone and small pieces of wood as well as a number of fragments clay pipe stems and glass. A stone filled drain was noted running north towards the river. The upper layers consist of rubble and hard core capped with a 10cm thick layer of concrete.

The plot probably post-dates 1600 with the majority of the site consisting of redeposited, unstratified soils.

SITE 6:

RPRAP 26
Tobergal Lane   **Moffitt**

The site, to the rear of Moffitt's, O'Connell Street, (Fig. 1) takes the form of a roughly rectangular area measuring some 15m by 12m. It fronts out onto the north side of Tobergal Lane.

An 11m long trench, parallel to Tobergal Lane, was machine excavated down to bedrock. The bedrock sloped upwards from east to west, ranging in depth from 2m to 1m BGL. The lowest layer was a continuous 10cm thick layer of slits and sands with small fragments of weathered bedrock. Over this lay a layer of black, highly organic soil, consisting of small twigs, leaves, matted grasses and roots. The layer was of variable thickness but averaged some 20cm. On this layer lay a thick deposit of grey or dark grey clay loams which contained isolated fragments of shell, some animal bone and small pieces of timbers. This deposit measured 50cm deep to the east but was down to 30cm towards the west end.

Towards the centre of the cutting, and effectively within this layer, was uncovered a small dump of leather fragments, consisting of waste pieces, uppers and soles. These pieces have been dated to the 17th century (Daire O'Rourke pers. comm). The leather-bearing layer was overlain by a fairly homogenous deposit of grey brown clay loam which ran from west to east across the cutting, getting thicker across the exposed 11m. A large, 1.3m wide and 1m deep, stone filled drain was cut into this layer. No dating evidence was found in association with this feature.

A further deposit of mortar-flecked clay had been deposited over the area, prior to the construction of two substantial cross walls, both of which appeared to run perpendicular to the line of Tobergal Lane. The eastern example was set within a 1.4m wide and 50cm deep foundation trench and consisted of large, angular, roughly hewn, sandstone blocks, bonded with a gritty, grey mortar. The wall stood 50cm high in total and 60cm in width. Only the slight remains of a foundation trench survived of the western example. The upper 50cm of the section consisted of a mixture of rubble and hard core over which a concrete floor had been laid.

SITE 7:

RPRAP 23
Tobergal Lane   **Carraig Donn**

The site lies on the S side of Tobergal Lane (Fig 1) close to the junction with O'Connell Street. The proposed development area measured no more than 5m E-W by 10m N-S. A single 3.5m long and 75cm wide machine cut trench was excavated running perpendicular to the line of the Tobergal Lane. Bedrock lay at a depth of 75cm BGL. It was very uneven with patches of blue grey boulder clay lodged in the crevices. Over this lay an homogenous dark grey silt clay with a high humic content and many pieces of animal bone and sea shell. A small fragment of a clay pipe stem was the only significant archaeological find. The surface of this layer had small areas of well laid cobbles surviving, presumably representing an old floor or yard surface. Above this was modern hardcore and concrete.

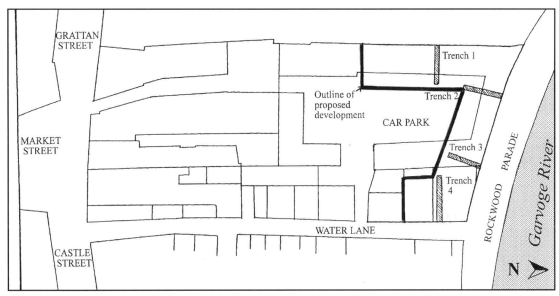

Fig. 4 - Location of trenches in Site 8, Blackwoods Yard, also showing outline of photos to the rear of castle street.

SITE 8:

RPRAP 9 & 14
Blackwood's Yard, Rockwood Parade
& Water Lane   O'Dowd & Rippon

This development (Fig 1) has the largest area of the ten sites. It lies south of the River Garvogue and west of Water Lane. The open space within it, known as Blackwood's Yard, was surrounded by multi-story warehouses.

Four trenches were machine excavated down to bedrock which was noted to slope down to the E towards the river, varying in depth between 1.8m to 2.4m BGL. Generally speaking the soil profiles examined in all four trenches were similar, consisting of smooth shelving bedrock, overlain by some 30cm of blue grey riverine silts and muds, over which lay a brown organic deposit of twigs, leaves and grasses. These in turn were covered by up to 1.8m of redeposited soils which contained a wide variety of ecofacts and artifacts, ranging from sea shells and animal bones to clay pipes and roof tiles. The upper 40cm consisted of modern rubble and concrete flooring.

Trench 1 at the W end of the proposed development area ran E-W for a distance of 8.5m. Two walls were noted in this cutting one at the extreme western end of the trench and the other some 6m to the E. Interestingly both of the walls were of similar form, being some 0.6m wide and consisting of angular, roughly hewn, blocks, on average 25cm thick, and bonded with a light-grey, gritty, mortar. In both cases the walls were founded on bedrock with the foundation trench cut through the redeposited soils. Bedrock here varied in depth between 1.8m BGL at the W and 2m BGL at the E.

Trench 2 ran perpendicular to the proposed Rockwood Parade frontage and for a distance of 10m. Two features of note were revealed, firstly a substantial stone filled drain was uncovered at the northern end of the trench and secondly a cross wall ran E-W across the cutting some 5m from the S end. This wall coincided with one of the walls which comprised the Blackwood's Yard buildings. Unlike the walls noted in Trench 1 it was not founded directly on bedrock but rather on a loose deposit of stones which in turn sat on bedrock.

Trench 3, located parallel to, and some 14m to the E of Trench 2, exhibited a sloping bedrock floor which varied between 1.9m BGL at the S end down to 2.3m BGL at the N. The junction of two walls were noted at the S end, the configuration of which does not apparently relate to the buildings of the yard recorded on the O.S. 4th edition map. However, the wall running N-S was founded on the bedrock while the wall running E-W was not, even though in their upper courses they were apparently keyed together. Some fragments of red brick, roof tile and clay pipe were recovered from the redeposited soil in this cutting.

Trench 4, was located at the E of the area and ran for the full width, some 10m, of the proposed buildings along this side. The E end of the trench abutted Water Lane. The wall which was revealed along this edge consisted of angular, roughly hewn, blocks, on average 25cm thick, and was bonded with a light-grey, gritty, mortar. It was apparently founded on bedrock which was some 2.4m below the ground level. Rising water levels within the cutting made it very difficult to discern details. It was clear however that the presence of bedrock at such a depth, and the overlying depth of natural silts and muds as well as redeposited soils created severe difficulties for the construction of the buildings of Blackwood's Yard.

A series of wooden piles, located some 4 ft. apart in a grid pattern, were driven down to the bedrock. On each of these piles rested the corners of stone filled wooden boxes, roughly 4ft square and 4ft in depth. It was these which formed the solid ground on which the cobbled yards of the buildings were laid. This feature was noted before in the Rockwood Parade area, specifically in the development at 25A Tobergal Lane, where similar boxes were used as the foundations to a yard, which overlay a particularly marshy part of the site.

The picture which emerges from the Blackwood's Yard is that the walls running N-S noted in Trenches 1, 3 and 4 are all original plot divisions. Each is of the same construction and dimension and, most importantly, are founded on bedrock. They continue the boundary walls of the plot divisions existing in Grattan St., thought by Bradley and Dunne (1987) to be medieval in date, across the area of reclaimed ground.

The other feature of note is the line of Water Lane. A number of facts, the bedrock slopes down from W to E in this area, rather than from N to S towards the river, allied to the depth of natural silts and muds and that during trenching the water flowed remarkably quickly into the trench from the S, suggests that there was and possibly still is, a flowing stream running down the present line of Water Lane.

SITE 9:

RPRAP 25A
Tobergal Lane   Caliendo

The site lies on the N side of Tobergal Lane (Fig 1) some 40m east of the junction with O'Connell Street. The proposed development area measures no more than 8m E-W by 15m N-S. A single 10m long and 1m wide machine cut trench was excavated running perpendicular to the line of Tobergal Lane. Bedrock lay at a depth of 2m BGL. It was immediately overlain by some 20cm of coarse sand and clays with abundant shell fragments mixed throughout. This in turn was covered by up to 50cm of red brown organic matter consisting of roots, grasses, twigs and pieces of unworked timber. Above this was over 1m of an homogenous dark grey silt clay with a high humic content and many pieces of animal bone and sea shell. The surface of this layer had small areas of well laid cobbles surviving, presumably representing an old floor or yard surface. Above this was modern hard-core, 60cm thick, and concrete. Cross walls were encountered at the extreme southern end of the trench and at the mid point, both were founded on bedrock and represent the original walls to the buildings on Tobergal Lane.

SITE 10:

Junction of Tobergal Lane and Rockwood Parade.

The results of monitoring of the digging of a pad hole at junction of Tobergal Lane and Rockwood Parade suggested that this part of Tobergal Lane did not pre-date the standing buildings on either side and therefore it most likely dates here to the 17th. century. This does not exclude the possibility that the line of Tobergal Lane is much older, possibly medieval in date.

DISCUSSION

The archaeology of the Rockwood Parade area of Sligo as revealed in the ten sites archaeologically examined is relatively consistent.

The bedrock shelves down from O'Connell Street northeastwards towards The Garvoge River. Pits 1 and 2 in Site 1 (Callery) and the small trench in Site 7 (Carraig Donn) all revealed that bedrock lay a mere 50cm to 75cm below present ground level. The surface of the bedrock close to O'Connell Street is very rough and uneven with patches of boulder clay surviving in the small grikes. This boulder clay could not have survived if the river washed this area.

However, the western end of the Site 6 (Moffitt) trench and Pits 3 and 4 in Site 1 (Callery) reveal a marked change in the nature of the underlying rock. In these cuttings, and indeed all the cuttings to the east of this line, the bedrock is quite smooth and gently shelving downward from west to east towards the river.

In the trenches closest to the river the nature of the bedrock was difficult to discern due to the high level of ground water and water seeping in rapidly from the river. Nonetheless it was possible to see that the bedrock was not only quite smooth, as the bed of The Garvoge is, but the there was also a layer of silts and sands immediately overlying the rock. These deposits could be traced in the trenches in Site 3 (Kilcawley NBA), Site 4 (Bagnell) and Site 8 (O'Dowd & Rippon) as well as over much of the length of trench 3 in Site 2 (Bishop). However, more interestingly was the fact the these deposits of silts and sands were almost absent from Sites

5 (Martin) and 9 (Calliendo), replaced here by an organic deposit of leaves, twigs and rushes. Site 6 (Moffitt) in turn had some silts and sands but these were, by and large, replaced by a layer of weathered bedrock and a thick organic layer consisting of leaves and grasses. As mentioned above these deposits were totally absent in Site 7 (Carraig Donn) and west of Pits 3 and 4 in Site 1 (Callery).

The interpretation of this evidence is that the original course of The River Garvoge was different or greater in width than that which exists to-day. O'Connell Street is on a natural ridge from which the ground falls away towards the river to the east. The smooth bedrock, noted in all of the trenches east of Site 7 (Carraig Donn) and Pits 1 and 2 in Site 1 (Callery), is a product of weathering and erosion and the most likely agency of such erosion is the river. It is probable that the bend in The Garvoge once extended almost to the line of O'Connell St. The rough bedrock and boulder clay deposits in Site 7 (Carraig Donn) and at the west end of Site 1 (Callery) show that the river never extended beyond this line. The deposits of weathered bedrock, grasses and twigs in Sites 5 (Martin) and 6 (Moffitt) suggest a foreshore area, which may have been flooded on a regular basis and was probably tidal, at least occasionally. The deposit of shells noted at the base of the Site 9 (Calliendo) trench may confirm this though most openings of the ground in Sligo reveal some deposis of sea shells at varying depths. To the east of Site 9 (Calliendo) the ground was probably constantly under water. The organic deposits of reeds, rushes and twigs in Site 3 (Kilcawley NBA) and trench 3 of Site 2 (Bishop) suggest this. Further east the organic deposits become less apparent with a corresponding increase in the depth of natural silts and sands indicating a constant flow of quite deep water.

The earliest known detailed map of Sligo town, dated to 1689, (Wood-Martin 1889, fig. 14, opp. 134) shows a street running north-south, represented to-day by O'Connell Street. From the time the first site testing took place in 1992 Martin A. Timoney had being carrying out documentary and cartographic research work with the help of John McTernan, then Sligo County Librarian, and Derry O'Connell but had failed to discover any pre-mid-19th. detailed maps of the town. McTernan (1994) provides a listing of all those maps of Sligo town known to him.

Bradley, however, suggests that the unusually long burgage plots on the west side of O'Connell St. hints that it, like Wine Street, was laid out in the 17th century. This expansion of the town to the north and west may have been the spark which lead to the desire to have the flow and course of The Garvoge regularised. Such a project would have had the additional benefit of reclaiming the entire east side of O'Connell Street, which up until that time had been an inter-tidal/riverine marsh. In order to reclaim this area and make it serviceable, the ground level west and south of the line of Rockwood Parade had to be raised above the flood level of the river. To achieve this vast quantities of soil, stone, etc., were deposited here. This material contained a mixture of soil, organic and general midden matter. This episode showed up in the archaeological record as up to 2m of redeposited soils which were noted in many of the cuttings. While this may have been done by walling the river on both the east and west banks, either piecemeal or as an overall project, we have no written or cartographic records to establish this actually happened. However, as pointed out below, there are archaeological hints that this was done, at least in parts. The 17th century developers had, however, in order to achieve solid foundations just like the developers to-day, to dig down to bedrock. Hence almost all of the original walls running from O'Connell Street to the river were found on bedrock.

Evidence for leather working industry, in the form of two tanning pits, was uncovered in Site 2 (Bishop). The pits consisted of the fragmentary remains of wooden boxes, clay lined in order to make them water tight. Examination of the primary fills proved to be wood bark, probably oak, a common source of tannic acid which gives its name to the process. In essence, mashed oak bark was placed in increasing concentrations in a series of water tight pits. The fresh hides were placed in the weakest solution first and then transferred to increasingly stronger tanning liquids until the process was complete. This process could take from months to years depending on the thickness of the hide. A location close to a renewable water source was essential and the area to the east of O'Connell Street, slightly removed from the town centre, indeed probably outside the medieval town, would have been excellent. The discovery of tanning pits in the St Patrick's Street and Dean's Street area in Dublin forms an interesting parallel. In both cases there is a renewable water source close by, in Dublin it was the Poddle, and in both the tanning industry was located outside the main area of settlement.

TOBERGALL LANE AND WATER LANE

The two small thoroughfares which cross the area were examined in passing.

There was no evidence in the case of Tobergal Lane of a history earlier than the formation of O'Connell Street. The single cutting which was dug into the Tobergal Lane showed clearly that, although there was evidence for a series of cobbled surfaces, the earliest rested directly on the sort of redeposited material found on the adjoining sites.

Water Lane was somewhat different. The archaeology of this area was not examined directly. However, the layers at the eastern end of trench 4 in Site 8 (O'Dowd & Rippon), suggested that the Water Lane might once have been, as the name may also suggest, the course of a small stream. The evidence for this was secondary in that the bedrock and silts at the eastern end of trench 4 in Site 8 (O'Dowd & Rippon) sloped away quite steeply suggesting some sort of a gully running N-S. During excavation of this trench water flowed into the cutting from the south, rather from the Garvoge to the north which would have been expected. If this is so the stream would be draining water from the high ground in the area of High St.

CONCLUSIONS

The archaeology of the Rockwood Parade area suggests that originally the course of the Garvoge spread further to the west, almost as far as the present line of O'Connell Street. With the expansion of the town in the early years of the 17th century the river was probably contained and the course established as it appears today. The area between O'Connell St. and Grattan St. and the river was reclaimed by the deposition of massive amounts of material, which brought the ground level above the flood plain of the river. The area was quickly developed and one of the industries which became established was leather working. Tobergal Lane dates to this period. Water Lane, however, may have been the course of an old stream which flowed from the heart of the medieval town.

ACKNOWLEDGMENTS

I acknowledge the help of the following. The developers and their workers who assisted where possible. Martin A. Timoney for on-site help on several locations and providing freely of his knowledge of Sligo town and of two sites in particular, No. 3 (Kilcawley & NBA) and Site 1 (Callery), whose engineering test pits he had examined prior to my involvement. John O'Dwyer of Sligo Corporation. Daire O'Rourke for her comments on the leather working.

APPENDIX

Some Notes on the Rockwood Parade area.
Martin A. Timoney.

1: Many of the standing buildings, warehouses, walls, passageways, *etc.*, of the various development plots were photographed individually from both outside and inside and in their settings. This photographic recording continued as the sites were cleared of buildings, the site testing trenches were opened, the new buildings rose from the cleared sites and were completed and became occupied. This recording, in B&W and colour, was mainly done by Martin A. Timoney with supplementary work by James McHugh of Sligo County Council who also made Video footage.

2: The premises on the nine sites are active as residential or business premises. The business premises include clothes, shoes, books, sports, computer, photography, recorded music, antiques, nostalgia, fancy goods, jewelry and crafts, a bookmaker, a coffee shop, a variety of restaurants and two public houses. Tobergal Lane and Rockwood Parade have been resurfaced and provided with enhancements. The official opening was by Mr. Brendan Howlin, T.D., Minister for the Environment on 12th. May, 1997. With these streets completed Sligo is no longer turning its back to the river. Rockwood Parade has become a new focus of activity in Sligo. The north bank of the river has also been developed.

3: The new development, Rockwood Court, on Site 3, RPRAP 25B, at the junction of Tobergal Lane and Rockwood Parade, designed by Sligoman Mr. Derry O'Connell and jointly developed by Kilcawley and The National Building Agency received the Irish Planning Institute/ First National Building Society Urban Infill Award for 1996. In the acclimation Rockwood Court is described as representing the successful combination of town planning, urban design and architectural skills in opening up backlands at the river end of the Tobergal Lane leading from Sligo's main street, O'Connell St. to the River Garvogue and establishing a strong relationship with the river.

4: The actual location of the well that the name Tobergall Lane derives from has been the source of much interest during the work along the Lane itself.

The early O.S. maps of this area of Sligo show a well on the north side of Tobergall Lane within the area of Site 9, RPRAP 25A. One of the construction team there told me that there was a very strong flow of water from a well in this area.

Late in 1996 Mr. John McTernan, former Sligo County Librarian, came across a reference in *The Sligo Independent* of November 1943 to the discovery of a well at the rear of Messers O'Connor Brothers premises on the south side of Tobergal Lane. This would be Site 5, RPRAP 21A, Tobergal Lane. The well, whose location was at that time known by tradition, was discovered in the floor of a store that was being resurfaced. Its cover of rotted planks was 18" under the surface. The well, seven feet in diameter and approximately eleven feet in depth, was surrounded by neatly done and perfectly preserved stonework and the water was crystal clear, as its name would imply.

Again, there was a strong flow of water at a number of locations within this site when it was being prepared.

It would seem, therefore, that about half-way down Tobergall Lane from O'Connell St. there is a spring line. From one of these wells Tobergal Lane got its name.

In the National Library of Ireland, Dublin, there is a series of maps of the Palmerston Sligo Estates. These were made by James Williamson in 1813-1814 at a scale of 20 Irish Perches to 1 inch. Regrettably the map for Sligo Town, of which only the west half exists, is not very detailed and omissions need not represent reality. Water Lane seems to be shown but is not named. Tobergall Lane is not indicated at all. The National Library of Ireland call number for the Palmerston Maps is 16F17 while the Sligo Library Local History Archive call number for the Sligo Town sheet is 1047.

REFERENCES

Anon 1995: *Record of Monuments and Places, Co. Sligo*, Dublin, Office of Public Works. Limited distribution.

Bennett, Isabel, Ed. 1994: *Excavations 1993: Summary Accounts of Archaeological Excavations in Ireland*, Bray, Wordwell

Bennett, Isabel, Ed. 1995: *Excavations 1994: Summary Accounts of Archaeological Excavations in Ireland*, Bray, Wordwell

Bergh, Stefan, 1995: *Landscape of the Monuments, A Study of the Passage Tombs in the Cuil Irra Region, Co. Sligo, Ireland*, Stockholm, Riksantikvarieämbetet Arkeologiska Undersökningar, Skrifter nr 6.

Bradley, John, and Dunne, Noel, 1987: *Urban Archaeological Survey, Part XXI*, County Sligo. Dublin, Office of Public Works. Limited distribution.

Bradley, John, 1997:

Gallagher, Fiona 1987: *Sligo Town Street Names and Their Origins*, Sligo, Limited distribution.

Gibbons, Michael, Alcock, Olive, Condit, Tom, Tunney, Mary, and Timoney, Martin A., 1989: *Sites and Monuments Record County Sligo*, Dublin, Office of Public Works, Limited distribution.

Gunning, Paul, and Feehily, Padraig, 1995: *Down Gallows Hill, An Illustrated History of Sligo from 1245 to 1995*, Sligo, Sligo Heritage Group.

Halpin, Eoin, 1994: "Rockwood Parade Development, Sligo", in Bennett 1994, 72-73.

Halpin, Eoin, 1995: "Rockwood Parade Development, Sligo", in Bennett 1994, 79-80.

Kilgannon, Tadgh 1926: *Sligo and its Surroundings*, Sligo, Kilgannon. Reprint 1988 Sligo, Dodd's Antiquarian Books

McTernan, John, 1994: *Sligo: Sources of Local History*, Sligo, Sligo County Library.

O'Connell, Derry, 1992: *Rockwood Parade Recommended Action Plan*, Dublin, Urban Design Unit, National Building Agency. Limited distribution.

O'Connell, Derry, 1995: "Rockwood Parade's Development", in Gunning and Feehily 1995, 171.

O'Dowd, Mary 1991: *Power, Politics and Land, Early Modern Sligo 1568-1688*, Belfast, Institute of Irish Studies.

Office of Public Works 1968: *Mainistir Sligigh - Sligo Abbey*, Dublin, Office of Public Works.

Ordnance Survey Letters: Co. Sligo 1836: Typescript, Bray, 1928.

O'Rorke, Terrence, 1889: *The History of Sligo: Town and County*, Dublin, James Duffy, Reprint, Sligo, 1986, Dodd's Antiquarian Books.

Wood-Martin, William Gregory 1882: *History of Sligo County ahd Town from the Earliest Ages to the close of the Reign of Queen Elizabeth*, Dublin Hodges Figgis & Co. Reprint Sligo 1990, Dodd's Antiquarian Books.

Wood-Martin, William Gregory 1889: *History of Sligo, Accession of James I to the Revolution of 1688*.

Wood-Martin, W.G., 1892: *The History of Sligo, County and Town, from the close of the Revolution of 1688 to the Present Time*, Dublin, Hodges, Figgis & Co.; Reprint, Sligo, 1990, Dodd's Antiquarian Books.

Pl. 7 - Millstone found at The Garvoge end of Site 1. Photo. Martin A. Timoney.

Pl. 8 - Looking upriver along Rockwood Parade from Hyde Bridge when several buildings were under construction. The shelving bed of the river is barely covered with water. Photo. Martin A. Timoney.

Pl. 1 - Tobergall Lane looking towards The Garvoge in 1992. Photo: Martin A. Timoney.

Pl. 4 - Water Lane looking towards Castle St. in 1992. Photo: Martin A. Timoney.

Pl. 2. Tobergall Lane looking towards The Garvoge in 1992. Photo: Martin A. Timoney.

Pl. 5 - Looking upriver along Rockwood Parade from the junction with Tobergall Lane in 1992. Photo: Martin A. Timoney.

Pl. 3 - Tobergall Lane looking towards O'Connell St. in 1992. Photo. Martin A. Timoney.

Pl. 6 - Looking downriver along Rockwood Parade from the junction with Tobergall Lane in 1992. Photo. Martin A. Timoney.

Sligo Antiquarian Society and Sligo Field Club

Robert Kirwan

Patrick Tohall

John P. and Kathleen Moran

Queenie Dolan

Eithne Dolan

Guy Perrem

Mary F. Ryan

Sheila Kirby

Sean Daly

Noel Murphy

Briga Murphy

Pat Kitchin, Liam Horgan and Michael C. Cahalane.

Tom McGettrick

Joyce Enright

Mary B. Timoney

Patrick E. O'Brien

SILVER PENNIES OF EDWARD I FROM TUBBERCURRY, CO. SLIGO

*Michael Kenny,
Art & Industry Division, National Museum of Ireland, Dublin.*

Silver pennies of King Edward I, II and III are found throughout every part of Ireland in hoards, single finds and excavations. Coins of Edward I are particularly common and issues of the king's English mints predominate. English mint output far outstripped that of the struggling and embattled Irish colony and after 1302 the Irish series came to an almost complete halt. The majority of Irish hoards are therefore comprised largely, sometimes exclusively, of English coins. It has been estimated that the total production from Edward I's English mints was close to £1.5 million, compared to a paltry £50,000 from his Irish mints (Dolly 1967-1968, 235, 252) which helps to explain the relative proportion of English and Irish issues in Irish hoards. The majority of Irish pence from Edward's reign have been found in hoards concealed outside the country, indicating that "the prime function of these mints..... was not to serve the needs of the colony but to supplement the output of Edward's English mints" (Dolley 1972, 14).

Many of the Irish finds are fairly small and in such cases it would be difficult to suggest any particular reason for their deposition. Accidental loss rather than intentional, pre-meditated concealment, would appear the most reasonable explanation, which raises the question of whether the term "hoard" should be used in such cases. The little find discussed in this short note is a case in point.

Unfortunately we do not possess any precise information on the manner in which the coins were recovered. We know only that they were found in Tubbercurry, Co. Sligo, in September 1941 and lodged in the National Museum at some point afterwards. Since they were not of any major numismatic significance, they were not regarded as meriting registration. The Museum records do not note an actual find-spot such as a ford, fort or habitation site, which might provide a clue as to the cause of deposition.

The silver pennies, six in number, date to the reign of Edward I. They are all English and were struck at the mints of London, Canterbury and Bristol. The coinage of Edward I, struck between 1279 and his death in 1307, is divided into ten main groups, with numerous sub-groups and varieties. The groups are distinguished from each other by stylistic differences. Features such

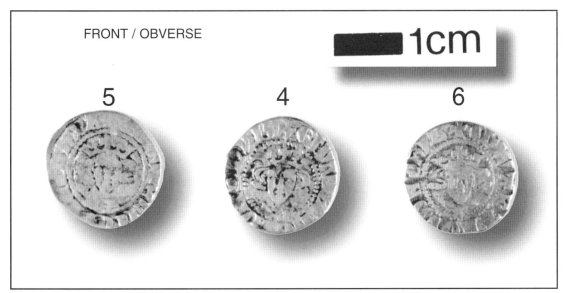

Fig. 1

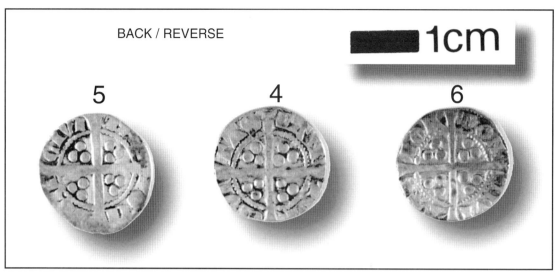

Fig. 2

as the number of fleurs in the king's crown, the contraction of the king's name (EDW, EDWA, EDWAR), and variations in the style of lettering, help to identify the phases in the series, although this can be extremely difficult when the coins are worn. The standard obverse legend reads, EDW, R, ANGL, DNS, HYB. (Edwardus, Rex Angliae, Dominus Hyberniae = Edward, King of England, Lord of Ireland). The reverse legend carries the name of the mint - CIVITAS LONDON, VILLA BRISTOLLIE (City of London, Town of Bristol)

The Tubbercurry coins are as in the table below. The dates for the different phases in the series are approximate and are occasionally revised as new numismatic evidence comes to light. The latest Tubbercurry coin belongs to Class 10. The date range traditionally accepted for this class was 1302-7 but in more recent times specialists in the series have assigned to it the date range 1302-10 (North 1975, Vol. II, 24), bringing it possibly into the early years of Edward II. The hoard may well have been deposited during the unsettled period of the Bruce Invasion, but such is its size that it may have been totally unconnected with contemporary military on political events.

References

Dolley, Michael, 1967-1968: 'The Irish Mints of Edward I, in the light of the coin hoards from Ireland and Great Britain', in *Proc. Royal Irish Acad.*, 66.

Dolley, Michael, 1972: *Mediaeval Anglo - Irish Coins* London.

North, J.J., 1975: *English Hammered Coinage,* London.

Edward I (1272 - 1307) ENGLAND

Number	Legend	Mint	Class
1	Obv: EDW R ANGL DNS HYB Rev: CIVITAS LONDON Barred A, reversed N, wedge contractions	London 2	(Jan- May, 1280)
2	As no. 1	London 2	(Jan- May, 1280)
3	Obv: EDW R ANGL DNS HYB Rev: VILLA BRISTOLLIE	Bristol 3g	(1280 - 1281)
4	Obv: EDW R ANGL DNS HYB Rev: CIVITAS CANTOR	Canterbury	4b (1282-1289)
5	Obv: EDW R ANGL DNS HYB Rev: CIVITAS LONDON	London 9b	(1300-1302)
6	Obv: EDWA R ANGL DNS HYB Rev: CIVITAS LONDON	London 10 c/e	(1302-1310)

IRISH DOMINICAN MEDIEVAL ARCHITECTURE

Patrick Conlan, O.F.M.
St. Francis, Cork

ABSTRACT: An overview of Dominican architecture in Ireland from the first foundation in Dublin in 1224 to the last at Ballindoon, Co. Sligo, in 1507 is presented. Twenty-six priories, mainly larger buildings in towns and cities serving the pastoral needs of the greatest possible number of people, pre-date the Black Death. Fourteen, mainly smaller buildings away from centres of population representing the need for quiet, prayer and contemplation, post-date it.

The Dominicans were one of the most important orders in medieval Ireland. This article provides an overview of the remaining buildings, putting them in an historical and artistic context. Before the Black Death, these were usually large churches with a priory to the north. Many of the churches were extended during the fifteenth century. Small houses were built in more remote country areas.

INTRODUCTION:

Interest in Irish medieval church architecture has increased over the last forty years. Two comprehensive overviews of individual orders have appeared: Canice Mooney for the Franciscans[1] and Roger Stalley for the Cistercians[2]. Daggert and O'Keefe have writte on the Augustinians[2a.] Some excellent monographs on individual sites have appeared under Stalley's guidance. This article provides an overview of Dominican houses, intermediate between that of Mooney and my own Franciscan publications, on the basis of personal visits and research[3]. Architecture changes by decade rather than by year, so simple foundation dates suffice[4]. The Irish Dominicans remained under the control of the English province almost up to the Reformation[5]. This association may account for the richer window styles in Dominican houses when compared with other orders, in particular the Franciscans.

There are three types of medieval church sites in Ireland: diocesan [cathedral, parish], monastic [Benedictine, Cistercian, Augustinian Canons] and mendicant [Dominican, Franciscan, Carmelite, Augustinian]. Monks lived in monasteries which were usually in the countryside. Friars of mendicant orders lived in friaries which were initially in or near towns. The size and shape of town burgage plots were not normally sufficient for a friary within town walls. By the fifteenth century, friaries were often in remote areas which allowed greater quiet and prayer. Superiors of non-Franciscan mendicant houses are called priors, with the result that these are often called priories.

Unless it was protected by town walls, the immediate area around a medieval monastery or friary was surrounded by a wall or rampart with a large entrance gate. The church normally ran east to west. The eastern end contained an altar, with a lavabo or piscina, sedelia, tomb niches and choir stalls for friars or monks. A large east window let in the rays of the rising sun. This gave plenty of light for morning worship and was a symbol of the Risen Christ. The north or south walls of the choir had a series of windows to admit more light. The western end of the church was the nave for the laity, with a main door in arched gothic style. Aisles were sometimes added to increase capacity. Monastic churches were large with two big transepts, giving plenty of room for side altars for extra masses and statues. Friary churches were long narrow buildings, often with a side or transept chapel. Parish churches had a residential tower at the western end. Monastic churches had squat towers of square cross-section over the transept crossing. Friary churches had towers carried on haunches within the church and dividing choir from nave. The base was as wide as the church. The towers were either narrower than the church, and thus of square cross-section, or the full width of the church and of rectangular cross-section. The Franciscan ruin, with its tall narrow tower decorated with string courses, has become the stereotype of the medieval friary. Towers were belfries and thus had few windows except at the level of the bells. Preaching in the church was done from a gallery, called the rood loft, on the lower western face of the tower. Major

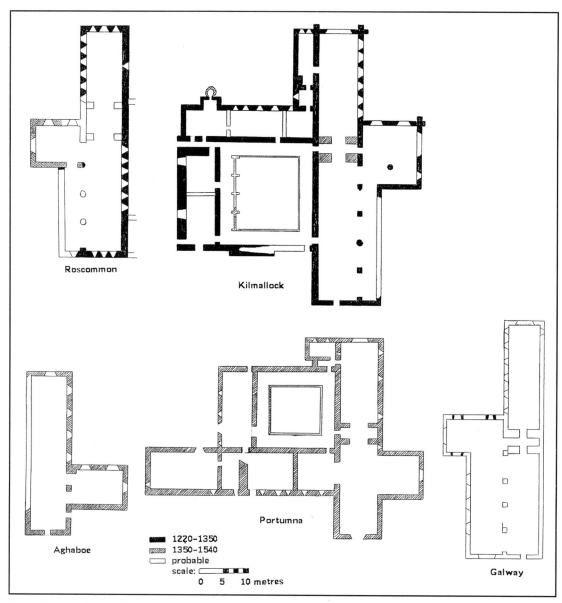

Fig. 1 - Plans of nine Dominican Priories in chronological sequence of Waterford, Cork, Athenry, Sligo, Roscommon, Kilmallock, Aghaboe, Portumna, Galway. These plans are drawn to a common scale by the author, based on personal observation as well as the following sources: Aghaboe: Thomas Flynn, O.P., *The Dominicans of Aghaboe,* Dublin 1975; Athenry: Harold G. Leask, *Irish Churches II,*, Dundalk 1966 and observations by Prof. Etienne Rynne; Cork: Plans prepared by and discussion with Maurice Hurley, Cork City Archaeologist, to whom due acknowledgement is made; Galway: Drawn from 1651 description edited in Eustace Ó Heideáin, O.P., *The Dominicans in Galway . . .*, Galway 1991; Kilmallock: Daphne D. C. Pochin Mould, *The Irish Dominicans*, Dublin 1957 and Arlene Hogan, *Kilmallock Dominican Priory*, Kilmallock 1991; Portumna: Michael MacMahon, *Portumna Priory;* n.d., Roscommon: Luke Taheny, O.P., *The Dominicans of Roscommon*, Tallagh 1990; Sligo: *Mainister Sligigh, Sligo Abbey,* Dublin, O.P.W., 1968, and observations by Martin A. Timoney; Waterford: Hugh Fenning, O.P., *The Waterford Dominicans . . , Waterford* 1990.

benefactors were buried in the choir, or later in the nave. There is evidence of medieval burials in the cloister area of Dominican priories.

Buildings could be erected as a unit, or have parts added or changed. Churches could be given new towers or chapels. Windows could be replaced. Window styles are a good indication of the age of a building. Lancets are typical of the thirteenth century. Mullions dividing windows into two, three, five or seven lights arrived before the fourteenth century. While earlier examples are known, tracery, either switch-line or switch-line-and-bar, is typical of the fifteenth century.

Flowing or reticulated tracery, often with cusps in a Dominican context, occur from the mid-fifteenth century. Thirteenth century choir sidewindows consisted of a series of lancets. Later the most easterly one was enlarged to let in more light. A series of large windows with tracery became the norm for choirs early in the fourteenth century.

The cloister or residential part of Irish monasteries, be they Augustinian, Benedictine or Cistertian, was normally to the south of the church. Following the Franciscan stereotype, friary cloisters were usually to the north. They

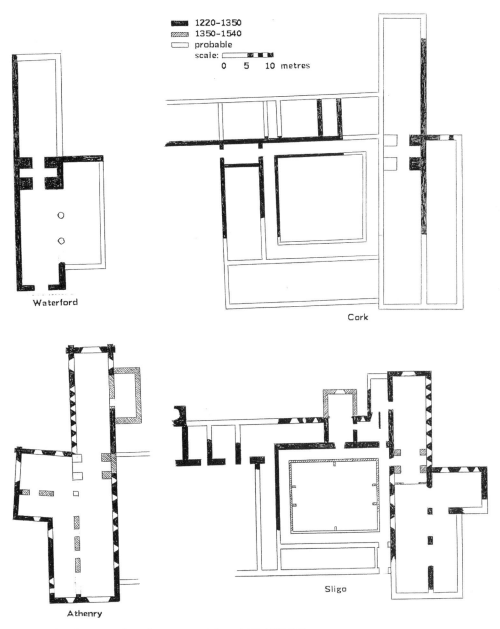

consisted of a kitchen and refectory, with dormitories over, as well as various workshops and stores. A stream supplied water and took away sewage. The buildings were in ranges around the quadrangle of the cloister garth. A walkway around this was marked out by the cloister arcade, which was either integrated with the building, carrying the first floor walls, or free-standing with a lean-to roof. The lean-to could be of the same date as the other buildings, or a later addition. The arcade can be considered as a series of windows of small [Athassel, Co. Tipperary], or medium [Burrishoole, Co. Mayo] size, or a set of windows divided by mullions [Timoleague, Co. Cork] or with tracery [Killmallock, Co. Limerick], or a genuine arcade [Mellifont, Co. Louth]. Early mullions were two simple pillars [Mellifont] which evolved into single pillars with a dumbbell or later an hexagonal cross-section.

THE SITES

Nothing remains of the Dominican priory in DUBLIN, founded in 1224 on the north bank of the Liffey just across from the walled town.

The earliest surviving ruins in Ireland are in DROGHEDA, founded in 1224. The priory was on the northern side of the town and was included within the walls when these were built. The tower would have provided an excellent lookout point for defenders. The cloister was probably to the north of the church, between it and the town wall. The tower is of the narrow friary type, inserted within the church, with a string course half way up. As with a number of other Dominican towers, the lower part lacks a stone floor and the vaulting is higher up. There is an external stairs, which looks like a truncated chimney, battlements and no trace of a rood loft. The windows are two lights foliated beneath a quadrifoil, suggesting an early fourteenth century date. This was been proposed as the earliest stone belfrey in an Irish, and possibly an English, friary church[6].

The next priory is that at KILKENNY, founded in 1225. It lay just outside the west corner of the town walls, with the cloister to the north of the church. The remains, consisting of nave with south aisle, transept with west aisle, and tower, present major problems of interpretation and dating. The aisles give a very spacious effect which is rare in medieval churches. The tower, donated by the Shorthall family early in the sixteenth century, is squat, of square section, with an internal stairs and topped by four pinnacled turrets. It is carried on pillars which over-lap the transept. This is unusual in Irish medieval churches, where the transept normally joins the nave by the western face of the tower, but is found at a number of Dominican sites. The transept is dominated by the huge south window. This and the east window were thirteenth century triple lancets. The original south window was replaced late in the fourteenth century by one of five lights with switch tracery, the top part containing a mixture of trefoils and quadrifoils. This suggests an Irish version of English fourteenth century decorated designs. The same applies to the four [originally five] smaller windows in the transept[7]. What looks like a residential tower at the western end of the church is a small castle or residence which predates the arrival of the friars. The windows in the north wall of the nave and the east face of the tower are neo-gothic, dating to nineteenth century rebuilding.

The Dominicans came to WATERFORD in 1226. A ten year delay in building enabled them to get a vacant site within the town walls where there had been an old tower[8]. The cloister was to the north of the church. The ruins, enclosed by other buildings, consist of the tower, part of the north wall of the choir, the north and west walls of the nave and part of a transept or aisle. No details remain of the choir. The tower, with two string courses and simple two light windows, is of rectangular section and nearly as wide as the church. It was added to the original building towards the end of the fifteenth century. Doors indicate the presence of a rood loft. The northern wall of the nave was originally lighted by four windows, now blocked. The western gable has a rare round-headed doorway with an empty window over. While the door is original, remaining stonework indicates that the west window was a later addition. The southern wall of the nave consisted of three arches in Caen (French) stone indicating the presence of an aisle at an early stage. The section of wall remaining to the south of the tower is insufficient to decide whether it was the east wall of a transept or of an aisle. Considerations of space seem to exclude the former.

The friars came to LIMERICK in 1227 and settled outside the northern corner of the Englishtown walls. The priory was included when the walls were extended. The northern wall of the church still stands, containing one window with switch tracery and some short lancets. The existence of a cloister to the north of the church has been confirmed by excavations. These failed to reveal further details about the church, including the tower for which there is cartographic and documentary evidence[9].

The Dominicans came to CORK in 1229. Like Dublin, they settled near the Viking area on an island across the Lee from the south walls of the town. The cathedral and old monastic site were nearby, just across another branch of the Lee. Recent excavations have revealed almost the entire groundplan, as well as parts of the wall which surrounded the Dominican property[10]. The church ran east to west, parallel to the river and the hills above. As in Waterford, the indications are that the foundations to the south of the church are those of an aisle rather than a transept. A tower was added later, overlapping the transept/aisle as in Kilkenny. The cloister was built on infill to the north of the church, between it and the main river. The refectory, complete with evidence for seating and a reader's desk, has been located in the northern range. There is some evidence for a chapter room in the middle of the eastern range, which extends to the north of the northern range as in Sligo.

Nothing remains abovr ground of the foundation in MULLINGAR in 1237.

ATHENRY, in mid-Galway, welcomed the friars in 1241. The priory was included within the town walls when these were built early in the fourteenth century. The building was accidentally burned in 1423 and underwent a long period of reconstruction. The ruins now consist of church and transept. The tower fell in 1845 and the cloister south of the church has been built over. A typical thirteenth century series of lancet windows occupy most of the northern wall of the choir. The choir was extended eastwards early in the fourteenth century, but the east window of that period, based on switch tracery of five lights, was replaced by a smaller one with switch-bar tracery. The two windows on either side of the choir walls are two-light, typical of the early fourteenth century, but with complicated use of cusps to give a multifoiled circle in one and a hexafoiled triangle in the other. Then or soon afterwards an aisle and a transept chapel and

Fig. 2 - East window of Athenry Priory, Drawing courtesy of Dúchas –The Heritage Service.

aisle were added to the north of the nave. The smaller windows here are again two light foliated with quadrifoil centers. As in all the other windows, they have a lightness of construction not usually found in Ireland during this period. The north wall of the transept is a mass of tracery, with a set of nine arches under the window, which is itself of four foliated lights topped by three multi-foliated spherical triangles. The west window, now partially blocked, is of switch-bar tracery with cusps giving quadrifoils on top. The tower, probably inserted in the early fifteenth century, had a lower storey as wide as the church which narrowed to give a top storey of square section. There is evidence of an external stairs on the south side and of a wooden rood loft on the western face[11].

The friars arrived at CASHEL, Co. Tipperary, in 1243, settling near the Rock, eight years before the town wall was built. The remains consist of a typical long narrow church with tower, and a south transept. The nave had a southern aisle and the transept a western one, giving a good feeling of open space. The cloister buildings were to the north. The church started as a classical mid-thirteenth century building: an east window of three lancets, with a series of lancets on either side of the choir and three lancets on the south gable of the transept. An unusual feature is the placing of niches between the choir lancets. The tower is of rectangular section across the full width of the church. There is some evidence for a rood loft under the tower. Extensive rebuilding took place following a fire before 1480. The new east window mixed elements of flowing and reticulated tracery typical of the late fifteenth or early sixteenth century and used cusps, to which the Dominicans were becoming attracted. The new transept window is in flowing style, like the bigger east window at Kilcooly, Co. Tipperary. The aisle window is a small two light. The west window is of switch-bar tracery with a central quadrifoil almost identical with two contemporary Franciscan windows at Moyne, Co. Mayo. Except for the choir windows, the church was transformed into a classic late fifteenth century building[12].

Only a few stones remain of the priory founded at TRALEE in 1243 and nothing of COLERAINE founded in 1244.

As with Cashel, the priory founded at NEWTOWNARDS, Co. Down, in 1244 underwent major modifications. The rectangular thirteenth century church had a cloister to the south. The eastern gable has collapsed. Early in the fourteenth century, a northern aisle was added to the nave, which itself was extended westwards. The west wall proved unstable and was rebuilt in the fifteenth century. The priory was burned by O'Neill of Clandeboye in 1572 after the community had been expelled. Lord Montgomery re-roofed the aisle for Protestant use. A tower and doorway were added later. There is no evidence for an earlier tower. The building is now in a dangerous condition and contains little interesting medieval material other than the four arches between nave and aisle[13].

The Dominicans came to SLIGO in 1252 and settled near the recently constructed castle, the precise location of which is a matter of much debate. The remains consist of the church with a priory to the north. Parts date to the thirteenth century. Reconstruction took place after a fire in 1414. The church began as a long narrow building, with a triple lancet on the east wall, a series of eight lancets on the south wall of the choir and three two light windows on the north wall of the nave. The east window was replaced by a reticulated window, with cusps, in the fifteenth century. Re-building in the early fifteenth century may include the impressive stone rood loft, the transept and the southern aisle to the nave with its pillars of unusual octagonal section. The tower, of square section with just one string course, was inserted after the

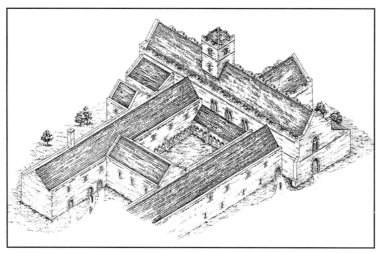

Fig. 3 - Isometric view of Sligo Abbey. Drawing courtesy of Dúchas - The Heritage Service

Fig. 8 - Carving under tower of Sligo Abbey. Photo. Martin A. Timoney.

Fig. 4 - Sligo Abbey at the east side of Sligo town as seen in Thomas Phillips Prospect of Sligo of 1685. Courtesy National Library of Ireland.

Fig. 7 - Right inside of east window of Sligo Abbey. Photo. Martin A. Timoney.

Fig. 5 - Drawing of Sligo Abbey in 1849 or 1850 by an anonymous artist, from NLI Sketchbook 2003TX (See Elizabeth Kirwan, History Ireland, 3:2 (1995), 48-52). Courtesy National Library of Ireland.

Fig. 6 - Rib-vaulting of the room in the tower of Sligo Abbey. Photo. Martin A. Timoney.

Fig. 9 - Two-light window, Rathfran, Co. Mayo. Photo. Martin A. Timoney.

rood loft. The church still has its fifteenth century altar and the excellent early sixteenth century O'Crean tomb in flamboyant style. Three sides of the cloister arcade exist to the north of the church, all integrated with the main building and dating to the second half of the fifteenth century. The eastern, and presumably the western, arcades had eighteen arches with one butress, the southern and northern ones had sixteen arches with two butresses. A bas-relief of Saint Dominic is found on one pillar. The eastern range contains the sacristy and a chapter hall, with dormitories over and indications of a necessarium. The northern wing possibly contained the kitchen, with the refectory over, as indicated by a reader's desk built into the cloister wall. Some wonder whether there was a second cloister to the north. This is unlikely in a medieval context. Extra cloisters are usually seventeenth century military additions[14].

The friary at STRADE, Co. Mayo, originally Franciscan, was given to the Dominicans in 1252. It was burned in 1254 and was restored in the mid-fifteenth century. The ruins consist of the church and an outline of the cloister area to the south, all in relatively poor condition. The choir is thirteenth century with a series of six lancets in the north wall. The east window, probably a triple lancet, was replaced in the fifteenth century by one now missing its tracery. An arch at the west end of the choir has two excellent finials, one of a pelican, the other of a bird. The arch may be part of a tower, but this seems unlikely since it would not fit in neatly with the other fifteenth century additions, a south aisle to the nave and a transept. Only one small window remains in the transept. It is of two lights with cusped flamboyant tracery above. It is closely related in style to the tracery of a magnificent late fifteenth century tomb in the choir, which has quadrifoil openings flowing like leaves on two stems. This tomb has eight weepers. Two other weepers and a Pieta have been placed on another tomb in the choir[15].

The friars came to ATHY in 1253. Only a few stones remain.

Felim O'Connor welcomed the Dominicans to ROSCOMMON in 1253. The church was consecrated in 1257, burned in 1270, struck by lightning in 1308 and restored in the second half of the fifteenth century. The remains consist of most of the church, with a northern aisle to the nave and a transept. One pillar remains of the cloister to the south of the church. The tower, now gone, seems to have been of the wide type as in Waterford and Cashel. The thirteenth century church had the usual triple lancet east window. Parts of a series of six lancets remain in the north wall of the choir, as do a similar series of lower windows in the south wall of the nave. The effigy of the tomb of Felim O'Connor dates to the end of the thirteenth century and is now guarded by eight fifteenth century gallowglasses. Both transept and aisle date to the fifteenth century. The tracery of the new east and west windows has gone, but reconstructions show them to date to the end of that century. Of flamboyant style with cusps, they are reminiscent of the tomb screen in Strade[16].

Nothing now remains of the priories of TRIM (1263) and ARKLOW (1264).

The ruins of the Dominican house at ROSBERCON, Co. Kilkenny, founded in 1267, were pulled down c.1817. Illustrations show it with a tower as wide as the church. It had a southern aisle to the nave, implying a cloister to the north of the church[17].

The friars came to YOUGHAL, Co. Cork, in 1268. Little remains of their house, the North Abbey. The west window of the church is divided into three lights by mullions. These continue to the top of the frame, giving two small triangular lights above the side lights. This is a rare example of a window intermediate between the late thirteenth century simple division of a window by mullions into narrow lights and fourteenth century switch tracery. Part of a second west window indicate a southern aisle to the nave. A pillar with parts of arches suggests a fifteenth century transept to the south. The cloister would have been to the north[18].

The priory at LORRHA, Co. Tipperary, was founded the year after Youghal. The church is long, but wider than usual, with the cloister to the north. The design is of late thirteenth, if not early fourteenth, century. The date is indicated by a large east window, divided into five lights by mullions. There are six pairs of lancets on the south wall of the choir designed to give a line of six embrasures on the inside. Foundations in the middle of the church probably mark the site of a rood loft and possibly a screen rather than a tower[19].

The friars came to DERRY in 1274. Nothing remains.

RATHFRAN priory, Co. Mayo, was also founded in 1274. It was a large building with traces of two cloister rectangles to the north of the church. The choir is typical of the late thirteenth or early fourteenth century with an east window of three lights and a series of five paired lancet windows on the south wall, as at Lorrha. There are interesting arched tomb recesses alongside a piscina and a sedelia. A small aisle was built to the south of the nave in the late fifteenth century, as indicated by a small two-light flamboyant window with cusped tracery. There is a late Crucifixion over the west door[20].

One of the most extensive Dominican sites is at KILMALLOCK, Co. Limerick, founded in 1291 across the river from the walled town. The late thirteenth and early fourteenth century church was a typical long narrow building. The east window of five lights with piped shafts is, like those at Ennis and Kilkenny Franciscan churches, an intermediate type between thirteenth century grouped lancets and fourteenth century tracery. The south wall of the choir has a row of six two-light windows with switch tracery. Three windows on the north side of the nave are of the same type, while the west window over the door is of three lights with switch tracery, implying that this part of the church was finished early in the fourteenth century. A south transept with a west aisle was then added, to judge by the rare ball-flower ornament on one pillar. The east windows in the transept are small, of two lights with switch tracery, confirming the fourteenth century, as does the small ogee-headed window in the aisle. The south window is an excellent example of late fifteenth century reticulated racery with inset cusps, giving many quadrifoils. The transept and parts of the church contain many good examples of carved heads and other decorations, as well as a piscina, a sedelia and several fifteenth century tombs. A tall narrow tower, with two string courses and battlements, was inserted into the church in the mid-fifteenth century. Unusually, as in Drogheda, the bottom floor of the tower was not vaulted. At some stage, possibly early in the fifteenth century, a southern aisle was added to the church. Two ranges of the cloister still exist. There is a small sacristy beside the choir. The ground floor of the east range contained the kitchen, complete with oven, with what may have been the refectory or chapter room over, as indicated by a large three light window. The north range may have been used for stores, possibly with a refectory or dormitory over. The only sign of a western range is an internal staircase. The arcade was of the integrated type. One of the four arcade windows on the north face has been reconstructed with two lights, each topped with four cusps with a quadrifoil in between[21].

BALLINEGAUL, Co. Limerick, a dependency of Kilmallock, was founded in 1296. The ruins consist of a small rectangular east-facing church which lacks datable features. The tracery of the east window has vanished. Stairs inset in the west wall indicate that there was a loft, possibly a small living quarters, at that end of the church. The building is more like a medieval parish church than a priory[22].

The Dominicans were invited to CARLING-FORD, Co. Louth, in 1305. The ruins consist of a long narrow church with no datable stonework. The east window has vanished and was probably of five lights. The choir and nave have several small windows high in the walls. The tower is the full width of the church, vaulted, not very deep or tall, and is integrated with the church walls. The west end of the church has a pair of turrets, a bartizan and is crenellated. The building gives the impression of conversion into a fortress, possibly during rebuilding after 1423 because of damage done by enemies and robbers. There are remains of domestic buildings to the south of the church[23].

The Black Death arrived in Ireland in August 1348 and killed many. Religious communities, particularly those of friars involved in helping the poor in towns and villages, were badly hit. The religious orders ceased to grow for half a century. Then some accepted any applicant, no matter what their quality, to fill vacant seats in monasteries. Friars committed to reform tended to go to the more isolated parts of the west and north. Thus the Dominicans of Portumna talked about choosing a place remote from the noise and turmoil of the world, in order to serve the Most High in a life of regular observance. The Franciscan order split into two, Conventuals and Observants, because of this reform. The Dominicans remained one united order, but containing a strong observant branch. The Franciscan Third Order Regular emerged in Ireland during the fifteenth century based on a life of quiet and contemplation. While no such independent Dominican order arrived in Ireland, equivalent groups sprang up[24].

Nothing now remains at NAAS, founded in 1356 just after the Black Death.

In 1382 the Dominicans were invited to the old Irish monastic site at AGHABOE, Co. Laois. The ruined church there dates to the second half of the fifteenth century. It is long and narrow, with the cloister area to the north. The east window, in a simple flamboyant style, without cusps, is like the Franciscan examples at Dromahair, Co. Leitrim, Kilconnell, Co. Galway, and Lislaughtin, Co. Kerry. It resembles two lighted candles beside each other. The west window, in the same style, lookes more like leaves on a branch rather than candles. There was a series of four windows on the south wall of the choir and a piscina near the altar. There is no evidence for a tower. A transept chapel was added, possibly in the early sixteenth century. Its south window, now believed to be at nearby Heywood House, was of three lights with flamboyant tracery and cusps. The other windows in the transept seem to have been of similar style [25].

The friars came to CLOONSHANVILLE, Co. Roscommon, in 1385, but again the building seems to belong to the second half of the fifteenth century. It was a relatively small church, with a nice piscina in the sanctuary, a slim tall tower rising on well-dressed arches with rose finials, a transept to the north and presumably a cloister to the south. There is also a piscina, decorated with entwined animals, in the transept. Indications are that the east window was of flamboyant style with cusps [26].

There had been a Cistercian cell at PORTUMNA, Co. Galway, which was abandoned before the Dominicans were invited there in 1414. It seems that they adapted the older chuch before building their own late in the fifteenth century. The remains are among the most complete of any Irish medieval Dominican site. A small church has a central tower with a transept to the south. A northern transept may be a type of aisle or a later adaptation when the building was used by the Church of Ireland. A number of round-headed single or double-light windows in the choir, nave and over the door, as well as the piscina, may have come from the Cistercian church. The unique east window is a late variety of switch and bar tracery, with a second inverted bar and cusps. Its closest relative is in the parish church at Callan, Co. Kilkenny. Its use of cusps to give a cross effect is found at the Franciscan church at Moyne, Co. Mayo. The stonework of the south window in the transept is in flamboyant style, with cusps making the lights look like commas. Heavy in execution, it is signed "Johanne", a name repeated on the rood loft at Clontuskert, Co. Galway, also in the diocese of Clonfert. The tower is too damaged to determine its original height or width. The inverted head on the jamb of the sacristy door, a feature also found in the Franciscan friary in Ennis, raises many a puzzled smile. There is some evidence for a porch outside the west door. The sacristy has an unusal circular quadrifoil window. The cloister area lies to the north of the church. The east range is missing, the north range contained the refectory and the west range various stores and the enigmatic transept. The freestanding cloister arcade has been partially reconstructed. Each side consisted of seven or eight segmental-pointed arches with hexagonal mullions [27].

LONGFORD was a place apart, hardly even a village, when the friars came about the year 1420. Nothing now remains.

TOOMBEOLA, Co. Galway, rises on a windswept headland in south Connemara. The Athenry Dominicans came there in 1427, presumably as a place for rest and recollection. The original building was dismantled in the sixteenth century, but the site is marked by a mass of stones. There is a small chapel, possibly of the eighteenth century, with two slit windows in the north wall, a niche in the east wall and a crude doorway in the south wall.

The next house was founded at URLAUR, Co. Mayo, in 1434. The remains consist of a long narrow church, with an aisle to the north and a small domestic east range to the south. There is no evidence for a tower. Except for the aisle, this L-shaped layout corresponds to many contemporary houses of the Franciscan Third Order Regular such as Ballymote, Co. Sligo, Clonkeenkerrill, Co. Galway, Friarstown, Co. Limerick, and Kilmacrenan and Magherabeg, both Co. Donegal. The east window was in cusped flamboyant style. The west window, of two lights, cusped and surmounted by a quadrifoil light, tops a good gothic doorway. There are two ogee-headed two-light windows in the choir. The aisle east window has vanished.

KILCORBAN, Co. Galway, is the one place where there is mention of a Dominican Third Order group. An existing house was given to the Dominicans in 1446. Like Toombeola, it became a dependency of Athenry. The ruins consist of most of the north, west and east walls of a small church, as well as the north transept. The living quarters were probably to the south of the church [28]. The east window was reconstructed during restoration and is an excellent example of the transition from switch-bar to flowing tracery. The bars to the two lights are segmental pointed with cusps. The lights over are also cusped, not unlike the west window in Cashel. The transept has a good arch, with a female head over and a north window with simple switch-bar tracery. There are several wooden statues associated with Kilcorban, including an Enthroned Madonna, a Calvary group [Cross, Our Lady, John the Evangelist] and St. Catherine of Alexandria.

The Dominicans came to TULSK, Co. Roscommon, in 1448. The remains are those of a medium-sized church with a transept to the south. This implies that the residence was to the north. The east end has been changed into a type of tower, probably when Sir Richard Bingham repaired the building in 1595. A double arch leads into the ruined transept. Most of the north wall of the church has fallen, but there are still remains of tombs and vaults in it [28a].

After so much work in the west, the

Dominicans now went south. The church of simple design at GLANWORTH, Co. Cork, founded in 1475, still stands, but the cloister to the north has vanished. Early Ordnance Survey maps indicate that this may have been a small one range residence. The tall tower is the width of the church and of rectangular cross-section, with evidence for a rood loft on its west face. The east window has simple switch-bar tracery. The south wall of the choir has three small two-light ogee-headed windows. There is a lancet on the south wall under the tower, with a round-headed lancet and a two-light ogee-headed window on the south wall of the nave. There is a piscina near the site of the altar. The church door was probably in the south wall of the nave.

The friars now returned to the west, to BURRISHOOLE, Co. Mayo, in 1486. Like Portumna, the ruins are a miniature of a big priory and church with the cloister to the north. The church is complete with a wide low tower and a transept to the south. The tower overlaps one of the arches leading to the transept, showing that it is a later addition, and has corbels indicating a wooden rood loft. The east and south windows have switch-bar tracery. There are two long windows on the south wall of the choir, two small two-light ones on the east wall of the transept and a small single light one over the west door. The cloister ranges were of two-storey integrated type. The eastern arcade of round-headed windows seperated by solid pillars has been restored[28b].

The Dominicans came to GALWAY in 1488. Nothing remains of their large house, but it is possible to deduce a certain amount from a description of the church before it was pulled down in 1651[29]. It was situated just across the Corrib from the walled town, protected by its own wall and gate. The church ran east to west, with an east window of five lights and the usual tower in the middle of the church. There was an aisle, almost certainly to the north of the nave, and divided from it by four arches, and also a transept chapel to the north. The living quarters were to the south of the church. There was a lazar house nearby, but its relation to the church is unclear. There seems to have been three three light windows on the north wall of the aisle and one each of the same type on the west walls of nave and aisle. There was a two light window in the south wall of the choir and a series of six one light windows in the north wall. The north window of the chapel was of three lights, as were the other three windows there. The top of the walls were decorated with battlements.

In that same year of 1488 friars, probably dependent on Sligo, arrived at CLOONA-

Fig. 10 - Cloonameehan, Co. Sligo. East end of church and part of North range. Photo. Martin A. Timoney.

Fig. 11 - Cloonameehan, Co. Sligo. East window. Photo. Martin A. Timoney.

MEEHAN, Co. Sligo, and built a small priory. It has the plan and style of many Franciscan Third Order houses. The church now has a small two-light east window, with each light having four cusps on top. This may be a replacement for a larger window. The central mullion has an extra piece for holding the shuttering in place. The west wall is solid, with no sign of a door or window. A two-storey residence jutted out at right angle to the north eastern part of the church.

The last medieval Irish Dominican foundation

ERRATA

The flow lines of the Stokes Family Tree were inadvertently omitted and the complete diagram printed here should be inserted at page 248

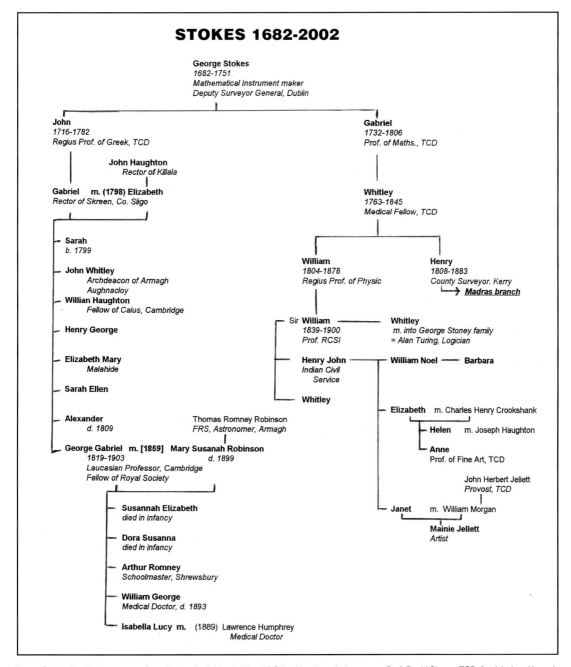

Fig. 2 - Stokes Family Tree, 1682-, Compiled by Prof. Alistair Wood, DCU, with acknowledgments to Prof. David Simms, TCD, for right-hand branch.

The captions to the illustrations on page 126, that indicate a lingering of Pagan Celtic traditions well into Christian times, should be transposed.

ADDENDUM

We acknowledge the pre-purchase by Sligo County Library of several copies of the book.
We acknowledge the contribution by Aidan Mannion,
The Record Room, Grattan St., Sligo, towards the launch of the book.

Fig. 12 - Ballindoon, Co. Sligo. Aerial view from northeast.
Photo. Martin A. Timoney.

was at BALLINDOON, Co. Sligo, in 1507. The small church has a tower and a transept to the north, but there is no indication of the site of a separate residence. Doors in the south wall of the church open to an area where the ground falls steeply away to the adjacent lake. Both east and west windows have simple switch-bar tracery. The north wall of the choir has a single and a double light windows. The church door was in the north wall of the nave. The glory of Ballindoon is its unique tower. Covering the full width of the church, it is not very deep. Access was by stairs on the outside of the south wall of the church, then by an internal stairs. The top of the tower is stepped, with the central third a storey higher than the outer sections. Looked at from the nave, the tower has three arches over three others. Those on the ground floor provide a central arch for access to the choir, and two niches, probably for side altars. The top three provide an open arch for a rood cross and possibly a rood loft, with two niches, probably for statues of saints[30]. When roofed and viewed from the outside, it would probably have looked like the tower at Athenry.

ANALYSIS: PRE-BLACK DEATH SITES

Eighteen of these Dominican ruins pre-date the Black Death. Except for Ballinegaul, these were all substantial buildings in the cities and towns of Leinster, Munster and East Ulster, with only a few in the west. Waterford was within the town wall. Others were included when the walls were extended [Drogheda, Limerick, Athenry], or near the walls [Cashel, Kilkenny, Kilmallock] or just across the river from the walls [Cork, Dublin]. Twelve of the cloisters were to the north of the church, five to the south and one unknown. Thirteen churches had aisles to the naves. Seven - all with aisles - had transepts. In three other cases [Waterford, Cork, Youghal], there is insufficient evidence to decide whether there was a transept as well as an aisle. Four priories had aisles added to the transepts. In two of these cases [Cashel, Kilkenny], aisles to both nave and transept produced a huge area for the congregation with a groundplan of two overlapping squares rather than the usual medieval one of two joined rectangles. Towers existed in the middle of at least thirteen churches [Newtownards tower is not medieval]. Five of the towers were the full width of the church, small in length and not very tall [Waterford, Cashel, Roscommon, Rosbercon, Carlingford]. Three were of the slim friary type [Drogheda, Sligo, Kilmallock]. Two [Athenry, Kilkenny] are impossible to classify. Normally the east wall of the transept joined the wall of the choir at or near the west face of the tower. This is true of at least four Dominican sites, but at five others [Kilkenny, Waterford, Cork, Athenry, Kilmallock], the east wall joins at or even east of the east face, leaving one leg like a pillar in the church.

Turning to window styles in these early priories, five had triple-lancet east windows [Cashel, Kilkenny (also south window), Roscommon, Sligo, Strade] and five had lancets in series on the choir wall [Athenry, Cashel, Roscommon, Sligo, Strade], all typical thirteenth century features. Four have east windows intermediate between lancets and tracery [Kilmallock, Lorrha, Rathfran, Youghal (west window)]. The extension to Athenry put it in the intermediate stage of choir windows [a big window at the east end of a series of lancets]. The next developement was a series of grouped choir windows as found at Lorrha and Rathfran. The series of switch tracery windows at Kilmallock bring us well into the fourteenth century. Other series of tracery windows more properly belong to after the Black Death.

ANALYSIS: AFTER THE BLACK DEATH

Remains of eleven Dominican houses survive from the time after the Black Death. The plan of a twelfth, Galway, can be reconstructed. With the exception of Glanworth, they are in the more isolated parts of the Midlands and the West. Again with the possible exception of Glanworth and now-vanished Galway, there are no large fifteenth century houses like the Franciscan friaries at Ardfert, Co. Kerry, Moyne, Co. Mayo,

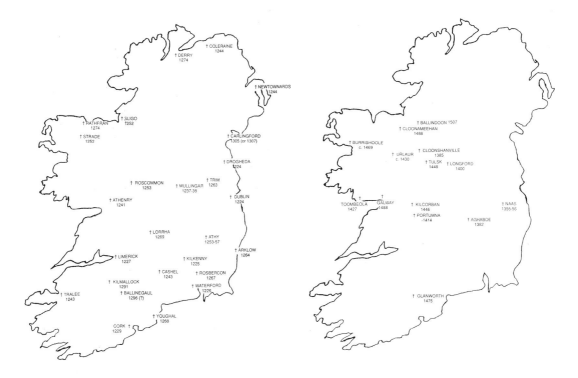

Fig. 13 - Distribution of Irish Dominican Priories with dates of foundation: Phase I, Pre Black Death.

Fig. 14 - Distribution of Irish Dominican Priories with dates of foundation: Phase II, Post Black Death.

Muckross, Co. Kerry, and Quin Co. Clare. The new Dominican houses are compact, like those of the Franciscan Third Order Regular. Some are mini-friaries [Ballindoon, Burrishoole, Cloonshanville, Portumna]. Others are small churches with one residential range [Cloonymeehan, Kilcorban, Toombeola, Urlar and possibly Glanworth]. On the other hand, much effort went in to improving or extending earlier houses.

The new houses kept the ratio of two-to-one in favour of the cloister to the north of the church. Similarly half [seven] had transepts. Unlike the earlier ones, only one [Urlaur] had an aisle. Two had towers of the wide squat type [Burrishoole, Glanworth], one of the slim type [Cloonshanville] and one indeterminate [Ballindoon, which when roofed, would have looked like Athenry].

Only one [Aghaboe] of the new houses had a series of windows in the choir wall. Including replacement windows in earlier priories, you can find examples of all styles: simple switch tracery [Kilmallock] or the same with cusps [Kilkenny]; switch-bar tracery [Athenry, Ballindoon, Burrishoole, Cashel, Glanworth] or same with cusps [Athenry, Portumna]; reticulated with cusps [Cashel, Kilmallock, Sligo]; simple flamboyant or flowing [Aghaboe], or with cusps [Aghaboe, Cashel, Cloonshanville, Portumna, Roscommon, Urlaur]. If there is one thing which distinguishes later Irish Dominican medieval windows, it is the extensive and imaginative use of cusps, possibly under English influence. Their Franciscan contemporaries went for simplicity and purity of line in window tracery.

CONCLUSION

Irish Dominican medieval architecture splits into two parts on either side of the Black Death. The thirteenth and early fourteenth century foundations were in or near cities and towns in the east and south. Churches were orientated, with the high altar under an impressive east window. Initially this consisted of three lancets, but later had five lights divided by mullions. One wall of the choir had a series of lancets, or later grouped lancets. A tower belfrey carried on arches divided the choir from the nave. This was usually the full width of the church, but not very deep, and had a rood loft for preaching on its western face. Occasionally the width of the top of the tower was narrowed to give a small slim effect. However the squat broad tower of rectangular cross section is a feature of the Dominicans in medieval Ireland. An aisle to give extra room was almost always built, usually to the south of the church. A transept was added to the nave in about half of the churches, and an aisle added to the back of the transept in four of these. In Dominican churches, the transept joined the choir at the east face of the tower more often than at the west face. The main door was at the west end of the church under an elaborate window. The residential area was around a cloister garth to the north of the church with a refectory in the north range. An arcade surrounded the ambulatory.

Three things happened after the Black Death.

(1) Few large churches were built, but existing ones were extended and improved. The latest styles in window tracery, making extensive use of cusps, were used. Again let us remember that it is the use of cusps which distinguishes Irish Dominican medieval windows.

(2) Smaller houses were built in the west, away from populated areas. Sometimes these were miniatures of the older priories, but more often they were small churches with a residential range at right angles.

(3) They represent a different view of religious life - the need for quiet, prayer and contemplation replacing the pastoral needs of the greatest possible number of people. The same dicotomy still exists today and has been a perennial problem for all mendicant orders, be they Carmelite, Franciscan, Augustian or Dominican!

Notes

1. Mooney, Canice, O.F.M., "Franciscan Architecture in Pre-Reformation Ireland", in *J. Roy. Soc. Antiq. Ireland*, 85 (1955), 133-173; 86 (1956), 125-169; 87 (1957), 1-28, 103-124.

2. Stalley, Roger, *The Cistercian Monsteries of Ireland*, London 1987. Britta Kalkreuter, *Boyle Abbey and The School of The West*, Bray, Wordwell, 2001.

2a. Dermot Doggett, "The Medieval Monasteries of the Augustinian Canons Regular", *Archaeology Ireland*, 10:1 (1996), 8-11; complete article in *Archaeology Ireland*, 10:2 (1996), 31-33; Tadhg O'Keeffe, *An Anglo-Norman Monastery, Bridgetown Priory and the Architecture of the Augustinian Canons Regular in Ireland*, Cork County Council ~ Kinsale Gandon, 1999.

3. Conlan, Patrick, O.F.M., *Franciscan Ireland*, 2nd. ed., 97-102, Mullingar 1988.

4. Gwynn, Aubrey, and Hadcock, R. Neville, *Medieval Religious Houses: Ireland*, 218-32, Dublin 1970.

5. In theory the Irish Dominicans became independent of England in 1484, but actual control remained confused: see Flynn, Thomas, O.P., *The Irish Dominicans 1536-1641*, 8-11, Dublin 1993.

6. Leask, Harold G., *Irish Churches and Monastic Buildings, II*, 132-134, Dundalk 1960.

7. Leask, II, 128-129, implies that the transept windows date to the 1340s. It is true that English prototypes for the smaller windows can be found as early as 1310. My instinct tells me that the whole transept is too rich for the fourteenth century and more properly belongs to the second half of the fifteenth century when Irish architects, with more financial resources behind them, became quite innovative.

8. Fenning, Hugh, O.P., *The Waterford Dominicans*, 6-8, Wateford 1990.

9. Information supplied by Dr. Elizabeth Shee-Twohig, University College, Cork.

10. I wish to thank Maurice Hurley, Cork City archeologist, for access to the excavation reports on the Dominican priory prepared by him and Catherine Sheehan. Hurley, Maurice F., and Sheehan, Cathy M., *Excavations at the Dominican Priory, St. Mary's of the Isle*, Cork, Cork Corporation, 1995.

11. Leask, II, 93-94 and 126-128; Peter Harbison, *'Our Treasure of Antiquities', Bereanger and Bigari's Antiquarian Sketching Tour of Connacht in 1779*, 2002, 167-169.

12. Leask, II, 93, and III, 123-124, Dundalk 1960.

13. *Archeological Survey of County Down*, 245-246, Belfast 1966.

14. *Mainistir Sligigh; Sligo Abbey*, Dublin 1968. M.H. Gaffney, *Seventh Centenary, 1252-1952, The Story of Sligo Abbey*; Hugh Fenning, 2002: *The Dominicans in Sligo*, Sligo. For a beautiful lit-up at night view of Sligo Abbey see *Sligo County Council Annual Report 1999*, 52. For a W.F. Wakeman view of Sligo Abbey see *Sligo County Council Annual Report 1994*. Wakeman, W.F., 1866: "Abbey of the Order of St. Dominick, Sligo", *Dublin Saturday Magazine*, 2:67, 1. Harbison 2002, 13-42.

15. Leask, III, 168; Harbison 2002, 124-128.

16. Leask, III, 127-128; Taheny, Luke, O.P., *The Dominicans in Roscommon*, Tallaght 1990; Harbison 2002, 186-191.

17. Flynn, Thomas, O.P., *The Dominicans of Rosbercon*, Tallaght 1981.

18. Personal observation.

19. Leask, II, 115.

20. Leask, II, 117-118 and III, 125-126.

21. Hogan, Arlene, *Kilmallock Dominican Priory*, Kilmallock 1991.

22. Flynn, *The Irish Dominicans ...*, 23-24.

23. Leask, II, 146-147.

24. On the Observant movement among the Dominicans in Ireland, see: Flynn, *The Irish Dominicans ...*, 3-8.

25. Flynn, Thomas, O.P., *The Dominicans of Aghaboe*, Dublin 1975; Leask, III, 131.

26. Leask, III, 181; there is a photograph of the east window in Pochin-Mould, Daphne, *The Irish Dominicans*, Dublin 1957. Harbison 2002, 178-181.

27. Leask, III, 120, 128 and 185.

28. Stanley, Cathal, ed., *Kilcorban Priory*, Kilcorban 1987.

28a. Harbison 2002, 184-185.

28b. Harbison 2002, 130-132.

29. O Heideain, Eustace, O.P., *The Dominicans in Galway*, 1241-1991, 62-64, Galway 1991; the reconstruction on pp 41 & 45 should be treated with caution; the author seems to have based his positioning of the lazar house and a south transept on the well-known map of Galway in 1651.

30. Leask, III, 54-5; Harbison 2002, 75-76.

APPENDIX

Dates of foundation of Irish Dominican houses and some other key dates as regards alterations.

Foundation	Year	Notes, events, alterations, *etc.*
	1203	Dominic begins his life of active preaching
	1215	Foundation of the Dominicans as a diocesan congregation
	1216	Papal approval of the Dominican Order
Dublin, Drogheda	1224	Arrival of Dominicans in Ireland
Kilkenny	1225	
Waterford	1226	
Limerick	1227	
Cork	1229	
Mullingar	1237	
Athenry	1241	
Cashel, Tralee	1243	
Coleraine, Newtownards	1244	
Sligo, Strade	1252	
Athy, Roscommon	1253	
Trim	1263	
Arklow	1264	
Rosbercon	1267	
Youghal	1268	
Lorrha	1269	
Derry, Rathfran	1274	
Kilmallock	1291	
Ballinegaul	1296	
Carlingford	1305	
	1310?	Drogheda tower built
	1310?	Newtownards nave extended and aisle added
	1325?	Athenry choir extended, transept and aisles added
	1330?	Kilmallock transept with aisle added
	1340?	Kilkenny transept built
	1348	The Black Death
Nass	1355	
Aghaboe	1382	
Cloonshanville	1385	
Longford	1400	
Portumna	1414	Sligo rebuilt after fire, transept and aisle added
	1425?	Athenry tower built, nave and aisle arches changed
Tombeola	1427	
Urlaur	1434	
	1440?	Kilmallock tower and N. range, ?followed by new cloister arcade
Kilcorban	1446	
Tulsk	1448	
	1461	Sligo rood loft, followed by tower
	1470?	Sligo cloister arcade
Glanworth	1475	
	1480	Cashel rebuilt after fire, new E. and S. main windows
	1480?	Strade tower, aisle and transept added
	1480?	Portumna rebuilt, including S. window in transept
Burrishoole	1486	
Galway, Cloonameehan	1488	
	1490?	Roscommon aisle and transept added, new E. and W. windows
	1490?	Rathfran aisle added
	1495	Ahgaboe rebuilt or finally finished
Ballindoon	1507	Present Kilkenny tower
	1536	Irish Dominican province finally becomes independent

ARCHAEOLOGICAL SITE ASSESSMENT WEST OF THE GREEN FORT

Eoin Halpin Archaeological Development Services, Dublin and Belfast

ABSTRACT: In advance of Phase 1 of a housing development to the south-west of The Green Fort a total of 103m of section face was examined in three trenches in 1993. Nothing of archaeological significance was recorded except a shallow pit from which no datable finds were recovered.

HISTORY OF THE GREEN FORT

Sligo town was attacked in 1641 by Royalists under MacDonagh but the castles of O'Crean and Lady Jones held out. It was again attacked and captured in 1645 by a Parliamentary army under Sir Charles Coote which held the town until October 1649 when it was retaken by the Confederates under the Marquis of Clanricarde. By the start of the Williamite wars the town lacked a garrison. However one was hastily formed by the local Protestant Association which immediately marched out seeking the greater protection of Enniskillen, leaving the town to Lutterell, the Jacobite commander. Believing false reports of approaching armies he abandoned the town to the Williamites who were in turn ousted by Sarsfield in 1690. He kept control of the area until his defeat in September 1691.

In 1646 the sum of £270 was allocated for the fortification of Sligo and Roscommon. It is generally accepted that some of this money was used to construct the Stone Fort in Sligo town, the site of which is now occupied by the Town Hall. It has also been suggested that the construction of the Green Fort may also date from this time. It is described as an earthwork in poor condition and is recorded on the Down Survey map of the barony of Carbury, both sources dating to about 1656. The fort features again in the Williamite wars, when it was defended by Teige O'Regan for the Jacobites. At the end of the 19th century the site was described as being almost one acre in extent and consisting of a large bastion and a platform at each corner. Access to the interior was gained via two gates with the whole site surrounded by a large fosse. The fort is located at the presumed north-east corner of the town with banked and ditched defences running due west and south of the site. See Wood-Martin 1889, (fig. 14, opp. 134) Bradley & Dunne 1987 (35-36 and fig. 2) and Kerrigan (1995, passim, with refs.) for further information on The Green Fort.

ARCHAEOLOGICAL SITE TESTING

Phase 1 of a housing development (Fig. 1) lies some 120m to the south-west of the fort, and 50m to the south of the projected line of the town defences. In all, three trenches were machine excavated (Licence No. 93E0119) down to, and through undisturbed sub-soil. Each of the trenches ran approximately north-south, extending the full width of the development area. A total of 103m of section face was examined in detail and nothing of archaeological significance was recorded. However, towards the northern end of the western trench a shallow pit was noted. In section it was 1m wide and round bottomed, measuring at most 20cm in depth. The dark grey brown clay-loam fill contained some small flecks of charcoal. However, as the feature did not extend across the width of the cutting and no datable finds were recovered, it is an isolated and undatable feature.

At the southern end of the two westernmost trenches, an ash spread was noted, delimited to the north and south by two shallow gullies 12.5m apart. Each gully was 30cm wide and 20cm deep and was filled with a mixture of topsoil and white ash. Close examination of the section between the two gullies revealed that the ash was spread very thinly and intermittently across the full 12.5m. A number of small fragments of red brick and late 19th century wares and pieces of bottle glass were recovered from this ash deposit, suggesting it to be quite a late feature. Nothing of archaeological note was recorded either in plan or section in the eastern trench, Trench 3.

REFERENCES

Bennett, Isabel. 1994: *Excavations 1993: Summary Accounts of Archaeological Excavations in Ireland*, Bray, Wordwell

Bradley, John, and Dunne, Noel, 1987: *Urban Archaeological Survey, Part XXI, County Sligo*. Dublin, Office of Public Works. Limited distribution

Halpin, Eoin, 1994: "Rockwood Parade Development, Sligo", in Bennett 1994, 72.

Kerrigan, Paul M., 1995: *Castles and Fortifications In Ireland, 1485-1945,* Cork, The Collins Press.

Wood-Martin, William Gregory 1889: *History of Sligo, Accession of James I to the Revolution of 1688,* Dublin, Hodges Figgis; Reprint, Sligo, 1990, Dodd's Antiquarian Books.

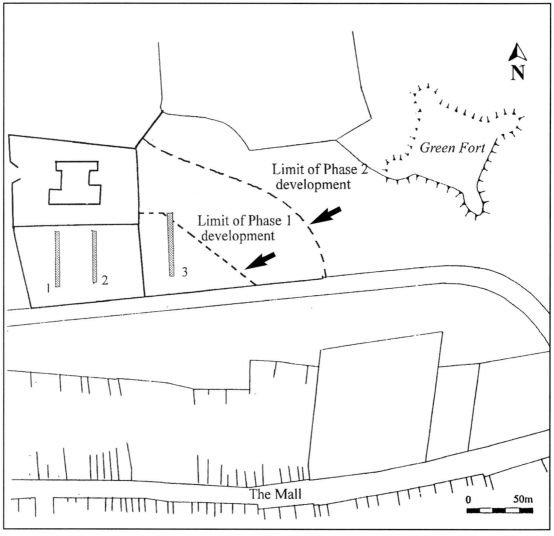

Fig. 1 - Location of trenches in the development area of the SW of the Green Fort

A CELEBRATION *OF* SLIGO

DOWNING'S DESCRIPTION OF COUNTY SLIGO, C. 1684

Nollaig Ó Muraíle
Department of Celtic, The Queen's University of Belfast

ABSTRACT: One of a series of descriptions of Irish counties collected by William Molyneux in the early 1680s, the account edited and annotated here was the work of a rather mysterious writer named R. Downing. It concentrates largely on the physical features and antiquities of Co. Sligo, but also contains some fascinating remarks on aspects of Sligo history and on some of the great families of the county.

INTRODUCTION

This text, which has not been printed heretofore - nor, to the best of my knowledge, commented upon in print recently other than by myself last year - is one of a series of accounts of more than twenty Irish counties (in whole or in part) which were collected by the Dublin writer William Molyneux in the years 1682-1685.[1] Molyneux (1656-1698) - who is best remembered as the author of a work in support of parliamentary independence for Ireland, *The Case of Ireland Stated* (1698) - had been engaged to contribute a description of Ireland to an ambitious work, *The English Atlas*, being planned by a London bookseller, Moses Pitt.[2] The project collapsed when Pitt ran into financial difficulties and was declared bankrupt in 1683; he fled to Ireland but was arrested in April 1685 and imprisoned for debt. Molyneux had planned to base his 'Description' on the material he had gathered, but, following Pitt's arrest, he burnt what he himself had written. Fortunately, however, he preserved the work of the other contributors.

Molyneux had begun by publishing a questionnaire in May 1682. He then engaged some of his relations to help him. These included a brother-in-law, Sir William Domville, who was able to furnish him with a very brief draft of an account of Co. Carlow and Queen's Co.,[3] while a cousin, Nicholas Dowdall, reported in August on his fruitless efforts to get someone to describe Roscommon and Westmeath; Dowdall himself later penned an account of Co. Longford.[4] In September 1682 Molyneux obtained, through another brother-in-law, Bishop Anthony Dopping of Meath, a revised version of an account of Westmeath which Sir Henry Piers had written some years before.[5] Several accounts were ready by the spring of 1683, but a well-known description of Iar-Connaught (*i.e.*, west Co. Galway) by the Galway scholar Roderick O'Flaherty was not completed until 5 April 1684[6] - some three weeks after John Keogh's account of Co. Roscommon, 'March 14th 1683/4'. Further accounts arrived in the summer of 1684, but some of Sir Richard Cox's material on Co. Cork did not reach Molyneux until November 1685.[7]

Some of the items, the present one among them, are difficult to date with certainty; but, in view of the fact that Molyneux wrote in March 1684 to John Keogh of Strokestown, asking for suggestions as to who might provide him with descriptions of Cos. Mayo and Sligo,[8] we can take it that Downing's accounts of those two counties may date - at the earliest - from mid-to-late 1684.

A further and most pertinent reference to a man named Robert Downing has recently come to light. In the *Irish Statute Staple Books, 1596-1687*, the alphabetical list of debtors includes, under the date 13 December 1680, one Robert Downing of 'Castlelaygy,' Co. Mayo[19]. His occupation is described as 'gentry: gent' and the amount of his debt is the quite considerable sum of £4,000. (The MS No. is given as BL 15,637 f. 44a and the Ident. No. as 3927.) The placename, Castlelaygy, with which he is associated appears to represent the townland of Castlenageehy in the parish of Kilcummin, barony of Tirawley, in north Mayo – a strikingly similar form of the name in another seventeenth-century source is Castlelegie[20].

WHO WAS R. DOWNING?

An additional problem attaching to the present work concerns the identity of the author. The assumption that it was in fact the work of a person called Downing is simply based on the fact that the description of Co. Sligo is in the same hand as that which penned the earlier of the two TCD copies of the description of Co. Mayo ascribed (in the later copy) to 'R. Downing.' Apart from his name we know very little for certain about him. Among the things we do know are that (i), in addition to the present text, he also wrote accounts of Cos. Clare, Down, Louth and Mayo (and possibly Longford),[9] and (ii), at his request, Roderick O'Flaherty in January 1682 addressed to him a tract entitled 'Observations on Dr. Borlace's Reduction of Ireland.'[10]

One authority, William O'Sullivan, former Keeper of Manuscripts in the Library of Trinity College, Dublin, has ventured the opinion that the individual in question may be identified as a certain 'Richard Downing who graduated from TCD in 1691',[11] but I find this somewhat implausible. It would seem odd that Downing should have written descriptions of five widely-scattered Irish counties, Down, Louth, Sligo, Mayo and Clare, some seven years before graduating, and even earlier been in communication with O'Flaherty. There is also the fact that he is referred to as *Robert* Downing by the nineteenth-century writer James Hardiman.[12] It is worth noting that there are two additional instances of his being called 'Robert':

(i) 'in Thorpe's curious Catalogue of the Southwell MSS., A.D. 1834, No. 348', in relation to the autograph of O'Flaherty's aforementioned 'Observations' - the notice begins: 'These observations were transmitted to Mr. Robert Downing ...';[13]

and

(ii) in an 'endorsement, twice repeated, "County of Lowth, by Robert Downing" written on 'one of the two blank leaves, now mutilated (evidently the original outer wrapper)', which were attached to five leaves containing an account of Co. Louth which R.A.S. Macalister published in 1917. (He adds: 'There are three different handwritings in these endorsements.')[14]

The Co. Louth tract is very similar to Downing's other works, but for some reason it was not preserved along with them in TCD Library. Instead, it was for many years 'imprisoned' in England, in the library of Sir Thomas Phillipps. It was later acquired by a London bookseller, from whom Macalister bought it a short time before publishing it in 1917. I do not know its present whereabouts. Macalister confessed that he could not 'find anything as to who, Robert Downing may have been', adding that 'the name "Robert Downing, Gent." occurs in a deed'; dated 1687, but there is no evidence to link him with the author of the MS. 'From the absence of any honorific prefix or suffix to the name in the endorsement of the MS.', declares Macalister, 'I suspect its writer to have been a person comparatively unimportant - possibly a clerk, writing for so much a page', and he concludes: 'The people referred to in the text as living at the time, so far as they can be identified, date the document to about 1670-1680 ...'[15]

Another piece of evidence which may shed some light on Downing's identity is a reference to 'Robert Downing, Gentleman, Deputy Ulster [King of Arms]' in a funeral certificate of Elizabeth St Leger, dowager Countess of Inchiquin, dated 22 November 1685.[16] A few years ago the late William O'Sullivan kindly drew my attention to the fact that there is mention of one 'Robert Downeing, gent.' as a landowner in the parish of Desertlyn, Co. Londonderry, in the so-called 'Census of 1659';[17] could this, perhaps, be our author - or maybe his father? Mr O'Sullivan also made an interesting alternative suggestion to me in private correspondence: that Robert Downing may have been related to the brothers Joshua and Emanuel Downing from Suffolk who came to Ireland early in the seventeenth century. The two, both lawyers, held positions respectively in the Court of Exchequer and the Court of Common Pleas in Dublin and Emanuel, who married a sister of the historian Sir. James Ware, became involved *c.* 1620 in a government-sponsored plantation at Mountrath, Co. Laois. However, against the suggestion that our Robert Downing might have been descended from one or other of this pair is the fact that both returned to England within a few years, Joshua by 1619 and Emanuel in 1625; the latter soon afterwards became involved in founding the Massachusetts Bay colony in New England.[18]

A further and most pertinent reference to a man named Robert Downing has recently come to light. In the *Irish Statute Staple Books, 1596-1687*, the alphabetical list of debtors includes, under the date 13 December 1680, one Robert Downing of 'Castlelaygy,' Co. Mayo.[19] His occupation is described as 'gentry: gent' and the amount of his debt is the quite considerable sum of £4,000. (The MS No. is given as BL 15,637 f. 44a and the Ident. No. as 3927.) The placename, Castlelaygy, with which he is associated appears to represent the townland of Castlenageehy in the parish of Kilcummin, barony of Tirawley, in north Mayo – a strikingly similar form of the name in another seventeenth-century source is Castlelegie.[20]

The work printed here occurs in TCD MS 888/1 (formerly I.4.17) and, as mentioned above, is in the same handwriting as Downing's description of Co. Mayo in TCD 888/2 (formerly I.4.19); that same handwriting occurs also in the descriptions of Cos. Clare and Down attributed to Downing. Later, and much more easily legible - but very inaccurate! - copies of the Mayo tracts are to be found in TCD MS 883.1 and 883.2; there appears to be no similarly late copy of the work on Co. Sligo. (Those later copies of Downing's writings were apparently the work of a clerk who transcribed them, as well as other texts, for William Molyneux's son, Samuel, who planned to publish a 'Natural History of Ireland'.[21])

Downing's manuscript is not a very satisfactory piece of penmanship: some of it is roughly written in what can almost be characterised as a scribble and overall it resembles the handwriting of an earlier period. Some parts of the text are virtually indecipherable. Also notable are the numerous deletions, interlineal additions, examples of dittography (*i.e.*, erroneous repetition) and the often rather strange syntax. In this context it is interesting to consider some of Macalister's comments on Downing's account of Co. Louth; referring to a 'curious mistake' and a 'clumsy correction', he remarks that they 'suggest that the document was merely a draft meant for a more finished report: the whole has an air of disorder, as though Downing had put down things as they came into his head, intending later to arrange them systematically.'[22]

Finally, we may note that, to judge from his other tracts, Downing appears to have had some familiarity with the Irish language.

THIS EDITION

For convenience, I have divided the work into numbered paragraphs or sections, and after each of these (in square brackets) I have inserted appropriate annotation or commentary. The latter makes no pretence to being exhaustive but - it is hoped - will help elucidate certain textual references. There remain some references which quite escape me (notably the name of the sea, 'Virginian', in §17, the form 'Smecourte' for Abbey Court in §26, the word immediately following the name Keon Ô Hara in §28 or the location of the place called Doon Pallar, ?near Ballinafad, in §45 - not to mention the problematical readings in §3). Any suggestions which might shed light on such puzzles would be most welcome.

While I have faithfully reproduced the orthography of the original text, I have taken the liberty of bringing punctuation and capitalisation into line with modern practice. Initial 'ff' has been written 'F' where appropriate.

Most abbreviated words are silently expanded: 'ye' and 'yt' (as 'the' and 'that' respectively); 'sd' ('said'); 'nxt' ('next'); 'wch' ('which'); '&c' is written '*etc.*' Editorial insertions (*e.g.*, of words or letters accidentally omitted by the scribe) are enclosed in square brackets. Empty square brackets indicate missing or illegible material.

A. PUBLISHED EDITIONS

This and the following list indicate respectively the portions of the Molyneux survey which have hitherto appeared in print and those which have not yet been published. (A bracketed county-name indicates that only part of that county is included.)

1a. Co. Antrim, R. Dobbs (G. Hill, *MacDonnells of Antrim* (1873), 377-386).

1b. [Co. Antrim] Carrickfergus, R. Dobbs (ibid. 386-389).

2. Co. Clare, R. Downing; (B. Ó Dálaigh, *The Strangers Gaze: Travels in County Clare, 1534 - 1950*, (1998), 61-68; H. Brigdall (ibid., 68 - 72).

3. Co. Cork, R. Cox (S.P. Johnston, *JRSAI* 32 (1902), 353-363; + nn. on pp. 363-376).

4. [Co. Down] Ards, W. Montgomery (R.M. Young, *Old Belfast* (1896), 138-143).

5. [Co. Galway] Iar Connaught, R. O'Flaherty (J. Hardiman, *H-Iar Connaught* (1846), 1-122).

6. Co. Kerry, J. Kennington, E. Curtis and unknown author (W. O'Sullivan, *JKAHS*, 4 (1971), 35-47).

7. Co. Kildare, T. Monk (E. MacLysaght, *Irish Life in the Seventeenth Century* (1969), 313-319).

8. Co. Leitrim, T. Roddy and unknown author (J. Logan, *Bréifne* 4/14 (1971), 325-334).

9. Co. Longford, N. Dowdall (R. Gillespie, G. Moran, *Longford: Essays in County History* (1991), 207-211).

10. Co. Louth, R. Downing (R.A.S. Macalister, *PRIA* 33 (1917), 495-499).

11. Co. Mayo, R. Downing (Ó Muraíle 1998, 242-261).

12. Co. Westmeath, H. Piers (*Collectanea de Rebus Hibernicis* 1 (1774), 1-126).

13a. Co. Wexford, S. Richards, R. Leigh; *JRSAI* 7 (1862), 85-91 [Richards]; *JRSAI* 5 (1859), 451-467 [Leigh].

13b. [Co. Wexford] Forth, -- Sinnot (*JRSAI* 7 (1862), 57-84).

B. HITHERTO UNPUBLISHED PORTIONS

1. [Co. Armagh] Oneilland, W. Brooke;
2. Co. Carlow & Queen's Co., W. Domville;
3. Co. Donegal, ?;
4. Co. Down, R. Downing;
5. Co. Limerick, D. Hignet;
6. [Co. Londonderry] Magilligan, T. Beck;
7. Co. Longford, ? [distinct from A 8, above];
8. Co. Monaghan, ?;
9. Co. Roscommon, J. Keogh;
10. Co. Sligo, R. Downing - printed herein;
11. Co. Waterford, A. Stanhope.[23]

ACKNOWLEDGEMENTS

Before I conclude, I wish to record my gratitude to the Board of Trinity College, Dublin, for permitting me to reproduce Downing's account from a manuscript in their possession. I must also thank the editor of this volume, Martin A. Timoney, for many valuable suggestions which have markedly improved the present paper, while my colleague, Dr John Curran, Department of Ancient History, QUB, helped me with some of the problematical Latin passages.

PLACENAME-INDEX BY BARONY
Numbers indicate the paragraphs of this edition

CARBURY 1-15
Sligo 1-7, 9-10
Lough Gill 7
Garvoge River 7-8
Sligo Harbour 11
Knocknarea 12
Drumcliff, Glencar 13
Belladrihid, Duff River 14
Ardtermon, Collinsford, Grange 15

COOLAVIN 46-49
Moygara 47
Lough Gara, Killaraght 48
CORRAN 32-36
Keshcorran 32
Ballymote 33-36

LEYNY 23-31
Bellahy 23, 30
Achonry, Templehouse 24
Ballysadare 25
Abbey Court 26
Banada 27
Ballyara 29
River Moy 31

TIRERAGH 16-22
Ardnaree, River Moy, Ox Mountains 17
Rathlee 18
Ardnaree 19
Castleconor 20
Rathmulcah 21
Aughris 22

TIRERRILL 37-45
Ballindoon 37-39
Collooney 40
L. Arrow,
Unshin, Owenmore, Ballysadare 41
Killamoy, Kilross 42
Ballinafad 43
Dún Balair 45

NOTES

1. See maps (indicating the areas covered in the accounts) in *NHI* 3 (1976), 456, Map 11, and Emery 1954, 269. The maps are somewhat inaccurate, however see n. 3, below.
2. O'Sullivan 1971, 28; Logan 1971, 320-322; Simms 1982, 34-36; also Hoppen 1970, 62.
3. William O'Sullivan (1971, 30) says the draft account was of the Queen's County, while the county attributed to Domville in the map in *NHI* 3 is Carlow. In fact, both are partly right: Domville deals, albeit sketchily, with both counties in his account.
4. See Gillespie and Moran 1991, 207-211.
5. O'Sullivan 1971, 30; Emery 1954, 271.
6. *H-Conn.* 122.
7. Emery 1954, 272-273.
8. Logan 1971, 322; the letter is in RIA MS 12 W 22 (p. 9).
9. Some further details of the accounts of Mayo and Louth are given later on in this Introduction and of Mayo in Ó Muraíle 1998.
10. *H-Conn.* 431-4.
11. O'Sullivan 1971, 33, n. 21.
12. *H-Conn.* 4n, 251.
13. *H-Conn.* 422.
14. Macalister 1917, 499.
15. Macalister 1917, 499.
16. Ó Muraíle 1998, 238.
17. Pender 1939, 136.
18. See Loeber 1998.
19. Ohlmeyer and Ó Ciardha, 1998, 211. I am most grateful to Conleth Manning, Dúchas, for bringing this reference to my attention.
20. O'Sullivan 1958, 156.
21. O'Sullivan 1971, 33.
22. Macalister 1917, 500.
23. There are no descriptions for any of Cos. Cavan, Fermanagh, Kilkenny, King's Co. (now Offaly), Meath, Tipperary, Tyrone or Wicklow.

Barony Map of Co. Sligo.

ABBREVIATIONS

AConn.	*Annála Connacht, The Annals of Connacht* (ed. A.M. Freeman, 1944)
ALC	*The Annals of Loch Cé* (ed. W.M. Hennessy, 2 vols., 1871)
AU	*The Annals of Ulster* (to AD 1131) (ed. S. Mac Airt & G. Mac Niocaill, 1983)
bar.	barony
Bk. Fen.	*The Book of Fenagh* (ed. W.M. Hennessy & D.H. Kelly, 1875)
BSD	Book of Survey and Distribution, Co. Sligo [MS in National Archives, Dublin]
CP	*Complete Peerage*
DHA	*De Hibernia et Antiquitatibus Ejus* (Sir James Ware, 1654)
DPH	*De Praesulibus Hiberniae* (Sir James Ware, 1665)
Eccl. Tax.	Ecclesiastical Taxation of diocese of Killala, *Calendar of Documents, Ireland* 5 (1886) 217
EP	*Burke's Extinct Peerages* (1866)
FM	*Annals of the Kingdom of Ireland by the Four Masters*, 1-7 (ed. J. O'Donovan, 1848-51)
H-Conn.	*A Chorographical Description of West orH-Iar Connaught, AD1684, by Roderic O'Flaherty, Esq.* (ed. J. Hardiman, 1846)
Hy-F	*The Genealogies, Tribes and Customs of Hy-Fiachrach* (ed. J. O'Donovan, 1844)
JGAHS	*Journal of the Galway Archaeological and Historical Society*
JKAHS	*Journal of the Kerry Archaeological and Historical Society*
JRSAI	*Journal of the Royal Society of Antiquaries of Ireland*
MRHI	*Medieval Religious Houses: Ireland*, (A. Gwynn & R.N. Hadcock, London, 1970)
NHI 3	*New History of Ireland* 3 (ed. T.W. Moody *et al.*, London, 1976)
NHI 9	*New History of Ireland* 9 (ed. F.J. Byrne *et al.*, London, 1984)
OS	Ordnance Survey (usually in connection with OS six-inch maps)
par.	parish
PRIA	*Proceedings of the Royal Irish Academy*
RIA	Royal Irish Academy
TCD	Trinity College, Dublin
tld	townland
tn	town
UJA	*Ulster Journal of Archaeology*

SOURCES

Barnard, Toby, Ó Cróinín, Dáibhí, and Simms, Katharine, eds., 1998: *A Miracle of Learning. Studies in Manuscripts and Irish Learning. Essays in Honour of William O'Sullivan*, Aldershot, Ashgate.

Bergh, S., 1995: *Landscape of the Monuments. A study of the passage tombs in the Cúil Irra region, Co. Sligo, Ireland.* Riksantikvarieämbetet, Stockholm. Arkeologiska Skrifter nr 6.

Bieler, L., 1979: *The Patrician Texts in the Book of Armagh.*

Byrne, F.J., 1972: 'Rathmulcah: an historical note', *JRSAI*, 102, 73-76.

Conlan, P., 1991: 'The Franciscans in Ballymote', *The Corran Herald*, 21, 4-6.

de hÓir, [Éamonn], ... 1967: 'Cúil Mhuine, Cúil Mhaine, Cúil Áine', *Dinnseanchas*, 2, 76-80.

Emery, F.V., 1954: 'Irish geography in the seventeenth century', *Irish Geography*, 3, 263-276.

Gillespie, R., & Moran, G., 1991: *Longford, Essays in County History.*

Gray, E.A., 1982: *Cath Maige Tuired: The Second Battle of Mag Tuired.*

Gwynn, E.J. 1924: *The Metrical Dindshenchas*, IV.

Herity, M., 1970: 'Rathmulcah, Ware and MacFirbisigh: the earliest antiquarian description and illustration of a profane Irish field monument', *UJA*, 33, 49-53.

Hoppen, K.T., 1970: 'Samuel Molyneux's tour of Kerry, 1709', *JKAHS*, 3, 59-65.

Kerrigan, P.M., 1995: *Castles and Fortifications in Ireland, 1485-1945.*

Knox, H.T., 1917-1918: 'The Bermingham family of Athenry', *JGAHS*, 10, 139-154.

Lewis, S., 1837: *A Topographical Dictionary of Ireland*, I-II.

Loeber, R., 1998: "Preliminaries to the Massachusetts Bay Colony: the Irish adventures of Emanuel Downing and John Winthrop Sr." in Barnard *et al.*, 1998, 164-200.

Logan, John, 1971: 'Tadhg O Roddy and two surveys of Co. Leitrim', *Bréifne*, 4:14, 318-334.

Lough Gara Cultural Resources Project, 1994: *Map of Lough Gara Cultural Resources.*

Lynn, C.J., 1985-1986: 'Some 13th-century castle sites in the west of Ireland: notes on a preliminary reconaissance,' *JGAHS*, 40, 90-113.

Macalister, R.A.S., 1917: 'Robert Downing's History of Louth', *PRIA*, 33 C, 499-504.

Macalister, R.A.S., 1956: *Lebar Gabála Érenn: The Book of the Taking of Ireland*, V.

Mac an Bhaird, A., 1991-1993: 'Ptolemy revisited', *Ainm*, 5, 1-20.

McDonnell, T., 1976: *The Diocese of Killala from its Institution to the End of the Penal Times.*

McGarry, J., 1993: *Collooney,* 2nd ed.

MacHale, E. 1985: *The Parishes in the Diocese of Killala*: IV - *Tireragh.*

McKenna, L., 1951: *The Book of O'Hara: Leabhar Í Eadhra.*

McTernan, J.C., 1992: *Memory Harbour. The Port of Sligo.*

McTernan, J.C., 1993: *At the Foot of Knocknarea,* 2nd ed.

McTernan, J.C., 1994: *Sligo, Sources of Local History*, 2nd ed.

Morris, H., 1927: 'Where was Tor Inis, the Island Fortress of the Formorians', *JRSAI*, 57, 47-58.

Morris, H., 1928: 'The first battle of Magh Tuiredh', *JRSAI*, 58, 111-112.

Mould, D.D.C. Pochin, 1964: *The Irish Saints.*

Mulchrone, K., 1939: *Bethu Phátraic: The Tripartite Life of Patrick.*

Mulchrone, K., 1971: *Caithréim Cellaig.*

Ó Concheanainn, T., 1981: 'The Book of Ballymote', *Celtica* 14, 15-25.

O'Dowd, M., 1991: *Power, Politics and Land: Early Modern Sligo, 1568-1688.*

Office of Public Works, 1968: *Mainistir Shligigh, Sligo Abbey* [guidebook].

Ohlmeyer, Jane, and Ó Ciardha, É., 1998: *The Irish Staple Books, 1596-1687.*

Ó Muraíle, N., 1985: *Mayo Places: Their Names and Origins.*

Ó Muraíle, Nollaig, 1998: "A description of Co. Mayo *c.* 1684 by R. Downing" in Barnard *et al.*, eds., 236-265.

O'Rahilly, T.F., 1946: *Early Irish History and Mythology.*

O'Sullivan, William, 1971: 'William Molyneux's geographical collections for Kerry', *JKAHS*, 4, 28-47.

Pender, S., 1939: *A Census of Ireland, circa 1659.*

Rogers, N., 1994: *Ballymote, Aspects through Time,* 2nd ed.

Simms, J.G., 1982: *William Molyneux of Dublin.*

Timoney, Martin A., 1995: 'A Spa Well near Ballymote in 1684', *The Corran Herald*, 28, 10.

Timoney Martin A., 2002: "Aughris, Portavaud, Lackan and Kilcummin" in Timoney M.A. 2002.

Timoney Mary B., 2002: "St. Feichin's, Kilboglashy, Ballisodare, Co. Sligo: Discoveries and Rediscoveries" in Timoney M.A. 2002.

Wood-Martin, W.G., 1882, 1889, 1892: *History of Sligo, County and Town*, I-III (Reprint 1990).

THE COUNTIE OF SLIGOE,
OTHERWISE CALLED
EIGHTER CONNAUGHT
TCD MS 888/1 (FORMERLY I.4.17)

1. [34r] This countie of Sligoe from that aunceint towne soe called, which Sligoe is alsoe called by Ptolomei Slichnea or Slichneum (soe Ware, capto. x°). This towne stands in the Barony of Carbry.

[The reference is to *DHA* 54; see below, §7. In fact, there is no mention of Sligo in the *Cosmography* of Claudius Ptolemaeus (Ptolemy) - see Mac an Bhaird 1991-1993.]

2. But why soe called? [It] is said by the inhabitants there abouts that it takes its name from a longe stone near St. John's Church in that towne.

[I do not understand what word the name is here supposed to be derived from. The name *Sligeach* - *Slicech* in Old Irish - originally denoted the river now called the Garvoge - *An Gharbhóg*, 'the rough [river]': the latter name occurs, as the 'river of Sligo Garveoge' in Tadhg Ó Rodaighe's Description of Co. Leitrim, which was also written - like Downing's work - for William Molyneux (Logan 1971, 329). *Slicech* (or *Sligeach*) means 'place of shells' and is earliest attested in the Annals of Ulster at the year 543, *'bellum Slicighe'*. The editor has suggested to me that the long stone may be identified as the 'Sligo Stones' stated by Wood-Martin (1892, 122, 205) to have been marked near the Presbyterian Church on a 1766 map of Sligo and referred to in the 1783 Applotment Book as 'Back-Lane up to Sligo Stones'. Wood-Martin (1892, 122) also suggests that it is this stone circle which is depicted on the early Sligo Corporation seals. Over the years the stones got converted into shells - perhaps coming from the understanding of *Sligeach* as 'shelly place'. (The hare is depicted with his hind paw caught in one of the shells.) An archaeological interpretation might be that there was a standing stone set outside of a stone circle. I do not, however, see any connection between the 'longe stone' and the name *Sligeach*.]

3. This towne, though having but a soveraigne or provost magistratt thereof and haveing noe countie, yett it hath and still has a major and constable of the staple to (acknowledge) wood [?=word] and lake [?=take] cognizance or recognizance of any fame whatsoever. (?)

[The statement about the town 'having no county' presumably refers to an entity such as the 'County of the Town of Galway.' The second part of this paragraph does not make sense; the difficulty of deciphering some words does not help.]

Ballinafad Castle. Photo: Dúchas, The Heritage Service.

4. This priviledge belongs onelie to the abby lands in this towne, which abby is said by Sir James Ware to bee built by Maurice fz Gerald for the Order of Preachinge Fryers anno Domini 1252.

[See *MRHI* 229-230, where details are given of this Dominican foundation; see also *DPH* 264 and also Office of Public Works 1968.]

5. (Tralee Abby built for the same order by John fz Thomas de Geraldinis 1243, nine yeares before Sligoe.)

[*MRHI* 230. This passage is placed within brackets since it occurs in the left margin of the manuscript rather than in the body of the text.]

6. Here was a castle and bawne built by the said Fz Geralds in Sligoe afforesaid, and upon the building of the abby a monke made, as it's sayd, the ensueing verses:

Congeride lapidum varys constructa maximis
aut R[.]uet aut alter captor habebit eam.

[See O'Conor, this volume.

A - rather tentative - translation might be:

'(This building) put together from a huge mass of greatly varying stones will either collapse or another will take and hold it.']

7. [34v] Here is a lough about a mile above this town wherein are severall islands, lyeing southeast of the towne, called Loughgill, takeing its name from 'gile', whitenesse or clearenesse, but the river proceeding thence is called Garvoge, but by Ptolomeius, sayth Sir James Ware, Libninis or Livoeius fluvius (capto. x° Antiquit. Hiberniae Warei).

[There is an account of the supposed origin of the name *Loch Gile* in the medieval Irish *Dinnshenchus* (Gwynn 1924, 12-15) - lore of famous places. As mentioned above - §1 - the original name of the Garvoge was *Sligeach*. Ware's statement, *DHA* 54, that the river is called 'Libnius, al. Liboeus flu.' by Ptolemy seems to have little basis; it has recently been suggested that this latter name, LIBNIOS, denotes instead the River Laune, Co. Kerry - Mac an Bhaird 1991-1993, 4 and 6.]

8. Here is a salmon in season in this river for all seasons of the yeare. This river is neither verrie varied or slowe; it empties it selfe into the sea at a place called Inismoylclohy, about three myles below Sligoe. The flood in all springe and nipp tides flowes upon to the bridge of Sligoe.

[The place in question appears on the OS map as Inismulclohy or Coney Island, representing Irish *Inis Uí Mhaoil Chluithe*. The surname Ó *Maoil Chluiche* is nowadays generally anglicised Stone - of which there is a single instance in Griffith's *Valuation*, 1858, in the barony of Carbury.]

9. Out of this towne of Sligo (is) the Lords[hip] of Scudamore of HamLacy in Hereford shire is dignified.

[See *EP* 483 on the Scudamore family of Holme Lacy, Herefordshire: - 'John Scudamore, Esq., of Holme Lacy, ... was created a baronet, 1620, ... and was created Baron of Dromore, and Viscount Scudamore, of Sligo, by letters patent, 2 July, 1628.']

10. This towne and superioritie of the countie till 1641 did belonge to a sept of the O Connors of the race of Cataldus Crowderge, King of Connaught, brother to Roderick, last monarch of Ireland, of which Ó Connor of late was called O Connor of Sligoe, but a[ ]nter was called the lord of [35r] (of - *dittography*) the countrye below Curlew Mountaine which is all that countie of Sligoe.

[The family of O'Conor Sligo was not in fact derived from Cathal Crobhderg, king of Connacht, who died in 1224, but from a brother named Brian Luighnech who died in 1181 (see *NHI* 9, 158, 160). The suggestion here seems to be - and this is merely a guess - that the family's designation originally derived from the town of Sligo, but that later their title extended to the whole of the county established in the later sixteenth century. The Curlews - representing Irish *Corrshliabh*, anciently *Corrshliabh na Seaghsa* - are a well-known range of hills on the borders of Cos. Sligo and Roscommon. I am unable to make sense of the word which is sixth from the end of fo. 34v - there appear to be four letters between *a* and *nter* (?).]

11. Here is a fayre harbour and inroad for shipping of great burthen.

[For Sligo Harbour, see McTernan 1992.]

12. Here is a fayre sheere hill betweene Sligoe and the mayn ocean called Cnocknerea where there are great precipes of rocke and ayrie of hawkes.

[The name of this well-known hill, Knocknarea - located in par. Killaspugbrone - appears to represent Irish *Cnoc na Riabh*, 'the hill of the stripes/streaks', perhaps referring to the limestone layering of the mountain? It is called *Knocknarew* on the Down Survey map, Map 4 (= Map 21 old) from the 1650s and *Knocknereah Mountaine* on a map, (=map 21 old) of 1658 by William Boswell (cited in the Ordnance Survey Namebook for this parish). There have been several, sometimes quite fanciful, attempts at explaining this name. For details of this historic area, see McTernan 1993 and Bergh 1995.]

13. Within three myles thereof is Droumcleife, now a prebend and formerlie a bishop's seat and now and for many century past annexed or united to the see of Elphinn. In this Droumcliefe is a river running from Lough Dullane in Glancarbry called the Dullane or river of Droumclefe, where salmons are catched in the springe and sumer seasons.

[Tld Drumcliff Glebe, par. Drumcliff (*Droim Chliabh*), bar. Carbury and dioc. Elphin, was the site of an early Irish monastery founded by St Colm Cille - see *MRHI* 34-35. The Drumcliff River, flowing out of Glencar (Irish *Gleann an Chairthe*, rather than *Gleann Cairbre* - although the latter name appears on the Down Survey map of bar. Carbury, on the Co. Sligo side of the Leitrim border), is believed to have formerly borne the Irish name *Codhnach* - *IIy-F* 143 (and n. y), 278-279 (and n. j), 296-297 and 300-303. The other alternative names of the river and of the lake from which the river is said to flow (Glencar Lough) - as given by Downing - share an element with *Gleann Dalláin*, an alternative name for Glencar (*FM* V 1462-1463 & n. y, *FM* VI 1976-1977 & n. e, 2036-2037 & n. i - *sub annis* 1541, 1595 and 1597 respectively - and Bk. Fen. 402-403 & n.); they are *An Dallán* and *Loch Dalláin* respectively.]

14. This Barony of Carbry in which this towne stands is excellent good lande, only (?) where theirin extending in length from Belladrohidd three myles southwest of Sligoe to the River of Bunduvy about fifteen myles, but in former times in [*recte*, it] extended all to the River of Erny eight myles further.

[The places mentioned are, respectively: bar. Carbury; tld Belladrihid (par. Ballysadare, bar. Tirerrill); the Duff River (forming the boundary between Cos. Sligo and Leitrim); and the River Erne. Belladrihid (Irish *Béal an Droichid*) was known in ancient times as *Droichead Martra* - in the Middle Irish tale *Caithréim Cellaig* (Mulchrone 1971, 1, line 28; 32, line 37) and down to the earlier seventeenth century. The Duff (*An Dubh*) is called 'flumen quod dicitur Niger' in the writings of the late seventh-century bishop Tírechán (Bieler 1979, 160); its Irish form, *Dub*, occurs later in the same work (180) and in the ninth-century Vita Tripartita (*do Dúib* - Mulchrone 1939, 89); it occurs as *Bondufe river* in Tadhg Ó Rodaighe's account of Co. Leitrim, 1683 (Logan 1971, 329). The syntax immediately following *only (?)* is very puzzling; I am not at all sure that I have deciphered it correctly.]

15. This [35v] Barony of Carbry did belong to Ô Connor Sligoe as his demeasnes of his house of Sligoe, or else to his officers, as Ô Harte of Ardtarmun, Bradcullen, Ô Harte Grandge or Knocknesamur, or to others of the Ô Connors that were younger brauthers.

[The genealogies of Ó hAirt of *Ard Tearmainn* (tld Ardtermon, par. Drumcliff), *Brághaid Choillighe* (= tld Collinsford, par. Drumcliff, according to the index to *AConn.*, s.a. 1536.16) and *An Ghráinseach* (apparently representing Grange in par. Ahamlish, but see further below) are given in Dubhaltach Mac Fhirbhisigh's mid-seventeenth-century 'Book of Genealogies' (*Leabhar Genealach* - UCD Add. Ir. MS 14), 316. In relation to the last name(s) mentioned by Downing ('Grandge or Knocknesamur'), there are two townlands in the county called Knocknashammer - one in bar. Carbury and the other in bar. Coolavin. The first of these - called Knocknashammer or Cloverhill (a reasonable translation of *Cnoc na Seamar*) - lies (in par. Kilmacowen) east of the Carrowmore megalithic cemetery, and immediately east of four townlands (in par. Killaspugbrone) on the slopes of Knocknarea that contain the element 'Grange' - Grange East, North and West, and Primrosegrange. These are on record in the Fiants of Elizabeth, *e.g.* Fiant no. 1455 (AD 1569): *the Grange of Cowllhyrrye*, followed immediately by a reference to 'a new castle built by Hugh O'Harte', together with two further citations, *Cowleyrre and Tulskyrre*; the same names are repeated, in slightly different orthography, in Fiant 4407 (AD 1587): *the Graunge of Cowlehirrie ... a new castle built by Hugh O Hartie, and lands in the Graunge in same country ... Cowleycre or Cowlirrie*. (I am indebted to Patrick E. O'Brien and Martin A. Timoney for their interesting suggestions in relation to Grandge or Knocknesamur.)]

16. [36r] Tireragh Barony, Ô Dowde's Countrie. Next barony to this of Carbry, i.e., southwest thereof, is the barony of Tireragh or Ô Dowde's Country - this word Tirerhagh signifieing vulgarlie the westerne country, but it was rather Tirfechragh or Feaghra's various familia, of whom is descended Ô Dowdas afforesaid, Ô Shaghnussy, Ô Hine, and other lesser families in Connaught. See Sir James Ware, De Praesulibus, of the bishops of Kilmaduagh, or Duacensis, concerning this familie of Faghreavii.

[The explanation of the name of this barony, as *Tír Fhiachrach*, is correct; the alternative 'explanation' reflects the phonetic form of the name and is held to represent *Tír Iarthach*, which would arguably be a development of *Tír Iartharach* ('western country'). For details of the leading families of Uí Fhiachrach - Ó Dubhda, Ó Seachnasaigh, Ó hEidhin - see *Hy-F* 110-144, 56-58 and 64-68 respectively; the text of that work derives from Dubhaltach Mac Fhirbhisigh's *Book of Genealogies*. The final reference is to Ware's book, *DPH* 280: 'familiâ, Hy-fiachriorum'.]

17. This barony consists of twentie foure myles in length, from Balliassidarra Bridge to Ardnary nere the River of Moay. There is at every [?] miles, and of [?] and in this barony, a castle of greater or lesser note, and a river of [*recte*, or] rivulett of water of this bounded about two myles broad from the mountaynes of Slewgaffe in the east and the Virginian (??) sea in the west.

[The places mentioned are Ballysadare Bridge (at Ballysadare - *Baile Easa Dara* -tn, tld and par. in bars. Leyny and Tirerrill); Ardnaree (*Ard na Ria* - tn Ardnaree and td Ardnaree or Shanaghy, par. Kilmoremoy, bar. Tireragh); River Moy (*An Mhuaidh*) and Slieve Gamph or The Ox Mountains (*Sliabh Gamh*). The final name, referring to the sea, is very doubtful, some letters being difficult to decipher. If the name be as I read it, it no doubt refers to the North American colony of Virginia which in the seventeenth century was much more extensive than the present states of Virginia and West Virginia - The Virginian Sea, then, would represent an attempted alternative designation for the Atlantic. Finnes Moryson refers to Ireland as "this famous island in the Virginian Sea" in his *An Itinerary*, London, 1617. (I am grateful to Patrick E. O'Brien, Hon. Sec., Sligo Field Club, for his suggestions in relation to this last name.)]

18. This barony soone after the English invasion was enjoyed by the Lord Bermingham, Baron of Athenry or Atridei (?), but upon the disorder of the warrs of the houses of Yorke and Lancaster was totallie routed and rooted out thence by the Ô Dowdes, but one branch of that familie of the Bermingham since called Albanaghes or Scott, continued some lands called Rathleehy till 1641.

[For details of the presence of the de Berminghams in Tireragh see Knox 1917-1918 and Wood-Martin 1882, 201. The genealogy of the *Albanach*/Scott family is given by Dubhaltach Mac Fhirbhisigh in his 'Book of Genealogies', 824. He refers to them in his shorter genealogical work, the *Cuimre* (RIA MS 24 N 2, 399), as '*Albanuigh Ratha Shligheadh i tTír Fhiachrach Muaidhe*' - the placename corresponds to Downing's 'Rathleehy' and both represent tld Rathlee, par. Easky. The family also features prominently in the 1641 Depositions relating to the outbreak of rebellion in that year in Co. Sligo. The alternative name-form for Athenry (*Áth an Rí*), Co. Galway, looks more like one of the earlier forms of Ardee (*Áth Fhirdhia*), Co. Louth - 'Atherdee' or the like.]

19. [36v] Here is on the extreame south bonde of this barony of Tireragh with the countie of Mayo stands the abby called the abby of Ardnary of the order of the Eremitae of St. Augustine; it [is] generallie reported to bee built by the Berminghams afforesaide, but the founder is not mentioned by Sir James Ware.

[Ardnaree (in Co. Sligo until 1898, when it was transferred to Co. Mayo - see §17, above): see *MRHI* 295-296; also McDonnell 1976, 83-85; *DHA* 264.]

20. Here is within two myles upon the River of Moay afforesaid a most delicatt seat and castle called Castle-Connor, latelie Ô Dowde's mansion house, but said to be built by the said Berminghams, but by the Ô Dowdes said to bee built by them.

[Tld and par. Castleconor, bar. Tireragh. See Ó Muraíle 1985, 45. Also *Hy-F* 172-174.]

21. Here is about an English [mile] north east of Castle Connor afforesaid a great mount or mote called Rathmoylcaha which is hollow underneath for a great length and is said to bee a seat of the Flaineus (?) or place of worshipp in there time, where some urnes were found, as is said.

[On this notable ringfort see Herity 1970, 49-53, and Byrne 1972, 73-76. It is worth noting that only in the present document and in Dubhaltach Mac Fhirbhisigh's 'Book of Genealogies', 11, penned in 1650 in Galway, is the structure named; in the latter the name occurs as *Ráith Maoilcatha*. (This gave rise to the form employed by the Ordnance Survey - Rathmulcah.) The word which I read, rather
tentatively, as 'Flaineus' is a puzzle to me; perhaps the author intended a reference to the Fiana - or to the *Filí*?]

22. In this barony of Tireragh is the priory of the Canons Regulars of St. Augustine of Akeras als. Kilmaltin als. de Echrois, whereof Molaisse sive [=or] Lazarianus of Loughlin was first abbott and founder thereof, sayeth Sir James Ware.

[Tld Aughris (*Eachros*), par. Templeboy: *MRHI* 158; there now appears to be no trace of an ecclesiastical foundation in this townland; see also Timoney. M.A., 2002, Appendix II. The alternative designation, *Kilmaltin*, also occurs as *Kylmultin* in a document of 1584 (McDonnell 1976, 79). This place is referred to as *Lassariani* in a papal document of 1198 (McDonnell 1976, 12). Molaise was also associated with Kilglass, a parish in Tireragh, whose name is derived from *Cill Molaise* (see McDonnell 1976, 14); we get the form *Kilglass alias Kilmolaisse* in late sixteenth- and early seventeenth-century documents, but the apparently corrupt form occurs - as *Killoglass* - as early as Eccles. Tax. 1306; see also MacHale 1985, 57 *et seq*. I am unaware of Molaise's association with 'Loughlin' - perhaps *Loch Glinne* in Tirawley (par. Crossmolina - see *Hy-F* 240-241 n. k). Ware's reference to this place occurs in *DHA* 264.]

23. [37r] The Barony of Leichnia, Leyny, olim dict. Magher Leyney or Ô Harae's Countrie.

This barony containes from Balliassadarra Bridge to Bellahy about sixteene myles from north to south or south west, the northerne parte whereof verrie good limestone lands called Ô Hara Buy his country, and the south somewhat courser which was called O Hara Reavagh's Countrey.

[This territory bears the name of an ancient population-group, *Luigne*. (There is mention of *Machaire Luighne* in *FM* VI 1880 - sub anno 1589.) Another branch of this people gave name to the barony of Lune, Co. Meath. The Luigne, according to the early Irish genealogies, were closely related to a people called the Gailenga who gave name to the barony of Gallen in east Mayo (and also to the barony of Magheragallion - *Machaire Gaileang* - Co. Meath). Bellahy - *Béal Lathaí*, 'mouth or entrance to [the] muddy place' - is the tn and tld in par. Achonry, bar. Leyny, which adjoins Charlestown, Co. Mayo. On the families of Ó hEaghra Buí and Ó hEaghra Riabhach see McKenna 1951, xi-xxvii.]

24. In this northerne Lichnea or Liny stands the Cathedrall Church of Achonry, in Latine Achadensis or Achadense, now united to Killala or Alladensis. Within three or ffoure miles of Achonry in the same north territorrie or halfe barony is the auncient houses called Teatempla or Templehouse, formerlie belonging to the Knights Templars untill theire overthrow and dissolucion in anno 1313, and after there dispersion (?) in King Edward the Second's reigne it was made a praecentorie of the Knights of Hierusalem, [37v] and soe continued till the generall dissolucion in King Henry the Eighth's reigne.

[Achonry (*Achadh Conaire*): *MRHI* 60. In the Established Church (Church of Ireland) administrative system - which is what Downing has in mind here - the dioceses of Achonry and Killala were united since the time of the famous (or infamous) pluralist bishop Miler Magrath (c. 1522-1622). Templehouse (*Teach an Teampla*), par. Kilvarnet: *MRHI* 331, 342, and McKenna 1951, xxx-xxxi. King Edward II reigned 1307-1327 and Henry VIII 1509-1547. See *DHA* 265-266.]

25. In this barony of Liny is the monastery or abby of Assadara als. Ballyassadarra of the order of the Cannons of St. Augustine's built by Sanctus Fechinus (of the familie of the Haraes) in the seaventh ayre or century of Christ; this great saint dyed the 20th of January (16 - *partly written over*) DCLXV (?), sayth Sir James Ware. Hee was after abbott or founder of Foure in the countie of Westmeath where hee dyed the day and yeare abovesaid. This St. Fechinus is said to bee sometime abbott of Conge, so Sir James Ware.

[Ballysadare (*Baile Easa Dara*) *MRHI* 160. For a brief account of the life of St Féichín, see Mould 1964, 151-154. The saint's death - of the plague called *Buide Conaill* - is recorded in *AU* 665.3. Ware's reference to Féichín occurs in *DHA* 257, 265. See also Timoney, M.B., 2002.]

26. In this barony of Liny is likewise the house of ffrierie of Court, als. Smecourte, of the Third Order of St. Francis built by the said Ô Haraes.

[Court: *MRHI* 270. See Ware, *DHA* 265. The name occurs as *Coorte Abby*, par. Achonry, Pender 1939, 599; it appears on the OS map as *Abbey Court* just north of tld Lavagh (OS 32). The variant form *Smecourte* is a puzzle.]

27. [38r] In this barony of Liny, in the southwest parte thereof, is the priory of Benada Liny of the order of the Ermite of St. Augustine built by the familie of the Ô Haraes; it lyes in that division that was called Ô Hara Reaugh's Countrie.

[Tld Banada, par. Kilmacteige: *MRHI* 296; *DHA* 265.]

28. In this barony is the auncient house of Ô Harae Buy being demolished, the proprietor whereof was in 1641 Keon Ô Hara E..an (?), head of that familie or clann, the onelie mere Irish man who kept his estate in the late troubles in that province of Connaught.

[On Kean O'Hara (Cian Ó hEaghra mac Taidhg), who died in 1675, see McKenna 1951, xiv. The principal seat of the O'Haras was in tld Annagh More (or Annaghmore), par. Kilvarnet, bar. Leyny, and par. Ballysadare, bar. Tirerrill. I can only partly decipher the word following 'Keon Ô Hara'; it is written above the line and is a complete puzzle to me.]

29. Here was another auncient castle and house in this south parte of this barony called Bally Ô Hara or Ballyara belonging to Ô Hara Reagh afforesaid.

[Tlds Ballyara or Falduff and Ballyara (Knox), par. Achonry.]

30. Here is now reputed in this barony a ffort called the ffort of Belaky built in the late times; it is sometimes reputed parte of the countie of Mayo.

[Belaky: Bellahy - see §23, above. According to Kerrigan (1995, 97 and 102) the fort at Bellaghy, Fort Cromwell, was under construction in 1656 at a cost of £2,200 and was for one hundred men. (I am grateful to Martin A. Timoney for this reference.)]

31. [38v] In this barony of Liny begins the River of Mooey and so runns through the barony of Gallen and in the countie of Mayo.

[River Moy (*An Mhuaidh*): see Ó Muraíle 1985, 66.]

32. [39r] The Barony of Corren. This barony takes it[s] name from a fayre hill so called; the hill is likewise Ceas Corran. From this hill was Sir John Taaffe created Lord Viscount about the yeare 1628. His now Majestee, King Charles the Second, conferred the title of Earle of Carlingford on his son, Theobald Taaffe, Lord Viscount Corren and Lord Baron of Ballymote.

[The Irish names of the barony and hill are respectively Corann and Céis Chorainn. On Taaffe's title, see *CP* XII 595: 'John Taaffe, created Viscount Taaffe of Corren ... 1628'; *ibid*. III 28: Theobald, created Earl of Carlingford 26 June 1661.]

33. The chiefe towne herein in [*recte*, is] Ballymote afforesaid a qua the Lord Taaffe and Earle of Carlingford is Lord Baron.

[Tn. Ballymote, par. Emlaghfad, bar. Corran]

34. In this Ballymote is a verrie [ ] castle and ffoure towers on the great and high bawne built by Lord Ralph Ufford in King [ ]. Other sayde it was built by the familie of the Bourke whereof the Redd Earle is said to bee the man thereof that built it. [It] was mended and repaired by Sir George Bingham Kt., sometime Governor of Connaught, whose armes is on one of the said towers, engraven about 1580, to this day; it belongs since Queen Elizabeth's reigne to the heires of Sir William Taaffe, [39v] father of Sir John Taafe, Lord Viscount Corren and Baron thereof, but before that time it did belonge to a familie of the McDonnoughs called McDonnough of Corren.

[Ralph Ufford was appointed justiciar of Ireland in 1344 and died in 1346. Sir George Bingham, a brother to Sir Richard (*c*. 1528-1599), the controversial governor of Connacht, was not himself governor of Connacht but was military governor of Co. Sligo; he was ancestor to the earls of Lucan. There is now no trace of the arms to which Downing refers on any of the towers nor of any other record of it known to either the writage or the editor. Sir William Taaffe died in February 1631; his son, Sir John, created Baron of Ballymote and Viscount Taaffe of Corran in 1628 (see §32, above), died in January 1642. The family of Mac Donnchaidh an Chorainn was based at Ballymote; the famous late fourteenth-century manuscript known as the Book of Ballymote (*Leabhar Bhaile an Mhóta*) was written - at least in part - *c*. 1391 in the house of Tomaltach Mac Donnchaidh, lord of Corran, who died in battle in the autumn of 1397 (see Ó Concheanainn 1981). See Rogers 1994 for a modern description of the town.]

35. This familie built a ffrierie in this towne for the Third Order of the Franciscans.

[Ballymote (*Baile an Mhóta*): *MRHI* 268; *DHA* 265; see also Conlan 1991.]

36. Here is latelie found a virtuous well or spaw neere this towne which is much resorted (in mensibus non quibus R.)(?).

[I have not, as yet, located the spa well in question, but a published query by M.A. Timoney (1995, 10) elicited local knowledge of three spa wells - none any longer in use as such - in the vicinity of Ballymote. The three were respectively located in the townlands of Rathdooney More, Cloonkeevy and Bellanascarrow, all on OS 33. The Latin phrase appears somewhat corrupt; perhaps the intended suggestion is that the well in question was only resorted to in months whose names do not include the letter 'r' - May, June, July and August? The final letter in the phrase is written there as a Capital 'R'.

37. [40r] The Barony of Tirrerill or McDonnough of Tirrerill's Countrie. The chefe towne in this barony was Ballindoone, the house of abode of McDonnough afforesaid.

[The reference here is to the family of Mac Donnchaidh Tíre hOilealla. There are numerous references to *Baile an Dúin* in *AConn*.; see also next paragraph. There is no town, nor even a village, at Ballindoon today.]

38. Here was a priorie of the Order of ffryers Preachers or Dominicans built by the said ffamilie but [not?] mentioned when by Sir Ja. Ware.

[Ballindoon (*Baile an Dúin*), par. Killadoon: *MRHI* 222; *DHA* 265.]

39. Here was an auncient castle and bawne of the said McDonnoughs.

[In tld Barroe South, par. Killadoon, south of the Dominican priory. There are remnants of the castle at the corner of a grass covered bawn.]

40. Here is likewise in the barony the towne of Coloony, a qua the Lord Baron Coote of Coloony dignified, formerlie belonging to another branch of this familie.

[The placename Collooney (*Cúil Mhuine*) is discussed and elucidated in de hÓir (1967). See *CP* III 415-416: Richard Coote (1620-1683) was created Baron Colloony 6 September 1660. See McGarry 1993 for a modern description of the town.]

41. Here is nere the towne of Ballindoone afforesaid a great lough called Lough Arwaugh, from whence flowes the River of Funshinagh which runns downe to Coloony and where it meets the River of Avonmore but which [ ] into theire ocean at the fall of Ballissadarra.

[Lough Arrow: *Loch Arbhach*, *FM* VI 1886 (*sub anno* 1590); *Loch Farbach*, *AConn*. 1398.6; *ALC* II 82 (*sub anno* 1598). See also *Innsi Locha Arbach*, *AU* 1053.1; *ALC* I 50 (*sub anno* 1053). Unshin River (*An Fhuinseanach*): there are references to the river as *Teora hUinseanna Ua nOilealla* ('The three

Unshins of *Uí Ailealla'*) in *FM* I 32 (*anno mundi* 3503) and in the medieval *Lebar Gabála* ('Book of Invasions' Macalister 1956, 170). Owenmore (*An Abhainn Mhór*) is mentioned in *Bk. Fen.* (1516) 396 and *FM* VI 2016 (*sub anno* 1597); called *Owenmore* in a document dated *c*. 1635 in Wood-Martin 1885, 186.]

42. Here are two small houses of the order of the Crotched ffryers or Praemonstratenses or the order of the Holy Trinitie for the redemption of captives [40v] imprisoned by pagans; the one whereof called Kilamoy or the other Kilras - both which were coells belonginge to the Abby of the Holy Trinitie of Loughkoea in Moylurge or McDermott's Countrie in the countie of Roscomon, built by Clarus McMailin, archdeacon of Elphinn, who dyed on Pentecost Sunday 1251. This Clarus McMaylin built an abby of the same order of the Trinitarii in Lough Oughter in the countie of Cavan in 1249 (see Sir J. Ware).

[Athmoy: *MRHI* 204; Kilross, *ibid*. 205; Loughkey, *ibid*. 205. *Kilamoy & Kilras* in *DHA* 265 (see *Killamoy*, par. Kilmactranny, Pender 1939, 606; *Kilrasse* - par. Kilross - *ibid*.). The name Killamoy is now apparently obsolete. The death of Clarus Mac Maílín is recorded in *AConn*. 1251.2; see also a reference to the same individual in relation to Loch Uachtair in Bréifne, *AConn*. 1250.11; *DHA* 224.]

43. Here was likewise in this barony of Tirrerill an aunciect castle and great fortifications called Belanafadd, which place belonges to the Archb[ishop] of Tuam.

[Tlds Ballinafad (*Béal an Átha Fada*) and Gortalough, par. Aghanagh.]

44. This barony is generallie verrie [ ] lands, especiallie for grasinge.

45. Here is in this baronie a (verrie) place called Doon Pallar, a Balthazaro or Ballar, King of Norway, who built this fort (or [41r] dunum by the Latines). This Balthazar is said to have invaded Ireland before the incarnation of Christ and to bee killed by Lue, Loz or Lozh (Lugh Lafadda), so called from the eacesume (?) length of his armes which this Lozh, expelling the Danes out of the northerne and northeast parts of Ireland, it is said that they did not them make any thourow conquest till DCCXCVIII in Ireland.

[The name *Dún Balair* occurs in the medieval Irish tale *Cath Maighe Rath* (apparently in relation to Tory Island); there appears to be no instance of such a name in medieval or early modern Irish-language sources relating to Co. Sligo. Not having exhaustively searched all other available sources, I cannot say categorically that no such name is attested in Co. Sligo, but I would be far from surprised should it turn up. After all, the celebrated mythological tale *Cath Maige Tuired* - dating probably from the ninth century and relating to a supposed 'Second Battle' of that name - was set in tld Moytirra, par. Kilmactranny, in this barony of Tirerrill; and one of the tale's principal protagonists was Balor mac Dóit, leader of the Fomoire, who was - as Downing correctly states - killed by Lug Lámfhata of the Tuatha Dé Danann. For details of this mythical battle see O'Rahilly 1946, 388-390, *etc*.; and for a modern edition of the text, see Gray 1982. (See also Morris 1928, 111-127 - although O'Rahilly dismisses this article as 'lengthy, but unconvincing (and not always accurate)'.) The equation of the Danes and Fomoire is interesting. (The word followed by a question-mark appears to represent 'awsome'; the date in Roman numerals is 798.)]

46. [42r] The halfe barony of Colovine or Garae's Countrie. In his halfe barony or territorie is the house of mendicants said to be built by the said familie, it being but barelie mentioned by Sir James Ware and marked FC, id est fratruum (*sic*) mendicantium coenobium.

[Bar. Coolavin (*Cúil Ó bhFinn*): *t*erritory of Ó Gadhra. The religious house referred to is called "Knockmore Abbey' on OS map 44 of Co. Sligo - in tld Mountirvine *alias* Knockmore, par. Kilfree. See *MRHI* 290 and *DHA* 265.]

47. Here is but (?) territorie Moyogarra an auncient house of that familie.

[Tld Moygara (*Maigh Uí Ghadhra*), par. Kilfree.]

48. Here were seaven townes of this territorie beyond Lough Ô Gara now in the countie of Roscomon; in these seaven formerlie belonging to Ô Gara stands the house of nunns of Killaraght, properlie Kilatract from Athracta for whom St. Patricke built this house, sayth Sir James Ware.

[The townlands in question are the portion of the parish of Kilaraght which lies to the southeast of Lough Gara (*Loch Uí Ghadhra* - anciently *Loch Teichead*); that area is now divided into sixteen townlands. Killaraght (*Cill Athracht*): *MRHI* 320-321; see *DHA* 262. For details of St. Athracht, see Mould 1964, 31-32. The Lough Gara Cultural Resources map shows the area in question.]

49. This territorie beyond the lough that is now in the countie of Sligoe thereof is generalie woody tourfe (?) and mountaynous.

[The third last word is very difficult to decipher; my reading is accordingly very tentative. The lough in question is Lough Gara.]

THE ANTIQUITIES OF SLIGO IN 1779
AS SEEN BY LEWIS IRWIN OF TANREGO HOUSE

Peter Harbison
Loughshinny, Skerries, Co. Dublin and Royal Irish Academy

ABSTRACT: Lewis Irwin of Tanrego House, Beltra, Co. Sligo, wrote in March 1779, presumably to Col. William Burton, in response to a letter from Gabriel Beranger seeking help as regards proposals to sketch the antiquities of Co. Sligo and surrounding counties. In the letter Irwin offer help and in June and July 1779 he accompanied Gabriel Beranger and Angelo Maria Bigari on their tour.

When Col. William Burton[1], Col. Charles Vallancey[2], the Rev. Edward Ledwich[3], the famous Connacht antiquary Charles O'Conor of Belanagare and others assembled in Dublin in February 1779 to found the Hibernian Antiquarian Society[4], they kindled a new interest in Irish antiquities which fortunately still burns spiritedly in many a breast today. One of the aims of this Society, was to publish volumes of engravings illustrating the 'Antiquities and Curiosities of Ireland'[5] in order to make the country's monuments more widely known and appreciated. Sadly, the project never came to fruition, but some of the material collected for the purpose eventually found its way into Grose's *Antiquities of Ireland*, which was edited by Ledwich and published in two volumes during the 1790s.

William Burton, who was a man of influence and taste in the Irish Ascendancy society of his day, prepared his ground well by sending around what today we would call a brochure to his friends and contacts throughout the length and breadth of the land, asking for their help not only in identifying antiquities worth recording in their locality, but also in providing guidance for the artists whom he intended sending on tour to execute the necessary drawings. Of the two artists whom he sent to Connacht in 1779, one was an Italian named Angelo Maria Bigari[6], and the other was Gabriel Beranger, whose cause Sir William Wilde was to champion in the 1870s[7].

In the case of County Sligo, the contact would seem to have been made by Beranger himself who, in a communication which has not survived, asked assistance for the project from Lewis Irwin of Tanrego House near Beltra, whose acquaintance Beranger appears to have made previously. He could not have chosen a better contact, for Irwin obviously already had an intimate knowledge of the antiquities of his native county, and proved to be a most enthusiastic supporter of Burton's aspirations. His initial reaction to the request for assistance has been preserved for us in a long letter, written presumably to Burton, and preserved for us on pages 149-154 of Manuscript 1415 in the National Library of Ireland in Dublin. As the letter gives us considerable insight into those antiquities of the County which were of interest to an enthusiastic dilettante of the period, it is worth publishing here in full as on offering for this volume commemorating many years of fieldwork, outings and lectures of the Sligo Antiquarian Society and its successor Sligo Field Club.

This is the letter:

Tanrego, March 26th, 1779

Sir,
I this day received a Letter from Mr. Beranger, as he informs me by your Directions, to acquaint me that the Antiquarian Society had wished my assistance for the Artists to be employed by them, as also a communication of such particulars as my mean Capacity may be deemed worthy of Notice.

In this County, the Barony of Tireragh seems most replete with objects worthy the attention of an Antiquarian, not that the rest are destitute of Vestiges not to be overlooked, but that being maritime retains the traces of the earliest Inhabitants. Should the artists begin their Progress from the northward by Ballyshannon, thro Carbury Barony, which also lies on the sea, the first and greatest Object is the Island now known as Innismurray, and perhaps always as dedicated to the Virgin, altho Usher or rather Author of the Addenda spells it Inis Comera (see the Dublin Edition *de Primordiis Ecclesiarum* AD

1639, page 1066) this lies about three leagues in the Sea between that coast and Killibegs and as the first asylum of Columbkille after the battle of Clundarub[?] is really the Mother Church of the famous Island Hy or Iona in Scotland, so celebrated by Johnson and other Travellers. It is full strange rude antiquities and superstitious Legends, to long here to enumerate, next in that Barony on the Shore is Drumclief said once to have contained fifty religious Houses, many traces of edifices are visible, but nothing to throw any distinct Light; it was formerly a distinct bishoprick, but now incorporated with Elphin. The Abbey of Sligo is next in Place, and near the town up the river two large cairns, or cromlech, and westward a Number of small circles of large stones surrounding three others supporting a still larger, just beyond those on Top of a great Hill, the immense cromlech, by much the largest I ever saw. about five or six miles up the river is the old castle of Drumahaire, where the Famous Hall wherein O'Rorks noble Feast was celebrated, is to be seen, and the ruins of an old abbey beautifully situated over a fine water fall. higher up the country in that direction nothing interesting is to be seen. pursuing the sea coast westward the five Waterfalls at Ballisadare present themselves and some Ruins of an old Augustine Abby. two miles farther is a large strand, to this day called Cuchullen Strand, and a Burial place shown for his on a Rock, and all the Denominations environing it correspond with the names recorded in [Macpherson's] *Fingal*. crossing that Tireragh is entered, I think more fertile in old remains than any country I ever saw; it is a narrow stripe four and twenty miles long, and not three broad between the ridge of mountains and the Sea, at each miles end runs a River and stands a Castle, and the Vestiges of old circular Forts called Danish, with subterraneous caves, stand as thick and close almost as the Foundations of Houses in many cities; some considerably large, some of those circular arrangements of stones already mentioned like Stonehenge, but much smaller, here and there some structures which appear to me like some Druidical alter or place of Worship, they general Consist of six large stones, sometimes four, of a vast size near six feet above ground, placed three on aside enclosing an Area of perhaps ten feet by six, open at one End, on the other nearly closed by an odd stone of the same size, sufficient however to afford Entrance for a man, just before this stone placed another with a flatt face uppermost above the Height of the Knee; this supposed was the altar and the apperture an Entrance for the Priest, whilst the other extreme was open to the assisting Congregation. in one place, on a high Hill is a large rock, which I cannot avoid conjecturing to be a Rocking stone, it is as I recollect about six feet Diameter, irregularly roundish, and supported on the Point of a Rock, on one side elevated above two feet from the surface, and the other gradually declining a little, without any such near it; Nature could not form it there, chance could not stop, nor Art without violent Efforts, stop any Efforts in a progressive Motion there, and for what other Purposes Men could erect it there, I am not sufficiently informed to decide. in this Barony and apart almost inaccessible for Bogs and Morasses, stands Fin Mac Coils Gridle as called by the common people, eight long narrow flag shaped stones, thin but sufficient to support the incumbent Weight, and fixed on the End in the ground, on the outside where the soil has grown up they are visible for about four feet, within where sheep have worn away the soil for shelter, above five; on these is placed on the convex side a larger, about nine feet in length, and six feet in breadth, having the appearance of a perpendicular and lesser segment of a cylinder, not through the axis but the third of the Base, with the plane Surface layed upwards and horizontally on these four stones, having in fact the Appearance of a Gridle, it can scarcely be doubted to be an altar, and probably for some druidical Holocaust. this process through this Barony terminates the County at the influx of the river Moy, which separates it from the County of Mayo, on the opposite Banks of which are the ruins of the fine Abbeys of Moyne and Rosserk, with the old tower of Killalla, with these limits also my Information Ends. farther than that the inland Baronies of the County of Sligo offered little that I have perceived for the Antiquarian Enquirer, some danish Forts excepted, a Crumleach at Heapstown, the Castles of Ballymote and Moigara, and the Abbeys of Court and Banada; Boyle Abbey tho in another county is so near, it is worthy inspection I have seen two views of the latter but none interesting farther than an Ancient Ruin; whereas the Style of Gothick architecture is peculiar and the most airy and elegant, with more real Strength than I ever saw; from the high surrounding Walls this is only discernible at the Inside, and to be communicated by an internal perspective of the Edifice; I have twice lately when there unfortunately interrupted by heavy Rains, but shall repeat my Attempts till I succeed, should not the artists employed by the Society anticipate me. This is said by Cambden to be built in 1152.

As I wished to communicate the earliest Information of the particulars that the Society did me the honour to demand I have as briefly as the Space for and Compass of a Letter permits acquainted them with such particulars as in the short Period occurred to my Recollection, many I know I have omitted, and many not sufficiently dwelt upon, but which will all occurr in the trail I have prescribed, which I think had best commence either from the Westward by Ballina in the Barony of Tyrawley in the County of Mayo, or from the Northward by Ballishannon; as the county of Roscommon is sterile in Matter, the Castles of Roscommon, & Ballintober, the Residence of our last Monarch of Ireland & a very few others excepted. For many obvious reasons maritime Counties or Districts were most thickly inhabited, and most subject to Invasion, consequently most fitted with indigenal, as well as foreign Antiquities. indeed from Circumstances and Geographical Probabilities as well as such Vestiges, I cannot avoid conjecturing that this county if not the first, at least the most frequented Avenue of Danish incursions. of the proper Rout however the Society will be the best Judges from their other Informations and objects, I must however beg that you may assure them, that on proper Notice some days previous to their Artists entering the County, and at what approach, I shall meet them and afford every assistance and protection in my power. one thing I must beg leave to promise, that a clerk conversant in the Irish language will throughout be a very necessary attendant on the Party and such Books as can aid them or the Gentlemen of the County through which they pass, from the matters therein suggested, to make further Enquiries from those Inhabitants where such Places have stood, of the particulars worthy remarking.

Mr. Berenger in his Letter seems to imply that you yourself propose making a tour of this County, when you are determined on the time it shall take Place, I must entreat that you will honour me with the earliest notice of the time and from what quarter, as I shall do myself the Pleasure to wait on you before you enter it, to offer my Services as a Guide, on which Occasion I shall only premise that altho you may find more qualified and Respectable, you will not find a more assiduous or attentive Conductor. from a person totally unknown, this Profession may seem extravagant and outrée, but the gentleman who has avowed not only the Patron, but acts as the first Spring in so laudable Enterprize, which had I powers or Abilities, it would be my Pride to emulate, must receive my Applause and Esteem, with high Sentiments of both I therefore subscribe myself
Sir
Your most obedient and most humble servant
Lewis Irwin

Time would scarce permit me to write, & cannot read over this. Your own good Understanding must supply Defects, it will of course excuse

COMMENT

William Burton probably never managed to tour the antiquities of County Sligo, but the two artists, Bigari and Beranger, spent most of the period from June 19th to July 11th, 1779, happily sketching them - and with what great success can be judged by Beranger's diary (now lost) of the trip, from which William Wilde published lengthy extracts[8]. The same National Library manuscript album containing Lewis Irwin's letter transcribed above also preserves a series of unpublished letters (pp. 75-101) in which Beranger tells the recipient [presumably Burton] about his travels in Connacht, though these duplicate to a considerable extent the diary extracts published by Wilde. A further letter in the volume (pp. 61-74) written some years later (1785) to Col. Vallancey and recently reproduced *in extenso* in *Ireland of the Welcomes* magazine[9] gives a fascinating account of the trip to Inishmurray, where Irwin, Beranger and Bigari, encountered 'Irishmen in the true state of nature, hospitable, innocent and merry'.

Faithful to his word, also expressed in a further letter in the same volume,[10] Irwin accompanied the two artists throughout their 'Expedition' to County Sligo, and proved to be invaluable. Beranger found him to be not only 'an excellent guide but a good ingenier & helps us with infatigable aclarity in taking ye plans of the antiquities'[11]. The artists became 'so expert under the command of Capt. Irwin that at one view we discover what was antique and what was added tho' some centuries ago'[12]. Beranger found Irwin to be a 'man made of steel'[13] and when at last they had to part company with him at Newport (-Pratt) in Co. Mayo, because Irwin got a pain in his foot (which Wilde, the surgeon, was able to diagnose as gout), Beranger expressed 'sorrow in being deprived of him, he not only was an agreeable Companion but an excellent guide and assistant in planning & measuring, in all our Collateral Excursions'[14]. The cost of the whole trip, hospitality included, was paid for entirely by Irwin, and so it is not surprising to find Beranger concluding on one occasion that 'Our table is rather too elegant, but such is the man un tres galant homme, zealous in the cause'[15].

May his zealous spirit long live on in the capable hands of his spiritual successor - The Sligo Field Club!

Acknowledgement

I would like to express my thanks to the Trustees of the National Library of Ireland for their permission to reproduce Capt. Irwin's letter from their Ms. 1415.

Notes

1. C.E.F. Trench, 'William Burton Conyngham (1733-1796)', *Journal of the Royal Society of Antiquaries of Ireland*, 115, 1985, 40-63.
2. Vallancey was then the Chief Engineer of Ireland.
3. At the time, rector of Aghaboe in Co. Laois, and later to become the author of *Antiquities of Ireland* (1790; second edition 1804).
4. Walter D. Love, 'The Hibernian Antiquarian Society', *Studies* 51, 1962, No. 203, 419-431.
5. The description comes from a letter of March 15th, 1779, written by Thomas Campbell, probably to Burton, and preserved on p. 131 of the manuscript album 1415 in the National Library of Ireland in Dublin.
6. He was an architect and theatrical scene painter from Bologna.
7. Wilde wrote a number of articles about Beranger during the 1870s in what is now the *Journal of the Royal Society of Antiquaries of Ireland*, and these were reprinted, together with a final article which Wilde did not live to see, in a volume produced after his death by his widow, the poetess 'Speranza', entitled *Memoir of Gabriel Beranger, and his labours in the cause of Irish Art and Antiquities, from 1760 to 1780* (Dublin 1880). In his Memoir (pp. 51-52), Wilde pointed out that one of the drawings made during the tour - M'Dermott's Castle in Lough Key - was not attributed to Beranger by the book's editor, Edward Ledwich, though it should have been. Otherwise, all the drawings from the tour engraved in Grose were by Bigari.

Original drawings by Beranger in the Royal Irish Academy and the National Library of Ireland in Dublin respectively have been published in two books edited by Dr. Peter Harbison: *Beranger's Views of Ireland* (Dublin, Royal Irish Academy, 1991) and *Beranger's Antique Buildings of Ireland*, Dublin Four Courts Press in association with the National Library of Ireland (1998). The Irwin letter which forms the focus of this article is now also reproduced in the author's book 'Our Treasure of Antiquities', Beranger and Bigari's Antiquarian Sketching Tour of Connacht in 1779, where more detail is provided for the background of this letter.

For a photograph of Tanrego House see Martin Wilson, "Tanrego" in O'Horo, Michael, ed., 2000, *Skreen & Dromard, Past & Present, History & Heritage*, Skreen, Skreen & Dromard Parishes, 45.

8. Wilde, Memoir (n.7).
9. Vol. 42, No. 5, September - October 1993, 30-33. See also John C. McTernan, *In Sligo Long Ago*, (Sligo, Avena, 1998), 9-13.
10. National Library of Ireland Ms 1415, pp. 155-156.
11. *ibid.*, p. 79.
12. *ibid.*
13. *ibid.*, p. 87.
14. *ibid.*
15. *ibid.*, p. 80.

APPENDIX

Monuments in Cos. Sligo, Leitrim & Roscommon Drawn by Beranger and/or Bigari, June & July 1779, according to NLI Ms. 4162.

JUNE:

17	Stayed in Manorhamilton, Co. Leitrim.
19 & 20	Abbey of Sligo
22	Abbey of Drumahare, Co. Leitrim.
22	Church Island, Lough Gill
22	O'Rourke's Hall, Dromahaire
23	Cromleagh, etc., Carrowmore
23	Misgan Mewe, on Knocknarea
24	Drumcliffe
24 & 25	Ennismurray Island (Inishmurray)
26	Stayed at Inn in Sligo
28	Abbey of Balisadare (Augustinian)
28	Balisadare church
28	Balydoon Abbey (Ballindoon)
28	Carn Oliolla or Heapstown
28	Stayed in Boyle, Co. Roscommon
28 & 29	Abbey Boyle, (Cistercian)
28 & 29	Ennisnacreeny (Inchmacnerin)
28 & 29	McDermot's Island, Lough Key
30	Ballimote Castle
30	Ballymote Church (Franciscan)
30	Stayed at Tubbercurry

JULY

1	Abbey of Banada (Augustinian)
1	Abbey of Court (Franciscan)
1	Castle of Ballynafad
4	Cuchullin's Tomd (Ballisodare Bay)
5	Stayed at Tanrego
6	Clogg Glass
7	Cloghmorkit (rocking stone)
7	Hill of Skrine (Farranyharphy/Carrowculleen)
7	Stayed at Tubberpatrick
8	Finnmacool's Griddle (Tawnatruffaun)
8	Knockmallagrish (rath).
8	Stayed at Fortland
10	Rosslee Castle (Bunowna)
11	Rathmulcagh rath (Rinroe)

Beranger (NLI Ms 4162, f. 15) records that Cloghmorkit rocking stone is at the foot of the Hill of Skrine and that Knockmallagrish can be equated with Lishangan, or, in English, Fortland.

George Gabriel Stokes, A Sligo Born Scientist

John O'Dea
School of Science, Institute of Technology, Sligo.

Ireland is a country where any stone or grave is upturned to find famous or infamous sons and daughters that might bring prestige and indeed commercial advantage to a county. Thus Sligo is synonymous with the name Yeats given that one brother was a literary figure of world renown and the other an artist of European significance. Yet there is another who remains almost totally anonymous in the county where he was born and raised and is a person of world stature in his chosen field. Maybe it is a reflection of the relative positions that the Irish assign to literature rather than science and mathematics that George Gabriel Stokes, born in Skreen in 1819 remains such an unknown.

The Stokes family has been traced back to 14th century Gloucestershire with the Irish branch originating in the 17th century when John Stokes came here as an engineer in the service of the Deputy Surveyor General. It was a family that were more intellectually endowed than wealthy and had a long history of service to the church and education in Trinity College, Dublin. George was the youngest son of Gabriel Stokes, the Anglican rector in Skreen, County Sligo, a man who is remembered by an inscription in Skreen rectory as having been mild, sincere and pious. His father was considered taciturn and his mother, Elizabeth Haughton, daughter of the rector in Killala, beautiful but stern. He was largely raised by his older sister Elizabeth who claimed that while George had quite a temper he never told a lie.

George lived his first 13 years under the shadow of the Ox mountains in what his daughter Isabella described as "rustic simplicity". Here he was educated in the classics by his father and in mathematics by the parish clerk, George Coulter. He then studied in Dublin for three years where his exceptional ability with mathematics attracted attention. His father died in 1834 but his mother, despite her meagre circumstances and with the assistance of some friends, was able to allow him complete his second level education in Bristol. The family moved to Malahide and it appears that George never returned to Sligo.

From here he matriculated to Cambridge where he graduated in 1841 as a prize student and thus began an illustrious career at Cambridge where he was immediately elected a fellow of his college, Pembroke. By 1849 he was elected Lucasian Professor of Mathematics a chair held by Isaac Newton and presently by Stephen Hawking, author of 'A Brief History of Time'. Despite this being a position with a prestigious past it was, however, poorly endowed thus making it necessary for the holder at the time to supplement his imcome by other means such as teaching elsewhere.

His life was one of enormous achievement in mathematics and science which was duly acknowledged in the long list of awards and positions of importance he attained. These include Fellowship of the Royal Society (1851), Secretary (1854) and President (1885) of same, MP for Cambridge University 1887 and

Fig. 1 - Sir George Gabriel Stokes. Photo: © The Royal Society.

STOKES 1682-2002

George Stokes
1682-1751
Mathematical Instrument maker
Deputy Surveyor General, Dublin

John
1716-1782
Regius Prof. of Greek, TCD

Gabriel
1732-1806
Prof. of Maths., TCD

John Haughton
Rector of Killala

Gabriel m. (1798) Elizabeth
Rector of Skreen, Co. Sligo

Whitley
1763-1845
Medical Fellow, TCD

Sarah
b. 1799

William
1804-1878
Regius Prof. of Physic

Henry
1808-1883
County Surveyor. Kerry
<u>Madras branch</u>

John Whitley
Archdeacon of Armagh
Aughnacloy
Willian Haughton
Fellow of Caius, Cambridge

Sir William
1839-1900
Prof. RCSI

Whitley
m. into George Stoney family
= Alan Turing, Logician

Henry George

Henry John
Indian Civil Service

William Noel   **Barbara**

Elizabeth Mary
Malahide

Whitley

Elizabeth   m. Charles Henry Crookshank

Sarah Ellen

Helen   m. Joseph Haughton

Alexander
d. 1809

Thomas Romney Robinson
FRS, Astronomer, Armagh

Anne
Prof. of Fine Art, TCD

George Gabriel m. [1859] **Mary Susanah Robinson**
1819-1903   d. 1899
Laucasian Professor, Cambridge
Fellow of Royal Society

John Herbert Jellett
Provost, TCD

Susannah Elizabeth
died in infancy

Janet   m. William Morgan

Dora Susanna
died in infancy

Mainie Jellett
Artist

Arthur Romney
Schoolmaster, Shrewsbury

William George
Medical Doctor, d. 1893

Compiled by Prof. Alistair Wood DCU, with acknowledgements
to Prof. David Simms, TCD, for right-hand branch

Isabella Lucy m. (1889) Lawrence Humphrey
Medical Doctor

Fig. 2 - Stokes Family Tree, 1682-, Compiled by Prof. Alistair Wood, DCU, with acknowledgments to Prof. David Simms, TCD, for right-hand branch.

knighthood in 1892. The greatest recognition is surely that of one's peers and the fiftieth jubilee of his tenure of the Lucasian chair was celebrated by an impressive collection of the world's foremost scientists. The photographic record of the gathering includes such notables as Becqueral who discovered radioactivity and Helmholtz who formulated the general law of the conservation of energy.

In Cambridge he belonged to a prestigious triumvirate who established for Cambridge the predominant position and reputation in the world of mathematical physics. The other two were William Thomson (Belfast born and known as Lord Kelvin) who established much of modern thermodynamics and has given his name to the scientific temperature scale and James Clerk Maxwell from Scotland whose contribution to electricity and magnetism parallels Newton's accomplishments in mechanics. Unfortunately Maxwell died at the relatively young age of forty eight but Stokes and Kelvin continued to share the keenest interest in the advancement of scientific discovery and a lifelong friendship.

Stokes always remained a student, continually pondering over mathematical problems and the causes of natural phenomena. He was noted as a silent but formidable man. Along with his reticence went an over cautious nature which made him reluctant to draw conclusions from his work and slow to publish it. It is now acknowledged that many ideas attributed to others had previously been mooted by Stokes. In 1859 Kirchoff and Bunsen announced an exciting discovery on how the analysis of light (spectra) from the sun and the stars could reveal much information of their composition and nature. Kelvin soon claimed that Stokes had in 1852 recognised such a possibility.

Fig. 3 - Stokes Monument at Skreen with Skreen Rectory of 1960s in the background. Photo: M.B. Timoney

Despite such reticence and caution Stoke's contribution is still prodigious and he is honoured in having a law of science called after him. His first published papers in the early 1840s were on the motion of incompressible fluids (liquids) and the internal friction in fluids (viscosity). Galileo's famous dropping of the stones from the leaning tower of Pisa displayed that falling bodies continue to accelerate (get faster) when in free fall. These same stones dropped into a liquid would soon reach a steady speed (terminal velocity) and Stokes produced a simple equation (F = 6prhv) that related this terminal velocity to other relevant variables such as the size of the object and the viscosity of the fluid. This equation is now known as Stoke's Law.

His interests and areas of enquiry were wide ranging and included, how the wind effects the loudness (intensity) of sound, how clouds are suspended in the air, how ripples and waves on water subside, the flow of water in rivers and canals, the respiratory function of haemoglobin and geodesy.

Later in the forties he turned his attention to the study of optics which was to become his major interest. Just as sound cannot travel through a vacuum it was assumed (since Newton) that the propagation of any wave motion needs a medium and in the absence of an observable one for the propagation of light it was assumed that one called the *aether* existed. Stokes developed mathematical equations for the propagation of vibratory disturbances through this aether. Further work in optics involved the study of the aberration and polarisation of light. He discovered that certain materials such as flourspar emitted visible light when illuminated by ultraviolet radiation (which is invisible) and accordingly named this phenomenon fluorescence. As a by-product of this work he also discovered that whereas ordinary glass is opaque to ultraviolet light (therefore you do not get a suntan in a conservatory) one could use quartz prisms and lenses to disperse and focus UV light.

The bulk of Stoke's work concentrated on straight physics topics. More than half of his written output of over one hundred papers and memoirs concerned optics with about a quarter relating to hydrodynamics and acoustics. Even though only one tenth of his writings were purely mathematical it is important to realise the extent to which he brought his astounding mathematical ability to bear on the analysis of physical problems. He was very interested in the mathematics of convergent and divergent series, exponentials and asymptotics. Much of his work in asymptotics was ignored by his contemporaries but has more recently been resurrected and re-interpreted. Appropriately a six month workshop of this area of mathematics was held in 1995 in Cambridge. One of his interesting accomplishments was to "unweave the rainbow" (Keats) by producing the complex mathematical equations that explain the faint light patterns, called supernumeraries, that one can sometimes observe around the central rainbow (originally explained by Newton's prism experiments). He also has a mathematical equation, Stoke's Theorem, erroneously called after him. This theorem was actually discovered by Kelvin but first saw the light of day when Stokes included it on an examination paper in Cambridge. Although, in keeping with the scrupulous character of the man, he always acknowledged its true authorship of the theorem, it continues to bear his name.

The copious output of Stokes in the early years slackened in his midlife as he became involved in various administrative and facilitative duties in Cambridge and the Royal Society. It is widely recognised that he was very generous in his help and assistance to those who requested it and that his editorial advice frequently added to memoirs at the Royal Society. While in the Royal Society he was in commumication with many Irish scientists and he edited many of the Irish papers submitted to the Society. Thus he was well informed of the work of his Irish comtempories and not as remote from his native island as is sometimes thought. He was also the scientific adviser to Ireland's most prestigous manufacturers of scientific instruments, the Grubb Company who availed of his great knowledge of optics. His generosity in assisting and encouraging others was acknowledged in *The Times* obituary which noted that Stokes was remarkable for his freedom from all personal ambitions and petty jealousies.

Stokes was a man of quiet disposition and a deep religious conviction who occasionally went to print on theological matters. In an era when ideas on evolution and the age of the planet abounded he was very concerned that science and religion should not be at loggerheads. In 1857 he married Mary Robinson daughter of the Armagh astronomer Arthur Romney Robinson. They had two sons and a daughter Isabella. She ascribed his legendary silence, especially in Parliament, to advice from his brothers when leaving for college in Bristol, not to give "long Paddy answers". In her eyes he was an Irishman, a Unionist and an Anglican. His legendary silence followed him into Parliament where he was referred to as the silent Irish member speaking on only three occasions. When in Parliament he sat with the Conservatives and supported them on the Irish Question and against Home Rule for Ireland. It would appear that he found parliamentary life uncongenial and did not seek re-election.

He paid many summer trips to Ireland mainly visiting his sister and life-long friend Elizabeth in Malahide and his wife's family in the north of Ireland. He did not return to the north west to glimpse the white Atlantic rollers visible from the three story rectory of his youth. Living in the ivory towers of Cambridge he was able to maintain an image of the land of his birth far removed from the realities of 19th century Ireland. Yet he frequently longed for the peace and solitude of the shores of west Sligo.

The advances made by this Sligo scientist and mathematician, especially in the fields of optics and fluid dynamics, are universally acknowledged as milestones in the history of 19th century science. George Gabriel Stokes, one of the most celebrated and exceptional Irish men of the last century, died in Cambridge at the age of 84 in 1903 and is buried in the Mill Road cemetry in that town whose reputation he greatly enhanced.

The first steps in addressing the lack of recognition of such a major scientific figure in the county and country of his birth were taken in June 1995 when the inaugural Stokes Commemoration Weekend was held at RTC, Sligo. It consisted of a series of lectures on the

Fig. 4 - Stokes Monument at Skreen with Anne Crookshank, Prof. of Fine Art, TCD, at the 1995 unveiling. Photo: M.B. Timoney

life, work and times of George Gabriel Stokes and was attended by academics from six different countries. A series of general talks on the great scientist were also held for the general public and on the afternoon of Saturday, June 10th, 1995, Skreen's most famous son was acknowledged by the people of that area with the unveiling of a memorial in his honour outside the old rectory grounds. There is a note on the event, with a photograph of the monument, in *Physics World*, November 1995, page 64.

The Inaugural Stokes Summer School was held at Skreen, Co. Sligo, in 1995. On that occasion a commemorative monument made by Peter, "Petie", Diamond of Sheeanmore, Skreen, Co. Sligo, was unveiled by Ray McSharry, former European Commissioner for Agriculture. There is a note on the event with a photograph of the monument in *Physics World*, Nov. 1995, 64. There have been intermittent Stokes Summer Schools since then.

The inscriptions on the monument read

George Gabriel Stokes	Mathematical Physicist
Born in the Old Rectory	Laucasian Professor of
Skreen Aug. 13 1819	Mathematics at Cambridge
Died Cambridge Feb. 1 1903	President of Royal Society

Unveiled by
Ray McSharry
Former
European
Commissioner
For
Agriculture
June 10 1995

Sir George Gabriel Stokes
• 1819   + 1903

The new building, opened in May 2002, housing the School of Engineering at the Institute of Technology, Sligo, has been named The Stokes Building in his honour.

A Northern Scholar in County Sligo

Ernan Morris
Retired Librarian, Bray.

ABSTRACT: Henry Morris, born in Co. Monaghan in 1874, was a noted Gaelic scholar, antiquarian, folklorist, and educationalist. He was the Divisional Inspector of Schools in Sligo from 1923 to 1932. He collected Gaelic poems, songs, proverbs and folktales, most of which were published afterwards under various titles. He also contributed to learned journals and periodicals; he sometimes became involved in newspaper controversy. His death occurred in 1945.

HENRY MORRIS

People of older generations will probably remember the name of my father Henry Morris (Enrí Ó Muirgheasa) who served as Divisional Inspector of Schools in Sligo, from 1923 to 1932. Promoted to be Deputy Chief Inspector in 1932, he then moved with his family to Howth Road, Clontarf in Dublin, where he resided until his death in 1945.

For most of his life he had been a tireless worker in the sphere of Irish scholarship; the language, literature, early history, archaeology, folklore and placenames being his special interests. By his unremitting study and toil in these fields, he advanced the knowledge and understanding of our national heritage. The list of some of his published Sligo material reproduced in the appendix provides evidence of his dedication over the course of half a century; the full list, covering the years 1894 to 1941, was published by Ó Muirgheasa and Ó Casaide in *A Man of Farney* in 1974, pp. 21 - 28.

GAELIC ACTIVITIES

The Irish language was not widely spoken in Carrickmacross, Co. Monaghan, when Henry was born there in 1874. However, he started to learn the native tongue on his own initiative, and later became a founder member of the Gaelic League in the barony of Farney. Soon he commenced the collection of Gaelic poems, songs, proverbs and folktales, taking them down from the lips of the fast disappearing population of native speakers. Most of this rich material was afterwards reproduced in printed form under various titles.

PUBLICATIONS AND WRITINGS

In 1901 he published the first issue of Greann na Gaedhilge[1]. This booklet and the others which followed were produced annually until 1907. They consisted of short stories and anecdotes suitable for children beginning to learn Irish. The series was highly acclaimed by Conradh na Gaedhilge as serving an urgent need at the time. *Céad de Cheoltaibh Uladh*, which appeared in 1915, was the first book of modern Irish Ulster poetry ever to be published. Among other volumes which followed were *Amhráin Airt Mhic Cubhthaigh* (1916), *Seanfhocla Uladh* (1931), *Amhráin na Mídhe* (1933), *Dhá Chéad de Cheoltaibh Uladh* (1934) and *Dánta Diadha Uladh* (1936).

Apart from his published books and brochures he made numerous contributions to learned journals such as the *County Louth Archaeological Journal, The Irish Book Lover, Béaloideas, Dublin Historical Record and Journal of the Royal Society of Antiquaries of Ireland*. He was a founder member of the Louth Archaeological Society in 1903 and became first editor of the Journal. During his years in Sligo, a good deal of his writings and research related to that county and the surrounding areas. He frequently corresponded with the local newspapers, particularly the *Sligo Champion*, on a variety of subjects. One of the most valuable tourist guides of the county is probably *Sligo and its Surroundings* by Tadhg Kilgannon. Henry was closely involved in the production of this publication. There are pictures of him in the book[2] and they illustrate his active interest in the discovery of some prehistoric graves in County Sligo. Respecting the discovery of ancient remains it is important to point out that Enrí Ó Muirgheasa was no dilettante. He was in fact meticulous about the treatment of prehistoric material. Every single item had to be

Énrí Ó Muirgheasa
1874-1945

accurately described, marked, measured and photographed before being touched and removed for scientific examination. Another matter that concerned him greatly was the damage done to ancient monuments by ignorant people hoping to find a buried crock of gold. In a letter to the *Roscommon Herald* on 23rd June, 1928, he deplored such vandalism and pointed out that there was no coined money in this country until after the coming of the Danes, that is about four hundred years following the introduction of Christianity. Christians were usually buried in graveyards attached to churches. Single or isolated monuments were almost certainly pre-Christian, and related to a time when there were no coins in this country. About the last place where money could be found would be an ancient tomb. In his letter he asked teachers to explain this to their pupils.

ST. PATRICK

Henry Morris might well be described as a revisionist of his day, because concern for historical truth and accuracy was always of supreme importance to him. It was this that prompted him to question the authenticity of the familiar image of St. Patrick with the flowing beard, anachronistic vestments, mitre, and crozier[3]. His contention that the patron saint was clean shaven started a lively debate in the national and local newspapers which continued for quite some time. There was sound historical evidence to sustain his claim, and he had the support of some well-known scholars, including that of L.S. Gogan of the National Museum of Ireland. In 1930 he published an important little booklet entitled *St. Patrick in County Sligo*[4]. Although not directly connected with the controversy, it provides some fresh information about the saint and his missionary activities in the county.

LOCAL HISTORY AND FOLKLORE

Enrí Ó Muirgheasa was very keen on the teaching of local history in schools. At the National Teachers Congress in Galway in 1927, he read an important paper on the subject stressing its significance in the proper education of children. In 1922 he had proposed to the Chief Executive of the Department of Education that the school children be involved in the collection of folklore. Nothing was done at the time and many years were to elapse before the scheme was implemented. The result of a single year's work astonished Prof. Delargy of the Folklore Commission. When the Folklore of Ireland Society, An Cumann le Béaloideas Éireann, was founded in 1927 Henry became a member and was a frequent contributor to its publication *Béaloideas*. Later on, when the Society became the Irish Folklore Commission and the collection of folklore was organised on a more systematic basis, he continued to support it.

ARTEFACTS

When travelling through the country on school inspections he was always alert for information about any stone age or bronze age artefacts that might be discovered during turf cutting, road making and other such activities. Over the years he accumulated quite a collection of stone axes, bronze spears, swords and other objects which he housed in show cases in his home. It was his custom to talk to the schoolchildren on the significance of these finds. The results were often quite positive and he would be put on the track of some recent discovery, and enabled to retrieve it from possible loss or damage. On one occasion when travelling in the West he came upon a farmer cutting back a hedge with a bronze sword. 'An old implement I found in the bog', he was told! The sword is now with the rest of his collection at the National Museum of Ireland.

THE FOMORIANS

It was the belief of Henry Morris that all the prehistoric invasions of Ireland took place in the Sligo area. The incursions of Lady Caesar,

Partholan and the Nemhedh were all located there. In this connection it is interesting to note that he deprived Tory Island off the Donegal coast of its doubtful distinction of being The stronghold of the Fomorians, and instead, identified their fortress on a rocky isle off the Sligo coast. In an erudite, closely argued, and well authenticated paper read to the Louth Archaeological Society in May, 1927[5] he put forward the view that Tor Inis, for long identified by historians as the home of these ferocious sea-raiders, was in fact Derinish, near Grange in the parish of Ahamlish, about eight miles south of Bundoran, and not Tory Island as had been believed. In support of this claim he cites *An Leabhar Gabhála*, *The Book of Leinster*, *The Annals of the Four Masters* and other well known sources.

DUBHALTACH MAC FHIRBHISIGH

There is a wayside monument in the parish of Skreen, Co. Sligo, erected to commemorate the distinguished scribe and historian Dubhaltach Mac Fhirbhisigh. It was through the exertions of Henry Morris and a few others that this memorial was mounted in 1931, in an effort to rescue from near oblivion, the fame of an important Gaelic Scholar of the 17th Century. A sandstone flag from the locality was prepared by a local sculptor, a Mr. Diamond, and set up in Doonflinn near the spot where Mac Fhirbhisigh met a tragic death in 1670. Regrettably over the intervening years the monument has suffered and is now in a poor state of repair.

THE ENVIRNONMENT

Linked to his interest in local history was a deep concern for the environment. In this respect he was well in advance of many of his contempories. He had a great love for trees, plants, birdlife, and all creatures of the wild. Of the many books in his possession were included several authoritative works in these fields which he often consulted. Ringforts and ancient earthen mounds always attracted his attention. With hills and mountains he invariably had an urge to scale their heights. One of his Sligo publications was

a pamphlet entitled *Benbulbin in History and Literature* in which he told something of the story of that legendary mountain[6]. According to the leaflet the correct name of Benbulbin should be Beann Gulban Guirt Mhic Mhaeilghaeibh or the mountain peak of Gulban Gort.

LIBRARY

Henry Morris was a great collector of books, and during his lifetime he managed to assemble a valuable library of books and journals relating mainly to Ireland, its history, literature, folklore, language and antiquities. He also possessed a number of manuscripts. After his death his family decided to dispose of the collection by sending it to Coleraine University. Most of his papers were donated to University College, Dublin. His more personal notes and a collection of letters remain with the family. One item retained is a cartoon by V.L. O'Connor, and presented to him at the instigation of H.G. Tempest of Dundalgan Press. It dates from the 1920s. Henry is depicted talking to schoolboy. It is reproduced here with the kind permission of the Dundalgan Press (W. Tempest) Ltd., Dundalk.

GAELIC LEAGUE

His life long interest in the native language has been mentioned, but we have no information of his activities in this regard during his years in Sligo. We do know, however, that he was Chairman of an enthusiastic meeting convened in the Town Hall, Oct./Nov. 1929, for the purpose of reorganising the Gaelic League in the town.

SLIGO

During his sojourn in Sligo, Henry lived with his wife and seven children in a house called Mountshannon, about two miles outside the town near the old Bundoran road. It was a lovely old building, surrounded by trees, in sight of Knocknarea, Benbulbin, the Ox Mountains and the sea. While there is no evidence that Henry was an active member of any archaeological or historical society in Sligo, it is clear from his outlook that any such society would have had his full support but none existed.

FOUR MASTERS

He had his triumphs and disappointments during his long career, but one of his most notable achievements was to pinpoint the place at Rossfriar on the Leitrim side of the River Drowes, Co. Leitrim, where the Four Masters had their habitation, and where they compiled the famous Annals in the 17th century. A commemorative monument was unveiled on Kinlough Bridge in 1975 by the late President Cearbhall Ó Dálaigh. It had always been believed that the Annals were assembled in Co. Donegal and when Henry challenged this belief it led to a vigorous controversy in the pages of the *Irish Independent* which continued over many weeks in the Summer of 1936.

BELFAST DEGREE

Henry Morris was, indeed, a remarkable man, of whom it could be said that he lived before his time. Some of his ideas and endeavours were, perhaps, not always appreciated while he lived but it gave much pleasure to his friends, and undoubted satisfaction to himself, when in 1936, the Chancellor of Queen's University, Belfast, bestowed on him an Honorary Degree of Master of Arts in recognition of his work for Irish scholarship.

ÉIGSE

In the Spring of 1974 an Éigse was held in Carrickmacross[7] to celebrate the centenary of his birth. This consisted of a programme of lectures, discussions, services in Irish in all the local churches, an historical tour, and the unveiling of a plaque on the Morris family home in Cashlan, Carrickmacross. The proceedings were attended by some distinguished scholars, including the late Cardinal Tomás Ó Fiaich, who played an active role in organising the Éigse. A useful biographical booklet entitled *A Man of Farney* was also produced[8]. The function was a great success and a fitting tribute to the memory of Enrí Ó Muirgheasa who died almost sixty years ago.

References:

1. Morris, H. 1901-1907: *Greann na Gaedhilge*, Baile Átha Cliath. Pts. 1-7.
2. Kilgannon, T. 1926: *Sligo and its Surroundings*, Sligo; reprint Sligo 1988, 290, 309-310.
3. Morris, H. Sept. 25th, 1930: Did St. Patrick wear a beard, *Irish Independent*, Dublin.
4. Morris, H. 1930: *St. Patrick in County Sligo*, Sligo.
5. Morris, H. 1927: Where was Tor Inis, The Island Fortress of the Formorians? *J. Roy. Soc. Antiq. Ireland*, 57, 47-58.
6. Morris, H., n.d. (c.1929): *Benbulbin in History and Literature*, Sligo.
7. Ó Casaide, P. 1974: *Enrí Ó Muirgheasa (1874 - 1945)*, Cathair na Mairt.
8. Ó Muirgheasa, P., and Ó Casaide, P., 1974: *A Man of Farney*, Dundalk.

APPENDIX

The Writings of Henry Morris Relating to Sligo[1]
Martin A. Timoney and Mary B. Timoney

1926: 'Researches in Local History: Ancient Corran', *The Sligo Champion*, 3/7/1926.

1926: 'Researches in Local History', *The Sligo Champion*, 17/7/1926.[2]

1926: 'Researches in Local History: Some of our Local Names', *The Sligo Champion*, 7/8/1926.

1926: 'Researches in Local History: Lough Gill', *The Sligo Champion*, 21/8/1926.

1926: *'Review of Sligo and its Surroundings'*, *The Sligo Champion*, 11/9/1926.

1927: 'Where was Tor Inis, the Island Fortress of the Formorians?', *J. Roy. Soc. Antiq. Ireland*, 57, 47-58.

1927: 'Researches in Local History: Ros Ceide', *The Sligo Champion*, 31/12/1927.

1928: 'Ros Ceide', *The Sligo Champion*, 11/2/1928.

1928: 'Researches in Local History: Maugherow', *The Sligo Champion*, 25/2/1928.

1928: 'St. Assicus', The Patron Saint of Elphin Diocese; Unravelled after Patient Research; Confused with St. Assach, His Feast Day Obscured, *The Roscommon Herald*, 25/2/1928.

1928: 'The O'Dalys as Irish Bards: Murray O'Daly, The Lissadell Poet', *The Roscommon Herald*, 17/3/1928.

1928: 'Researches in Local History: Drumcliffe', *The Sligo Champion*, 31/3/1928.

1928: 'St. Fechin', Born near Ballisodare, Co. Sligo, Interesting Story of his Great Career. His Name Associated with Churches in Ireland, Scotland and France', *The Roscommon Herald*, 2/6/1928.

1928: 'Important Discoveries of Ancient Graves in Sligo and Roscommon', *The Sligo Champion*, 23/6/1928.[3]

1928?: 'The Hill of The Great Defeat, An Idle Evening at Boyle', *The Roscommon Herald*.[4]

1928: 'A Prehistoric Grave at Ballymote', *The Roscommon Herald*, 17/11/1928.[5]

1928: 'The First Battle of Magh Turedh', *J. Roy. Soc. Antiq. Ireland*, 58, 111-127.

1929: 'Ancient Graves in Sligo and Roscommon', *J. Roy. Soc. Antiq. Ireland*, 59, 99-115.

1929: 'Drumcliffe and Dun na mBarc', *The Sligo Champion*, 2/11/1929.

1929: *Benbulben in History and Literature*, 26/10/1929.[6]

1929: 'Local History: The "Green Fort", Sligo', *The Sligo Champion*, 30/11/1929.

1929: 'A County Sligo Tradition', *Bealoideas*, 2, 138-139.[7]

1932: Letter relating to The Battle of the Curlews.[8]

1930: *St. Patrick in County Sligo*.[9]

1930: Two letters, *The Sligo Champion* 22/2/1930.[10]

1931: 'The Ballyduane Skeleton', *The Western People*, 9/5/1931.[11]

1931?: 'The McGoldrick Family'. *The Sligo Champion*.[12]

1932: 'Dualty MacFirbis - Monument Erected at Doonflinn', *The Sligo Champion*, 6/2/1932.[13]

1933: 'Dún na mBárc and the Lady Ceasair', *J. Roy. Soc. Antiq. Ireland*, 63, 69-87.

1933: 'Some Western Prehistoric Monuments in Ireland', *Proc. Belfast Nat. Hist. & Phil. Soc.*, 1931-1932, 22-29.

1940: 'Ancient Burial in Co. Sligo,' *J. Roy. Soc. Antiq. Ireland*, 70, 200-202.[14]

1940: 'Associated Finds of Bronze from Sligo and Armagh', *J. Roy. Soc. Antiq. Ireland*, 70, 94.[15]

Notes

1. Compiled from the bibliography in Ó Muirgheasa, P., and Ó Casaide, P., *A Man of Farney*, 20-28, and Sligo Library Local History Archive, Nos. 2, 3, 6, 22, 27, 32. There are many additional notes by Henry Morris on the copies in Sligo Library Local History Archive.

2. On mythology.

3. Moylough, Co. Sligo, and Corry, Co. Roscommon.

4. Date not recorded; on Knock-a-doo-brisleach, near Boyle, Co. Roscommon, probably to be equated with Knockadoobrusna, for which see Condit, Tom, 1993, 'Ritual Enclosures near Boyle, Co. Roscommon', *Archaeology Ireland*, 7:1, 14-16.

5. Stonepark.

6. 10 pages; reprinted from *The Sligo Champion*.

7. On a burial custom.

8. On a letter of 1599 by Sir John Harrington to Mr. Combe of Trim taken from *Anthologia Hibernica*, 1793. Date not recorded but post Sept. 1929, probably between May 1931 and Feb. 1932.

9. 34 pages.

10. Reply by letters to an anonymous piece entitled 'St. Loman and Lough Gill'.

11. Reference to Ballogan, *recte* Ballyogan, near Culleens, Co. Sligo. OS 17, See *NMI Ann. Rept.*, 1930-1931, Pl. 2:2.

12. Signed 'E Ó M'.

13. This lists the subscribers, mostly teachers, who paid £10 in total for this monument in 1931. The idea of a monument was that of Morris and John Mulligan, N.T., Doonflin, "A master of the type that should be in every school in Ireland" was the local driving force. The stone was cut by Mr. Diamond. See also Nollaig Ó Muraile, *The Celebrated Antiquary Dubhaltach Mac Fhirbisigh, (c. 1600-1671), His Lineage, Life and Learning*, Maynooth, 1996, 301, fn. 81, 335.

14. Kilglass.

15. Knockanbawn, Co. Sligo, and Ballinliss, Co. Armagh.

A CELEBRATION *OF* SLIGO

SLIGO FIELD CLUB

Eve O'Kelly, Claire O'Kelly, Estie Calahane and Sheela Kitchin at Newgrange.

John Troddyn

Eileen Lambert

Michael Hopper

Kay Raftery

Margaret Mc Brien & Pat Hurley

Jim Hughes & Pat Kitchin

Aodhán O'Higgins

Jack Flynn, Brendan Rooney, Martin Wilson, Larry Mullin, Mary B. Timoney, Aidan Mannion and Pat O'Brien at Tanrego, May 2000.

A CELEBRATION *OF* SLIGO

THE ARRIVAL AT SLIGO
EARLY APPROACHES TO SLIGO IN THE 19ᵗʰ CENTURY

Derry O'Connell
Head of Dept. of Regional and Urban Planning, U.C.D.

ABSTRACT: The realignment of approaches to Sligo has dramatically altered the way in which the town has been entered from north and south over the last two hundred years. The effect of such realignment is examined, focusing in particular on the creation of the great Victoria and Albert Lines in the middle of the nineteenth century.

BACKGROUND

As the twenty-first century begins, Sligo is due to receive a new main entry road from the south which will change totally the view and comprehension of the town for anybody first entering it.

Rather like moving the front door from one side of a house to the other, a change in the entry position alters the whole perception of a town for those who use it either as residents or visitors. But this has happened to Sligo before. In fact on at least two occasions in as many centuries, entries to the town have been completely redirected by single engineering works.

BACKGROUND

From early maps we know that entries to Sligo from both north and south followed natural routes associated with dry ground and easy river crossings (Taylor and Skinner 1778, maps 65, 211 and 226). The north and south entries were probably always more important than were those from east or west, because of Sligo's significance as a river crossing on the busy coastal traffic route.

The first Ordnance Survey map of 1838 (1:10560 (6-inch)) is interesting as on it we can see the strongest route from the north entering via Holborn Hill, with the route from Cartron via Barrack Street being clearly secondary.

From the south, Gallows Hill and Old Pound Street have similar characteristics. It is likely that Gallows Hill was originally the more important entry as its route outside the town shows a long established line from Ballydrehid Bridge, the next route constriction to the south, at the inner end of Ballisodare Bay. When Mail Coach Road was laid out, however, in the early nineteenth century it seems to have become the new entry, eliminating much of Old Pound Street, the line of which is still visible today behind houses to its west side. In doing so, it moved the main southern entry eastwards to more level lower ground.

The early routes focus on a river crossing somewhere about Water Lane, close to the position of the present footbridge.

However, all of these routes were to be completely upstaged in 1846 when two of the most impressive transformations ever considered for the town were introduced.

As part of distress relief works the Victoria Line and the Albert Line were proposed, later to become respectively Markievicz Road and Pearse Road.

Relief works were an early form of public-private enterprise which combined investment by inhabitants of the town with public funds to provide public works, the construction of which provided employment for the poor in the famine stricken economy. They were described as "necessary and useful".

It was in the early 1840s that the population of Ireland was at its highest, before being reduced by famines and associated emigration. Market towns such as Sligo, serving a dependent hinterland as central places of trade, were at their most congested and one can assume that at that period the entrances to towns were areas of periodic traffic chaos no different to today. In Corporation debates, Pound Street is consistently referred to as impassable and chaotic (*Sligo Journal*, 25 Sep. 1846)

The Victoria Line and the Albert Line were proposed to improve the approaches to the town. The Victoria Line was to be a new grand level road from Hudson's at Duck Park to Victoria Bridge (now Hyde Bridge). This would replace the route over Gallows Hill North, into the town via Holborn Street, which was hilly. The Albert

A CELEBRATION OF SLIGO

Fig 1. Ordnance Survey Map of Sligo, 1:10560, 1838.
From the South, Mail Coach Road has taken over as the primary approach, but entry is still via Pound St. to High St.
Map Permit No. 6785

Line was to create a new straight descending route from the southern end of the present Mail Coach Road to the Courthouse. Both approaches were commenced at the same time in 1846.

The Albert Line took just two years to construct. Although more extensive in length than the Victoria Line, it was straightforward, involving only minor engineering works. It was simply a wide road requiring a level surface with a long shallow gradient. Victoria Line, on the other hand, was a serious engineering scheme, requiring the construction of an embankment wall that to this day remains a mammoth piece of work. It was completed in 1852 and opened on the 26th June of that year.

It was proposed at the same time, on September 17th 1846, to run a new short road from the north end of Pound Street to connect High Street to the new Albert Line. This would "be of great benefit to the people of Pound Street which suffered from congestion due to parked carts"! It would be called Burton Street.

The cutting down of Cartron Hill was also proposed in order to improve the secondary approach from the north.

Although often taken for granted by those of us who know them, both approaches are unusually impressive as entrances to a town, but each in a totally different way.

THE ALBERT LINE

The Albert approach, descending northwards from Markievicz Park to the Courthouse, makes full use of the setting of the town against its scenic backdrop with the distant Mall buildings particularly prominent. Although the southern section, from Markievitz Park to Mail Coach Road, was already there as part of the earlier Mail Coach Road approach, it appears, if we examine our maps, to have been widened and slightly realigned in the 1846 works.

The new approach presumably gave that long descent described in 1849 by Carlyle as a "beautiful descent into a beautiful town altogether" (Kilgannon 1926, 99-100).

It consists of two long shallow-graded straights, separated by a slight change in direction at the junction with Mail Coach Road. Though dropping over 200 ft. in just under a mile, the gradient is constant, in order to ease the burden on upward-bound horse-drawn traffic.

Because Vernon Street (now St. Brigid's Place) was already there and lined with buildings, the new road had to conform to a specific level at this point which it then maintains northwards for a short distance. North of Burton Street the most dramatic final descent then begins.

Here, from a relatively open townscape, with little sense of enclosure, the road suddenly drops at a gradient of almost 1 in 20 into the tightly enclosed townscape of Teeling Street, in an

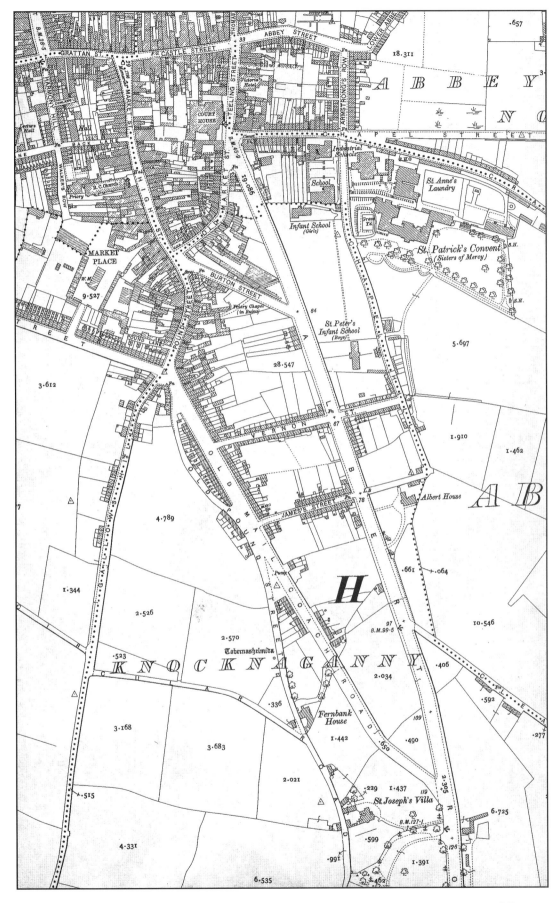

Fig. 2. Ordnance Survey Map of the south side of Sligo, 1:10560, 1910. Much of the Albert Line still runs through open fields
O.S. Map Permit Number: 6785

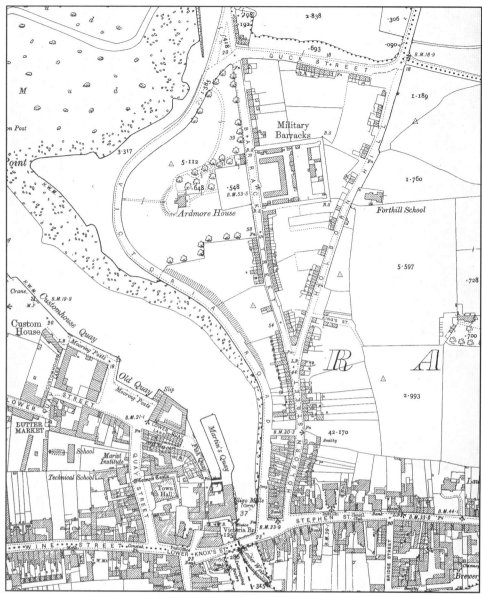

Fig. 3. Ordnance Survey Map of the north side of Sligo, 1:10560, 1910. The great sweep of the Victoria Line serves the main northern entry.
O.S. Map Permit Number: 6785

experience, which could be described as the final touchdown after the long approach.

In the first years of the Albert Line an older courthouse stood in Teeling Street, to be replaced or refaced by the existing building in 1878. The 1878 building makes maximum use of its terminal position by placing its tower on axis with the Albert approach and developing from that the composition which has made its façade so successful as a flagship building on the entry to the town.

Apart from the construction of some terraces of houses north and south of Vernon Street, the town never extended out to face the edges of the Albert Line with buildings. The road never became a street. Perhaps this had more to do with land ownership than with the size of the town. At the northern extremity of the Albert Line, an open field in fact existed right up to the early 1960s, now occupied by the Mercy College Schools. Some residential development by Sligo Corporation in the early 20th century has helped to fill the edges, albeit at a very low density.

THE VICTORIA LINE

The Victoria Line, or Markievicz Road, is a very different entry. Here there was no gradient to challenge. The new road simply took a longer route to avoid the steep gradient from Ballytivnan over Holborn Hill to Stephen Street, which was quite obviously a major obstacle for heavy horse-drawn vehicles.

The sequence of entry by which the town is revealed on this approach is striking. The road rises slightly southwards from Duck Street before beginning its slow dramatic curve to the east through which it unveils the town, and its then bustling quays, with the high grounds of Forthill on one shoulder and the deeply curving sweep of the estuary on the other, focussing finally on the enclosed end of Stephen Street, where the façade of the Barton Smith building terminated the route at Victoria Bridge (now Hyde Bridge).

Like the Courthouse, the new Ulster Bank building responded to this pivotal corner position with its prominent palazzo in 1863. A number of buildings fronting on to Stephen Street between Holborn Street and the River had been demolished to make way for the connection between the Victoria Line and the Bridge. The bridge was constructed in 1852 at the same time as the Victoria Line, replacing an earlier bridge.

Fig. 4. The enormous embankment wall of the Victoria Line, 150 years old in 2002. Photo. Derry O'Connell.

As with the Albert Line however, the town never extended its quality buildings out to enclose The Line. Land ownership, topography and in particular site depth may have made such enclosure unattractive.

It is the Victoria embankment wall that stands out as a serious engineering work. The wall, close to 30 ft. high, runs in a single sweep of almost 1000 ft. in squared limestone, with a slight batter to take the thrust of the busy road which it had to support. Its only articulation is a cut-stone string course at pavement level. The scale and simplicity of this work gives a striking base line to the town from its northern approach.

It had been contemplated that the Victoria Line might be terminated at the small slip road which emerges from Holborn Street, just opposite the present Connaughton Road, which ran to the river. There were concerns about the difficulties of building the section between here and Stephen Street, where the river flowed slightly broader, making construction more difficult (*Sligo Journal*, 25 September 1846). If we examine the 1838 maps we can see that there were also many buildings established in the area facing both Stephen Street and Holborn Street which presented an obstacle to the route.

These concerns however were obviously overcome in the final decision to link the line to Victoria Bridge, creating the great sense of arrival that this junction has had to this day.

THE VICTORIA LINE

The effect which the Victoria and Albert Lines had on the perception of entry to Sligo must have been significant at the time. For a town of Sligo's size, the creation of new approaches along completely new routes, from edge to town centre, must have had an enormous impact on the image and operation of the town. This would have been particularly so on the south side where the transfer of activity was probably responsible for the beginning of the decline of Pound Street and later High Street, a decline which continued into the 20th century.

In 1943 the Victoria Line and Albert Line were renamed as Markievicz Road and Pearse Road respectively. Householders in the area were petitioned by the Gaelic League who put a proposal to Sligo Corporation for the renaming of the routes, among many other routes in the town. In the case of the Victoria Line and the Albert Line proposal there appears to have been a conspicuous reluctance by councillors to discuss the renaming, which suggests that the degree of public support was not overwhelming. The renaming was however adopted and certified by Manager's Order on December 18th 1943.

To this day Pearse Road continues to be called "The Line" by many as indeed Burton Street continues to be called "The Short Line".

REFERENCES

NEWSPAPERS:
Sligo Journal, 9 September 1842.
Sligo Journal, 18 September 1846.
Sligo Journal, 25 September 1846.
Sligo Journal, 25 June 1852.
Sligo Champion, 22 November 1943.

MAPS:
Ordnance Survey 1:10560 (6-inch) series, 1838.
Ordnance Survey 1:10560 (6-inch) series, 1910.

PUBLICATIONS:
Andrews, John, 1964: "Road planning in Ireland before the railway age", *Irish Geography*, 5, 1-6.
Kilgannon, Tadgh, 1926: *Sligo and its Surroundings*, Sligo, Kilgannon; Reprint, Sligo, 1988, Dodd's Antiquarian Books.
Taylor, George, and Skinner, Andrew, 1778: *Maps of the Roads of Ireland*, Reproduction Dublin, Irish University Press, 1969.

Some Sligo Architecture

Grange Beg medieval Castle & Church, Templeboy, Co. Sligo.

Bridge carrying Sligo-Ballina road over Owenbeg River, west of Dromore West, Co. Sligo.

Spanish Armada monument at Streedagh, Grange, Co. Sligo.

THE ORIGINS OF TECHNICAL EDUCATION IN SLIGO TOWN, 1904-1912

Larry Mullin
Past President, Sligo Field Club, Ballinode, Sligo.

ABSTRACT: The beginnings and early development of Technical Education in Sligo are examined. From its origins in 1904 its growth and flowering up to 1912 are outlined. This brief survey ends in that year at it was marked by the death of the first Chairman of the Board and lifelong supporter of Technical Education, Most Rev. Dr. John Clancy, Bishop of Elphin, and by the departure of Mr. J. H. Smith, its first Headmaster and guiding light.

With the passing of the Agricultural and Technical Instruction (Irl) Act of 1899 Technical Education took on its first formal structure in Ireland. At local level country boroughs and councils were empowered to set up statutory committees and raise a level of local finance (ld to 2d in the Pound on the rates) to fund technical instruction. This was supplemented by a grant from the Dept. of Agriculture and Technical Instruction to help local schemes with capital costs. Local funding had to be forthcoming before the Department provided money from central funds.

The Catholic Hierarchy, who were an important voice in education then, accepted this secular-controlled and rate-supported form of education. This was due mainly to the influence of Dr. Walsh, Archibishop of Dublin, and, as we will see later, the strong support of Dr. John Clancy, Bishop of Elphin, for the Sligo initiative. The work of the new Department was guided in its early years by Horace Plunkett, Vice President of the Education Board, and by T. P. Gill, Secretary.

Sligo Corporation was one of the first local authorities to become involved in technical education. At its meeting in January 1904 it appointed a Technical Instruction Committee for the Urban District with a brief to prepare a scheme for the town. The committee consisted of 16 members representing the Corporation, the Clergy and the business community. The Town Clerk, John McGovern, acted as secretary for the initial meetings. The names of some of the Committee would still be remembered in the town - P.A. McHugh, M.P., Rev. Dr. Clancy, Bishop of Elphin, Dr. Keilty (President of Summerhill College), Clr. John Jinks, Canon Ardill, Rector of Calry, and Fr. John Hynes, later President of U.C.G.

The first meeting of the Committee was held in the Town Hall on 11th February 1904 and Bishop Clancy was appointed Chairman. Dr. Clancy, a Sligo man, born in the parish of Sooey, had been Bishop of Elphin since 1895 and had a abiding interest in Technical Education. Indeed a few years previous to 1904 the Marist Brothers had, at his urging and financing, established a carpentry class in a room at their premises in Quay St. Dr. Clancy was now the principal guiding force behind the new committee and

Fig. 1 - Mr. J. H. Smith, first Headmaster.

was instrumental in preparing the first scheme for the school year 1904 - 1905.

As yet the scheme had no premises, no principal and no staff - but this was soon to be remedied. A premises in High St. belonging to Messrs. J. & M. Mulligan was rented for classes at £30 a year. In subsequent references it was always called the "High St. premises" and is believed to have been the building known in later years as "Carroll's Auction Rooms".

In October 1904 one George H. Smith, who previously taught in Tullamore, was appointed Headmaster and he took up duty on 1st November. Miss Janet Wallace of Drumshambo was appointed teacher of Cookery, Laundry and Housewifery and John R. Tracey who was on the staff of Summerhill College was appointed part-time teacher of Commercial Subjects. With this limited staff and he himself teaching full-time Mr. Smith set about organising classes. A prospectus was prepared by the Headmaster and some committee members who seem to have been very involved in the promotion of the school. At the December 1904 meeting, which was considering the prospectus, a committee member (one Clr. Edward Kelly) offered his resignation because his name was omitted inadvertently from the list of members published in the prospectus. This did not, however, slow down unduly the progress of the school and the first classes opened on 12th December with an enrolment of 76 pupils. Classes were held in the afternoon and evening and were attended by young or mature adults.

The occupations of students attending classes varied from saddler, telegraph messenger, cartwright apprentice and tailor for males to, domestic assistant, milliner, monitress and 'no occupation' for females.

The classes were obviously meeting a demand because when school re-opened after Christmas the total enrolment had risen dramatically to over 200. Classes for ladies were just a well attended as those for men. This was a spectacular beginning and a lot of the credit for it must go to the Headmaster, Mr. Smith. By any standard his workload was onerous. As well as being Headmaster and Secretary to the Committee he taught over 30 hours per week - subjects such as science, art, carpentry and geometry. His remuneration was £200 per annum which was a sizeable sum in those days.

The school was formally opened by Mr. T. P. Gill, Secretary of the Department of Agriculture and Technical Instruction on 1st. February 1905 in the presence of the assembled dignatories of the town. An excellent start had been made and throughout 1905-1906 classes continued to grow

Fig. 2 - Most Rev. Dr. John Clancy, Bishop of Elphin, first Chairman of the Board.

and diversify. Requests from local trades for special classes in carpentry and joinery, painting and decorating, dress-making and crochet were met if accommodation was available. In 1906 Mr. John McDermott of Glencar was appointed Trades Teacher and Rev. Thomas O'Kelly of Summerhill College part-time teacher of Irish.

By early 1906 it became apparent to the Committee that the premises in High St. was inadequate to cater for all the classes requested. Through that year the committee kept pressing vigorously for the provision of new premises for the school but to no avail. As yet the Department was providing no finance for building Technical Schools. However in November 1906 His Lordship, Bishop Clancy, came to their assistance and offered a lease on a building in Quay St. known as "The Old College" to the Committee. This building had been formerly the Bishop's residence and in 1862, when the Marist Brothers came to Sligo, they used part of it as a primary school. However the Brothers withdrew from Sligo in 1880 following a dispute with Bishop Gillooly and Summerhill College was transferred to the Quay St. premises until the new College was built in 1892. Hence the Quay St. building became known as "The Old College".

It was part of this premises that Bishop Clancy leased to the Committee at a rent of £60 for the 1907-1908 school session. In March of 1907 he offered them further accommodation in the Marist Brothers residence beside the Old College. The Brothers had been invited back to Sligo following the appointment of Dr. Clancy as Bishop and they returned in 1898 to their former premises in Quay St. There they took over the running of a junior and senior primary school.

There were surplus rooms in their residence which were then given over for Technical Education.

With this extra accommodation it was decided to move the school completely from High St. and centre it in Quay St. from September 1907. Thus began a long and fruitful association of Technical Education with the Quay St. premises. This continued for over 60 years, down to June 1971, when classes were moved to a new school at Ballinode, beside the Regional Technical College. The VEC Administrative offices are still located in the Quay St. premises and VEC meetings take place there. The Sligo Teachers' Centre was based there from 1972 to 2000 and it was in this centre that Sligo Field Club held its public lectures from about 1975 to 2000. Indeed the wheel has almost gone full circle because at present VTOS students - young adults - are getting a second chance at education in this premises as their predecessors did in the 1900's.

With increasing numbers and more accommodation in Quay St. the Committee were able to appoint two new teachers in 1907. Mr. J. P. Quigley was appointed teacher of Painting and Decorating and Mr. James Fitzgerald teacher of Tailoring.

The type of courses offered by the school in its early years was of a trade, commercial or craft nature for young or mature adults. Classes were held in the afternoons or evenings; mainly evenings for men as most of them would be working during the day. The high attendance at evening classes may be due in part to lack of attractions elsewhere as well as a desire to learn new skills. The relentless eye of the TV screen or the alluring comforts of the modern lounge bar were not there in those years. Although there were weeks when attendance dropped seriously - due, the minutes of the day record, "to the Annual Parish Mission".

The question of providing courses in full-time continuing education for young people who had completed their primary education was being examined regularly by the Headmaster and Committee from 1906 onwards. Such education was badly needed at the time as only 2% of those leaving primary schools in the town went on to secondary school.

In September 1908 what was known as a Day Trades Preparatory School for boys was opened at the Quay St. premises with the assistance of a £200 grant from the Department. The object of this course was "to provide for boys, who had completed the ordinary National School course, a special training for two years which would enable them to be apprenticed to any skilled trade and to take up their work intelligently from the commencement". They were admitted to the course following an entrance test in English, Arithmetic and Drawing. From the beginning the Committee awarded eight scholarships on the results of this test and those who did not get a scholarship paid a fee of £1 per year. On successful completion of the course students were awarded a certificate. The course flourished

Fig. 3 - The Technical School, Quay St., Sligo.

and was later developed into the Manual Trades Group Certificate after Irish Independence. This "Group Cert", as it was commonly known, continued in Technical schools and was also taken in some Secondary Schools until it was absorbed into the Junior Certificate of the Department in 1992.

In the years that followed the introduction of the Day Trades preparatory courses the school continued to grow. More accommodation was required and in 1911 Bishop Clancy again came to the aid of the Committee by offering more rooms in the Quay St. building for classes. By that year the staff of the school had increased from the original three to ten. One staff member acted as a badly needed assistant to the overworked Headmaster. This teacher - Dominic McHugh - must hold the record for service to Technical Education in the town. He was a student on the very first classes organised in 1904-1905 and remained on as a teacher until his reitrement in 1954 - an association of 50 years. He died in 1962.

A few more features of the early years are worth recalling here. Apart from the enormous contribution made by Mr. Smith and Bishop Clancy to the early development of the school the input from members of the Committee was considerable. A visiting sub-committee called to the school each week and inspected registers. Committee members gave their services as supervisors at exam time and organised social evenings for students and parents. Above all, the Committee never took "No" for an answer when dealing with Department officials. A refusal to sanction anything considered important for the school was answered by an even firmer request at the next meeting.

Another feature of the early days was the close co-operation which existed with the local secondary school - Summerhill College. Mention has already been made of college teachers Mr. Tracey and Fr. O'Kelly, who taught commercial subjects and Irish respectively on a part-time basis in the school. Mr. Smith and other Techncial teachers took classes in Summerhill also. Evening classes were organised in other centres in the town, such as in Forthill N.S., in the Mercy Convent N.S. and in the Grammar and High Schools.

What was the cost of education on the public purse in those far off pre-inflationary days? The scheme for the first year cost about £1,000; by 1912 this had risen to £1,400 - due mainly to employing extra teachers. As regards teachers' pay a full-time teacher could expect £70 a year rising to £100 by 1912. Lady teachers seem to have fared worse than their male colleagues. A part-time teacher of dress-making and cookery got 2/6 an hour while a part-time male teacher of science, commerce or manual instruction got 4/- an hour.

In June 1912 Mr. Smith resigned as headmaster to take up a position in England and in October of the same year Bishop Clancy died. The efforts of those two men together with an enthusiastic commmittee were responsible for laying the foundation of Technical Education in Sligo in those early years, an achievement for which we should be justly proud.

SOURCES:

Primary

Sligo Committee of Technical Instruction 1904 - 1912: Minutes of Meetings of Borough of Sligo Committee of Technical Instruction, 1904 - 1912
  The Sligo Champion, 1906-1912.
  The Sligo Independent, 1906-1912.

Secondary

Canning, Rev. Bernard, 1987: *The Bishops of Ireland, 1870-1987*, Donegal, Donegal Democrat.
  Coolahan, John, 1981: *Irish Education - History and Structure*, Dublin, I.P.A.
  Hoctor, D., 1971: *The Department Story*, Dublin, I.P.A.
  Kilgannon, Tadgh, 1926: *Sligo and Its Surroundings*, Sligo, Kilgannon; Reprint, Sligo, 1988, Dodd's Antiquarian Books
  Marist Brothers, 1962: *Marist Brothers Centenary Journal*, Sligo, Marist Brothers.
  Ní Leitháin, Íde, 1999: *The Life and Career of P. A. McHugh, A north Connacht Politician, 1859-1909, A Footsoldier of the Party*, Maynooth Studies in Local History: No. 23, Dublin, Irish Academic Press.
  O'Beirne, Francis, ed., 2000: *The Diocese of Elphin, People, Places and Pilgrimage*, Blackrock, Columba.
  West, Trevor, 1986: *Horace Plunkett, Co-Operation and Politics*, Washington.

ENVIRONMENTAL EDUCATION AT THE INSTITUTE OF TECHNOLOGY, SLIGO

Dr. Billy Fitzgerald,
Head of Department of Environmental Science, Institute of Technology, Sligo

Although the upsurge in general concern for the environment did not take place until the late 1980s, the Institute of Technology, Sligo, had long established itself as the main centre for providing Third Level education in the environmental sciences. As far back as 1975, the School of Science received approval to offer a National Diploma in Environmental Science, now known as the National Diploma in Environmental Protection. This course was particularly strong in the area of environmental analysis and waste management. Approximately five hundred students have graduated from this course, many of whom have progressed to degree level and higher.

The introduction of the Local Government (Water Pollution) Act in 1977 increased the environmental responsibilities of local authorities and industry particularly in relation to the licensing of effluent discharges. The School of Science took cognisance of the requirement for higher technical skills, and in 1982 commenced the four-year B.Sc. (Hons) Degree in Environmental Science and Technology. To-date about three hundred and sixty students have qualified with degrees from this course.

With increasing environmental controls being introduced through national and European legislation during the 1980s, an educational gap became apparent with regard to graduates and technologists from other science and engineering disciplines requiring environmental training. The School of Science in association with FÁS and the Environmental Services Department of Enterprise Ireland developed a two-year Postgraduate Diploma in Environmental Protection by distance learning. This course which commenced in 1989 is aimed at graduates and technologists in industry and State Bodies who have environmental management responsibilities but lack formal environmental training. As a follow-on to the Postgraduate Diploma, approval was granted for a M.Sc. in Environmental Protection incorporating a further year of study by distance learning. This represented the first taught M.Sc. to be approved by the NCEA. These courses have attracted participants countrywide from varying types of organisations. The distance learning mode of delivery provides an opportunity for people to further their technical skills with minimum disruption to normal employment. To-date over two hundred participants have qualified from these postgraduate courses.

Further expansion of environmental courses included a B.Sc. (Hons) Degree in Environmental Chemistry and a diploma and degree in the related area of Occupational Safety and Health, all of which commenced in September, 1995.

In September 2001, the Department commenced the first full-time taught M.Sc. in the Institute. It focuses on the area of Environmental, Health and Safety (EHS) Management and the ways in which these issues are integrated into the general management of organisations. Many organisations are now implementing standardised systems to manage their EHS affairs in a pro-active rather than a reactive manner in line with ISO 14,000 and ISO 18,000 series as well as the EU Eco-Mamagement and Auditing Scheme (EMAS).

A new B.Sc. Degree in Applied Archaeology is planned to commence in September 2002, subject to approval. The emphasis of the course is on developing applied skills for field based

Fig. 1 - A postgraduate research student monitoring laboratory-scale waste water treatment plants.

archaeologists and in the application of scientific methods of analysis, such as, surveying, excavation, analysis of artifacts, scientific skills, field work, computing, human and animal osteoarchaeology, deterioration and conservation of materials, *etc*.

The Department of Environmental Science is committed to becoming actively involved with the local community and provides many part-time courses to encourage continuing and advanced education. Part-time/night courses on offer include, Organic Gardening, Occupational Safety and Health, and First Aid.

The staff are actively involved in environmental research programmes which enable post-graduate research students to progress to the awards of M.Sc. and Ph.D. The research interests of the academic staff include environmental microbiology, toxicology, sludge and biosolids, water analysis, wastewater treatment, mining and hydrogeology. Much of the research is grant aided and has involved research into environmental problems as well as the development of environmental products on behalf of industrial partners.

Major research studies have been completed on the 'Vulnerability of Groundwater to Pollution in the West of Ireland' in association with a number of local authorities under the European "Stride" programme and also in the development of a 'Management Plan for Lough Gill' under the European "Life" programme. The latter study involved the development of a long term management strategy for the lake in terms of water supply, tourism, angling, wild life, *etc*. and engaged all interested groups such as local authorities, the fishery boards, Sligo Field Club, angling associations, farmers, *etc*.

A postgraduate research scholarship was awarded to the Institute by the NCEA in commemoration of Padraigh MacConamhna from Belderrig, Co. Mayo, who first identified and understood the significance of the 5,000 year old field system under bogland in north Mayo. The research involves an assessment of the environmental and economic impact of the Céide Fields.

The Department is also engaged in research, funded by the EPA, into the recently arrived zebra mussel in Ireland and its proliferation and spread throughout the Shannon catchment and other aquatic systems. The Higher Education Authority (HEA) has also provided funding of one million euros for research into a study of 'Life Cycle Analysis in Sustainable Waste Management' encompassing a diverse range of projects with particular emphasis on municipal sludge and biosolids. The programme involves ten separate projects with nine other partner institutions including universities in Ireland and the UK as well as Teagasc and Enterprise Ireland.

The School of Science has recently established the Centre for Sustainability. The purpose of the Centre is to bring together all the research at the Institute that is involved in issues of sustainablity. It is intended that the Centre will also act as a focus and a source of information for local, regional and national interests with regard to sustainability.

A large proportion of those employed in the environmental sections of industry, local authorities, fisheries, EPA and other state bodies are graduates of some kind from IT Sligo. This has enabled a two-way liaison to continue between such organisations and the Institute. The varied careers followed by these graduates is evidence of the balanced approach of the courses towards concern for the natural environment and the role of industrial development in the creation of employment.

The School of Science is proud of the contribution it has made over the years to Sligo, Ireland and beyond, and will continue to respond to the environmental education and training requirements of various sectors. The expertise of the staff is well recognised and the Institute is keen to maintain its reputation as the foremost Institute in Ireland for providing environmental education.

Fig. 2 - Undergraduate students sampling for freshwater invertebrates.

ARCHAELOGICAL SURVEY IN SLIGO

Olive Alcock and Mary Tunney
Archaeological Survey of Ireland, Dúchas - The Heritage Service

ABSTRACT: The rich archaeological heritage of Co. Sligo has consistently attracted the attention of scholars and researchers. An account of the Sites and Monuments Record and Field Survey for the county is given here along with a list showing the range and diversity of site types encountered.

THE COUNTY SMR

The Sites and Monuments Record (SMR) Office was established in 1985 by the Office of Public Works in response to increasing threats posed to our archaeological heritage by urban growth, the development and up-grading of motorways and roads, land improvement schemes, housing in rural areas, quarrying and afforestation. Its brief was to compile a record of all known, suspected or destroyed archaeological sites in sixteen counties which had not been officially recorded previously. The work was almost entirely office-based with provision for only occasional field inspections. Initial SMR work on the sixteen counties was completed by 1992.

Once research was concluded, each site noted was given an individual identification number referring to a file containing all the relevant documentation. This SMR number also accesses a record on the computer database, thus resulting in an effective information storage and retrieval system which can be easily up-dated on an ongoing basis. On completion of each county an edited version of this information, consisting of 6-inch Ordnance Survey maps (known as constraint maps) showing the locations of sites, along with accompanying computerised check-lists, was issued to various government departments, county planning offices and development agencies, thus enabling these authorities to monitor how proposed developments would affect a monument or area of archaeological importance.

Work took place on the Co. Sligo SMR over a 20-month period in 1988 and 1989. A wide range of cartographic, documentary, photographic and local sources were consulted. As well as the various editions of the Ordnance Survey 6-inch maps, the Down Survey maps of 1650 in Sligo County Library were checked, and various estate maps in the National Library of Ireland, all revealing a percentage of 'new' sites. The main archaeological journals were consulted along with the Ordnance Survey Letters (1838), regional and county histories and Office of Public Works and National Museum of Ireland files. Regarding antiquarian accounts, the Rev. William Henry's Natural and Topographical History of Sligo, dated 1739, was of particular importance as it includes a very interesting description of the Carrowmore megalithic tombs and also an account of Knocknarea. Material published by renowned antiquarians such as Petrie, Wakeman, Wood-Martin and Macalister were also major sources of information, as well as more recent publications by Burenhult, on his excavations and field surveys at Carrowmore and the surrounding areas, and Heraughty's book on Inismurray. John McTernan's *Sligo: Sources of Local History* (1988) proved to be a very valuable checklist.

With regard to aerial photography, the SMR office pioneered the systematic use of both vertical and oblique photography as an integrated part of its research programme. The main reference collection used was the high altitude vertical photography taken for the Geological Survey of Ireland (GSI) between 1973 and 1977. Lower altitude vertical photographs taken by the Irish Air Corps and the Ordnance Survey were also examined. These were supplemented by a collection of some three hundred oblique photographs taken by Dr J.K. St Joseph of Cambridge University between 1963 and 1971. The aerial photographs recorded many sites not marked on the Ordnance Survey maps thus making a very important contribution to the archaeological record. In Sligo a large number of sites were identified in this way, the most spectacular being the hillfort at Knocknashee. Some thirty house sites and two

The Archaeological Record-Classifications for Co. Sligo, 1995

PREHISTORIC
(NEOLITHIC, BRONZE AGE, IRON AGE)
c. 4000 BC – c. AD 400)

Archaeological complex	16
Barrow	112
Barrow group	3
Bell-barrow	2
Boulder-burial	3
Bowl-barrow	30
Cairn	78
Ceremonial enclosure	5
Cist	36
Court tomb	60
Crannóg	137
Field bank	6
Field system	54
Field wall	44
Fulacht fiadh	65
Fulachta fiadh	5
Habitation site	5
Hearth	1
Henge	2
Hillfort	2
Hilltop enclosure	2
Hut hollow	1
Hut site	182
Kerb cairn	1
Linear earthwork	1
Long cist	3
Megalithic structure	72
Megalithic tomb	52
Midden	64
Mound	69
Passage tomb	82
Pit burial	3
Pond-barrow	1
Portal tomb	11
Post row	10
Promontory fort	20
Ring-barrow	9
Ring-cairn	3
Ring-ditch	3
Rock art	3
Saucer-barrow	43
Settlement hearth	1
Settlement platform	13
Settlement	1
Short cist	1
Stone alignment	1
Stone circle	6
Stone pair	4
Stone row	3
Standing stone	29
Urn burial	2
Wedge tomb	38

EARLY MEDIEVAL
(c. AD 400 – c. 1100)

Bullaun stone	31
Burial ground	1
Cashel	345
Cemetery	9
Church	88
Cliff-edge fort	9
Clochan	2
College	1
Cross-inscribed pillar	10
Cross-inscribed stone	6
Cross	14
Cross-slab	21
Earthwork	48
Ecclesiastical enclosure	9
Ecclesiastical remains	100
Enclosure	830
Graveyard	77
Graveslab	17
High cross	2
Holed stone	2
Holy stone	3
Holy tree	1
Holy well	112
Inscribed stone	3
Leacht cuimhne	5
Ogham stone	1
Oratory	2
Penitential station	3
Rath	2
Ringfort	1620
Ringfort – raised	83
Round tower	1
Shrine	1
Saint's tomb	2
Souterrain	408
Wellhouse	1

THE ARCHAEOLOGICAL RECORD-CLASSIFICATIONS FOR CO. SLIGO, 1995

MEDIEVAL AND POST-MEDIEVAL
(c. AD 1100 – c. 1700)

Abbey	12
Altar-tomb	2
Altar	22
Architectural fragment	10
Bawn	2
Brick kiln	2
Bridge	7
Building	26
Castle	77
Chapel	3
Children's burial ground	9
Corn-drying kiln	2
Crucifixion plaque	4
Cultivation ridge	1
Deerpark	1
Dovecote	1
Dwelling	7
Effigy	1
Exhibitionist figure	1
Fish pond	1
Fish-breeding pond	1
Folly	1
Font	10
Ford	2
Fortified house	1
Friary	4
Garden feature	1
Gateway	1
Gatehouse	1
Hospital	3
House	86
House - 17th century	3
Kelp-drying kiln	2
Kiln	6
Lime kiln	12
Mansion	4
Mass rock	2
Moated site	38
Motte	1
Motte and bailey	2
Nunnery	6
Oratory	2
Plantation castle	2
Priory	1
Rectangular enclosure	42
Ridge and furrow	3
Ringwork	1
Road	26
Saltworking	2
Settlement - deserted	6
Star-shaped fort	4
Stone sculpture	12
Tomb	2
Tower	4
Tower house	9
Town	1
Tree ring	7
Village	1
Weir	3

OTHER

(includes sites which could date to more than one section)

Annex	2
Ash pit	2
Barrack - Infantry	1
Battlefield	1
Boundary stone	1
Burial	13
Cave	8
Clearance cairn	4
Linear feature	1
Mill	13
Millpond	1
Mill race	2
Millstone	2
Mineworking	4
Miscellaneous	41
Monument	1
Natural cave	1
Non-antiquity	136
Pond	1
Potential site - aerial photograph	13
Potential site - name	1
Potential site - tradition	1
Quarry	39
Quernstone	19
Rectilinear enclosure	2
Stone sculpture - iconic	1
Sweathouse	25
Well	7

cairns had already been identified there but on close scrutiny the photographs revealed an ancient rampart around the entire hilltop.

The SMR for Sligo was compiled by Michael Gibbons, Olive Alcock, Tom Condit and Mary Tunney with assistance from Martin A. Timoney. Local input to the SMR was considerable. A network of contacts was built up and our attention was drawn to many important sites that would otherwise have gone unnoticed. Invaluable aid was given by the Sligo Field Club which passed on information on all 'new' sites noticed over the years by their fieldwalkers, in particular Finlay Tower Kitchin better known as Pat, Michael Cahalane, Des Smith, Paddy Heraughty, Jack Flynn, Aodhán O'Higgins, John McTernan, Brían Ó Súilleabháin, Martin A. and Mary B. Timoney. These sites are incorporated into the SMR record. Also, the results of some of Major R.B. Aldridge's fieldwalking in west Sligo, which had been passed on to the Sligo Field Club, were added to the files. A total of 4,500 sites were noted and apart from unlocated sites, they were all marked up on the constraint maps. Because of the importance and density of sites in the Carrowmore megalithic cemetery, a special insert of the 25-inch map for this area was included.

THE ARCHAEOLOGICAL FIELD SURVEY

Following the completion of the SMR, initial field survey work was undertaken for the Archaeological Survey of Ireland by Victor Buckley, Charles Mount, Jane O'Shaughnessy, Kieran D. O'Conor, Ellen O'Carroll, Mairead Weaver, Ailish McGuinness and Markus Casey. Many new sites were recorded, locations were found for some previously unlocated sites and a number of sites listed in the original SMR were reclassified. The field survey is at present being completed hand in hand with the writing up of the inventory entries. The inventory will be published in two volumes: North Sligo, being written up by Patrick O'Donovan and South Sligo, being written up the Archaeological Survey Office in University College Cork. The inventory format allows for a short description of each site with appropriate measurements and specific locational information. The sites are grouped by classification in a broad chronological sequence and the volume will include some maps and photographic material.

RECORDED MONUMENTS LISTINGS

Recent legislation (National Monuments (Amendment) Act 1994) required the Minister for Arts, Heritage, Gaeltacht and the Islands to establish an up-to-date record of monuments for each county comprising a new list and a set of location maps. Newly found sites were added, some classifications were changed while some sites were found on field inspection not to merit inclusion. These new maps and lists, referred to as the 'Record of Monuments and Places' and issued for Sligo in 1995, are available for consultation through the planning authorities and county libraries.

SITE CLASSIFICATIONS

The following list gives a chronological breakdown of the 175 classifications used in the archaeological record for Co. Sligo. The aim is to provide a general overview of the classifications used. The use of chronological sections is quite arbitrary as classifications such as 'enclosures' or 'ecclesiastical remains' may include material dating to more than one such section. Some terms cover more than one individual site. 'Archaeological complex', for example, is used when three or more related elements occur together. The term 'ecclesiastical remains' covers sites with churches, graveyards, ecclesiastical enclosures, crosses, bullaun stones, *etc*. Again, it is generally used where three or more elements occur.

It should be noted that fieldwork since 1995 has turned up some more 'new' sites. These now form part of the Sites and Monuments Record which remains the core record for all counties.

Castlebaldwin Castle

A Practitioner's Perspective on the Development Conflict

John O'Dwyer
Senior Executive Officer, Sligo Corporation.

ABSTRACT: Development is briefly examined from the constraints, opportunities, conflict, balance, objections, sustainability, roles and structures points of view. The essential recognition is that development is all about resolution.

DEVELOPMENT - CONFLICT

This essay is not intended to be scholarly or academic but is rather intended to inform the public from a practical viewpoint of the constraints and opportunities proposed by development. The essential recognition is that development is all about conflict resolution. There are many sides: those wishing to remain static for commercial reasons, i.e., to avoid competition: those wishing to oppose competition: those concerned at the impact of development on the greater Environment; developers wishing to make optimum use of site potential and finally the planning authority desirous to secure development on the basis of the legal cited 'requirement in the proper interest of orderly development'.

DEVELOPMENT - BALANCE

The broad principle of 'sustainable development', *i.e.*, development aimed at not adversely affecting the quality of life of future generations, is an attempt to balance conflict but is always a difficult concept to achieve. Planning is and will always be a subjective process, subject to the policy directions of an elected Council.

The introduction of professionals does not necessarily ease or change the process and conflicts in planning as issues such as Whose town or city is it?, When and what stage must objections be seriously entertained?, Is employment a factor?, still remain to be resolved.

DEVELOPMENT - OBJECTIONS

It is always difficult to propose or permit development that encounters local objection. It could be argued with some justification that a democratically defined local objection should be sufficient to prevent development or ameliorate its worst elements at least. How practical can this be? Take for instance the need to provide residential halt sites, landfill sites, heavy industry, road infrastructure, reservoirs, etc. Few will argue on their merit. All see the need, provided they can be provided at locations somewhere else. The problem is where, and who decides, and what right is there to decide in the face of concerted local opposition.

Local Authorities are now experiencing enormous difficulty given the increased level of local and community awareness on the adverse impact of some developments. It must be accepted that all development has some adverse and almost irreversible environmental impact. It is not only desirable but essential that local authorities now have to engage in public consultation.

DEVELOPMENT - SUSTAINABLE

At the Earth Summit on the Environment in Rio de Janiero in 1992 the broad principles of sustainable development and what is now called 'Agenda 21' emerged as -Development today must not undermine the development and environment needs of present and future generations.

In order to achieve sustainable development environmental protection shall constitute an integral part of the development process and cannot be considered in isolation from it. Environmental issues are best handled with the participation of all concerned citizens. The inherent dynamic proposal is that the services delivery mechanisms must change. It will no longer be acceptable for local authorities to decide policy and execution on the basis of a Development Plan. The principles of community participation, empowerment and partnership emerge. This challenges the democracy of existing delivery, it is being challenged and questioned in a manner that calls for a consultative partnership with the Community.

All this emerges side by side with the 'bottom up' approach enshrined in the Community Support framework which forms the funding basis for most major projects.

DEVELOPMENT - ROLES

Communities are now organising and defining their own local needs. This is occurring without any real leadership or thought. There is almost a role reversal, public authority records on consultation and devolution stand indicted, the new Community Order is now setting the agenda and yet these new organisations are failing to consult upwards. What is therefore happening is the creation of a demand expectation that cannot be met by supply provision. This is potentially damaging and could destroy local initiative.

Communities must be seen as a resource. Public bodies offer a wealth of provision experience matched by an organisational capacity with perpetual existence. This latter factor is vital as community dynamic centers on objective achievement in the short term without consideration of maintainance in the long term. The questions to be posed are What happens when the funding runs out?, What capacities and resources will remain?, What will the negative community impact mean?, Were there any exit strategies?, How real was the need and the market?, etc.

DEVELOPMENT - STRUCTURES

This calls for a structured approach involving the public authorities, business and community leaders. Otherwise development opportunities will become log-jammed in a senseless power struggle, forgetting the reason why services are provide, i.e., to meet 'people' needs. The provision agency remains unimportant but what is vital is that the service can be delivered efficiently and in a manner that will enhance the receiver and the environment in which he resides. Only through real-partnership involving all sectors can any semblance of consensus emerge. This calls for the release and sharing of power by those in whom it now is vested.

BIBLIOGRAPHY

E.C. Commission - *Towards Sustainability: A European Community Programme of Policy and Action in relation to the Environment and Sustainable Development.*

Ireland - Community Support Framework, 1994-1999.

Keating, Michael, 1993: *The Earth Summit's Agenda for Change - A Plain Language Version of Agenda 21 and the Other Rio Agreements,* Geneva, Centre for Our Common Future, 1993.

Local Government (Planning and Development) Act, 1999.

Our Common Future - Report of the World Commission on Environment and Development (The Brundtland Report), London: Oxford University Press, 1987.

Planning and Development Act, 2000.

SLIGO ANTIQUARIAN SOCIETY, 1945-1946
AND
SLIGO FIELD CLUB, 1946-1947, 1954-2002

Martin A. Timoney and Patrick Heraughty
Sligo Field Club

ABSTRACT: Sligo Antiquarian Society was founded in 1945. It changed its name to Sligo Field Club in 1946 and had a public existence until mid-1947 after which it was moribund until a Revival in 1954. Since then it has been in continuous existence, arranging lectures and outings and encouraging preservation of our heritage but has not published until now. This history of Sligo Antiquarian Society and Sligo Field Club, their Officers, Committee, some members and some outsiders who influenced its direction, was compiled from Sligo Field Club minute books and files, local newspapers and the personal archives and recollection of several members and fellow antiquarians.

INTRODUCTION

Sligo Antiquarian Society was founded in 1945. It changed its name to Sligo Field Club in 1946. There is no record of any public activities from mid-1947 until it was revived in 1954. Since then it has been in continuous existence, arranging lectures and outings, assisting students of all stature and publicising and encouraging preservation of our heritage. This history of Sligo Antiquarian Society and Sligo Field Club, their Officers, Committee, some members[1] and also some outsiders who influenced its direction or were of like mind, was compiled from Sligo Field Club minute books and files, local newspapers and the personal archives and recollection of several members and fellow antiquarians. The backgrounds, ideals, successes, failures, contacts and publications of those involved, mainly members but also some outsiders, are described as we feel that they may not otherwise pass on to the next generation. There is considerable overlap between the history of SAS & SFC on the one hand and the history of archaeology in Co. Sligo on the other[2]. This volume is its first publication though many of its members have individually published articles and books.

THE TRADITION OF ANTIQUARIAN STUDIES IN SLIGO

Antiquarian studies have a long tradition in Sligo. Dúbhaltach MacFirbisigh described Rathmulcagh in the mid-17th. century (Ó Muraile 1996). Edward Lhuyd visited Sligo in 1699 and 1700 (Ó Nualláin 1989, [3]). Rev. William Henry wrote on monuments and natural events in Co. Sligo in 1739 (NLI Ms. 2533). Lewis Irwin of Tanrego made the arrangements for Gabriel Beranger's visits to monasteries, castles and Carrowmore in 1779 (Wilde 1880; Harbison 2002a; 2002b). Late eighteenth century drawings by Austin Cooper of Inishmurray, Drumcliffe and Banada were recently published by Harbison (2000). R.A. Dukes of Newpark was collecting antiquities early in the last century (NLI Ms 794, No. 657; Wood-Martin 1888, 207).

Roger Chambers Walker, 1806-1854, of Rathcarrick was in many ways Father of Sligo Archaeology, though some of his methods were not the best. By 1828, at the latest, he was with his life-long friend George Petrie on Knocknarea (NLI Ms 794, No. 657). His very informative letters to Petrie are in the National Library of Ireland and his Account Book is in Sligo Library Local Studies Archive. He had a land surveyor make a map of the Carrowmore cemetery [NLI Ms 794, no. 657] and he dug many of the tombs there. In 1837 Petrie wrote a detailed description of Carrowmore at Walker's house at Rathcarrick (Ordnance Survey Letters, Co. Sligo). Wood-Martin (1888) used Walker's work as the basis of his work on Carrowmore. Walker had designs on digging Misgaun Maedbh (NLI Ms 794, no. 659). He was an avid collector and went so far as to steal a cross from a churchyard3 in September 1837, though he got the wrong one on the first attempt (NLI MS 794, no. 660). This is now in the National Museum of Ireland (Wood-Martin 1889, 304; Harbison 1992, 73-74, No. 81). He sold his collection of antiquities to the Duke of Northumberland at Alnwick Castle in 1851. In 1990 the National Museum of Ireland purchased back gold objects from this collection including the Carrowmore gold ribbon torc (Eogan 1983, no. 45, fig. 29). The gold filigree panel and a coin from an Irish crannóg now at Alnwick (Whitfield 2001) may have been in his collection. Walker's sister, Letitia, discovered 'a Danish fort with three Cromlecks on the top of it' on the Cummeen Demesne (NLI MS 794 no. 661) though Kitchin maintained that it must be a folly like the others on that demesne (McTernan 1990, 50-52, 69). Wood-Martin was in possession of at least one diary of his (Wood-Martin 1895, 658)[4].

Rev. Constantine Cosgrave, P.P., Keash, was the first person with a Connacht address (Timoney and Timoney 2001, 12) to join the Kilkenny Archaeological Society, (later to become the Royal Society of Antiquaries of Ireland, hereinafter RSAI), which had been founded in 1849. He reported many of his discoveries to RSAI (Cosgrave; Wood-Martin 1888, 206). In the late 1870s and early 1880s Edward Cooper of Markree had William F. Wakeman make drawings of antiquities throughout the county of Sligo and adjoining areas[5].

In the latter nineteenth century came Sligo's two most prolific antiquarian authors, O'Rorke and Wood-Martin. Dr. Archdeacon Terence O'Rorke, D.D., P.P., (1819-1907) (McTernan 1994, 150-154) wrote two volumes, *History of Sligo* (1889 & reprint 1986) and *Ballisodare and Kilvarnet* (1878).

William Gregory Wood-Martin , 1847-1917, (McTernan 1995, 161-164; Ireland 2001 with a bibliography of his works and of the reviews of some of them) wrote on the archaeology and history of Sligo, publishing nine volumes between 1880 and 1902. He wrote on latchets and dress fasteners (Wood-Martin 1903; 1904; 1905).

Wood-Martin was very active in the Royal Society of Antiquaries of Ireland in the 1880s. He joined as a fellow in 1882 (*JRSAI*, 21, lists) and was appointed Editing Secretary of its *Journal* in June 1887 (Proceedings JRSAI 18, 100) but by January 1889 he had resigned that post. He resigned from the Society in 1892. His grandson, Richard 'Dickie' Wood-Martin, recounts that he had not the desire for organising a society and that, combined with the time he devoted to the Royal Society of Antiquaries of Ireland and his duties as Major in the Sligo Artillery, left little time for organising a Society[6].

In 1904 the Field Club Union met in Sligo, the multy-author report is in Volume 13 *of The Irish Naturalist* (Anon 1904), but left no permanent organisation behind it[7].

Tadgh Kilgannon drew heavily on the works of Wood-Martin and O'Rorke and added material giving the story of Sligo in synoptic form up to 1926 (1926 & reprint 1988).

Henry Morris[8] (Morris, this volume), National Schools Inspector in Sligo from 1923 to 1932, devoted his energies to writing and fieldwork. The elder author[9] was examined by him in Inishmurray N.S. in 1928 or 1929 and Tim Kelly in Kilross NS. The Mousterian controversy relating to discoveries at Ballyconnell, Rosses Point and Coney Island of the late 1920s (Woodman, this volume, wherein Mousterian is explained) seems to have passed over the heads of Sligo people at the time though it has resurfaced for various reasons on a number of occasions over the last two decades (Finnegan 1977, 42-47, 81-85; Clarke 1985, 7). Despite being a Founder member of the Louth Archaeological & Historical Society in 1903 and its first editor he, like Wood-Martin, did his own thing. His son Brendan, and his wife Phil are current members of SFC.

The minute books of Sligo Town Vocational Education Committee for the period April 1934 to August 1943 do not contain any references to Royal Dublin Society extension lectures nor any cultural matters whatsoever, being more concerned with building the new Technical School in Quay St., later the home of Sligo Teachers' Centre and hence of SFC and Sligo Historical Society. The Ballina Historical and Folklore Society, which spanned the years from 1936 to 1944 (McHale 1987-1988, 40), may have had members from west Sligo. Two major excavation of the Creevykeel court tomb in 1935 pre-dates our founding.

Throughout the nineteenth and the first half of the twentieth century many local societies were established in Ireland[10]. All the Sligo antiquarian activity up until the mid-1940s seems to have been individual in nature; it may not be surprising then that it was not until 1945 that Sligo got its first such society, the Sligo Antiquarian Society[11].

We are almost entirely dependent on the Sligo newspapers for record of the early years[12], particularly of the first two phases, 1945-1947 and 1947-1954. Even by 1968 there was confusion as to founding date and the people involved. There are among the Sligo Field Club papers some notes made by Michael Cahalane for a ten-minute talk to the Sligo Rotary Club in which he writes "Founded 1937 (Tohall, Moran and Kirwan), lapsed during the War years, revived after the War". This is incorrect in a number of ways as will be seen below. We know nothing as to how long some people were members before becoming committee members.

Our County Library has an excellent Local Studies Archive to which there is a thorough guide (McTernan 1988; 1994) but even this has failed to elucidate the story; our County Library was not fully used as a repository in the 1940s and 1950s[13]. How much harder it will be to reconstruct our present history because of use of the phone!

In January 1944 the Sligo National Monuments Advisory Committee held its first meeting. Those present were Martin Mulligan, Jr.[14], T.H. Blackburn, Headmaster in The Grammar School, Canon J. Feeley, Adm., Fr. O'Hara, O.P., and Br. John; none of the clergy figure later in this history. A list of one hundred and twelve monuments by Mulligan and a list of forty-seven holy wells were forwarded to the Corporation with a recommendation that they be declared National Monuments. They also recommended that three houses in front of the Abbey be removed to enhance its setting. Later that year, in March, Prof. F.E. Stephens, M.A., lectured in the Technical School on "Local History and its Place in Education". Carrowmore, Deerpark and Inishmurray were mentioned in the lecture. D.A. Mulcahy, C.E.O., suggested that the time had come when they should form their own local Committee or Antiquarian Society and also that they should start moves towards a museum and art gallery. Those recorded as being present were Harry de Pew[15], J. McKenna[16] and Seamus Rossiter a teacher in the Technical School who lived in Bridge St, and D.A. Mulcahy. The idea of a museum for Sligo came from Patrick Tohall who made the initial push for it in the early 1952.

FOUNDATION OF SLIGO ANTIQUARIAN SOCIETY

On 29th January, 1945, Michael V. Duignan, then of the National Museum of Ireland, Dublin, and later Prof. of Archaeology at UCG, gave a lecture in Sligo entitled 'Life and Work in Ancient Ireland'. This was organised by Co. Sligo VEC whose CEO at the time was Thomas McEvilly. For a long time we worked on the premises that this was under the auspices of the Royal Dublin Society[17], as reported in the local newspapers of February 1945, though this seems now to have been RSAI.

During discussions after the Duignan lecture there was general agreement that there was need for a local society or club to arrange the specialised activities best suited to the locality.

The Sligo Independent of. 3rd February 1945, report includes the comment that "In a county like [Sligo] . . . there was no field society" and, even though the piece is headed 'Call for a Revival' there is no mention in the report of a pre-1945 Antiquarian or other Society in Sligo. *The Sligo Champion* records that Patrick Tohall proposed that there be a local Antiquarian Society and that, pending the appointment of a permanent secretary, those interested should contact him at No. 6, High St., and that those interested in joining RSAI should contact Robert Kirwan at Ard na Veigh. We take it that the press reporter got confused between the RSAI, of which Tohall, and Morris before him, were local secretaries, and the proposed Sligo Antiquarian Society.

Those recorded as being present at the meeting include Very Rev. V. Hanly, Adm., Mr. D.A. Hegarty, Co. Manager, Dr. Michael Kirby, County M.O.H., Mr. Mulcahy, C.E.O., Dr. T. Foley[18], Ald. Michael Nevin of The Magnet, High St., Ald. Andrew J. Dolan of Stephen St, Mr. P. Sliney, Herbert Quinton [19], Fintan A. Raftery[20], Robert J. Kirwan and Patrick Tohall.

On 17th April 1945 a **preliminary meeting** was held in the Imperial Hotel on Corcoran's Mall, now The Embassy on Kennedy Parade. Robert Kirwan was appointed Chairman, Dr. J.P. Moran as Vice Chairman and Patrick Tohall as Hon. Secretary. Also present were Anthony, he prefers to be called Tony, Toher, chemist, Austin G. Jennings, engineer, Bernard F. Rhatigan, architect, Frank McLoughlin, of the Royal Bank and from Buncranna, T.P. Ó Catháin, B.E., B.Sc., Land Commission, Nora Niland, who had recently taken up the position of County Librarian, and Mrs. Elizabeth Tohall.

On 24th April 1945 the **inaugural meeting** was held in the Imperial Hotel. The three officers, Chairman, Robert J. Kirwan, Vice Chairman, Dr. J.P. Moran, and Hon. Secretary, Patrick Tohall, were present; Frank McLoughlin was added as Hon. Treasurer. New members who joined on that occasion were Mrs. Eileen Lambert, Miss Margaret Willis, Headmistress, Sligo High School, Miss Glasgow, Miss E.G. Mitchell, Gertrude Healy, a National Teacher living in Wolfe Tone St., Nora Richards, Maureen Regan[21], Dr. Thomas J. Murphy, Robert Browne of Scarden, J.C.F. Giles[22], Christopher A. McCormack, B. Agr. Sc. (Forestry), Dept. of Lands, Alfred McHugh of The Sligo Champion, Mr. T.P. Monaghan [Monahan], solicitor, and Fintan Raftery.

Letters of encouragement and advice from Dr. Farrington, on behalf of the Royal Irish Academy, Dr. Joseph Raftery, on behalf of the National Museum, and the Ordnance Survey were read.

The first outing was on 8th May 1945 when thirty-four people went to Deerpark. Tony

Toher's photograph of the group in the court-tomb[23] shows only 23 of these, of which 15 can now be identified. They are 1 Edith Mitchell, Sligo High School; 2 Mrs. Elizabeth Tohall; 5 James Rigney, N.T., Rosses Point[24]; 6 T.P. Toher, M.P.S.I., father of Tony; 7 Dr. T.J. Murphy; 9 Christopher A. McCormack; 14 Patrick Tohall; 15 Frank McLaughlin, Manager, Royal Bank[25]; 16 R.J. Kirwan, B.E., County Surveyor; 18 Miss Margaret Willis, Headmistress, Sligo High School; 19 T.P. Ó Catháin, B.E., B.Sc.; 20 Mrs. Margaret Toher; 21 **Queenie** Dolan; 22 Nora Niland, B.A.; 23 Maureen Rhattigan.

On May 13th SAS went to Carrowmore. The earliest surviving document of the Sligo Antiquarian Society is a folder entitled "The Monuments of Cuil-Irra Peninsula, County Sligo. Usually called the Carrowmore Monuments". On the cover is written "This folder is issued by Sligo Antiquarian Society as Membership Card for its Inaugural Year 1945". Inside, below the map of Carrowmore, is written "Copied from Wood-Martin's Works for Sligo Antiquarian Society 1945". It is signed and dated "Patrick Tohall 21 May 1945". The two page spread has a map of the Carrowmore Cemetery at a scale of four and a half inches to the mile and, on the opposite page, a list of the monuments with brief comments on what was found in them and when.

On 5th June T.P. Ó Catháin, B.E., Land Commission, lectured to them on "The Ice Age". On June 10th they went by cycle to Maugheraboy, The Glen and Carrowmore. Austin G. Jennings lectured on geology on 5th January 1946.

The older members of Sligo Field Club, many of whom have since passed to their eternal reward, have been repeatedly questioned over the years about the origins of our Sligo Field Club. Some think that there may have been 'some loose organisation before the War'. There are clear recollections of going out on bicycles at a time of petrol scarcity but, as to whether that was before, during or after the war, was not clear. The elder author says that there were no pre-World War II activities; the earliest remembered outing was on bicycles to Maugheraboy, The Glen and Carrowmore. Tohall is always mentioned in connection with founding SAS, but as he did not come to Sligo until on 27th February, 1942, this founding could not be before this. This, we think, rules out a pre-World War II founding.

We do not know why this year of 1945 but, lest anyone think that it had anything to do with the 700th anniversary of the founding of Sligo Castle in 1245 (O'Conor, this volume), we have not seen any reference to Sligo Castle nor to 1245 in this context, nor did SAS go in 1945 to the only surviving medieval building in the town, the Dominican Priory, better known as Sligo Abbey. On 2nd November 1944 RSAI established a sub-committee to take the Society of Antiquaries to the country by arranging popular lectures. There is confusion over this because the Proceedings (JRSAI 1946, 113) record that a committee was established to organise a public lecture scheme on 15th March 1945, even though three such lectures had already been held in Dublin and one in Sligo.

Prof. Seán P. Ó Ríordáin gave a lecture on 'Irish Field Antiquities' in November 1945 as part of the Thomas Davis Centenary. This lecture under RSAI was offered to the Davis Centenary Week Committee[26] by Tohall who suggested some orchestral music, but not high brow, at all lectures. At intervals in the lecture music was provided by the Centenary Week Orchestra directed by Jennie Balantine-Koss. Ó Ríordáin, who was accompanied by Mr. Rory de Valera, said he was in Sligo five years previously with Prof. Childe of Edinburgh who later lectured in Dublin on his survey of Sligo. Robert Kirwan and Ó Ríordáin both mentioned the 'local society'.

Tony Toher's lecture to SAS on the work done on pollen analysis of the Swedish bogs was reported on in *the Sligo Independent* of 5th January 1946. The elder author may have joined SAS by the time of this lecture. For a while geology was to the fore with SAS. Austin G. Jennings lectured on 5th January 1946 on geology. T.P. Ó Catháin, B.E., B.Sc., lectured in late January 1946[27] on the Geology of Ireland. The newspaper report gives his name as G.P. Keane. In early February 1946 Patrick Tohall lectured on The Carboniferous Limestone Age and later in the month Robert Kirwan lectured on the Geology of Sligo. The drift from the main antiquarian theme, as implied in the name SAS, was already under way. The catalyst may have been an RDS extension lecture in late February 1946 in the Technical School arranged by D.A. Mulcahy, Sligo Borough CEO, and presided over by Mrs. Flannagan, Mayor. The lecture was by Dr. Dermot F. Gleeson, D.J., of Nenagh, on 'Antiquities of an Irish Parish' or 'Historic Monuments of an Irish Parish'. He praised the existence of the local society, encouraged additions to the OS maps by fieldwalkers and discouraged the changing of street names. Kirwan, 'Chairman of the SAS' proposed the vote of thanks and Tohall, in seconding it, asked people to join RSAI, or at least SAS at the nominal fee of 5 shillings. Dr. Gleeson responded to the acclamation by "laughingly warning those assembled not to let Tohall lead SAS to specialise in prehistory and overlook vanishing historic houses, weirs, quays, roads and streets". His 'fears', as we see later, were unfounded[28].

The next event following Gleeson's lecture was the AGM held on 12th March 1946. The newspaper report headed "Sligo Field Club (Formerly Sligo Antiquarian Society)" heralds the change of name[29]. At this meeting "Owing to the development of the scope of the Society's activities the meeting unanimously decided to change its name to SFC[30]. As well as geology many of the members are interested in birds, wild plants and nature generally." Curiously there is no mention of antiquarian considerations perhaps it was felt unnecessary to mention it. At this first AGM Robert Kirwan was elected Chairman, Dr. John Moran Vice-Chairman, Mr. C.A. Giles[31], Provincial Bank, Collooney, Treasurer, Patrick Tohall Secretary; James Rigney and P. McGuinness for the Committee. B.J. Dowling, Mr. Lanigan, Mr. H. Depew are the only others mentioned as being in attendance, and there were apologies from C.A. McCormack, Herbert Quinton, Mr. Mulreaney and Miss Margaret Willis. There were proposals to visit the barytes mines, Carrowkeel with tea at Hollybrook, to cross from Gleniff to Glencar, to visit Aughris for the birds, Pollacheeney for the submerged forest, "Slieve da Eun" for geology, and Lugnagall by cycle. The first Monday of each month was set for a meeting at 8 PM when the two outings for that month would be arranged. The report includes the comment that "The prime object is a pleasant ramble amid beautiful scenery and the development of a culture based on an appreciation of earth and sea."

The reason the name 'Sligo Field Club' was adopted was that the number of persons then interested in matters solely antiquarian would be insufficient to maintain an Antiquarian Society, so 'Field Club' allowed us to embrace several outdoor activities, archaeology, botany, geology, natural history, history and ornithology, in combination. The cross fertilisation between people of different disciplines, so well exemplified elsewhere in the life and work of Prof. G. Frank Mitchell of T.C.D., benefited members tremendously. Sligo Field Club joined the Royal Society of Antiquaries of Ireland on 29th May 1946[32] on the proposal of Patrick Tohall. In April 1946 SFC went to Lugnagall visiting a cashel with a souterrain and a lios, in May to Creevykeel and also to Mullaghmore, to Aughris, Carrowkeel and "Cnoch-na-Riach" that year. *The Sligo Independent* report on the Creevykeel outing states "The prime object, however, is a pleasant excursion, and in this the Society has been most fortunate heretofore". The outing to Aughris was with five motor loads, Mrs. Finnegan made them tea in her house there and they had a great look at the sea cliffs from a boat belonging to Gallagher Bros. [33] of Owey, Co. Donegal. Sea conditions were so good that they got the boat into a cavern in the Aughris cliff and watched two seals playing there. Yet again there is a call to arms with a comment about them "creating a public spirit". The report on SFC activities in 1946 in *The Sligo Independent* of 4th January 1947 includes the statement that "SFC supersedes SAS, founded two years ago". The proposed outings to Aughris and Pollacheeney are not in the list though they did go to Aughris. The submerged forest at Pollacheeney was mentioned at a lecture in Kilmacowen by Tohall in 1952, but we can find no mention of the outing taking place.

Even in those early days Tohall's reputation for having the local knowledge was respected in the County Council. When Staff-Sergeant Robert Spencer arrived from Canada to the Council in May 1946 looking for his wife's Ormsby ancestral home at Cummeen, Tohall was contacted. Tohall took them into his care and showed them the demesne. Tohall's report in the newspaper points out that not only are there two prehistoric sites there but also three fakes, a tower of water-worn blocks known as The Hermit's cell, a fake gable of a monastic church, and finally, a wall complete with battlements and embrasures to represent a feudal fort. There was an outing in Summer 1961 to Church Island in Lough Gill led by Paddy Heraughty and John Troddyn. This produced an "unexpected thrill when several members found themselves waist deep in water" and that "finally decided the Committee against all such aquatic operations in the future."

He was responsible for the wooden scoop-like vessel from Cartrontaylor, Ballintogher, being lodged in the National Museum of Ireland, NMI IA 1959:22.

In July 1946 Stuart Piggott and Terrence G.E. Powell visited several megalithic tombs in Sligo and Achill but there is no mention in the report of Sligo Antiquarian Society or Sligo Field Club or any of its members being of assistance[34].

On a pleasant day snatched from a wet September 1946 Moran, Murphy and McEvilly provided transport to Carrowkeel followed by tea at Hollybrook.

On 26th October 1946 the entire Sligo staff of the Land Commission, including Patrick Tohall and Eithne Dolan, visited Inishmurray to report on a possible evacuation of the island. Cathríona MacLeod of NMI was with them, possibly on the invitation of Tohall; presumably she was putting the finishing touches to her article on the medieval wooden statues including that of St. Molaise (MacLeod 1946). In January 1947 the Land Commission were still trying to solve the problem. The Co. Co. did evacuate the last eight families to Carns in 1948. There is a poignant mention of the repeated pleas for a simple solution, a breakwater which would make the natural harbour, Classeymore, safe for use in almost all sea conditions[35].

In early winter 1946 there were "simple talks by members on the elementary side of one of the natural aspects of the locality"; Kirwan spoke on the 'Geology of Sligo from a Beginners Standpoint' and Toher spoke on 'Some Special Features of the Botany of Co. Sligo'. The idea was to have a meeting every Tuesday at 8 PM.

T.O. Ruttledge lectured to SAS in February 1947 on the topic of Lambay Island. Afterwards Herbert Quinton suggested that Inishmurray should be declared a bird sanctuary now that there were proposals to abandon the island. In April 1947 Dr. Gerald P. Laferty, a newcomer to Sligo living in Rathedmond, spoke to SFC on Animal Instincts based on examples from abroad.

Progressing through the newspapers for Spring 1947 one was fearing that SFC had already closed down. The snows of February and March 1947, the fear in April 1947 that Sligo Grammar School would be closed, the contrasting standards of Féis Ceóil and Féis Shligigh and the financial problems of the SLNCR were topics of concern in the newspaper. We feared these may have pushed SFC activities out of the newspaper. Happily we find a report on 21st June 1947 that they had been to Streedagh in May, and recently to Mullaghmore, and to Killeenduff at Easkey, all for to examine the natural vegetation. The subtle preaching, "unconsciously picking up knowledge . . . from the few enthusiasts who form the power behind the Club" continued. There was no forewarning of these three outings in the newspaper and no mention of proposed events either.

In November 1947 only a dozen or so people came to hear Dr. Dermot Gleeson, D.J., of Neenagh on 'Manuscript Materials for Local History'. This lecture in the Technical School was arranged by the VEC and was presided over by Mrs. E. Flannagan, T.C. D.A. Mulcahy, Borough CEO, explained away the small crowd by saying there were other things on in Sligo that night. Kirwan proposed and Mulreany seconded the vote of thanks. The preaching in the newspaper this time reads "Educated people should feel the obligation to investigate the history of their parish" and "A vast store of valuable information was lying to a great extent neglected in the old books and manuscripts"[36].

A reasonably thorough search of the newspapers has been made and only these references to individual members or to SFC in general are to be found.

THREE FOUNDER MEMBERS

Whatever the reason for the founding of SAS it is clear that three people, Kirwan, Tohall and Moran were the main protagonists. Kirwan and Moran were interested on their own for themselves but the elder author believes that it was Tohall who got Sligo Antiquarian Society going.

Robert Kirwan, BA, BE, (or CE), was a native of Tuam, Co. Galway. He studied at the College of Science, Dublin, and transferred to UCG when in went into mechanical engineering. There he headed the examination lists. He was a kindly man but, in all things, an accurate observer and a dedicated student of botany.

On leaving college he took up a position as an engineer on the construction of the Galway-Clifden railway line and wrote a most exact paper on the geology of cuttings between Oughterard and Recess (Kirwan 1895; Mohr 1994, 146). He worked with the Congested Districts Board in Mayo. Later, about 1917, he took a private interest for three years in the Ballisodare Abbeytown mines with two partners; they considered the possibility of asbestos mining in the Aughamore Mountain region and mica in the Killery Hills though he found the vein to be too narrow to be economically mined.

He made the maps, plans and photos for T.B. Costello's article on Tuam Raths and Souterrains (Costello 1902; 1903). He then became involved in the development of the Congested Districts Board working in Castlebar. He became Sligo Co. Surveyor, as the Co. Engineer was known then, in 1907. The story of how Sligo nearly did not have Kirwan is recounted by McTernan (2000, 18-19). He married Lydia Gaynor of Calry. He pointed out after the severe snow of February and March 1947, that the tropical plants in his extensive garden at Ard-na-Veagh House, to which he had moved in 1914, had survived while all the Temperate Zone plants had been killed. His explanation was that the tropical plants had an inherent facility to adjust to extremes of temperature. He first joined RSAI in 1928. He retired from The County Council in 1942 (Photo in McTernan 2000, 87) and was succeeded by P.J. Haugh. He died on 23rd October 1949, in his eightieth year; but this had nothing to do with his fall on Inishmurray earlier that year. Bishop Doorly, assisted by many leading clergy, presided over his funeral mass.

Much of Kirwan's work in Sligo was in repairing bridges destroyed during The Troubles; he took a personal interest in all roadworks[37]. He was interested in botany and geology but not in devoting time and energy to starting a local society. He lectured to Sligo Antiquarian Society on geology; this text is in the SFC files.

Like the proverb, Sligo Antiquarian Society, and its successor Sligo Field Club, is the wit of one and the wisdom of many. The wit was that of Patrick J. Tohall, a native of The Moy, Co. Tyrone, very much the 'father figure'. He was born in 1887, graduated with B.E. and B.A. from Queen's University, Belfast, in 1911, worked with the Congested Districts Board in Castlebar and may have known of Kirwan at this stage. He joined the 5th Connaught Rangers in 1914 or 1915. He survived the Kabor Kuyu covering party, as did the Sligo Alderman John Fallon. He suffered a shattered thigh in Gallipoli. He joined the Royal Engineers and spent two and a half years in Macedonia and Bulgaria working on waterworks, roads and railway buildings, and organising large groups of native labourers. There are many myths regarding Sligo Field Club and its members. One regarding Tohall is that after he was wounded in the War he was put on a ship home with the normal proviso to be buried at sea, when the inevitable happened. Of course it did not, and he went on to live a very productive life for almost another sixty years.

After the War he worked with the Congested Districts Board and later the Land Commission, first in Co. Roscommon, then Co. Leitrim from 1934, and finally, from August 1940, with the amalgamated Cos. of Leitrim and Sligo where he was Resident Engineer. He became an Associate Member of the Institute of Civil Engineers in 1923. He married Elizabeth McTiernan of Tarmon, Co. Leitrim, in 1919 and had three daughters, Elis, Martha and Maeliosa. He moved from Roscommon town to Carrick-on-Shannon in 1936 and then to Sligo on 27th February, 1942, living for a while in the second house on the north side of the Strandhill Road outside of the railway bridge. He soon moved to No. 6, High St., opposite the Dominican Priory, to be nearer his office in Thomas St. He built a bungalow on the Mail Coach Road, the third from the south end on the west side, in 1951. Tohall joined RSAI in 1944 (JRSAI 1945, 124). He retired on 26th July 1952, but lived in Sligo until 1961; Mr. & Mrs. Patrick Tohall moved to Newbridge on 28th March 1961; he died in Newbridge on 25th June, 1973, aged 86. Mary Ryan left Sligo at bout the same time. Dr. Patrick Heraughty, Pat Kitchin, Tom McEvilly, Mrs. Sheila Kirby and Michael Cahalane made presentations on behalf of SFC on the occasion of their departures.

His father, Henry, a pharmacist, hardware and food shop owner[38], had written an article on the Battle of Benburb[39]. In 1913 he made a survey of the Charlemont Fort site for Rev. W.J. Kerr. Francis J. Biggar, the archaeologist, was a frequent visitor to the house. After World War I he went to an Irish College in Co. Donegal. Thereafter, in Roscommon and elsewhere, he worked through the Irish language. He studied geology as part of his B.E. Degree. These all gave him a background well suited to antiquarian pursuits. In addition, his work with the Congested Districts Board and the Land Commission had him out in the archaeological laboratory, the fields and the bogs, the mountains and the lakes, with the farmers telling him of their discoveries. He was an agronomist and once wrote an article on farm classification by rateable value instead of area (Tohall 1953). His enthusiasm was infectious! He travelled by motorbike. His association with the agricultural life of Connacht convinced him that the vain-glory of warriors is shabby compared with to the unremitting fortitude of the men and women who developed the open heaths of Connacht into tillage fields[40].

He was an extremely intelligent but also a most practical man, experienced in the ways of the world. He guided us with a firm hand, like an understanding father, and if correction were required, it was given in a kindly, almost allegorical, manner. When an impasse seemed imminent, Patrick could lighten the cloud with perhaps a remark such as to how well the colourful dress of the lady members toned in with the sunny day and the delightful scenery.

As everyone knows, much has changed in archaeology since those days. But for the time, his aligning of the building of the three main types of prehistoric tombs with the dates of the Old Testament Prophets, Abraham with Court Tombs at 1,800 B.C., Joseph with Passage Tombs at 1,600 B.C., Moses with Wedge Tombs at 1,400 B.C., was a then a useful mnemonic, but would be millennia, never mind centuries, out of line with current thinking. He used to say that the primary purpose of an outing was not scientific investigation but enjoyment of the countryside.

He joined RSAI in 1944 and was Local

Secretary for some years. He attended the RSAI Centenary Dinner and outing in July 1949.

Kirwan and Tohall were informed of a find by Michael 'Soldier' Healy[41] in Summer 1947. He found a Beaker period, then c. 1,800 BC, stone wrist-bracer (Mitchell 1976, 145, b) 9ft down in a bog near the Carrowkeel passage tomb cemetery. Kirwan was responsible for the find being properly recorded and sent to the National Museum of Ireland and he helped G. Frank Mitchell on pollen analysis work at Carrowkeel. The full-column report, which makes mention of the megalithic tomb sequence, varying past climates and I-Breasil and laments the sewn shoes found in the bog on another occasion not having been saved, says finds should be reported to the Guards or to Kirwan at Ardnaveigh; there is no mention of SFC nor of Tohall, though the text is certainly in Tohall's style.

Tohall was a man of very independent views. He did not always agree with Department instructions, particularly as regards the houses of the landed gentry, Hazelwood being a notable example. He was instrumental in its being retained and it was later used by the Mental Hospital[42]; since 1969 the house has been owned by Snia, an Italian fibre company, and more recently Seehan Media, a Korean videotape manufacturer. Tohall's assistant engineer, T.P. Ó Catháin, saved at Hazelwood House a collection of three hundred and four deeds, addresses and rent books of the period 1694 to 1836 of the Hazelwood Estate and a mid nineteenth century botanical scrapbook with 49 different grasses in it by David Moore, Curator of the Botanic Gardens. Tohall copied the documents into a scrapbook and sent the originals to the National Library43. Tohall was a member of Sligo Show.

Perhaps because of family commitments in the post war years[44] and because of designing and building his own house in 1951 he had not time to devote to the Sligo Field Club. He retired from The Land Commission on 27th May 1952. There were only a few communications from Tohall to the NMI from mid-1947 to late-1952. We will return to Tohall's involvement below.

The third in the founding hierarchy was Dr. John Patrick Moran, M.B., B.Ch., B.A.O, of Stephen St., Sligo. He was born in Terratick House in Ballintogher in 1892. While in UCD he became associated with Tom Kettle and the Irish Historical Society. He qualified in 1914, graduating from the Mater Hospital in 1916. He joined the British Army Medical Corps in 1916 (Henry 1995, 112) and landed on a beach in the Dardanelles in 1916. He got scarlet fever. He recounted to the elder author seeing the country people in France continuing to work undisturbed in the fields whilst the shells passed overhead. He worked in Kilteegan and London. He was appointed Medical Officer for Carney Dispensary in March 1919 and lived in Carney from 1919 to 1923. His 1923 bicycle certificate was given to Sligo Museum. He was on the Library Book Selection Committee. He was a very clear-minded thinker with an uncanny facility to bring one to the practical basis of 1945 AD or 1,500 BC. He was a keen reader with an unusual ability to retain what he had read and he did lecture to us in 1954. His interests were mainly parish history and archaeology; his wife Kitty, long time Secretary of The Yeats Society, was interested in bees and birds. He joined RSAI in 1945. From 1943 until his death in 1959 he was Coroner for North Sligo and the Borough of Sligo, Registrar of Births, Deaths and Marriages, and he was Medical Officer for the Gardaí. He was Captain of The Co. Sligo Golf Club in Rosses Point. His, boat, The Nanette, was a converted lifeboat from the *Lusitania* and he used to take SFC members from Rosses Point to Inishmurray and archaeological sites in Sligo and Donegal Bay in it. In his obituary he is credited with several donations to Sligo Museum and with being a valued member of SFC. He died on 11th December 1959. Bishop Hanley presided as his funeral mass. There is no mention of SFC or related themes in his obituary in the newspaper. His wife, Kitty Moran, as Secretary of The Yeats Society continued the academic liaison between our two organisations for many years. His nephew, Des, is a member of RSAI since 1993. He left a quernstone from Inishmurray to Sligo Museum.

Two sisters who still hold detailed memories of Sligo in the early years of SAS and SFC have been of great assistance to us in putting this text together. Queenie *alias*, Gerardine, *alias* Gearóidín, Dolan worked in the Housing and Health sections of Sligo County Council, of which Robert J. Kirwan was the County Surveyor. She has put some of her memories on record elsewhere (Ní Dhubhláin 1998; Dolan 2000). Her sister, Eithne Dolan, was a Civil Servant who held an appointment in the Land Commission in Sligo where she worked with Patrick Tohall. She was preceded in that office by Maureen Regan (No. 14 in the 1945 photograph)

Very junior in years to Dr. John Moran, but even then an expert in his knowledge of botany, was A.A.P. Toher, better known as Tony Toher, a chemist, who is still happily with us and still contributing to the proceedings of the Field Club. He first joined the Committee after the Revival in 1954 but it was not until 1996 that he became an officer, being chosen as Vice President; he was President from 1998 and 1999. On his return from post-graduate work in London in May 1946 he was invited by his neighbour[45], Dr. Moran, to join the Field Club outing and to speak on botanical matters[46]. Not only did he speak on botany but also on geology. Though he now claims he was ill-qualified to do so, he lectured to the Field Club on 5th December 1946, on "Peculiar Aspects of the Botany of County Sligo". On another occasion Mr. Tohall asked him to lecture to the Field Club on Dr. Gunner Erdtman's paper, a copy of which Tohall had got, on pollen analysis of the Swedish bogs done in 1916 and the significance of this development; this lecture at the Thomas St. venue of the Society was reported on in *The Sligo Independent* of 5th January 1946. Frequently he gave talks on the wild flowers of Co. Sligo based on a series of Kodachrome transparencies of all of the rare and unusual plants (excepting *Dryasoctopetala*). Most regrettably, mould action has destroyed these slides. He gave the first lecture after the SFC Revival on "The Wild Flowers of Co. Sligo". The only photo of Sligo Antiquarian Society, that of the first outing to Deerpark in 1945 was taken by him; it is reproduced herein and on the back cover. He lectured on penicillin to the CYMS Club in March 1947. He has been a committed field walker as regards nature and he has given of his knowledge in a book of walks for Sligo and north Leitrim (Toher 1994). He was involved in the founding of the Sligo-based Connaught Camera Club in October 1955[47]. The Field Club honoured him with Honorary Life Membership at the 2002 AGM.

The story of how a map of the locations of a series of thirty-eight photographs[48] of scenery of Co. Sligo from 1947 to 1949, entitled *The Yeats Country*, on sale at Toher's the Chemists of Sligo led to the foundation of the Yeats Summer School after Prof. T.R. Henn saw the map in Toher's window in 1958 is detailed by McGarry (1990, 8)[49]. He is desirous of establishing a Geological Study Group in Sligo.

Austin G. Jennings, a native of Craughwell, Co. Galway, manager and engineer at the barytes mines on the mountain between Gleniff and Glencar (Jennings 1946-1947) was somewhat involved in the early years. He lectured to SAS on "Elementary Geology" in 1946 and to SFC in 1955 on geology.

1947-1954 A MORIBUND SOCIETY

We can find no Sligo Field Club document to tell us what happened in the second quarter of 1947; we do not know if there was an AGM in 1947. We have no mention of SFC activities until 4th March 1954, the date of the Revival. In this period there are a few references and letters and a few people remember that members continued to assist visitors in those intervening years and those mentioned in the newspaper are mentioned below.

The Irish Vocational Education Authority met in Sligo in June 1949. For this Michael Connaughton, NT at Forthill NS, after whom Connaughton Rd. was named, prepared an article on 'Historic and Beautiful Sligo', and Paddy Downey, NT, wrote on 'Lough Gill and Creevelea'. In the former, regarding the cromlechs, it says "Arrange for a guide from Sligo Field Club". None of the three stalwarts are mentioned, and SFC only once.

In June 1949 Kirwan took Richard Hayward from Belfast and others to Inishmurray. Hayward with his artist, Richard Piper, was on circuit, like Beranger two centuries earlier, gathering information for a book on Mayo, Sligo, Leitrim and Roscommon (Hayward 1955[50]) and also doing preparatory work for the Belfast Naturalists Field Club trip to Sligo in September that year.

In a follow-up letter of 28th July 1949, Richard Hayward wrote to Kirwan. Tohall is mentioned but Hayward says of Kirwan's proposed talk "Of course it's you I want to hear, and not members of the Sligo FC, as you know" and emphasises that the outing was to be run jointly between them. He hopes that Kirwan, 'a grand man, bedad', was none the worse for his fall on Inishmurray. In the draft reply to Hayward, Kirwan says he has given circulars to "Tohall and the other former members of our moribund Field Club", continues a discussion about there being passage tombs at Carrowmore and adds the happy news that his knee "is quite better now and I feel fit for anything".

In September 1949 fifty members of the Belfast Naturalists Field Club spent two days in Sligo. Kirwan's draft plan for one of the outings suggested that it would last 9 hours and 40 minutes! Their own guide was Richard Hayward. Kirwan, Murray and Tohall are recorded (Adams and Carrothers 1950) as being members of Sligo Field Club who were guides. Kirwan also gave them a talk, and Murray showed them colour films, "W.B. Yeats - A Tribute", "Reburial of Yeats" with the commentary by Miss Jill Noone, and "Prehistoric Monuments of Sligo", captioned and arranged by Patrick Tohall.

Eithne Dolan and Tohall brought Louise Cedarchöld of Stockholm to Carrowmore and Carrowkeel in 1949.

In another draft reply of late 1949 to a letter to an unidentified person, though probably Richard Hayward, Kirwan says he was Chairman of the Sligo Archaeological Society; Kirwan was thinking of a major interest, archaeology, not another change of name.

Kirwan died on 23rd October 1949, in his eightieth year, and so ended the first phase of our history.

In January 1950 T.H. Blackburn, MA, Headmaster of The Grammar School, presided over the Sligo National Monuments Advisory Committee, which had three vacancies. Martin Mulligan, Jr., was Hon. Secretary. The main consideration was Sligo Abbey about which three points were raised, getting it improved, better access on Sundays and getting copies of the guide booklet[51].

Tohall does not show in record of two events in Abbeyquarter, the erection of the statue, by A. Barnardi of Cork, of Our Lady at Garvoge Villas in "an old fort" in November 1951 nor the celebrations for the 700th anniversary of Sligo Abbey in August 1952. These were altogether local residents initiatives and here is the first mention we have of Michael Hopper of Abbeyquarter. The elder author gave a long talk in the Abbey following religious ceremonies in Holy Cross.

The finding of a stamp for linen or strong calico, *Alexander Perceval Strong Dowalas*, gave 'Gleaner' the opener for agitating for a museum in the Congregational Church in the newspaper in January 1950. Again, in October 1952, he uses a piece entitled "150 year old document for money" as the line of attack. In May 1952 'Gleaner' congratulated Thomas O'Connor, Town Clerk, on proposals for a museum. Who was 'Gleaner'? Was it a name for a group of journalists at the *Sligo Independent*? Whoever this was there was a regular contribution on several archaeological and historical pieces per month during the late forties and early fifties to the newspaper. They are so wide-ranging and so accurate that one wonders if in fact they are from the pen of Tohall. He describes Jack Kilfeather, NT. "as a very genial personal friend". Some older members have suggested that Paddy McDonagh, brother of the artist Bernard McDonagh, wrote of SAS or SFC activities for *The Sligo Independent* but we can not recognise these. Gertrude McHale, nee O'Reilly, who worked with McDonagh as a journalist does not think that this was so. There were periodic notices of finds from the Lough Gara excavations in the 1953 and 1954 newspapers.

Tohall retired from the Land Commission in 1952 and was succeeded by John T. Troddyn who served on the Sligo Field Club committee from 1959 to 1974.

There is no mention of Sligo Field Club *in Sligo, The Yeats Country, The Official Guide, City* and County, published in 1952 by the Sligo Tourist Development Association which was founded in June 1950[52], even though Tohall has an article in it on ancient monuments entitled "Pre-history and Purple Heather, Notes of Antiquities of Co. Sligo"; the section on general information lists some organisations of a cultural nature, but not Sligo Field Club[53]. There is no change in the 1953 edition. Perhaps SFC was by then even more moribund!

Tohall gave a talk to Kilmackowen Muintir na Tire on 18th December 1952. This was organised by Fr. Michael O'Beirne; Jack Kilfeather and Michael Gillagan. Subsequently Tohall wrote up his views in the newspaper on the dating of megaliths, antler picks for mining, a spear shaft, bog layers with sunken pines at Owneykeevaun and Pollacheeney, the Culleens Griddles, Listooghil, Corlona and much more. If the newspaper report is anything to go by then Tohall was back, and in full flight. We have not really seen or heard from Tohall for many moons, but this was one lecture we all should have been at!

Sligo did not have a museum and in 1952 moves were afoot to establish one. The first meeting of the Sligo Corporation[54] sub-committee to establish a municipal museum in Sligo was held on 27th May 1952. Several people involved two years later in the revival of Sligo Field Club were on the sub-committee. These were Nora Niland, Patrick Tohall, D.A. Mulcahy of Oakfield, Tom McEvilly, Sean Carroll of High St., Guy Perrem of Cleveragh Drive, Thomas M. O'Connor the Town Clerk[55], Charles Tyndall, Rev. Tom Hanley. Later J.C. McDonagh, Michael Hopper and Patrick Heraughty became involved. Mayor Leo Hunt, Councillors J.C. Cole, Nevin and Pilkington were involved, as was Mr. A. Toher from Sligo Tourist Board. Notice of the opening of a museum in the Harbour Master's Offices from Easter Monday, 6th April, to 25th April, 1953, was made in the newspapers as was a long wide-ranging list of desirable objects. Opening times were from 7 to 9.30 PM on weekdays and 3 to 5.30 PM on Wednesdays, Saturdays and Sundays. Notice of temporary closing of the museum, together with hopes of a permanent museum, was given in late April 1953. J.C. McDonagh gave a lecture, sponsored by the Museum Committee, on 'Old Sligo' which received a long report in the newspaper. Kevin Murray's three films, 'W.B. Yeats - A tribute', 'Reburial of Yeats' and

'Prehistoric Monuments of Sligo', were shown. Tohall is mentioned at end of the report and so also a film on 'Inishmurray' by Jim Hughes though the latter was not shown.

At the time of the first An Tostal in 1953 Mr. P. Tohall, in helping to set up Sligo Museum, gave the finds from O'Connor's Island a shelf to themselves. There is mention in *The Sligo Champion* of 27/2/1954 of the "newly created Sligo Museum" and of "the recent creation of a municipal museum." Perrem, in a letter of August 1954 to Liam, perhaps to Liam S. Gogan of the National Museum of Ireland, a cousin of Mrs. Guy Perrem, rather than to the historian and archaeologist Liam de Paor, writes "Sligo museum premises and showcases [are] now ready so that we should be able to open in a couple of months." It was officially opened in 1955 by the Mayor, Stephen Bergin, and Dr. Gerard A. Hayes-McCoy, Professor of History at U.C.G. and a college friend of the elder author, gave the keynote speech. Was it to be the focal point for archaeology and history or a home of dead flies! In September 1959 Paddy Hartnett wrote to Michael Cahalane 'museum open but without a flourish of trumpets'.

Perrem, Tohall, Moran, McEvilly and Heraughty were voluntary guides who attended in rotation for the two hour opening of the museum each Monday and Thursday. D.M. Candy, County Manager, recommended that the three ground floor rooms of the dwellinghouse attached to the Congregational Church, which had just been acquired as the permanent County Library[56] building, be made available to the recently established Sligo Museum Committee.

In 1953 Willem Van Zeist, the internationally famous Dutch paleobotanist, visited Sligo Field Club at the suggestion of Frank Mitchell of Trinity College, Dublin, and was "kindly received by Mr. Tohall and other members of Sligo Field Club" and "was a guest of the Field Club". It may have been on this occasion that Van Zeist took a section of Owenykeevaun Bog for palynological examination[57].

It seems then that there was a group of people interested in archaeology, *etc.*, who were continuing the work of the 1946 SFC and it was only a matter of time until a formalisation of all this effort led to a Revival. Regrettably there are no antiquarian entries in Tohall's diary which is still in the possession of the Tohall family for 1954 nor 1955 to help us so we do not have any information on the Revival of Sligo Field Club prior to the minutes of the first meeting.

We now turn briefly some of those who helped considerably in the 1950s, Kevin Murray and Tom McEvilly.

Kevin Murray, a native of Co. Meath where he was well acquainted with archaeological monuments including the Loughcrew passage tomb cemetery, purchased the D.M. Hanley premises in 1944. His great interest in life was machines, cars, engines and flying. When the ESB were planning for the power station in the Claudy valley in Donegal about 1953 they needed an accurate recording of the land use and ownership. Kevin devised a system[58] for his plane whereby he accurately vertically strip photographed the area, much to the satisfaction of all. Flying out of Rosses Point he took aerial photographs in 1955 and of Carrowkeel in 1957, co-ordinating them with the 25" OS map. He also took aerial photographs of Tara for Seán P. Ó Riordáin. He was declared the first Hon. Life Member of The Connaught Motor Club in Dec. 1953 and was elected first President of the Sligo-based Connaught Camera Club in October 1955. There is a photograph of him is in the Marist Brothers Centenary publication (1962, 99).

Tom McEvilly was an organiser in the Gaelic League and interested in art. After serving as a Vocational Teacher he became County Sligo CEO. His son, Ronan, now runs Sligo Art Gallery.

Joe and Betty McGlynn were interested in history, local history, archaeology and botany, **Joe McLynn**, was a temporary teacher of Irish in the Grammar School while they sought a qualified Irish teacher.

1954 REVIVAL

The earliest specific indication of a desire to revive the Field Club is in *The Sligo Champion* of 27th February 1954 and it reads "A small representative group of Sligo people wish to revive the Field Club, which had a comparatively brief spell of active life in Sligo some years ago". The indication from Harry O'Rorke (see below) is that no Field Club existed in 1952, even though the letter from Van Zeist implies that the Field Club existed in 1953. The situation must have been that no formal arrangement existed but still the like-minded people worked together for the advancement of Sligo's heritage when the need arose.

The minutes and newspaper reports of a meeting held in the Imperial Hotel[59] on the night of 4th March 1954 are headed 'Revival of Sligo Field Club'. Fourteen of the fifteen 'new and former members' present were Rev. Fr. Charles Kelleher, later President of Summerhill College, Mr. Patrick Tohall, Dr. John Moran, Dr. Patrick Heraughty, all described as members of the 'old Field Club', Mrs. Hannigan, of Chapel St. whose husband was in the Dept. of Agriculture, Mrs. T. Toher, Mary F. Ryan, Miss Imelda Farry, a National Teacher living in High St., Thomas A. Kerin, Guy C. Perrem, Mr. Hopper, Michael Cahalane, Mr. Ó Neachtáin and Mr. Stapleton, both of The Custom Ho.[60]

Tohall was elected as Chairman, Kerin as Treasurer and Perrem as Secretary; the subscription was set at 5/-. Mr. Tohall handed over money, recorded in the Minutes as £2.12.0 "ex old Sligo Field Club" and £2.12.0 in the Hon. Treasurer's report as "Dormant Credit Balance outstanding in former 'Field Club' Account received from Mr. P. Tohall for credit of the Funds of the present Club". Mr. Sheridan of the Imperial Hotel kindly offered the use of the hotel for the immediate future. Mr. Toher suggested that time should be spent in winter in the way of research and the compilation of records and on the modern reassessment of the Sligo megalithic situation. Thus at this early stage the main theme for SFC activities was set.

The press were to be informed of 'the revival of the Sligo Field Club', of 'the scenic and other attractions of the club's activities', of 'the botanical and historical interests that the club intended to examine during their outings' and of 'the records which the Club hoped to compile in connection with Sligo's attractions'. *The Sligo Champion* wrote of what "history books seldom reveal".

The first outing after the Revival was to Creevykeel and Cashelbaun (*i.e.*, the cashel at Cashelgarran) on Sunday, April 4th 1954. The notice included notes on topography, archaeology, botany and bird life that may be seen on the outing. Castleore, Castledargan, Deerpark, Parke's Castle, Creevelea, Killery, Carrowkeel, Ben Bulben, The Ox Mts., Carrowculleen[61], Glenade, Maugherow, Staad Abbey, the Dromore West area, Streedagh and Cliffoney[62] featured among the sites visited on the other outings that summer. In all thirty-four sites were visited. Several of these places are referred to in the present volume. They held eleven outings in their first year and twelve in the following year[63].

The elder author recollects his wife's reaction to the enthusiasm of Tohall and himself on that outing to Cashelgarran on 4th April 1954. After Tohall had waxed eloquently on souterrains and their ingenious ventilation shafts he led the way to examine the souterrain itself and, giving good example, Heraughty followed him. While not in their Sunday best both were fairly respectfully dressed and just as Heraughty was about to disappear he saw Mrs. Tohall's pained look at his wife Julia with the unspoken assertion "See what we have to put up with!".

At the June preparatory meeting, members were given a pre-view of the Inishmurray slides. The commentary was spoken by Dr. Heraughty. Sound, recording and photography were by Mr. Jim Hughes. By 6th July 1954 they had made the local arrangements for the summer outing of RSAI of which Seán P. Ó Ríordáin was President at the time (see below).

By October a wide ranging programme of lectures had been arranged. The Café Cairo now Guckian~Mulreaney (Gunning and Feehily 1996, 125; Hunt 1999, 17), Wine St., was chosen as the place for winter meetings and remained a frequent venue for Sligo Field Club meetings for many years. Tony Toher gave the first lecture after the Revival, "The Wild Flowers of Co. Sligo", and A. G. Mason lectured on "Birds of the Sea Coast", Harold G. Leask on "Irish Castles"[64], Austin Jennings on Geology, Commandant David Beglin from Athlone on The Battle of the Curlews, Harry O'Rorke on "My Native Parish of Ballisodare", John Moran on archaeology, John Garvin (Garvin 2001, 80-83) on local history, Dr. Heraughty and Jim Hughes on Inishmurray and Rev. Denis Molaise Meehan on Ancient Rome. Films were hired from The National Film Institute of Ireland.

Perrem was not quite correct in writing on 24th September 1954 to Thomas Garvin that "The old SFC did not have a winter programme and was not as ambitious in its scope as the new one" but certainly they were much more active. They had at least fourteen indoor meetings, many of which were to arrange the next outing, which together with the eleven outings gives a total of at least twenty-five arranged activities in their first year.

By mid October 1954 numbers had grown to 8 family and 29 single members, making a total of 45 named people. The first AGM on 5th April 1955, was attended by twenty-eight people. There was a call for a more intensive study of ornithology, with Noel Murphy being suggested as the one to consult in this regard, and also of botany. The photographic recording of 'fast crumbling churches' and the seeking of permission to visit old country houses was recommended; though excavation was mentioned it was realised that caution was needed!

In addition to organising lectures and outings SFC members were already heavily into research. There is in the Sligo Field Club files an eight page hand-written document, titled "Megalithic Sites, Actual, Probable and Possible" which is dated 19/1/1954 though it seems from its position in the file that it should read 19/1/1955, after the turn of the year people quite often forget to increase the year. Though the heading suggests that Roscommon, Mayo and

Leitrim were to be included they were not. There are references to more than megaliths and there are many references to Wood-Martin's *Rude Stone Monuments, Sligo and the Island of Achill* and his *Traces of The Elder Faiths in Ireland*, and to O'Rorke. Descriptions and mythology are included. There is a list of castles and abbeys, a list of crannogs, liosanna, cairns, forts & souterrains and circles.

The receipts for this first year, 1954-1955, came to £28-14-6 leaving a balance of £12-17-9. They had eleven family members and thirty-six single members according to the end of year's Hon. Treasurer's report[65].

We now return to **Patrick Tohall.** He retired on 26th July 1952, and became very active again, continuing to serve SFC for another decade. Not only was Tohall a founder member but he was also a re-founder member in 1954, its Chairman for three years and became its first President in 1957 when that title was established; that position he held for four years until he moved from Sligo to Newbridge in 1962 where he died in on 25th June, 1973, aged 86.

Tohall published many articles[66] such as those on Dug-out canoes from Corry, Lough Allen, Co. Leitrim, (Tohall 1945), the 'Dobhar-Chú' story (Tohall 1948), on 'team work' on a rotary quern from Dromore West (Tohall 1951) and notes of antiquities for a Sligo guide (Tohall 1952). Tohall was the local contact for Dr. Van Zeist of Groningen, Holland, whom he brought to, among many other sites in Sligo and Leitrim, the three-quarter mile long 'oaken viaduct' or ancient bog roadway on two rows of piles or stilts at Corlona, Kiltoghert, Co. Leitrim, where Hl. de Vries took samples for the first (Eogan pers. comm.) radiocarbon dating in Ireland (Tohall *et al*. 1955). Tohall's newspaper report, dated 29th January 1953, is from Mail Coach Road. He was now living in his new house.

Tohall was involved in the Sligo *An Tostal* celebrations and the founding of Sligo Museum in 1953. The establishment of Sligo Art Gallery, a separate but closely related entity, is set out by Hegarty (1998, 5-6).

Several members were involved in a Muintir na Tire illustrated talk in the Waverly Hotel in Strandhill on 28th September 1956. Jim Hughes showed stills of glaciers, Tohall spoke on the economic value of the Carrowmore gravels[67], Kevin Murray showed his films on Deerpark, and Egypt 'whose Pharoe tombs were aped in the passage tombs', Jim Hughes' cine-colour film of the dolmens of Cuil Iorra and Kevin Murray's sound picture on life in Spain. Then Tohall spoke on how it all tied together

Tohall made pencilled additions[68] about the ancient divisions of modern Maugheraboy to the copy of the First OS Sheet 14 in SLLSA on 26th October 1956.

Tohall designed, among other things, the monument to St. Asicus at Ballintra, Co. Donegal, Cloonaquin Bridge on the Bonet River, the stream layout at the Holy Well at Tobar an Alt and the corkscrew road up onto the mountain over Glencar. Apparently due to his strong advocation, Bord Fáilte gave a grant of £2,000 to Sligo County Council for the improvement of the accommodation road to the Carrowkeel passage tomb cemetery in 1957.

The second surviving SFC handout from Tohall is that of The Bricklieve Passage-Graves. It is based on Macalister, Praeger and Armstrong's *Proc. Royal Irish Academy* paper of 1912; it is signed and dated *Patrick Tohall, Mail Coach Road, Sligo, Sept. 1957*. In April 1962 he sent three articles under the collective title *The Surroundings of Truskmore* to Telefís Eireann with the idea that they be used in a programme about the area surrounding the mountain where Telefís Eireann had just erected a TV mast. Telefís Eireann chose not to use the scripts but we publish it elsewhere in this volume (Tohall this volume). In them Tohall does not refer to the complex of fieldwalls, hut sites, cairns and megalithic tombs on the mountains that Brendan Rooney brought to notice in the mid 1980s (Rooney 1991, 105-106; see also under Br. Alphonsus Maxwell below).

Tohall had his own opinion of the name of Carrowmore No. 51, 'Listohil. In a letter to Cahalane in December 1962 he wrote "If the word [Listohill] has not been tampered with it should mean the reversed (or mis-formed) liss". One's first idea of 'tohill' as a name must be discounted, for in this case the 'Tohill' would have the 't' aspirated to sound as a 'h'. On the monument was a tremendous cairn of stones untill around 1840, the most conspicuous feature of the plain, . . . the 'Liss is more likely to have been alongside the monument on the grassy plane (*recte* plain)". How close Tohall was to the truth; there is a site only to be seen in cropmarks on the east side of the monument (Sl 14:209-23; Bergh 1995, 120). Tohall was interpreting the name not as in its literal translation, 'left handed', but as 'odd'. He realised the need for the vernacular in dealing with placenames to avoid such pitfalls as the misinterpretation of Moytragh (Maghtrach) for Magh Tuire[69] and published articles on families and placenames (Tohall 1944; 1960). The elder author takes Listoghil to mean the "unusual liss".

The Royal Society of Antiquaries of Ireland held their Summer outing to Sligo on 6th to 10th

July 1954, with Patrick Tohall, Dr. Ruaidhrí de Valera and Mr. A.T. Lucas guiding the party of 74 people to Drumcliff, Creevykeel, Cashelbaun, Lisnalurg, Deerpark, Park's Castle, Dromahair, Heapstown, Moytura, Carrowkeel, Ballymote, Slieve Gamh, Gortakeeran, Cabragh, Ballysodare, Carrowmore and Sligo Abbey. Stephen Bergin, Mayor, welcomed the party to Sligo and the Field Club entertained the group at the Technical School. The outing dinner was attended by 103 people. Dr. Patrick Heraughty, Sligo Marist Brothers and Major R.B. Aldridge, Mount Falcon, Ballina, joined RSAI that year.

Guy C. Perrem, whose ancestors were from Newton Abbot, came from Carrick-on-Shannon[70] to Sligo as manager of the Sligo Guinness Depot soon after it opened in Feb. 1950[71] and he lived in one of the three Guinness houses, Doonie Rock, 3 Cleveragh Drive. His interest was mainly military history but Mary F. Ryan recollects his definition of SFC as 'being covering everything from gathering mushrooms to exploring archaeological sites' and he gave a number of swords and a revolver from Michael Collins, to Sligo Museum, of which he was, with others, a founder member of the Sligo Museum Committee. Mollie, his wife, was a cousin of Liam S. Gogan of the National Museum of Ireland. He was one of the main driving forces behind the Revival, so much so that **Mary F. Ryan** and Harry O'Rorke thought he was the originator of a new SFC. Before he really got SFC into action he was transferred to Ballinasloe and resigned from SFC as of 3rd May 1955. After Ballinasloe he worked in Tullamore and Waterford where he retired in 1970 and died in 1980 but does not seem to have had any active Society involvement other than in Sligo.

Mary F. Ryan, from Bruff, Ballinahinch and Knocklong, Co. Limerick, came to Sligo in 1950. She worked with Perrem in the Guinness Depot which opened in Sligo in 1950. Her interest was and is modern history. She was elected as a Joint Secretary with Perrem in 1955. She was a highly efficient Hon. Secretary and some say she would have been involved even if she did not work with Perrem. She was also Hon. Secretary of an Art Group guided by Tom McEvilly. She succeeded Perrem as Secretary when he was transferred about June 1955 to Ballinasloe; all secretarial letters earlier than 11th May 1955 are by Perrem, after which they are by Mary F. Ryan. She left Sligo in 1960, weeks before the Yeats Summer School. She now lives in Kilfinnane and though of considerable age she is actively involved with a similar local society in the Barony of Coshlea, Co. Limerick.

There is not agreement, yet again, on who was responsible for the 1954 Revival. Mary F. Ryan, Joint Secretary with Guy C. Perrem credits Perrem with the 1954 event, which she considers to have been a Founding. She informs us that she was not aware of any pre-1954 SFC activity, organised or otherwise. This octogenarian's memory of many things and people of her time in Sligo in the 1950s is incredibly clear. The elder author credits Patrick Tohall with the 1954 event. It seems to the younger author that SFC was so moribund that not even those newcomers to Sligo town who were interested in SFC topics were aware of the individual interests of a small dedicated group who were quietly getting on with heritage.

No matter who was responsible, from the time of the Revival there seems to have been a strong bond between members and a strong desire to succeed; if ever there was a major rift there is no record of it in the minutes. Sligo Field Club has continued unbroken since then, providing quality lectures, outings and enjoyment, and getting research work done.

The idea of a Sligo Field Club publication of lectures was mentioned by Guy Perrem and Mary F. Ryan in the first Annual Report on April 5th 1955 but was not proceeded with for financial reasons. This may have arisen from John Garvin's asking if his lecture would be published by SFC; it was published in *The Sligo Champion*. The topic of publication was again raised at the second AGM, 16th April 1956. This time the proposed *Sligo Independent* "Centenary" publication being prepared by William Peebles, its Owner~Editor, who had given prominent and extensive coverage to SAS and SFC in the early days, was the reason for deferral[72]. Tohall had provided a substantial triple-titled article, totalling almost two full pages over two issues, for Peebles on "A Survey of Old Sligo, Sligo of 1855 and 1855-1955" which was published in the newspaper in November 1955 and was reprinted later. The Donegal Historical Society was founded on 21st December 1946 (Cookman 1996[15]), a year and a half after we were founded, with J. C. McDonagh (McTernan 1977, 139-142; 1994, 139-142) from Ballymote being the driving force. It began publishing, first a Journal, of which four issues appeared between November 1947 and 1950, and then *The Donegal Annual* in 1951. One wonders had McDonagh been transferred from the Bank of Ireland in Dublin to Co. Sligo, as opposed to Ballybofey in 1940 (McTernan 1994, 40), would his enthusiasm for local history have led to the founding of a Sligo Historical Society. *Cumann Seanchais Clochair*, serving Monaghan, Fermanagh, south Tyrone and south Donegal began publishing *The Clogher Record* in 1953 though it was printed in 1952. The Armagh Diocesan History Society was founded in 1953 and began publishing *Seanachais Ard Macha* in 1954. The Meath Society was founded 1937 but did not begin publishing *Ríocht na Midhe* until 1955. The local society serving Cavan and Leitrim, *Cumann Seanachais Bhreifne,* began publishing its Journal, *Breifne*, in 1958, the year of its revival, having been founded in 1920.

At the AGM on April 15th 1959 Mary F. Ryan again suggested a 'publications fund' with the idea of producing a *Journal*. A quotation in February 1959 of £20 for 500 copies of a twelve page 8" by 10" Journal had been received from Frank Wynne of Sligo Stationery Depot. In April another quotation of £70 for 500 copies on the same style as the *Old Kilkenny Review* had been received from Wynne; this quote did not include cost of illustrations or blocks and was 'for matter only without advertising'. The quote *from The Drogheda Independent* was £120 for 500 copies of 84 pages plus cover, selling at 5 shillings, no advertisements and blocks costing an additional £10 each. Supposedly for financial reasons, though we think more likely because it would take time from fieldwalking, publication of a *Journal* was not pursued with. Ryan was transferred to Cork in 1960[73] and one wonders if she remained in Sligo would she have succeeded in starting a Journal. The possibility of a SFC publication was raised at the 1989 AGM.

Despite the many and close contacts with eminent scholars there seems to have been no further attempt to publish until the current one. There are occasional subsequent references to publication of a *Journal* in the minutes and a 1966 note by Cahalane of the publication of a Field Club *Journal* but nothing ever happened. In 1969 Etienne Rynne suggested that Sligo Field Club order offprints of articles on Sligo, such as that on his investigations of a cist at Treanmacmurtagh (Rynne 1969, 145-150). In 1975 the cost of £950 for 500 copies of *The Old Athlone Society Journal* was noted.

Frank Wynne, of Adelaide St., owned Sligo Stationery Depot in Market St. He was very active in the social life of Sligo. He was a founder member of Strandhill Golf Club, was prominent in Sligo Chamber of Commerce and was very much involved in founding The Yeats Society. His wife, Georgina Wynne, has been active Secretary of the Yeats Society for many years.

Thomas A. Kerin, Manager of the Hibernian Bank, now the GHQ building opposite the P.O., had left Sligo by April 1959 having been Hon. Treasurer for five years.

Br. Alphonsus Maxwell, from the Swinford area of Co. Mayo, first came to Sligo in 1923, returned in 1946 and was moved to Ballina in April 1956, two years after the Revival of SFC (*Marist Brothers*[74] 1962, 23). He served on the committee in 1954 and 1955. He was a keen long distance walker and he told the elder author of seeing, while walking from Gleniffe to Glencar, a prehistoric megalithic tomb on the mountain above Glencar. Regrettably neither passed the information to higher authority and so it was not until Brendan Rooney (see below) mentioned a megalithic tomb up there to Michael Gibbons of the SMR that the importance and extent of the monuments here was realised[75].

Harry O'Rourke of The Sally Gardens in Ballisodare and a grand-nephew of Archdeacon Terrence O'Rorke, came to live in Sligo town in 1952. He had a shop in Castle St. perhaps the first self-service shop in Sligo, and later a laundrette. He was greatly influenced by his schoolmaster, Seán Devaney, NT, a native of Billa, the birthplace as St. Fechin, who often gave post-3 o'clock tuition in local history. Once Harry was seriously late back to school after lunch but the genuine reason of having taken a classmates around the church ruins in the graveyard was more than acceptable! In the 1950s he similarly took great satisfaction at the way the Field Club got people out to sites on Sunday afternoons.

When I talked about the founding of the Field Club in 1997 Harry O'Rorke was very surprised at the fact that there was SAS and SFC in the mid-1940s and later. Harry came into Sligo town in 1952 and was quite clear that there was no active archaeological society in Sligo at that time. Furthermore he believed that the 1954 Revival was in fact a Founding of the Field Club. Clearly then SFC was more than 'moribund' by 1952.

Robert Browne, of Scarden, was a member of the O'Donovan and Brown coach building business at the corner of John St. and Adelaide St. He was a horse owner, trainer and amateur jockey. A nephew of Frazer Brown, TD, he claimed a relationship with W.B. Yeats through his mother who was Jackson; he wrote some poetry. He served on the committee in 1962 and his name does arise in listings for 1945 and in 1954.

Jim Hughes was a native of Newry, lived in Cleveragh Rd. where he maintained an excellent flower garden. He was a ladies hairdresser, with his premises where Joseph Martin later had a tailoring business adjacent to the Clarence Hotel in Wine St. He was on the Committee from 1954 to 1971. He was a taker of good photographs rather than a good man at photographically recording monuments, perhaps too fussy at getting the right angle when there were scores of other monuments to record, and so he would be left behind by the search party! There are still some slides taken in the 1950s though most of Hughes' slides, including his before and after restoration work photographs at Sligo Abbey were destroyed by fire in his flat. He took SFC on a guided tour of the Abbey after he had shown those slides and also Cumman Bhreifne. He may have helped Kevin Murray in filming. Having seconded its foundation he was elected first Hon. Secretary of the Sligo-based Connaught Camera Club in October 1955. Together with Tohall he is acknowledged in the National Museum of Ireland for the recovery of bones and slag from a souterrain at Bunduff, NMI 1955:97:a-c.

Anne O'Gorman, who also served on the Committee in 1967, worked in The Tourist Office. She was a daughter Paddy O'Gorman and granddaughter of Dr. Thomas Rouse, GP, Wine St.

Rev. Dr. Owen Francis Traynor, of a large family, long serving P.P. in Dromahaire, was active in matters historical. He joined RSAI in 1943. He was in Dromahaire by 1953. He communicated with many members, particularly Eileen Lambert, Michael Cahalane and Pat Kitchin, all of whom found visits to him to be most elevating academically speaking. In July 1964 he led an important outing to St. Farnan's Shrine, between Dromore West and Easkey, and compiled a description of Drumcliffe. He could not be persuaded to serve on the Committee and he never published. His 1963 unpublished review of Bishop Charles Tyndall's *The Ancient Parish and Church of St. John the Baptist, Sligo, from Early Times to Disestablishment*, which runs to twenty typed pages, is well worth reading for more than its historical content! Tyndall was enthroned in 1956. The younger author was overawed when introduced to Traynor by Eileen Lambert in the Library. He was transferred to Mullagh, Co. Cavan, in 1969.

Two of the longest serving early members, Patrick Heraughty and Eileen Lambert, were active both before and after the Revival.

Patrick Heraughty, a sixth generation descendant of Domhnall Heraughty who settled on Inishmurray in 1802, was born in Cliffoney in 1912 and lived on Inishmurray until 1924[76]. In 1926 while a First Year student at St. Nathy's College, Ballaghaderreen, he was involved in cataloguing Archdeacon O'Rorke's library there. He returned to Sligo as a medical doctor in 1940, married Julia Kelly of Allihes, Co. Cork, in 1942 and has been active in heritage matters since 1945. He joined SFC in 1945 after Tohall had suggested it to him; he was a member before Austin Jennings' Jan. 1946 lecture, and perhaps before Tony Toher's botany lecture late in 1945, though he can not be sure. He joined Royal Society of Antiquaries of Ireland in 1954 after Tohall had suggested it to him. He was involved in the Revival of the Field Club in 1954. He was President of Sligo Field Club from 19th April 1961, to 20th April 1983, the longest run by anybody in any one position in SFC. His particular interest was in geology, the building bricks of our planet. This interest led inevitably to an interest in stone monuments and his interest in history to man's place and development. He has frequently lectured on Inishmurray and on geology and also spoke on geology on many outings77. He has spoken on the nesting sandmartins at Carrowmore and the fossils at Streedagh. At an international level, Ur of the Chaldees is of more than a little interest to him and he lectured on it in the early days in the Cafe Cairo and recently in The Teachers' Centre in Quay St.

Almost as vulnerably available in his medical practice as Michael Cahalane was in Blackwood's Shop, on the corner of O'Connell St. and Wine St., he was a ready target for interested visitors. Like many other members his local knowledge saved visitors time and energy and got them to see more of the heritage of the county than would normally have been possible. On the occasion of the visit of a Dutch prehistoric society to Inishmurray, one Dutchman remarked when passing his ruined home "When first you come back here you are sad because this was your home; now you need no longer be sad because it is your very own family ruin".

As medical doctor he, like Dr. T.B. Costello[78] of Tuam, brought matters antiquarian to his patients with no little success. As County Coroner he could not get away from archaeology, having Walter from Owenbeg[79] in his garage for several weeks and hosed him down regularly[80] to keep him and this major find of clothes fresh. Needless to say Walter at this stage had been dead for centuries. He was found on a raft of birch twigs in a bog hole in Tawnamore on the north side of the Ox Mts. (Ó Floinn 1995, 231, No. Sl.3). Walter, a middle-aged male, was clothed with a hat, coat, doublet, open breeches, knitted worsted stockings, garters and leather shoes, all of which is of great importance in that they show a degree of acceptance of foreign fashion and smooth fabrics of the middle classes in the late seventeenth century. Detailed descriptions were published in 1972 (Lucas 1972, 215-222) while more recently

Dunleavy (1989, 64, 81-83) has written of its context in the history of Irish dress and she illustrates the garments at a common scale (1989, 82). The elder author now believes that Walter laid down to sleep on the birch twigs and died of unknown causes rather than him having been buried in the bog (Dunleavy 1989, 81). Heraughty was also called on when several skeletons of young males and a horse tooth were found at Shannon Eighter on the line of the new Bundoran Rd. [81], and when bones found in the sand dunes at Strandhill were thought to be human.

Some recent research on Inishmurray is worth mentioning. Jenny White Marshall and Grellan D. Rourke have considered the possible secular origin of the monastic enclosure wall (2000a, 30-34, Figs. 5 and 6; 2000b, Ch. 9). Francke (1999; see also *Avenue* 1, 53) has an excellent aerial photo of the cashel and lake and Somerville-Large's section has very informative five aerial photos as well as an accurate description (1999, 44-49 and back cover photo) based on the elder author's book (Heraughty 1996). James Charles Roy, an American historian of Moyode tower house near Athenry, Co. Galway, since 1969, produced a book on islands linked to St. Colmcille; the first chapter (1991, 7-136) contains much that is of Inishmurray, and much that is not, though some points are worth a second consideration. Joe McGowan (1998) produced a compact handbook for Inishmurray. Rainer Berger (Berger 1995, 170-171) has extracted small samples of charcoal from mortar of two buildings for dating purposes. The calibrated date of AD 660-980 was derived from the older architectural phase of the Men's Church while Teach Molaise gave a date of AD 690-980. James P. Whittal (Whittal 1991) has attempted to read the inscription on the holed pillar-stone at *Teampull na mBan*. Rodney Lomax and Joe McGowan are now the main boatmen for Inishmurray. Gerry O'Sullivan has recently been excavating several sites on Inishmurray, interim reports are to be found in *Excavations Bulletin* for the years in question, and making an overall re-assessment in the light of his findings. In May 2002 Archaeology Ireland published *Inishmurray, An Island off County Sligo*, the eighteenth in its series of Heritage Guides; contributions are by O'Sullivan, Niamh Connolly, Marie Heraughty and Don Cotton.

At Julia Heraughty's suggestion in November 1978 we began holding a special lecture for beginners; new members are welcome at all of our activities. On that and subsequent occasions a number of members gave short talks on topics of interest to the Field Club. The idea was to provide enough information to encourage beginners and new members, to update long-standing members in present interpretations and new methods and to encourage active support.

Eileen Lambert was Dublin born, though her father was from Sligo, and she lived in Sligo from the age of eleven until her death in 1985. She received much of her education in Kerry, the native county of her mother, Julia O'Brien. She married Jack Lambert, the youngest County Librarian in the country, when she was nineteen. Jack collected rare First Editions of Yeats. He died at the age of 35 leaving Eileen with three children, the ventriloquist and puppeteer Eugene, Jackie and Miriam. She worked in Sligo Library for 27 years, from 1944, and rose to be Assistant Librarian. It was in this capacity that she was very influential. She did much private research on the commercial and social history of Sligo and had begun card index of publications relating to Sligo. Her knowledge of what was available of Sligo culture, history, archaeology and literature was shared with so many students whom she nurtured; the younger author has many happy memories of this sharing of knowledge and frequently Library rules were bent to allow the loan of Wood-Martin, *etc.*, for copying when the Library did not have its own copier! Rev. Owen Traynor was a frequent visitor to her in her enormous upstairs back room office in the Library.

She was at the Sligo Antiquarian Society meetings in 1945 and the Sligo Field Club Revival meeting in 1954, was a committee member for 23 years from 1954 to 1984, five of them from 1978 to 1982 as Assistant Secretary. She joined RSAI in 1980.

In 1979 Eileen wrote a very strong letter to Sligo Co. Co. concerning its destruction of archaeological layers at Drumcliff early monastic site[82]. This work which had been going on for three weeks for a tourist facility was discovered by Dr. John Waddell of UCG and reported to SFC by Prof. George Eogan of UCD, both of whom had been *monumenting* in Co. Sligo. She was the last surviving member of the original committee formed in 1930 to revive Feis Shligigh after a lapse of twenty years and was its President at the time of her death in January 1985. She helped form the Yeats Society in 1959 and was elected Secretary; in 1982 she was its first female to be President.

Bernard McDonagh, a local artist, won the Taylor Art Award in 1947 and 1948 and the Higgins Art Award in 1949. In 1952 he had an exhibition of watercolours and oil-paintings of Sligo, Spain and Italy, and several other exhibitions down the decades. Historical events have been the major theme of his works. We have heard him lecture and paint at the same time. He produced a booklet with drawings of Lough Gill (MacDonagh 1977), a booklet of his reconstruction drawings of the Spanish Armada events of 1588 (MacDonagh 1978), a card showing nine architectural towers of Sligo in 1993 and a card showing the 'Norman de Burgo Road' in 1999.

James P. McGarry was involved with Sligo Field Club but his interest in Yeats drew him more into an active position in The Yeats Society. He has published several books and booklets on local history, the placenames in Yeats' writings, the story of The Yeats Society, his native Collooney, the O'Connor family and the establishment by Nora Niland of Sligo Art Gallery (McGarry 1971; 1976; 1980; 1990; 2002). He also published several pieces in *The Corran Herald*. In 1977 he was involved in the founding of Sligo History Society with Dr. T.A. Finnegan, President of Summerhill, and Aodhán O'Higgins.

1955-1958

SFC suffered a major upheaval at Guy Perrem's leaving Sligo. Into his shoes, in partnership with Mary F. Ryan, stepped **Michael Cahalane,** who with Pat Kitchin, were to be major influences in SFC for over two decades.

In March 1956 Michael Cahalane, a native of Cork, took over as Joint Hon. Secretary with Mary F. Ryan. He was present at the 1954 Revival meeting. He was Manager of Blackwood's Corner Shop on the corner of O'Connell St. and Wine St. We are not certain of when he came to Sligo but he was in Sligo by January 1946 when he attended the first joint staff social as a guest of the Grattan St. Blackwood's branch. His vulnerable availability as Manager of a grocery shop in the main street of Sligo[83] was gladly accepted by him with his unfailing good humour and charming sense of fun. His home at No. 5, Hanly Tce. was available, at all times, under the welcoming hospitality of his wife Estie[84], as a meeting place for officers of the Field Club. He was active in St. Vincent de Paul, Merville Tennis Club and County Sligo Golf Club, and was a founder member of Sligo Rotary Club. This may have been where he became aware of Des Smith's photographic talents.

Michael put more work into and gave more time to the Field Club than anyone else in the 1950s and 1960s. He introduced information sheets on sites to be visited on an outing. He often acknowledged acknowledgements to his letters. He was a member of the national National Monuments Advisory Council by co-option and was Vice-President for Connacht of the Royal Society of Antiquaries of Ireland. His work was inexorably intertwined with that of Pat Kitchin. He entertained many foreign groups and Des Smith recollected a Norwegian group demanding payment of 1d. for a hunting knife that they were giving him as a present, such was their adherence to their National customs and tradition.

With Mary F. Ryan and Patrick Tohall he provided texts for plaques at eleven National Monuments in the county by March 1959. He assisted Lord Mountbatten with archaeological sections of the booklets on Classiebawn Castle and Inishmurray.

The Prehistoric Sligo leaflets, though not SFC publications, were written by people who were members; some versions are unaccredited and undated. Thomas J. Hamilton of STDA sent his voluntarily written draft text of a proposed **Archaeological Leaflet** to Michael Cahalane in December **1961**. Seventeen sites or locations of all periods were detailed. Regrettably later drafts are neither credited nor dated so the development of the publication of this most basic and useful information leaflet has not been reconstructed. Michael Cahalane and Pat Kitchin jointly reworked the text, concentrating more on the megalithic tombs, and completed the first[85] Prehistoric Sligo leaflet in early 1962 with Seán Ó Nualláin doing the map and Ruaidhrí de Valera checking the content. This brochure for the Sligo Tourist Development Association described the megalithic sites of the county. It was so successful that there were complaints by the middle of the 1963 tourist season that not enough copies had been produced. Several updates have been produced, the most recent being by Timoney (Timoney, M.A. 1984).

In 1956 SFC helped Mayo Historical Society, which at that stage had sixty members at their meetings, with information. In 1957 they gave £2-2-0 for the Hungarian Relief Fund.

In April 1968 Cahalane discovered that a stone in the shed adjoining the former Cloverhill schoolhouse had concentric circles and a cup mark on it. When it was removed from the wall in 1986 several sets of concentric circles were discovered on the back of it. It is now in Sligo Museum. It may have come from the Cloverhill Monument (Wood-Martin 1888, 92-99, figs. 77-81) or the barrow dug in 1977 (Timoney 1984, 324; 1987-1988, 77) or as tradition passed on by Pat Kitchin records, from some unspecified monument to the south.

1958-1959

There were many others who were active in SFC, many as Officers and who gave service above and beyond the call of duty.

Michael 'Mickey' Hopper, 1913-1974, worked for 46 years from 1928 in The House for Men, beside *The House for Wines*, in O'Connell St.[86] His interests were local history and archaeology. A most loveable character he was renowned as a walker and a talker. It was said of him that if you went in to buy a handkerchief you would come out having bought a perfectly fitting suit or overcoat and having the added bonus of a mind converted, if you were not already, to local history and archaeology. His family had lived in Riverside for generations carrying down the traditions of that area along the south side of the Garvogue and much of Lough Gill he committed to paper. He was co-opted onto the Museum Committee. Once during an outing to Aughris he remarked to an old native woman as to the quality of the griddle she was baking on whereupon she gave it to him for the museum. Not having a car he became less involved as his children were growing up during the late 1950s.

J.R. McWilliam, Agent at the Bank of Ireland, Chairman and Vice-President in the early 1960s, was the first to contact Belfast for weather predictions for outings. He moved from Sligo to Derry in 1964.

Liam Horgan of Cork was Inspector, and later Commissioner, of Taxes; afterwards he was a Financial Consultant. He Chairman in 1965 at which time he moved to Dublin. He was more interested in the social aspects of SFC. There is a photograph of him standing up in the boat in Classeymore harbour on Inishmurray.

Captain, or Commandant, **Larry Corr**, from the midlands, an Officer in charge of the F.C.A. in Ballymote, joined us in 1965. He was Chairman in 1966 and 1967 and was a good Irish scholar and was interested in placenames[87].

Though **Herbert Calvert,** Manager of Gouldings Fertilisers in Sligo, was Chairman as recently as 1968 and 1969 and **George Collier** was Assistant Secretary in 1967, we know nothing of their backgrounds or interests.

There was, for a while, the Ladies Committee which was often called on to provide sustenance on special occasions.

Jack Noone had the grocery that later became Blackwood's Corner Shop opposite the Post Office and he had a Public House around the corner on Wine St. His great interest was in matters maritime and in particular the port of Sligo. **Peggy Noone** was interested in local history and botany. At several AGMs she raised the lack of commercially produced slides of Sligo heritage. **Joe McGlynn** taught Irish in The Grammar School.

Jill Tritton lived for some time in the Inishcrone area and later at Moneygold and later near Bristol. Her ability to see small things has to be experienced.

Thomas J. Kennedy, a native of Galway, was Sligo County Engineer from 1959 to 1971, a big man in attitude and outlook, very quiet but practical, and known affectionately as "the little man" (Reidy 2000, 52). One of Tom's big contributions to Co. Sligo was the setting up the Planning Department in the County Council following on the Local Government Planning and Development Act of 1963 (Harney 2000, 59) with Jimmy Harney preparing the Development Plans. He served on the committee for nine years, 1962 to 1970, six of them as Vice-President. Kennedy was responsible for the saving of the Ballyeeskeen tumulus near Doonycoy which was under threat due to road widening. The tumulus was later excavated by Peter Danaher (Danaher 1964). One of the myths of SFC is that Kennedy may also have been responsible for the pointing of the walls of Rosslee castle at Easkey to as far as the available ladders would reach! He had drafted a manuscript on Sligo placenames which was passed to Tom McGettrick soon after he died in 1971; Lucas had seen it in 1971[88]. For an outing to Knocknarea he proposed measuring the cairn to see how much it had changed as compared with earlier surveys. More recent work by Bergh (1995, 89-94) indicates that the early surveys of Maeve's Cairn were of their time[89].

1961

Cahalane, with the appreciated guidance of Corkman Paddy Hartnett of the Office of Public Works and the help of Pat Kitchin, organised the very successful visit of The Prehistoric Society in 1961. Over one hundred members of this premier world-wide society came. On Carrowkeel the late Patrick Healy, who had worked with Macalister, Praeger and Armstrong on the excavations there in 1910, told us that when a slab that was difficult to move was encountered during the excavations, the cry was 'Healy, the sledge'. He had the elder author take a photograph of the three CIE buses which had been skilfully manoeuvred to just below the monuments. The coup of a very hot Summer day, in the heather covered bog of north Mayo, was not the monuments but the photographing of the world renowned and reputedly very conservative archaeologist Graham Clark drinking Guinness, from the bottle; Clark was then President of the Prehistoric Society. For this visit Sligo Field Club had got some signposting done up in Carrowkeel for which Bord Fáilte granted £68 for site clearance and signposting.

Our final dinner was at the Downhill Hotel in Ballina; 37 Sligo members attended. The original menu, of Ptertydactyl Soup, Sphagnum Salad, Roast Brontosaur, Amber Honey Cake and Heather Beer was unavailable, much to the vociferous regrets of the visitors. However, things changed for the second course. It being a Friday in pre-Vatican II times meat was not allowed to Roman Catholics. The true menu had chicken and salmon, with the expectation that the fish would be available for the native Roman Catholics. Needless to say, the visitors all went for salmon, leaving the Catholics to dispense themselves and have the chicken.

Finlay Tower Kitchin, a legal man and a most learned and most witty Cumbrian, joined us about 1959[90]. Pat, as we knew him, claimed that had not Brian Boru expelled his ancestors from Dublin, he might have been born there. He married Sheela O'Hara of Newpark, one of the native families of the county who claim ancestry going back into the Early Bronze Age. Apparently Kitchin had been trading with Blackwood's Corner Shop for many years and knew Michael Cahalane only as an excellent shop manager before the penny dropped and they discovered their common interest in things antiquarian. Cahalane and Kitchin are remembered as a most felicitous and scholarly partnership which greatly enhanced the Club. Indeed Tony Lucas of N.M.I. wrote of them in 1969 "What a pleasure it is to be dealing with sober efficient people with pure hearts and no axes to grind. The pure hearts and absence of edged tools leave ample scope for taking a cool objective view on problems and the working out of their solutions without fear or favour. Pardon the philosophising but it wells up from a grateful heart."

Kitchin delighted in telling the story of a visit to Carrowmore of an international group when academic axes were ground. The national expert who was to speak to the illustrious group was ill and so an understudy was sent in to bat, so to speak. After the understudy had said his piece the professor from a different school of thought asked "Will you give us one good reason why this is a passage grave?" at which the understudy's friends were seen to get very agitated. A senior member of SFC was heard to remark "I see the old war-horses are smelling the smoke!" The debate continues even now and regrettably axes are still being ground.

His wife **Sheela O'Hara**, of one of the most ancient Sligo families, that of O'Hara of Annaghmore, went on many of those field walking expeditions. She found those enclosures at Portavaud and later at Aughris, and possibly others at Ardnaglass on the north slopes of Benbulben (Kitchin this volume; Timoney this volume). She is fondly remembered as a great hostess in Newpark and Ballisodare. She has executed paintings of Sligo antiquities. Her watercolour of Carrowmore illuminates the card presented to those who supported in advance this publication. Sheela's granddaughter, Rachel Moss, continues the interest as an art historian with a particular interest in the Medieval period (Moss 2000; 2002).

Pat's veterinary surgeon, **Alfie Gallagher** of Ballymote, already had an interest in antiquarian matters, he being the first to report the Lough Gara crannogs to the National Museum of Ireland (Gallagher and Raftery 1952, 182)[91]. Local teacher Gerry McLoughlinn had been finding objects along the recently exposed shoreline. With Lucas and Kitchin he visited monuments and brought some farmer's discoveries to light.

The trio of Cahalane, Kitchin and Kennedy did tremendous **fieldwork**, checking known monuments, discovering "new" monuments and "rediscovering" others. Pat regularly advised the hip flask as a major aid in field walking, not mainly for self-rectification but as a means of loosening the tongue of an otherwise reticent farmer. Their successes were widely reported and it was rumoured that they discovered five megalithic tombs in one day. One Sunday in February 1964 they did discover two unrecorded tombs in the Ballintrellick area and another at Drum. Their discoveries were welcomed by the professional archaeologists. In May 1992 Ruaidhrí de Valera cried out across a Dublin street to Paddy Hartnett "Cahalane has found a bute". This was no female but yet another megalithic tomb! Besides Pat and Sheela, their son Anthony was also involved and in a letter of thanks to Cahalane he tells of how he looked forward to further *monumenting* with them. In a note of at least 1966 they record that they had found 18 megaliths in the previous six years[92]. Their contact with owners served to preserve monuments and educate people as to their heritage.

Finlay Tower Kitchin, Sheela Kitchin, J.R. McWilliam, Jim Hughes and Michael C. Cahalane went out in various combinations photographing monuments in the 1960s. We have detailed record of their outings in the very cold month of January 1963 and on four of the five Sundays in March 1968. Cahalane made notes on access, condition, weather, and occasionally an observation on folklife such as the lid of a saucepan seen nailed to a tree at St. Patrick's Well at Dromard in 1963 and presumed to be used as a gong.

Besides taking their own photographs two people, Reginald J. Wiltshire and Elinor V. O'Brien of The Green Studios, recorded some of our monuments. They had a camera mounted on a pole 24ft. long that could be extended to 32ft. and the camera could be operated from the ground. Photographs of Creevykeel and Deerpark court-tombs taken in this way were used on the *Prehistoric Sligo* leaflet and were issued as colour slides.

In 1962 SFC held a buffet which was attended by about 100 people. There were 91 members plus 4 guests at the 1963 buffet but only 37 members and 13 guests at that for 1964. This led to the idea of such an event being deferred and quietly forgotten. There were 49 family at 20 shillings, 57 single members at 10 shillings, and 4 Life Members at the end of the 1963-1964 year. There were 38 family, 61 single members and four Life Members at the end of the 1967-1968 year.

In 1962 Paddy Hartnett and Seán Ó Nualláin were instrumental in getting a set of Ordnance Survey 6" maps of the county for SFC, provided the OS had access to the extra information added by Sligo Field Club. Many features depicted as rock outcrop on the maps were discovered to be unrecorded monuments, mainly megalithic tombs. In 1962 the fieldwork for the Megalithic Survey of Sligo began under Ruaidhrí de Valera and Seán Ó Nualláin. Many of the discoveries were published in 1989 as *The Megalithic Survey of Ireland: Vol. V, Co. Sligo*. As that volume includes the first national inventory of megalithic tombs the 20th century, wherein some 1488 tombs are listed, it is a much sought after and much used volume, giving international publicity to the major aspect of our county's heritage.

On a snowy January day in the early 1960s SFC had a visit from the French Archaeologist, P.R. Giot. Having barely made our way to Carrowkeel, the group continued to Moygara where Cahalane and Kitchin had discovered that one feature depicted as rock outcrop was a megalithic tomb. The company included Prof. Michael O'Kelly of Cork, Prof. Ruadhrí de Valera of Dublin and Seán Ó Nualláin of the Ordnance Survey. We could feel their thoughts as we approached the site and read them as 'they are a decent bunch of lads and how can we let them down easily when we reach the mare's nest' but as we neared the location Ruadhrí de Valera dived through the thicket from the northwest and Seán Ó Nualláin did likewise from the east. Thus was the now famous Moygara court tomb (Ó Nualláin 1989, 79, fig. 53) with twin galleries brought to academic attention. Deerpark, Co. Sligo, (Ó Nualláin 1989, 32-33, fig. 37) and Malin More, Co. Donegal, (Lacy 1983, Pl. 3) are the only two other examples of this twin gallery subtype of court tomb (Ó Nualláin 1976, 107).

Kitchin devoted much of his archaeological energy to Carrowmore and published a synoptic article on it in *Proceedings of the Prehistoric Society* in 1984 (Kitchin 1984). He wrote a short manuscript on the earthen enclosures at Aughris and Portavaud; it is published elsewhere in this Volume. On the Sunday following his death a small fieldwalking party consisting of Des Smith, Brían Ó Súilleabháin, Jack Flynn, Aodhán O'Higgins and Martin A. and Mary B. Timoney, visited Aughris to look at the archaeological complex there (see Kitchin this volume; Timoney this volume). Jack Flynn suggested we should commemorate his work for SFC and that of his close academic and fieldwalking companion Michael Cahalane by having an annual Cahalane-Kitchin Memorial Lecture and each year one lecture is so designated[93].

John Thomas Troddyn, 1908-1979, came to Sligo in 1949 or 1950, via Donegal and Monaghan from his native Dublin. His father was a senior Civil Servant with the Land Commission in Dublin. John was associated with the founding of *The Bell* literary magazine in 1940 before coming to Sligo and later with its liquidation. When he was an engineering student he spent time on archaeological work in the Ballymote area, perhaps the Keash caves excavations. He lived in Cranmore House. He worked with Tohall and succeeded him in the Land Commission Office in Sligo in 1952. His work included new roads, drainage and housing, particularly of the Cooper estate in the Dromore West area of the Ox Mts. He did some fieldwork for A. T. Lucas of the National Museum of Ireland on houses with a *cúlteach*, a bed outshoot, in the Tireragh area. He served on the Sligo Field Club committee for sixteen years, 1959 to 1974, including years as Chairman and Vice-President. He had an interest in Roman Scotland and did lead outings. Apparently he was quite a character and spoke eloquently on matters scientific and historical, and his interest in archaeology was only outweighed by his interest in world religions. He read widely but never published. He retired about 1971, died on 23rd Aug., 1979, and is buried in Dromard where he served as Churchwarden.

Col. **Oliver Wagstaff** (1908-1976) married Elizabeth L'Estrange from Lisnalurg, a granddaughter of Owen Wynne of Hazelwood (Guthrie Jones 1995). Again we are not sure of when he joined though it was subsequent to Kitchin joining us. He served as Hon. Treasurer from 1960 to 1973 and extracted membership fees with military precision; he was of The Royal Marines. He made illustrations of St. John's Cathedral which were published in Bishop Tyndalls's booklet (Tyndall 1962).

Violet Maud Dodd was Wagstaff's Assistant Treasurer from 1960 to 1963. She was born about 1902, was originally from The Mall and served in the Women's Royal Air Force. She retired from Lyons Ladies Fashion Department about 1972 at which time she was living in Lyons' Terrace. Wagstaff was succeeded as Treasurer at very short notice by **Joe Feeney**.

By 1961, when Tohall left Sligo, most of those originally actively involved had passed on or had left Sligo. Exceptions were Tony Toher and Eileen Lambert, and also Patrick Heraughty, who was President until the Constitution was introduced in 1983.

Sean Daly, from Kerry, headmaster in Ballyshannon Secondary School, lived in Cliffoney. He purchased some excellent onions in 1962. On enquiring where they were grown he suspected that the description fitted that of a megalithic tomb. On inspection he discovered that what was marked on the 6" O.S. sheet as a ringfort with a bit taken out of it was in fact the fine Bunduff court tomb (Ó Nualláin 1988, 9, fig. 9, Pl. 1) with its original drystone walling to the court still intact. Such a discovery was rewarded with the positions of Chairman and Vice-President! He died in May 2002.

Mrs. Dianna Campbell-Perry was interested in botany; her husband, Ronald Campbell-Perry of the milling firm in Union St., an actor on the London stage, was described in the Minutes when he died in 1963 as having been a founder member.

Sheila Kirby, of the Flannagan coal and salt merchants family of High St., was the first, and only, lady to be Chairman of Sligo Field Club. She scripted "Women in the Story of Sligo and its Surroundings", an entertainment in music and verse, for the Sligo Town Association of the ICA. The ICA Guild in Sligo town developed a slide show on places associated with Yeats for the 1958 An Toastal celebration. This was presented by Sheila Kirby[94]. A period of being confined to bed led to her writing *The Yeats Country* (Kirby 1969). We have not traced a copy of her notes or article on Sligo Abbey (Hildegard O'Connor pers. comm.). She died in 1975. Her husband, Dr. **Michael Kirby**, from Athlone, was the first Medical Officer of Health for Co. Sligo and died in office in 1964. He is described in the Annual Report for 1964 as having been 'a founder member'; he was at Duignan's lecture in 1945. **Hildegard Kirby**, their daughter, served on the Committee in 1972 having joined the previous year. She initially studied archaeology at UCD.

Nora Niland, from Co. Galway, was County Librarian from 1945 until just before McTernan took over in 1979. She was a leading light for the art gallery in its early days. She devoted her energies to building up a very fine collection of Yeats paintings and memorabilia (Tinney 1998, 4; Hegarty 1998, 5-6; McGarry 2002).

John W. Trotter, a quiet stocky sub-agent in the Hibernian Bank, O'Connell St., or the Bank of Ireland, Stephen St., retired to Cork about 1960[95], having been Hon. Treasurer in 1959 and 1960.

Arthur Henderson[96], gave us a copy of the first edition of *The Shell Guide* in 1961 and in 1964 Mrs. Sheila Cosgrave, a brother of Dr. Tim Foley, of Brewery House, off Bridge St., gave us a Visitors Book. The former has probably gone into somebody's personal library but the latter has had a chequered history. It was first used in 1965 for a visit of the Route Naturalist Field Club from Co. Antrim. There are five entries for 1967 and then it was mislaid until 1984, to be first used again on the occasion of another visit to Sligo of the Route Naturalist Field Club. Since then it has been used to record those present at the AGM each year, those lecturing to us through the years. In 1995 year, our 50th Anniversary year in one sense, all those present at the lectures and outings were invited to sign as a record of their presence.

1971-1974

The year 1971 was a very sad one for the Field Club; Kennedy died in Spring and Cahalane in the Autumn, bringing to an end a phase of our past.

In 1963 **Des Smith**, 1926-2002, BE, a Dubliner, joined the telephones section of the Department of Posts and Telegraph in Sligo. In 1971 he took over as Hon. Secretary at the untimely passing of Cahalane who had been unwell for over a year. He is first mentioned in 1966 in the minutes as a photographer. His photographic recording of sites over twenty years, mainly of megalithic tombs, with a professional skill has added to our library of slides. His photographs of Teampul na mBan on Inishmurray, with its east gable cracked from top to bottom and a wooden buttressing aspiring to keep it from falling, were shown to all and sundry until such time as the State decided to rebuild it. He was involved in recording the Earlier Bronze Age cist burials at Brougher[97], near Ballinafad, and Ballygrania, near Collooney. He served on the County National Monuments

Advisory Committee along with Pat Kitchin and Paddy Heraughty and, at a later stage, with John McTernan. He was slide projectionist at Field Club lectures since Jim Hughes' time and also at the Carrowmore Conference. With Pat Kitchin he logged our slide collection and Bernie Doyle typed up those lists in 2001. His technical expertise in making slides from illustrations and in replicating programmes has been to the benefit of all. The screen formerly in the Sligo Teachers' Centre is of Russian origin having been acquired by Smith. He arranged automated back-projected slide presentations at the Carrowmore Conference and the Inishmurray Symposium. The Field Club honoured him with Honorary Life Membership at the 2002 AGM shortly before he died in February 2002.

Tom McGettrick, a native of Ballymote, was a National School teacher in Carrigans and Ballymote. He had a strong interest in history and placenames. His persistent agitation and work led to Ballymote castle, that built by Richard de Burgo in 1300, being taken into full State care in 1976. He was responsible for the handpin, a type of early first millennium A.D. pin, from Treanmacmurtagh (Duignan 1973) in the Bricklieves reaching the National Museum of Ireland. He was an active member of The Ballymote Heritage Group. He published many articles on a wide range of topics in *The Corran Herald*. Besides matters of heritage he was an actor (*Actors* 1993, 82) something that showed through in his presentations on outings, involved in the GAA, golf, tennis, fishing, the INTO, the VEC and St Vincent de Paul. Under his Irish name, T. MacSitric, he reported to NMI on the discovery of a souterrain. His daughter, Mary McGettrick, was Assistant Secretary in the early 1970s. Tom McGettrick, Patrick Heraughty and Jim McGarry were classmates in St. Nathy's in Ballaghaderreen, and thankfully all are still with us.

The Field Club had the good fortune to have the expert and always willing guidance down the years of **Noel Murphy**, 1909-1991, and his wife, **Briga**. Noel was recommended as early as November 1954 as the one to consult in matters of birdlife. He was on the Committee just after the Revival and again from 1970 to 1982, being Chairman in 1974 and 1975. He worked in Sligo ESB offices, went on cycling and camping trips in Mayo and Donegal, built a boat at an early stage and loved the sea, Coney Island and Rosses Point, joined the Irish Naval Reserve in 1940 and was commissioned with the rank of Ensign in 1948. This outdoor life boosted his knowledge of nature. He regularly talked of duck, geese and swan counts that he had been doing and philosophised on what the fluctuations in numbers meant as to what we are doing to the environment. Under the influence of Major Robin Ruttledge, 1899-2002, the founder of the Irish Wildbird Conservancy, and David Scott, a well known ornithologist and conservationist, Noel took his interest further and became involved in detailed observations of birds for *The Atlas Of Breeding Birds* from 1968 to 1972.

Due to Noel's successes and enthusiasm the Ornithology Section of Sligo Field Club was formed on 22nd. April, 1970. Some of his knowledge was committed to paper in the form of several hundred articles, accompanied by his own drawings, on birds in The *Angelus*, the Elphin Diocesan newspaper, over twelve and a half years. Besides drawing birds he photographed many of them and used his photographic skills for counting flocks of birds. He was a National Council member of the Irish Wildbird Conservancy in the late 1970s. The Sligo Branch of the Irish Wildbird Conservancy erected an information board in 1993 dedicated to the memory of Noel Murphy at Cartron Marsh on the Rosses Point Rd. This has paintings of the birds at Noel's beloved Carton Marsh by Phil Brennan. It was erected with financial support from Sligo Corporation and Abbott (Ireland).

Noel's wife, **Briga Murphy**, nee O'Flynn from Annaghdown, Co. Galway, came to Sligo in Sept. 1935, she was for many years our Hon. Treasurer, and her meticulously kept account book details our activities from 1978 to 1983. She has a strong interest in wild flowers and feeds the many birds that come to her garden.

Their house[98] is adjacent to Sligo Cathedral and as much to their surprise as anyone else's the arm of the high cross from Cloncha, Co. Donegal, (Colhoun 1970, 242-243) was found in 1976 in the Cathedral grounds; it certainly was not brought there by the Cathedral's resident peregrine falcon! It had been removed from Cloncha to Sligo Cathedral about three years before the Colhoun article was written.

Joe Sweeney, from Kilkenny, a National Teacher in Cloontia, Co. Mayo, lived in Gurteen, Co. Sligo. Joe is a polymath; archaeology, history, painting and Irish music are all active parts of his make-up. Noel Murphy realised that Joe's knowledge of birdlife was worth making use of and so Joe was added to the Committee. Joe counted birds on Lough Gara and encouraged the people of south Sligo in matters of Irish culture in the broadest sense. He told Patrick F. Wallace of the Carrowntemple slabs in 1973 (Wallace and Timoney 1987; Timoney 1992)[99].

Frank O'Connor is a native of O'Connor's

Island[100], Streedagh. He returned to Sligo from Dublin in 1971 when OPW opened a depot in Park's Castle. He was Clerk of Works for O.P.W. in the northwest and later District Inspector for the northern half of the Republic. During his twenty years with O.P.W. many National Monuments were made more presentable to the public. Following excavations by Claire Foley from 1972 to 1974, Park's Castle was transformed from a local depot in a ruinous castle into a very fine tourist facility, presenting to the public a good impression of what a 17th century castle looked and felt like[101]. The carpentry, particularly the spiral staircase, is a testimony to local craftsmanship under Frank's guidance. He was succeeded at Dromahaire by John Corcoran.

Dr. Ben Farrell, Assistant Co. Medical Officer, was interested in nature.

Ernest Johnston, B. Agr. Sc. (Forest) B., discovered the habitation layers in the sandhills at Streedagh that hurricane Debbie exposed in 1962; finds included a number of whale intervertebrate discs and a bone pin. He was transferred to Dublin in 1979 but rejoined SFC when he returned and was recently instrumental in making contact with the descendants of Henry Morris, one of whom has set down Morris' story as regards his involvement in Sligo antiquarian matters (see Morris this volume). His own interests are ecology and field studies, especially botany

In June 1960 Sligo Field Club began to assist the Yeats Society with their embryonic Summer School. Cahalane and Ryan were co-opted to the Social Activities Committee. At first transport was all that was involved but soon Sligo Field Club members were taking foreign students on tour to some of the ancient monuments of Co. Sligo. Soon it became a formal arrangement with Cahalane and Kitchin leading an outing. Carrowmore, Carrowkeel and Culleenamore have been the standard locations until dwindling numbers, because of the greater attraction of a trip to Thor Ballyllee and Coole Park in Co. Galway, caused a change from a Sunday trip to a Thursday one and only Carrowmore[102] is now officially visited. They went to Maugherow in 1965. After Cahalane's death in 1971 Kitchin was joined by Tom McGettrick, at least for the mythology of the Sligo landscape as seen from Carrowkeel, and by Des Smith. Timoney took over from Kitchin in 1979 and was assisted by Smith; in the 1980s and 1990s Frank Kerrin, who had been our Field Officer from 1955 to 1959, came along as Yeats Society chaperone to the students[103]. For several years now, Jack Flynn has taken on that onerous task and we manage to show students from all over the world the best of Carrowmore in three hours. There is no knowing just how many people around the world saw photographs of Sligo's monuments taken by students of literature on those occasions.

Carrowkeel was for many years the highlight of the outing. One could crawl into the confined passage of a tomb, see the corbelling and the side chambers and emerge to see the extensive scenery of north Connacht. There are many holes in the limestone and in warning any group of visitors, we tell the story from the 1960s of the lady from a dominant world power. When the bus was about to return to Sligo the lady had not returned. She was reported to have been seen walking down from the region of Cairn O in a northerly direction. We returned to the area and, with dark rapidly falling, we surmised that she possibly headed for a small house[104] visible some distance below. Anthony Kitchin took his fathers new car down to the main road and back up the very narrow laneway from the Lough Arrow side. Never before had a car travelled that laneway! Cahalane, Pat Kitchin and the elder author watched with great apprehension for the new car, more so than for the lost lady. Sure enough the lost lady was there. Anthony, having collected the lady, reversed for a considerable distance before he could turn the car. It being a very hot day and being distracted by the natural beauty of the landscape the lady had failed to keep up with the party. She saw Lough Arrow below and thought this would be a good place to paddle her aching feet! On reaching the first inhabited house she inquired if she could use the telephone to call for a taxi. The house in question, like most this far up the mountain, did not have electricity never mind have a phone!

Cahalane and Kitchin made contact with Prof. **Michael J., 'Brian', O'Kelly** about 1963. That association with the Field Club lasted until O'Kelly's death in 1982. His wife, **Claire**, was also involved in no small way. For many years O'Kelly was a major academic inspiration to Sligo Field Club. He was instrumental in Göran Burenhult's involvement in Carrowmore. Kitchin had tried in 1968 and 1969 to interest one particular Irish archaeologist in Carrowmore but with no success. When Burenhult came to Newgrange to see the megalithic art as a comparative for the Swedish rock art that he was studying for his Ph.D., O'Kelly immediately seized the opportunity and sent him to Carrowmore to see the tombs that were thought by some to have Swedish parallels (Daniel 1981; Burenhult 1979; 1984).

After O'Kelly discovered that the rising sun shines through the roof-box into the chamber at

Newgrange on the shortest day of the year (O'Kelly 1982, Col. Pl. VIII) he suggested to Cahalane and Kitchin that they should try out Carrowkeel for a similar phenomenon at sunset at mid-summer. Weather normally hampered the observations with the cloud descending to well below the level of the cairns; since 1985 only 1995 (see below) has proved suitable from a visibility point of view. Even on a good day the north-western horizon was so full of moisture that one could not clearly see the sun set. Furthermore the trampling over the years of cairns, K and G particularly, has left the outer passage stones exposed to the extent that light is getting in between them at so many places that scientific decisions can not be made as to where there may have been a constructed way in which light was designed to enter the chamber. Kitchin was quite satisfied that the image of the light of the sun through an opening over the passage entrance of cairn G was co-extensive with the left upright of the back chamber. It is part of the mythology of Sligo Field Club that Kitchin and Tom McGettrick were separately and unbeknownst to each other in cairns G and K hoping for a sighting; Sheela Kitchin was also up there on occasions. From 1975 on the younger author frequently, and once with Joe Sweeney, tried; we saw the co-extensive image noted by Kitchin at cairn G. The summer of 1995 really began on June 23rd with brilliant sunsets for several evenings

Minutes for February 1964 record the receipt of a plan of the passage graves on the Bricklieve Mountains from Mr. J. Hally, County Engineer, Waterford, who had worked with Sligo Co. Co. for about two years; regrettably no copy of this survives in the SFC files nor do we know why he did it.

O'Kelly was not the only national academic to have a close relationship with the Sligo Field Club. Richard Hayward of Belfast, G. Frank Mitchell of Trinity College, Dr. A. T. Lucas, Dr. Joseph Raftery, A. Brendán Ó Riordáin and Etienne Rynne of the National Museum of Ireland, Seán Ó Nualláin of the Archaeological Branch of the Ordnance Survey, Ruaidhrí de Valera, George Eogan and Michael Herity of University College, Dublin, Patrick Hartnett of Bord Fáilte, E. Estyn Evans and Robin Glasscock of The Queen's University, Belfast, were all part of a two-way communications system on matters of archaeological importance.

Prominent members of local societies or local activists such as Major R.B. Aldridge of Mount Falcon, Ballina, Carmel Hughes, Christy Lawless and Thomas Hennigan from Mayo, Louis and Kathleene Emerson of Ballyshannon, Billy English, Harman Murtagh, Brendan O'Brien and Alfie Faulkner of Athlone, Margaret Phelan of Kilkenny, and Frank Tivnan and Albert Siggins[105] from Roscommon were in contact with us down the years. Over the years local Irish societies from Antrim, Armagh, Fermanagh, Longford, Donegal, Athlone, Cork, Kilkenny, Limerick and Roscommon visited us. In 1974 The Ulster Architectural Society visited Sligo and in 1976 The Group for Irish Historical Settlement came.

Some of those national contacts lead to **international contacts**. John Coles, Chris Scarre and Joan Taylor from England, George Boon of Cardiff, Ian Fisher from Scotland, Willie Groenman-van Watteringe and Lisabeth de Jong from Holland, Louise Cedarchöld, Göran and Monica Burenhult, Mats Malmer and Stefan Bergh from Sweden, Knut E. Henriksen of Oslo, Emanuel Anati of Barcelona, Martin Hoder of Lisbon, F.C.J. Los of Hilversum, Roger Joussaume from France and Pierre Rolland Giot from Brittany, and not just individuals but groups from Oxford, Cambridge, Sheffield, Nottingham, Derby, Southampton, Liverpool, Chippenham, Hanover, Amsterdam and the USA have likewise been guided around many Sligo sites. Prof. Arriba of Barcelona had a five-day visit to us in the 1950s. Scholars from many countries, Ireland, England, Wales, Denmark, Sweden, Germany and Majorca, attended the Carrowmore Conference in 1982[106]. Like the story of his predecessor Prof. Graham Clarke drinking stout from the bottle, Prof. Colin Renfrew carrying his briefcase to examine the hutsites on the karstic platform of Donaveragh has gone into our store of legends.

The **campaigning** energies of the Field Club were directed in the 1960s and 1970s to Carrowmore, **Inishmurray** and Ballymote castle. Inishmurray (Heraughty 1983; 1996) had been abandoned in 1948 and, with greater ease of access, there was fear for the Early Christian monuments. **Ballymote** castle, the most substantial surviving castle in Sligo (Sweetman 1985), if not in Connacht, took "thirteen years, seven months and eighteen days" to be declared as a National Monument; the joy at that success was immense. Since then OPW have invested a lot of time and money on conserving this building.

By 2nd March, 1965, they had compiled a letter to the Commissioners of Public Works on the subject of preserving about **one hundred monuments** by having them taken into Care at various levels. The four appendices dealt with Inishmurray and Carrowmore, both of which were in State Care, twenty of the best monuments in the county that should be taken into full State Care and these at very little expense since many were megalithic tombs, and finally 132 sites in need of Listing. They provided the results of considerable research work as to importance, publication and ownership. Several years of work that should be done by state officials was handed on a plate to OPW. The reply that there were already 15 monuments in State care and 3 Listed monuments in the county only served to draw out an even stronger reply. In January 1967 a supplementary list of 120 sites in need of Listing Orders was forwarded. Undaunted they continued and by January 1969 ninety-three of the 270 or so monuments had been listed. Michael Healy had been made caretaker of Carrowkeel, all of which was in State Care by April 1970; Carrowmore was left unattended locally. Ardtermon Castle and the holy wells at Tullaghan, Clogher and Kilturra had been rejected. Perhaps no one took note that at each there was more than a holy well and one, Tullaghan, was classified among the *Mirabilae Eireann* in the Middle Ages!, and the 17th century Green Fort did not get the status we thought, and still think, it deserves![107]

The **Foras Forbartha** "Preliminary Report on Sites of Archaeological Interest in County Sligo" was compiled by Joyce Raftery, now Joyce Enright, having been given three weeks to complete the mammoth task in January 1973[108]. This time constraint, even when she expanded it to six weeks, did not allow for original research or fieldwork. She did however carry out six days fieldwork and drew heavily on SFC members Sheila Kirby, Dr. Paddy Heraughty, Des Smith and, particularly, Pat Kitchen for information. She was given the SFC list of sites compiled in the 1960s referred to above and she was brought to see many stone age sites not then officially recognised or marked on the OS maps.

The report for Sligo Co. Council's Planning Office was accompanied with a set of six-inch maps of the county, on which the selected sited were encircled in the same manner as on the current Recorded Monuments and Places maps. She recommended 438 sites for preservation. These belonged to about 25 monument types. Seventy-eight of the then estimated 1500 ringforts were included. The highest proportion of all sites listed were megaliths and other prehistoric burial sites, considered by her to be the most vulnerable site type. Megaliths, the earliest type-site, were given a starting point of 3,500 BC, the date then in vogue.

As a result of this Foras Forbartha report, commissioned by Sligo Co. Council, the number of monuments recommended for preservation was increased from 274 in the 1972 County Development Plan to 438 in the 1979 Plan. This was a major step forward, yet it meant that less than 10% of the pre-1700 AD monuments in the county were included; see Alcock and Tunney (this volume) for current statistics.

Special consideration was given to sites in the vicinity of Sligo town, to Inishmurray and to Carrowmore, the three areas considered most at risk from development. For Carrowmore Raftery provided a map with lines suggesting the extents of areas to be protected around the passage-tomb cemetery. These lines were to have major implications during the Carrowmore 1983 High Court and 1988 Supreme Court Case (Timoney, M.A., 1990; 1992).

Raftery (1974, 16-19) indicated the prevailing attitudes to preservation in the early 1970s. An important result of the report, even before it was released, was that the Council declared Carrowmore to be an unauthorised gravel pit in 1973. This decision followed on consultations between the then County Secretary, Patrick Doyle and Joyce Raftery. In 1985 she wrote a piece on putting Carrowmore in context (Enright 1985b).

SFC has always been involved, **actively involved**, in the material heritage of this county. Back in 1955 a survey of early Irish churches and mills, the latter perhaps because of friendship with Dr. A. T. Lucas, was mooted. If it got under way there is no record of any results in the SFC files. The Field Club's megalithic survey was going so well by 1976 that they were contemplating an Archaeological Survey of all monuments in the county. The new blood in the Field Club came from different Universities and were interested in a fuller range of monuments. The number of megalithic tombs left to be discovered was very small[109]. The full archaeological survey of nearby Co. Donegal was getting underway (Lacy 1983). However our own survey did not get underway because a number of other things drew our attention and by 1980 it was no longer being reported on[110]. Our archaeological survey was done, if at all, on a very individualistic format. The younger author, prompted by two things, five years spent in east Clare which has so many castles and later the work of Mary O'Dowd for her Ph.D. on the history of early modern Sligo (O'Dowd 1983; 1991; 1994), visited and photographed many castles and castle sites throughout the county accompanied by his father and Tim Kelly from 1974 to 1980. In 1988 survey work was begun officially by the Office of Public Works as part of the national SMR and this has been followed by fieldwork which is incorporated in the Recorded

Monuments and Places Record (Alcock and Tunney this volume)[111].

John Devlin, from Toomebridge, Co. Antrim, came from Donegal to Dromahaire in 1955 and married Ann Craig in 1959. He worked with the Dept. of Agriculture as Land Projects Officer in Carrick-on-Shannon and in Sligo. His interests were history and 'things old'. He was Chairman in 1976 and 1977 and Vice President in the following two years. He died in 1996.

Frank Mahon, from Mohill, Co. Leitrim, came to Castlegal, Glencar, as a blacksmith on the Gleniff barytes mines. Just around the corner from Noel Murphy's house in John St. he had a metal worker's yard in Adelaide St. and his son is the third generation of the family to be metalworkers. Frank had worked his land for decades and his observations on the location of sites in relation to the land and its quality were very clear-sighted. It was Noel Murphy who introduced Frank to the Field Club in the early 1960s. He claimed that an 'illegal' excavation in 1930 that he worked on at Sheemore, Co. Leitrim, was in no small way responsible for the actual bringing of the 1930 National Monuments Act onto the Statute Books. He died in May 2002 in his 91st year.

Terry McGowan was born in Kiltyclogher in 1916. He joined SFC in the 1960s through Paddy Heraughty. He has a great interest in the Black Pig's Race which he was brought out to see by Henry Morris.

1974

Up until the early 1970s none of the members had formal training in archaeology, they were just totally dedicated devotees. Today we look back in admiration at the successes of a dedicated small group, uninhibited by their lack of professional training but constantly encouraged by archaeologists of national standing. Then in the 1970s some people, with archaeology or history as part of their degrees, joined and influenced the direction of Sligo Field Club more towards archaeology, perhaps with all the other disciplines being part of the backdrop for man's existence in Sligo.

Joyce Enright, a daughter of a long-standing member Kay Raftery of Finisklin, joined in September 1973, though with her mother and the Kirbys she had often been at SFC events in the 1960s. Joyce graduated in Archaeology and Early Irish History from UCD in 1970 and followed this with a Diploma in Librarianship in 1971. She worked both on excavations and as a research assistant for OPW and as chief assistant to the late Tom Fanning on excavations at Kells Priory in Ossory and Reask Early Christian Monastic site on the Dingle Peninsula for much of 1972 and 1973. She also worked as a consultant archaeologist for Foras Forbartha completing reports on Cos. Waterford and Sligo. She remained on their panel of consultants until they were disbanded about 1981. She returned to Sligo as Assistant Co. Librarian in Sligo Co. Library in September 1973 (on Eileen Lambert's retirement) and was the first Sligo Regional Technical College Librarian. In 1974 she married Martin Enright from Dingle.

She has directed two excavations (Enright 1985d). She was one of the earliest non-public-service archaeologist to be contracted by OPW to carry out excavations on their behalf. In 1982 she carried out excavations at Ardtarmon Castle, the seventeenth century semi-fortified Manor House on the Maugherow peninsula, prior to its restoration by Erica and the late Holger Schiller. Joyce directed excavations of archaeological domestic deposits north of the High Cross at Drumcliffe Monastic site[112] for six seasons, 1980 and 1982 to 1986, (Enright, 1984b; 1985c; 1985d; 1986; 1987a; 1987b) and a full report of this very complex area is in preparation.

Joyce served as joint Hon. Secretary of SFC with Des Smith for 1975 and 1976. From 1977 until 1983 she served as Hon. Secretary. She initiated the production of a twice-yearly programme of SFC events of summer outings and winter lectures as opposed to the issuing of individual lecture notices. From the outset she was keen that the SFC would produce an annual Journal, but this has not yet come to fruition, though this volume may be an initial step. She helped to draw up the SFC Constitution with Pat Kitchin and Jack Flynn in 1983. Since 1998 she has served as Hon. Treasurer. Joyce conceived the idea of a *Newsletter* to inform Sligo people of the SFC activities and has produced one issue in Summer 1998.

She summarised the archaeology of Co. Sligo in the Sligo ASTI 1978 Congress Magazine (Enright 1978), for the Bord Fáilte guide to Sligo (Enright 1984a) and in the Irish Association of Quaternary Studies Conference in Sligo handbook in 1985 (Enright 1985a). She has a special interest in Inishmurray (Enright 1989), particularly its Early Christian slabs.

Since 1973 she has worked on and off as a Consultant Archaeologist and Heritage Advisor, fulfilling diverse contracts with a variety of clients in various parts of Ireland. Drawing on their experience of guiding various groups, Joyce and her husband, Martin, began a tourism business in 1987 under the name of Wild Rose Tours. This offered guided bus tours of Sligo's rich heritage combining diverse aspects of the Sligo landscape from archaeology to Yeats. In 1998 the venture focused as an Incoming Tour Operator specialising in Irish heritage and culture but has not operated since 2000.

She has given many lecture courses and individual lectures to a wide variety of groups. These include Adult Education from 1976 to 1983, UCG Extra Mural from 1977 to 1981, Elderhostel at St Angela's, Clogherevagh, Co. Sligo, from 1990 to 1998, and In-Service Courses for Primary Teachers from 1988 to 2000 in Sligo, Dingle and Dublin and for Sligo Institute of Technology Art students in 1999 and 2000. The origins of the Ballymote Heritage Group (see below) lie in five lecture courses she gave in Ballymote between 1978 and 1983. In 1999 she was invited to join the INTO panel of Heritage Experts and develops a sense of place in the Primary Schools pupils.

She was active on various national organisations in the 1970s and 1980s. In her undergraduate days she was class spokesperson seeking to negotiate changes in the Archaeology Department at UCD. She was an active member of the UCD Archaeology Society from 1966 to 1973, and on the committee in 1969 and 1970. From its inception in 1968, she actively participated in the Association of Young Irish Archaeologists. This association was set up to promote interaction between the students in the University Archaeology Departments, north and south. She was the UCD representative on the National Committee of AYIA in 1971 and 1972. It was to this group that she gave her first lecture in 1970; the theme was the importance of Irish Annals and other MSS as a source of information to archaeology. From 1970 she was a member of the Group for the Study of Irish Historic Settlement, and served on the National Committee for about ten years from the early 1970s. She was the local organiser for their annual weekend conference in Sligo in 1976. In the early 1980s she was Treasurer of the Sligo branch of An Taisce. In 1983 she was a founder member of the Organisation of Irish Archaeologists and a National Council member of OIA for several years[113]. Since 1984 she has been a member of the Medieval Academy of Ireland.

She has carried out archaeological and cultural heritage inputs in Environmental Impact Statements in various parts of Ireland, for example for the Arklow, Co. Wicklow, Bypass (Enright 1992a; 1992b; 1993) and in relation to the proposals for a hotel and leisure complex at Lough Key, Co. Roscommon, (Enright 1990).

Recently she has noted several hundred circular features, possibly hut sites, that seem to pre-date the bog in the wetlands valley between Ballinadrehid and Lough Gill. They lie along the eastern boundary of Burenhult's "model for seasonal circuit of the megalith-building population of Carrowmore" (Burenhult 1980, facing 6). These features deserve trail trenching and a detailed examination by a range of specialists.

Joyce and Martin have both been unstinting in their generosity with providing information to the many who have requested their help with research in the Sligo area over the years for a multitude of projects, from undergraduate and graduate theses, to a variety of school and youth work projects to radio and T.V. programmes. Indeed both have appeared on T.V. and been interviewed for radio programmes including Donnacha's Sunday and Radio na Gaeltachta.

Martin Enright, from Dingle, married Joyce Raftery in 1974. He is a National Teacher, with a BA Degree from UCD, in Archaeology and Irish. His special interests are in Archaeology, Ornithology and the Traditional Arts. As a National School Teacher he has inculcated in his students a sense of place. His students in the classrooms of Carraroe and Coolbock National Schools have achieved local, regional and national success for diverse projects based on Sligo and its surroundings. Martin served on the committee for eighteen years, being President in 1988 and 1989.

From the time of his arrival in Sligo Martin was particularly influenced by the late Noel Murphy. Noel, being the ornithological secretary of the SFC, formed the Sligo branch of the Irish Wildbird Conservancy in February 1982 (now BirdWatch Ireland). Martin is currently chairperson of the Sligo Branch of BirdWatch Ireland.

His other interests are varied. He was a founder member in 1975, as was his wife, Joyce, of the Sligo town Branch of Comhaltas Ceoltóirí Eireann. Since 1993 he has been the Co-ordinator of the James Morrison Traditional Music Festival in Riverstown. He is an active Committee member of the Yeats International Summer School. He was the Co-Treasurer, with Larry Mullin, of the Co. Sligo Famine Commemoration Committee (1995-1997). He was active on the INTO committee that compiled The *National Schools of Co. Sligo, 1831-1999*, the Co. Sligo INTO Millennium Project. Martin is a Member of the Co. Sligo Heritage Forum (representing, with Aidan Mannion, the heritage groups of Co. Sligo) and he is the chairperson of the Natural Heritage sub-committee.

With his wife Joyce, he has been involved in

their Wild Rose Tours activities as guide and lecturer on courses since 1987. He particularly enjoyed his involvement in the In-Service Courses for Primary Teachers. He regularly shares his knowledge and enthusiasm for Sligo's rich cultural heritage with local and visiting groups.

Meetings were held on occasions in the Land Commission Offices, the Imperial Hotel, the Cafe Cairo, Lyons Cafe, Toher's Shop, The Great Southern Hotel, The Columban Club, the Regional Technical College, Ballinode Technical School, The Yeats Memorial Building and The Teachers' Centre.

Pat Hurley, from Tuam, came to teach in St. John's N.S., Sligo, in 1958. About 1972 **Sligo Teacher's Centre** was established, with Pat Hurley and Padraig Foran being the main forces at that stage. In 1974/1975 its Director, Pat Hurley, invited SFC to use the premises for lectures and meetings and also provided facilities for us. Pat thinks that the link may have been Tom McGettrick, NT, who was SFC Vice-President in 1974 and 1975. 'In return' we provided adult education in archaeology, local history, birdlife, *etc*. In the 1980s Hurley arranged a number of Summer courses in these topics for National School teachers and several SFC members did the lecturing and outings. He guided the new SEC development on the Institute of Technology campus in 1999-2000 and when Sligo Teacher's Centre became Sligo Education Centre and moved from Quay St. we moved with them. The last lecture in Quay St. was by Dr. Stefan Bergh and Eamon P. Kelly of NMI lectured on the night of the last AGM in Quay St. We may have influenced the most helpful and efficient caretaker at the Quay St. Teachers' Centre, **Martin Dunbar,** to delve deeply into his family roots.

Unfortunately no event notices of the 1940s are known to us other than mentions in the local newspapers. In the days of cheap postage a **programme** per lecture was the norm. Cahalane often added comprehensive site notes on the outing notices of the 1950s and 1960s. From the mid-1970s the year's activities was announced on two or three programmes. From 1981 to 1985 these were hand-written and decorated by **Catherine McConville.** From 1985 on programmes were typed up on a word processor by the younger author and illustrations related to the lectures added.

Dr. J.K. St. Joseph of Cambridge begun taking **aerial photos** of Sligo sites in 1964 and continued until 1971, taking almost 300 photos in total. In September 1966 SFC proposed purchasing a set but may not have done so. Kitchin examined the prints in NMI but with failing eyesight deferred the duty to the younger author. Fifty pounds was spent on prints in the mid-1970s and these have been used to assist us on site and to aid further study. While examining the photos in NMI the younger author recognised the presence of an enclosure around the cairn on Keash (Condit, Gibbons and Timoney 1991, 62; Timoney and Timoney 2001, 13 and 16). Daphne D.C. Pochin Mould took seven aerial photos over Co. Sligo in the 1960s.

Tim Kelly, 1913-1995, a farmer who had worked the lands of Carricknagat, Ballintogher, eased out of farming in the mid 1970s and armed with his bicycle and Peter Harbison's *Guide to National Monuments* discovered a new life for himself. He regularly travelled by train, with the bicycle, to distant counties and then cycled to the major National Monuments, encountering many farmers along the way and regaling them with descriptions of comparable monuments throughout the country. Enlightened by his travels he clearly could distinguish between what was 'ancient', *i.e.*, pre-historic, and what was 'modern', *i.e.*, of historic times. He also recognised the earthworks that were not ringforts, sending some of them into the 'ancient' category. He repeatedly shared folklore information with members and recollected the visit of Henry Morris (Morris this volume) to Kilross National School, because the greater part of the day was spent investigating the earthen burial mound on the hill behind the school. For many years, after the ending of the official outing, he would 'drag' some of the more willing members to extra sites. One trip to north Mayo ended near Culleens about 10.30 PM on a summer's evening, having seen seven extra sites, two of which were not on the OS map and had been discovered by Kelly some months previously. On another occasion the younger author passed through the National Museum of Ireland *en route* home from England to discover Kelly examining, somewhat reluctantly, some treasures in glass cases. Nothing that he had sent to the National Museum of Ireland was on display and anyway he would prefer to be out in the field. We offered him a lift to Sligo, but before Kinnegad he had us decide that the way home was going to be through Westmeath and south Longford, with several mandatory diversions into ancient sites; Carricknagat was reached by midnight plus![114] He presented some objects to Sligo Museum, including what he believed to be an ink well dated 1724, though probably the date stone for a house.

Carrowmore (Wood-Martin 1888; Kitchin 1983; Bergh 1980; 1984; 1997; this volume; Burenhult

1980; 1984; 1995; 2001) is a megalithic cemetery in the Passage Tomb Tradition. It is built on gravel deposits which were worked, over the years, for building and road materials, a process which increased in the 1960s and 1970s, resulting in the scarring of the landscape and the loss of some of the passage tombs. The latter half of 1970, just five years after the SFC letters, was crisis time for Carrowmore with fresh quarrying and offers of land for sale for housing. The persistence of Sligo Field Club as a watchdog[115], perhaps occasionally as a hound, prevented the destruction of even more. In 1983 Sligo County Council proposed establishing a landfill site in the, by now, considerable quarry east of the Clockwell Road that goes south through the cemetery. A local group took legal action to prevent it and were supported by members of SFC. In the action, referred to as McGarry and others at the Relation of the Attorney General v. Sligo County Council, both authors were called as learned witnesses (Timoney, M.A. 1990, 3; 1992, 23-25). The many lines drawn, by Raftery (1974) and others, around Carrowmore to indicate its extent were severely tested during the Carrowmore High Court and Supreme Court Case (Timoney, M.A., 1990; 1992; Supreme Court 1985 No. 118/133, ILRM 1989, 768-777) and, following a precedent in the Hanrahan v. Merck, Sharp and Dohme case (O'Callaghan 1992) this non-legal technical expert was allowed to explain them at the Supreme Court appeal. The Supreme Court decision ruled against the dump and stated the need for a fallow area around ancient monuments, in the case of Carrowmore the cemetery extends over a very large area, that Development Plans form an environmental contract between the Planning Authority and the Community and that it should consult with that Community. That Supreme Court decision of 1989 "regarding the Neolithic passage tomb cemetery at Carrowmore, Co. Sligo, further strengthened the (archaeological) legislation" (Eogan 2002, 477). In 1987 OPW began the purchase of the cemetery and established a Visitor Centre in a renovated cottage. Much remains to be done for Carrowmore but see Bergh (2001, 5).

The early dating of the Carrowmore tombs and the consequent debate as to their cultural background has given unexpected world-wide publicity to Carrowmore. See for instance the reviews by Kaul (1985) and Ryan (1982) and two pieces by Daniel (Daniel 1980, 7; 1981, 82-84). When one looks at the chart of C14 dates produced by Burenhult (2001, 15) there is a clear and confident concentration of dates from 4,750CalBC to 2,800CalBC from the excavations of the tombs. The dating of the many other samples gathered during the excavations would be costly but rewarding in sorting out the internal dating of Carrowmore.

The **results of many years fieldwork** on megalithic tombs are to be seen, duly and rightly acknowledged, throughout the pages *of The Megalithic Survey of Ireland: Vol. V, Co. Sligo*, published in 1989 under the authorship of our Honorary Life Member Dr. Seán Ó Nualláin. When the Sites and Monuments Record Office turned its attention to Sligo in 1988 many of the Sligo Field Club fieldwork discoveries were incorporated into the SMR. The benefit of the basic fieldwork of the 1960s and 1970s does not end there. In 1991 when the Ordnance Survey began to issue the 1:50,000 Rambler Series OS maps of Co. Sligo they used the SMR maps as their archaeological guide and these Sligo Rambler Series maps, which were among the first to be issued, were to set the standard for the national series. Furthermore the younger author scrutinised the first versions of these 1:50,000 Discovery Series OS maps and suggested amendments and additions for the later editions.

A number of papers deriving from the Sites and Monuments Record have been published (Condit, Gibbons and Timoney 1991; Condit and Gibbons 1991). Startling results include the discovery of hundreds of sites from aerial photographs, the recognition of the greater extent of many sites, some to the extent that we have to consider areas of archaeological interest, the discovery of some hill-top enclosures and the increased number of Medieval rectangular moated sites from four in 1971 to at least forty, if not considerably more than that (Timoney and Timoney, 2001, 22). See Alcock and Tunney (this volume) for the statistics. An unexpected by-product was the meeting of Joe Burke of Mullin who worked on excavations on Knocknashee about 1971.

In 1988 the **Armada 400** was marked by an international gathering in Sligo (Gallagher and Cruickshank 1990); the elder author lectured in Grange and the younger author took some of the participants on a field trip to monuments in north Sligo. Sligo County Council republished Allingham and Crawford's 1897 edition of Captain Cuellar's account of that time in 1988 and another version (Stapleton and de Cúellar 2001) was issued recently; see also Carville (1990). The Grange people continue to hold a commemorative weekend. Devins (2000, 56) records that Michael O'Donnell of Sligo Co. Co. designed the replica ship's prow monument at Streedagh to commemorate the 1588 disaster. Gunning and Feehily (1995, 14-15) have illustrated some of the recent work and discoveries at Streedagh. The High Court Judgement of 1994 by Justice Barr and the Supreme Court Judgement of June 1995 by Justices Hamilton, O'Flaherty, Egan, Blaney and Denham are legal statements of international importance; the former also contains historical information on the Armada.

At the AGM on 14th March 1988, arising out of the perennial argument as to which AGM it was and the consequent discussion as to our date of foundation, 1938, 1939, 1944 or 1945, Des Smith suggested we pick a date and celebrate so many years of our existence. Joyce Enright proposed and Dr. Patrick Heraughty seconded that we celebrate 1995, our 50th Anniversary year in one sense, with a commemorative volume of essays. Martin A. Timoney was nominated to be Editor. The aspiration during 1993 was that our celebration would link in with the Sligo 750, the commemoration of the founding of Sligo's first castle in 1245[116]. Yes, we are somewhat late! But then 2002, the year of this publication, is the 750th Anniversary of the founding of Sligo Abbey. It may be a lame excuse to ask what is a few years in comparison with the millennia on settlement in Sligo? The increased knowledge of Sligo and the more detailed evaluation if will be of benefit to us all.

Sligo Regional Technical College, now The Institute of Technology, Sligo, was opened in September 1970. Due to the interest of several staff members courses in environmental sciences (FitzGerald, 2002) were quickly established[117]. Dr. Don C. F. Cotton joined that team in 1981 and has brought to us all in Sligo, not only his expertise in botany, ornithology and natural science, but also, a comprehensive knowledge of the ancillary sciences and again their use in combination.

Don is interested in anything that creeps or crawls, flutters its feathered wings or anything that is rooted to the ground. He has been compiling a computer database of all that is known about the flora and fauna of Sligo and Leitrim and is compiling a bibliography of written papers and notes in the same academic area with the addition of the earth sciences. Don's ultimate ambitions are to publish books on the Birds of Sligo and Leitrim and eventually on the Natural History of these two counties. A book on the birds is currently underway and his bibliography of published works may be converted to a searchable database. He has written about twenty-five scientific articles on the wildlife of Sligo and Leitrim, most of which have been published in *Irish Naturalists' Journal* and Irish Birds, publishing therein several species not previously recorded in Ireland. He arranged a seminar on Inishmurray in 1987 and edited the proceedings (Cotton 1989).

By 1981 **Irish Wildbird Conservancy** numbers had grown to such an extent that they formed a branch in Sligo in February 1982. This was the culmination of many years work by Noel Murphy. This voluntary organisation, now known as BirdWatch Ireland, takes care of ornithology and other wildlife matters. They hold ten field outings and about six indoor lectures each year. They have made yearly counts of ducks, geese and swans and they have pressed for better conservation status of wildlife habitats including the establishment of the Lissadell goose field as a National Nature Reserve, wintering grounds of the Barnacle goose. They did the bird counts for all of Sligo and Leitrim for *The Atlas of Winter Birds* (Lack 1986) in these islands; Don Cotton edited the Sligo and Leitrim sections of it. They have co-ordinated many other national surveys such as those of the corncrake, peregrine falcon, whooper swan and wetland birds. BirdWatch Ireland have moved their lecture venue to the Institute of Technology.

Don Cotton was a major figure in the very innovative Lough Gill Environmental Management Project which is concerned with the entire catchment area of Lough Gill. Its meetings are a forum for the mingling of people and ideas from many organisations, including Sligo Field Club, Sligo and Leitrim County Councils and the people of the catchment area. The goal is to manage the catchment area so that the natural resources, waters, woodlands, wildlife and heritage are used in an environmentally sustainable manner (Thompson, Ryan and Cotton 1998). Don wrote nature trail leaflets for Hazelwood and Dooney Rock and contributed on the flora and fauna for The Miners Way & Historical Trail booklet. He has many other publications to his name (*e.g.*, Cotton 1992) and also in this volume.

Besides SFC there have been other groups in the county that had overlapping interests with us. The **Ballina Historical and Folklore Society**, which spanned the years from 1936 to 1944 (McHale 1987-1988, 40), may have had members from west Sligo. **The Lough Gara Historical Society** came into existence on 7th October 1969 under the influence of Michael Garvey of Ballaghaderreen and for a few years served the needs of north Roscommon and south Sligo; it was semi-dormant by 1974; the younger author may have been the last to lecture to in 1975. Since November 1970 the **North Mayo Historical and Archaeological Society** have served the interests of people in west Sligo. Based in Inishcrone **The MacFirbis Society** has since 1971 celebrated the life and works of that 17th century family from nearby Lackan (See Ó Muraíle 1996 for the life of Dubhaltach Mac Fhirbhisigh, c. 1600 - 1671). **The Roscommon Historical and Archaeological Society** was reactivated in 1982, having been originally founded in 1905 (Anon. 1986, 5). **The Flannery** families from Tubbercurry, who have devoted much time to drama (Actors 1993, *passim*).

Based in Sligo town the Sligo History Society spanned the years 1977 to 1987 and so history ceased to be covered by SFC for a few years. When active they sponsored local history projects. Many people simultaneously served on the committees of Sligo History Society and SFC and after its demise SFC took upon itself to have one history lecture each year[118].

Aodhán O'Higgins, a native of Lahinch, Co. Clare, came to Co. Sligo in 1972. He married Patricia O'Gara from Ballisodare. Most of his teaching was with The Town of Sligo V.E.C. Matters of local, social and gentry family history of the last three centuries are his forte. He was awarded an MA in 1983 for his thesis on The Sligo Borough Improvement Act of 1869. He joined RSAI in 1983. He was a major force in Sligo Historical Society founded on 17th November, 1977. He has lectured widely, including to Teacher's Summer Courses and has led several of our outings.

Kay Raftery, daughter of the poet R.J. Milne from Knocknarea, lived most of her life in Sligo, except when she trained in the Mater Hospital and worked as a nurse. She married George Raftery of Finisklin in 1935. She was skilled in many traditional crafts and she passed on her knowledge though the Irish Countrywomen's Association. She was the first President, 1951-1953, of the ICA in Co. Sligo and set up guilds around the county in the 1950s. See under Sheila Kirby (below) for activities related to our interests that the Sligo Guild undertook during her period of activity with the ICA.

She was on Sligo Agricultural Show Committee in the 1950s and 1960s and was active for a time with the Irish Country Markets movement. She was an active member of the Yeats Society and a committee member of the Sligo Art Gallery for many years. She was active in the SFC in the 1950s and she was a Committee member from 1975 to 1982. She and Eileen Lambert were active members of the Royal Society of Antiquaries, attending lectures in Dublin, and often travelling together on week-end outings and trips abroad.

In the late 1960s the elder author sent a patient's son, the younger author, who was then studying archaeology at University College, Galway, to see Cahalane. Cahalane, after giving much attention to the youth, asked him if he would join the Field Club, but the youth had much less than the subscription rate in his pocket. A small sum was accepted and, hopefully, the balance has been repaid in effort since or, as Capt. Lewis Irwin informed Beranger's party on July 21st, 1779, his "portion of the account had been lost" (Wilde 1870, 152). Thus the younger author, the 'barking dog' sent forth by Etienne Rynne to check a souterrain at Culleenamore, began a long-term active involvement with SFC.

Martin A. Timoney, being a native of the Cuil Iorra peninsula[119], made an undergraduate study of this peninsula which includes Knocknarea and Carrowmore. This meant that he has walked in almost every field on the peninsula, something that was to stand to him later when the Swedish Expedition to Carrowmore took place from 1977 to 1981 and also in the Carrowmore landfill site case in 1983.

In 1968 Stephen O'Connor[120] of Breeoge noticed a group of stones in the corner of a field in Breeoge and told the younger author who, being unaware of the SFC told his lecturer at UCG, Etienne Rynne. Rynne accompanied by Patrick F. Wallace, Tom Fahy and the younger author came to see the site and confirmed it as a wedge-tomb and then went on to meet with Cahalane, Kitchin, Smith and Hughes at the Primrose Grange court-tomb[121]. Looking back on it now the younger author has mixed feelings at finding a wedge-tomb in *their* county, particularly so near Sligo town, even if the finder was a native of the next townland. The tomb was hastily drawn by Etienne Rynne that day and photographed later but regrettably it was bulldozed into a corner of the field in 1972. When the ground on which it stood was subsequently excavated in 1972 cremated and skeletal human remains were found (Rynne and Timoney 1973; 1974-1975). He excavated the Knocknashammer burial mound (Timoney, M.A. 1984; 1987-1988), which contained the remains of three skeletal burials, since no State body would try to save it from falling into a gravel quarry. He has since done several pre-development test excavations including that for the Irish National Field Study Centre at Ballinafad. With his wife Mary they have an archaeological research consultancy business.

He attended one SFC meeting in early Summer 1974 with very muddy shoes, to the horror of the ladies. On being reprimanded by one of them, Kay, he asked just how many sites she had visited that day, or even that week. Silence! He had just been searching the Finisklin area for a *fullacht fiadh* marked on the 6" O.S. map without much satisfaction.

His teaching career in Clare, 1969-1974, and Roscommon, 1974-1997, has led him into research, lecturing and publications (see bibliography) in those counties and he has served on the Roscommon National Monuments Advisory Committee of Roscommon Co. Co. He joined RSAI in 1968 and was its Vice President for Connacht from 1984 to 1986. He has lectured in every county west of the Shannon. He has been a member of about twenty archaeological societies including The Prehistoric Society, and of Irish societies in Limerick, Galway, Athlone and Roscommon. He has done specific study in museums and libraries here and on the Continent.

His contributions include the discovery of many previously unknown rectangular Anglo-Norman sites in Sligo, the hilltop enclosure on Keash, the recovery of the Early Christian Carrowntemple decorated grave slabs (Wallace and Timoney 1987; Wallace, 2000, No. 42, p. 47) in 1986 with Dr. Patrick F. Wallace of the National Museum of Ireland[122] and his involvement in 1983 and 1988 in the defence of the Carrowmore Passage Tomb Cemetery from the unwelcome intrusion of domestic and industrial waste of Co. Sligo. In addition to all that he has been a member of the committee without a break since 1975, serving the Sligo Field Club in every capacity.

He has written several local archaeology articles, and has dabbled in Radio, TV and Video in relation to archaeology. Several of his Hon. Secretary's Annual Reports have been published in the Federation or Local History Societies *Local History Review* in the 1990s.

He assisted NMI on more than one occasion as regards the scourge of metal detector operators. He was instrumental in having the Glen[123] Later Bronze Age Hoard (Eogan 1983, 150-151) deposited in the NMI.

He also has studied Early Christian slabs of mainland Sligo (Timoney 1966-1971; 1987; 1988; 1989; 1992; Wallace and Timoney 1986). He is working towards publishing the Early Christian slabs of mainland Sligo[124].

He suggested the use of Carrowntemple No. 4 as our **logo** (Wallace and Timoney 1987; Timoney this volume). Carrowntemple was not the only Early Monastic Site to have one part of its **heritage removed** (Timoney M.A. 2002). In 1991 a fine cross-slab from Keelty Early Christian site was recovered from Germany by the younger author with the individual assistance of several members of the SFC, unbeknownst to each other, and the guidance of Dr. Michael Ryan of the National Museum of Ireland, over a period of a year. We have had no such luck as regards the four cross-slabs from the nearby graveyard at Knockmore, *alias* Mount Irvine, also missing since about 1984 (Timoney 1997[125]). On a happier note was his recognition that two decorated stones discovered within Drumcliffe Church of Ireland church, when Terry Gannon pointed out to Rev. Canon Ian Gallagher that the old dry lining had to be removed, were two sections of the shaft of a major high cross (Timoney 1999; 1999-2000). The large roadside cross illustrated in an unsigned drawing of Drumcliffe, probably by Bigari, (Harbison 2002b, Fig. 30) looks as if it could have been the cross the shaft of which was exposed within Drumcliffe Church of Ireland church.

John Flynn, a native of Laughill, near Ferbane, Co. Offaly, became Chief Agriculture Officer for Sligo in 1975. He was a valued addition to the field walking team, questioning the age and function of many oddities. He discovered the Carrowculleen Romanesque stone (Timoney this volume), brought the Corkagh Beg ogham stones to our attention in 1976 (Swift this Volume) and told the younger author of the removal of the Keelty Early Christian slab to Germany[126]. He served two periods as President, the first following the introduction of the constitution on 23rd April 1983. He published an article on the management of the land of Inishmurray (Flynn 1989) and another encouraging the owners of most of our monuments, *i.e.*, the farmers, to preserve our field monuments (Flynn 1995). The Field Club honoured him with Honorary Life Membership at the 2002 AGM. He joined RSAI in 1978 and served on its Council and as Vice-President for Connacht for three years.

Jack Flynn's bemoaning his failure to read a 18th century weathered headstone in Corcoran's Acres graveyard prompted a group of us[127] to begin the work of recording the pre-1880 headstone inscriptions and their artwork in May 1984. The major by-product so far of this work was the recognition by Mary B. Timoney that Kitchin had not got the full story as regards the Diamond box-tombs and this she developed into a Masters thesis.

Brían Ó Súilleabháin, came to work in Sligo, having grown up in Dublin. He soon became involved in a number of local organisations, including SFC. He has been President of Sligo Historical Society and of *Cumman Gaelach Shligigh* and served on the Council of the Yeats Society for a number of years. A Veterinary Officer with the Department of Agriculture, he was concerned, while on a visit to Inishmurray, to come across a large number of dead and dying seagulls. He later had the condition diagnosed as Botulism. He is currently Chairman of the Veterinary History Society of Ireland and has had papers published on that subject. Some of his poetry in Irish has also been published. He served as President of SFC in 1984 and 1985.

Mary B. Timoney, nee Murphy, from Waterford city, came in 1979 to teach with Sligo V.E.C. at Easkey and later at Coola; she married the younger author in 1985. She served as Hon. Treasurer in 1983 and as Hon. Secretary from 1984 to 1987. She joined RSAI in 1983. She has opened up a new field of interest for us since May 1984 in the recording and study of Sligo memorials of the dead of the last three centuries particularly the artwork on them. Besides encouraging us all to appreciate the artwork of generations of family memorials her desire is to get the people of Sligo to properly maintain the graveyards without resource to machinery or weed-killer, sheep and goats being more graveyard-friendly as has been seen at Drumnacillin near Curry.

In particular she has studied the work of the Skreen School of Stone Masons, the best known being Frank Diamond who carved the Black and Scott box tombs in Skreen graveyard (Timoney, M.B., 1986; 1988; 1992; 1993; 1996). She received an MA for her thesis on the Skreen School in 2001. The decorated box-tombs are now recognised in graveyards from Drumcliffe to Emlaghfad and across to Moygownagh, Co. Mayo, as the work of the related families of Diamond, Flannelly and McGowan. Kitchin may not have been fully aware of the importance of the box-tombs in Skreen graveyard[128].

She has frequently published articles on memorials in *The Corran Herald* and elsewhere (see Bibliography). Mary was one of four editors of the Keash and Culfadda parish history (Higgins *et al.* 2001) and contributed an article on the parish graveyards to it and a joint article with the younger author on the archaeology of the parish (Timoney M.B. 2001). She has designed the cover for this volume and has been an indispensable research assistant in its production.

Catherine M. Timoney, of the next generation, has developed two articles from computerising some Keash and Culfadda National School registers (Timoney, C.M.H., 2001) and has drawn attention to 20th century wooden crucifixes in bottles (Timoney, C.M., 2002-2003). Catherine and her schoolmate Orla Cryan have drawn attention to Ballymote street furniture, including the weigh-bridge in the street pavement at the Market House which was broken on removal in May 2002 (Timoney and Cryan 1999-2000).

Göran Burenhult's involvement in Carrowmore passage tomb cemetery has now completed its second campaign, the first having lasted from 1977 to 1982. Ten Carrowmore tombs[129], 1, 3 (= 4), 7, 13, 19, 26, 27, 51, 55a, 56, and several settlement sites have been at least partly excavated. The strange megalithic tomb at Primrose Grange (*National Geographic*, 192:3 (1997)) had inhumations, the same date range as Carrowmore but had different artefacts. Burenhult has published two editions of his illustrated guide to Carrowmore (1995; 2001); some of his articles, which publicise Sligo, are in the bibliography. Work has begun towards a reconstruction of No. 51. One major regret that we have is that the spaces between the tombs have not been excavated[130].

During the 1978 excavation season Kitchin brought Malcolm Billings to interview Burenhult. This was the first of several such interviews that brought knowledge of the excavations to the world via the BBC World Services' *Origins* programme.

It is worth correcting the record as regards the discovery of the hut-sites on Knocknarea. In 1949 George Eogan and G. Frank Mitchell discovered several hut sites on the shoulders of Knocknarea. Later they had Dr. J.K. St. Joseph of Cambridge take aerial photographs of these. The younger author showed Burenhult some of these photographs and he had Stefan Bergh, Henry Bengtsson and Ingar Osterholm excavate two of the hut sites in 1981 and 1982 (Bengtsson and Bergh 1984; Osterholm 1984). Some of Burenhult's students, Bergh and Fredengren, have studied Irish archaeology for themselves.

Derry O'Connell from Larkhill Rd., Sligo, has opened our eyes to the architectural wealth of Sligo buildings, private as well as public, some of which he has published (drawings in Rothery 1975; drawings in Finnegan and O'Connell 1978; 1989; 1992). His illustrative talents are to be seen in his book on the street furniture of Dublin (O'Connell 1975) and in works by himself and others (Craig 1976; Rothery 1978; O'Connell 1978; 1989; Williams 1995). Some of his ideas on town planning are set out in his *Tending the City* (O'Connell 1991) and are to be seen in reality in the Rockwood Parade - Tobergall Lane - Water Lane urban renewal development of the centre of Sligo. Rockwood Parade showed the archaeological standards required[131]. He won major awards in 1996 for the building at the north-east end of Tobergall Lane. His town walks have opened our eyes to the architectural details that we would normally pass by without noticing.

Larry Mullin, a native of Kilconly, Tuam, came to Sligo in 1964 having studied archaeology and Irish at UCG. He has been a member of both SFC and of RSAI since 1964 and a leading figure in the running of the Field Club and also the Sligo Historical Society. For many years the write-up article for *The Sligo Champion* have been done by him. He has studied the history of The Town of Sligo VEC with whom he teaches (Mullin this volume). He has ably served as Hon. Treasurer, Vice-President and President and often has undertaken some aspects of the secretarial work of SFC while the younger author has been working on this volume. He was an active member of the Famine and the Markievicz Commemorative Committees.

John McTernan, Dip. Soc. Econ. Sc. U.C.G., M.A. and Fellow of the Library Association of Ireland, of Drumlaheen and Graigue, Co. Sligo, entered Library service in Sligo in 1950. He was assistant Librarian in Cork from 1958 to 1968, and County Librarian in Kilkenny from 1968 to 1979 and in Sligo from 1979 to 1994. As Librarian he built up a comprehensive Local History Archive in Sligo and published two editions of an indispensable guide cum bibliography to it (McTernan 1965; 1988; 1994b). He has published several books on local history (McTernan 1990; 1992; 1995a, 1998, 2000; 2002), biographies of prominent people of Sligo down the centuries (McTernan 1977; 1994a), Sligo G.A.A. (McTernan 1984; 1986). He had a major involvement in the millennium history of the Diocese of Elphin (Beirne 2000). He has lectured regularly on various aspects of Sligo's more recent past and has contributed many articles to a wide range of periodicals. Though unaccredited in many cases he has assisted others with their own writings on local history of Co. Sligo. McTernan retired in 1994 and was succeeded as County Librarian by Donal Tinney. McTernan is a Director of the County Sligo Heritage and Genealogical Society and currently its Hon. Secretary. He lives, like Kirwan did, in Ard na Veigh. He served on the committee from 1985 to 1995, being President in 1992 and 1993. The Field Club honoured him with Honorary Life Membership at the 1998 AGM in recognition of his major single-handed contribution to the local history collection in Sligo Library, his many publications on Sligo's past and his activities on behalf of SFC.

Nicholas Prins, a farmer from Ballinlig, Beltra, has represented An Taisce in Sligo since 1989 and has won many planning battles in that capacity. He was agent for Lisadell House and estate. He has a great enthusiasm for the conservation and restoration of heritage buildings.

Stefan Bergh has studied the landscape and the megalithic tombs of the Cuil Iorra Region for his Ph.D. (Bergh 1995) having earlier published a paper on the court tombs as well as passage tombs of Sligo, (Bergh 1987). Bergh excavated at other Sligo sites, Primrose Grange (Bergh 1986, 35-36), Glen Passage-tomb (Bergh 1986, 34-35) and Cairn M of the Carrowkeel Passage tomb cemetery (Bergh 1987, 32)[132]. Since coming to settle in Co. Sligo in 1999 he has spent months walking Knocknarea and discovering one of Sligo's largest monuments which we have been walking over without seeing it (Bergh 2000).

Christina Fredengren, one of Burenhult's Second Campaign students, is devoting her energies to crannogs in general and to Lough Gara in particular (2000, 7; 2000, 26-28; 2001, 24-25).

Patricia Curran-Mulligan, of Cummeen and now of Carrowmore, was Secretary to the local group who opposed Sligo County Council's proposed landfill site at Carrowmore. She joined RSAI in 1983. She is an art teacher in Sligo RTC, has on occasion devoted her art skills to ancient monuments (*e.g.*, Bergh 1995, cover photograph; postcards) and was Irish Assistant to the Second Swedish Carrowmore Campaign[133]. For a number of years she has ran the OPW Carrowmore tourist facility where her slides have been shown to thousands of tourists. From one of these slides of Carrowmore No. 51, Listoghill, (Bergh 1995, 198-199) Michael B. Roberts of Dún Laoghaire discovered (Roberts 1994, 34) art on the east face of the chamber capstone (Curran-Mulligan 1994). This faint carving of a series of arcs is best seen between 2.15 and 2.50 PM from May to August or by torchlight, though the current plans for the reconstruction of this site may change this. The pattern of arcs here, it was pointed out at the Stones and Bones conference in Sligo in May 2002, is reminiscent to some Neolithic rainbow design such as on the Folktone chalk drums. She took photos in 1993 for the Federation's "Our Own Place" photographic project. She was responsible for bringing the Dernish Island burial (Buckley, Buckley and McCormack this volume) to attention in 1990.

Richard Thorn joined Sligo Regional Technical College in 1982. He has brought to us all in Sligo his expertise in geology, particularly that of limestone and the importance of maintaining the quality of our groundwater. He edited the IAQUA field guide to Sligo and west Leitrim (Thorn 1985) and has written widely on (Thorn this volume). He was Director of Galway-Mayo Institute of Technology at Castlebar before becoming Director of the Institute of Technology, Sligo.

In 1984 we affiliated to **Federation of Local History Societies**[134]. For their Local History Week we arranged folklife and history material for exhibition in Lyons', Wood's, Keohane's and First National shop windows, displays reflecting their own trades. In 1990 and 1991 the Federation set about replicating one thousand photographs taken by or for William Lawrence about 1900. John Mulligan, Mary B. Timoney and the younger author found that it was not as easy as seemed at first to photograph from the exact same spot due to the enormous growth of trees at some locations. Patricia Curran-Mulligan took photos in 1993 for the Federation's "Our Own Place" photographic project. Copies of the photos from both projects have been lodged in the Local History Archive of Sligo Library.

Since 1985 **The Ballymote Heritage Group** have been active in the centre of the county and beyond; they hold an August weekend of lectures and outings and have produced thirty-four issues of *The Corran Herald*, under the editorship of **James Flannagan**. This is a publication containing history, folklore, archaeology, *etc.*, by an extensive range of authors. **Eileen Tighe**, now a retired National Teacher, Chairperson of Ballymote Heritage Group[135] co-founded by Una Preston and herself in May 1984, has been a member of SFC since the mid-1970s after Tom McGettrick told her of a great outing to Carrowkeel. Nuala Rogers, sister of Eileen, has produced two editions of a booklet on Ballymote (Rogers 1993; 1994) and an article on the folklore of Keshcorran (Rogers 1996).

Paddy and Chris Tuffy from Lackan, Inishcrone, keep a watchful eye on that part of the county. Paddy has published one article (1987-1988).

Brendan Rooney, from Glencar, reported the prehistoric field system complex of fieldwalls, hut sites, cairns and megalithic tombs high up on the Dartry plateau at between 500 and 1,400 ft. above sea level (Rooney 1991, 105-106) to the professional archaeologists[136] and recently produced a booklet on his native area of Glencar (Rooney 1996). Following on his two years as immediate President he took over as Hon. Secretary for a year and thus allowed the younger author to begin to get back to editorial work, a deed very much appreciated.

Berta Money, a resource teacher, originally from Santa Barbara in California, came to Sligo from Dublin in 1975. She joined SFC after completing one of Joyce Enright's Autumn Courses in Archaeology in the Regional Technical College. She has helped by arranging lectures and outings for two years. She was the major initial player in the recovery from Germany of the Keelty Early Christian cross slab. Joe McGowan, from Mullaghmore, compiled a substantial informative book on north Sligo (McGowan 1993), a convenient handbook for Inishmurray (McGowan 1998) and one on folklore and traditions (McGowan 2001). His is one of the boats to Inishmurray. He was a major figure in the Famine and the Markievicz Commemorative Committees. The evacuation of Inishmurray in October 1948 left the island without a presence to protect the heritage but the two Mullaghmore boatmen, Rodney Lomax and **Joe McGowan**, have been unpaid guardians, ensuring that those who do get to the island bring away only good memories

Dr. **Paul Money**, Barta's husband, a medical practitioner from Zimbabwe, came to Sligo from Dublin in 1975. He was introduced to the SFC in 1978, and went on two outings that summer, that to the Ballintrellick area and the exhausting one to the Ballyhaunis area led by the younger author and Bernie Freyne. He has identified some 'new' monuments in Cartronwilliamoge and Ardnaglass on the lower slopes of Benbulben. He arranged Heritage Day outings for SFC for two years in the north Sligo area.

Sandy Perceval has written about his house, Temple House, and its people (Perceval 1995).

Allison English, is a niece of Billy English, 1922-1978, the founder of the Old Athlone Society.

Br. Angelo Stewart (Marist Brothers 1962, 101, 107, back left, 113, top) served on the committee 1988 to 1991.

Kevin Dodd, from Ballydoogan, republished six of the most frequently used early volumes on Sligo, those by O'Rorke, Kilgannon and Wood-Martin, between 1986 and 1990.

It is worth stating that so many members of SFC have at one time published on the heritage of this county. How come then it has taken until the mid-1990s to get this publication under way? The story of the delay until 2002 for publication will be told in a later volume. Much of the Sligo material in the St. Patrick's Day Annual of *Ireland's Own* for 1989 was written or provided by SFC members. Others outside the Field Club have actively served the county in heritage matters and their publications are listed by McTernan (1988; 1994).

For several years the printed tourist guides we can trace had little content of our interests. We do no know who wrote the piece on Megalithic Burial Tombs in Co. Sligo in those of the 1970s. In 1980 Junior Chamber Sligo asked for entries and Patrick Heraughty provided one on Geology, Briga Murphy on Flora, Noel Murphy on Wild Birds and Martin A. Timoney on archaeology tours of north Sligo, a circuit of Lough Gill, Knocknarea and Carrowmore. Gradually these were whittled down and by 1988 some of the material was still being included though in an edited form and was no longer being credited[137].

The Field Club files contain references to a great variety of topics that received attention down the years[138].

Many of those interested in Co. Sligo[139] have drawn on our talents down the years. However some have chosen otherwise. There are many pieces of Sligo religious artwork and sculpture, The Moylough Beltshrine, Carrowntemple, Drumcliffe, Inishmurray, Sligo and other abbeys, that could have been used to illustrate the wonderful book of prayer entitled *Sligo at Prayer* (Higgins and McElhone 1995) for Sligo's 750th commemoration. Instead nine illustrations used for Hospitals Trust newspaper advertisements of 1947 were included. The only Sligo related piece is the Fiacle Pádraig. An Inishmurray slab was used as the commemorative cross. Sometimes when requested to get involved in a major project, for example a Civic Trust for Sligo, we have not had the energy nor the time to respond. At other times when requested, Castleconnor (Castleconnor 2000), we have been bypassed. Things are improving in the new millennium; Sligo Co. Co. and Dúchas have recently been in serious consultations with us on matters of mutual interest, the Co. Sligo Heritage Plan and Carrowmore.

Good work is also being done by people at or beyond the fringes of SFC which deserves to be published. This would include Fiona Gallagher's 1984 work on street names of Sligo town, Conor MacHale's 1985 history of Eniscrone, John Bradley's Urban Survey of Sligo, Timoney's trail of Sligo Abbey, O'Higgins's trail of the area surrounding that same abbey, and the Inishmurray Symposium. Perhaps a Sligo publishing house is the answer! For an internationally published photographic feast of some Sligo heritage, landscape, botany, geology and archaeology see Bunn (1997).

People are generally reluctant to lecture if they are expected to provide a written text for publication. An exception was Jack Johnson whose September 1999 lecture on Sligo material in the Public Record Office of Northern Ireland was published in *Spark* (Johnston 2000, 3-9). Bob Curran lectured to us in 2001 on Dracula. A publication of this (Curran 2000, 12-15) does not allude to the fact that Bram Stoker's Mother was from Sligo (Gunning and Feehily, 1995, 38-41).

In addition to the financial support of our members, we have received support from ESB, Telecom Eireann now Eircom, Sligo Co. Co., Sligo Corporation, Sligo Teachers Centre, Sligo Education Centre, Sligo Regional Technical College, The Royal Dublin Society Extension Lecture System and Foras Éireann - The C.F. Shaw Trust.

The IFCU held its seventh "triennial" conference in Sligo in the Sligo Institute of technology in August 2000[140]. SFC members Dr. Patrick Heraughty, Jack Flynn, Mary B. Timoney and Martin A. Timoney spoke. While SFC today does not have as much a nature orientated a remit as most Field Clubs, though these tend to call themselves Naturalists' Field Clubs, the deficiency in that regard was made up by Dr. Don Cotton.

Throughout the 1990s numbers on outings, with the exception of the mid-week evening outings, were dwindling. Partly to counteract this and also to reduce the demands on the Timoney and Enright members who were possibly suffering from burn-out because of regularly being required to lead outings the younger author initiated a series of 'training' outings[141]. These were for the Committee, though a few of the stalwart fieldwalking non-committee members came along also. The idea was that a Committee member would organise access to some sites in their own area and that the younger author would speak to those assembled, totally unprepared, even totally unaware as to what sites we were going to.

Aidan Mannion, from Sligo, is currently our Vice President. He has a Diploma in archaeology from NIU Galway. He was a major figure in the Famine and the Markievicz Commemorative Committees and was Chairman of the Archaeological sub-committee of County Sligo Heritage Forum which helped devise the Sligo Heritage plan. His father, Gerry, was a tenant of a major part of the lands of the Carrowmore Cemetery for forty years. Today his Record Room[142] in Grattan St., filled with the Sligo music of Westlife, Dervish and Colm O'Donnell, is our on-street clearing house for matters historical and archaeological just as Blackwood's Corner Shop, filled with the aromas of herbs, spices and coffee, was in Cahalane's day. His record label, Sounds Records, has produced two videos showing some of the treasures of Sligo and over fifty music albums. He has a large collection of old photos, postal history and postcards of Sligo. He, like the authors, devotes much energy to bringing greater attention to various aspects of Sligo.

Martin Wilson, from Tullylin, Co. Sligo, is a builder living in Larkhill, Beltra. His appreciation of what we have around us came in a curious way from his clients. His work is varied and takes him to meet some very interesting people from all walks of life who have come from many countries to settle in this part of the country. From talking to these he began to develop an awareness and greater appreciation of what we have around us that so many of us natives tend to take for granted. He felt embarrassed at their wealth of knowledge in comparison with what he felt he should know and he did something about it. He involved himself with a small heritage group in Skreen but someone directed him to the younger author for advice. A phonecall to him about 1989 was responded to by the provision of some previous SFC AGM materials. In 1995 he alerted us to the threat from forestry to the magnificent Larkhill cashel and its surrounding archaeological landscape high up on the slopes of the Ox Mts. and was provided with contact numbers which he made use of and so saved the setting of the cashel. He joined the Committee in 1999. He has published several articles on his own area (Wilson 2000a to 2000e) and in so doing is creating a local awareness of what we have. He sees this commitment of the present generation as insuring the heritage of future generations. He also brought to our attention a long lost leaf shaped spearhead from his parish. He was local organiser for the first Committee training outing and set a standard to be followed. His wife, Moya, has come to our assistance on occasions.

Patrick E. O'Brien, a native of Limerick city, came to GWI in Collooney as an industrial engineering manager in 1974. Though aware of SFC since the late 1980s he did not join until 1995 or 1996. He became aware of archaeology through SPOR lecture on his excavations at Lough Gur but more so through Raftery's excavations at Lough Gara in the early 1950s. His history teacher, Fr. Pat O'Donnell, C.Ss.R., had him cycling to sites within twenty miles of Youghal in the late 1950s and then regaled O'Brien's classmates with the story of how he 'stood on the spot'. He was awarded a Certificate in Local History Studies by NUI Maynooth in 2001 for his work on his adopted parish, Kilross, and is currently researching Castledargan Demesne and Ballydawley townland. He has published an article on the Flynn family of blacksmiths from the Riverstown area (O'Brien 2001). He became Hon. Secretary in 2001 and his note on SFC is to be found in Heritage Matters, 2:3, 3. His son, Maghnus, computerised the content of the cover of this book.

In 1999 Sligo Co. Co. appointed **Siobhán Ryan** as its first **Heritage Officer**. She was a member of the Lough Gill Environmental Management Project team and is an SFC member. Her ideals are set out in McTernan (2000, 4-5). Some of the published works emanating from her office are *Heritage Matters*, a quarterly newsletter, the Environment and Heritage information brochure and the *Windows of Sligo leaflet*. She organised a museums and community heritage initiatives training course for local Sligo societies in 2000 and a Field Fences Project for schools in 2001; see www.sligofieldfences.com.

She has developed the Co. Sligo Heritage Plan 2002-2006 which proposes partnerships between committed interested parties, public, private and voluntary, for key actions in the areas of archaeology, built heritage, nature and landscape. Aidan Mannion and Martin Enright, both members of SFC, are representatives from the Heritage Groups of the county and were Chairmen of the archaeology and natural heritage working groups respectively.

Margaret McBrien, a native of Drumduff, Co. Leitrim. She was Chairperson of STC for many years. She was co-opted at the enlargement of the SFC Committee from ten to twelve in 2000. She taught in England, Leitrim and Sligo. Her father, Harold, worked under Patrick Tohall as a Land Commission supervisor on the Friarstown estate, where they tried to save the plaster-work, Belhavel House, and on bog roads on Burke's Mountain, where Tohall applied archaeological knowledge to building a road over the soft bog by putting in heather as a base just as in crannogs. She has helped take SFC ideals to teachers through STC summer courses and having SFC as guests at STC for many years. Margaret conceived the idea of a bookmark for insertion in this book as an appreciation of advance support of its production.

Mai Neary, a native of Belmullet, began teaching Home Economics at St. Angela's college of education, Cloghereva, in 1959. Soon after her arrival in Sligo she joined the SFC at the invitation of the Heraughtys and so her memories of those involved spans four decades. Her interests are wide ranging in the beauties of nature, archaeology, language, mythology and poetry. She holds a Masters degree in Food Science from the University of Reading. She joined the Committee at the 2001 AGM and will help us maintain our old enthusiasm and high standards.

At the AGM in January 2002 three members new to the committee were nominated. **Frank McGill**, from Glenties, has taught in Kilanummery N.S. since 1975. **Sam Moore**, from Dublin, has worked with Highwood Resource

Centre and has been involved in some parish histories and has published some archaeological guidebooks and also editions of Macalister (1912) and Sharkey (1930). He was involved with the embryonic National Field Study Centre at Ballinafad and is currently studying archaeology at NUIG. Domhnail O'Connor, a farmer, lives next door to where Guy Perrem used to live in Cleveragh. Domhnaill recollects being brought to Creevykeel in the 1950s by his father, Dr. Michael O'Connor, a long-term member of SFC.

FINAL THOUGHTS

Sligo Field Club has acted as the **antiquarian and heritage presence** in the county. Our approach to conservation is educational and then it is conciliatory rather than confrontational. Our hope would be that without further delay the authorities would provide an official presence in the county for the protection of our heritage, a heritage that has 8,000 sites, monuments and buildings spread over 700 square miles of landscape rich in natural history and scenery. We have brought to the attention of those who live in and administer Co. Sligo, the wealth of monuments and the related talents we have within the county without the need for distant experts. We need a County Archaeologist and a County Museum with a fulltime Curator to use this heritage wisely for the benefit of Sligo people today and into the future and hopefully the Heritage Plan for Sligo will deliver these in the immediate future. A Museum for Sligo is badly needed; we should be concerned to keep our heritage in Sligo and not have it taken from these shores.

Those members who have been active in the Field Club have come from many counties as well as from our own, hence "Whence this Motley Crew". Many of those who were involved were linked by relationship, by occupation, by being neighbours, by county allegiance or by place of business as well as a common academic interest. They have come from a wide range of backgrounds. Some have served for long periods, others have stayed only a while. Activities reflect the interests of active members. To them we tender our thanks in the knowledge that Sligo has benefited culturally, socially and economically from their efforts.

We have **passed on** much to the academics, archaeologists, historians, geologists, botanists, ornithologists, natural historians and calligraphers, who have been so kind to the Field Club in giving of their time to listen to us, to lecture to us and lead outings for us a motley crew of mostly amateurs untutored in the wonders to which they introduced us, with a few professionals in more recent years, though all of us students of this county, willing to learn of their specialities. In return we have been the eyes and ears in Co. Sligo for these academics stationed in far off offices or universities. We are not just enjoying sites but the fruit of the labours of those we have helped or inspired to study our county. Our county is better known and better understood, nationally and internationally.

ACKNOWLEDGEMENTS

This history of Sligo Antiquarian Society and Sligo Field Club has been compiled from the SFC minutes for the years since 1954, the files of Sligo Field Club and newspaper reports, *The Sligo Champion*, The Sligo Weekender but particularly The *Sligo Independent*. Much information was retrieved, perhaps extracted, from memories of members and their descendants. We thank Tony Toher, Sheela Kitchin, Queenie and Eithne Dolan, Briga Murphy and Pat E. O'Brien for their comments on earlier drafts of this article and likewise Mary B. Timoney who has also been research assistant. We thank Elis Ó Muire for information from her Tohall family papers, Amanda Phelan and John Phelan for family information on Michael Cahalane, Deirdre Vickers and Lydia and Jim O'Halloran for information from their Kirwin family papers, Sióbhán de hÓir for information from the Royal Society of Antiquaries of Ireland. We thank Mary F. Ryan, Eithne and Queenie Dolan, James P. McGarry, Kevin Murray, Francis Hopper, Harry O'Rorke, Dr. Don C. F. Cotton, Martin and Joyce Enright, Des Smith, Dr. Patrick Henry, Orna Sommerville, Ronan McEvilly, Martin Coleman, Prof. Etienne Rynne, Dr. Harman Murtagh, Michael Keohane, Eileen McCaffrey, Frances Higgins, Lidia O'Halloran, Fr. John Geelin, Maura Scanlon, Mary Cahill, Stephen O'Connor, Nora McDonagh, Bernard McDonagh, Gertrude McHale, John Troddyn, *The Sligo Champion*, Stephen Stokes Books, Margaret Pilkington, James McHugh, Georgina Wynne and Kevin Colreavey for various sources, pieces of information or advice and illustrative material published with this article. Some photos are from the SFC archives.

Notes

1. Eighty-eight people have served as Officers or on the Committee since 1945. While only twenty-three of these were female some of these made up for the deficiency in numbers. The sequence of pen-pictures of members relates somewhat to their joining the Committee, though some were active in SFC before being elected joining the Committee. Photographs of many, particularly the Officers, are to be found in this volume.

2. The context for much of what is included is that if it is not saved from the passage of time now, and questions asked about by those that are, Thank God, still with us, it will be lost forever. We have benefited from the memories of those who were actively part of Sligo life in the formative years of SAS and SFC. Perhaps we are too close to the people and events of the last decade to give as balanced a view as we have of the earlier periods. However we feel that it is better to put the present on record than for someone to have to reconstruct it, with far less written correspondence to work from since we use the phone so much nowadays. Many current members do not know of the people and events of the 1980s in the same way as in the late 1960s the story of our origin just twenty years earlier had become garbled. The article includes many facts and anecdotes relating to the interests of members, individually and collectively, and are a glimpse at some of the social life of Sligo through the second half of the twentieth century. The topics detailed are not necessarily by or for SFC members but certainly are part of what we are and what we stand for.

3. We suspect Drumcliff, as he later had portions of a high cross from Drumcliffe at Rathcarrick.

4. Wood-Martin (1895, 658) refers to Walker finding a crannóg at Frenchford. This Frenchford can be equated with an area where the road bends to cross a river in Sessuecommon and Tullyvellia townlands on the south slopes of the Ox Mts.; Walker owned property in Tullyvellia. The crannóg may be the adjacent Sl.31:35 (Christina Fredrengren pers. comm.).

5. The original drawings are in Sligo County Library Local Studies Archive. See de hÓir (1990, 117) for Wakeman's thoughts on Beranger. See Ireland (2001, 5-6) for the Wakeman family.

6. He did take the Louth Archaeological Society around Carrowmore in 1915 (Anon 1912-1915, 288).

7. The programme of events was republished by Nunn (2000, 39-50) for the Sligo Revival meeting.

8. He was instrumental in the 4th Harvard Expedition going to dig at Creevykeel, though it was Dr. Sean F. Keenan, M.D., G.P., Ballinalee, Co. Longford, that re-discovered it when on holidays at Mullaghmore.

9. The 'elder author' is Dr. Patrick Heraughty;

the 'younger author' is Martin A. Timoney.

10. See Townley (1976), Ireland (1982), Cookman (1996), O'Halloran (2001) for some histories of local societies.

11. Dr. Patrick Heraughty gave an outline history of Sligo Antiquarian Society and Sligo Field Club under the title "Whence This Motley Crowd" on 24th February 1995 as the second lecture in our 50th. anniversary year. The content of that lecture was the basis of this article to which the younger author has added considerable research. The sequence of Officers and Committee members are charted herein.

12. A search of the minute books of the Town of Sligo Municipal Technical Schools revealed no reference to any cultural matters whatsoever. Likewise searches by John McTernan, Mary B. Timoney and the younger author through The *Sligo Independent* revealed no mention of SAS or SFC though there are pieces by Duignan and Leask on the importance of heritage.

13. Records of societies, clubs, businesses, public bodies, *etc.*, should be offered to the local Library rather than consigning them to the dump. The personal archives as well as the recollection of several members have enabled us to fill out this story.

14. Martin Mulligan of the Calry Bar on The Mall did Trojan work for Sligo's past. He would have been born about 1913 or 1914. In March 1947 'Martin Mulligan, Jr., Sales', were in Teeling St. *The Sligo Champion* of April, 1953, has a notice of 'Martin Mulligan's Sales' at an address at 7, Thomas St Later Mulligan had a very successful public house in Kilburn, London.

15. Of John St., a builder, his daughter Alice married Tom Giffney; she was a teacher in Carraroe N.S.

16. Probably Seamus McKenna, a Schools Inspector.

17. Duignan gave this lecture to the Royal Society of Antiquaries on March 7th. 1944 and it was published in their Volume for that year (Duignan 1944).

The inaugural lecture of our 50th. anniversary year was given by Prof. Etienne Rynne, the successor in the Chair of Archaeology at University College, Galway, to Michael V. Duignan who gave the founding lecture in 1945. The title was "The Irish in War and Peace during the Early Christian Period" and though it covered the same time-span the content was radically different (see Rynne this Volume).

The Royal Society of Antiquaries sub-committee, which was formed on 15th March 1945, arranged a public lecture in Sligo in 1945 but they do not have details; this is later than Duignan's lecture in Sligo.

18. He went to Kerry after he retired from being chief doctor in the Mental Hospital.

19. Herbert Quinton, LDS, was a dentist in Wine St. whose interests were fishing and bees.

20. He lived on Cleveragh Rd. and was a journalist with and later with RTE.

21. The newspaper report says Maureen Dolan, but Eithne and Queenie Dolan tell us that this should be Maureen Regan, later the wife of Bernard Rhatigan.

22. He may have worked in a Bank or in the Model School.

23. The landscape around Deerpark in 1945 was open and free of the horrendous conifers that have blocked out the views to and from this major national monument for decades until their recent clearance. See Wood-Martin (1895, fig. 70) and Ireland (2001, 4) for a late-19th century photograph of this location.

24. Later Professor of English at St. Patrick's Training College, Dublin.

25. McLaughlin was from Buncranna. The Royal Bank is now The Yeats Memorial Building at Hyde Bridge.

26. The sub-committee for the lecture consisted of Tohall, Moran, Giles, Flattery, Mulcahy and J. Hunt. See McTernan (2000, 578) for further mention of the Thomas Davis Centenary. Seán P. Ó Ríordáin also gave an RDS Extension lecture, "The Arts in Early Ireland", in Ballymote in October 1946. Though we can not be certain only Tom McEvilly of the Sligo town group came out.

27. Rev. T.A. McElfatrick (Mac Giolla Padraig), 1874-1950, presided. He was Presbyterian Minister in Sligo from 1930 to 1947, after which he retired to Belfast. None of his interests in local culture or historical societies are specified. He was Vice-Chairman of the County Library Committee

28. Tohall's interests were wide ranging. Tohall lectured to SFC and the general public on "Old Sligo 1595 to 1800" in October 1955 and he saved Hazelwood House from demolition

29. We have occasionally incorrectly been called The County Sligo Field Club and Sligo Historical Society particularly while such a titled Society existed.

30. The only other Field Club in the Federation of Local History Societies is that for Mallow, Co. Cork, founded in 1952 as Mallow Field Club, Historical & Archaeological Society. John Caplice, their Hon. Sec. inform us that local history is their main theme; nature is not part of their interests.

31. C.A. Giles and J.C.F. Giles are variously given, though consistently of Collooney.

32. SFC subscribed to *National Geographic* for a while. In 1956 SFC joined the Geographical Society of Ireland. In April 1964 we cautiously agreed to join the Regional Tourist Association. In November 1965 SFC joined An Taisce, but for how long we do not know. In the 1950s they hired out films from the National Film Institute. We are currently members of the Federation of Local History Societies and of the Border Counties History Collective.

33. John Gallagher (Hayward 1955, 149) traded via sea and Inishmurray to Killybegs.

34. This joint effort on Sligo may have been planned when Piggott and Powell were working together under Glynn Daniel with the Central Photographic Interpretation Section, Hyderabad House, New Delhi, during the Second World War. See Daniel 1986 for photo of some of the CPIS staff including Daniel, Piggott and Powell. Powell later gave a talk on English Long Barrows to SFC. One wonders if Tohall and Moran were drawn together to start the SAS through their common First World War background.

35. Presumably if Inishmurray had any strategic possibilities a solution would be found.

36. This is even more true in these days of surfing the Internet.

37. Hayward (1955, 150), probably using information from Kirwin, credits Kirwan with constructing the road around Mullaghmore Head.

38. See Public Record Office Northern Ireland D 1116, Account of grocery and hardware business in Moy, Co. Tyrone, of the Tohall Family, 1889-1894. The father's name was originally Henry T. Nailer Toall.

39. He was writing on military history at an early stage; see Public Record Office Northern Ireland D 328, *Collection of letters describing Charlemont Fort from W. Kerr and P. Tohall with some tracings and a map of the fort by Patrick Tohall, 1913*. Kerr was Rev. W.J. Kerr, Rector of Irchester, Bedfordshire, who had been born inside Charlemont Fort before its demolition in 1854 and was interested in the mathematics of 17th and 18th century fortifications.

40. *The Sligo Independent and West of Ireland Telegraph,* Nov. 19, 1955, p. 3.

41. Healy worked with Macalister on the Carrowkeel excavations in 1911.

42. An article in *The Irish Times* of 12th. January 1946, bemoaning the proposed demolition of the house suggested that few Sligo people, W.J. Tolan, Senior Alderman, excepted, cared about its preservation. Tohall is not mentioned in newspaper reports of May 11th 1946 that the Mental Health Committee were going to take over the building. See also Guthrie-Jones 1994 (91-93).

43. See *Hayes Catalogue: Manuscripts*, Vol. 8,

281-282, for Wynne papers. The copy he made is in private possession.

44. Élis got married in 1947, Martha and Maeliosa in 1950.

45. See Gunning and Feehily (1995, 143 and 147) and Hunt (1999, 35) for photographs of Toher's chemist shop in Stephen St. on which site now stands The Irish National Bank.

46. On a 1954 outing up Gleniff, when the climbing was getting quite severe and the Alpine and Arctic plants had not yet been reached Tony was heard to comment that their destination was an area where the goats can not get to, hence their survival! More than one member wondered how people would reach it, if the goats could not!

47. The initial meeting was courtesy of Mr. Caliendo at his Ritz Café, now Liber Books, in O'Connell St. A three-column newspaper article of Aug. 31st 1946 by James Wilson making a plea for a camera club ends with a note by the editor that there was a Sligo United YMCA Camera Club in Sligo in the early 20th century.

48. Some of these may be those published in the two editions of the Sligo Tourist Development Association in 1952 (11, 24, 31) and 1953 (12, 25, 29).

49. A series of photographs produced over the years 1947 to 1949 was entitled 'The Yeats Country' and the accompanying map appeared for a number of summers in the window of Toher's The Chemists, beginning in 1950. (Information from Tony Toher and McGarry 1990, 8). The Guide to Sligo, subtitled *The Yeats Country*, edited by Tony Toher and Thomas J. Hamilton, was published by Sligo Tourist Development Association in 1952 and 1953 and included some of these photos. The earliest notice of a lecture on W.B. Yeats that we have traced was that by Miss Dorothy Macardle in December 1947. Hopes were then expressed for the return of the body and for the erection of a commemoration plaque.

50. In the book Hayward (1955, 106) refers to Kirwan and Tohall as "two old members of the moribund SFC" and lauds Kirwan most particularly for being their guide for a week or more and taking part in strenuous activities like squeezing into the chamber of Carrowmore No. 52, a feat even for one of twenty. Hayward (1955, 156) describes the concluding events of his tour of Sligo as follows "Robert Kirwan was there and Patrick Tohall, to bring back the atmosphere of the old SFC, and Kevin Murray, too, to whose house we later repaired to see his excellent coloured film of the antiquities of the Sligo Countryside." A nice sketch by Piper (Hayward 1955, 138) shows these two gentlemen on the way to Inishmurray. Between them Hayward and Kirwan were responsible for sixty-four pages of excellent publicity, with almost a score of sketches, for Sligo (Hayward 1955, 94-158); this was Kirwan's major contribution to publication of Sligo heritage. Hayward later wrote (1955, 106) Kirwan's "subsequent sudden and peaceful death fell upon me heavily".

51. About 1928 The Board of Works issued a guidebook under the authorship of Robert Cochrane and Harold G. Leask; the third edition, printed in March 1937, is credited to Cochrane but revised by Leask and a 1953 edition is again credited to Cochrane revised by Leask; The Office of Public Works produced a new guidebook in 1964 but no author is given. Dúchas produced *Sligo Abbey Visitor's Guide*, a six page fold-out, in 2002. In this 750th anniversary year of Sligo Abbey there are two other publications about the Sligo Dominicans. Fr. Hugh Fenning, has written *The Dominicans in Sligo* and there is a book celebrating the greater Sligo community.

52. T.P. Toher, MPSI, was then President of the Chamber and Thomas J. Hamilton was Secretary. They had a bureau in Quay St. The earliest notice of M. Cahalane speaking that we have seen is in the newspaper for 22/9/1951was at a STDA meeting when he asked that the child's copybook visitors book be replaced with a new and presentable book. The STDA had a bureau at 13, Quay St.

53. The detailed information on many other sites in Sligo, town and county, could have been written up by Tohall or have been derived from the Irish Tourist Authority Survey of 1943.

54. The museum was begun under the Corporation, not the County Council, with the initial displays being in The Harbour Master's Office.

55. He married a sister of Gladys West who was a long term SFC member.

56. In 1880 Mayor J. Walsh opened a Reading Room and Public Library in The Town Hall. The Library was established in Sligo in August 1923 with S.J. Maguire as Organising Librarian for Co. Sligo and R.N.D. Wilson as Assistant Librarian.

57. In a letter from Willem Van Zeist to the younger author, Feb. 11th., 1997. There is a copy of the resulting pollen diagram in the Tohall papers. It may be published in a future Sligo Field Club volume. The Owenykeevaun Bog site location in the Dromore West area is on OS Sligo 6" Sheet [17]. Dodson and Bradshaw (1987) have studied the influences of fire, man and climate on the Lough Gill region.

58. His motto might well be *'Occupation Conquers All'*.

59. Throughout the years meetings have been held in The Land Commission Offices in Thomas St., The Imperial Hotel, The Café Cairo, Lyons Café, Toher's in O'Connell St., The Great Southern Hotel, The Columban Club in Castle St, Sligo Teachers' Centre in Quay St. and Sligo Education Centre adjacent to the New business Innovation Centre on the Sligo Institute of Technology Campus in Bellanode. Meetings in The Cafe Cairo were held in a room reached through the shop and down a passage to the café.

60. Though not listed in relation to the Founding nor to the Revival Mrs. Violet Crichton of Carrowgarry is described at her passing in 1961 as having been 'a founder member'; this was probably of the 1954 Revival. Our files contain a long series of letters from and to her on the subject of attempting to rid Ballymote and Manorhamilton castles of ivy. Her son, Aleck, and his wife, Joan, have published notes on aspects of their parish (Crichton, A., 2000; Crichton, J., 2000).

61. There was a newspaper report of this outing to Carrowculleen and also of the 1963 outing to this location. On neither occasion was the Romanesque sculpture in the wall of a house beside the lane to the hill noticed.

62. Possibly St. Bridget's Well, pillar and Early Christian site in Ballinphull.

63. SFC responded to the threat of Foot and Mouth disease in 2001 by cancelling all outings except the Yeats Summer School one.

64. The Correspondence of Autumn 1954 says SFC had slides of the McDonagh castle at Castledargan and the O'Dowd castle of c. 1600 at Ardnaglass. Apparently Leask was already interested in both these castles.

65. Those recorded as having attended the 1955 AGM were Chairman Patrick Tohall, Secretary Guy Perrem, Treasurer Thomas A. Kerin, Michael Cahalane, Herbert Greene, Tony Toher, Tom McEvilly, Michael Hopper, Jim Hughes, Frank Kerrin, Bro. Alphonsus Maxwell, Dr. John Moran, Mr. and Mrs. Ronald Campbell-Perry of Lyons Tce., Mrs. Sheila Cosgrove, Dr. and Mrs. Tim Foley, Mr. and Mrs. Rory Hannigan, Miss. Frances Wall, Miss Violet Dodd, Miss Nora Niland, Miss Frances Flynn, a Theatre sister in the hospital, Miss Mary F. Ryan, Mrs. Eileen Lambert, Bernard McDonagh, Paddy McDonagh, and Master Dermott McEvilly. Apologies for non-attendance were received from Harry O'Rourke and Dr. Paddy Heraughty. Others named in a September 1954 list of 45 members include Dr. Nora Murphy of Weston House, John and Mary Quirke of Wine St., Kevin Cosgrove of Market St., Betty McGlynn of Old Market St., Fr. Kevin McDermott, Mr. and Mrs. Alexander of Drumcliff, Frank Armstrong of Teeling St., Maeve and Phil Dowling of Temple St., Alice Gallagher of Burton St., Margaret Casey of O'Connell St., Miss R. O'Beirne of Cregg Ho., Michael Beirne of Connolly St., Fr. Tom Foy, Aileen Kerin, Mrs. C. McCarthy of The Mall, Douglas Taylor of Manorhamilton and Violet Crichton of Carrowgarry. Herbert Greene is described as being of Fernbank, probably the house behind Tohall's on Mail Coach Rd., rather than Fernbank in Finisklin.

In 1954/1955 there were 11 family and three single memberships. The rate was 5 shillings. In 1963/1964 there were 38 family and 61 single memberships and four Life Memberships. The rate was 10 shillings.

66. There are fourteen items under his name in the Hayes Catalogue of *Articles in Irish Periodicals, Persons*, V, 329.

67. Looking back on it now this encouragement of quarrying in Carrowmore was in total contrast to what many of us have fought for over the last thirty years.

68. These additions read as follows:

[1] Probable position of townland of Knockatowell or Knockatohill as mentioned in 1733, *etc*.

[2] Conor Kelly as scaled from Down Survey

[3] By elimination and by association with Rushine this is probable location of townland of Farranmacadownie (=Farranmac Devany?)

[4] Knockatóófil local name of hill 1956

[5] Rusheen local name 1956

[6] Probable position of Rushine townland as mentioned 1733, *etc*.

Nos. 1, 4, 5 and 6 are down the east side of Maugheraboy with Nos. 2 and 3 down the west side.

He also has switched the names of Knappagh More and Knappagh Beg townlands.

69. *The Sligo Independent and West of Ireland Telegraph*, Nov. 19, 1955, p. 3.

70. Could Tohall and Perrem have been personally acquainted with each other from both having worked in Co. Leitrim?

71. Mr. Kelly was manager of the Guinness Depot which opened in Sligo in 1950, Guy Perrem was assistant manager, Peter Carroll and Cecil Ewing also worked there as did a number of secretarial staff including Mary F Ryan.

72. See Gunning and Feehily (1995, 87) for an early photograph of his *Sligo Independent* Office and herein for a photo of Hopper passing it.

73. She was given a watercolour of Mullaghmore by Lynn Hope. Lynne Hope shared accommodation with her in Rowlett's Hotel, at the west end of Wine St. Hope had an exhibition of paintings in Nov. 1951.

74. This book, like many others cited herein, does not name an editor; in this case we have used Marist Brothers in the citations.

75. Brendan Rooney did mention "some stones on the mountain" to the younger author but he did not get around to going up there and see for himself.

76. That evacuation of Inishmurray in 1948 was painful to many, considering the pleas to Dublin for a simple solution. The natives saw that all that was needed was for a breakwater opposite the natural harbour of Classeymore to make safe for use in almost all sea conditions. The pleas of the locals were ignored, as many of our current pleas are. This evacuation could have caused the eradication of memories of life on the island.

77. He helped Francis Synge with his geological work in the 1960s and Gerard Remmele with his Ph. D. study of the geology of the Dartry Mountains (Remmele 1985).

78. Costello published the pin from O'Connor's Island which our Past President's mother, Alice O'Connor, found in a sod of turf about to be put on the fire.

79. The site location in Tawnamore townland, Kilmacshalgan parish, south-west of Dromore West. National Grid Reference G.39.26.

80. This was done on the advice of Dr. Seamus Caulfield, a brother of Dr. Brendán Mac Conamhna, former Director of Sligo Regional College, a major sponsor of this publication.

81. He wonders if this was the location of the 13th century Battle of Credran Cille between O'Donnell and FitzGerald. Col. Oliver Wagstaff, who lived at nearby Lisnalurg, often told him of having seen bones in the soil in this area.

82. Joyce Enright subsequently carried out excavations in this area for six seasons, 1980 and 1982 to 1986, (Enright 1986, 34; 1987, 32).

83. For years we badly lacked a street presence in the town but now we have Aidan Mannion's Record Room in Grattan St. as a contact point.

84. Quite often the spouse did much background work, such as providing hospitality, taking messages, *etc.*, which has gone unrecorded. When Honorary Life Membership was constitutionally established in 1985 it was agreed that spouses would be included.
Honorary Life Membership was bestowed on Mr. and Mrs. Guy Perrem and Mr. and Mrs. Patrick Tohall in the 1950s and 1960s. In more recent times those so honoured were Dr. Patrick and Julia Heraughty, Michael J. O'Kelly, Pat and Sheela Kitchin, Noel and Briga Murphy, Estie Cahalane, Seán Ó Nualláin, Michael Gibbons, Tom Condit, Mary Tunney, Olive Alcock, Frank McGarry, Paddy O'Hara, Neal Cremmin, John Hamilton, Patricia Mulligan, John McTernan, Des Smith, Jack Flynn and Tony Toher.

85. Patrick Tohall may have produced a leaflet on Prehistoric Monuments but we can not find a copy. Hopper found the juxtaposition of these two shop nameplates, *The House for Wines* and *The House for Men*, a little amusing, if not annoying! Was one to buy men in his premises?

86. See Gunning and Feehily (1995, cover, left) for a photograph of these adjacent premises in earlier days on the east side of O'Connell St.

87. His explanation of the name Benwiskin was that it is from Ben Fhoiscín, the word for a 12-month old female goat.

88. Devins (2000, 56) mentions that Kennedy satisfied himself as to the meaning of all Sligo Townland names, Raughley and Moodoge proving the most difficult. The elder author thinks Raughley may be from *Reachtáil*, a current; Moodoge could be from *Mudhadh*, a site of destroying or killing.

89. The Cairn referred to in one Board of Works document as Uiscaun Cave, *recte* Misgaun Maedbh, Co. Sligo, was deemed on examination to be impossible to protect and impossible to injure (Lohan 1995, 122, citing OPW 730/85).

90. Finlay Tower and Sheela Kitchin came to live permanently in Sligo in 1950. We are not quite sure when Kitchin joined Sligo Field Club, he first appears at the 1959 AGM when he became Vice-Chairman. The earliest programmes in his own files, those of 1957, could have been given to him by Cahalane. Regrettably only intermittent membership lists have been preserved.

91. Publication of the excavations by Dr. Joseph Raftery in the 1950s is currently in preparation by his son Prof. Barry Raftery. Scott (1968, 19) gives a photograph of the excavation of one of the crannogs and O'Sullivan (1997, 120, Pl. 1) gives a photograph of a Late Bronze Age wicker 'firebasket' from Crannog 61, Rathinaun, Lough Gara.

92. Kitchen, and perhaps the others, had a theory that the capstones on many portal tombs slipped down because of the earthquake that formed Lough Achree in 1490. If so should we not have recorded mention of collapsing churches and castles; perhaps it was an earlier earthquake.

93. Normally we do not have a Vote of Thanks after a lecture, though it may happen at the Memorial Lecture; it used to happen in the early days of SFC; we are unsure as to when it ceased or for what reason!

94. It was one of the cultural developments in the period prior to the establishment of the Yeats

International Summer School, which began in 1960 and is now the longest running Summer School in Ireland. McGarry, the only surviving founder member of the Summer School has set out the story of the foundation (1990, 8).

95. Mr. W. Trotter is mentioned in October 1955 as Treasurer of the Chess Club and W. Trotter is given in the SFC 1959-1960 Annual Report.

96. He was proprietor of Henderson's Garage and a Director of Blackwoods, the grocery retail and wholesale firm that Cahalane was a manager with; he lived in Ballincar. He resigned in 1965 on retiring to Dublin.

97. See *The Corran Herald*, No. 28, 21, for Des Smith's photo of the Lynch family of Brougher at the cist grave on their land.

98. Bishop Gilhooley lived in this house before the building of The Cathedral in 1875 and later Fr. Pa Hynes had a Youth Club for girls here.

99. Sweeney had been rebuffed as to their importance some years earlier when he told a National School's inspector of them.

100. Frank's mother, Alice O'Connor, donated many of the items, including a ringed pin, she had found on O'Connor's Island to Sligo Museum. His father James also found a pin, now in the NMI, on O'Connor's Island (Costello 1919-1920; Warner 1998). The design was used on wedding rings in 1985, an idea inspired by Lisnacroghera scabbard designs decorating wedding rings of another Field Club family.

101. Foundations of the earlier castle, a tower house, were found within the courtyard.

102. In 1889 William Butler Yeats writes of this landscape in *The Wanderings of Oisin*.
"And passing the Firbolg's burial-mounds,
Came to the cairn-heaped grassy hill
Where passionate Maeve is stony-still".

103. See Gunning and Feehily (1995, 185) for a photograph of his premises known as Young's Medical Hall. Frank Kerrin was elected first Hon. Treasurer of the Sligo-based Connaught Camera Club in October 1955.

104. This was the house of William Healy who had worked with Macalister, Armstrong and Praeger on the Carrowkeel excavations.

105. See Siggins (1995) for a note on a Sligo token.

106. Commemorative pottery mugs made by Michael Kennedy, specially marked the occasion. A second conference, Stones and Bones, was held in Sligo in May 2001; Sligo Field Club was not involved in its organisation, though many of our members attended.

107. The frequently published drawing of The Siege of the Green Fort (*e.g.*, Wood-Martin 1882, Frontispiece; Gunning and Feehily 1995, 26) is not of Sligo at all but was taken by A. Schoonebeek in 1689 from a drawing of the Siege of Bonn by J. Tangena of Lyden (O'Neill 1966). Apparently variations of this drawing has been used to illustrate many sieges throughout Europe. See Halpin (this volume) for a note on test excavations adjacent to this site.

108. The need for this survey arose from the 1963 Planning and Development Act, and, as OPW did not have the manpower, it fell on Foras Forbartha, the National Planning Institute for Physical Planning and Construction Research, to develop a Conservation and Amenity Service to fulfil this need for the Planning Offices of each County Council.

In 1979 Joyce Enright compiled the Foras Forbartha report for Leitrim County Council. The brief included a recommendation of a selection of sites to be taken into care by the Council; County Councils have under the 1954 National Monuments (Amendment) Act the same statutory powers as OPW / Dúchas in this regard. As a result car parks, access, site presentation and signposts were completed for about twenty-five archaeological sites throughout Leitrim.

109. There are still undiscovered monuments and the younger author's Sligo fieldwork adds six to ten per year, rejects a few as well and often it is a case of reinterpretation. Recently the Timoneys have found a wedge tomb in Murhy on the south-east slope of Keash.

				15	37	39	
				7	168	62	
				39	194	61	
32	132	125	115	268	128		
80	93	95	234	268	118		
24	10	3	163	170	167	23	
	2	63	228	203	249	122	
	69	108	138	156	229	54	
		31	3	92	19		
				53	98		

110. Dr. Göran Burenhult's Carrowmore excavations campaign from 1977 to 1982, the Carrowmore dump crisis (Timoney 1990; 1992) in 1983 and the Drumcliffe excavations from used up considerable time that might have otherwise been diverted into survey work.

111. The approximate distribution of Recorded Monuments in Co. Sligo, for 1995 as per 6" O.S. sheet, is as follows.

112. The story of the saving of the archaeological area north of the High Cross prior to these excavations is given above under Eileen Lambert. In 1980 Sligo Co. Council financed the excavations. From 1982 to 1986 they were financed jointly by OPW and the Dept. of Labour and FÁS schemes. The Drumcliffe Development

Association, under the Chairmanship of Rev. Maurice Sirr, Treasurer Vincent Blighe and Secretary Eileen Blighe, were instrumental in obtaining the Dept. of Labour schemes without which much less ground would have been excavated.

113. In the late 1990s most of the members of The Organisation of Irish Archaeologists joined the Irish Association of Professional Archaeologists and in 2001 IAPA became the Institute of Archaeologists of Ireland.

114. Even of longer duration was a trip made to the Burren in June 1969; after a full day walking that stony landscape the medieval town of Athenry, or at least some of it, was examined and departure time for Sligo was 3A.M.! Today we struggle to get further than the distance of the Collooney Gap with a group of any significant size.

115. Jimmy Harney at Sligo Co. Co. was always quick to respond to our pleas to prevent the expansion of the adjacent 1971 quarry. Officers of SFC at times of prolonged absence from the county advise their fellow officers so that if, and when, a crisis arises we know who is around to call on. These crises tend to arise at Bank Holidays or during major sporting events; once we were informed that a heavy earth-moving machine was on a megalithic tomb just as an All Ireland Hurling Final was starting.

116. This is not the castle built by Richard de Burgh in 1310 which was depicted in 1685 by Thomas Phillips in his Prospect of Sligo and is discussed in detail in this Volume by O'Conor. The first time that Phillips' Prospect may have been seen in Sligo, since 1685, was when Dr. John A. Claffey showed it during a lecture to SFC in 1978, since when there has been considerable agreement that the castle was on the Town Hall site. Eóin Halpin, excavating for Sligo Corporation, found walls in May 2002 under the Stone Fort walls which were under The Gate Lodge of The Town Hall which may well be of the 1310 castle. The location of the 1245 castle has not been established (but see Timoney and O'Brien, this Volume).

117. Dr. Brendán Mac Conamhna, Director, has had planted 8,000 trees and shrubs in eighteen clumps as a parkland development at the Institute. The chosen tree-types are those associated with each of the eighteen letters of the Irish Alphabet as set out by Ballymote-born Canon Andrew Dunleavy, 1694-1765, in his 1742 bilingual *Teagusc Críostaidthe*. The word Sligeach over the reception is of the appropriate timber types.

118. There have been debates, as for instance in 1966 and 1997, as to how much of each discipline, or even how many disciplines, we should be catering for. A look at the lecture programme for some years shows a very broad range of themes indeed! Perhaps we are over-stretching ourselves! A possible solution is to have more lectures over the Winter season. People regularly travel from as far away as Donegal town, Westport and Ballyhaunis to our lectures. Our membership has come from all walks of life, commercial and professional, some from the religious fraternities, Ursuline & Mercy Orders, Dominican Community, with many retired enjoying our activities in their restful years. The late Alderman James Gannon seems to be the only politician that was involved in SFC.

119. While living in Cuil Iorra he gave his address as Knocknarea or Knocknahur, both equally incorrect as his father's house, in a field on its own and demolished in 1985, was in Seafield but the front wall was in Breeoge.

120. Stephen O'Connor and Eileen Lambert were first-cousins. A casual comment by O'Connor about a discovery, probably in 1946, of a long stone cist burial in Carrowmore led to a publication by the younger author (Timoney 1966-1971) which has recently been brought to the attention of Dúchas in relation to their proposed works at Carrowmore.

121. Jim Hughes was present, but in a very discrete way.

122. Noel Cassidy from Lisacul, Co. Roscommon, but living in Waterford, was the last fieldwalker to photograph some of the Carrowntemple slabs on site before their unauthorised removal in 1984.

123. The find-spot was where Woodpark , just below Glen, not in adjacent Lufertan.

124. For a list of Sligo slabs published in 2001, see Herity, Kelly, and Mattenberger (1997, 80-124).

125. There were two printings of the article on the missing Knockmore slabs; that with the slabs numbered is the correct one.

126. Arising from a discussion between the younger author and Dave McEllin about the return to Ireland of this Keelty slab, another Early Christian slab, one from Inishbofin in Lough Ree came to light in the store at Newtown Cashel Garda Station, Co. Longford, from where took it to NMI; it had previously been rescued from an ominous position on the island's shore.

127. Des Smith, Brían Ó Súileabháin, Aodhán Ó Higgins, John McTernan and Martin A. Timoney helped clear the many overgrown graveyards allowing the recording of the memorials by Jack Flynn and Mary B. Timoney.

128. Nor was anybody locally aware that Rev.

Martin Sherlock, the colourful later 18th century Protestant cleric and author was buried in Skreen. If Mrs. Margaret Diamond, a member of SFC, was on an outing to Skreen in June 1966. This may be the source of Kitchin's knowledge of the Diamond box tombs, the Incumbent of Skreen at that time being totally unaware of the artistic riches in his graveyard.

129. The numbering of the Carrowmore tombs was originally set out by George Petrie in 1837 in a letter from Roger Chambers Walker's house at Rathcarrick. Mapping errors unfortunately crept in at a number of places, 2-6, 10a-11a, 48-49, 53-55, in Wood-Martin's 1888 publication. Bergh (1995, 179-180, 254-256) details the errors and reverts to Petrie's numbering. The most controversial tomb of all, Carrowmore No. 4 (Wood-Martin 1888, 21-30; Burenhult 1980, 68-82; Bergh 1995, 182) should be No. 3.

For many years in the 1980s we entertained visiting University Archaeological groups from these islands and mainland Europe who wanted to see this controversial megalithic cemetery.

130. The work outside of The Giant's Ring, within which there is a Carrowmore-type passage tomb, at Ballynahatty, Co. Down, (Hartwell 2002) has revealed a ritual complex which whets the appetite for what may be found to fill out the spaces between the tombs at Carrowmore.

131. "In areas of archaeological sensitivity it is necessary to comply with both the National Monuments and Planning Acts, regarding excavations and the finding of artefacts. The principle which applies is that any area which is disturbed or exposed must be declared available for the extraction of archaeological information in the course of that disturbance" (Rockwood Parade Recommended Action Plan 1992, 44).

132. The hand emerging from the vault under a box tomb in Kilmacowen graveyard on the cover *of Att Överleva Döden*, edited by Peter Brookesmith, is that of Bergh!

133. In the period between the two Carrowmore campaigns Burenhult studied the building of megalithic tombs in Melanesia which continues there into the 20th century AD. Burenhult includes several illustrations of Sligo folklife and archaeology in his publications of this work (Burenhult 1992, 16-18, 24-25, 30-31, 38-41) as well as in his overall view of Stone Age man (Burenhult 1981, 122-170).

134. The Minutes record the suggestion of a national meeting of Archaeological Societies in Athlone in Autumn 1964.

135. Other active members of the BHG are John & Betty Conlan, Gerry & Ester Cassidy, Stan & Tilly Casey, Paddy Horan.

136. See above under Br. Alphonsus Maxwell.

137. Images of Sligo archaeology grace the cover of several archaeological works (Rynne, ed., 1987; O'Kelly 1989; Brindley 1994; Clinton 2001).

138. These concerned a 1956 call for repair of damaged stonework at Deerpark, a 1960s proposal to demolish Athlone castle, a vote of 25 to 4 to support a resolution from Kilkenny Corporation on the restoration of the Irish language, the moving of national monuments to the 1967 ROSC exhibition, the preservation of North Bull Island and of Wood Quay, Sligo airport in 1977 because of Killaspugbrone court-tomb and church, the proposed drainage of the Owenmore catchment in 1988, Rockwood Parade in 1992, the long running problem of Killaspugbrone church and the precariously positioned Dominican Ballindoon Abbey This unique structure is illustrated in the Sligo County Council Annual Report 1999, 43, the building of a house adjacent to the cairn at Heapstown which possibly covers a passage-tomb, threats to Roslee Castle at Easkey and The Green Fort in 1980, a proposed World Heritage list, bypass roads, the care of graveyards and seeking the help of the Bishops in 1984 in that regard, the sandblasting of graveyard monuments, advising OPW of when tracts of land with monuments were coming on the market and encouraging them to purchased land such as at Carrowmore, Knocknarea and Carrowkeel, assisting Ken Hannigan of the National Archives in 1980 to acquire business records, the destruction of archaeological levels just north of the high cross at Drumcliffe, providing texts and other help for Junior Chamber visitor guides, the Chamber of Commerce and Industry video, copy material supplied to the Irish Architectural Archive, attention drawn in 1984 to the Magheracar passage-tomb's precarious position on the top of a vertical sea cliff face which called for archaeological excavation Initially a marine engineer was sent to examine the site! Later Eamon Cody of The Ordnance Survey excavated the site, the disturbance around Keelty church in 1984, the presentation of the Ballydrehid bridge stone by Billy Brown who discovered it built into the porch of his house in nearby Drumiskabole, the Harper-Campbell buildings in Sligo in 2000 and the Lough Gill Environmental Management Project Committee.

In September 1966 our only response to a request from Sligo Corporation regarding the proposed erection of information plaques on historic buildings was to suggest The Abbey and The Green Fort as possible locations; today we would suggest buildings associated with academic, historic and literary personages.

The tree threatening the Eugenius MacDonnell monument of 1591 at Skreen was removed because of our persistence. See photograph by the younger author in O'Dowd (1991, Pl. 4). The entry in the Annals of Lough Cé translates as "The Kallends of January 1599. Benmhuan Óg Ni Duíbhgennain, daughter of Maelechlainn, son of Dúbhaltach Óg, son of Dúbhaltach Mór, erected this tomb of hewn stones which is over the great well of the Scrin, for the soul of her husband, *i.e.*, the Vicar MacDomhnaill; and Eóghan MacDomhnaill was the same vicar's name". This contradicts what the inscription on the monument says, *i.e.*, that it was Vicar Eóghan, Eugenius, MacDomhnaill himself who had the monument erected.

139. These include the British Girls' Exploring Society in 1963, Gary Huckle, Elizabeth de Jong, David Drury, Dave Keeling, George Eogan, Etienne Rynne, Brendán Ó Ríordáin, Peter O'Connor, Malcom Billings, Caroll Gleeson for Irish Landmark Trust, Collette Harper of North West Enterprise Group, Peter Collins for Christian Heritage Promotions in 1997, John Higgins, Jimmy Foran (Foran 1983), Máire Nic Domhnaill Gairbhí (2000). Marian Dowd (Dowd 2001), Peter Woodman and Nicky Milner (Milner and Woodman, 2001) on shell middens, Dáithí Ó hÓgáin, the authors in this book, Niamh Whitfield on a piece of filigree at Alnwick castle (Whitfield 2001), Aideen Ireland on Roger Chambers Walker. NMI, NLI, Dúchas, Coilte, Sligo Co. Co., Gardaí, *The Sligo Champion*, Sligo Weekender, *The Irish Times*, RTE, NWR, Channel 4, BBC. Donal Tinney & SLLSA & Museum.

140. The first conference was in Galway in 1895, the sixth in Rosapenna in 1910, with Sligo having the fourth in 1904. For the Sligo 1904 programme see Nunn (2000, 39-50).

141. Martin Wilson arranged the first for the Beltra area, but it did not quite work out as planned. We soon discovered that we had an already well-informed guide who delivered a hitherto unsuspected wealth of local knowledge. Larkhill cashel and Knocknarea mountain were examined at a distance, and then four sites down the lane to Tanrego castle. The banks and walls west of Tanrego court tomb were examined and were considered not that recent. For three hours we entertained each other with information and questions after which discussion continued until midnight while Moya Wilson plied us with tea and cake. Sligo Field Club was back doing fieldwalking. When the younger author told Briga Murphy of the event she said "That is what we started at and it was so enjoyable, Kirwan on his bicycle". The next outing arranged by Pat O'Brien for the Kilross area was washed out at the first site but when reconvened was again a tour-de-force. The fourth outing, arranged for Lugnamacken by Aidan Mannion. Lugnamacken is a 'high-density low-level of information archaeological landscape' north-west of Collooney. The fifth was a dry-run for Martin Wilson and the younger author's Ballymote Heritage Weekend outing. The threat of Foot and Mouth disease prevented the continuation of this most enjoyable style of outing in 2001, but we have had ad hoc outings such as the boat trip to check the doubtful Church Island ogam stone (Swift 2002).

Beltra on May 3rd Martin Wilson, Larry Mullin, Aidan Manion, Pat O'Brien, Brendan Rooney, Martin A. Timoney, Mary B. Timoney, Jack Flynn. Kilross 1 AM, LM, P O'B, MAT, MBT, Margaret McBrien. Kilross 2 AM, LM, P O'B, MAT, MBT, MMcB, Joyce Enright, Martin Enright. July 3rd 2000 Lugnamacken AM, LM, PO'B, MAT. July 10th 2000 Dromard MW, MAT, AM, P O'B, MMcB.

142. See Gunning and Feehily 1995, 184-185, for a photograph of this premises when it was The Grosvenor Hotel.

ARCHIVES

Sligo Field Club Papers
Kirwan Family Papers
Tohall Family Papers
Cahalane Family Papers
Kitchin Family Papers
Timoney Family Papers and Notebooks

NEWSPAPERS

The Sligo Champion
The Sligo Champion Sesquintenial
The Sligo Independent and West of Ireland Telegraph, 1945-1955, 1959

REFERENCES

Actors ?1993: *The Actors Are Come Hither, A History of The Western Drama Festival, Tubbercurry*, 1944-1993,

Adams, G.B., and Carrothers, E.N., 1950: "News from Societies. BNFC", Irish Naturalists J., 10, 26-27.

Allingham, Hugh, and Crawford, Robert, 1897: Captain Cuellar's Adventure in Connacht and Ulster, AD 1588, *etc.*, Reprint 1988, Sligo, Sligo Co. Co.

Anon. 1904: "Irish Field Club Union. Report of the Fourth Triennial Conference and Excursion, held at Sligo, July 12th to 18th, 1904", *The Irish Naturalist*, 13, 173-224.

Anon. 1912-1915: "Our Annual General Excursion", Co. Louth Archaeol. J., 3, 288-291.

Anon. 1986: "Our Society", *J. Roscommon Historical and Archaeological Society*, 1, 5.

Anon. 1995: *Record of Monuments and Places, Co. Sligo*,

Dublin, Office of Public Works.

Bairead, Brian, 1943: *Glór Shligigh .i. Leabhrán in-ómós agus in-onóir Féile Leathchead an Chonnartha Ar n-a chur amach ag Chraobh Shligigh*, (Sligeach), Conradh na Gaeilge.

Banks, Tommy, 2000: *A Brief History of Christianity in Ransboro / Strandhill*.

Barceló, Juan A., Briz, Ivan, and Vila, Assumpició, eds., 1999: *New Techniques for Old Times CAA 98*, BAR International Series 757.

Beirne, Francis, ed., 2000: *The Diocese of Elphin, People, Places and Pilgrimage*, Blackrock, Columba.

Berger, Rainer, 1995: "Radiocarbon Dating of Early Medieval Irish Monuments", *Proc. Roy. Irish Acad.*, 95C4, 159-174.

Bergh, Stefan, 1986a: "Glen", *Excavations* 1985, 34-35.

Bergh, Stefan, 1986b: "Primrose Grange", *Excavations* 1985, 35-36.

Bergh, Stefan, 1987: "Carricknahorna East", *Excavations* 1986, 32.

Bergh, Stefan, 1987: "Court Tombs, Passage Tombs and Social Contexts in North Sligo", in Burenhult *et al*. 1987, 241-255.

Bergh, Stefan, 1995: *Landscape of the Monuments, A Study of the Passage Tombs in the Cuil Irra Region, Co. Sligo, Ireland*, Stockholm, Riksantikvarieämbetet Arkeologiska Undersökningar, Skrifter Nr 6.

Bergh, Stefan, 1997: "Design as Message: Role and of Irish Passage Tombs", *O Neolítico Atlántico E As Orixes Do Megalitismo, Actes Do Coloquio Internacional, Santiago de Compostella, 1-6 de Abril de 1996*, 141-150.

Bergh, Stefan, 2000: "Transforming Knocknarea – the Archaeology of a Mountain", *Archaeology Ireland*, 14:2, 14-18.

Bergh, Stefan, 2001: "Chamber of Horrors", *Archaeology Ireland*, 15:1, 5.

Bernelle, Agnes, 1992: *Decantations, A Tribute to Maurice Craig*, Dublin, Lilliput.

Brindley, Anna, 1994: *Irish Prehistory, An Introduction*, Dublin, Country House / National Museum of Ireland.

Brookesmith Peter, ed., 1988: *Att Överleva Döden, Teorier Om Ett Liv Efter Detta, Det Oförklarliga*, Höganäs, Bokorama.

Buckley, Victor M., Buckley, Laureen, and McCormick, Finbar, "A Curious Inhumation Burial from Dernish Island, Co. Sligo" in Timoney 2002.

Burenhult, Göran, 1980: The Archaeological Excavations at Carrowmore, Co. Sligo, Ireland: Excavation Seasons 1977-1979, *Theses and Papers in North-European Archaeology 9*, University of Stockholm.

Burenhult, Göran, 1981: *Stenåldersbilder, Hallristningar och Stenåldersekonomi*, Stockholm, Sureförlaget AB.

Burenhult, Göran, 1984: The Archaeology of Carrowmore Environmental Archaeology and the Megalithic Tradition at Carrowmore, Co. Sligo, Ireland. *Theses and Papers in North-European Archaeology* 14, University of Stockholm.

Burenhult, Göran, Carlsson, Anders, Hyenstrand, Åke, Sjovold, Torstein, 1987: *Theoretical Approaches to Artefacts, Settlement and Society, Studies in Honour of Mats P. Malmer*, Brit. Archaeol. Reports, International Series 366.

Burenhult, Göran, 1992: *Sten Männen, Megalitbyggare och Människoätare*, Hoganas, Wiken.

Burenhult, Göran, 1981: *Stenåldersbilder,* 122-170

Burenhult, Göran, 1992: *Sten Männen,* 16-18, 24-25, 30-31, 38-41

Burenhult, Göran, 1995: *The Illustrated Guide to The Megalithic Cemetery of Carrowmore, Co. Sligo*, Ynglingarumsgården, Burenhult.

Burenhult, Göran, 1997: "Different Tombs, Different Folks", *National Geographic*, 192:3, introductory page.

Burenhult, Göran, 1999a: "Megalithic Symbolism in Ireland and Scandinavia in light of new evidence from Carrowmore", in Cruz and Oosterbeek 1999, 49-108.

Burenhult, Göran, 1999b: "KARTAGO as a viewer of GIS- and Multivariate Archaeological data in the Ajvide and Carrowmore Projects – the Full Concept", in Barceló, Briz and Vila, eds., 1999, 97-102 and figs.

Burenhult, Göran, 2001: *The Illustrated Guide to The Megalithic Cemetery of Carrowmore, Co. Sligo*, 2nd ed., Ynglingarumsgården, Burenhult.

Burenhult, Göran, 2001: "Cultural Interactions in Europe and the Eastern Mediterranean During the Bronze Age (3000-500BC), in Werbart 2001, 47-66.

Burenhult, Göran, 2002: Remote Sensing, Vol. II, *Theses and Papers in North-European Archaeology* 13:b, University of Stockholm.

Bunn, Mike, 1997: "Splendid Sligo", *The World of Hibernia*, 3:2, 146-166.

Canning, Paul, and Dalby, Barry, 1998: *The Sligo Way Map Guide*, Sligo, Sligo Co. Co.

Carville, Geraldine, 1990: "A Cistercian Grange and adventures of Captain Cuellar", *Donegal Annual*, 1990, 49-60.

Castleconnor 2000: *Castleconnor Parish, An Historical Perspective – Pre 1900*, Corballa, Castleconnor Parish Development Group.

Caulfield, Seamus, 1983: "The Neolithic Settlement of North Connaught", in Reeves-Smyth and Hammond, eds., 1983, 195-215.

Clark, Grahame, 1985: "The Prehistoric Society: From East Anglia to the World", *Proc. Prehist. Soc.*, 51,1-13.

Clinton, Mark, 2001: *The Souterrains of Ireland*, Bray, Wordwell.

Colhoun, Mabel R., 1970: "The Missing Stones Conwall and Cloncha", *Donegal Annual*, 9, 241-243.

Condit, Tom, and Gibbons, Michael, 1991: "A Glimpse of Sligo's Prehistory", *Archaeology Ireland*, 5:3, 7-10.

Condit, Tom, Gibbons, Michael, and Timoney, Martin A., 1991: "Hillforts in Sligo and Leitrim", *Emaina*, 9, 59-62.

Cookman, E.W.R.,1996: "Achievements", *The Donegal Annual*, 48, 15-20.

Costello, T.B., 1902, 1903-1904: "Tuam Raths and Souterrains", *J. Galway Archaeol. & Hist. Soc.*, 2, 109-116; 3, 1-10.

Costello, T.B., 1919-1920: "Find of Bronze Pin with La Tène Ornament", *J. Galway Arch. Hist. Soc.*, 11, 76

Cotton, Don C. F., 1989: *The Heritage of Inishmurray*, Sligo, Regional Technical College.

Cotton, Don C. F., 1992: " Sligo' Undiscovered Wild Places", *Living Heritage*, 9, 26.

Cotton, Don C. F., Timoney, Martin A., McDermott, C.V., 1999: *The Miners Way & Historical Trial Map Guide*, Ballyredmond, Leitrim, Sligo and Roscommon County Councils.

Craig, Maurice, 1976: *Classic Houses of the Middle Size*, Architectural Press.

Crawford, Harriet, 1979: *Subterranean Britain, Aspects of Underground Archaeology*, London, Baker.

Crichton, Aleck, 2000: "Skreen/Dromard Co-Op. Agricultural Society" in O'Horo 2000, 29.

Crichton, Aleck, 2000: "Carrowgarry Cheese" in O'Horo 2000, 29.

Crichton, Aleck, 2000: "Christ Church Dromard" in O'Horo 2000, 76-77.

Crichton, Aleck, 2000: "Roads and Transport" in O'Horo 2000, 156.

Crichton, Joan, 2000: "Beltra ICA" in O'Horo 2000, 42-43.

Cruz, A.R., and Oosterbeek, L., eds., 1999: *Perspectiva em Diálogo. 1.o Curso Intensivo de Arte Pré-Histórica Europeia*, Tomo I, Arkeos 6. Tomar.

Curran, Bob, 2000: "Was Dracula an Irishman", *History Ireland*, 8:2, 12-15.

Curran-Mulligan, Patricia, 1994: "Yes, but it is Art!", *Archaeology Ireland*, 8:1, 14-15.

Danaher, Peter, "A Prehistoric Burial Mound at Ballyeeskeen, Co. Sligo", *J. Roy. Soc. Antiq. Ireland*, 94, 145-158.

Daniel, Glynn, 1980: "Megalithic Studies in Ireland, 1929-79", *Ulster J. Archaeol.*, 43, 1-8.

Daniel, Glynn, 1981: Editorial, Antiquity, 55, 81-89.

Daniel, Glynn, 1986: Some Small Harvest, The Memoirs of Glynn Daniel, London, Thames & Hudson.

De hÓir, Siobhán, 1990: "A Letter from W.F. Wakeman to James Graves in 1892", *J. Roy. Soc. Antiq. Ireland*, 120, 112-119.

Devins, John Pat, 2000: "Memories", in McTernan *et al.*, 2000,54-56.

Dodson, John R., and Bradshaw, Richard H.W., 1987: "A History of Vegetation and Fire, 6,600 B.P. to Present, County Sligo, western Ireland", Boreas, 16, 113-123.

Dolan, Queenie, 2000: "Memories", in McTernan *et al.*, 2000, 50-51.

Dowd, Marion, 2001: "Archaeology of the Subterranean World", *Archaeology Ireland*, 15:1, 24-29.

Duignan, Lasairíona, "A Hand-pin from Treanmacmurtagh Bog, Co. Sligo", *J. Roy. Soc. Antiq. Ireland*, 103, 220-223.

Duignan, Michael V., 1944: "Irish Agriculture in Early Historic Times", *J. Roy. Soc. Antiq. Ireland*, 74, 124-145.

Durand, Stella, 2000: Drumcliffe, the Church of Ireland Parish in its North Sligo Setting, Manorhamilton, Drumlin.

Enright, Joyce, 1978: "The Archaeology of Co. Sligo" in O'Callaghan, ed., 1978, 83-86.

Enright, Joyce, 1984a: The Sligo Guide, Dublin, Bord Fáilte.

Enright, Joyce, 1984b: "Summary of Excavations at Drumcliffe, Co. Sligo, Ireland, 1980-83", Medieval Archaeology, 28, 257.

Enright, Joyce, 1885a: "Archaeology", in Thorn, 1985, 44-55.

Enright, Joyce, 1985b: "Carrowmore in Context", Public Eye, March 26th, 4. (private circulation)

Enright, Joyce, 1985c: "Summary of Excavations at Drumcliffe, Co. Sligo, Ireland, 1984", Medieval Archaeology, 29, 215-216.

Enright, Joyce, 1985d: "Administrative and Contractual Aspects of Archaeological Excavations at Two Sites in Co. Sligo: summary of paper read at O.I.A Seminar, Dec. 1984", O.I.A. *Newsletter*, No. 2, March, 1985, 1-2.

Enright, Joyce, 1986: "Drumcliffe South", Excavations 1985, 34.

Enright, Joyce, 1987a: "Drumcliffe South", Excavations 1986, 32.

Enright, Joyce, 1987b: "Drumcliffe: Part 1 - Yeats and Columcille", *The Corran Herald*, No. 8, February, 1987, 10.

Enright, Joyce, 1989: "Some Aspects of the Archaeology of Inishmurray in the Context of a Management Plan" in Cotton, ed., 1989, 75-86.

Enright, Joyce, 1990: "Archaeology and Recent Architectural & Cultural Heritage inputs", in EIS on Hotel and Leisure Complex at Lough Key, Environmental Consultancy Services.

Enright, Joyce, 1992a: "Archaeology and Recent Architectural & Cultural Heritage", in Arklow Bypass EIS, Route Selection Report, May 1992, E.S.B.I. / Atkins.

Enright, Joyce, 1992b: "Archaeology and Recent Architecture & Cultural Heritage", in Arklow Bypass EIS, Final Report, June 1992, E.S.B.I. / Atkins.

Enright, Joyce, 1993: "Archaeology and Recent Architectural & Cultural Heritage", in Arklow Bypass EIS, 2nd ed., Dual Carriageway, April 1993, E.S.B.I. / Atkins.

Eogan, George, 1983: The Hoards of the Irish Later Bronze Age, Dublin, University College Dublin.

Eogan, George, 1986: Knowth and the Passage Tombs of Ireland, London, Thames and Hudson.

Eogan, George, 1983: "Ribbon Torcs in Britain and Ireland" in O'Connor and Clarke, 1983, 87 – 126

Eogan, George, 2002: "Archaeology in Ireland during the last 50 years: an outline", Antiquity, 76, 475-484.

Finnegan, Thomas A.,1977: Sligo, Sinbad's Yellow Shore, Sligo, Keohane & Dublin, Dolmen

Finnegan, Thomas A., and O'Connell, Derry, 1978: A Signposted Walking Tour of Sligo City, Sligo, Donegal-Leitrim-Sligo Regional Tourism Organisation.

FitzGerald, William, 2002: "Environmental Education at The Institute of Technology, Sligo" in Timoney 2002.

Flynn, Jack, 1995: "Preserving Field Monuments", *The Corran Herald*, 28, 39.

Flynn, John, 1989: "Land Management Options for Inishmurray" in Cotton, ed., 1989, 72-74.

Foran, James, 1983: The Megalithic Tombs of Ireland, A Bibliography, unpublished

Francke, Klaus D., 1999: Ireland, Aerial Photographs, ?, Dewi Lewis.

Fredengren, Christina, 2000: "Iron Age Crannogs in Sligo", *Archaeology Ireland*, 14:1, 7.

Fredengren, Christina, 2000: "Iron Age Crannogs in Lough Gara", *Archaeology Ireland*, 14:2, 26-28.

Fredengren, Christina, 2001: "Poor People's Crannogs", *Archaeology Ireland*, 15:4, 24-25.

Gallagher, Alfie, and Raftery, Joseph, 1952: "Crannog Finds from Lough Gara", *J. Roy. Soc. Antiq. Ireland*, 82, 182.

Gallagher, P., and Cruickshank, D.W., 1990: God's Obvious Design: Papers for the Spanish Armada Symposium, Sligo, 1988, London.

Garner, William, & Craig, Maurice, 1976: Buildings of Architectural Interest in Co. Sligo, A Preliminary Survey, Dublin, An Foras Forbatha, Limited Distribution.

Garvin, Thomas, 2001: "John Garvin" in Higgins, Timoney, Connolly and Kielty, 80-83.

Gibbons, Michael, Alcock, Olive, Condit, Tom, Tunney, Mary, and Timoney, Martin A., 1989: Sites and Monuments Record, Co. Sligo, Dublin, Office of Public Works.

Gilligan, Mary, ed., 2001: A Moment in Time, Sligo Folk Park, Riverstown, Co. Sligo, Riverstown.

Gunning, Paul, and Feehily, Padraig, 1996: Down Gallows Hill, An Illustrated History of Sligo from 1245 to 1995, Sligo, Sligo Heritage Group.

Guthrie-Jones, Winston, 1994: The Wynnes of Sligo and Leitrim, Manorhamilton, Drumlin.

Halloran, Martin, ed., 2000: Templeboy 2000, Templeboy, Templeboy.

Harbison, Peter, 1992: The High Crosses of Ireland, An Iconographical and Photographic Survey, 3 vols., Bonn, Rudolf Habelt.

Harbison, Peter, 2000: Cooper's Ireland, Drawings and Notes from an Eighteenth-Century Gentleman, Dublin, O'Brien.

Harbison, Peter, 2002a: "The Antiquities of Sligo in 1779 as seen by Lewis Irwin of Tanrego House" in Timoney 2002.

Harbison, Peter, 2002b: 'Our treasure of Antiquities', Beranger and Bigari's Antiquarian Sketching Tour of Connacht in 1779, Dublin, Wordwell in association with the National Library of Ireland.

Harney, Jimmy, 2000: "Memories", in McTernan *et al.*, 2000, 58-60.

Hartwell, Barrie, 2002: "A Neolithic ceremonial timber complex at Ballynahatty, Co. Down", Antiquity, 76, 526-532.

Hayward, Richard, 1955: This is Ireland, Mayo, Sligo, Leitrim and Roscommon, London, Barker.

Hegary, Fran, 1998: "Niland Gallery" in Tinney, 1998, 5-6.

Hencken, H. O'Neill, 1939: "A Long Cairn at Creevykeel, Co. Sligo", *J. Roy. Soc. Antiq. Ireland*, 69, 53-98.

Henry, Patrick J., 1995: Sligo Medical Care in the Past, 1800-1965, Sligo

Heraughty, Patrick, 1978: "Inishmurray – Island of Muirdeach" in O'Callaghan, ed., 1978, 67-73.

Heraughty, Patrick, 1982: "Inishmurray, Ancient Monastic Island, 1st ed., Dublin, O'Brien.

Heraughty, Patrick, 1982: "The Geology of County Sligo", Sligo Visitors Guide '82, 75-77, Sligo, Junior Chamber Sligo. (Repeated in Guides until 1984).

Heraughty, Patrick, 1989: "Some Recollections of Land Management and Wildlife of Inishmurray from before 1948", in Cotton, ed., 1989, 65-71.

Heraughty, Patrick, 1996: "Inishmurray, Ancient Monastic Island, 2nd ed. Dublin, O'Brien.

Heraughty, Patrick, 1993: "Inishmurray - Sligo's Sacred Isle", Ireland of the Welcomes, 42:5, 27-33.

Herity, Michael, Kelly, Dorothy, and Mattenberger, Ursula, 1997: " List of Early Christian Cross Slabs in Seven North-Western Counties", *J. Roy. Soc. Antiq. Ireland*, 107, 80-124.

Higgins, Chris, and McElhone, Patricia, 1995: Sligo at Prayer, Sligo, ???

Higgins, John, Timoney, Mary B., Connolly, Br. Thomas, and Kielty, John, 2001: Keash and Culfadda, A Local History, Culfadda, Keash ~ Culfadda History Committee.

Hunt, Mary, 1999: Looking Back at Sligo's Past, Photographs and Reminiscences of Old Sligo, Sligo, Sligo Family Centre ~ Sligo Active Retirement Association.

ICA 2000: Random Memories, 1950-2000, Sligo, Sligo Federation ICA.

Ireland, Aideen, 1982: "The Royal Society of Antiquaries of Ireland", *J. Roy. Soc. Antiq. Ireland*, 112, 72-92.

Ireland, Aideen, 2001: "Colonel William Gregory Wood-Martin, Antiquary, 1847-1917", J. Irish Archaeol., 10, 1-11.

Jennings, Austin G. 1946-1947: "Barytes Development in Sligo", Bulletin of the Institution of Civil Engineers of Ireland, 73, 185-222.

Johnston, Jack, 2000: "The Sligo Archive in the Public Record Office of Northern Ireland", *Spark*, 14, 3-9.

Kaul, Flemming, 1985: Review of Burenhult 1980, J. Danish Archaeol., 1, 198-202.

Kilgannon, Tadgh, 1926: Sligo and its Surroundings, Sligo, Kilgannon; Reprint, Sligo, 1988, Dodd's Antiquarian Books

Kirby, Sheila, 1962: *The Yeats Country*, Dublin, The Dolmen Press.

Kirwan, Robert J. 1895: "Geological Notes from West Galway, The Galway and Clifden Railway", Irish Naturalist J., 4, 151-161.

Kitchin, Finlay Tower, Various dates: *Prehistoric Sligo*.

Kitchin, Finlay Tower, 1983: "The Carrowmore Megalithic Cemetery, Co. Sligo", Proc. Prehistoric Soc., 49, 151-175.

Lack, P., 1986: The Atlas of Wintering Birds in Britain and Ireland, ?, BTO/IWC.

Lacy, Brian, 1983: Archaeological Survey of County Donegal, A Description of the Field Antiquities of the County from the Mesolithic Period to the 17th. Century A.D., Lifford, Donegal County Council.

Lambert, Eileen, 1978: "Dominican Abbey Sligo" in O'Callaghan, ed., 1978, 57-60.'

Lohan, Rena, 1994: Guide to the Archives of The Office of Public Works, Dublin, The Stationery Office.

Lucas, A.T., 1972, "National Museum of Ireland Archaeological Acquisitions in the Year 1969", *J. Roy. Soc. Antiq. Ireland*, 102, 181-223.

Macalister, R.A.S., Armstrong, E.C.R., and Praeger, R.Ll., 1912: "Report on the Exploration of Bronze-Age Carns on Carrowkeel Mountain, Co. Sligo", Proc. Roy. Irish Acad., 29, 311-347.

Marist Brothers, 1962: Marist Brothers Sligo Centenary, 1862-1962, Sligo, Marist Brothers.

Marshall, Jenny White, and Rourke, Grellan D., 2000a: "The Secular Origin of the Monastic Enclosure Wall of High Island, Co. Galway", *Archaeology Ireland*, 14:2, 30-34. Fig. 5 and fig. 6

Marshall, Jenny White, and Rourke, Grellan D., 2000b: High Island, An Irish Monastery in the Atlantic, Dublin, Town House and Country House.

McDermott, C.V., Long, C.B., and Harney, S.J., 1996: A Geological Description of Sligo, Leitrim, and Adjoining Parts of Cavan, Fermanagh, Mayo and Roscommon, to Accompany the Bedrock Geology 1:100,000 Scale Map Series, Sheet 7, Sligo-Leitrim, with Contributions by K. Claringbold, D. Daly, R. Meehan and G. Stanley, Dublin, Geological Survey of Ireland.

MacLeod, Catríona, 1946: "Some Medieval Wooden Figure Sculptures in Ireland. Statues of Irish Saints", *J. Roy. Soc. Antiq. Ireland*, 76, 158-161.

McCurtain, Margaret, and O'Dowd, Mary, 1991: Women in Early Modern Ireland, Dublin, Wolfhound.

MacDonagh, Bernard, 1977: Lough Gill: Lake of Legends and Literature, Sligo, Sligo School of Landscape Painting.

MacDonagh, Bernard, 1978: Spanish Armada: Illustrated Account of the Francisco De Cuellar Story from Paintings and Drawings by Bernard MacDonagh, Sligo, Sligo School of Landscape Painting

McGarry, James P., 1971: The House of O'Connor, Collooney, McGarry

McGarry, James P., 1976: Placenames in the Writings of W.B. Yeats, London

McGarry, James P., 1980: Collooney, Collooney, McGarry

McGarry, James P., 1988: "The Eagle of the North", Donegal Annual, 1988, 84-89.

McGarry, James P., 1990: The Dream I Knew, Thirty Years of the Yeats International Summer School, Sligo, Collooney, McGarry.

McGarry, James P., 2002: A Memoir of Nora Niland, 1913-1988, Collooney, McGarry

McGowan, Joseph, 1993: In The Shadow of Benbulben, Anecdotes and History of North Sligo, Aeolus.

McGowan, Joseph, 1998: Inishmurray, Gale, Stone and Fire, Sligo, Aeolus.

McGowan, Joseph, 2001: Echoes of a Savage Land, Cork, Mercier.

McGowan, Joseph, Mullin, Larry, and Reynolds, Paula, eds., 1997: Co. Sligo Commemoration of the Great Famine, Sligo.

McElhone, Patricia, 1994: Lift the Latch, Memories of Old Rosses Point,

McHale, E. 1987-1988, "Details on Ballina Historical

and Folklore Society", North Mayo Hist. Archaeol. J., 2, 40-52.

McTernan, John C., 1965: Historic Sligo: A Bibliographic Introduction to the Antiquities and History, Maps and Surveys, Mss. and Newspapers, Historic Families and Notable individuals of County Sligo, Sligo, Yeats Country Publications.

McTernan, John C., 1977: Here's To Their Memory, Profiles of Distinguished Sligonians of Bygone Days, Cork, Mercier.

McTernan, John C., 1978: "Sligo and Its Surroundings" in O'Callaghan, ed., 1978, 29-33.

McTernan, John C., 1984: Sligo G.A.A.: A Centenary History, 1884-1984, Sligo, Coiste Chontae Shligigh.

McTernan, John C., 1986: Coolera: A Centenary Record, 1886-1896, Kilmacowen, Coolera/Strandhill G.A.A Club.

McTernan, John C., 1988: Sligo: *Sources of Local History, A Catalogue of the Local History Collection, with an Introduction and Guide to the Sources,* Sligo, Sligo County Library.

McTernan, John C., 1990: *At The Foot of Knocknarea, A Chronicle of Coolera in Bygone Days,* Sligo, Avena.

McTernan, John C., 1992: *Memory Harbour, The Port of Sligo: An Outline of its Growth and Decline and its Role as an Emigration Port,* Sligo, Avena. Reprint with additions 2002.

McTernan, John C., 1994a: *Worthies of Sligo, Profiles of Eminent Sligonians of Other Days,* Sligo, Avena.

McTernan, John C., 1994b: *Sligo: Sources of Local History, A Catalogue of the Local History Collection, with an Introduction and Guide to the Sources,* New Edition, Sligo, Sligo County Library.

McTernan, John C., 1995a: *Olde Sligo, Aspects of Town and County Over 750 Years,* Sligo, Avena.

McTernan, John C., 1995b: "Memorials of the Dead, Emlaghfad", *The Corran Herald,* 28, 26-29.

McTernan, John C., 1998: *In Sligo Long Ago,* Sligo, Avena.

McTernan, John C., et al., 2000: *Milestones and Memories, Sligo County Council Centenary Record,* 1899-1999, Sligo, Sligo County Council

McTernan, John C., 2000: *A Sligo Miscellany,* Sligo, Avena.

Miller, Liam, 1979: "Yeats's West", *Ireland of the Welcomes,* 28:3, 17-32. Landscape and monuments

Milner, Nicky, and Woodman, Peter, 2001: "Mesolithic Middens – from Famine to Feasting", *Archaeology Ireland,* 15:3, 32-35.

Mitchell, G. Frank, 1976: *The Irish Landscape,* London, Collins.

Mitchell, G. Frank, 1986: *The Shell Guide to Reading the Irish Landscape,* Dublin, Country House.

Mohr, Paul, 1994: "John Birmingham of Tuam: A Most Unusual Landlord", *J. Galway Archae. Hist. Soc.,* 46, 111-155.

Moss, Rachel, 2000: "A Medieval Jigsaw Puzzle: the Ancient Stones of Christ Church", *Archaeology Ireland,* 14:2, 20-23.

Moss, Rachel, 2002: "Tales from the Crypt: the Medieval stonework of Christ Church Cathedral, Dublin", *Medieval Dublin III,* 95-114.

Mount, Charles, 1994: "'From Knoxspark to Tír na nÓg'", *Archaeology Ireland,* 8:3, 22-23. Photo reversed

Mount, Charles, 1996: "The Environmental Siting of Neolithic and Bronze Age Monuments in the Bricklieve and Moytirra Uplands, County Sligo", *J. Irish Archaeol.,* 7, 1-11.

Mount, Charles, 1998: "Ritual, Landscape and Continuity in Prehistoric County Sligo", *Archaeology Ireland,* 12:3, 18-21.

Mount, Charles, 1999: "Excavation and Environmental Analysis of a Neolithic Mound and Iron Age Barrow Cemetery at Rathdooney Beg, County Sligo, Ireland", *Proc. Prehist. Soc.,* 65, 337-371.

Mountbatten, Louis, n.d.: *Classiebawn Castle Guidebook,* Privately published

Mountbatten, Louis, n.d.: *A Short Guide to Inishmurray,* Privately published

Mulligan, Martin, 1943: *Topographical Survey of County Sligo, Parish by Parish,* Typescript, Sligo County Library Local History Archive, No. 1266.

Mullin, Larry, 1978: "The Origins of Technical Education in Sligo Town", *Spectrum, Sligo,* An Cheard Scoil.

Mullin, Larry, 2002: "The Origins of Technical Education in Sligo Town, 1904-1912" in Timoney 2002.

Murphy, Briga, 1980 to 1986: "Flora of Co. Sligo", *Sligo Visitors Guide* 1980, 41-43, Sligo, Junior Chamber Sligo. (Repeated in *Guides* until 1986).

Murphy, Noel, 1980 to 1986: "Wild Birds in Co. Sligo", *Sligo Visitors Guide* 1980, 79, Sligo, Junior Chamber Sligo. (Repeated in *Guides* until 1986).

Nic Domhnaill Gairbhí, Máire, 2000: *A Traditional Music Journey, 1600-2000, from Erris to Mullaghban,* Manorhamilton, Drumlin.

Ní Dhubhláin, Gearóidín, 1998: *Ag Féachaint Siar,* Coiscéim, Baile Átha Cliath.

Nunn, Julia, D., 2000: *Irish Field Club Union Sligo Meeting,* 18-23 August 2000, Belfast, Irish Field Club Union.

O'Brien, Patrick E., 2001: "The Flynn Family of Blacksmiths" in Gilligan, ed., 2001, 104.

O'Callaghan, Austin, ed., 1978: *A.S.T.I. 56th Annual Convention Sligo – 1987,* Sligo, Sligo ASTI.

O'Callaghan, Jerry, 1992: The Red Book, *The Hanrahan Case against Merck, Sharp and Dohme,* Swords, Poolbeg.

O'Connell, Derry, 1975: *The Antique Pavement, An Illustrated Guide to Dublin Street Furniture,* Hardwicke and An Taisce.

O'Connell, Derry, 1978: *Guide to the Buildings of Sligo,* Bord Fáilte

O'Connell, Derry, 1989: *Tending The City, A Handbook of Urban Principles,* Dublin, An Taisce.

O'Connell, Derry, 1992: "Sligo - Surprisingly Intact", *Living Heritage,* 9:1, 18-20.

O'Connell, Derry, 1995: "Rockwood Parade Development" in Gunning and Feehily 1995, 171

O'Connor, Anne, and Clarke, D.V., 1983: *From The Stone Age to The 'Forty Five, Studies Presented to R.B.K. Stevenson,* Edinburgh, Donald.

O'Dowd, Mary, 1983: "Land Inheritance in Early Modern County Sligo", *J. Irish Econ. Soc. Hist.,* 10, 5-18.

O'Dowd, Mary, 1991: "Women and War in Ireland in the 1640s", in McCurtain and O'Dowd

O'Dowd, Mary, 1991: *Power, Politics and Land: Early Modern Sligo,* Belfast, Institute of Irish Studies.

O'Dowd, Mary, 1994: "Sligo", in Simms and Andrews 1994, 142-153.

Ó Floinn, Raghnaill, 1995: "Gazetteer of Bog Bodies in the British Isles: 2 Ireland" in Turner and Scaife, 221-234.

O'Halloran, Joe, 2001: "'By Time Everything is Revealed': The Galway Archaeological and Historical Society, 1900-1999", *J. Galway Archaeol. Hist. Soc.,* 53, 162-182.

O'Horo, Michael, ed., 2000: *Skreen & Dromard, Past & Present, History & Heritage,* Skreen, Skreen & Dromard Parishes.

O'Kelly, Michael J., 1982: *Newgrange, Archaeology, Art and Legend,* London, Thames and Hudson.

O'Kelly, Michael J., *Early Ireland, An Introduction to Irish Prehistory,* Cambridge, Cambridge University Press.

Ó Muraíle, Nollaig, 1996: *The Celebrated Antiquary, Dudhaltach Mac Fhirbisigh (c. 1600-1671), His Lineage, Life and Learning*, Maynooth, An Sagart

O'Neill, T.P., 1966: "Dutch Engraving of the Williamite Wars 1689", *Irish Book*, 1:3, 1-4.

Ó Nualláin, Seán, 1976: "The Central Court-tombs of the North-West of Ireland", *J. Roy. Soc. Antiq. Ireland*, 106, 92-117.

Ó Nualláin, Seán, 1989: *The Megalithic Survey of Ireland: Vol. V, Co. Sligo*, Dublin, Stationery Office.

O'Rorke, Terrence, 1889: The History of Sligo: Town and County, Dublin, James Duffy, Reprint, Sligo, 1986, Dodd's Antiquarian Books.

O'Rorke, Terence, 1878: *History, Antiquities, and Present State of the Parishes of Ballisodare and Kilvarnet, in the County of Sligo, with Notices of the O'Haras, the Coopers, the Percevals, and other local families*, Dublin, Duffy.

O'Sullivan, Aidan, 1997: "Interpreting the Archaeology of Late Bronze Age Lake Settlements". *J. Irish. Archaeol.*, 8, 115-121.

Perceval, Sandy, 1995: "Temple House", *The Corran Herald*, 28, 30-31.

Piggott, Stuart, and Powell, T. G. E., 1947: Notes on Megalithic Tombs in Sligo and Achill, *J. Roy. Soc. Antiq. Ireland*, 77, 136-146.

Prins, Nicholas, 2000: "Farming in Tireragh Two-Hundred Years Ago" in O'Horo 2000, 26-27.

Raftery, Joyce, 1974: *Preliminary Report on Sites of Archaeological Interest in County Sligo*, Dublin, An Foras Forbatha. Limited distribution.

Reeves-Smith, Terence, and Hammond, Fred, Eds., 1983: *Landscape Archaeology in Ireland*, British Archaeological Reports, International Series, 116.

Reidy, Frank, 2000: "Memories", in McTernan *et al.*, 2000, 52-53.

Remmele, Gerhard, 1985: *Massenbewegungen an der Hauptsschichtstufe der Benbulben Range*, Tubingen, Instituts der Universitat Tubingen.

Roberts, Michael, 1994: "New Expierence", *Archaeology Ireland*, 8:2, 34.

Rogers, Nuala, 1993: *Ballymote*, Aspects *Through Time*, Ballymote, Rogers.

Rogers, Nuala, 1994: *Ballymote, Aspects Through Time*, 2nd edition, Ballymote, Rogers.

Rogers, Nuala, 1994: "The Legend of the Enchanted Fort of Keshcorran", *The Corran Herald*, 29, 8-9.

Rooney, Brendan, 1991: "Prehistoric Sites in Leitrim", *Leitrim Guardian Magazine*, 23, 105-106.

Rooney, Brendan, 1996: *St. Osnat's Church, Glencar, 150th. Anniversary, 1846-1996*, Glencar, Glencar Anniversary Committee.

Rothery, Sean, 1976: *Everyday Buildings of Ireland*, Dublin, Bolton St. College of Technology.

Rothery, Seán, 1978: *The Shops of Ireland*, Dublin, Gill & McMillan

Rothery, Sean, 1997: *A Field Guide to The Buildings of Ireland, Illustrating the Smaller Buildings of Town & Countryside*, Dublin, Lilliput.

Roy, James Charles, 1991: *Islands of Storm*, Chester Springs, Delfour.

Ryan, Michael 1982: review of Burenhult 1980, *Proc. Prehist. Soc.*, 48, 536-537

Ryan, Michael, 1998:*Irish Antiquities, Essays in Memory of Joseph Raftery*, Bray, Wordwell.

Rynne, Etienne, 1969: Cist-burial in a Cairn at Treanmacmurtagh, Co. Sligo, *J. Roy. Soc. Antiq. Ireland*, 99, 145-150.

Rynne, Etienne, and Timoney, Martin A., 1974: "Breeoge Wedge-tomb", *Excavations* 1973, 30

Rynne, Etienne, and Timoney, Martin A., 1974-1975: Excavations of a Destroyed Wedge-tomb at Breeoge, Co. Sligo, *J. Galway Archae. Hist. Soc.*, 34, 88-92.

Rynne, Etienne, 1992: "Dún Aengus and Some Similar Celtic Ceremonial Sites" in Bernelle 1992, 196-207.

Scott, Dermot, 1968: *Caisleán Éireannacha*, Baile Átha Cliath, An Foras Riarácháin.

Sharkey, Patrick A., 1930: *The Moyturra Record*, Dublin, Brown & Nolan.

Sherlock, Martin, 1779: *Letres d'un Voyageur Anglois . .*, Privately printed: Londres, [Geneva?] 1779. 8o.

Sherlock, Martin, 1780: *Letters from an English traveller ... Translated from the French original printed at Geneva and Paris, With notes, A new edition, revised and corrected*, London, Nichols, 1780. pp. xv, 190, 8o.

Sherlock, Martin, 1780: *Letters from an English Traveller, Translated from the French original printed at Geneva..*London, 1780. 4o.

Sherlock, Martin, 1781: *New Letters from an English Traveller, written originally in French, ... translated ... by the author.*

Sherlock, Martin, 1802: *Letters from an English traveller, written originally in French. Translated, with original letters on several subjects and a fragment on Shakespear, by the same author. New Edition.* 2 vols., London, 1802. 8o.

Siggins, Albert, 1995: "A Ballymote Token", *The Corran Herald*, 28, 16-17.

Simms, Anngret, and Andrews, J.H., 1994: *Irish Country Towns*, Cork, Mercier.

Somerville-Large, Peter, 1999: *Ireland's Islands, Landscape, Life and Legends*, Dublin, Gill & Macmillan. 44-49 and photo on back cover.

Sprinks, Neil Whitby, 2001: *Sligo, Leitrim & Northern Counties Railway, An Irish Railway Pictorial*, Hinckley, Midland.

Stapleton, Jim, and de Cúellar, Francisco, 2001: *The Spanish Armada 1588, The Journey of Francisco de Cúellar, Sligo to the Causeway Coast*, Grange & Causeway,

Stokes, W. 1868: *The Life and Labours in Art and Archaeology of George Petrie*, Dublin.

Sweetman, P. David, 1985: Archaeological Excavations at Ballymote Castle, Co. Sligo", *J. Galway Archae. Hist. Soc.*, 40, 114-124.

Swift, Catherine, 2002: "Ogam Stones in Sligo and their Context" in Timoney 2002.

Swords, Liam, 1997: *A Hidden Church, The Diocese of Achonry, 1689-1818*, Blackrock, Columba Press.

Thompson, Enda, Ryan, Siobhán, and Cotton C.F., 1998: *Management Plan for Lough Gill Catchment*, Sligo, Sligo County Council.

Thorn, Richard, 1985: *Irish Association for Quaternary Studies, Field Guide No. 8, Sligo and West Leitrim*.

Thorn, Richard, 1989: "Position, Geology, Soils and Climate of Inishmurray", in Cotton, ed., 1989, 8-15.

Timoney, Catherine M., 2001: "Early National School Registers from Keash and Culfadda, Co. Sligo", in Higgins *et al.*, 143-156.

Timoney, Catherine M., 2002-2003: "God in the Bottle", *The Corran Herald*, 35, 28.

Timoney, Catherine M., and Cryan, Orla, 1999-2000: "Some Street Furniture in Ballymote", *The Corran Herald*, 32, 46-47.

Timoney, Martin A., 1966-1971a: "A Cross-inscribed Slab from Kilmacowen, Co. Sligo", *J. Galway Archae. Hist. Soc.*, 32, 80-88.

Timoney, Martin A., 1966-1971b: "A Long Stone Cist at Carrowmore, Co. Sligo", *J. Galway Archae. Hist. Soc.,*

32, 90-91.

Timoney, Martin A., 1970: "A Halberd from Clonloum Bog, Co. Clare", *N. Munster Antiqarian J.*, 13, 3-5.

Timoney, Martin A., 1971a: "A Stoup from Clonlea, Co. Clare", *N. Munster Antiqarian J.*, 14, 76-77.

Timoney, Martin A., 1971b: "Ancient Monuments in the Neighbourhood of Broadford, Co. Clare, Compiled by Lieutenant-Colonel William Audrey Bentley", *N. Munster Antiqarian J.*, 14, 3-16.

Timoney, Martin A., 1972: "Moin Na Gaoineach Tower-House, Drimmeen, Co. Clare", *N. Munster Antiquarian J.*, 15, 13-16.

Timoney, Martin A., 1979: "Archaeology: A Wander Through The Past", *Reflections 1979*, 19-20.

Timoney, Martin A., 1980a: "Two Stone Crucifixion Plaques From East Connacht", in Murtagh 1980, 142-146.

Timoney, Martin A., 1980b: "Archaeology Tours, North Sligo", *Sligo Visitors Guide 1980*, 15, Sligo, Junior Chamber Sligo.

Timoney, Martin A., 1980c: "Circuit of Lough Gill", *Sligo Visitors Guide 1980*, 73, Sligo, Junior Chamber Sligo.

Timoney, Martin A., 1980d: "Knocknarea Peninsula", *Sligo Visitors Guide 1980*, 73, Sligo, Junior Chamber Sligo.

Timoney, Martin A., 1980e: "Carrowmore and Knocknarea", *Sligo Visitors Guide 1980*, 81-82, Sligo, Junior Chamber Sligo.

Timoney, Martin A., 1982: "Roscommon Crucifixion Plaques - A Detective Story", *Roscommon Association Yearbook 1982*, 8-9 (ed. Michael Fitzmaurice).

Timoney, Martin A., 1983: "Archaeological remains, Knocknarea and Carrowmore", *Sligo Visitors Guide 83*, 14-15, Sligo, Junior Chamber Sligo. Repeated in *Guides* until 1986.

Timoney, Martin A., 1984a: "Earthen Burial Sites on the Carrowmore Peninsula, Co. Sligo", in Burenhult, ed., 1984, 319-325.

Timoney, Martin A., 1984a: *Prehistoric Sligo*, Sligo, Donegal-Leitrim-Sligo Tourism.

Timoney, Martin A., 1987: "Where was 'Gluinaragh or St. Atracta's Knees'?", *The Corran Herald*, 9, 11.

Timoney, Martin A., 1987-1988: "Knocknashammer", J. Irish Archaeol., 4, 77.

Timoney, Martin A., 1988: "A Carrowntemple Slab on Eurovision 1988", *The Corran Herald*, 15, 1-2.

Timoney, Martin A., 1989a: Edited Sligo entries of 3rd edition of *The Shell Guide* to Ireland by Peter Harbison.

Timoney, Martin A., 1989b: " Where was 'Gluinaragh or St. Atracta's Knees'?", *The Corran Herald*, 17, 1 & 3.

Timoney, Martin A., 1990a: "Carrowmore Megalithic Cemetery, Co. Sligo: The Dump Crisis 1983-1989", *Past*, 8, 3.

Timoney, Martin A., 1990b: "The Changing Landscape Around Tarmon, Co. Roscommon", *Tarmon N.S. Centenary 1890-1990*, Ed. Martin Lavin, 13-16.

Timoney, Martin A., 1991: "Earthen Burial Mounds On The Knocknarea Peninsula, Co. Sligo", *The Corran Herald*, 19, 10-11.

Timoney, Martin A., 1992a: "The Carrowmore Court Case, 1983-1989", *Living Heritage*, 9, 23-25.

Timoney, Martin A., 1992b: "The Replica Grave Slabs at Carrowntemple, Co. Sligo", *Echoes of Ballaghaderreen*, 7, 10.

Timoney, Martin A., 1992c: "Sligo Field Club Report", *Federation of Local History Societies Local History Review*, 5, 68-70.

Timoney, Martin A., 1993a: "Three Crucifixion Plaques At Ballinakill. Co. Galway", *The Church in Glinsk, 1843-1993*, 27-30.

Timoney, Martin A., 1993b: "Three Crucifixion Plaques At Ballinakill. Co. Galway", *The Church in Glinsk, 1843-1993*, 27-30.

Timoney, Martin A., 1993c: "Tarmon - The Remains Of Our Past", *Living Heritage*, 10, 19-20.

Timoney, Martin A., 1993d: "Rebuilding 'Misgaun Maedbh, Knocknarea, Co. Sligo", *Excavations 1992*, 64.

Timoney, Martin A., 1994: "Sligo Field Club Report", *Federation of Local History Societies, Local History Review*, 7, 95-96.

Timoney, Martin A., 1995a: "Sligo Field Club Report", *Federation of Local History Societies, Local History Review*, 8, 101-104.

Timoney, Martin A., 1995b: "Landscape And Archaeology, Clooncan, Co. Roscommon", *Clooncan School Reunion*, ed. Mary Nolan, 7-9

Timoney, Martin A., 1996: "Sligo's Ancient Burial Monuments, Sculptures And Dwelling Places", in eds. Gunning & Feehily, 174-175

Timoney, Martin A., 1997: "Where Are They Now, The Knockmore Early Christian Slabs", *The Corran Herald*, 30, 3-4.

Timoney, Martin A., 1999: "Substantial Archaeological Discovery in Drumcliffe, Co. Sligo", *The Church of Ireland Gazette*, 23rd July 1999, 8-9.

Timoney, Martin A., 1999-2000: "Recently Discovered High Cross at Drumcliff, Co Sligo", *The Corran Herald*, 32, 41-43.

Timoney, Martin A., 2002: "Carrowntemple, Co. Sligo, A Review", in ed. Timoney 2002.

Timoney, Mary B., 1986: "An Eighteenth Century Memorial Cross in the Franciscan Abbey", *The Corran Herald*, 4, 12.

Timoney, Mary B., 1988: "A Late 18th. Century Headstone", *The Corran Herald*, 14, 2.

Timoney, Mary B., 1992: "The Black Monument", *Living Heritage*, 9, 29.

Timoney, Mary B., 1993: "Cloonameehan Graveyard 1993", *The Corran Herald*, 25, 10-11.

Timoney, Mary B., 1994: "Killaraght Graveyard", *On The Record (Killaraght & Cloonloo Parish Magazine)*, 5, 11.

Timoney, Mary B., 1995: "Bronze Age Food Vessels from the Ballymote Area", *The Corran Herald*, 28, 21.

Timoney, Mary B., 1995: Review of FitzPatrick, ed., 1995: The Care and Conservation of Graveyards, *N. Munster Antiquarian J.*, 36, 182-183.

Timoney, Mary B., 1996, "Diamond Memorials at Emlaghfad, Co. Sligo", *The Corran Herald*, 29. 22-26.

Timoney, Mary B., 1999-2000: "A Blacksmith's Headstone in Templemore Graveyard", *The Corran Herald*, 32, 40.

Timoney, Mary B., 2000: "Two Diamond Box Tombs In Skreen and Dromard" in ed O'Horo, 2000, 53-55.

Timoney, Mary B., 2001: "The Headstone to Charles Flynn, Blacksmith, in Templemore Graveyard, Co. Sligo", in Gilligan, ed., 66-67.

Timoney, Mary B., 2002-2003: "Concrete Memorials in Carrownanty Graveyard, Ballymote, The Work of Martin and Brian WImsey", *The Corran Herald*, 35, 6-11.

Tinney, Donal, ed., 1998: *Jack B. Yeats at The Niland Gallery Sligo*, Sligo, Sligo County Library.

Tinney, Donal, Gannon, Pat, and Hegarty, Fran, 1999: *The Yeats Brothers and Sligo, The Influence of the Sligo Landscape on the Yeats Brothers*, Sligo, Sligo County Council.

Tohall, Patrick 1944: "Measgra. Some Connacht Traditions. Munster Families in Co. Leitrim, Group Movements from Ulster to Connacht, The MacManus Family .. Tadgh O'Flynn", *Béaloideas*, 14, 289-291.

Tohall, Patrick J., 1945: "Two Dug-out Canoes from Co. Leitrim", *J. Roy. Soc. Antiq. Ireland*, 75, 59-60.

Tohall, Patrick J., 1948: "The Dobhar-Chú Tombstones of Glenade, Co. Leitrim", *J. Roy. Soc. Antiq. Ireland*, 78, 127-129.

Tohall, Patrick J., 1948: "Supplementary note on a Dug-out Canoes", *J. Roy. Soc. Antiq. Ireland*, 78, 181-182.

Tohall, Patrick J., 1951: "Team work on a Rotary Quern", *J. Roy. Soc. Antiq. Ireland*, 81, 70-71.

Tohall, Patrick J., 1952: "Pre-history and Purple Heather, Notes of Antiquities of Co. Sligo", in *Sligo, The Yeats Country, The Official Guide, City and County*, Sligo, Sligo Tourist Development Association Ltd., 12-14.

Tohall, Patrick J., 1953: "Pre-history and Purple Heather, Notes of Antiquities of Co. Sligo", in *Sligo, An Illustrated Guide to The Yeats Country*, 2nd ed., Sligo Tourist Development Association Ltd., 13-15.

Tohall, Patrick J., 1953: "Farm Classification in Economic Geography. A Plea for Classification by Rateable Value Instead of Area", *Irish Geography*, 2, 227-229.

Tohall, Patrick J., 1958: "The Diamond Fight of 1795 and the Resultant Expulsions", *Seanchas Ardmacha*, 3:1, 17-50.

Tohall, Patrick J., 1960: "Notes on Some Gaelic Place Names (mostly as a Background to Pollen Diagrams)", *J. Roy. Soc. Antiq. Ireland*, 90, 82-83.

Tohall, P., de Vries, Hl., and van Zeist, W., 1955: "A Trackway in Corlona Bog, Co. Leitrim", *J. Roy. Soc. Antiq. Ireland*, 85, 77-83.

Toher, Tony, 1994: *Exploring Sligo and North Leitrim, 70 Walks in the Yeats Country*, Sligo, Sligo Chamber of Commerce and Industry.

Toher, Tony, and Hamilton, Thomas J., 1952: *Sligo, The Yeats Country, The Official Guide, City and County*, Sligo, Sligo Tourist Development Association Ltd.

Toher, Tony, and Hamilton, Thomas J., 1953: *Sligo, An Illustrated Guide to The Yeats Country*, Second Edition, Sligo, Sligo Tourist Development Association Ltd.

Townley, Christopher, 1976: "The Galway Archaeological and Historical Society, *J. Galway Archaeol. Hist. Soc.*, 35, 5-11.

Traynor, Owen Francis, 1963: *Review of The Ancient Parish and Church of St. John the Baptist, Sligo, from Early Times to Disestablishment*, Privately circulated.

Tuffy, Paddy, 1987-1988: "The Parish of Kilglass", *North Mayo Historical Journal*, 2:1, 64-71

Turner, R.C., and Scaife, R.G., 1995: *Bog Bodies: New Discoveries and New Perspectives*, London, British Museum Press.

Tyndall, Charles, 1962: *The Ancient Parish and Church of St. John the Baptist, Sligo, from Early Times to Disestablishment*, n.p., n.p.

Wakeman, W.F., 1866: "Abbey of the Order of St. Dominick, Sligo", *Dublin Saturday Magazine*, 2: 67, 1.

Wakeman, William F., 1883: *Drawings of Antiquities on the County of Sligo. By W.F. Wakeman, M.R.H.A.I., made in the years 1878, 1879, 1880, 1881, 1882 for Colonel E.H. Cooper, Markree Castle*. Original illustrations bound London 1883.

Wallace, Patrick F., 2000: *A Guide to The National Museum of Ireland*, Dublin, Town House ~ National Museum of Ireland.

Wallace, Patrick F. and Timoney, Martin A., 1987: "Carrowntemple, Co. Sligo, and its Inscribed Slabs", in Rynne, ed., 1987, 43-61.

Warner, Richard, 1998: "An Iron Age Lead Pin from County Donegal" in Ryan 1998, 111-122.

Warner, Richard, 1979: "The Irish Souterrains and their Background", in Crawford 1979.

Webart, Bozena, ed., 2001: *Papers from a Session held at the European Association of Archaeologist Sixth Annual Meeting in Lisbon 2000*, BAR International Series 985.

Whitfield, Niamh, 2001:, "A Filigree Panel and a Coin from an Irish Crannog at Alnwick Castle, with an Appendix on the Discovery of Crannogs at Strokestown, Co. Roscommon", *J. Irish Archaeol.*, 10, 49-72.

Whittall, James P., Jr., 1991: "The Teampull-na-mBan Inscribed Monolith, Inishmurray, County Sligo, Ireland", *Early Sites Research Society Bulletin*, 18:1, 43-46.

Wilde, William, 1870: "Memoir of Gabriel Beranger, and his labours in the cause of Irish Art, Literature and Antiquities, from 1760 to 1780, *J. Roy. Soc. Antiq. Ireland*, 11, 121-152.

Wilde, William, 1880: *Memoir of Gabriel Beranger, and his Labours in the Cause of Irish Art and Antiquities, from 1760 to 1780*. Dublin 1880.

Williams, Jeramy, 1995: *Irish Architecture in the Nineteenth Century*, Blackrock, Irish Academic Press.

Wilson, Martin, 2000: "Our Ancestors and How they Lived" in O'Horo 2000, 24-25.

Wilson, Martin, 2000: "Beltra Show" in O'Horo 2000, 30-33.

Wilson, Martin, 2000: "Derk Coastguard Station" in O'Horo 2000, 48.

Wilson, Martin, 2000: "Tanrego" in O'Horo 2000, 45.

Wilson, Martin, 2000: "Historic Beltra Strand" in O'Horo 2000, 140.

Wilson, Martin, 2000: "Construction at Holy Hill" in O'Horo 2000, 144-145.

Wood-Martin, W.G., 1880; *Sligo and the Enniskilleners, 1688-1691*, Dublin.

Wood-Martin, W.G., 1882: *The History of Sligo, County and Town, from the Earliest Ages to the Close of the Reign of Queen Elizabeth*, Dublin, Reprint, Sligo, 1990, Dodd's Antiquarian Books.

Wood-Martin, W.G., 1886: *The Lake Dwellings of Ireland: or Ancient Lacustrine Habitations of Erin, Commonly called Crannogs*, Dublin, Hodges Figgis; Reproduction Dublin, Crannóg.

Wood-Martin, W.G., 1888: *The Rude Stone Monuments of Ireland, (Co. Sligo and the Island of Achill)*, Dublin, Hodges Figgis

Wood-Martin, W.G., 1889: *The History of Sligo, County and Town, from the Accession of James I to the Revolution of 1688*, Dublin, Hodges Figgis; Reprint, Sligo, 1990, Dodd's Antiquarian Books.

Wood-Martin, W.G., 1892: *The History of Sligo, County and Town, from the Close of the Revolution of 1688 to the Present Time*, Dublin, Hodges Figgis; Reprint, Sligo, 1990, Dodd's Antiquarian Books.

Wood-Martin, W.G., 1895: *Pagan Ireland, An Archaeological Sketch, A Handbook of Irish Pre-Christian Antiquities*, London, Longman Green.

Wood-Martin, W.G., 1902: *Traces of the Elder Faiths of Ireland, A Folklore Sketch, A Handbook of Irish Pre-Christian Traditions*, 2 vols., London, Longman Green.

Wood-Martin, W.G., 1903, 1904, 1905: "Bronze Serpentine Latchets, and other cumbrous Dress fasteners", *Ulster J. Archae.*, 2nd Series, 9, 160-166; 10, 12-20; 11, 33-39.

A CELEBRATION OF SLIGO

SLIGO ANTIQUARIAN SOCIETY & SLIGO FIELD CLUB OFFICERS AND COMMITTEE 1945 TO 2002

```
44      555555 66666|66666 77777|77777 88888|88888 99999|99999 00000|00000
56      456789 01234|56789 01234|56789 01234|56789 01234|56789 01234|56789
CC                                                             KIRWAN Robert
cc      nfmmmm                                                 MORAN John P.
SS      CCCPPP P                                               TOHALL Patrick
T                                                              McLOUGHLIN Frank
nT                                                             GILES C.A. (or J.C.F.)
m                                                              RIGNEY James
m                                                              McGUINNESS P.
        TTTTT                                                  KERIN Thomas A.
        SS                                                     PERREM Guy
        nSSSSS S                                               RYAN Mary F.
        nFFFFF                                                 KERRIN Frank
        nf                                                     MAXWELL ALPHONSUS Br.
        nfm                                                    FOLEY Tim
        nfmCCp pPPPP PPPPP PPPPP PPPPP PPPm                    HERAUGHTY Patrick
        nfm                                                    HOPPER Michael
        nfmmmm mmmmm mmmmm mm                                  HUGHES Jim
        nfmmmm mmmmm mmmmm mmmmm mmmss sss m                   LAMBERT Eileen
        nfm           mmccC Cpp00 000                          MURPHY Noel
        nfm                                                    O'ROURKE Harry
        nfmmmm mmmmm mmmmm mmmmm      mmm    m m mppPP mm      TOHER TONY
        n SSSS SSSSS SSSSS SS                                  CAHALANE Michael C.
        n  mmm ttttm mmmmm mm                                  DODD Violet
        n  ccC ppmmm mm                                        McEVILLY Tom
        n  mm                                                  MURRAY Kevin
        n  mmm m                                               TOHER Monica
           c   Cppmm mmmmm mmmmm mmmmm mmm                     KITCHIN Finlay Tower
           m   cCppm mmmmm mmmmm                               TRODDYN John T.
        n  T   T                                               TROTTER John
           m   TTTTT TTTTT TTTTc c                             WAGSTAFF Oliver
           m   mmmmm                                           WYNNE Frank
               mmmmm mmmcc CCpp                                KIRBY Sheila
               mmm                                             NILAND Nora
n       n      cCpp  mmmmm m                                   DALY Sean
               mmmmm mmmmm mmmmm                               WEST Gladys
n       n      m                                               BROWNE Robert
               mcC   ppppp p                                   KENNEDY Tom
               cCp                                             McWILLIAM J.R.
               mc    C                                         HORGAN Liam
                     cCC                                       CORR Larry
                     ccCC                                      CALVERT HERBERT
                     s                                         COLLIER George
                     m                                         O'GORMAN Anne
                     mm    ccSSS SSScc CCpmp pPPmm   m mmmmm m SMITH Des
                           mmCCp pmmmm mmm                     McGETTRICK Tom
                           ssssS                               McGETTRICK Mary
                           mmmmm mCCpp mmm                     DEVLIN John
                           mTT   Tm                            FEENEY Joe
                           m                                   KIRBY Hilda
                           mmm   mmmmm mm                      MAHON Frank
                           mmm                                 RYAN Nicola
                           mm    mmm                           TRITTON Jill
                           mm    mTTTT TTT                     MURPHY Briga
                           mm    mmmmm mmm   mpp  PPm          O'CONNOR Frank
                           m                                   SWEENEY Joe
                           m  mm                               ALVEY Reginald J.
                           m  SSSSS SSSSm    mmm mmmTT TTT     ENRIGHT Joyce [1]
                              mmmmm mmram mppPP mmm            ENRIGHT Martin
                              mmm                              FARRELL Ben
                              mmmmm mmmmm m       mmm          O'HIGGINS Aodhán
44      555555|66666|66666 77777 mmmmm mmm                     RAFTERY Kay
56      456789 01234|56789 01234 mccCC pprRT TTTSS SSSSS SSSSS ppP  TIMONEY Martin A. [2]
                                 mmmmm ccCPm mm     ppP  Pm    FLYNN John
                                 mm                            COX Kathleen
P:  President: since 1957        mm   mmcpP Pm                 Ó SÚILLEABHÁIN Brian
p:  Vice President                    mmm                      RIPON Tony
C:  Chairman
c:  Vice Chairman                     mmmTS SSS    mmmmm m  mm mmm TIMONEY Mary B. [3]
T:  Tresurer                          mmmm mmmTT TTTTT TTTpp PPm MULLIN Larry
t:  Assistant Treasurer                    mmmm  ppPPm         McTERNAN John C.
S:  Secretary                              m     mmmmm         CURRAN-MULLIGAN Patricia [4]
s:  Assistant Secretary                    m                   DODD Kevin
a:  Acting Secretary                       mm                  ENGLISH Alison
O:  Ornithological Secretary            mmm m     m            JORDAN Vincent
F:  Field Officer                       mm  mm                 STEWART Angelo Br.
m:  Member                              mm  mmmmp pPPmm S      ROONEY Brendan
f:  Field Outings committee             m                      DUIGNAN Mary
R   PRO                                          mm mmm        MONEY Berta
r   Joint PRO                                    m             McGOWAN Joseph
n:  Named in early records                          mm         O'CONNOR Vincent
                                                 mmm  m        MONEY Paul
                                                      m        SMITH Tim
1. Nee Raftery                                        m  mmp   MANNION Aidan
2. Editor 1995-2002                                   m  mmm   WILSON Martin
3. Nee Murphy                                            mmm   McBRIEN Margaret
4. Nee Curran                                            mSS   O'BRIEN Patrick E.
#   SAS became SFC in March 1946                         mm    NEARY Mai
#   Rules decision 1965 not implemented.                 m     McGILL Frank
#   1983 Constitution committee of 10.                   m     MOORE Sam
#   2000 Amendment set it at 12                          m     O'CONNOR Domhnail

44      555555 66666|66666 77777|77777 88888|88888 99999|99999 00000|
56      456789 01234|56789 01234|56789 01234|56789 01234|56789 01234|  © M.A.T. Nov. 2002
```

Out In The Field

Patrick Tohall emerging from a souterrain, Cooladrumman, Cashelgarran, April 1954. Photo: Tony Toher

A landowner expounding on his monument to Sheila Kirby and Joe McMorrow.

Two members of the Green Studios with Pat Kitchin and Michael Cahalane mounting a camera at Creevykeel, June 1964.

A CELEBRATION *OF* SLIGO

PAST TO PRESENT

L-R: Professor Michael J. O'Kelly, Pat Kitchin and Michael Cahalane, Newgrange, Co. Meath.

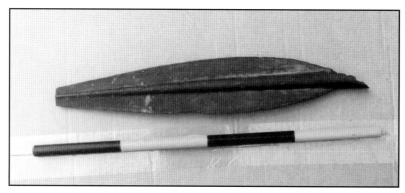

Spearhead found at Carrowvard, Beltra, Co. Sligo about 50 years ago and recovered recently by Sligo Field Club member.

After the last Sligo Field Club Lecture in the Teachers' Centre, Quay St., Sligo - May 2000

Back Row L-R: Pat O'Brien, Tony Toher, Brendan Rooney, --, Berta Money, Paul Money, Jack Flynn and Aidan Mannion.
Middle Row L-R: Brendan McKeon, Joyce Enright, Larry Mullin, Des Smith, Bernie Doyle.
Front Row L-R: Mary B. Timoney, Margaret McBrien and Brother Angelo.

A CELEBRATION *OF* SLIGO

AUTHORS

Olive Alcock, M.A., M.I.A.I., Archaeological Survey of Ireland, Dúchas – The Heritage Service, Harcourt Lane, Dublin 2 A member of the Sites and Monuments Record team for Sligo. She edited several of the County Archaeological Inventories and was joint author of the *Archaeological Inventory of Co. Galway, Vol. 2.*

Stefan Bergh, Ph. D., Culleenamore, Co. Sligo, formerly of Stockholm from which University he holds his Ph.D., *Landscape of the Monuments,* on the Neolithic of Sligo. Since settling in Sligo in 1999 he has done a major study of Knocknarea. He is currently Programme Director of MA course in Landscape Archaeology at Dept. of Archaeology, NUIG. Specialise in Neolithic and Bronze Age landscape studies.*

Jason Bolton, Faculty of the Built Environment, Dublin Institute of Technology. Specialises in work towards the long-term preservation of stonework. He was joint author with Sara Pavía of *Stone Monuments Decay Study 2000* and *Stones, Bricks and Mortar.*

Laureen Buckley, M.A., M.I.A.I., Paleopathologist, 25 Ard-Rí Drogheda, Co. Louth. She has applied her knowledge of Medicine and Analytical Chemistry to the archaeology of burials, and has studied over 7,000 burials from over 180 sites dating from the Neolithic to the 18th century. She has a wide range of publications on life and death of past Irish populations.

Victor M. Buckley, M.A., M.I.A.I., Senior Archaeologist, Dúchas – The Heritage Service, Harcourt Lane, Dublin 2. He was Director of the Sligo Field Survey and has published widely, including the *Archaeological Survey of Co. Louth* (with P. David Sweetman). He specialises in the landscape and popularising the past.

Fr. Patrick Conlan, B. Sc., B. Ph., S.T.L., O.F.M., The Friary, Rosnowlagh, Co. Donegal. He specialises in Irish Franciscan history and archaeology and has published two editions of *Franciscan Ireland.* He has published a complete short title catalogue of Irish Franciscan material in the archives of the Order in Rome.

Don C. F. Cotton, B. Sc. (Hons), Ph. D., M.I.Biol., Rahaberna, Sligo. Senior Lecturer in Ecology, Institute of Technology, Internationally recognised expert on the flora and fauna of Sligo and Leitrim. He has extensively published on these topics and his help is acknowledged in many more. He has prepared several environmental impact assessments and is currently a sectional editor of *Irish Naturalists' Journal.**

Jean Farrelly, M.A., M.I.A.I., Dúchas – The Heritage Service, Harcourt Lane, Dublin 2. Hhe was previously with the Sites and Monuments Record Office of the Office of Public Works, now Dúchas. She was joint author of the *Archaeological Inventory of Co. Tipperary Vol. 1.*

William FitzGerald, B. Sc., Ph. D., Head of Environmental Science, Institute of Technology, Sligo. He is a Lecturer in Waste Management at the Institute of Technology, Sligo. His research interests are mainly in the area of biological wastewater treatment.

Hans Göransson, Ph. D., Ibsberga, Pl 809, Ljungbyhead, Sweden S-260 70. International paleobotanist.

Eóin Halpin, M.A., M.I.A.I., Archaeological Development Services, Westlink Enterprise Centre, Distillery St., Belfast. He is a Contract Archaeologist who has done several major excavations in Sligo town.

Peter Harbison, Ph. D., M.R.I.A., 5, St. Damien's, Loughshinmny, Skerries, Co. Dublin. Formerly archaeologist with Bord Fáilte, now Hon. Academic Editor with the Royal Irish Academy. Author of over twenty books, from popular to thoroughly academic, the most recent of which is his publication, *Our Treasure of Antiquities,* a tour of Connacht in 1779 by Beranger and Bigari.

Dr. Patrick Heraughty, Past President, Sligo Field Club, of which he has been a member since 1945. His particular interest is geology, man's place and development.*

Margaret Keane, M.A., M.I.A.I., Dúchas – The Heritage Service, Harcourt Lane, Dublin 2. works in the Planning and Development Unit of Dúchas, the Heritage Service. She moved to the Office of Public Works, now Dúchas, in 1994 from the Irish Archaeological Wetland Unit.

Michael Kenny, M.A., Art and Industry Division, National Museum of Ireland, Dublin. He is an expert in Irish numismatics and Irish history of more recent centuries on which he has frequently published.

Finlay Tower Kitchin†, Past Vice-President, Sligo Field Club. Diligent defender of Carrowmore.*

Finbar McCormick, M.A., Ph. D., Department of Archaeology, The Queens University, Belfast. He specialises in quantifying food consumption from excavated animal bone, the Early Christian period and funerary monuments of recent centuries.

Christopher Moriarty, Ph. D., Zoology Department, Trinity College, Dublin. Formerly Research Scientist at the Government's Fishery Research Centre at Abbotstown. Author of several walking and cycling publications.

Ernan Morris, BA, Dip. Librarianship, Retired Librarian, Bray. He was librarian at several locations, the longest term being for 33 years at Athlone. He wrote a history of Athlone castle and a guide to Clonmacnoise.

Charles Mount, M.I.A.I., M.A., Ph. D., The Heritage Council, Kilkenny. He was one of the team who did the field survey for the Sligo Recorded Monuments and Places.

Larry Mullin, B.A., Bellanode, Sligo, Past President and former Hon. Treasurer of Sligo Field Club, of which he has been a member since 1964. He was awarded a Certificate in Local History Studies by NUI Maynooth in 2001. He was a member of the Famine and the Markievicz Commemorative Committees and was Chairman of Sligo Historical Society.*

Nollaig Ó Muraíle, M.A., Ph. D., Reader in Irish and Celtic Studies, Queen's University, Belfast. Expert on Irish Placenames and on Dubhaltach Mac Fhirbhisigh. His edition of Mac Fhirbhisigh's *Great Book of Irish Genealogies* is due for publication in summer 2003.

Patrick E. O'Brien, Hon. Sec., SFC, Ballygawley, Co. Sligo. Former industrial engineer and project manager, awarded a Certificate in Local History Studies by NUI Maynooth in 2001 and is currently involved in historical research.

Maghnus O'Brien, B., Design in Interactive Media, Dip. Design in Communications, Ballygawley.

Derry O'Connell, Dip. Arch., M.R.U.P., Dept. of Regional and Urban Planning, UCD, previously Head of Urban Design at the National Building Agency. Wide range of publications on Irish towns.*

Kieran D. O'Conor, M.A., Ph. D., Dept. of Archaeology, National University of Ireland, Galway. He is a direct descendant of the mid-13th century Phelim O'Conor who 'altered Sligo Castle in his day'. He specialises in medieval rural settlement and published the pioneering *Medieval Rural Settlement in Ireland.*

John O'Dea, M. Sc., M. Ed., M. Inst. P, Circular Rd., Sligo, a lecturer in Environmental Physics at the Institute of Technology in Sligo. He was an organizer of the inaugural Stokes Commemoration Weekend. He has a number of academic publications in topics ranging from environmental radioactivity, including *Exposure* on living with radiation in Ireland, to teaching science in Nigeria.

John O'Dwyer, Senior Executive Officer, Sligo County Council. He was a founder member and first national President of the Housing Institute of Ireland. He was Development Co-ordinator for Urban Renewal Programmes in Sligo since 1994, including the Rockwood Parade Area Development and the proposed Wine St. Retail Development.

Sara Pavía, Dept. of Engineering, Trinity College, Dublin 2. She was joint author of *Stone Monuments Decay Study 2000* and *Stones, Bricks and Mortar,* and she specialises in preservation of stonework.

Etienne Rynne, M.A., M.R.I.A., F.S.A., Professor Emeritus in Archaeology, Galway. He was Assistant Keeper in the National Museum of Ireland. He is a prolific writer and editor of several volumes of essays and of *North Munster Antiquarian Journal.* He is both an academic and a popular lecturer. Many of students hold key archaeological posts in this country.

Catherine Swift, M. Phil., D. Phil., Department of History, National University of Ireland, Maynooth – She has held posts in several universities in these islands and is also attached to the Centre for the Study of Human Settlement & Historical Change in University College Galway.

Richard Thorn, B.A., (Mod), M.A., Ph. D., Director, Institute of Technology, Sligo. He was previously Head of Dept of Environmental Science, IT, Sligo, and Head of Castlebar Campus, Galway-Mayo IT. He has published one hundred and fifty writings from papers to books covering subject areas as diverse as environmental and earth sciences, travel and management.*

Martin A. Timoney, F.R.S.A.I., M.I.A.I., Keash, Co. Sligo. President, Sligo Field Club. He was a Secondary Teacher. He now specialises in research into Sligo's past on which he has widely published.*

Mary B. Timoney, M.A., M.I.A.I., Keash, Co. Sligo, former Hon. Treasurer and Hon. Secretary of Sligo Field Club. She specialises in the study of Sligo memorials of the dead of the last three centuries, particularly their artwork, on which she frequently published.*

Patrick Tohall†, Past President, Sligo Field Club. A founder member of Sligo Antiquarian Society in 1945.*

Mary Tunney, M.A., M.I.A.I., Archaeological Survey of Ireland, Dúchas – The Heritage Service, Harcourt Lane, Dublin 2. She was a member of the team who compiled the Sites and Monuments Record for Sligo. She has edited several of the County Archaeological Inventories.

Peter Woodman, M.A., Ph. D., Professor of Archaeology, National University of Ireland, Cork specialising in the Mesolithic, on which he has several publications including reports on his major excavations at Mount Sandle and Ferriter's Cove.

• *Biographical details are to be found in the article by Timoney and Heraughty herein.*

A CELEBRATION *OF* SLIGO

TABULA GRATULATORIA

SPONSORS

Institute of Technology, Bellanode, Sligo
Sligo County Council, Riverside, Sligo
Sligo Corporation, The Town Hall, Quay St., Sligo
Dúchas - The Heritage Service, Harcourt Lane, Dublin 2
Sheela Kitchin, Ballisodare, Co. Sligo
Town of Sligo Vocational Education Committee, Quay St., Sligo
The Morris Family, Sligo and Dublin
Sligo Field Club Members' Account, Sligo
Archaeological Development Services Ltd., Westlink Enterprise Centre, Distillery St., Belfast
The Dean's Research Fund, Faculty of Arts, University College, Cork
Ulster Bank, Sligo
Hopper & Pettit, Castle St., Sligo
Abbott Ireland Pharmaceutical Operations, Ballytivnan, Sligo
Galway-Mayo Institute of Technology, Castlebar, Co. Mayo
Patrick F. O'Donovan, Larkhill Rd., Sligo

SUBSCRIBERS

Michael Archer, Aughacarna, Corrigeenroe, Boyle, Co. Roscommon
Tom and Maura Armitage, Strandhill, Co. Sligo
Brian Armstrong, Millenium Ho., Stephen St., Sligo
Fiona Beglane and Edward Wiazewicz, Glenborin, Donegal Town
Linda Beirne, "Alder Villa", Roosky, Carrick-on-Shannon, Co. Leitrim
Malcolm Billings and Bridget O'Hara, Gower St., London
John Bodley, London
Tim and Jaqueline Boland, Tanrego, Beltra, Co. Sligo
Imelda Brady, Ballygawley, Co. Sligo
Councillor Declan Bree, 1, High St. Sligo
Drs. Vivian and Ann Brennan, Athenry, Co. Galway
Peter Burke, Spurtown, Bunninadden, Co. Sligo
Rita Ann Burke, Skreen, Co. Sligo
Rory and Mary Callaghy, Rosses Point, Co. Sligo
Joseph Carter, Howley Carter & Co., Wine St., Sligo
Stephen T. Carty, "Lyndoo", Ballydoogan, Sligo
Stan and Tilly Casey, Teeling St., Ballymote, Co. Sligo
Eoin Clerkin, Skreen, Co. Sligo
Michael Conmy, Plan Design Associates, Bury St., Ballina, Co. Mayo
Shaun Connor, Upper Rosses, Rosses Point, Co. Sligo
Miss Peg Corcoran, 12, Short Walk, Bellanode, Sligo
Alec and Joan Crichton, Carrowgarry, Beltra, Co. Sligo
David and Aideen Daly, Cliffoney, Co. Sligo
Greg and Aine Daly, Carrowcrory, Ballinafad, Co. Sligo
Andy Dodd, Sr., Ballyglass, Calry, Co. Sligo
Eithne and Queenie Dolan, 'Marlbruff', Pearse Crescent, Sligo
Rev. Fr. Gerard Dolan, Rosses Point, Co. Sligo
Martin and Joyce Enright, "Raheen", Kilmacowen, Ballysodare, Co. Sligo
Dermott and Brid Fallon, Sligo Gate, Collooney Roundabout, Co. Sligo
Joseph P. Fenwick, Bunoghanaun, Corrandulla, Co. Galway
Shane Flannagan, GHQ, O'Connell St., Sligo
Bishop Thomas Flynn, Bishop of Achonry, Ballaghaderreen, Co. Roscommon
Patricia FitzSimons, Two Mile Hill, Calry, Co. Sligo
James Foran, The Library, Institute of Technology, Sligo
Padraig and Ann Foran, Calry, Fivemilebourne, Sligo
The Franciscan Friary, Rosnowlagh, Co. Donegal
Ben and Marie Healy, Ardowen, Sligo
Joseph Henry, Bohalas, Ballaghaderreen, Co. Roscommon
Mary Henry, 24, Queen St., Clonmel, Co. Tipperary
Declan Hegarty, Millenium House, Stephen St., Sligo
Dr. Patrick Heraughty, Nazereth House, Malahide Rd., Dublin 3
Frank Hopper and Catherine Pettit, Castle St., Sligo
Audrey Irwin, Doomore House, Beltra, Co. Sligo
Mairead Jennings, 8, Pearse Crescent, Sligo.
J. Ernest and Irene Johnson, Rathonoragh, Strandhill Rd., Sligo
Keenan and Marie Johnson, Ballymote, Co. Sligo
Bishop Christopher Jones, St. Mary's, Sligo
Mark Keane, Gortarowey, Drumcliffe, Co. Sligo
Fr. Desmond Kelly, P.P., Castleconnor, Corballa, Co. Sligo
Eileen and P.J. Kelly, Hazelwood, Sligo
Joseph and Angela Kelly, Oranmore, Co. Galway
Michael and Rosaleen Keohane, Easky, Co. Sligo

Sheela Kitchin and family, Ballisodare, Co. Sligo
Leo Leyden, Cloghboley, Maugherow, Co. Sligo
Richard and Wendy Lyons, Camphill, Collooney,
   Co. Sligo
Conleth Manning, Dúchas, Dún Scéinne,
   Harcourt Lane, Dublin 2
Aidan and Dympna Mannion, The Record Room,
   Grattan St., Sligo
J. H. Martin, Ballisodare, Co. Sligo
Leo Mattimoe, Lecarrow, Strandhill Rd., Co. Sligo
Columb McBride, 11, Rosehill, Sligo
Margaret McBrien, 20, Crozon Park, Sligo
Gerry McCanny, McCanny & Co., Solicitors,
   Wine St., Sligo
Roger McCarrick, Tubbercurry, Co. Sligo
Sylvia McCarrick, 10, Howard View, South Ham,
   Bassingstoke, RG22.LF6
Conor McDermott, Dept. of Archaeology,
   University College, Dublin 4
David McDonagh, "Truskmore", Strandhill Rd.,
   Sligo
Martin McGettrick, Ballymote, Co. Sligo
Frank McGill, Dromahaire, Co. Leitrim
McGovern, Walsh & Co., 33, Chapel St., Sligo
Gerald S. McGowan, Killargue, Dromahaire,
   Co. Leitrim
Terry McGowan, Faughts, Co. Sligo
Conor McHale, 30, Lakelands Drive, Stillorgan,
   Co. Dublin
Neill McHugh, "Wincanton", Minster Rd., Foxrock,
   Dublin 18
Brendan McKenna, Lisnalurg, Co. Sligo
Fr. Austin P. McKeon, P.P., Tulsk, Co. Roscommon
Brendan McKeon, 20, Neville St., Durham City
Mrs. Felicity McNab, The Boat House, Raughley,
   Co. Sligo
Raymond and Elaine McSharry, Pearse Rd., Sligo
Joe and Anna Meehan, Lecarrow, Strandhill,
   Co. Sligo
Paul and Berta Money, Barnaribbon, Carney,
   Co. Sligo
Dr. Desmond and Siobhán Moran, Wheatrock
   House, Ballyweelin, Co. Sligo
Brendan and Phil Morris, 8, St. Joseph's Tce., Sligo
John Mullaney, Mullaney Bros., O'Connell St., Sligo
Larry Mullin, Bellanode, Sligo
Paddy Mullrooney, Gortarowey, Carney, Co. Sligo
Briga Murphy, 2, John St., Sligo
Prof. Aoibhín Nic Donachadha, Dublin Institute of
   Advanced Studies
Seósamh Ó Luana, Faughts, Clogherevagh,
   Co. Sligo
Ann and John O'Neill, Carrowconnor Rd.,
   Dromard, Co. Sligo
Eugene O'Neill, Rooney O'Neill Architects, Flynn's
   Tce., Sligo
Brendán Ó Ríordáin, Burgage More, Blessington,
   Co. Wicklow
Nan and Harry O'Boyle, The Mall, Sligo
Patrick E. and Ann O'Brien, Ballygawley, Co. Sligo
Dr. Michael O'Connell, Dept. of Botany, National
   University of Ireland, Galway.
Brian F. and Mary O'Carroll, Eagle Lodge,
   Convent Rd., Roscommon

Conor O'Connor, Adelaide, South Austalia
Donald and Anita O'Connor, Cleveragh, Sligo
Dr. Michael O'Connor, Rosses Point, Co. Sligo
Frank and Betty O'Connor, Moneygold, Grange,
   Co. Sligo
Garry O'Connor, O'Connor Construction,
   Castlegal, Cliffoney, Co. Sligo
Gerald O'Connor, Skreen, Co. Sligo
Seamus and Patricia O'Dowd, Rosses Point,
   Co. Sligo
Dermot O'Hara, Annaghmore, Collooney, Co. Sligo
Aodhán and Patricia O'Higgins, Strandhill,
   Co. Sligo
Fr. Michael O'Horo, P.P., Skreen, Co. Sligo
Jerry O'Sullivan, Castletaylor, Ardrahan,
   Co. Galway
Sandy and Deb Perceval, Templehouse, Co. Sligo
Marie and John Perry, T.D., Ballymote, Co. Sligo
Jan and Pat-Ann Prins, Ballinlig, Beltra, Co. Sligo
Nicholas Prins, Ballinlig, Beltra, Co. Sligo
Vincent and Catherine Raftery, "Grallagh",
   Strandhill Rd., Sligo
Willie Regan, Regan Plant Hire, Gurteen,
   Ballintrellick, Co. Sligo
James and Mairead Reidy, Ballyhaunis, Co. Mayo
Teresa Rock, 104, Rathedmond, Sligo
Nuala Rogers, Carrigeenmore, Ballymote, Co. Sligo
Aideen Rynne, "Liosnarianna", Athenry,
   Co. Galway
Bernadette Scully, 35, Rathedmond, Sligo
Stephen Stokes, Stokes Books, Georges St. Markets,
   Georges St., Dublin
Greg Tansey, Tansey & Co., Ballymote, Co. Sligo
Michael and Helen Tarmey, Ballymote, Co. Sligo
Prof. Charles Thomas, Truro, Cornwall
Dr. Richard Thorn, Director, Institute of Technology,
   Sligo
Aidan and Geraldine Tighe, Strandhill, Co. Sligo
Eileen Tighe, Carrigeenmore, Ballymote, Co. Sligo
Francis and Bernadette Tivnan, Cornameelta,
   Boyle, Co. Roscommon
Tony and Ray Toher, Rosses Point, Co. Sligo
John Troddyn, Graigue, Cloverhill, Co. Sligo
Prof. John Waddell, National University of Ireland,
   Galway
Tony and Ita Wherly, O'Connell St., Sligo
David and Mary Willis, 18, Charleville Rd.,
   Rathmines, Dublin 6
Martin and Moya Wilson, Larkhill, Beltra, Co. Sligo
Richard J. and Elizabeth Wood-Martin, Seamount,
   Mullaghmore, Co. Sligo

~~~~~~~~

Ballinode College, Bellanode, Sligo
Dept. of Archaeology, National University
   of Ireland, Galway, bis.
Dept. of Archaeology, University College, Cork
Ionad Múinteóirí, Sligeach, Institute of Technology
   Campus, Sligo
St. Angela's College, Lough Gill, Sligo